CADOGAN
guides

Richard Lloyd Parry

JAPAN

D0921332

Cadogan Books plc
London House, Parkgate Road, London SW11 4NQ, UK

Distributed in North America by
The Globe Pequot Press
6 Business Park Road, PO Box 833, Old Saybrook,
Connecticut 06475–0833

Copyright © Richard Lloyd Parry 1995
Illustrations © Satoshi Kambayashi 1995
Shrine architecture illustrations © William Schenck

Book and cover design by Animage
Cover illustrations by Animage
Maps © Cadogan Guides, drawn by Map Creation Ltd

Series Editors: Rachel Fielding and Vicki Ingle

Editing: Helena Gomm
Proofreading: Jacqueline Lewin
Indexing: Isobel McLean
DTP: Jacqueline Lewin and Kicca Tommasi
Production: Rupert Wheeler Book Production Services

A catalogue record for this book is available from the British Library

ISBN 0–94–7754–72–5

Output, printed and bound by WSOY, Finland

Please Note

The author and publishers have made every effort to ensure the accuracy of the information in the book at the time of going to press. However, they cannot accept any responsibility for any loss, injury or inconvenience resulting from the use of information contained in this guide.

About the Author

Richard Lloyd Parry first visited Japan in 1986 after winning a holiday on a TV quiz show. Since then he has spent 18 months in the country as a teacher, journalist, and unsuccessful model. He has written for the *Daily Telegraph*, *Sunday Times*, and *Modern Review*, and contributes to the weekly *Intelligent Cod* column to the *Funday Times* comic. He presently lives in Japan as Tokyo correspondent of the *Independent*.

Acknowledgements

Like most people who spend time in Japan, I've encountered more kindness there than I'll ever be able to repay or acknowledge: my sincere apologies to all those whose names I've missed or whose *meishi* I have mislaid.

This book's been a long time in the pipeline, and would never have come through at all without the generous assistance and help of several organisations. Nippon Travel Agency provided railcards, invaluable introductions and moral support: special thanks must go to Mr Yamaguchi in London, Isao Matsuzawa in Tokyo, Renato Pisa, and Jeremy Hale. Japan Airlines came up with the all important flights, thanks to Joe Brett in London and Geoffrey Tudor in Tokyo. Several generations of employees of the Japan National Tourist Organisation gave tireless answers to factual queries (and more railcards): in London I'm indebted to Simon Halewood, Patrick Wilson, Louise Hooper and Sian Evans; in Tokyo, to Messrs Tsukamoto and Nishikawa. Mr Hiro Takemura arranged a warm welcome courtesy of the Tōkyū Hotel Chain.

Several journalist friends contributed greatly to this guide, either by furnishing me with information or by paying me to write for them. I thank especially Andrew Marshall and Greg Starr of *Tokyo Journal*, John Ashburne and David Jack of *Kansai Time Out*, and the staff and members of the Foreign Correspondents' Club of Japan. Thanks to Nigel Reynolds, Robert Winder and Tom Shone for commissioning articles about obscure aspects of Japanese culture; to Margot Wilson, Paul Cemmick and the *Funday Times* for keeping alive the Intelligent Cod; and to Vicki Ingle, Rachel Fielding and Helena Gomm, my editors at Cadogan Books, for their inexhaustible patience.

For hospitality in Japan, I salute Kathleen Morris and Jonathan Annells in Tokyo, Rupert Naylor in Okawa, Al Ruxton and St Catherine's College in Kōbe, Mark Coutts-Smith and the Kōdo Drummers in Sado, Andrew Allen in Bitchu-Takahashi, and Lesley Parkinson in Nagoya. For friendship, support and advice, thanks to Jim Bennett, Steve Clemons, Jim Davis, Guy Delauney, Dave Jones, Kaori Kawada, Akane and Mrs Kawakami, Terue Kojima and family, Mike and Henrietta Linsell, John Lyon, Yoshiko Magari, Tom McGeehan, Mark Gill, John Lyon, Nick Midgley, Hiroko Ofuchi, Megumi Omori, Andrew Oros, Rod Pryde, Robert Stern, Teruko Takahashi, Professor and Mrs Ryozo Tanaka and Ayako, Sachiko Tamashige, Take Tanioka and the Shinjuku Intellectuals, Tom La Tourette and Seto Inland Sea Lines, Aleks Weiler, Yuka Kunita, and Barry Webb. Steve Kremer and Dylan Tanner of Intermatrix advised me on the Business Section and much else, Robert Whitehouse and Kodansha International supplied books, and Hotei Tomoyasu and the IRC2 Corporation—especially Senji Kasuya, Ken Sugaya, Lennie Zakatek, and Victoria Hodgson—enabled me to see Japan like a rock star. And here's to Bob Holness, for making it all possible.

Thanks to my family for their love and support, and to my friends, particularly Alex, Julia, and Fiona, for living with this book (or the idea of it) over the years, and with the mood swings which it has from time to time provoked.

My greatest debt of thanks in Japan is to Miyoko Hayakawa and her family, especially Shinjiro, who were like a second family. Without their kindness and hospitality I could never have written this book or visited Japan so often and for so long.

To the great sadness of everyone who knew him, the friend who did most for this guide and its author is not alive to see its publication. This book is affectionately dedicated to the memory of Philip Young, and to his wife and daughter, Kanako and Sarah.

Contents

Maps

It's a peculiarity of conversations about Japan that almost everyone, no matter how scant their knowledge or experience, knows *exactly* what they think about the place.

Japan (you will hear) is a beeping, neon, sci-fi wonderland where high-tech gnomes inhabit soaring skyscrapers and labyrinthine subways, and where even the lavatory seats have control panels. Someone else will entertain images of misty mountains and rice paddies tended by old men in pointy hats. Many older people remember the war, and the tales of

Introduction

samurai fanaticism and cruelty brought back by surviving prisoners of war. Others have tales of shyness, courtesy and almost embarrassing kindness. Each one of these generalizations is true, in its way, but none reflects more than a fraction of the whole picture. Few countries—certainly none as influential as the second richest nation in the world—are so burdened by hearsay and cliché. One of the best reasons for visiting Japan is simply to go see what it's really like.

Even then, it depends—on where and when you go, how you travel, and what you choose to do when you get there. A glance at an atlas confirms the quality that most surprises first-time visitors to Japan—its variety. The northernmost capes have a Siberian climate and, in winter, pack ice clogs the ports of the Sea of Okhotsk. Eighteen hundred miles south are subtropical islets from which, on a fine day, you can see Taiwan. Linking these extremes is an uncountable string of mountainous islands. The upper slopes have volcanoes, hot springs, hiking, deer and bears; the lowland plains contain some of the biggest, densest and most exciting cities in the world.

The culture fostered by this striking geography is no less varied. Among Japan's Buddhist temples are the oldest and biggest wooden structures anywhere; 20th-century architects have created bold and bizarre modern buildings in steel and glass. The corporate offices, department stores and entertainment districts of the big cities are monuments to secular consumerism, but within a few hours' train ride are Shinto shrines and Buddhist monasteries where priceless images of the gods have been worshipped for centuries.

Between these extremes there are a thousand different holidays to be had, and a comprehensive and unfailingly efficient public transport network makes travelling long distances a pleasure. In one well-organized fortnight, it would be possible to begin with skiing in Hokkaidō, followed by hot spring bathing in Tōhoku, *kabuki* theatre in Tokyo, temple architecture in Kyoto, modern history in Hiroshima, and a cruise across the Inland Sea to wind up sunbathing on a volcanically heated beach in Kyūshū.

Japan is not the place for a budget holiday, but neither need it be ruinously expensive, and compared to the bedlam of many East Asian destinations, standards of service and safety are unsurpassed. Some of the best bargains—the homely *izakaya* restaurants, and traditional *ryokan* and *minshuku* inns—are cultural experiences in their own right, and even the most cash-strapped traveller will find accommodation that is always clean and secure, trains which always run on time, and food and refreshment that will never give you a bug. No one who visits Japan will be disappointed, even if they come away less sure what to make of it than when they arrived.

The Best of Japan

Art Collections:	National Museum, Nijō-jō (Kyoto)
	National Museum (Tokyo)
	Tokugawa Art Museum (Nagoya)
	Museum of Oriental Ceramics (Ōsaka)
Sculpture:	Tō-ji, Sanjūsangen-dō, Kōryū-ji, Byōdō-in (Kyoto)
	Hōryu-ji, Kōfuku-ji, Nara National Museum, Tōdai-ji (Nara)
	Daibutsu, National Treasure Hall (Kamakura)
Buddhist temples:	Kiyomizu-dera, Nishi Hongan-ji, Daitoku-ji, Sanjūsangen-dō, Byōdō-in (Kyoto)
	Hōryu-ji, Tōdai-ji, Yakushi-ji, Tōshōdai-ji (Nara)
	Mt Kōya
	Zenkō-ji (Nagano)
Shinto shrines:	Ise
	Izumo
	Inari Taisha (Kyoto)

	Tōshōgū (Nikkō)
	Tsuruoka Hachiman-gū (Kamakura)
	Sacred Mountains of Dewa (Tōhoku)
	Miyajima
	Meiji Jingū (Tokyo)
Castles:	Himeji
	Nijō-jō (Kyoto)
	Matsumoto
	Matsuyama
Islands:	Sado
	Hirado
	Kinka-san
	Rishiri-to and Rebun-to
Cities:	Tokyo
	Kyoto
	Kanazawa
	Hiroshima
	Nagasaki
Samurai Houses:	Chiran
	Nijō Jinya (Kyoto)
	Aizu-Wakamatsu
	Kanazawa
Villas and Palaces:	Katsura Rikyū, Shūgaku-in Rikyū (Kyoto)
	Tokyo Imperial Palace
Towns and Villages:	Okayama International Villas
	Tsumago and Magome in the Kiso Valley
	Takayama
	Kurashiki
Gardens:	Saihō-ji moss garden, Ryōan-ji, Ginkaku-ji, Daisen-in
	(Daitoku-ji), Heian Jingū (Kyoto)
	Ritsurin Kōen (Takamatsu)
	Kenroku-en (Kanazawa)
Hot Springs:	Kamuiwakka waterfall (Hokkaidō)
	Ibusuki
	Ebino Kogen
Volcanoes:	Osore-zan
	Mt Fuji
	Mt Aso
	Shōwa Shin-zan
Festivals:	Kanda (Tokyo, May)
	Kangen-sai (Miyajima, June–July)

	Gion (Kyoto, July)
	Nebuta (Aomori, August)
	Hiroshima Peace Festival (August)
	Okunchi (Nagasaki, October)
Nightlife:	Kabukichō, Roppongi (Tokyo)
	Namba (Ōsaka)
	Susukino (Sapporo)
The Bizarre:	Takarazuka
	Mummies of Dewa San-zan
	Shōwa Shin-zan volcano

Guide to the Guide

The book covers all four of the main Japanese islands from north to south.

Hokkaidō, the most northerly, has a chapter to itself. Honshū, the biggest, most populous and most important island is divided up into five regions and two cities. **Tōhoku** is the remote and craggy 'Deep North'. Then comes **Tokyo**, the capital, with a chapter to itself, and **Kantō**, the region in which it lies. **Chūbū** is the mountainous centre of the island, and west of it is the **Kansai** district, the ancient heartland of which the old capital **Kyoto** has a chapter to itself.

Next is the smallest of the big islands, **Shikoku**, tucked underneath **Chūgoku**, the narrow western arm of Honshū. The last chapter describes **Kyūshū**, the semitropical south island.

Within each chapter, the towns and attractions are described broadly north to south or, in central Japan, east to west.

Travel

By Air

Japan is comprehensively connected by air to most of the major cities of Europe, Asia, Oceania and North America, almost all of which have direct non-stop flights. The days of the 18-hour haul over the North Pole from London to Tokyo, with the obligatory stop at Anchorage Airport, are past; nowadays, with favourable weather, it takes little more than 11 hours.

Remember that if you plan to conduct most of your sightseeing or business in the Kansai area (Ōsaka, Kyoto, Nara), you will save time and money by flying to the new **Kansai International Airport** rather than to Tokyo's inconvenient **Narita**. If Tokyo is your destination, investigate the possibility of flying in by **China Air Lines**, especially if you're coming from Asia. They remain the only carrier still flying into the old (and much handier) Tokyo airport, **Haneda**, a mere taxi or monorail ride from the centre of Tokyo.

From the UK

British Airways, Virgin, Japan Air Lines and All Nippon Airways fly non-stop from Heathrow to Narita and Kansai, and British Airways goes twice a week to Nagoya. The advanced purchase PEX fare (from two weeks to three months; no option to change your flight) is about £1000 off peak, but this is considerably reduced when bought through an agent.

It's cheaper—but more time-consuming—to take an indirect flight. Numerous national carriers will fly you from London to the home capital, and from there to Japan. Among the more respectable carriers are KLM (via Amsterdam), Finnair (via Helsinki), and Scandinavia Air Lines, all quoted at a little more than £600. Cheaper still are Airlanka, and the budget traveller's favourite, recently tarnished by a poor safety record, Aeroflot.

Bucket shops (look in the classified ads of a Sunday newspaper or a magazine like *Time Out*) are cheapest of all: several quote return fares for under £500.

It may be worth investigating a courier flight, where the traveller carries a parcel of documents from airport to airport. Contact British Airways Travel Shop, World Cargo Centre, Export Cargo Terminal, Heathrow Airport, Middlesex TW6 2JS, ✆ (0181) 562 6213. Flights cost about £550 return in high season and £450 low season, and there is a maximum stay of six weeks.

From the US

The following American cities have flights to Tokyo Narita only: Atlanta, Boston, Calgary, Cincinnati, Dallas, Houston, Memphis, Miami, Minneapolis, Nashville, Orlando, Salt Lake City, San Diego, San Jose, Seattle and both the Washingtons.

Chicago, Detroit, Los Angeles, New York and San Francisco connect directly with Narita and Kansai International Airport, Portland with Narita and Nagoya.

From Honolulu you can fly to Narita, Kansai, Fukuoka and Sapporo.

From Canada

From Toronto you can fly to Narita and Kansai; Vancouver connects directly with them too, as well as with Nagoya.

From Europe

The following cities connect directly with Narita only: Athens, Brussels, Geneva, Madrid, Helsinki, Milan, Munich, Rome, Stockholm and Vienna.

From Paris and Frankfurt you can fly to Narita, Kansai and Nagoya. Moscow is connected to Narita and Nagoya.

From Australia and New Zealand

Darwin, Melbourne and Perth connect directly with Narita only; Brisbane and Christchurch with Narita and Kansai; Sydney and Auckland with Narita, Kansai and Nagoya. From Cairns you can fly direct to Narita, Kansai, Nagoya, Fukuoka or Sapporo.

From Asia

Most Asian capitals, apart from obvious political mavericks like Pyongyang in North Korea, have direct flights to Narita and Kansai, and often the regional airports too.

airlines in Japan

British Airways, Sanshin Building, 4–1 Yūrakuchō 1–chome, Chiyoda-ku, Tokyo 100,
   ℃ 03 3593 8811.

Virgin Atlantic Airways, 5–2–1 Minami Aoyama, Minato-ku, Tokyo 160,
   ℃ 03 3499 8835.

Japan Air Lines, Daini Tekko Building, 1–8–2 Marunouchi, Chiyoda-ku, Tokyo 100,
   ℃ 03 5259 3777 (near Tokyo Station).

All Nippon Airways, Yanmar Tokyo Building, 2–1–1 Yaesu, Chūō-ku, Tokyo,
   ℃ 03 3272 1212.

By Sea

A few cruise companies offer fly and sail packages: jet out from Europe or North America and begin your cruise in Asia.

Costa Ocean Cruise Lines presently run two 14-day cruises in the spring and summer: **Classical Japan**, which starts in Seoul and begins at £2295 per person, and **China, Japan and Korea** from £2595. 10 Frederick Close, Stanhope Place, London W2 2HD, *℃* 0171 723 5557.

Orient Lines runs a 22-day **China and Japan** holiday, including a 14-day cruise, from £2950. 38 Park Street, London W1Y 3PF, *℃* 0171 409 7500/2500; or, in the US, 1510 SE 17th Street, Fort Lauderdale, FL 33316, *℃* 305 527 6660.

ferries

Various ferry services connect Japan with mainland Asia and Russia. Among the more useful are: the Vladivostok to Niigata service (one way fares begin at ¥31,400); and the ferry (¥8500) and jetfoil (¥12,400) which connect Fukuoka (Hakata) and Pusan in Korea.

Other possibilities include: Tianjin to Kōbe, Shanghai to Kōbe, Ōsaka or Yokohama, Pusan to Shimonoseki, Kōbe or Ōsaka, and Naha (in Okinawa) to Kaohsiung or Keelung.

By Land

You can't go all the way of course, but from Moscow it's possible to take the Trans-Siberian railway as far as Vladivostok and then take a ferry. Agencies which specialize in the Trans-Siberian include:

In the UK

Intourist Travel, Intourist House, 219 Marsh Wall, London, E14 9FJ, ✆ 0171 538 8600.

In Japan

Japan-Russia Tourist Bureau, Head Office, Kamiyachō Bldg, 3F, 12–12 Toranomon 5-chome, Minato-ku, Tokyo, ✆ 03 3432 6161.

STA Travel, Head Office, 4F Nukariya Bldg, 1–16 Minami Ikebukuro, Toshima-ku, Tokyo, ✆ 03 5391 2889.

Package and Specialist Holidays

Package holidays to Japan are proliferating, and for those with limited time, or anxieties about getting by in a non-English speaking country, they offer convenience and good value. But weigh up the pros and cons. Package tours are still in their relative infancy, and operators tend to turn their customers over to English-speaking Japanese guides who may offer a rather bland interpretation of their own country: unimaginative itineraries, characterless Western-style hotels, and inane non-stop commentary.

Tours offered one year may not always be repeated the next, so you should check details. Among the most interesting are the following:

Nippon Travel Agency, ✆ 0171 437 2424, offers a number of imaginative deals: recent examples have included a Sapporo Snow Festival package, and five nights in Tokyo and Kyoto, including bullet train and coach tours, for just £995. For independent travellers there's a Discover Japan package for £820: it includes a return flight from London to Narita on ANA, a 7-day Japan Rail Pass, and your first night's accommodation in Tokyo, Kyoto or Ōsaka. In the US they can be contacted at Suite 901, 120 W. 45th Street, New York, NY 10036, ✆ 212 944 8660.

The Japan Experience is the only British operator to publish a brochure dedicated to Japan. Packages include the main cities, a national parks tour, southern Japan, and two-country tours which take in Bali, Hong Kong, Singapore or Bangkok. Individual itineraries are also arranged. Kingfisher House, Rownhams Lane, North Baddesley, Hampshire, SO52 9LP, ✆ 01703 730830.

Creative Tours Ltd (run by Japan Air Lines) runs specialist tours. Recent brochures have included a bonsai tour and a cycling tour, visiting out of the way places and staying in simple *minshuku*. 2nd Floor, 1 Tenterden Street, London W1R 9AH, ✆ 0171 495 1775.

British Museum Tours, ℭ 0171 323 8895, organize occasional holidays with a cultural bias.

Club Med, ℭ 0171 581 1161, run 7-day skiing packages in Hokkaidō for £1020 per person, excluding flights.

Other companies offering tours including (or based exclusively in) Japan include:

Airwaves, 10 Bective Place, London SW15 2PZ, ℭ 0181 875 1188.

The Asia Experience, 83 Mortimer Street, London N1 7TB, ℭ 0171 636 4343.

Asia World, 230 Station Road, Addlestone, Surrey KT15 2PH, ℭ 01932 820050.

Finlandia, Regent Street, London W1R 8PD, 0171 409 7334.

Jasmin Tours, High Street, Cookham, Maidenhead, Berkshire SL6 9SQ, ℭ 01628 531121.

Kuoni Travel, Kuoni House, Dorking, Surrey RH5 4AZ, ℭ 01306 740719.

Premier Holidays, Westbrook, Milton Road, Cambridge CB4 1YQ, ℭ 01223 311103.

Silverbird, 4 Northfield Prospect, Putney Bridge Road, London SW18, ℭ 0181 875 9090.

Speedbird Worldwide (British Airways), Pacific House, Hazelwick Avenue, Three Bridges, Sussex RH10 1NP, ℭ 0181 741 3369.

Virgin Holidays, Ground Floor, The Galleria, Station Road, Crawley, West Sussex RH10 1WW, ℭ 01293 617181.

Travel Agents

Two of the biggest Japanese agents are **Nippon Travel Agency** (NTA) and **Japan Travel Bureau** (JTB). They have thousands of branches throughout Japan, with English-speaking staff in the big cities. The foreign branches listed below are all authorized sales outlets for the Japan Rail Pass.

Nippon Travel Agency (known in Japan as *Nihon Ryōko*)

Japan: Foreign Tourist Department, 3rd Floor, Shimbashi Ekimae Building 1, 2–20–15 Shimbashi, Minato-ku, Tokyo 105, ℭ 03 3572 8743, 🖅 03 3572 8766.

UK: Academy House, 161–167 Oxford Street, London W1R 1TA, ℭ 0171 437 2424, 🖅 0171 437 2954.

US: 120 W. 45th Street, New York, NY 10036, ℭ 212 944 8660, 🖅 212 944 8973; 3 Twin Dolphin Drive, Suite 100, Redwood City, CA 94065, ℭ 415 508 2077, 🖅 415 591 7634.

Canada: 1075 W. Georgia Street, Suite 2600, Vancouver, BC V6E 3C9, ℭ 604 662 8002, 🖅 604 688 4767.

Australia: Level 9, 135 King Street, Sydney, 2000 NSW, ℭ 02 221 8433, 🖅 02 223 8907.

Japan Travel Bureau

Japan: International Travel Division, 1–13–1 Nihonbashi, Chūō-ku, Tokyo 103, ✆ 03 3276 7803, ✉ 03 3271 4134.

UK: 3rd Floor, 10 Maltravers Street, London WC2R 3EE, ✆ 0171 836 9367, ✉ 0171 240 8147.

US: 11th Floor, Equitable Tower, 787 7th Avenue, New York, NY 10019, ✆ 212 489 1834, ✉ 212 307 0612; 333 S. Alameda Street, Suite 222, Los Angeles, CA 900013, ✆ 213 617 2222, ✉ 213 620 9633.

Canada: Suite 2300, Four Bentall Centre, PO Box 49317, 1055 Dunsmuir Street, Vancouver, BC V7X 1L3, ✆ 604 688 0166, ✉ 604 669 5849.

Australia: 46th Level, Nauru House, 80 Collins Street, Melbourne, Victoria, 3000, ✆ 03 650 6088, ✉ 03 650 6450.

Entry Formalities

You must have a passport valid for the duration of your stay and you must have a visa. If you're going to earn Japanese currency during your stay you're required to have a working visa. There are various different types and the process of applying for them can be complicated and time-consuming. Consult your nearest Japanese embassy or consulate as far in advance as possible.

Tourists and anyone studying or doing business in the short term (usually less than three months) only need a temporary visitor's visa. Almost everyone can get one of these stamped in their passports as they pass Immigration in Japan.

Citizens of Austria, Germany, Ireland, Liechtenstein, Mexico, Switzerland and the UK will get a 90-day stamp which they can later extend for another three months. To get an extension you'll need to fill out a form, supply photographs, pay a fee, and satisfy the immigration office that you're not illicitly working.

Travellers of many other nationalities, including those from Belgium, Canada, Denmark, Finland, France, Greece, Italy, Luxembourg, the Netherlands, New Zealand, Norway, Portugal, Spain, Sweden and the US, will get a three-month stamp which can't be extended (you must leave the country and then re-enter).

Everyone else must obtain a visa before entering Japan. A temporary visitor's visa usually takes only a few days. Australia is the most notable country to lack a visa exemption agreement. However, Australian, New Zealand and Canadian nationals aged 18 to 25 are eligible for working holiday visas, extendable up to 18 months (the age limits and duration may change from time to time). Contact your local consulate or the **Japan Association for Working Holiday Makers** in Tokyo, ✆ 03 3389 0181.

By Air

All Japan's significant cities have airports, well served by several domestic carriers. The fares are close to those of the *shinkansen* (bullet train), so if you need to get round fast and haven't got a railcard, it's almost as cheap to fly as to go by bullet train. This is especially true when travelling outside Honshū. Note, however, that on short to medium length journeys the time taken up by travelling out to the airport, and travelling back into town at the other end, may tip the balance back in the *shinkansen*'s favour.

By Sea

Ferry services connect all the inhabited islands of Japan. For comprehensive information, ask at a tourist information centre. A second-class berth is roughly two-thirds the price of the *shinkansen*. Among the most useful long-distance services are the following:

Tokyo to Tomakomai (Hokkaidō): 30 hours ¥11,840

Tokyo to Kōchi (Shikoku): 21 hours ¥13,910

Tokyo to Kokura (Kyūshū): 36 hours ¥12,000

Services between the smaller islands, and the ferries between Honshū, Shikoku and Kyūshū across the Inland Sea are described under the appropriate region.

By Train

The quickest, most comfortable and most convenient means of getting from one place to another will usually be the train. Since 1872 when British engineers laid the 27km stretch between Tokyo and Yokohama, 26,500km of track have been constructed, from Wakkanai in northern Hokkaidō to Yamagawa in southern Kyūshū. Of these, 13,000km belong to Japan Railways, the former nationalized corporation, privatized in 1987 into seven regional networks. The rest are operated by 14 smaller private companies, like Kintetsu and Odakyū, who tend to operate in busy commuter and resort areas; their trains are often cheaper and faster than the loss-making JR which dutifully serves the unprofitable, outlying regions.

You could spend weeks travelling in Japan, using nothing but the trains. They are unfailingly clean, spacious, punctual and safe and, in the shape of the Japan Rail Pass, they represent one of Japan's few authentic travel bargains.

timetables

JNTO publishes an abridged railway timetable in English, adequate for most purposes: it includes JR *shinkansen* and limited express times, a few of the major private lines, along with fare and mileage tables. If you need more up-to-date detail, look out for the bilingual *JTB Speed Jikokuhyō* (¥330), sold in big stations, bookshops and travel agencies.

Any tourist information centre, or JNTO's Japan Travel Phone, will supply you with fare and timetable information. JR East runs an English information service, **JR East Infoline**, ✆ 03 3423 0111.

Even in out of the way places, all station employees can be coaxed into a few words of English. The facts you need to convey are: where you are travelling from and to, and what kind of train you wish to travel on. If you are making a seat reservation, state the date and time of your journey and whether you want a smoking or non-smoking compartment. If simple spoken English fails, then write the details out in capitals on a piece of paper. Ideally, have someone write your ticket request out in Japanese.

Most tickets are sold through automatic dispensing machines. Insert coins, notes or a pre-paid card, press the button corresponding to your destination, and tickets and change are dispensed automatically. Diagrams of the network, indicating the fare to each station, are generally displayed above the ticket machines; however, these seldom include much English. Ask station staff or passers-by for help.

Travel agents like NTA and JTB sell tickets for express trains, and big stations have travel centres where you can also pay by credit card. Otherwise expect to pay in cash. Unused tickets which are still valid can be refunded, minus a handling charge.

Guriin-sha (Green Cars) are first-class coaches, correspondingly more expensive: more leg room, comfier seats and a better class of punter. Second class is *futsu-sha* (Ordinary Car).

Certain trains become very crowded on weekends and holidays, even the *shinkansen*. Sitting on your luggage for hours at a time is no fun so, if in doubt, make a reservation (*yoyaku*) which only adds a few hundred yen to the fare. Useful vocabulary: reserved seat is *shiteiseki* (pronounced 'shtay-secky'); unreserved seat, *jiyūseki* ('gee-you-secky'); non-smoking car, *kin-en-sha*.

types of train

Trains of different speeds often depart from the same platform; you can waste time by getting on the wrong one, so be prepared to ask station staff and fellow passengers.

Futsu is a local train, stopping at every station. **Kaisoku**, usually translated as rapid train, is a bit faster, stopping at fewer stations. These are aimed at commuters and rarely have reserved carriages. **Kyūkō** is an express, **tokkyū** is the faster limited express. The quicker the train, the more expensive and comfortable the journey.

The famous bullet train (no one in Japan calls it that; get used to saying **shinkansen**, 'new trunk line') is no longer the fastest super express in the world, but it's certainly the oldest, the most famous and the most comprehensive. The Tōkaidō line between Tokyo and Ōsaka opened for the Tokyo Olympics in 1964. Since then the network has been extended to Fukuoka in the southwest, Niigata in the north, and Yamagata and Morioka in the northeast. The *shinkansen* is one of the reasons why Japan sometimes seems a small country. On the fastest *nozomi* service, the 1700km journey from Kyūshū to northern Tōhoku takes about nine hours.

In 30 years of high-speed travel there hasn't been a single fatality. The trains run so smoothly in fact that, once the novelty of moving at 170km/h has worn off, it can actually be rather a dull experience, with more of the blandness of the international flight than the romance of the railway. Bowing hostesses dispense snacks and drinks, chimes and taped voices politely announce each station as it approaches. Stations and scenery belt by, but so silently and frictionlessly that they could almost be on video: aficionados of smoke and grime and clanking points will be disappointed. But for ease, speed and security it's unmatched: everyone, especially holders of the Japan Rail Pass, should use the *shinkansen* as much as possible.

If you haven't got a pass, it's expensive, almost as much as a domestic flight. Fares are based on the standard price, with a fat surcharge on top of that—there's a price list in the JNTO railway timetable. Not all *shinkansen* stop at every station: check with the conductor that you're getting on the right one. On the Tōkaidō line, the *kodama* is the slowest, followed by the *hikari*. The *nozomi*, which began in 1993, is the fastest and most expensive of all: all seats are reserved, and the Japan Rail Pass can't be used.

If you're getting on at the first station, the chances are that you'll find an unreserved seat. Otherwise, reservations cost ¥500, free to rail pass holders.

Japan Rail Pass

This is essential for almost anyone planning to travel extensively around Japan. It allows unlimited travel on most JR services, including ferries and buses, for a fixed period of time.

	Ordinary	Green
7 days	¥27,800	¥37,000
14 days	¥44,200	¥60,000
21 days	¥56,600	¥78,000

Children aged 6 to 11 pay half the adult price.

At first glance this may not look cheap at all, and a little arithmetic may be necessary to work out whether the pass will save you money. On local and ordinary express trains you would have to travel a very long way in a short time to make it worthwhile. In general, visitors staying in a single region or city of Japan will be better off buying individual tickets—in areas like Kansai, for instance, the non-JR lines (on which you can't use the pass) are quick and cheap. The pass comes into its own, however, on the *shinkansen*. A return from Tokyo to Kyoto, with reservations, costs ¥25,940—only ¥1860 less than a rail pass for the whole week. A return to Hiroshima is ¥35,400, to Hakata in Kyūshū ¥42,600. Add to these the cost of ordinary trains, the convenience of not having to buy tickets in advance (and being able to break your journey at any point), and the advantages become clear. Rail pass holders can also make reservations for nothing, although you must do this in person and in advance.

The Japan Rail Pass can only be obtained outside Japan. Buy one *before* you go. You can do this only at authorized agencies, like Nippon Travel Agency and Japan Travel Bureau (your nearest branch of JNTO will have a list). Pay in your own currency; in return you receive an exchange order which is valid for three months from the date of issue. This is exchanged for the pass itself at any JR Travel Service Centre. These are found only in the following stations:

In Tokyo: Narita Airport, Ueno, Ikebukuro, Shinjuku, Shibuya and Tokyo Station.

Outside Tokyo: Sapporo, Sendai, Misawa, Yamagata, Fukushima, Tsukuba, Niigata, Yokohama, Nagoya, Kyoto, Ōsaka, Shin-Ōsaka, Sannomiya, Hiroshima, Shimonoseki, Kokura, Hakata, Kumamoto, and Nishi-Kagoshima.

You must state the day you want the pass to begin, and show your passport. The rail pass is available *only* to those with temporary visitor visas.

other discount passes and tickets

Various discount tickets for different regions of Japan can be bought inside the country, such as *shūyū-ken* (excursion tickets) and *furii kippu* (free tickets). For a short period of travel within a fixed area, these are far more suitable than the Japan Rail Pass. Call the JR East Infoline, ✆ 03 3423 0111, or consult a local tourist information centre.

The *sei-shun ju-hachi kippu* (Youth 18 Ticket) is probably the cheapest way of getting round Japan, but very, very slow. They're designed for vacationing students and other impecunious types, and can only be used during the following periods: 20 Feb–10 April, 20 July–10 Sept, 10 Dec–20 Jan.

The tickets are sold in booklets of five; each booklet costs ¥11,300, and they can be split up and used by different people (tickets are often sold individually on student campuses).

On the day of travel, the date is marked on the ticket. For the rest of the day, until midnight, you can travel anywhere in Japan—but only on local (*futsu*) or rapid (*kaisoku*) trains. Thus, if you started early enough, it would theoretically be possible to travel from Tokyo to Hiroshima for ¥2260—but you would have to stop at virtually every station in between. Journeys can be broken at any time; the tickets are also valid for the ferry between Miyajima and Miyajima-guchi. Unused tickets can be refunded, minus a ¥210 handling charge.

By Bus

City buses take a little getting used to: timetables, destination panels and on-board announcements are almost never in English, and drivers speak only Japanese. Where relevant, specific bus routes are mentioned in the text; otherwise, seek local guidance from the nearest tourist information centre.

Inter-city buses are economical. They often depart at night, so you save not only on the fare (generally a third cheaper than the *shinkansen*), but also one night's accommodation. A few examples, all one-way fares from Tokyo:

Nagoya	6½ hrs	¥6300
Kyoto	8 hrs	¥8030
Ōsaka	8 hrs	¥8450
Kōbe	8½ hrs	¥8530
Nara	9½ hrs	¥8240

There are many different bus companies; again, ask a tourist information centre for details.

With such a choice of superlative trains, few short-term visitors to Japan will ever need to drive. In the cities, and on the urbanized Pacific coast of southern Honshū, you'd be mad to try: it's confusing, expensive and glacially slow. There are several rural areas, though, where sparse or slow public transport make driving the most convenient option, particularly for groups. Shikoku, the Japan Sea coast of western Honshū, southern Kyūshū, northern Tōhoku, and isolated escapes like Sado Island and the Noto Peninsula are all good driving territory. Best of all is Hokkaidō: fast, well-maintained, traffic-free roads, and beautiful countryside.

Outside the urban tangle, driving is fairly straightforward. Japanese motorists are generally cautious and polite, signposts on main roads are widely labelled in the Roman alphabet (*romaji*), and petrol costs about the same as in Europe.

The Japanese, like the British and Australians, drive on the left. Standard international rules of the road and signposting conventions apply. To drive in Japan you must have an International Driving Permit *and* your own national driving licence, but this arrangement only holds for six months—after that you must apply for a Japanese licence. Ask your national automobile asociation whether they have a reciprocal arrangement with an equivalent Japanese body—the chances are they'll be affiliated with the **Japan Automobile Federation** which issues an English-language booklet called *Rules of the Road* for ¥1860. It also has an English-language information line, ✆ 03 3436 2454. Various English road atlases are available in book shops: try to get a bilingual one so that you have a chance of recognizing the *kanji* characters even when the signposts are not Romanized.

Most roads have a **speed limit** of 50 km/h, although whether the traffic will permit you to go that fast is another matter. Expressways, which traverse all of the main islands, have a legal limit of 80 km/h. These are toll roads, and the tolls mount up: to drive from Tokyo to Ōsaka costs ¥10,000—not much less than a single ticket on the *shinkansen.*

The **police** are a discreet presence on the roads. Speed traps are mounted from time to time—the only sure way to avoid them is not to break the limit. If you're stopped for a minor offence, then profuse apologies and an inability to speak Japanese will often forestall anything stronger than a ticking off. Remember that, as well as your driving documents, you must carry your passport with you at all times.

car hire

For regional excursions, the most sensible thing is to take a train to the nearest town and hire a car there. There are rental companies all over Japan. Start looking in the station itself: 250 JR stations have their own **Eki Rent-a-car** offices. The going rate for a 1500cc car is between ¥12,000 and ¥15,000, plus ¥1000 insurance, for 24 hours. For English-speaking rental offices in Tokyo *see* p.185.

By Bicycle

This is a very pleasant and popular way of exploring both the countryside and the smaller cities. In bicycle-friendly towns, hire shops can usually be found near the railway station.

Youth hostels often rent out their own. These bikes are basic, usually gearless, and rather small, but adequate for a few hours of sightseeing. In towns, incidentally, it is perfectly acceptable to cycle on the pavement when the road is dangerous or unsuitable—even the police do it.

The small size of Japanese frames is more of a problem when you're planning to cycle long distances or over steep country. Multi-gear touring and mountain bikes in large sizes are hard to get hold of in Japan. If possible, bring your own: most airlines will carry them for you if you remove the pedals. The cheap and comprehensive delivery services (*see* 'Practical A–Z', p.38) make it very easy to send your bike around Japan. Bikes are allowed on trains for a few hundred yen, but must be transported in carrying cases—invest in one of these. Get hold of a bilingual road atlas, too, and plan your routes in advance. The secret of happy cycling is to keep clear of the main routes, with their snarl-ups and tunnels: even if the traffic doesn't bring you to a stop, the gathering fumes are very unpleasant.

Repair and maintenance shops can be found all over the country, although spare parts for unfamiliar models (like mountain bikes) may be hard to get hold of outside the cities: bring a spare tyre if your wheels are large.

Despite Japan's enviably low crime rate, bike theft is common: carry a good padlock and use it. Foreigners on bikes also seem unusually likely to attract the attention of the police, especially in cities. Cyclists should be doubly careful to carry their passports with them at all times, and some kind of proof that the bike isn't stolen.

The **Bridgestone Cycle Co Ltd** sells big frames and has an English-speaking overseas department in Tokyo, ✆ 03 3274 3411.

Hitch-hiking

Japanese people almost never hitch-hike, but for foreigners it's a nice way of travelling for nothing, and meeting the natives. Hitchers tend to fall victim to heartbreaking acts of kindness: stories abound of travellers being entertained and put up for the night by their lifts, or disembarking to find gifts of money tucked into little envelopes in their luggage. You'll feel less sheepish about this if you carry round a stock of token gifts—sweets, cigarettes, postcards from home.

Lifts aren't hard to come by, but you'll increase your chances by looking respectable and cheerful, and by holding out a card bearing the name of your destination in Japanese or, failing that, clear Roman capitals. Wave and smile rather than sticking out a thumb.

Japan is a safe country, but it is never advisable for a woman to hitch-hike on her own.

Practical A–Z

Addresses and Directions

With the exception of major thoroughfares, and a handful of cities built on a grid, like Kyoto and Sapporo, streets in Japan do not have names, and houses and buildings do not have individual or consecutive numbers. Postal addresses identify two-dimensional plots of land, like British post codes; with one of these, and a detailed map, you can narrow your search down to an area of a few hundred metres. But, unless you know the location of every individual building and household, you could spend hours plodding fruitlessly round the neighbourhood checking each name-plate and building name.

Everyone gets flummoxed once in a while by this Byzantine system, not just foreigners, and coping with it has become a way of life. Try to phone ahead for clear directions in Japanese as well as English, so you can show them to passers-by if you get lost (if necessary, have your hotel phone and do this on your behalf). Many establishments have a printed map of how to reach them, which they will post or fax. Often this will be found on the back of their business card: if you might want to find a place again, pick up one of these before you leave.

Get into the habit of noticing landmarks (police boxes, convenience stores, unusual buildings) as you walk around: these will enable you to retrace your steps on a return visit. Stop passers-by or ask in police boxes, local shops or hotels. Pronounce your destination clearly, write it down (point to the Japanese words in this book if necessary, and remember that everyone can read the Roman alphabet).

Don't be embarrassed to keep phoning until you have reached your destination. Call before you leave, call from the station, and call again if you are still lost. This will not raise eyebrows. Even the smallest restaurant or inn will often send someone out to meet you.

Allow time for getting lost.

Baths and Hot Springs

From Shinto ceremonies to the white gloves worn by subway drivers and shop assistants, rituals of purification and symbolic cleansing pervade Japanese society. Not surprisingly, 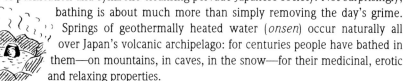 bathing is about much more than simply removing the day's grime. Springs of geothermally heated water (*onsen*) occur naturally all over Japan's volcanic archipelago: for centuries people have bathed in them—on mountains, in caves, in the snow—for their medicinal, erotic and relaxing properties.

The biggest difference between the Western and Japanese idea of a bath is that, in the latter, you don't do any washing at all. Soaping, scrubbing and rinsing of limbs and hair is performed outside the bath. Only when you are thoroughly clean do you enter the water to soak and relax and, as a result, the water is fit to be used by several people.

Baths, bathrooms and bath houses come in all shapes and sizes, but the standard arrangement consists of an outer room where you undress completely, leaving clothes and possessions in a basket or locker. Beyond here is the bath room itself (toilets are almost always housed separately), consisting of the tub, and a tiled and sluiced washing area.

There will be shower taps on the wall, low set mirrors and low stools on which you sit to douse yourself with water, and wash with soap, before rinsing off thoroughly. Buckets can be used to scoop up water from the tub to pour over yourself. You must be squeaky clean, and suds free, before moving onto the next stage.

The worst thing you can do is to get into the bath still dirty or soapy—in bath tubs made of cypress (the most expensive and desirable kind) the soap can stain and mar the wood. Individual tubs are deep, and you immerse yourself up to your neck. The temperature is often high, but don't cool it unless you are the last person in the tub. Soak for as long as you like, or until someone knocks on the door. In public baths (*sentō* and *onsen*), patrons often lounge around for hours, dipping in and out of baths of different temperatures and mineral contents, gossiping, preening and dozing.

It's common to make use of a little hand-towel for scrubbing and scouring. In public facilities, bathers who are uncomfortable about nudity can hold or dangle this above their private parts. These towels should never be taken into the bath itself, although bathers often sit with them folded on their heads, which is said to allay the wooziness induced by the high temperature. It can be very hot indeed, and feels wonderful afterwards. Move as little as possible once you are in, and you will feel the heat less.

Books and Media

Since the 'rediscovery' of Japan in the 19th century, libraries of **books** have been written on almost every aspect of Japanese culture, although high street book shops usually have only a small selection. Try the following specialists:

In the UK:

Japan Centre, 221 Piccadilly, London W1V 9LD, ✆ 0171 439 8035.

Fine Books Oriental, 46 Great Russell Street, London WC1B 3PA, ✆ 0171 636 6068.

In the US:

Kinokuniya, 10 West 49th Street, New York, NY 10020, ✆ 212 765 1461.

Paragon Book Gallery, 2nd Floor, 237 West 72nd Street, New York, NY 10023, ✆ 212 496 2378.

Zen Oriental Book Store, 521 5th Avenue, New York, NY 10017, ✆ 212 697 0840.

Kinokuniya, Japan Center, San Francisco, CA 94115, ✆ 415 567 7625.

Kinokuniya, ✆ 213 687 4480, New Ōtani Store, 110 S. Los Angeles Street, Los Angeles, CA 90012.

In Japan most big book shops stock at least a shelf of English-language books, although these may consist largely of dictionaries and abridgements of classics for Japanese students. The nationwide chains Maruzen and Kinokuniya are big importers of books with whole floors of foreign titles in their major stores, but their mark-ups are enormous: for everyday holiday reading, bring your own. Languages other than English are poorly represented.

In Tokyo, the Kanda-Jimbochō area is famous for its second-hand book shops, some of which specialize in foreign material.

The Japanese are voracious devourers of **newspapers** (*shimbun*), and the national dailies have the highest circulations of any in the world. Several of them also publish English-language editions, a digest of translated reports, syndicated news, and writing by foreign residents. Look out for the *Mainichi Daily News*, the *Daily Yomiuri*, the *Asahi Evening News* and, biggest and oldest of them all, the independent *Japan Times*. Like their parent organs, they tend towards the bland and colourless, although the *Mainichi* and the *Yomiuri* have some lively columnists. The *Nikkei Weekly* is a digest of translated financial news from the respected *Nikkei Shimbun*. The *International Herald Tribune, Asian Wall Street Journal* and *Financial Times* also publish in Japan, and can be found in Tokyo and Ōsaka, and in big book shops. In the big cities you might track down airmail copies of imported papers, at a big mark-up.

Time and *Newsweek* are the most widely available English language **magazines**. Of the many domestic publications produced by foreigners *Tokyo Journal* and *Kansai Time Out* are the liveliest and best, with features, comment and useful listings of events for their respective regions.

NHK **television** has a nightly bilingual news, available on special sets in some hotels; certain international films can also be listened to in their original undubbed version—consult the English language press for details of these. The bigger hotels often carry CNN.

Bilingual (part-Japanese, part-English) commentary is fashionable on FM **radio** stations, like Tokyo's J-Wave. The only exclusively English channel is the American military's moronic Far Eastern Network (FEN).

Budgeting

Fear of the expense, more than anything else, puts people off visiting Japan.

It's never going to be a bargain place to go on holiday. It's geographically remote, for a start, so getting there is costly. The soaring strength of the yen over the past ten years has slashed the buying power of foreign currencies. Principally because of the cost of permanent accommodation, Tokyo and Ōsaka consistently come out as number one and number two on a businessperson's index of the most expensive cities in the world. By the standards of the rest of southeast Asia, Japan is exorbitant: you could live for several days in India or Thailand for the cost of a half-hour taxi ride in Tokyo.

But this is the wrong standard to apply. Japan is the second richest country in the world, and it offers comforts and standards undreamed of in developing nations. Top hotels in Tokyo are no more expensive than their counterparts in London or New York, and, in terms of quality for cost, day-to-day eating is cheaper than in many European cities. Scandinavia and Switzerland are expensive countries, too, but travellers happily visit them. Japan does not deserve its unique reputation as a financial black hole. You will never save money by coming here; but there is no reason why, with a little cunning and forethought, you should haemorrhage it either.

Japan's problem is that it lacks obvious bargains to offset the stories of staggering excess that everyone's heard about (£100 melons, £6 cups of coffee, etc.). Things are either a regular price, or they are expensive. Here are a few suggestions for saving yen.

travel

If you are not tied to a particular departure date, look into courier tickets (*see* p.2).

Japan has one authentic bargain: the Japan Rail Pass. If you're going to do any substantial travelling then you must buy one—*before* you leave your own country.

If you don't have a pass, or on private lines where it cannot be used, be aware of the difference between various classes of train. For every express which gets you there in no time and costs a fortune, there will probably be a number of slower, cheaper services, from the *tokkyū* (limited express) down to the self-explanatory *kaku eki teisha* (every station stopping train).

On long inter-city journeys, travellers without rail passes should investigate the possibilities of overnight buses. Not only are these cheaper than the equivalent *shinkansen* fare, but they save you a night's accommodation.

If you plan to do a lot of travelling in a limited geographical area, ask JNTO about regional excursion tickets. The **Sei-shun Ju-hachi Kippu** is a very cheap but slow way of covering long distances (*see* 'Getting Around', p.10).

food and drink

Think twice about patronizing anywhere that immediately looks Japanese. Moss gardens, stone lanterns, waitresses in kimono, acres of *tatami* and private rooms with sliding screens are nice once in a while, but they come at a premium. Equally good, but unostentatiously presented food can be had at a lower price. The same goes for accommodation.

Certain everyday foods and drinks are especially expensive. Japanese sandwiches are always a big disappointment: tasteless cubes of cotton wool bread with soggy and inappropriate fillings. For a snack buy rice balls (*onigiri*) instead. Coffee in coffee shops is notorious: seldom less than ¥400 a cup and sometimes ¥1000 or more, with no free refills. Again, it's the atmosphere and the chance to sit down and relax which you are paying for. If you must have a regular caffeine fix, consider the following: cheap chain coffee shops, like Doutor, which charge as little as ¥180 a cup; hot can coffee from vending machines for ¥110 (it's always milky and sickly sweet); buying a jar of instant from a convenience store and making it in your room (all lodgings provide their guests with a thermos jug of hot water).

Go for lunchtime set menus (*teishoku*) which include a bowl of rice, salad, soup and a delicacy like *tempura* or *katsu* (cutlets). Treat lunch as the main meal of the day, and make do with a snack of noodles in the evening.

Take advantage of the inclusive dinner and breakfast offered by *ryokan* and *minshuku*.

The following is based on an actual budget for one person in Hiroshima—a very full day, with a lot of walking, and no extras like souvenirs. Costs of meals and accommodation include 3% consumption tax. This probably represents a realistic minimum for an active day of travelling. If you stayed in a good Western-style hotel and went by taxi instead of tram and foot, the total would be double.

Breakfast (included in last night's accommodation)	Free
Shinkansen (Kyoto–Hiroshima with JR Pass, normally ¥10,590)	Free
Tram (from the station to Peace Park)	¥200
Peace Memorial Museum (admission)	¥50
Lunch (tempura set)	¥1130
Castle (admission)	¥300
Drink (canned)	¥110
Museum of Contemporary Art (admission)	¥300
Minshuku (including tomorrow's breakfast)	¥4840
Dinner (ramen noodles)	¥650
Beer (one can)	¥450
Total	**¥8030**

Climate and When to Go

Japan's climate is broadly temperate, but, because the country is so long and thin, conditions at any one time vary enormously between Siberian Hokkaidō and sub-tropical Kyūshū and Okinawa. The four seasons, and the melancholy feelings associated with their passing, have been a theme of art and literature from the earliest times. Japanese people are very proud of them: you may even be told that Japan is the only country in the world that has four distinct seasons. Actually, it has five.

Winter is cold, but dry. In Hokkaidō, the mountains of Tōhoku, and the Japan Alps, there is heavy snow, but Tokyo and points south seldom freeze.

Spring is mild, and often rainy. In March the first cherry blossoms appear in Okinawa and southern Kyūshū, and pass in a wave across the country, reaching Kansai and Tokyo in April, the final flowers falling from the trees of northern Hokkaidō in May.

Summer months are the most difficult and enervating in Japan. The **rainy season** afflicts the whole country south of Tokyo: a wet blanket of warm rain and humidity from mid-June to mid-July (Hokkaidō and Tōhoku are largely exempt). Summer itself is hot and humid: mean August temperatures are around 18–27° but can go much higher. Kansai (Ōsaka and Kyoto) is slightly hotter than Tokyo. In late August and September typhoons bring more rain, and a handful of fatalities; for tourists, the greatest risk is that flights will be disrupted and vulnerable railway lines closed.

Autumn is the loveliest time of the year, and the best time to visit, especially in October and November, with clear mild days and cool nights, and stunning red autumn foliage on mountainsides and in parks and temples.

Apart from nasty weather, the most important thing to avoid when timing a visit is **public holidays** (*see* p.35) when offices close, and hotels, roads, airports and public transport become clogged with Japanese holidaymakers. At New Year in particular, the whole country shuts up shop and goes home.

Crime and Emergencies

Compared to other first world economic superpowers, crime rates are enviably low, but it would be wrong to describe Japan as crime-free. Take all the usual precautions: don't flash quantities of cash around; keep an eye on your belongings, especially in a crowd; keep purses and wallets in inside pockets.

Every neighbourhood has a *kōban*, a police box manned 24 hours, often indicated by a red lamp outside. **The national police emergency number is ☎ 110. For ambulances, or in case of fire, ☎ 119.**

With close to zero crime, the job of the neighbourhood policeman (*o-mawari-san*, literally 'Honourable Mr Walkabout') is not arduous. Never hesitate to ask for directions or assistance, but don't expect much English.

It is still an offence for a non-Japanese to venture out in public without a passport or (for longer term residents) alien registration card. Technically, you can be arrested for this, without the option of returning to your hotel to retrieve the necessary document. *Gaijin* are very unlikely to be stopped without good reason, although foreigners in cars or on bicycles are said to be particularly at risk—bike theft being one of the few growth areas of Japanese crime. Don't be caught out.

If you do ever find yourself on the wrong side of the law, the best strategy is to adopt an expression of crestfallen stupidity and apologise profusely. Charging a non-Japanese-speaking foreigner with a minor offence is a headache every policeman can do without.

Drugs

Possession of even small amounts of soft drugs is viewed harshly in Japan, as Paul McCartney found to his cost. At best, you will be deported and barred from re-entry; at worst, you will spend a long time in one of Japan's notoriously inhumane and disciplinarian jails. There are one or two spots in Tokyo where young foreigners might be offered illegal substances, almost always by other *gaijin*. The risks, as well as the prices, are high.

Earthquakes

Early in the morning of 17 January 1995 a huge earthquake, 7.2 on the Richter scale, struck the northern tip of Awaji island in the Inland Sea, and devastated the nearby city of Kōbe. It was the most powerful tremor to hit a heavily built-up Japanese city since 1923. In the days after the quake, television pictures and photographs of the stricken city were circulated all over the world. They seemed to show total devastation. Whole neighbourhoods burned; landfill islands were inundated and shaken to a sodden jelly; entire buildings toppled face down into the street; a lengthy section of the Hanshin overhead expressway fell sideways on its supports, which had snapped at their bases like concrete mushrooms. For a week the death toll steadily rose, as more and more bodies were extracted from the rubble. By the end of the rescue operation 5000 were confirmed dead, with many more injured and more than 50,000 buildings destroyed. Commentators made much of the apparent failure of Japanese earthquake precautions. How, they asked, could the world's most advanced technological society be so unprepared for the inevitable?

In fact, Japan was, and is, about as well prepared as it could possibly be. The aftermath of the disaster, with government relief agencies hesitating and fretting and failing to talk to one another, was an embarrassing shambles. But the 20 seconds of the quake itself showed how far construction technology has come in 70 years. It is impossible to know exactly how much worse the damage could have been, but strict building regulations introduced in the early 1980s undoubtedly saved many, many lives. When the initial period of shock and mourning had passed, plenty of people in Japan were able to find much reassurance in the Kōbe catastrophe, strange though that may sound.

Earthquakes have always been a part of daily life in Japan. The islands owe their existence to the interlocking tectonic plates which centuries ago thrust up the spiny archipelago of volcanic mountains from the bed of the ocean. Four of these plates join one another in the sea close to the centre of the main island of Honshū. As they press into one another, massive pressure builds up. When the contending plates shift or slip over one another, the pressure is released in the form of earth tremors.

There are thousands of these every week, most of them so weak as to be undetectable except on the most sensitive seismic instruments. Every few weeks come tremors which are strong enough to be felt, but which cause little or no damage. But every now and then, a large shift occurs. The damage caused depends on the depth of the tremor, the kind of rock in which it occurs, and its proximity to human habitation. At worst, a strong tremor causes landslides, tidal waves (*tsunami*), liquefaction of soft soil and coastal land, and shaking sufficient to destroy buildings and elevated roads, fracture gas mains and chemical storage tanks, and bring down live electric cables.

Although the theory of earthquakes is well understood, predicting them early enough to save lives is almost impossible. Some earthquakes seem to occur at regular intervals—since the 17th century, Tokyo, for instance, has been struck by devastating earthquakes at what seem to be 70-year intervals. The last one was in 1923, so the next 'Big One' would appear to be due any day. It's actually not that simple: the picture is immensely complicated by different types of quake, on different, overlapping cycles, which have at various times coincided and even triggered one another. The nature, scale and even existence of an imminent 'Big One' is hotly debated. But earthquakes in general remain a constant and unpredictable hazard.

What is known beyond doubt is that certain kinds of building stand up better to tremors than others, a fact that has profoundly influenced native architecture. Traditional Japanese buildings are wooden—plainly, stone or brick buildings would be suicidal. Timber, by contrast, yields to the strain of earth tremors, is cheaper to reconstruct and is far less deadly when it falls. The difficulty comes in cities, where large numbers of wooden houses are built side by side. In all the worst Japanese earthquakes, it has been fire, ripping through the tinder-wood of collapsed buildings, that has claimed more lives than any other single cause. In Kōbe, it was the older, poorer wooden neighbourhoods where the worst devastation occurred and where the great number of lives were lost.

Modern engineers have devised ever more cunning ways of compensating for the shaking of the earth, and all new construction above a certain height is required to incorporate earthquake defence measures. High-rises can be built with heavy weights attached to moving belts on their exteriors: when a shock is detected, they move automatically up or down the building, counter-balancing and neutralizing the shocks. Buildings are mounted on cushioning mattresses of springs, with skeletons of flexible girders which move with the building, absorbing and dissipating the stresses on it. During storms, the upper stories of such skyscrapers sway gently in the wind, a disconcerting effect for which one might be very grateful if the worst came to the worst.

In Kōbe, the new techniques and building codes underwent their first non-laboratory test and, by and large, they achieved what they were intended to achieve. The worst damage, as everyone had expected, was in old wooden neighbourhoods. Modern structures built more than 15 years ago, under the old building codes, suffered heavy, but lesser damage; most stayed up. The photographers and TV crews reporting on the disaster ignored the newest blocks: many of these suffered no significant damage whatsoever.

The life-saving effects of these measures are reflected in the death tolls of successive Japanese tremors. The 1923 Tokyo earthquake killed 143,000 out of a population of two million. A 1948 tremor killed 3900 in Fukui, a small city on the Japan Sea coast. In Kōbe, 5000 died, but out of a population of 1.5 million, in one of the most densely populated areas in the world. The most darkly apocalyptic projections of Tokyo's next Big One predict 60,000 dead—out of an affected population of 12 million.

It may seem a perverse conclusion to draw, but in modern Japan, in the most powerful kind of earthquake, victims have at least a 99.5% chance of surviving. In that, there is much cause for comfort.

Earthquake Safety

In seismically active zones like Tokyo, small earthquakes rattle the windows every few weeks. Almost all pass after a few seconds. If an earthquake appears to be serious, observe the following drill:

⚠ Turn off all gas taps and extinguish naked flames.

⚠ Take shelter in a safe spot. Best of all is in a ground floor doorway where you run the least chance of either becoming trapped or being struck by falling objects in the street outside. Next best is under a table. Keep clear of heavy pieces of furniture like bookshelves which could topple over and cause injury.

⚠ Evacuate as soon as it is safe to the designated spot, usually an open space like a park or playing field. In serious earthquakes, the majority of fatalities are caused not by the shaking itself but by the fires which follow.

⚠ If you are in a car, stop it immediately, trying if at all possible not to block the centre of the road. Switch off the engine, get out and take shelter.

⚠ If you are by the sea or on low-lying coastal land, evacuate to high ground to avoid the tsunami or seismic tidal wave which often follows a marine earthquake.

⚠ If you're planning to spend some time in Japan, be aware of dangers inherent in certain buildings. Wooden structures are the most vulnerable, especially those with heavy tile roofs (which could collapse and crush the occupants) in wooden neighbourhoods (unfortunately these include the most interesting parts of many Japanese towns). Concrete buildings over 15 years old may look solid, but are often less structurally sound than those built since 1980.

⚠ Wherever you are, make sure you know the route to be taken in an emergency (inns and hotels display maps indicating these) and have access to a torch (again these are obligatory in hotels).

Electricity

The standard current is 100 volts AC. Eastern Japan (including Tokyo) operates on 50 cycles, western Japan (including Nagoya) is 60 cycles. Plugs consist of two flat parallel prongs, identical to those in the US and Canada, and most American devices designed for 117 volts will work well enough. British 240 volt devices, however, require a transformer. Adapters, transformers and conversion plugs for most foreign gizmos can be found in the Akihabara area of Tokyo.

Embassies and Consulates

Australia: 2–1–14 Mita, Minato-ku, Tokyo 108, ✆ 03 5232 4111.

Canada: 7–3–38 Akasaka, Minato-ku, Tokyo 107, ✆ 03 3408 2101.

China: 3–4–33 Moto-Azabu, Minato-ku, Tokyo 106, ✆ 03 3403 3380.

France: 4–11–44 Minami-Azabu, Minato-ku, Tokyo 106, ✆ 03 3473 0171/9.

Germany: 4–5–10 Minami-Azabu, Minato-ku, Tokyo 106, ✆ 03 3473 0151/7.

Ireland: No. 25 Kowa Bldg., 8–7 Sanbanchō, Chiyoda-ku, Tokyo 102, ✆ 03 3263 0695.

New Zealand: 20–40 Kamiyamachō, Shibuya-ku, Tokyo 150, ✆ 03 3467 2271.

Russia: 2–1–1 Azabudai, Minato-ku, Tokyo 106, ✆ 03 3583 4224.

South Africa Consulate: Zenkyoren Bldg. 4F, 2–7–9 Hirakawachō, Chiyoda-ku, Tokyo 102, ✆ 03 3265 3366/9.

United Kingdom: 1 Ichibanchō, Chiyoda-ku, Tokyo 102, ✆ 03 3265 5511.

Consulate, Hong Kong-Shanghai Bank Bldg. 4F, 36–1 Awajichō, Chūō-ku, Ōsaka, ✆ 06 231 3355.

Consulate, c/o Nishi-Nihon Bank, 1–3–6 Hakata eki-mae, Hakata-ku, Fukuoka, ✆ 092 476 2353.

United States: 1–10–5 Akasaka, Minato-ku, Tokyo 107, ✆ 03 3224 5000.

Consulate, 2–11–5 Nishi-tenma, Kita-ku, Ōsaka, ✆ 06 315 5900.

Consulate, 2–5–26 Ōhori, Chūō-ku, Fukuoka, ✆ 092 751 9331.

Etiquette and Customs

Japanese society is a dense, invisible network of favour and obligation, exclusion and inclusion, to which there is no fixed set of rules or responses. An individual's relations with other members of the society depend not just on circumstances, but on the age, rank and sex of the parties and their relative place within the system. Foreigners (the literal meaning of the Japanese word *gaijin* is 'outside person') are largely exempt from all this. Good manners are the same all over the world, and for every sociological generalization there is an exception. Japan is a society based on reserve, fastidiousness and personal modesty—but walk down any city street on a weekend evening and you will see crowds of jolly drunks, singing, vomiting and urinating in the gutters. If there is a general rule, it is: don't stand out. Follow the lead of those around you, and you will never cause embarrassment.

There are, however, situations where knowledge of a few simple rules is necessary. Some of these are dealt with elsewhere in this chapter: Japanese baths (pp.14–15), table manners (p.32). For business etiquette *see* **'Business Culture'** (pp.97–108).

greetings

Japanese bow to one another when greeting, thanking and parting from one another. The depth of the bow depends on the relative status of the individuals. 'Greeters', the young women who welcome customers at the doors of department stores, are trained to calibrate their bows with special bowing machines: one angle for peers, another for senior staff members, a deep bow for members of the public. Foreigners tend to look (and feel) awkward attempting a full bow: a deep nod does just as well. Modern Japanese shake hands too, but the friendly continental-style peck on the cheek to acquaintances of the opposite sex may cause embarrassment: a kiss is still a largely sexual gesture.

shoes and slippers

In private homes, some offices, and anywhere containing *tatami* mats, outdoor shoes are removed. A transitional entrance area, called the *genkan*, just inside the front door, is the place for this: you'll recognize it by the rows of other shoes lined neatly up at one side. Slip out of your shoes and, without touching the floor of the *genkan* with your unsheathed feet, step inside and into the slippers which will be provided for your use.

These can be worn in all areas apart from two: on *tatami* mats which you should step onto only in stockinged feet; and the toilet, for which special toilet slippers are provided. Step out of your indoor slippers and into the toilet slippers; when you've finished, don't forget to change back into the indoor slippers. There's a powerful cleanliness/uncleanness, inside/outside taboo at work here; breaking the rules is very bad manners.

To summarize:

Outside: outdoor shoes only to be worn. Never pop out in indoor slippers and then come back inside.

Genkan: take off outdoor shoes, and step into indoor slippers.

Tatami: stockinged feet only.

Toilet: toilet slippers only.

All this stepping in and out of shoes raises practical points. Slip-ons, for a start, are much easier to get in and out of than lace-ups. Holes in socks, and smelly or unwashed feet, are obvious and embarrassing.

sitting

All offices and many restaurants have Western furniture, but on *tatami* one sits at low tables on the floor. Women should always (even on upright furniture) sit with their legs folded to one side, or on their heels. Crossed legs are for men only, but can be agonizing for those unaccustomed to it: nobody will mind if you sprawl a little bit.

tipping

Tipping is unnecessary anywhere. Good service is understood: to insist on a gratuity will cause embarrassment and is rude. In exceptional circumstances (if a taxi driver has tracked you all over town to return a lost wallet, say) you may want to slip notes into a plain envelope and present it discreetly. Even then don't press too hard. The gesture in itself will be appreciated. It is better to offer a gift.

gifts

Japanese people present one another with gifts at every opportunity although the gesture is often more important than the present itself. During the two great gift-giving seasons, summer and New Year, Japanese houses are piled high with identical bottles of whisky, melons, preserved local delicacies and golf accessories—many of them destined to be passed on unopened the next time around. If you are likely to enjoy hospitality in Japan (and everyone can arrange this, through the Home Visit system), then it is a good idea to buy a few simple souvenirs of home before you go. Picture books of your country or region, non-perishable foods like biscuits or sweets, small trinkets or mementoes will all go down well. Wrapping is all important: ribbons and glossy paper, preferably bearing the name of a famous shop or brand, can elevate even the humblest gift.

Food and Drink

For a picture of the range and weirdness of Japanese food, visit the basement food hall of a big department store or—harder to find these days—an old-fashioned local market. There you will see frothing gastropods, writhing octopi and bags of seaweed, alongside beef raised on beer, £100 melons, sweet potatoes and sour plums. The most surprising thing about Japanese cuisine is its variety—and the variety of prices. A *kaiseki* banquet can cost as much as a return air ticket to Korea. On the other hand, you can eat a new, strange and delicious dish every day for a week, and not spend more than ¥1000 a head. Whatever your other money worries, eating out need not be one of them.

Restaurants and eating places are classified in three categories, based on the approximate cost of dinner for one, including tax and service, but excluding drinks. These should be treated as rough guidelines; remember also that many restaurants offer lunchtime *teishoku* or sets which are much cheaper than the evening *à la carte* prices.

expensive	Above ¥5000
moderate	¥2500 – ¥5000
inexpensive	Under ¥2500

meals

The traditional Japanese **breakfast** is the only meal that many foreigners find they cannot become accustomed to, even after repeated exposure. Typically it will consist of a piece of broiled fish, pickles, a raw egg, green tea and rice, which the diner rolls up into little parcels between pieces of dried green seaweed. Somehow it's the rice that is the most unpalatable element: that dense volume makes you want to go straight back to bed, or leaves you feeling as if you're recovering from a heavy lunch at 8.30 in the morning. Many will prefer to eat in a *kissaten* (coffee shop) which can be found in most Western-style hotels and on every other street corner. Here you can get a *mōningu sābisu* (morning service) of coffee, toast and boiled egg for around ¥700.

Lunch is eaten early in Japan: 12 to 1 is the hour when restaurants are most crowded, rather than 1 to 2. Many restaurants, including the most expensive, do cheap lunch sets which can be an extremely reasonable way of sampling otherwise unaffordable food.

For businesspeople and young people out on the town, the **evening meal** is often little more than an accompaniment to alcohol. Set menus are fuller and much more expensive than at lunchtime.

rice dishes

Sticky white short-grained rice is the staple of every meal, even more so than bread or potatoes in the West. The Japanese words for breakfast, lunch and dinner (*asagohan, hirugohan* and *bangohan*) mean literally 'morning rice', 'afternoon rice' and 'evening rice'. Like many staple foods, the eating of rice has over the centuries acquired sacramental associations. Many of the Shinto legends and ceremonies are concerned with appeasement of the gods in order to secure a successful rice crop; bowls of boiled rice are offered in temples and shrines, and at household ancestral altars. Its polished whiteness and purity are essential, and the foreign taste for brown rice is considered very peculiar indeed.

For a bowl of plain boiled rice, ask for *gohan*. *Chahan* is Chinese-style egg fried rice, served in cheap restaurants as a meal in itself, but never eaten with other Japanese food.

Donburi is a kind of cheap snack, popular as a quick lunchtime filler. A large bowl (the literal meaning of *donburi*) is filled with hot boiled rice and various toppings: *ten-don* is rice with pieces of *tempura*, *unagi-don* is rice with strips of eel. Other common varieties are *tonkatsu-don* (deep-fried battered pork), *oyako-don* (literally 'parent and child', hence chicken and egg) and *gyū-don* (beef).

Onigiri is even more informal, the equivalent of a rice sandwich, eaten with the fingers, and the staple of picnics and packed lunches. A ball of rice, often shaped into a rough triangle, is wrapped in dried seaweed or rolled in sesame seeds, with a small piece of fish or pickle in the middle. Convenience stores sell 'instant onigiri', cleverly packaged so that the dry seaweed and damp rice come into contact only when they are unwrapped. *Umeboshi* (pickled plum) is the most common filling; they can also contain tuna, seaweed and fish eggs.

Kamameshi is a rice casserole, not unlike a simple paella: clams, chicken, vegetables or meat, cooked and served in an old-fashioned iron dish with a wooden lid.

noodle dishes

Noodles are the pasta of Japan—cheap, simple and versatile, and (like spaghetti) introduced originally from China. Every region of Japan has its own version of the main varieties, which inspire intense connoisseurship and local loyalty. Noodle partisans can debate for hours the relative merits of, say, Izumo and Tokyo *soba*.

As you will quickly gather on your first visit to a noodle restaurant, noodles are slurped. Hold the bowl in one hand and raise it towards your face before lifting a clump of noodles to your mouth with chopsticks; then suck, and don't worry about the noise. It's perfectly proper to raise the bowl to your mouth with both hands to finish off the tasty soup in which they are served.

Ramen are Japanized Chinese egg noodles, served in a variety of broths and garnished with morsels of pork, seafood, fish sausage and vegetables. In the smallest Japanese town, you will never be more than half a mile from a *ramen-ya*, sometimes a simple restaurant with a counter bar and a few tables, often a portable cart on wheels parked opposite the station, with a couple of stools and a canopy to keep off the rain. *Ramen* are served in a variety of broths. *Miso ramen* comes in a delicious salty, cloudy soup of fermented soy bean. *Shōyu* is thinner, based on soy sauce.

Soba and **udon** were also imported from China, but so long ago as to be considered thoroughly Japanized. The former are made from buckwheat flour and can vary in colour from off-white through brown to dark grey. *Udon* are made from wheat flour, and are plump and white, with a blander, more floury taste. Both are served in a broth which varies subtly over different regions, with or without a garnish. Popular *soba* and *udon* dishes include *tempura* (with a few pieces of battered fish), *sansai* (nutty mountain vegetables), *tsukimi* (with a raw egg) and *zaru soba/udon*, a summer dish, served cold with a separate sauce to which leeks and horseradish are added before dipping.

Other noodle dishes include *somen*, a thin form of *udon*, like vermicelli, and *champon*, a rich jumble of egg noodles, seafood and vegetables introduced from China via Nagasaki.

grilled dishes

Okonomiyaki (pronounced, almost, 'Economy-yacky') is a cheap, filling, fun food, something like a cross between a pizza and a pancake. Many *okonomiyaki-ya* feature DIY cooking. You sit down at a table with a hot griddle in the centre, and the ingredients—

cabbage and vegetables, egg batter, plus your choice of prawns, squid or meat—are brought to your table in a bowl which you mix up and pour onto the iron. Tamp it down with the spatula, and turn it over when one side is done. Then top with sweet sauce and writhing flakes of dried bonito fish. Someone will give a hand until you get the hang of it.

Yakitori (literally 'grilled bird') is another informal dish, very palatable to foreign tastes. Portions of dismembered chicken (they seem to have a use for every last giblet), plus vegetables and nuts, are pierced with wooden skewers, rubbed with salt or a sweet, soy-based sauce and cooked over a smoky barbecue. Two skewers generally constitute one portion, which costs a few hundred yen. In itself, a round of *yakitori* is insubstantial, so unless you stoke up with something heavier (try *yaki-onigiri*, grilled rice balls), you can find yourself spending a surprising amount of money before you're full. It's often less messy to prize the morsels off with chopsticks and eat them off the plate, than to gnaw them straight off the skewer. The following is a typical *yakitori* menu:

tsukune	chicken meatballs
tebasaki	chicken wings
rebā	liver
sasaki	breast
motsu	giblets
momoyaki	thighs
negi	leeks
asupara	asparagus
piiman	green pepper
shiitake	mushroom

Tonkatsu are cutlets of lean pork, deep fried, and served either on rice (*tonkatsu-don*) or in a set (*teishoku*) with rice, soup and pickles.

tempura

The word *tempura* is said, implausibly, to come from the Latin *tempora*, meaning Lent, and to have been introduced by Portuguese traders during the 16th century. When asked why they were eating fried fish instead of their usual meat, they replied that it was because of *tempora*, and the name stuck. Nowadays, the big pink prawns in their golden overcoats of spiky batter are a quintessentially Japanese food, but still one which foreigners find very easy to eat. A humble version of *tempura* crops up as a garnish on noodles and rice, but there are restaurants dedicated to it, some very expensive, with their own secret formulae for batter, oil and cooking time.

Tempura doesn't have to be fish: vegetables, nuts and leaves can also be dipped in the fine batter, deep fried in oil, and plopped on the table on white paper. A plate of tempura comes with a thin, light brown sauce into which you tip a pile of grated ginger and radish. Dip each piece in momentarily, and eat at once. It's often ordered in a set (*teishoku*). Common ingredients are *ebi* (prawn), *ika* (squid), *kakiage* (chopped shrimps and vegetables), *nasu* (aubergine), *shiitake* (mushroom) and *shiso* (a refreshing, aromatic leaf).

fish

The waters of the Japanese archipelago range from the iceberg-encrusted Sea of Okhotsk to the sub-tropical South China Sea; Tokyo-based factory ships range as far as the Antarctic and the deep Pacific. As a result, Japan is an icthyophagist's paradise, with the finest, freshest, and most hygienically prepared seafood in the world.

Sushi and **sashimi**, the famous Japanese 'raw fish', are not always raw and may not even be fish. *Sashimi* are mouth-sized morsels of seafood dipped into a mixture of soy sauce (*shōyu*) and grated green horseradish (*wasabi*); most are uncooked, but octopus (*tako*) *sashimi* is always boiled first, and prawns (*ebi*) usually are too. *Sushi* consists of balls of vinegared rice with pieces of raw or cooked fish or omelette pressed onto the top. *Maki* (wrapped) *zushi* are made by rolling up chopped vegetables and fish in a tube of rice, wrapped in dried seaweed, and chopping the long cylinder into small round pieces.

Foreigners are often revolted by the idea of eating raw fish, but the reality is seldom what they expect. Forget those images of fishmongers' shops, with limp carcasses lying on the slab all day, and flies buzzing round—Western restaurants *have* to cook their fish because it is allowed to sit around for so long. In Japan, only the finest and freshest cuts are used (so it's not cheap), and Japanese hygiene standards are the best in the world. The fishy tastes and smells which first timers dread are entirely absent. *Sushi* and *sashimi* are odourless and surprisingly mild in flavour—it is the texture of the different species, and the beautiful presentation of the ingredients on the plate (red tuna, pink prawns, yellow omelette, white rice) which excite and satisfy the appetite.

A few pieces of *sashimi* form a part of many traditional Japanese meals; some restaurants also offer a set menu including soup, rice and pickles for a reasonable price. *Sushi*, because it includes rice, is more of a meal in itself. At the top end, you can spend as much as you want, but an entertaining and inexpensive introduction to the dish can be found in *kuru-kuru-zushi* restaurants (literally, '*sushi* that keeps coming'). Here customers sit on the outside of a circular conveyor belt, onto which chefs place the *sushi* on little plates which are colour-coded according to the price of the dish. You sit down, watch the dishes coming round and, when you see one you fancy, lift it off. Eat as much or as little as you like and, at the end of your meal, present your stack of empty plates to be totted up.

At other establishments your *sushi* will be served on a board or placed on the counter directly in front of you. Put a little soy sauce (*shōyu*) into the separate dish and dip each piece, fish side down so the rice doesn't crumble. You can lift them with chopsticks, but it is perfectly acceptable to use your fingers.

Sashimi is served with a little pyramid of grated *wasabi* (horseradish) at the side. Using chopsticks, transfer a little of this into a saucer of *shōyu*. It's very strong: go easy until you know how much you like.

It's cheaper to order *nigiri moriawase*, a selection of eight or so different pieces. For *à la carte* orders, try the following:

maguro	tuna
toro	fatty tuna
ebi	boiled prawn

amaebi	raw sweet prawn
ika	squid
tako	octopus
anago	broiled sea eel
tai	sea bream
awabi	abalone
torigai	cockle
aji	herring
hamachi	yellowtail
ikura	salmon roe (*sushi* only)
tamago	sweet omelette (*sushi* only)

Unagi is broiled eel, barbecued over charcoal and steeped in a sweet sauce of *shōyu, sake* and sugar. Served on a bed of rice (*unagi-don*), or on its own, it's the opposite of austere, minimalist *sashimi*—rich, sweet, and indulgent.

Fugu is another dish which has achieved sensational fame outside Japan. The puffer fish (a.k.a. blowfish, globefish or swell fish) is an uncharismatic creature caught off the western coast of Honshū, with three unpleasant properties: it is extremely ugly, it can inflate itself into a spiny ball when threatened, and its liver and ovaries contain deadly toxins which can paralyse the respiratory and motor-nervous system within 20 minutes of ingestion. *Fugu* can only be served by chefs who are rigorously trained and licensed by the Ministry of Health and Welfare. The Imperial Family are forbidden by law from touching the stuff, but since the system was introduced there has been only one fatality: Bandō Mitsugorō, a *kabuki* actor, who was determined to sample the liver and suffered the consequences.

A *fugu* banquet consists of several stages. First warm *sake* is poured over the toasted fins of the fish, to produce a fishy aperitif. Then *fugu-sashi*, transparently thin slices of the flesh are eaten raw, dipped in a sauce containing *shōyu*, radish, pepper and bitter orange. Next comes *fuguchiri*, a hot-pot of *fugu* flesh boiled with vegetables. Finally, the soupy residue is boiled into a rice porridge. The flesh is white, mild, and—to the non-connoisseur—really nothing very special at all. It rarely comes cheaper than ¥4500.

stews and hot pots

Nabemono (things in a pot) are steaming casseroles, heated up on a flame at the table, and filled by the diners from plates of vegetables, leaves, *tōfu* and, sometimes, meat. *Chanko-nabe* is a high-protein version made famous by sumo wrestlers, who eat quantities of it to achieve and augment their distinctive waistlines. *Sukiyaki* and *shabu-shabu* are meat-based *nabe* dishes, both invented since the foreign popularization of beef in the late 19th century. The former is a rich, meaty dish of onions, mushrooms, *tōfu*, bamboo shoots and *konnyaku* (devil's root jelly), simmered in a suet broth with strips of thin, often fatty beef. *Shabu-shabu* can be made with pork as well: thin slices are dropped into boiling water with vegetables, allowed to cook for a few seconds, then dipped in a sesame seed sauce. 'Genghis Khan' is a novelty version served in Hokkaidō with lamb as the staple meat; it was allegedly invented by the notorious Mongolian warlord.

Oden is a basic, working man's food, an unglamorous but tasty brown stew of fish sausages, *tōfu*, cabbage, radish and vegetable jelly, dolloped out and eaten with mustard.

fruit

Japan produces delicious mandarin oranges (*mikan*), apples (*ringo*), watermelons (*suika*), peaches (*momo*), strawberries (*ichigo*), and grapes (*budō*), as well as two delicious fruit not familiar in Europe: the *kaki* or persimmon, a crisp, sweet, smoky fruit, the shape of a big tomato; and the *nashi*, a crisp, succulent autumn fruit, between an apple and a pear.

vegetarian cuisine

Vegetarianism has never caught on in Japan and it's notoriously difficult to explain to well-meaning hosts and puzzled waiters. The exception is in Buddhist, and especially Zen, temples where the injunction against taking the life of living creatures has led to the development of an ancient, delicate and sophisticated cuisine. A few city restaurants specialize in *shōjin ryōri*, as it's called, but the best place to sample it is in the restaurants adjacent to a big temple complex like Daitoku-ji or Nanzen-ji in Kyoto, or on Mt Kōya. The strictest Buddhist canons forbid even the use of garlic or onions, two of the 'Five Fragrant Vegetables' which are held to provoke an unhealthy lust for the food. Instead, wise and varied use is made of *tōfu, miso*, beans, vegetables, and plant extracts.

kaiseki ryōri

Kaiseki ryōri is the epitome of what many people think of as typical Japanese cuisine—fresh, natural ingredients, minimally cooked and flavoured, and exquisitely presented in tiny ceramic dishes arranged on lacquer trays. It began as a simple accompaniment to tea, and developed into a kind of culinary theatre in which the room, the hanging scrolls, the serving vessels, the view from the window, the demeanour and dress of the waitresses, the appearance and order of the dishes and their appropriateness to the season are as important to the connoisseur as the taste of the food which he finally digests. The food itself is elegantly simple—a series of short courses, including *sashimi*, cooked fish, vegetables, meat and rice. The ingredients are chosen for their seasonal freshness and, in Kyoto, are served with the minimum of seasonings. Kyoto chefs traditionally look down their noses at slobs from Tokyo—and abroad—who drown their delicately balanced meals in streams of soy sauce.

As you'd expect, this kind of experience doesn't come cheap. Having made your reservation (this must be done at least a day or two in advance), you'll be lucky to spend less than ¥10,000 per person for an authentic *kaiseki* meal in the evening. The alternative is to visit between 11am and 1pm when many restaurants serve lunchtime *bentō*—those lacquered lunch boxes with a morsel of food in each of their compartments—for under ¥5000; the experience is less elaborate, the portions smaller, but the food is exactly the same. Best of all, dine in a good Kyoto *ryokan*. The evening meal is included in the price, and the best *ryokan* are superb restaurants in their own right.

foreign and hybrid food

The influence of Chinese cooking has already been made clear, but every kind of national cuisine—from Balinese to Nigerian—seems to have a restaurant somewhere in Japan, most of them in Tokyo. International convenience foods like sandwiches (*sandoitchi* or *sando*), burgers (*hanbāgā*), spaghetti (*supagetti*), pizza (*piza*), and curry (*karii raisu*) are as much a part of the everyday diet as in the West. Even if you don't find any native dishes to your liking, there's no need to go hungry, or to resort to the ubiquitous *Makudonarudo* (McDonald's).

Japanese chefs have always been adept at tailoring foreign dishes to domestic tastes to produce often delicious half-breeds. *Mukokuseki ryōri* (no-nationality cooking) is the fashionable expression used to describe trendy hybrid restaurants, serving such delights as *gyōza* (Chinese dumplings) stuffed with mozzarella.

Restaurants

For Japanese food, the top of the range restaurants are the *ryōtei*, purveyors of *kaiseki* haute cuisine, and often beautiful examples of traditional tea house style architecture in their own right. Dining at a *ryōtei*, in the evening anyway, isn't a casual experience. They tend to tuck themselves away behind gardens and fencing shrubs; reservations must be made more than a day in advance so that the ingredients can be freshly ordered and prepared. The most exclusive *ryōtei* are like informal clubs, and may expect an introduction from an established customer.

Other establishments are classified according to the particular type of cuisine in which they specialize. It would be unusual to find a restaurant that served both *tempura* and *okonomiyaki*, for instance, so it's necessary to have some idea of what you want to eat as well as how much you want to pay. The suffix *-ya* means roughly 'business'—thus a *sushi-ya* is a raw fish restaurant, a *ramen-ya* is a noodle shop. Among the most congenial places for general relaxation and decent, non-gourmet eating are the thousands of little establishments classified as *nomi-ya* (drinking shops). These include *aka chōchin* (red lantern bars), humble working men's places with a few tables, a television and a trade-mark paper lantern hanging outside the door, and *izaka-ya*, which are a bit more up-market, but just as noisy and informal. Groups of diners usually order a number of individual dishes (and much alcohol) which are shared. *Robata-yaki* is hearty country-style grill cooking, performed in front of the diners, amid much smoke and sizzling. *Yatai* are outdoor carts, serving similar sorts of food, where customers sit on stools beneath an awning. Some *yatai*, like those in Fukuoka in Kyūshū, serve superb food at very reasonable prices.

One of the best places to get your culinary bearings is on the restaurant floor of a **department store**, usually near the top of the building. Big city stores may have half a dozen different restaurants, each serving a different kind of cuisine at very reasonable prices.

Styles of foreign restaurant are as varied as styles of foreign cuisine.

Kissaten are the ubiquitous coffee shops. The coffee is expensive; the simple snacks of pasta, pilaff and curry are cheap.

ordering

The chances of encountering English-speaking waiters decrease as you descend the price scale. Restaurants in the cities often have bilingual menus, and even in the smallest towns you will see window displays with plastic models of the various dishes, along with the prices. Simply lead the waiter outside, and point.

The most important skill you can master before coming to Japan is the use of chopsticks. Practise by picking up small objects with a couple of long pencils. Japanese chopsticks (*hashi*) are made of wood, sometimes lacquered, with pointed ends. Impaling food is a little indelicate, but friendly indulgence is extended to foreigners. Never transfer food from one set of chopsticks to another: the only time this happens is after a Buddhist cremation when relatives do this with the ashes of the deceased. Don't stick them upright in a bowl of food—again, this is reserved for offerings to the dead.

Apart from that, Japanese table manners are reassuringly relaxed and practical. Slurping food or rice is fine, indeed encouraged (it's said to improve the flavour), and it's quite all right to lift up your own bowl or plate of food to your chin and shovel the food in from there. Neighbours at table pour one another's drinks. When a bottle is proffered, place your hand on your glass to acknowledge the courtesy, and reciprocate afterwards. An empty glass is an invitation for a refill: if you want to stop drinking, leave it full.

Drinking

Lager (*biiru*) and **whisky** (*uisukii*) are popular. Domestic beer brands (Kirin, Sapporo, Asahi, Ebisu) are famously good, Japanese whisky (Suntory and Nikka) is notoriously rough. *Mizu-wari* is whisky, ice and water. Imported brands of both drinks are widely available, but more expensive.

Sake isn't one of the world's great drinks, but it's a pleasant accompaniment to a lot of Japanese food. Drunk hot, it's a delicious winter warmer. *Shōchū* is a white spirit, made from rice, potatoes, barley and whatever else was to hand at the time. It's cheap, rough and very intoxicating. Mixed with soda water and fruit cordial, it makes a refreshing, and deceptively mild-tasting, cocktail called *sawā—raimu sawā* (lime), *remon sawā* (lemon), and *ume sawā* (Japanese plum) are popular.

Health

You don't need any immunizations or certificates to enter Japan. Health and life expectancy in Japan are high, and medical treatment is good, if expensive. Tap water is safe to drink in all areas.

You may find yourself suffering from **stomach upset** but this is likely to be the result of a long flight, unfamiliar air, water and food, rather than specific germs. It should pass in a few days and can be relieved by a standard preparation like Kaolin and Morphine.

If you need **prescription drugs**, carry an adequate supply and a separate copy of your prescription, in case of loss. Make sure you know the full name of the drug rather than just its brand name which may not be the same in Japan.

Mosquitoes are not dangerous, but they can be a painful nuisance in the warm months: bring repellent. The most effective measure is the electronic mosquito repeller which is plugged into the mains and fuelled with small solid tablets. These are inexpensive and are widely available.

The **sun** can be surprisingly strong, so cover your head and wear a good sunblock. Remember that ultra-violet rays do damage even on overcast days—during the summer rainy season, for example.

Food, including raw sea fish, is safe to eat, but you should always refuse raw river fish, raw wild boar, raw bear, and raw chicken which can carry parasites. Avoid walking barefoot in **rice paddies** and drinking from **mountain streams** for the same reason.

Healthcare in Japan is good, and English-speaking doctors are not hard to find, but a serious accident or illness could quickly become ruinously expensive. Adequate **insurance** is essential, and you should arrange it before you go.

contraceptives

Bring your own supply of the **pill**: as a contraceptive it is dispensed only reluctantly in Japan. **Condoms** with names like 'Love Me Jelly' and 'Yes, Satisfaction!' are widely available, even from vending machines on the street. Foreign users often complain that differences in scale between the Western and Oriental anatomy make them uncomfortable and unreliable. You might want to bring your home brand of these as well.

Meeting the Japanese

Japanese people are compulsively, touchingly, almost painfully kind and welcoming to foreigners, but they can also be rather shy in their presence and, especially outside the internationalized cities, breaking through the diffident eye contact and embarrassed smiles can be a struggle. The best way round this is to take advantage of the many formal schemes established to promote contact between Japanese and foreigners. For anyone wanting to live for a while with a Japanese family, there are numerous **Home Stay** programmes in different parts of Japan. You should arrange this before you arrive: enquire at your nearest branch of JNTO for an up-to-date list of organizations.

More suitable for short-term visitors are the **Home Visit** schemes run in dozens of cities and towns. Via a tourist information centre, you make an appointment to spend a few hours with an English-speaking Japanese family (other languages are sometimes available). Usually there is no charge: your hosts' only motive is to practise their English and learn about the West. Arrive on time, take along some small gifts and photographs of your home and family, if you have them. Loyal and long-lasting friendships can begin in this way.

Volunteer Guides, often local university students keen to practise English, operate in several of the big tourist cities, including Kyoto and Nara. You pay for their entrance fees, transport, and lunch, if they are with you for the whole day; they guide and interpret for you as you tour the sights. Again, a small gift and a postcard when you get home are all that is expected.

Money

Notes come in denominations of ¥1000, ¥5000, and ¥10,000. Coins are ¥1, ¥5, ¥10, ¥50, ¥100 and ¥500. All display their value in Arabic as well as Japanese numerals, apart from the ¥5 coin, which is brass and has a hole in the middle.

Cash is still the most common medium of payment in most shops, restaurants and on public transport. Street robbery is very rare, so the only risk of carrying large amounts of cash is that you will lose them.

International **credit cards** like MasterCard (Access), DC, Visa and American Express are increasingly acceptable in city hotels, department stores, big restaurants and travel agents, but it is unwise to assume this unless you have checked in advance. Only the biggest railway stations accept cards in payment for tickets. They can also be used to withdraw cash directly from automatic teller machines in certain banks and department stores in big cities and international airports. Enquire at the nearest tourist information centre.

Traveller's cheques and **foreign currencies** like dollars and sterling can be cashed in major banks (which offer the best rates), *bureaux de change* and big hotels, but are almost never accepted in shops and restaurants. In smaller towns, not all the banks perform foreign exchange; stock up on yen before heading out to the sticks.

Banks open between 9am and 3pm, and close at weekends and on national holidays. Transactions can be time-consuming. If there is a queue, you may have to take a number from an automatic dispenser, wait for your number to be called, hand over your passport and cash or cheques, then wait for them to be processed. When this has been done behind the scenes, your name will be called and your currency handed over.

Museums

Museums and art galleries generally close over New Year and on Mondays, unless Monday is a national holiday, in which case they close on Tuesday.

Admission prices given in this book are for adults only. High school students (18 and under) almost always pay a cheaper rate, around half or two-thirds of the full ticket price.

Names

Japanese uses given names (what we call 'Christian' names) more reluctantly than English. It is quite usual for someone to introduce themselves by their family name alone (Mori or Watanabe, rather than Keiko or Noboru) even in an informal setting. In formal and business contexts, the form is to precede even the family name with the name of the company or institution: 'Toyota's Mr Nakamoto' or 'Tokyo University's Miss Higuchi'. Names are first and foremost a means of identifying the group to which the person is affiliated, not an individual handle. Among the young and Westernized, Western practice is very common, however. When introducing yourself, do what feels most natural in English.

Names are usually combined with some kind of honorific suffix. *-San* is the most common and neutral, being equivalent to Mr, Mrs, Miss or Ms. *-Sama* is formal and refers to the very honoured, including Shinto deities. *-Chan* is a pet, familiar form, used for young children, family members, very close friends and cute animals. Just as with English Mr and Mrs, one never employs a suffix in referring to oneself or one's own family or close circle.

Throughout this book names are given according to the Japanese practice: family name first, given name second. When one name is given, it is usually the family (i.e. the first) name. A few historical figures, writers and artists, however, are conventionally (and arbitrarily) referred to by their given names, in the same way that Van Gogh is sometimes referred to simply as Vincent. Thus the wartime Prime Minister Tōjō Hideki, and the novelist Mishima Yukio, are always Tōjō and Mishima. But the Meiji-period writer Natsume Sōseki and the 16th-century warlord Oda Nobunaga are often Sōseki and Nobunaga.

Confusingly, emperors are often referred to by more than one name. During his lifetime, the father of the present sovereign was known as Hirohito; posthumously, he is referred to as Shōwa, after the era name for the period of his rule.

National Holidays

On national holidays, banks and offices close, trains and hotels are booked up weeks in advance, and tourist spots become clogged with Japanese making the most of their free time. There are thirteen such days.

Note that three national holidays cluster at the end of April and beginning of May, a period known as **Golden Week** when most of the country takes a holiday and bookings are most difficult to obtain.

1 Jan	**New Year.**
15 Jan	**Coming of Age Day** honours those who will turn 20 in the next year.
11 Feb	**National Foundation Day** commemorates the date of accession of the legendary first emperor, Jimmu.
21 Mar	**Spring Equinox Day.**
29 April	**Green Day.** The birthday of the late Emperor Shōwa (Hirohito).
3 May	**Constitution Day.**
5 May	**Boys' Day.** Families fly colourful carp banners for their sons.
15 Sept	**Respect for the Aged Day.**
23 Sept	**Autumn Equinox Day.**
10 Oct	**Physical Fitness Day** in commemoration of the 1964 Tokyo Olympics.
3 Nov	**Culture Day.**
23 Nov	**Labour Day.**
23 Dec	**The Emperor's Birthday.**

The Japanese passion for classification ('Three Finest Scenic Views', 'Three Most Beautiful Gardens', etc.) is seen nowhere so clearly as in its museums. Every year, after vigorous vetting, a few more favoured statues, paintings and buildings are singled out for the cultural equivalent of the Oscars: as Important Cultural Properties or, for *la crème de la crème*, National Treasures.

The system has its roots in the 19th-century Meiji period when political victimization of Buddhist temples made it difficult for them to care for many of their finest art properties.

Large numbers of temple treasures were taken into custody by the government, and laws were passed concerning their care and preservation. Countless priceless works were destroyed in air raids during the Second World War, and in 1950 a revised law was passed which introduced the term Important Cultural Properties. Nowadays there are some 12,000 of these. One thousand of them are further designated National Treasures, including many of the finest oriental art treasures in the world. The classifications are made carefully by experts: if you hear of a National Treasure, it's almost always worth going out of your way to see it.

As well as honouring physical objects, the 1950 law created another category: Intangible Cultural Assets, such as weaving, pottery or traditional performance arts. Human 'Bearers of Intangible Cultural Assets', better known as Living National Treasures, are also named. There can be no more than 70 of them at any one time. Living National Treasures receive an annual stipend and, importantly, massive commercial interest in their work. Holders of the honour are almost always eminent, very elderly craftsmen, artists and performers; for the rest of their lives they can charge for their work virtually what they want.

Nuisances And Dangers

There are more of the former than the latter: Japan is still one of the safest countries in the world.

earthquakes

These are potentially the greatest danger. Small quakes which rattle the windows alarmingly are common; severe, life-threatening ones are rare but, as the Kōbe disaster of January 1995 showed, their consequences can be frightening. In the end, though, the number of tourists to have been killed or injured in Japanese earthquakes is so small as to be negligible. And, if the chances of natural disaster are higher than at home, the chances of robbery, assault or murder are much lower. It would be an exceptionally cautious person who avoided Japan solely because of the earthquake danger. For a full discussion of earthquakes and earthquake safety, *see* pp.19–22.

dangerous animals

Hokkaidō and mountainous areas of Honshū have populations of bears which can be dangerous in exceptional circumstances. *See* the **Hokkaidō** chapter (pp.115–6) for bear drill. Japan has a couple of poisonous snakes which give a nasty bite. Avoid walking barefoot through long grass. If anyone is bitten, keep them still and seek immediate medical help.

height

The Japanese are getting taller but their doorways and beams are not. In older homes and offices, castles and temples, and even some trains, anyone approaching the six foot mark will have to duck constantly to avoid cracking their head. After a while, the protective stoop becomes second nature; until you're used to it, beware.

lost property

Never give up on an item of lost property. Mislaid goods do get handed in, unplundered, and the systems for recovering them are straightforward and well-organized. Transport companies generally hold on to lost property for a few days, after which it is transferred to a local police station for one month, and finally to a central police station. In the first instance contact the taxi firm or bus or train station of the company which you travelled with; then go to the police. You might want to hand over a few thousand yen (depending on the value of the recovered item) as a reward for the finder.

In Tokyo, the following are useful numbers:

JR East Infoline, ✆ 03 3423 0111.

Tokyo Taxi Kindaika Centre, ✆ 03 3648 0300.

Metropolitan Police Department Lost and Found Office, ✆ 03 3581 4321.

You may need to ask your hotel to make some of these calls for you in Japanese.

Packing

Suits and ties are the rule for offices but, outside work, Japanese people dress casually (but smartly) even in grand restaurants and hotels, although obviously dirty or worn-out garments may be frowned on. Unless you have business to do, or very formal functions to attend, you can leave dressy clothes at home. There are few religious sensibilities to offend: Japanese tourists happily tramp round temples and shrines clad in shorts and mini-skirts and nobody minds.

If you're planning to travel the length and breadth of the country, then be prepared for a range of temperatures. In March, for instance, you can be sunning it in southern Kyūshū one day, and wading through snow in Hokkaidō, 48hrs later. Several layers of thinner clothing are more versatile, and just as warm, as a single heavy sweater: this is particularly important if you are likely to tackle big mountain climbs (like Mt Fuji) which you may begin in sunshine and conclude in a blizzard.

In the humid summers the most important garment is a lightweight waterproof, although you might prefer to make do with an umbrella, which you don't need to bring with you. They are cheaply available in every convenience store and souvenir shop.

Slip-ons make the complicated business of taking off and putting on footwear much easier. Bring strong shoes for hiking. Bear in mind that large foreign sizes of all clothes are expensive and difficult to get hold of in Japan.

Remember adapters and transformers if you're bringing over mains electrical equipment. A pocket torch can make all the difference in ill-lit temple halls and treasure houses.

Perhaps the most useful purchase which you can make before departure is the Japan Rail Pass. This can save you hundreds of pounds, but you must buy it before departure (*see* **'Getting Around'**, pp.9–10).

Post

The word for **post office** is *yūbin kyoku*. Its symbol is a red capital letter 'T' with a horizontal line over the top (〒), which also features in Japanese addresses to indicate the post code number.

Airmail letters under 10g cost ¥100 to North America and Oceania, ¥120 to Europe. Postcards are ¥70 worldwide, but there is a standard size; anything bigger is charged as a letter. Aerogrammes are the best value at ¥80. For parcels, pack printed matter separately and leave the envelope unsealed; it is charged at a lower rate. Post offices also send **faxes**, although it's usually quicker to do it from the reception desk of a big hotel.

Most post offices are open between 9 and 5, and closed at weekends and on holidays. **Tokyo International Post Office**, next door to Tokyo Station, is open for domestic and international mail 24 hours a day, 365 days a year.

For parcel deliveries in Japan, the cheapest and most efficient means of dispatch is one of the **courier delivery services** which operate out of convenience stores, rice and liquor shops. You can recognize these by their logos, all of which depict some kind of animal: **Perican-bin** (a pelican) and **Kuro-neko** (a black cat) are the most popular. From Tokyo you can send up to 20kg anywhere in Japan for less than ¥2000. This is an excellent way of dealing with bulky souvenirs, luggage, etc. which you don't want to lug around: send it c/o your Tokyo hotel and pick it up just before your departure.

Shopping

Shopping is the Japanese national pastime. For bustle, choice, affluence and expense, Knightsbridge and Manhattan have got nothing on the department stores of Tokyo's Ginza on a Saturday morning. During the economic bubble of the 1980s, when Japan had more money than it could flush into the Pacific, Tokyo became the consumer fetishist's dream. You could buy anything you wanted, and many, many things you never wanted at all— from mink lavatory seats, gold leaf noodles, to evening dress for dogs. All this cost a lot of money, naturally, but then that was all part of the fun. Compared to their counterparts in other first-world countries, Japanese consumers command little power in terms of choice and price, and all kinds of iniquitous monopolies and mark-ups flourish in the Byzantine distribution and retail networks. Since the bubble burst, matters have improved a little, with the spread of discount stores and the popularity of plain, workaday, non-designer goods. In general though, apart from uniquely Japanese items like crafts, you will find few bargains here, certainly when compared to other Asian cities. Instead, shop as the Japanese do—for the human drama, the attentive service, or the sheer pleasure of spending grotesque amounts of money.

Shopping etiquette is similar to that in the West, in other words, haggling is not expected (and may cause embarrassment) if the price is marked. A friendly shopkeeper may volunteer a discount, or throw in a free gift, but this is up to him. The biggest difference you'll notice is the attention paid to wrapping even the humblest items. The time this takes can add significantly to the length of your shopping trip—bear this in mind if you're in a hurry.

In general you get what you pay for: bargains are few, but so are obvious rip-offs, apart from those produced by the exchange rate and the genuine cost of living. As with restaurants, however, the more obviously Japanese a shop looks (sliding screens, assistants in kimono) and the more geared towards tourists, the more you are likely to pay.

Art and Antiques

Japanese art is prized all over the world—long gone are the days when you could pick up priceless statues for a few yen in a market because the stall-keeper didn't know what they were. Woodblock prints (*ukiyo-e*) were first shipped to the West as wrapping paper; now good impressions by famous artists cost millions of yen. Nonetheless, prints produced in editions are a good buy compared to 'original' works of art. Cheap but attractive versions of famous prints can be bought in tourist shops for a few thousand yen.

In Tokyo and Kyoto there are many shops specializing in one kind of art or another, often found in the vicinity of big Buddhist temples. Remember that whatever the art you are interested in, there is bound to be a museum somewhere specializing in it, where you can acquaint yourself with styles and techniques and train your eye.

Ceramics

Yakimono (literally 'baked things') are made all over Japan, in dozens of different local styles, some of them centuries old. They range from priceless and ancient tea bowls, to simple pots and cups produced by anonymous craftsmen for sale in local shops. Whatever you choose to spend, ceramics are among the most worthwhile souvenirs you can bring back from Japan.

There are over 100 pottery villages in Japan where traditional local ceramics are still made by hand. The most famous of these are Arita in Kyūshū, the home of Imari porcelain; the Bizen area, near Okayama, which produces an austere earthenware, much prized in the tea ceremony; the city of Kanazawa, for its gorgeous Kutani porcelain; Hagi, in Chūgoku, where a pinkish ware used in the tea ceremony is produced; and Kagoshima, in southern Kyūshū, where the white, porcelain-like Satsuma-yaki is made. Unfortunately, the demands of commercial production have turned some of these pottery towns into rather grimy and unattractive places. Mashiko, for instance, north of Tokyo, where the 20th-century folk potter, Hamada Shoji, had his workshop, has nothing worth seeing apart from its kilns and ceramic museums. Kilns are often rather inconveniently situated, away from the tourist sights on the outskirts of the towns. Most are happy to show visitors round but may prefer you to make an appointment. For serious pottery lovers, it's often a good idea to contact the local tourist office in advance, and set up a few meetings. Ask the tourist information centre in Tokyo or Kyoto for advice about this.

The most expensive of the handmade wares are works of art, prized by museums and collectors and priced accordingly. But even big name potters sell smaller items or kiln seconds at very affordable prices. Several pottery towns have a craft gallery, run by the potters, where a wide selection of items will be displayed, without big mark-ups. The best places to start shopping are often the craft floors of local department stores; the Maruzen chain of book shops also has a few of these. Even humble city supermarkets carry a range of teapots, plates and bowls for a few hundred yen each: they may not be collectors' items, but are designed according to the same ideals of elegance, dignity and simplicity.

Popular ceramics include teapots and bowls, *sake* sets (a flask and cups), dishes and serving bowls, vases and ashtrays.

Kimono: Visitors sometimes come to Japan with the idea of buying a kimono, only to come away disappointed. There are many different types of kimono (the word means simply 'thing worn') but the kind familiar in the West from woodblock prints and photographs is more than just a silk dressing gown. Properly worn, it's a complicated item of formal attire with strict rules governing the choice of patterns, the co-ordination of the colours, the length of the sleeves and the cut of the gown. Japanese women often attend classes in the art of wearing kimono; mastery of it can take years, and a hand tailored garment costs as much as any evening dress.

It's also peculiarly unsuited to the Western figure. Even young Japanese women, taller and fuller-figured than their mothers, find strapping themselves into one rather a struggle; then there's the problem of walking and breathing at the same time. Of course the image of the kimono-clad woman as a gorgeous parcel, waiting to be unwrapped, is all part of the allure, but perhaps this is easier to appreciate when you're not wearing one. The traditional kimono, at least nowadays, is also rather a formal garment. Opportunities to wear one are rare enough in Japan, let alone back home in the West.

Of course, there's no reason why a kimono gown shouldn't be worn casually, and there are all kinds of places where these can be picked up cheaply enough. Department stores are worth investigating. Tourist shops always have a selection, but marked up and not always of the best quality. The best value of all are second-hand kimono. There are a handful of shops in Kyoto and Tokyo which specialize in these—for the price of a nasty nylon job from a souvenir shop, you'll be able to pick up the genuine silk article. The monthly fairs held at many shrines and temples are another good place to look: check local press for details.

Far more practical are *yukata*: light, cotton kimono with simple patterns in blue or black, worn by both men and women. They are usually provided in inn and hotel rooms. In traditional *ryokan* and *minshuku* you can wear them around the inn and in bed, instead of pyjamas. During the summer, especially in hot spring resorts, you will see people wearing them outside, with *geta*, clumpy wooden clogs. They are inexpensive, cool, comfortable, excellent for drying off in after a bath or *onsen*, and make fine souvenirs. Your inn may be willing to sell the *yukata* from your room; otherwise try department stores.

Other clothes: Japanese people are astonishingly neat and elegant, and many beautiful clothes, including the world's best designer goods, are on sale. For foreigners the problems are size and price. The above average *gaijin* counts as outsize in Japan. There is no equivalent of the discount 24-hour tailors in other Asian cities. Unless you simply can't live without it, wait to pay less back home.

Crafts

Along with pottery, hand-made crafts are the best Japanese souvenirs. When buying them, the same advice applies: visit a Folk Art Gallery (*Mingei-kan*) to get an idea of quality and design; try craft galleries and department store craft floors, and expect to pay more in obviously tourist-oriented shops.

wood

For centuries, wood has been the principal medium of Japanese sculpture, architecture, and many of its finest crafts. The best forests were once as valuable and closely guarded as gold mines, with ferocious penalties for timber smugglers. These days there are almost as many styles of wood craft as there are of ceramics.

Northern Japan has some particularly interesting wood crafts. The Ainu people of Hokkaidō carve blocks of soft wood into long, streamer-like wood shavings. In Yamagata prefecture, the *itto-bori* ('one-knife carving') technique is used to produce the tails and wings of wooden cockerels and owls. All over Tōhoku you will see *kokeshi*, limbless wooden dolls, the shape of giant pegs, which are produced on a spinning lathe, their features painted in with simple brush strokes. Kakunodate in Akita prefecture is famous for *sakura-kawa-zaiku*, a method of covering boxes and tea caddies with flexible cherry bark in rich dark colours. Nearer to Tokyo, Kamakura is the home of *Kamakura-bori*—plates, trays and boxes with cloud and flower designs carved into the surface in low relief, then burnished with a deep red lacquer and charcoal. In the *Hakone-zaiku* style, from the hot spring area under the shadow of Mt Fuji, the flat surfaces of trays and boxes are covered with a mosaic pattern of tiny squares of different coloured wood, in geometric patterns.

When purchasing wood crafts, check that they are solid. Cheaper wares are often produced by affixing an outer veneer to lower quality wood, metal or plastic (of course, these hybrids often look just the same as the real thing). The small objects described above usually cost no more than a few thousand yen each. Antique Japanese furniture—low tables for *tatami*, the big hardwood chests called *tansu*, and ingenious items like steps with space-saving drawers underneath—are much more expensive and hard to get hold of.

paper

Japanese paper, called *washi* to distinguish it from Western *yōshi*, is more than just a material for writing. It's a building and craft material in its own right, as delicate as tissue paper or as tough as canvas and used, in its various different textures and strengths, for sliding screens, windows, umbrellas and lampshades, as well as for writing and painting. The manufacturing process is laborious. Mulberry branches are steamed and stripped to expose the softened pith within, which is heated, rinsed, purified and pounded with mallets into a fine pulp. The sheets are formed on fine screens of bamboo mesh, then dried and individually trimmed and coloured. Some shops specialize in *washi* products—envelopes, cards, notepaper, lampshades, fans and waxed paper umbrellas all make inexpensive, lightweight souvenirs.

lacquer

Much Japanese architecture and craft emphasizes the natural grain and unpainted beauty of the wood. Lacquering does the opposite. The wood is sealed forever beneath a thin but impenetrable glaze of hardened sap. It's an acquired taste: to the uneducated eye, an opaque lacquer might just as well be a highly polished piece of plastic. The weight, texture and heft of the lacquered object in the hand all contribute to the connoisseur's appreciation. Like certain porcelains, the finest lacquer suggests unfathomable depth and mystery beneath the opaque exterior.

The raw lacquer—a brown, smelly, poisonous gum—is tapped from the *urushi* tree, and coloured and thickened before being applied in thin, even layers to a prepared surface of wood, paper, leather, or even metal. Each layer is dried for up to a week in a warm, humid, dust-free atmosphere, then polished with charcoal before the next layer is applied. This process might be repeated as many as 90 times. Finally, a sealing layer is applied and polished with powder made from deer's horns. The famous *maki-e* lacquerware has powdered gold and silver sprinkled onto the wet lacquer to produce iridescent patterns. Mother-of-pearl and semi-precious stones can also be incorporated. When a certain thickness has been achieved, the lacquer itself can be carved into three-dimensional designs.

Gizmos

Surprisingly, given its status as a world centre of technological innovation, Japan is not a particularly cheap place to buy cameras, computers, electronics and hi-fi. Hong Kong is much better, and you can haggle there too. With present exchange rates, it may be cheaper to buy Japanese technology in Europe or America. If there's a special piece of equipment you're looking for, investigate prices before you leave home, and then compare them with those in an electronics district like Tokyo's Akihabara. Don't assume you'll save anything, especially for bigger objects which require shipping fees and insurance.

Where Tokyo does lead the way is in innovation: the latest Japanese models are on sale here first, and if novelty is more important to you than price, you have come to the right place. State-of-the-art gizmos may not be available in export models, however, which means that anything running off the mains will require adaptors and transformers. Satisfy yourself that you understand the operation of your gadget before walking away with an instruction book written only in Japanese, and bear in mind that guarantees, spare parts and service warranties may be difficult to invoke once you have taken your toy home.

Sport

In Japan, if you look hard enough, you can find almost any sport on the planet, plus several you've probably never heard of, from Ultimate Frisbee to Gateball, a curious croquet-clone played by very old people in white hats. Sumo is the *kokugi* or 'national accomplishment', though it's rivalled in popularity by baseball, and recently by the J-League, a professional soccer tournament launched, to tremendous public enthusiasm, in 1993.

The same rules apply to spectator sport as to all leisure activities in Japan: book early and try to avoid weekends and public holidays. One of the easiest ways to get hold of tickets (although you pay for the convenience) is through one of the nationwide booking agencies. **Ticket Pia** has an English language line, ✆ 03 5237 9999. **Ticket Saison**, ✆ 03 5990 9999, and **CN Playguide**, ✆ 03 3257 9999, offer only Japanese—but you might be lucky and get an English-speaking operator. These are a few of the main places to see the main sports in the main cities. For dates and times of matches, see local media such as *Tokyo Journal*, *Kansai Time Out* and the English language newspapers.

sumo

There are six tournaments (*bashō*) a year: Tokyo in January, May and September; Ōsaka in March; Nagoya in July; and Fukuoka in November. They begin around the 10th of the month and last for 15 days. The excitement (and most intense demand for tickets) mounts in the last few days of the tournaments, when the junior wrestlers have been filtered out and the big stars compete with one another for the highest honours.

It can be very difficult to get a seat, as tickets tend to be block-booked by companies who disburse them as corporate freebies. If you have connections, use them. Failing that, ask the local tourist information centre for advice. A few tickets are reserved for sale on the day but you will often have to queue very early in the morning to be sure of these. A heavy sumo habit can be expensive: seats vary from a few thousand yen to a few tens of thousands for the most expensive boxes. During the course of a tournament every TV and radio in Japan seems to be tuned in to the sumo. You will certainly have plenty of chances to see the excitement, even if you don't make it in person.

In Tokyo, the **National Sumo Stadium** (Kokugikan) is close by Ryōgoku, on the JR Sōbu line, ✆ 03 3263 5111. In Ōsaka, the **Prefectural Sumo Stadium** (Furitsu Taiikukaikan) is 10 minutes on foot from Namba subway station, ✆ 06 631 0121.

baseball

Baseball was introduced in 1872 by Horace Wilson, an American teacher at the forerunner of Tokyo University. By the turn of the century most schools and colleges had baseball teams, and a professional league began in 1934. During the nationalistic war years, when Western influences and foreign words were undesirable, English loan words in the sport were banned. Baseball itself was, and sometimes still is, known as *yakyū*.

There are two leagues with six teams each. Teams are sponsored by corporations. The Pacific League, for instance, includes the Seibu Lions, owned by the department store chain, and the Nippon Ham Fighters (proprietor: Nippon Ham). The Central League contains the Chunichi Dragons, Hanshin Tigers, Hiroshima Toyo Carp, Taiyō Whales, Yakult Swallows and—everyone's favourites—the Yomiuri Giants. The **Giants** play at the vast Tokyo Dome stadium (nearest stations Suidōbashi on the JR Sōbu line, and Kōrakuen on the Marunouchi subway line). Tickets cost between ¥1000 and ¥5600. In the Kansai area, the **Hanshin Tigers** play at Nishinomiya, between Ōsaka and Kōbe.

soccer

Whatever the quality of the football, the launch of the J-League in 1993 was one of the most successful marketing exercises in history. In its first year it generated ¥140 million revenue in advertising, sponsorship and—above all—merchandising. Attendance at a Japanese football match has none of the tribal elements of the European sport, in fact which team you support hardly seems to matter. Having the right J-League bag, J-League mascot and J-League anorak is much more important.

Verdi Kawasaki, ✆ 044 946 3030 (owned by the giant Yomiuri newspaper corporation) is based near Musashikōsugi Station on the JR Nambū line or private Tōkyū Toyoko line. Take a bus from outside the station (on match days there will be plenty of people going in the same direction) to Shiei Todoroki Guraundo-mae.

In Kansai **Gamba Ōsaka**, ✆ 06 396 2121, are your team. Take the Midōsuji subway line to Senri Chūō station, and change to the Ōsaka monorail for Bampaku Kinen Kōen station. The ground is a 20-minute walk away.

martial arts

Judō, aikidō and karate aren't the only ones—there are more than 20, including *kendō* (fencing with wooden staves), *kyūdō* (archery, using the traditional bamboo bow) and *naginata* (the art of the Japanese halberd). For long-term visitors there are many local clubs and associations offering classes. Many *dōjō* (martial arts halls) admit visitors to watch practice and competitions. The most famous in Japan is the Nippon Budōkan in Tokyo's Kitanomaru Park, north of the Imperial Palace. For information about tournaments, of which there are dozens each year, ring ✆ 03 3216 5139; for details of classes call ✆ 03 3216 5143, preferably in Japanese (or try the tourist information centre which keeps English language information on both).

skiing

The 1997 Winter Olympics, to be held in Nagaro in the Japan Alps, will bring worldwide attention to winter sports in Japan. You wouldn't come here especially to ski but for those with the inclination there are many ski resorts in the Japan Alps, Tōhoku and Hokkaidō. Most of them are small by European standards, and the Japanese approach to skiing is different too. Fortnight-long holidays are rare—the typical break will be a weekend, beginning on Friday evening with an all-night coach journey from Tokyo, and ending the same way early on Monday morning. Resorts are run along familiar lines, with lift passes and equipment hire—but foreigners of a larger-than-average size should expect to have trouble finding suitable boots and skis. Check in advance that these will be available, or hire them before leaving town. For current prices and information on where to find snow-laden slopes, ask at the Tokyo TIC. Two companies which offer ski packages are **Beltop Travel Service**, ✆ 03 3454 6331 and **IJ Travel**, ✆ 0462 51 4556. **Club Med** (in London, ✆ 0171 581 1161) offers week-long skiing packages to Hokkaidō.

Telephones

Public phones come in several types and colours. **Red, pink** and **yellow phones**, often located on the street and inside small shops, are the most basic. They take ¥100 or sometimes just ¥10 coins, and are good only for domestic calls. **Green phones** accept telephone cards but only work within Japan. **Green phones with gold plates** and **grey phones** (the Rolls Royce of phones) can make direct-dialled international calls. Buy **telephone cards** from shops, hotels or vending machines in the phone booths.

For English language assistance with overseas calls, or to reverse the charges, insert a coin or card and dial 0051 for the KDD International Operator. To call overseas direct, dial 001, followed by the country code, followed by your full phone number, minus the initial zero. Home Country Direct is a free service which puts you in direct contact with an operator in your home country: UK, ✆ 0039 441, USA, ✆ 0039 111, Canada, ✆ 0039 161, Australia, ✆ 0039 611, New Zealand, ✆ 0039 641, Hong Kong, ✆ 0039 852.

Time

Japan is 9 hours ahead of Greenwich Mean Time (London), and 14 hours ahead of American Eastern Standard Time (New York). It has no daylight saving time, so during British Summer Time the difference is 8 hours.

Toilets

Japanese toilet technology is the most advanced in the world. Self-flushing lavatories with heated seats, built in bidets, hot air 'dryers' and recordings of light music or running water (to mask embarrassing noises) are commonplace. The littlest room in the Japanese house frequently has a button control plan reminiscent of the bridge of the Star Ship *Enterprise*, and there are even plans for a new generation of 'intelligent toilets' which will automatically process and analyze waste and warn the householder in advance of any worrying medical problems. At the same time, an amazing proportion of Japanese homes, even in the cities, are not on a mains sewer: at regular intervals a man driving a big tanker calls round, shoves his tube down the hole, switches on his suction pump, and slurps. The lesson is to be prepared for anything.

In tourist facilities, Western-style sit-down toilets are the rule these days, but you will come across the traditional Asian squat models, especially in small rail and bus stations. These usually consist of an oval hole with a ceramic hood nearest the wall. Squat over the hole, facing the hood (gents can also stand and aim), steadying yourself if necessary on the pipes on the wall. This can be a uncomfortable position for the unsupple: skiing exercises are the best practice. The biggest hazard, for those wearing trousers, is that keys, change, etc. will tumble out of your pockets and into the abyss below. The consequences of this could be unspeakable. Loos of the Asian type can be unreliably stocked with paper: as always when travelling, a miniature packet of tissues is invaluable. Smaller establishments sometimes don't have both a ladies and gents, so don't be surprised if a member of the opposite sex barges in while you are washing your hands.

The character for ladies is 女 ; for gentlemen 男 . Toilet can be rendered お手洗, *o-tearai*, literally 'honourable hand wash'. In extremis, ask for *toire* (pronounced 'toy-ray'). *Benjo* is a bit vulgar, but will get you where you need to be.

Tourist Offices

The best of these are run by the estimable **Japan National Tourist Organisation** (JNTO) which has 16 overseas offices, including the following:

United Kingdom:

> 167 Regent Street, London W1, ✆ 0171 734 9638.

United States:

> Rockefeller Plaza, 630 Fifth Avenue, Suite 2101, New York, NY 10111, ✆ 212 757 5640.

> 401 N. Michigan Avenue, Suite 770, Chicago, IL 60611, ✆ 312 222 0874.

> 2121 San Jacinto Street, Suite 980, Dallas, TX 75201, ✆ 214 754 1820.

> 360 Post Street, Suite 601, San Francisco, CA 94108, ✆ 415 989 7140.

> 624 S. Grand Avenue, Suite 1611, Los Angeles, CA 90017, ✆ 213 623 1952.

Canada:

> 165 University Avenue, Toronto, Ontario M5H 3B8, ✆ 416 366 7140.

Hong Kong:

Suite 3606, Two Exchange Square, 8 Connaught Place, Central, ✆ 525 5295.

Australia:

Lv 33, The Chifley Tower, 2 Chifley Square, Sydney, NSW 2000, ✆ 02 232 4522.

In Japan JNTO runs four **tourist information centres** where you can find out anything you need to know about travelling in Japan. Maps, pamphlets, brochures, bulletins, lists and magazines are available, as well as personal advice from multi-lingual assistants. The centres also take bookings for the Welcome Inn group of hotels. They can get crowded, and for personal assistance you may be required to take a number and wait in a queue.

Tokyo: Near Yūrakuchō JR station, 6–6 Yūrakuchō 1-chome, Chiyoda-ku, Tokyo 100, ✆ 03 3502 1461.

Kyoto: Under Tokyo Tower, opposite the main JR station, Kyoto Tower Building, Higashi Shiokōji-chō, Shimogyō-ku, Kyoto 600, ✆ 075 371 5649.

Narita Airport: Two desks, in both Passenger Terminals 1 and 2, New Tokyo International Airport, Narita, Chiba 282. Terminal 1, ✆ 0476 32 8711; Terminal 2, ✆ 0476 34 6251.

Tourist information centres also operate the **Japan Travel Phone**, a nationwide service for those in need of English-language information and assistance. In Tokyo, dial ✆ 03 3503 4400; in Kyoto, ✆ 075 371 5649. You will be charged as if for a local call. Outside Tokyo these calls are free. For information on eastern Japan ring ✆ 0800 222800; for western Japan, ✆ 0800 224800. The service operates from 9am to 5pm daily.

Many prefectures, cities and towns operate their own tourist offices. These are principally aimed at Japanese tourists, but usually have some English-language information as well. They go under various names—tourist information office (*kankō annaijō*) or tourist association (*kankō kyōkai*). Almost all of them are located in or opposite JR railway stations.

Where to Stay

Japan's inns and hotels are among its biggest attractions. Top Tokyo hotels such as the Imperial and the Ōkura, and Kyoto *ryokan* like the Tawaraya, are as luxurious as anywhere in the world, but even in modest family-run inns, standards of service and courtesy are uniformly high, and rip-offs are almost unheard of.

The most important consideration, after price, is whether you want to stay in Western-style or Japanese-style accommodation. Even within these categories there are distinctions, but Japanese-style establishments will generally be in low-rise buildings (sometimes, but not always, made of wood), furnished with *tatami*, with shared Japanese baths. Guests take off their shoes, sleep on futon mattresses laid on the floor and eat Japanese food in their rooms. Western-style means you keep your shoes and sleep on a bed in a room which usually has a private bathroom. Some Western-style hotels have Japanese-style rooms or wings and vice versa. Nobody who visits Japan should miss the chance to stay at least once in a Japanese-style inn. The cheaper *minshuku* are not expensive: consider it as crucial a part of your holiday as travelling on the bullet train or tasting raw fish.

Western-style

International hotels range from one-offs like the Imperial and Ōkura in Tokyo, to nationwide networks like the Tōkyū, Ōtani, Prince, ANA, and Hilton. All have English-speaking staff, multiple restaurants and business facilities; many have pools, gardens, shopping arcades and gymnasia. **Resort hotels** are found in mountain and seaside locations, and are aimed at holiday-makers rather than businesspeople, with hot springs, golf links and often a floor of Japanese-style rooms. Prices generally begin at a minimum of ¥12,000 for a single, more in the big cities.

Business hotels are designed for convenience, compactness and low price. The basics of the standard hotel room—lavatory, bath, shower, sink, bed, TV, cupboard—are concentrated into an ingeniously small space. They seldom have much character, but are usually in good positions, close to railway stations and downtown. Nationwide business hotels, like the Tōkyū Inn, Washington and Sunroute chains, often rival the city hotels in terms of restaurants and facilities, with smaller rooms and lower prices (from about ¥6000).

Pensions are hardly Western-style at all, though they may think they are. They are found in ski, hot spring and resort areas and provide Western-style rooms (beds and carpets), home cooking and friendly family service. Many are purpose-built in an allegedly Alpine 'chalet-style'; interiors are often 'cute' (i.e. kitsch). From ¥7000 or so, including meals.

Japanese-style

A night in a traditional Japanese inn is a unique experience, a combination of theatre, architecture and gastronomy that may well be the high point of your holiday. Inns vary widely but fall into three principal categories.

Ryokan and **minshuku** overlap and the designation is often an arbitrary one. The biggest distinction is price: top *ryokan* are world-class restaurants housed in miniature palaces, and can cost ¥50,000 upwards per person. More modest ones, in regional towns, are as cheap as ¥8000. *Minshuku* are a bit like bed-and-breakfasts, run by families with whom you eat your breakfast and evening meal. Service is more informal—you may have to lay out your own bedding for instance, although someone will always be on hand if you're not sure what layer goes where. *Shukubō* are temples which provide *ryokan*-style accommodation. They are generally found near big Buddhist complexes and are principally intended for pilgrims, although non-believers are usually welcome.

a night in a Japanese inn

You'll be asked, when you make your reservation, what time you expect to arrive—try to keep to this, and phone ahead if you are likely to be significantly late or early. You'll be greeted in the *genkan* or entrance porch and, after removing outdoor shoes and donning slippers, escorted to your room by a maid. The Japanese guest expects to be fussed, almost mothered, and, compared to the invisible discreetness cultivated in grand Western hotels, *ryokan* service is hands-on. This can be off-putting if you're not used to it, but don't be surprised if your maid hovers around and pops repeatedly in and out, enquiring after your every need in incomprehensibly polite and formal Japanese—a nod and a smile are all that's needed to reassure her. No matter how solicitous she is, a tip is never necessary.

Slippers are removed before you step onto the *tatami* matting which covers the floors of your room. Before you unpack, your maid will serve green tea and sweet bean cakes at the low table in the middle of the room. After this, you will be asked when you wish to eat, though in a smaller inn or *minshuku*, the time may be fixed. *Ryokan* usually have a preferred period when they serve meals, often surprisingly early—from 6 to 8. It may a bit of a liberty to expect food after this time and, once again, you must keep to schedule. It may be assumed that, as a foreigner, you're unable to eat anything but pork chops and scrambled eggs—if this isn't the case, make a point of saying that you want Japanese food. You'll also be asked to fill in a form with your name, nationality and passport number. Next you'll be shown the facilities of the inn, including the toilet and bath. Japanese generally take a bath before eating, and dine in their rooms, wearing the *yukata*, a blue and white patterned cotton kimono, provided in each room. (You may be able to buy one of these before leaving.) Consult the sections on 'Baths and Hot Springs' and 'Toilets' for the etiquette appropriate to each of these rooms.

At the agreed time your food will be brought to you on trays, along with any drinks you have ordered. When the meal has been cleared away, your futon will be laid out on the *tatami*, and you will be left to your own devices. Posh *ryokan* would never be so presumptuous as to impose a curfew (smaller places might), but if you do intend to be out late, notify them of this, or request a late key.

Other types of accommodation

Youth hostels, both official and unofficial, are found all over the country, and are always the cheapest places to stay in the short term. They vary in quality. The best ones, often in mountain areas and national parks, can be beautiful buildings in their own right, run by enthusiastic volunteers who will have up-to-date and expert information on local hiking, cycling and skiing. The worst are grim detention centres run by embittered despots. JNTO publishes a guide map listing about 300 reliable hostels. Rates vary between ¥2000 and ¥4000, with or without meals.

Gaijin (foreigner) **houses** are cheap, urban lodgings for back-packers who are spending a few weeks in one place. They have a reputation for being rowdy and squalid, but are good places for gathering information about travelling and jobs.

The famous Japanese **capsule hotels** aren't nearly so ubiquitous as everyone seems to expect. Found near big urban transport termini, they offer a coffin-like bedroom with built-in TV and alarm clock, and a lounge area with machines vending noodles and drinks. Their clientele seems to consist entirely of single men: unaccompanied women might feel distinctly odd in one of these, or even be refused entry.

Love hotels are another Japanese phenomenon: rooms, rented by the hour or by the night, for amorous purposes. In a country of thin-walled houses and limited privacy, they're a blessing for married as well as illicit couples. There's nothing necessarily seedy about them, although theme love hotels may feature gaudy decor, whips, manacles and electric accessories. Bizarre though it may sound, they can be a very economical form of accommodation. Rates (higher at weekends) are generally no more than a business hotel, with the advantage that you pay by the room, not the person. In theory the whole family could bed down for as little as ¥10,000, as long as you don't mind a late check-in (nightly bookings begin after 10pm) and early check-out.

reservations

Reservations are advisable in most situations, especially for non-Japanese speakers. Japanese tourists book every night of their holidays months in advance, and at busy times (public holidays, during big festivals and the entrance exam season) your choice will be restricted if you don't think at least a few weeks ahead.

Arriving off a thirteen-hour flight into the bedlam of Tokyo or Ōsaka, it's certainly reassuring to know where you are going to lay your head. You can book from home through **travel agents** (see pp.5–6) like NTA or JTB, or through the foreign offices of big chains like Tōkyū and Prince Hotels. Overseas offices of the Japan National Tourist Organization (JNTO) provide leaflets and brochures, including information on the reasonable Japanese Inn Group and Directory of Welcome Inns (see below). Most lodgings in Japan have faxes.

In Japan itself, there are many options. Your hotel will often phone on your behalf to make reservations for the next night's accommodation. Agents often charge a commission. For cheaper accommodation use the free service provided by the **Welcome Inn Reservation Centre**, ✆ 03 3211 4201, 📠 03 3211 9009, or its satellite desks in the Tokyo, Kyoto and Narita Airport tourist information centres. Hundreds of small hotels, *ryokan* and *minshuku* are classified as Welcome Inns; all charge less than ¥8000 a night and are used to foreign guests. A similar service (for Japanese-style accommodation only) is provided by the members of the excellent **Japanese Inn Group** (book yourself in English; pick up a brochure from a tourist information centre or JNTO office).

If you find yourself getting off the train with nowhere to stay, go straight to the local tourist information centre, usually called the *kankō annaijo* or *kankō kyōkai*. Even the smallest towns have these, often located in the railway station. The chances are that someone there will have at least a few words of English. Explain how much you want to spend, how long you'll stay, and whether you want meals or not: they will phone round for you and point you in the right direction.

Alternatively, phone yourself. The chances of finding an English speaker increase proportionately to the cost of the establishment and its proximity to a big city. Small town *minshuku* owners are likely to get flustered by a foreign voice gabbling incomprehensibly on the end of a phone: If you have Japanese, use it; if not, don't be surprised if phones are hung up on you. Off the beaten track you may notice a reluctance on the part of proprietors to accommodate foreigners. Infuriating though this can be, it's based on a fear of misunderstanding rather than xenophobia, and a pervasive image of foreigners as gallumphing disaster areas liable to wear their shoes on the *tatami*, use soap inside the bath, and vomit at the merest sight of something uncooked. The onus is on you to be reassuring: smile and nod a lot, never lose your temper, and season your speech with phrases like *Nihongo o wakarimasu* (I understand Japanese), *Ofuro o wakarimasu* (I know how to use the Japanese bath), and *Ofuton/washoku ga ii desu yo* (Sleeping on a futon/Japanese food is absolutely fine).

Depending on the vicissitudes of the exchange rate, deluxe accommodation costs about the same in Japan as anywhere in the world. It is at the bottom end of the scale that choices become more limited. There simply is no equivalent of the £12 bed-and-breakfast. Even youth hostels rarely come cheaper than ¥2000 a night. There are bargains here and there but, on the whole, you get what you pay for. If a place seems unrealistically cheap there is probably be a reason (small rooms, poor transport links, inconvenient position, etc.)

The good news is that accommodation, certainly in the medium price bracket, seems to be getting cheaper. A combination of recession and stiff competition is causing hotels to drop their prices and good deals (big discounts, a double room for the price of a single) can be had. They're usually available only for limited periods, and aren't prominently advertised outside Japan; non-specialist agents may not know about them. Ask your nearest JNTO office and try phoning around the overseas offices of a few of the big chains.

In this book, prices for accommodation are banded according to the following categories:

luxury	above ¥30,000
expensive	¥15,000 – ¥30,000
moderate	¥ 8000 – ¥15,000
inexpensive	¥ 4500 – ¥ 8000
cheap	¥ 4500 and under

These categories are based on a single room (in Western-style accommodation) or a single night for one person (Japanese-style). Double rooms in hotels usually cost a bit less than two singles; in a *ryokan* or *minshuku*, however, even if several people share a room, they will generally all pay the full per person rate. Note, though, that Japanese-style accommodation almost always includes breakfast and dinner. Thus a moderate *ryokan* charging ¥8000 a head is actually a better bargain than an inexpensive single hotel room at ¥7000—as long as you are prepared to stay in for your Japanese meal and breakfast. If you don't want these, you can sometimes negotiate a lower rate at the less formal places. Note that the prices categorized above exclude service and a 3% consumption tax. In resorts and big cities, seasonal rates may apply.

Women Travellers

For a Japanese woman to travel extensively alone is considered unusual. Foreigners who do this can expect curious enquiries, but no unpleasant attention. The biggest cities have astonishingly low crime rates; even in a self-consciously seedy area like Tokyo's Kabukichō, it would be possible to walk around alone all night and suffer nothing worse than a few cat-calls and cheeky glances. Foreign women occasionally report being groped on crowded commuter trains. The perpetrator of this intrusion relies on the Japanese reluctance to draw public attention to oneself, whatever the circumstances; a Japanese girl would blush in silence and get off at the next station. Foreigners should feel no such compunction. Grabbing the offending hand in a vice-like lock, and announcing out loud that you have caught a *chikan* (pervert) should bring the incident to a swift conclusion.

History

Until the tragedies of the present century, Japanese history reads like a fantastic comic book, dense with grotesque heroes, baroque battles and gaudy detail—gripping for as long as you are immersed in it, but easy to forget once you've cast it to one side. Minamoto no Yoritomo, Oda Nobunaga, Tokugawa Ieyasu—the names are as exotic and meaningless to first-time visitors as Lex Luther and the Incredible Hulk. Who are these people? What have they to do with us?

The answer, a lot of the time, is nothing. In the late 1630s, less than a century after Japan's first, tentative contacts with the European world, the ruling shogun instituted a policy later known as *sakoku*—'closed country'. All Europeans, bar a handful of Dutch sailors in Nagasaki, were expelled within the space of a few years. Japanese nationals were forbidden any contact with the outside world; anyone who left the country was promised execution if they ever returned. The policy remained in force until 1853. In the rest of the world, kingdoms, empires and republics rose and fell, colonies were founded and lost, trade networks were established, industrialization spread across Europe and America, and unprecedented advances were made in the fields of science, philosophy, warfare and the arts. To all of this great intermingling of ideas and people and influences, Japan was oblivious.

For 250 years, the country was a sealed cabinet, a fable commemorated only in sailors' stories and on the edge of old maps. History (along with art, theatre, music, literature, science, religion and politics) was turned in on itself. Japan was (and still is, in many ways) like one of those freakish Oceanic islands, isolated from the continental mainstream by acres of sea, where nature is left to do its own thing, nurturing weird blooms and bizarre wildlife, a country of cultural platypuses and eucalyptus trees.

Periods of Japanese History

c. 10,000–c. 300 BC	Jōmon period	1333–1573	Muromachi period
c. 300 BC–c. AD 300	Yayoi period	1573–1600	Momoyama period
c. 300–c. 700	Kofun period	1600–1868	Edo period
538–645	Asuka period	1868–1912	Meiji period
645–710	Hakuhō period	1912–1926	Taishō period
710–794	Nara period	1926–1989	Shōwa period
794–1185	Heian period	1989–	Heisei period
1192–1333	Kamakura period		

Mythical Origins

The earliest account of Japanese history is the *Kojiki* (Records of Ancient Matters), an extraordinary chronicle compiled from traditional legends in the 8th century, which describes the sensational origins of the Japanese islands. They were formed by the incestuous union of **Izanagi** and **Izanami**, a brother and sister who came down from the Plain of High Heaven 'when the earth, young and like unto floating oil, drifted about medusa-like'. Unsure of where to make a landing, they dipped a jewelled spear into this primeval soup, and the brine which dripped off it coalesced into land.

Having established this first base, Izanami and her brother set about procreating first the other islands, and then the gods and goddesses of Japan. Not all of these were conceived in the conventional way. In fact, the divine couple could hardly scratch an itch without some new god or other springing into spontaneous life. The chroniclers gave them elaborate polysyllabic names, like the deity Heavenly-Water-Drawing-Gourd-Possessor, and the brother and sister team, Foam-Calm and Bubble-Calm.

During one particularly gruelling bout of child-bearing, Izanami had the misfortune to give birth to the fire god, an experience from which she never recovered. Even this tragedy brought forth new life, however, as new deities burst forth from her vomit and bodily fluids and her brother/lover's tears. Izanagi made the mistake of seeking out his loved one, by now rotting and infested with maggots, in the underworld. Fleeing from this horrible vision, he purified himself, and as he washed his eye, a new deity came into life. This was the sun goddess, **Amaterasu**, the most famous and revered of the ancient gods of Japan, whose shrine at Ise, near Kyoto, is the holy of holies of the Shinto religion.

Several generations of feuding, fighting and frantic copulation later, the descendants of the divine duo had spread throughout Japan. In 660 BC (on 11 February according to the legend, even today a national holiday), **Jimmu Tennō**, great-great-great-grandson of Amaterasu, celebrated his subjugation of central Japan by building a palace, and became the country's first emperor. Until 1946, when the late Emperor Hirohito formally renounced his divinity, all incumbents of the Chrysanthemum Throne claimed direct descent from Amaterasu Ōmikami, the Heaven-Shining-Great-August Deity.

Prehistory

Jōmon (10,000 BC–300 BC), Yayoi (300 BC–AD 300) and Kofun (AD 300–c. 700) periods

Splendid though they are, the *Kojiki* stories are not, of course, history; they are not even mythology. Their original function was political—propaganda designed to reinforce the authority and prestige of the imperial house, and to give form to the Japanese people's centuries-old conviction of their own uniqueness.

The inhabitants of Japan did not jump down from the clouds, and nor did their home. Until the end of the last ice age, around 11,000 BC, it was not even an island. Two great land bridges (later submerged by the rising sea) stretched to Siberia in the north and Korea to the west, and across these came waves of immigrants from China and Korea. The nature of these proto-Japanese is obscure; scholars make the best of an impenetrably murky prehistory by dividing it up into periods, based on archaeological finds.

The earliest known inhabitants were the Neolithic **Jōmon** (10,000 BC–300 BC), primitive hunter-gatherers who take their name from a style of pottery—striking, thick-rimmed earthenware decorated by pressing rope against the wet clay. Jōmon culture was concentrated in the north of the country; traces of it seem to have survived with the **Ainu**, a mysterious race of Siberian or even Caucasian origin, who underwent forced assimilation in the 19th century, but who still live in small numbers in present-day Hokkaidō.

Jōmon culture was supplanted by the **Yayoi** (300 BC–AD 300), a rice-growing people who imitated the bronze and iron instruments of their Chinese forebears, and spread into central Japan from their settlements in Kyūshū. It is during this period (perhaps the 1st century AD) that the historical prototype of Emperor Jimmu may have lived—one theory holds that he was a pirate-adventurer from Malaysia who united the bickering tribes, and imposed a form of central government based in the Yamato Plain, the site of present-day Nara. A Chinese chronicle of the late 2nd century describes the 'Land of Wa' (probably Kyūshū), ruled over by a shamaness-queen called Himiko or Pimiko, and details the habits of the people. 'They are much given to strong drink. They are a long-lived race, and persons who have reached 100 are very common. All men of high rank have four or five wives; others two or three. The women are faithful and not jealous. There is no robbery or theft, and litigation is infrequent.' Some of these generalizations hold true even today.

Large earth burial mounds, many containing elaborate bronze, glass and clay ornaments, give their name to the **Kofun** (tumulus) period (AD 300–c. 700)—in remote and unconquered parts of northern and eastern Japan, these tombs were being built as late as the beginning of the 8th century. By this time, the clans of the Yamato region were loosely united under the leadership of a dominant family, whose chieftain called himself emperor, and claimed divine descent. There was large-scale immigration from Korea and China, and much trade, mercantile and intellectual, was carried on with the Asian mainland, including two of the imports which have done most to shape the country as it exists today. The first was the adoption of Chinese ideograms in the writing of the (linguistically quite distinct) Japanese language. The second, also from China via Korea, was Buddhism.

The Rise of Buddhism
Asuka (538–645) and Hakuhō (645–710) periods

In the mid-6th century, a friendly Korean prince, angling for the loan of troops from his Japanese allies, sent to the emperor a Buddhist image, a collection of sutras and a letter commending the new religion, 'of all doctrines the most excellent'. The present provoked a rift in the Yamato aristocracy, between the powerful **Soga** and **Nakatomi** clans—the former champions of Buddhism, the latter hereditary high priests of Shinto. Successive emperors inclined first one way and then the other, but, by the end of the 6th century, temples had been built, more priests, statues and scriptures shipped over from Korea, and the new faith was firmly established—alongside Shinto which, despite the political rivalry between the different clans, it never sought to displace.

In 607 the great temple of Hōryū-ji, near Nara, was founded by the Prince Regent **Shōtoku Taishi** (572–621), an outstanding figure of Japanese cultural history, who—as a sculptor, artist, moralist, philosopher, teacher and scriptural commentator—did much to promote Buddhism, at least among the ruling classes. A coup headed by the rival Nakatomi family broke the power of the Soga clan. The emperor was deposed, a compliant rival crowned in his place, and in 646 the **Taika** (Great Reform) was promulgated, an ambitious new constitution which sought to abolish the clan system, replacing local chieftains with imperially appointed governors who would administer law and order and dispatch taxes to the central coffers. This ambitious and minutely bureaucratic centralized government, based on the Chinese model, was the work of the chief rebel, **Fujiwara Kamatari** (614–669). The imperial throne continued to pass smoothly from one emperor to the next, but in reality, for about 400 years, the Fujiwara family were the true rulers of Japan.

The Nara Period 710–794

The Taika reforms also made provision for the construction of a new permanent capital (until now the residence of the emperor had been moved after the death of the previous incumbent), but it wasn't until 710 that this was finally achieved. **Nara**, built on a geometric grid in imitation of the Chinese capital, Chang-an, was Japan's first real city, and the stability which it afforded to the imperial household fostered a vigorous artistic culture, much of it self-consciously emulating the glorious Tang dynasty. This was the time of the *Kojiki* (712), and a later volume of chronicles, the *Nihon-shoki* (720), both of them imitating Chinese histories. As well as the new palace (now an archaeological site), the great temples of Yakushi-ji, Tōshōdai-ji, Kōfuku-ji and, above all, Tōdai-ji (752), were built in Nara. Their halls were filled with statues and paintings from the workshops of the continental artisans who had been settling in the area for several generations; for the first time Japanese art began to take on a recognizably Japanese character. Gifts from visiting dignitaries, as well as touchingly personal everyday objects like toys and dolls, were stored in the Shōsō-in imperial repository where they can still be seen today.

The Heian Period 794–1185

The Nara temples were centres of education and art, but they were also crucial administrative bases, the collection points for the regional taxes levied by the Fujiwaras. The power and wealth of the bonzes eventually put them at odds with the aristocratic government. Some of the more worldly abbots even kept their own militias, and by 784 their threatening presence was causing unease among the Fujiwaras who moved the capital briefly to Nagaoka and then, in 794, to **Heian-kyō**, which remained the capital of Japan— later as Miyako, finally as Kyoto—until 1868.

The Heian period was one of the peaks of Japanese civilization although, even in Kyoto, pitifully few of its relics have survived to the present day. It began with a long and eventually victorious campaign against the Ainu 'barbarians' in the north, and ended in civil war, but for the greater part of nearly 400 years there was peace, under the firm stewardship of the **Fujiwara clan**.

They ruled by an ingenious system of 'marriage politics'. A young emperor, often no more than a child, would be married off to an older (i.e. teenage) Fujiwara daughter, of which there were many. He would remain on the throne for just long enough to father an heir, and then abdicate in favour of the child, who had a Fujiwara mother, a Fujiwara grandmother and, as often as not, a Fujiwara regent ruling in his name. There the cycle began again. The family trees of the time are dense circuit diagrams of criss-crossing relationships. The greatest of the chancellors, **Fujiwara Michinaga** (966–1027), managed to become father-in-law of two emperors, grandfather of a third, grandfather and great-grandfather of a fourth, and grandfather and father-in-law of a fifth.

This incestuous, inward-looking world bred one of the most delicate and appealing civilizations in history. With political power securely in the grasp of a single family, the emperor and his court were able to concentrate on the finer things in life: state ceremonial, contemplation of the beauties of nature, literature and art, and love affairs—which became a kind of art form in themselves, the subject of strict etiquette and forms of behaviour. In literature, the courtly poets perfected the delicate, gnomic 31-syllable *tanka*. More accessible to modern readers are the prose works of the period, many of them by women: tragic dewy-eyed stories of doomed lovers and selfless servants, gossipy diaries and feverish love letters—all of which are combined in Lady Murasaki's unique, and thoroughly readable, *Tale of Genji* (*Genji Monogatari*) written around AD 1000. Equally brilliant, but often anonymous, achievements in the visual and plastic arts—architecture (both secular and religious), painting (on silk, screen and scroll), lacquered boxes and furniture, calligraphy and sculpture—as well as the architecture and landscape gardening of the temples, shrines and palaces—made Kyoto one of the cultural treasures of Asia, a city as rich and multi-textured as Venice, Byzantium or Oxford.

After centuries of enthusiastic apprenticeship, Japan was outgrowing the influence of the Tang dynasty which, in any case, had internal problems of its own. Concepts and institutions, originally imported from China generations ago, were given unique, home-grown inflections—the familiar process of 'Japanization'. So, although Chinese characters, to this day, form the basis of the written language, scribes during this period developed the two *kana* syllabaries for spelling out Japanese pronunciations and indicating the grammatical function of individual words. Two monks, Saichō and Kūkai, returned from study in China to establish radically new schools of Buddhism—the **Tendai** and **Shingon** sects—which fused traditional teaching with the native gods and goddesses of Shinto. In 894 the official missions to Chang-an were terminated. For the next few centuries, Japanese culture stood aloof from the rest of the world, stewing confidently in its own rich juice.

But great changes were also in the offing. The Fujiwaras began running out of marriageable daughters and the emperors began to assert themselves. After centuries of successfully playing one regional clan leader off against another, the Fujiwara family, in the 12th century, became factionalized. The court had no military resources of its own, so the competing branches enlisted the support of certain regional clans among whom two arch enemies—the **Minamoto** and the **Taira**—were paramount. For a while the Taira, under their ruthless leader **Taira no Kiyomori** (1118–81), were victorious, and began the task of insinuating themselves into the royal dynasty as the Fujiwara had before them. But the sons of the defeated Minamoto renewed the struggle a generation later in an epic civil war, dramatized in plays, paintings and poems like *Tales of the Heike*, as central to Japan's culture as the Trojan war is to Europe's.

In 1185, the last of the defeated Taira threw themselves into the sea at the battle of **Dan no Ura** in the straits of Shimonoseki between Honshū and Kyūshū.

The emperor was allowed to remain in Kyoto, in powerless but untroubled luxury. But the true seat of power moved to the coastal town of Kamakura with the victorious general **Minamoto no Yoritomo** (1147–99).

The Kamakura Period 1185–1333

In 1192 Yoritomo was granted the title 'great barbarian subduing general', *sei-i tai-shōgun*, or *shōgun* for short. It was a profound change: for the next 800 years, military men, rather than civilian courtiers, wielded true power in Japan. They were the first samurai ('those who serve'), and it was during this time that the warrior code of service, obedience, and loyalty-to-the-death first found widespread expression. It was also a period of great artistic achievement: the large-scale rebuilding of the war-damaged temples of Nara and Kyoto fostered vigorous new schools of sculpture, and the austere **Zen sect**, which found particular favour with the samurai, brought with it from China fresh architectural techniques.

Yoritomo died in a riding accident in 1199 and within a few years his heirs had been usurped, in all but name, by another warrior family, the Hōjō. A bizarre system of government now existed, suggestive of those Russian dolls, each containing a smaller and still smaller replica. Japan's nominal ruler, the emperor, delegated authority to a Minamoto shogun, who was in turn a puppet of the **Hōjō regent**. All three titles were hereditary, and the picture was often complicated by the existence of a retired monk-emperor who effectively dictated the actions of his successor, after his formal abdication. Amazingly, thanks to the efficiency of the Hōjō, this system ran fairly smoothly for a hundred years.

The great crisis came in 1268 when the Kamakura government received a haughty letter from the great Mongol conqueror **Khubla Khan**. Addressed to 'the King of Japan', from 'the Emperor of Great Mongolia', it demanded tribute from the Japanese, and threatened war if none was forthcoming. When the demand was repeated a few years later, the envoys who carried it to Kamakura were beheaded. In 1274, therefore, 60,000 of the Khan's men sailed to Kyūshū in 450 ships. They made a great impression on the defending Japanese with their powerful long bows and rock-throwing artillery, but, after inconclusive fighting, storms arose and the fleet was dispersed with the loss of nearly a quarter of its men. Seven years later, Khubla Khan tried again, this time with a force of 150,000. In Japan there had been frantic preparations, including a defensive wall along the north coast of Kyūshū. Prayers for national deliverance were held in every temple and shrine across the country, and the Hōjō regent copied out sutras in his own blood.

Two separate armadas began to arrive in waves from the end of June 1281, and fighting continued for more than 50 days. Then another mighty storm arose and blew furiously for two days. It uprooted entire trees, and blew the Mongol boats far out to sea, or dashed them aground on the rocks. Less than half the original force limped back to the continent.

Yet again a 'divine wind', the original *kamikaze*, had been sent by the gods to save Japan. Actually the country remained on war alert for another 20 years and the cost of the crisis brought about the downfall of the Hōjō regency. After successful civil wars, the victor could reward his allies and supporters with enemy territory. The repulsion of the Mongols brought reprieve from slavery, but no material gain. Regional lords raised militias out of their own coffers, and peasants were conscripted to the detriment of the rice crop. In 1333 there was a serious dispute about the imperial succession. One of the candidates, **Emperor Go-Daigo**, mustered enough support to send an army to Kamakura. A number of the town's defenders defected to the other side and when the city fell, the last Hōjō regent, with 800 of his family and retainers, committed suicide in a mountain cave.

The Muromachi Period 1333–1573

For 60 years, two imperial factions—the **Northern and Southern Dynasties**—maintained bickering claims to the throne. In the end, the southern court, rivals of the late Go-Daigo, were victorious, but the real winners were another military family, the Ashikaga, who had themselves proclaimed hereditary shoguns from 1336. Kyoto was once again the administrative, as well as cultural, capital of Japan, but the emperors were no closer to real power than they had been a century before.

The rule of the **Ashikaga shoguns** was characterized by extremes of artistic distinction and political disaster. Culturally, it was one of the richest periods in Japan's history. Under Ashikaga patronage, many of the forms and genres considered today as quintessentially Japanese achieved their greatest expression. Zen Buddhism flourished, and Zen masters built superb meditation gardens, like the moss garden at Saihō-ji by the priest-artist, **Musō Kokushi**. New architectural forms also emerged, from the simple but artful huts built for the **tea ceremony**, to the exquisite villas built by the Ashikagas for their retirement, the **Golden** and the **Silver Pavilions**. Here the shoguns drank tea, watched performances of *nō* drama, and amassed priceless collections of ink paintings and ceramics, especially those of the Chinese Sung dynasty with whom relations had been resumed. The canons of taste established by the Ashikaga rulers—quietness, understatement, a taste for natural subjects and rustic simplicity—underpin Japanese aesthetics even today.

They were bitterly ironic ideals. Outside the temples and pleasure palaces, often in the streets of Kyoto itself, Japan was in a state of almost continuous civil war. Even after the succession dispute was resolved, battles between regional feudal lords, fanned by epidemics and famine, smouldered on in different parts of the country. From 1467 to

1477 the **Ōnin Wars** made a battleground of the capital itself. Shogunal authority was at an all-time low; the imperial court moved helplessly from place to place, as one palace after another was burned down. One emperor was even reduced to selling examples of his own calligraphy to buy food and fuel. The period from 1500 is known as *Sengoku jidai*, the Era of the Country at War.

The most interesting development of the 16th century came in 1542 when a crew of Portuguese sailors were shipwrecked on Tanegashima island, off southeast Kyūshū. Portuguese merchants and missionaries from China and Malaysia followed, and in 1549 the Spaniard **Francis Xavier** (later St Francis) was given permission to preach in Kyūshū and Yamaguchi where he gained many Christian converts. Even more significant, perhaps, was the other Western invention which the Portuguese brought with them: gunpowder and arquebuses, which were enthusiastically copied by local craftsmen. For centuries afterwards muskets were known in Japan as *tanegashima*.

The Momoyama Period 1573–1600

In the late 16th century, three great generals emerged from the mass of feuding samurai and between them brought order to the country. The first was **Oda Nobunaga** (1534–82), heir to a minor barony south of Kyoto, who attracted the attention of the emperor after a series of victories over technically superior armies. The Kyoto government was at its lowest ebb with the Ashikaga shogun a virtual refugee. Within a few years Nobunaga had supplanted him in all but name, and became the emperor's protector, rebuilding the Imperial Palace, as well as a personal stronghold, Azuchi-jō, the first of Japan's modern castles. He was extremely tolerant of the Jesuits ('These are the men I like,' he said, 'upright, sincere, and who tell me solid things.'), largely because he saw them as a means of breaking the power of the Buddhist orders which, with their large estates and private armies, contributed much to the bloodiness of the era. His most famous display of ruthlessness came in 1571 when he burned down the 3000 temples of Mt Hiei, northeast of Kyoto, and butchered their inhabitants. Two years later he imprisoned the last of the Ashikagas, and became *de facto* shogun. On his death, at the hands of a disaffected lord, he was master of half of the provinces of Japan, and all the most central and strategically important ones.

Nobunaga was succeeded by **Toyotomi Hideyoshi** (1536–98), one of his most brilliant lieutenants, who saw off the Oda heirs and cemented his authority with the construction of a massive castle at Ōsaka. Hideyoshi, a small, exceedingly ugly man, was born the son of a foot soldier and rose by sheer intelligence; he was a skilled diplomat as well as a warrior, and throughout his life showed a love of extravagance and display verging on megalomania. Hideyoshi's two palaces (one of them, at Momoyama, south of Kyoto, lent its name to the period) were as rich and gaudy as the Ashikagas' were austere and restrained, with profuse carvings of flowers, Chinese legends, and mythical monsters on gates, pillars and transoms; visionary screen paintings of mountain sides, peopled by sages and tigers, in bright colours and gold leaf; curving eaves and heavy tile roofs. Hideyoshi loved public spectacle: on one fabled occasion in 1597, he held at his palace a huge open-air tea ceremony to which everyone in the country, from peasants to lords, was invited.

The festivities went on for ten days. After his death the palaces were dismantled and distributed hall by hall among Kyoto temples like Nishi Hongan-ji where they were recon-structed and preserved to the present day.

By 1590, after the siege of Odawara, the remaining provinces yielded to Hideyoshi's control, but even this didn't quench his ambitions. Rather than consolidating his remark-able achievement—national peace, for the first time in 260 years—Hideyoshi set about the astonishing project of invading and subduing Korea and China. Two separate armies set sail, in 1592 and 1597. The first got as far as the Korean-Chinese border; the second was making slower progress when, in 1598, news came through of Hideyoshi's death, and the campaign was abandoned.

Tokugawa Ieyasu (1542–1616) was one of the trustees appointed by Hideyoshi to guar-antee the succession of his son, a trusted ally who had given loyal service to Nobunaga before him. A famous tale illustrates the differences in character between the three men. Nobunaga, Hideyoshi and Ieyasu, it is imagined, are presented with a nightingale, but nothing anyone can do will make it sing its famous song. Nobunaga approaches the bird. 'If you won't sing, little bird,' he says, 'I will kill you.' Hideyoshi tries next: 'If you won't sing, little bird, I will make you sing.' Last comes Ieyasu. 'If you won't sing, little bird,' he promises, 'I will wait.' This is how history remembers him. After the hot-blooded cruelty and unpredictability of his predecessors, he was a different kind of leader: cold, shrewd, with a reptilian patience which ultimately brought him the greatest prize.

Rather than jostling for position in central Japan, Ieyasu secured himself a base in the Kantō plain, and built an impressive castle at the small village of Edo. He managed to wriggle out of the Korean adventure, so that when his moment arrived, he was in a better position than many of his fellow lords to take advantage of Hideyoshi's death. Predictably, his master's will was not executed according to his wishes, and Ieyasu was soon at war with his fellow trustees. At the **Battle of Sekigahara** on 21 October 1600, they were decisively defeated. Enemy lords were stripped of their domains; Ieyasu's allies were richly rewarded, and in 1603 he himself was confirmed by the emperor as shogun. Ieyasu's headquarters, by now a booming city, became the administrative capital of Japan, and has remained so ever since, as Edo and, eventually, Tokyo.

The Edo Period 1600–1868

The defeat and death of Hideyoshi's son at the siege of Ōsaka in 1615 brought an end to nearly three centuries of civil war. The following year Ieyasu died, although, as shogun, he had already been succeeded by his son, Hidetada, in 1605. Although much of the ground-work had been laid by others, he had succeeded in the feat which eluded both of his predecessors: passing on his victory to the next generation. The dynasty he established was to rule unchallenged in Japan for 15 generations.

Shoguns came and went. Some were interesting and forceful characters; many wielded little more personal power than the emperors, and were the effective puppets of their advisers; it is more accurate, in speaking of these men, to talk of the work of the shogu-nate, rather than the shogun. Peace and stability were maintained by an autocratic government which sought, above all, to stifle change and prevent any alteration to the status quo. Hierarchy was all-important: society was divided into four classes—from samurai, through farmers and artisans, to the lowest rung, merchants—and strict rules governed the dress, duties and conduct of each rank. Freedom of movement was strictly curtailed, and contacts with the outside world were reduced almost to nothing. Even in the time of Hideyoshi, anti-Christian edicts had been promulgated and the Tokugawas, wary of the rivalry between different branches of the church, and fearful of their interference in Japanese internal politics, enforced these brutally, expelling or martyring many missionaries and their converts. Western books were banned, and by 1641 the only Europeans allowed in Japan were a group of Dutch merchants confined to an artificial island in Nagasaki harbour (although trade with China and other parts of southeast Asia was sustained intermittently throughout these years).

The cultural achievements of the period were largely associated with the city of Edo, and the 'Floating World' of teahouses, geisha houses and brothels which sprang up there. Woodblock prints (*ukiyo-e*) by artists like Hokusai and Hiroshige, *kabuki* drama and the Ōsaka *bunraku* puppet theatre, and the *haiku* and travelogues of the poet Bashō, were all products of these years. In the latter part of the period, the strains of the unbending Tokugawa system began to show in the economy. There were epidemics and famines, and discontent spread among the increasingly impoverished samurai whose military function was by now completely redundant. Nationalist intellectuals began to study the *Kojiki* and other Shinto-inspired histories, and to re-examine the role of the emperors who, throughout this time, lived on in Kyoto in powerless seclusion.

The Meiji Restoration 1854–1868

In the mid-19th century, while trains, factories and telegraph wires were appearing all over Europe, Japan was still effectively in its middle ages. Travel, on foot, horse or palanquin, over rough mountain roads, was slow and dangerous; medicine and science were crude and unenlightened; and the feudal hierarchy was strained near to breaking point by the rise of the merchant class and the switch from a rice to a cash economy. The shogunate was also harried by foreign worries: Russian and American vessels had been sniffing around Japan's territorial waters. Japan possessed no navy; if these incursions were to escalate to the point of an armed stand-off, there was no question who would be the loser.

Then, in 1853, **Commodore Matthew Perry** of the United States Navy steamed into Edo Bay at the head of four warships. He carried letters from President Fillmore requesting the opening of trade relations. After delivering them, he did a turn round the bay, much to the astonishment of spectators on the shore, and sailed away, with the promise of a return visit, with a bigger fleet of 'Black Ships', next year. A few months later a Russian admiral turned up in Nagasaki with similar demands.

The shogunate blustered and hesitated, even consulting the emperor who insisted that the barbarians be repulsed. Sea defences were erected but, on Perry's return, the Japanese had little choice but to accede to his demands and to open up the ports of Hakodate and Shimoda to American sailors. Further more comprehensive treaties followed, with Russia,

Britain, France and Holland as well as America, and in Japan the presence of the foreign diplomats and traders caused great unrest. An anti-shogunal faction emerged, led by samurai clans in western Honshū and Kyūshū, under the slogan, 'Revere the Emperor, expel the Barbarians!' This the shoguns seemed about to do, but the threat proved an empty one, and when a few zealots fired on foreign ships from shore batteries, they were quickly blasted into submission. At this point the anti-shogunal forces changed tactics. A number of young samurai from the rebel clans of Chōshū and Satsuma, including future prime ministers, were secretly sent abroad to Europe to study. Their samurai armed and organized themselves along Western lines.

By 1867, the shogun's hold on power was increasingly wobbly. Rebel forces entered Kyoto to 'free' the emperor, and defeated the shogunal army in a battle south of the city. Further skirmishes occurred in Tokyo, northern Honshū and Hokkaidō, but the shogun himself quickly abdicated and surrendered. In 1868 the 16-year-old Emperor, Mutsuhito, posthumously known as Meiji, entered Edo, and the following year he took up full-time residence there. The city was renamed Tokyo, 'Eastern Capital'.

The Meiji Period 1868–1912

The period of Meiji's rule was one of the most extraordinary in any country's history. Japan was weak when it began, divided and fearful of colonial incursion by the Western powers. By its end, she was an industrialized power, the victor of wars against both China and the mighty Russian Empire. Not only a military and industrial but also a social revolution had taken place. Foreign inventions (steam trains, Western dress, umbrellas, watches, gas lamps, horse carriages, bicycles, cameras, brick buildings and newspapers), foreign institutions (a Western-style educational system, parliament and armed forces), and foreigners themselves (teachers, missionaries, engineers, military attachés and advisers) were a fashionable part of everyday life. In less than half a century, Japan had bounded from the middle ages to the forefront of the 20th century.

The early years of Meiji were the time of greatest enthusiasm for things foreign, but by 1889 when the first Diet was inaugurated (the country had until then been ruled by an oligarchy made up of leaders of the Meiji Restoration) a certain insularity had taken hold. The **Meiji Constitution** was a conservative document, hedged around with vague qualifications of the limited freedoms which it guaranteed. Little more than one per cent of the population was entitled to vote for the Lower House of the Diet, which could be dissolved at any time: Japan was effectively still ruled by an oligarchy. The Imperial Rescript on Education of 1890 consolidated this authoritarian set-up, by enjoining the Confucian virtues of loyalty to emperor, family and state. Buddhism, tainted by association with the shoguns, was disestablished and many of the great temples suffered confiscation of their assets and privileges. In its place, Shinto was encouraged, particularly the aspects of it associated with emperor worship. The ancient and honourable tradition of syncretic worship was outlawed; hybrid shrine-temples were purged of their Buddhist elements.

Industrialization gathered pace in the 1890s and the great family combines, the *zaibatsu*, were formed (*see* 'Business Culture', pp.98–100). The Meiji forces' victory in the **Sino-**

Japanese War (1894) was scuppered by Russia, France and Germany who forced Japan to restore many of the territorial gains it had made on the Asian mainland. Tensions with Russia over control of Korea led to the Anglo-Japanese Treaty of 1902 which survived in various forms until 1921 and did much to boost Japanese self-confidence. In 1905 it was sent to dizzy heights by the **defeat of Russia**, especially the Battle of Tsushima, when the Japanese navy (equipped and trained by the British) sank or captured all but two of Russia's Baltic Fleet. By 1910 **Korea** had been fully annexed; it remained a Japanese colony until 1945. These victories created a tremendous prestige for the military and a growing mood of ultra-patriotism. At the same time a vocal socialist and anarchist movement emerged. In 1911, the year before his death from illness, a murder plot was uncovered against the Emperor, and this was taken as a pretext for a crack-down on all forms of left-wing dissent.

The Road to War 1912–1941

The short reign of the mentally ill **Emperor Taishō** (1912–26) was a breezy and optimistic period when the efforts of a few liberal minded statesmen seemed to have stifled the authoritarianism of the Meiji Constitution. During the First World War, Japan, as the ally of Great Britain, mopped up a few of Germany's possessions in China, and there was an inconclusive intervention in Siberia in the Russian Civil War of 1918. But on the whole, Japanese relations with the rest of the world were cordial. In the cities, students with bobbed hair or Oxford bags danced to jazz, and discussed Marxist ideas in the new beer halls and cafés. In 1921, the Crown Prince Hirohito, by now regent for his enfeebled father, made a famous visit to Britain. He was photographed wearing a tweed cap and plus fours, playing golf with the Prince of Wales. Tokyo was all but destroyed by the 1923 **Great Kantō Earthquake**, but it was quickly rebuilt, and the reign of **Emperor Hirohito** (1901–89) began in 1926 in a spirit of confidence and hope. It was given the official name *Shōwa*, 'Enlightened Peace'.

Depression, endemic throughout the world in the 1930s, struck Japan early, with a banking collapse in 1927. The suffering this caused among poor farmers provoked widespread anger, particularly in the army which was becoming increasingly powerful and independent. Young army officers, contemptuous of corrupt politicians and the self-seeking capitalists of the *zaibatsu*, toyed with the idea of a military coup, and several politicians were assassinated by fascist 'patriots'. In China, where Chiang Kai-shek's nationalist Kuomintang army was threatening Japanese interests, army officers took unilateral action, attacking and occupying the city of Mukden. Because the army had a veto over the appointment of army and naval ministers, it could effectively bring down the Cabinet whenever it chose. While Japanese politicians helplessly assured the League of Nations that their withdrawal was imminent, the army itself surged deeper into Manchuria to set up an 'independent' state under a Chinese puppet emperor.

At home, plots and coup attempts rumbled on. In February 1936, several members of the Cabinet were wounded or assassinated at their homes and two infantry regiments mutinied. The coup was quashed by the army itself but the incident stood as a grim warning to politicians who were now virtually dictated to by the military. In the same year

Japan signed the Anti-Comintern Pact with Germany. The country began to arm for a full-scale invasion of China. In December 1937, in one of the most notorious incidents in Japanese history, thousands of civilians were massacred in the Chinese nationalist capital Nanking by the rampaging army. But Chiang Kai-shek escaped, and the war lingered on.

When war began in Europe, Germany urged her Asian ally to attack the Allied colonies in the Far East. Japan held back, and Ribbentrop's Non-Aggression Pact between Germany and the USSR made it seem all the more likely that Japan would avoid involvement in the European war. But it was clear that, if fighting did spread to Asia, it could cripple the Japanese economy which relied so heavily on imported oil. War was developing its own momentum, and many in Japan had a lot to gain from it: the demand for munitions and the raw materials obtained from the conquered Chinese territories had already created a booming war economy. When Japanese forces in Indo-China threatened Malaya and the East Indies, economic sanctions were imposed by Britain, America and Holland. Japan was faced with a choice between economic disaster, a humiliating climb-down, or war.

Talks with the United States proceeded inconclusively. On 8 December 1941 Japanese planes made a devastating surprise attack on the US naval base in Hawaii's Pearl Harbour, and simultaneous assaults on Hong Kong, Malaya, Singapore and the Philippines.

The Pacific War 1941–1945

For four months Japan didn't put a foot wrong as, one after another, the colonial outposts of East Asia toppled before the imperial forces: Penang, Hong Kong, Manila, Singapore, Batavia, Rangoon and Mandalay. Massive new sources of raw materials were opened up; full-scale invasions of India and Australia seemed to be only a matter of time. But Japanese forces were repelled from New Guinea, and in June 1942 the US navy won a crucial victory at the Battle of the Midway. Thereafter, the whirlwind of early victories began to look more and more like beginners' luck, as the Japanese gains were first slowed, then halted, and finally, in battles of agonizing duration and ferocity, reversed. By mid-1943, Japan was losing the war. Any public articulation of this state of affairs was regarded as defeatist, and the activities of the military police, as well as domestic shortages, made life in Japan increasingly uncomfortable.

The country was far from defeated though; if Prime Minister Tōjō had been prepared to seek a peace at this point, he might have come away with treaty recognition for large portions of the conquered territories. Fanatical confidence in its invincibility was the greatest failing of the Japanese leadership, coupled with an arrogance and brutality in its treatment of prisoners of war which is a source of bitterness even today. Japan's pretext for the invasion of the European colonies—that it was liberating them from Western domination, in pursuit of an independent, self-determining Greater Asian Co-Prosperity Sphere—was taken seriously by nationalist groups in many parts of the continent. But the racism and cruelty of the occupying armies turned many potential allies into enemies, and contributed to Japan's eventual defeat.

The decisive loss came in June 1944 when American forces gained the Pacific island of Saipan, which put the Japanese mainland within reach of their heavy bombers. By the end of 1944, the imperial navy had been effectively destroyed at the Battle of Leyte Gulf, and General MacArthur was well on his way to winning back the Philippines. To anyone in a position to know, it was clear that Japan's decline was irreversible.

But it was glacially slow. In February 1945 the tiny island of Iwo-jima was taken after nine weeks and 20,000 American casualties; the Japanese garrison of 23,000 fought to the last man. The capture of Okinawa in June was similarly agonizing, and by now the airforce had started to employ the famous *kamikaze* pilots—young volunteers who dived onto Allied ships in planes loaded with explosives. Incendiary air raids on the mainland were burning out the wooden hearts of the Japanese cities, and supplies of food and raw materials, including oil, were perilously low.

From the outside, the Tokyo leadership seemed as far away as ever from a statement of surrender. However, from their deciphering of Japanese diplomatic codes, the Americans knew that Stalin was being asked to mediate a settlement on Japan's behalf. The Cabinet recognised that defeat was unavoidable; their one, insistent demand was that the emperor system should remain untouched. But in July 1945 Churchill, Truman and Chiang Kai-shek (Stalin was deliberately excluded) issued the Potsdam Declaration, demanding immediate and unconditional surrender. 'The alternative,' they asserted in an ominous phrase, 'is prompt and utter destruction.' Publicly, the Declaration was haughtily rejected; privately, the diplomatic wires revealed the anxiety of the Japanese high command.

On 6 August, an atomic bomb was exploded above Hiroshima. Communications between Tokyo and the west of the country were so bad that the full extent of damage was not immediately known by the leadership. Perhaps more significant than the second atomic attack on Nagasaki on the 9th, was the news of the day before—that Stalin's Red Army was invading Japan from the north.

At noon on 15 August, the entire country gathered around wireless sets to hear a remarkable broadcast. It was the Emperor, addressing his people for the first time in their history. Urging his people to 'endure the unendurable and suffer what is insufferable', he announced the government's acceptance of the Potsdam Declaration. At no point were the words 'defeat' or 'surrender' used. 'The war situation,' the Emperor nonetheless noted, 'has developed not necessarily to Japan's advantage.'

The Occupation 1945–1952

In contrast to the savagery, fanaticism and stupidity of the war itself, its aftermath was a model of calm and order, in Richard Storry's words, 'the most peaceful and, to outward appearance, most harmonious occupation of one great country by another that has ever been known.' A few responded to defeat in the traditional way, by committing ritual suicide, but the mass of the population, once the initial shock was over, welcomed the American forces, and the relief from suffering which they symbolized.

The Americans set about a comprehensive programme of political and social reform. In charge was the 'American Shogun', **General Douglas MacArthur**, the Supreme Commander for the Allied Powers and hero of the battle for the Philippines. Pre-war institutions held responsible for the war, such as the army and bureaucracy, were comprehensively purged. The *zaibatsu* were abolished, and a number of senior politicians, including the wartime Prime Minister, Tōjō, were hanged as war criminals. Right-wing organizations were banned, labour unions were established, and the old education system, with its emphasis on loyalty to the emperor, was liberalized. A **new constitution** was drafted, including a clause which renounced forever the use of force in resolving international disputes. Perhaps the most important decision related to the Emperor. His personal role in the build-up to war is still a matter of scholarly dispute, but at the time plenty of people would have been quite happy to see him put on trial alongside his ministers. MacArthur made the wise decision to let him stay. The peerage was abolished, and Hirohito's role was reduced to that of symbolic head of state. He issued a rescript explicitly refuting 'the false conception that the emperor is divine.'

With the outbreak of war in Korea and growing American fears of communism, a number of these reforms were reversed, or at least watered down. A large number of businessmen and bureaucrats were de-purged, and the *zaibatsu* re-emerged, in looser form, as the *keiretsu* collectives. The pacifist clause in the constitution which renounced Japan's right to air, sea and land forces became a particular embarrassment, and was quickly overcome by a form of words. In the shape of the 'Self-Defence Forces', Japan today has one of the biggest and best equipped military machines in the world.

The Economic Miracle 1952–1980

The Occupation brought large amounts of aid to devastated Japanese industry, but what kick-started the economy was the Korean War, and Japan's role as victualler and manufacturer to the anti-communist forces. With large numbers of American troops stationed in Japanese territory, it was, for a few years, as if the Occupation had never ended. Communist supporters organized noisy anti-American demonstrations and, in 1955, in reaction to the left-wing revival, the two principal right-of-centre parties amalgamated into the Liberal Democratic Party (LDP). Compared to the European or American idea of a political party, the LDP has always been a divided institution, a flag of convenience for a number of fiercely competitive individual factions. Nonetheless, for the next 38 years, it held on to power. Its politically stagnant, but stable, period of rule saw one of the most remarkable economic recoveries in history—perhaps the greatest since the reconstruction of the country during the Meiji period. In the 1950s the phrase 'Made in Japan' was synonymous with cut-price shoddiness. By the 1980s it signified reliability, value for money and innovation; few homes in the industrialized world are today without their Japanese car, TV, video, stereo or computer.

After a brief slump at the end of the Korean War, the economy—under the firm stewardship of the Ministry of International Trade and Industry (MITI)—achieved astonishing levels of unbroken growth, based on generous tax breaks, government subsidy of key industries and relentless encouragement of exports. Year after year, growth targets were exceeded: from 9 per cent in 1955 to 14.4 per cent in 1961. In 1960, Prime Minister Ikeda promised to double salaries before the end of the decade; the target was reached by 1967. As wages and the standard of living rose, Japanese families strove to acquire the 'three sacred treasures': car, refrigerator and colour television.

With the blossoming economy came a new mood of national self-confidence. The Tokyo Olympics in 1964, the first to be held in Asia, seemed to mark the symbolic end of Japan's period as an ailing, defeated, underdog nation. Hotels, roads, stadia and railways were built, including the first of the famous *shinkansen* bullet train lines. A cultural landmark of a different kind came two years later, when thousands of screaming fans turned out to see the Beatles at the Budōkan stadium. But there were social tensions, too, as a younger generation of Japanese grew up, with no direct memory of the war and less tolerance of the austere lives led by their parents. The construction of Tokyo's new international airport at Narita and the renewal of the US Treaty in 1970 became the focus for rioting among students and left-wingers, and for a few febrile months, change was in the air. The climax came in November 1970 when the novelist Mishima Yukio committed ritual suicide after a spectacularly bungled coup attempt.

In retrospect the incident marked the end of an era, as the restless students of the late 1960s became the obedient salarymen of the 1970s. It was a less spectacular decade than those which had gone before it, but remarkable in its own way. In 1974, the Lockheed bribery scandal brought down Prime Minister Tanaka Kakuei, and exposed publicly the institutional corruption of Japan's political system. The oil crisis of the same year cast a nasty cloud over a country almost entirely dependent on foreign fuel imports, but, miraculously, even this potential catastrophe was turned to Japan's advantage. With unerring discipline, the government and the country embarked on a systematic programme of energy conservation which minimized the recession, and allowed Japan to emerge from it even further ahead of her floundering international competitors.

The 1980s

At the end of the 1970s, Japan had the lowest inflation, lowest unemployment, lowest interest rates, and highest growth of any developed country—in other words, the strongest economy on the planet. By the middle of the next decade, Japan was not just beating the rest of the world in industries like steel, ship-building, cars, electronics and microchips, it was also bank-rolling its competitors. The seven biggest banks in the world were Japanese—in 1985, as the United States became the world's biggest debtor nation, Japan became its biggest creditor, largely through its purchase of US government bonds.

This extraordinary reversal had several consequences. Japan had long exported far more of its own goods than it ever imported from abroad, and the resulting balance of payments surplus rapidly began to infuriate its trading partners. Trade friction frequently threatened to flare into trade war; the danger has only recently begun to recede.

Increasingly, Japan's corrupt political head looked absurdly unsuited to its powerful economic body. The 1980s saw only one prime minister of any substance—Nakasone Yasuhiro, a statesmanlike and internationally-minded character who nonetheless caused unease with his nationalist sentiments and attempts to increase defence spending. Otherwise, party leaders were the usual LDP drones, the puppets of powerful, behind-the-scenes factions, embarrassingly prone to scandal and disgrace. In 1989 a prime minister was forced to resign after being implicated in a bribery scam. Two months later his successor followed him after saucy revelations about after-hours activities with a *geisha*.

But Japan looked and felt like a rich country. As the yen grew stronger, imported goods became cheaper, and luxury foreign labels flooded into the shops. Companies ploughed their profits into tax-free expense accounts and bonuses, and consumer industries boomed as their employees found ever more costly ways of entertaining themselves. All over the country, gleaming new offices and public buildings went up. Japanese corporations acquired a reputation abroad as voracious snappers-up of cultural icons, at prices that Western capitalism could no longer afford—from Impressionist paintings to Columbia Film Studios and New York's Rockefeller Centre.

The Heisei Era 1989 onwards

In January 1989, Emperor Hirohito died at the age of 88, and the Shōwa ('Enlightened Peace') period came to an end, having disgraced and lived up to its name in equal measure. Public grief was muted; the Emperor had been ill for months, and Japan soon had other things to think about. The new Emperor Akihito christened his ruling era Heisei, 'Accomplished Peace', but the first big issue to confront his country was the Gulf War. As a member of the United Nations (with hopes for a permanent place on the Security Council), Japan was under pressure to contribute troops to the international force being assembled for the liberation of Kuwait. On the other hand, the 1945 constitution expressly forbade the active employment of Japanese forces overseas. The issue paralysed the Japanese Diet; eventually a compromise was reached whereby Japan provided £4 billion in financial aid, and a token force of non-combat units.

In 1993 a sequence of events took place which seemed, at the time, startlingly dramatic, although history may prove them to be of limited significance. The LDP, wormy with corruption and riven by in-fighting, splintered. An important faction, grouped around the sinister and intelligent Ozawa Ichiro, quit the government and brought it down in a vote of confidence. By now the 'bubble' economy of the 1980s had burst. Unnaturally inflated asset growth had finally reached its ceiling and, although the recession caused few of the ugly consequences felt in other industrialized countries, growth was reduced and bankruptcies and unemployment rose. In the election that followed, the LDP's vote was split between several new parties founded by its former members; despite winning the largest number of seats, the Liberal Democrats lost control to a seven-party coalition which included these turncoat politicians and the old Socialist (renamed the Social Democratic) Party. Psychologically, this was a mighty coup: after 38 years of one-party rule, the LDP appeared to be out on its ear.

But, from the beginning, few believed the LDP leopards had changed their spots. The new prime minister, Hosokawa Morihiro, announced ambitious reforms, intended to inhibit the tendency among politicians to present voters with envelopes full of money. A move to raise taxes was less popular—combined with revelations about alleged financial improprieties, it was enough to bring down Hosokawa in April 1994. A stand-in prime minister attempted to hold the coalition together, but quickly yielded to a cynical re-configuration of the parties—an alliance between the LDP and the Socialists, old enemies throughout the post-war period. In early 1995, the Japanese government consisted of a cabinet dominated by old conservatives, with a socialist prime minister shorn of his socialism.

Culture

Art and Architecture

Beyond a vague familiarity with pagodas and woodblock prints, most first-time visitors arrive knowing very little of Japanese art and architecture, and many leave none the wiser. Everyone who has ever been on a guided tour of Kyoto is familiar with the condition known as 'temple fatigue'—after four hours and half a dozen different Buddha halls, you totter back to your lodgings with a roll of photographs but no cogent idea of what you have seen or what it means. This is nobody's fault: until the 20th century, the influence of Japanese art on the West was negligible, and its origins, history and conventions are as alien as can be.

One of the unswerving characteristics of Japanese art (with a few spectacular exceptions) is its simplicity. Plain, unpainted wood, and simple use of lines, form the basis of much architecture and painting. Differences in style are frequently ornamental, and can appear trifling to the non-connoisseur: the depth of the eaves on a shrine, or the glaze on a tea bowl, may be all that distinguishes entirely separate schools of architecture or ceramics. Obviously, this isn't something that can be picked up overnight—still, a little knowledge makes a big difference, and with preparation and reading you can greatly reduce your chances of culture-overload.

Don't try to do too much and, unless your time is limited, avoid guided group tours. Plan your temple and shrine visits and ascertain in advance the basic characteristics of the sites you will be visiting—age, historical significance, style and sect. In the Kyoto and Kansai region, for instance, it would be possible to spend a few days visiting the great architectural treasures of Japan, in chronological order, tracing their evolution from the Nara to the Edo period. Only specialists would want to follow such an itinerary strictly, but even casual tourists can add a lot to their appreciation by a little intelligent planning.

Detailed commentaries on individual buildings and collections are given in the regional chapters. The following descriptions are not comprehensive, but attempt to join the dots between various historical periods and genres.

Art

Prehistoric (*c.* 10,000 BC–*c.* AD 700)

The earliest inhabitants of Japan of whom traces survive are the **Jōmon** ('cord pattern') people (*c.* 10,000–300 BC), named after the pottery they produced. Damp clay, shaped by hand into pots and cooking vessels, was wrapped with ropes which left a distinctive imprint on the surface. Carbon dating shows the earliest fragments to be more than 12,000 years old. The most impressive items were made during the Middle Jōmon period (*c.* 3500–*c.* 2500 BC): the 'Flaming Jōmon' ware, so called because of the elaborate, rippling loops of inlaid clay which swirl and writhe over the surface and above the rim of the flat-bottomed vessels.

The size and ornateness of these jars suggests they were used for ritual offerings. Further tantalizing glimpses into the spiritual life of the proto-Japanese are provided by the *dogū*, clay figures with distorted bodies and stylized features. There's something simultaneously appealing and creepy about these mannequins. The writer Erich Von Daniken insisted that some of the later and more bizarre *dogū* provided proof that extra-terrestrials had visited and communicated with Jōmon man, and they do indeed look like astronauts, with little arms emerging from some kind of bulky suit or armour, round head-dress and slit eyes peering through goggle-like lenses.

Yayoi was the next artistic and cultural era (*c.* 300 BC– *c.* AD 300), the consequence of large-scale immigra-tion from the Asian continent. The invaders brought with them bronze, iron, wet rice agriculture, and an understanding of the potter's wheel. The new ceramics were smoother, more regular and symmetrical, and more varied in form: goblets, narrow-necked bottles, ewers and handled cups, as well as jars. Bronze was used to make striking bells called *dōtaku*, incised with meandering S-patterns. Comma-shaped jewels called *magatama* as well as polished mirrors and ornamental swords also survive from this time; mirror, jewel and sword are the three sacred objects of the imperial regalia.

The next distinct period, **Kofun** (AD 300–*c.* AD 700) takes its name from the huge burial mounds in the shape of bells or keyholes which dot the Kansai area. From these, many beautiful objects have been excavated, including crowns and helmets of bronze and gold, and *haniwa*, clay renderings of the creatures and objects which the deceased prince might find useful in the afterlife. There are clay houses, clay horses, deer, dogs and cattle, and many clay people—these seem to have been a humane replacement for living servants and warriors who would at one time have been sacrificed and buried alongside their dead lord. Many of them have great charm: simple, cheery faces, with elaborately detailed renderings of costume, jewellery and armour.

The best collection of prehistoric art is in the **Tokyo National Museum**.

Early (552–794)

From the introduction of Buddhism in the mid-6th up until the mid-8th century, Japanese art was heavily influenced by—and often copied from—foreign models. Religious trea-sures were imported from the continent, along with Chinese and Korean sculptors, painters and temple-builders who settled and established studios. Nonetheless, the **Asuka** (552–710) and early **Nara** (710–794) periods are among the richest eras of Japanese art. War and disaster have erased many of the Chinese and Korean originals; the Japanese works, tucked away in a few Nara monasteries, are some of the finest of their type in the world.

Statues and altars have fared better than paintings, and surviving examples of each show a freshness and grace, combined, in the earlier and more formal statues, with an archaic flat-ness and symmetry—the bronzes of the Korean master, Tori Busshi, for instance, in the magnificent collection of **Hōryū-ji** temple. Following the Taika (Great Reform) of 645, contact with Tang China became even more intense. Under the influence of Tang art, statues and painted figures became fuller and more three-dimensional, expressive of rhythm and motion.

In 710 the emperor and several of the early temples moved to a new capital—Heijō-kyō, today called Nara. Full-time workshops of artists and artisans were maintained by the state, and construction reached its peak in 752 with the consecration of the Daibutsu (Great Buddha), a 15m-high colossus of bronze in the great **Tōdai-ji** temple. Unsurprisingly, not much metal was left over for other purposes. In the statues created for the sub-temples of the Tōdai-ji complex, the sculptors were forced to turn to wood, clay and a technique known as dry lacquer which allowed for greater versatility and realism. In these beautiful portraits of deities and famous abbots (many of them preserved in the treasure house of Nara's **Kōfuku-ji** temple), Japanese art began to escape the influence of China, and assert a confident individuality of its own. As well as Tōdai-ji and its sub-temples, Nara period art is displayed in **Yakushi-ji**, **Tōshōdai-ji**, and the **Nara National Museum**.

Heian (794–1185)

The arrival from China of two new Esoteric Buddhist sects, Tendai and Shingon, introduced a whole new army of deities and religious iconography into the Japanese capital of Heian-kyō (Kyoto). Among the most popular were benevolent bogeymen like Fudō Myō-ō, a fearsome chastiser of evil, depicted with fangs, sword, lasso and a halo of flames, who appeared in statues and paintings, as well as in mandalas—concentric pictorial diagrams of hundreds of buddhas, bodhisattvas, demons and saints. These were intellectual and meditational tools as much as decorative works of art, a visual *Who's Who* of the complex hierarchy of Esoteric Buddhist icons.

Early Heian sculptures were rather heavy and brooding. Then, in the 11th century, popular worship came to focus on Amida, Buddha of the Western Paradise, a merciful being who offers salvation to all who invoke his name in a simple prayer. Amida halls enshrined seated statues of the saviour, surrounded by carvings and paintings of his heavenly attendants. A famous sculptor called Jōchō brought great finesse and variety to these figures by the perfection of a new technique. Instead of a clumsy single piece of solid wood, statues were composed out of several smaller blocks, hollowed out and joined together by apprentices, before being finished off by the master. The resulting carvings were lighter and less liable to warp and crack, permitting much greater detail and versatility than the old techniques. The **Byōdō-in** in Uji, outside Kyoto, contains the masterpieces of this style.

One of the most popular painted scenes was the *raigō*, the moment when Amida and his retinue descend from the clouds to welcome the dying soul into Paradise. It became fashionable for ailing aristocrats to lie on their deathbeds alongside a *raigō* picture. The dying man would chant Amida's name and hold a piece of cord, joined at the other end to the painted image, on which his soul would be tugged into Paradise.

But some of the most appealing remnants of Heian-kyō are secular, the products of the tiny, idle, introverted circle of courtiers and royalty. By the 10th century, contacts with the declining China of the Tang Dynasty had been cut off. Isolated from the rest of the world, Japanese artists began to respond to the landscape, language and emotions of their own country. In painting, the gentle, rolling hills of Yamato (the Japanese heartland containing Nara and Kyoto) replaced the beetling mountain tops and precipices of Chinese art. Exquisite narrative handscrolls (*emakimono*) depicting scenes from the *Tale of Genji* showed life in the *shinden* villas of the aristocracy, and reflected the preoccupations of the day—nature (especially in its transient and melancholy aspects), style (the subtle colours and contrasts of court kimono), and poetry (Heian-kyō was the birthplace of Japanese calligraphy, and the text of the narrative scrolls is often just as delicate and artistic as the images).

In the late 12th century, a very different style of narrative scroll was produced, depicting court intrigues, miracles from the lives of saints, and satires featuring anthropomorphic animals and cartoon-like demons and ghosts. The wars between the Taira and Minamoto clans inspired epic renderings of battles and armies.

The temples of **Kyoto** are the best place to view Heian art, especially **Tō-ji** for its Esoteric Buddhist statues, the **Byōdō-in** for its Amida Hall, and the **Kyoto National Museum**. The temples and treasure houses of **Mt Kōya** possess a huge collection of the art of the Esoteric Shingon sect.

Medieval (1185–1573)

Much of Nara was destroyed during the 12th-century wars. When the country had settled down, its new military rulers set about reconstructing its buildings and filling them with new statues, inspired by the old masterpieces. The shoguns of the **Kamakura period** (1185–1333) consciously dissociated themselves from the effete aestheticism of the court, encouraging an art that expressed their own ideals of spiritual alertness and martial virtue. Close study of the originals, plus the advantages of the multi-block technique, created a new style of unmatched energy and realism.

They were the first true portraits. Paintings and statues of Minamoto Yoritomo, victorious leader of the Genji clan, combine an almost abstract treatment of his billowing formal robes with a shrewdly realistic rendering of his cruel, haughty features. Even when portraits—of famous sages and monks, for instance—were posthumous, they looked and stood like living men, not sacred idealizations. Lumps of crystal were used for the eyes, and it was in the statues of Buddhist gods, particularly those of a fierce or grotesque character, that the Kamakura style found its most entertaining expression. Rippling, muscular torsos, flailing arms, flaring nostrils, manic grins and knotted brows expressed the divine anger of deities such as Emma-ō, King of Hell, who sit in judgement on mortal souls. The finest of these were created by a single studio of sculptors, a family descended from Jōchō of the Byōdō-in: Kōkei, Unkei, and Tankei, father, son and grandson. In the mid-13th century an unknown artist created another great Daibutsu in the town of Kamakura—

smaller than Nara's, but artistically superior and far better preserved. Japanese sculpture would never reach such heights again.

Zen Buddhism, which took root in Japan during the Kamakura period, became the conduit of renewed contact with China, especially in the arts. In the **Muromachi period** (1333–1573), most of the great developments in the arts—in painting, gardening, architecture, the tea ceremony, nō drama—took place under the auspices of Zen monks. More than other sects, Zen emphasized the transmission of knowledge between master and pupil, so it was only natural that some of the finest portraits should be created by its followers—highly personal, realistic and often grim and unflattering pictures of ageing masters. Just as its practice was based on strict discipline and epiphanic flashes of irrational insight, Zen pictures were austere and elliptical, painted in a few simple strokes of black ink (*sumi*), with rare use of colour. The subjects of Zen painting—landscapes half lost in wreaths of blank mist, tiny human figures dwarfed by looming trees and mountains—suggested ideas of timelessness and human insignificance in keeping with Zen thought. They were heavily influenced by Chinese models which were objects of enthusiastic connoisseurship during the Muromachi period—the master painter, Sōami (d. 1525), was curator of the collection of the Ashikaga shoguns, and the great shogun Yoshimitsu patronized an official painting academy in a Kyoto temple. Sesshū (1420–1506) created more solid, less ethereal compositions of flinty mountains, while a monk from remote Tōhoku, Sesson, created memorably turbulent images of storm-wracked seas and cruel birds of prey which seem to reflect the troubled character of the times.

The Pre-modern Period (1573–1868)

The **Momoyama period** (1573–1600) was dominated by a succession of military leaders who finally brought an end to the civil wars which had wracked the country for a century and a half. They raised castles at strategic locations, and asserted their personal authority by building themselves great fortified palaces, lavishly decorated with the finest and most expensive materials. Rooms were wide and high, and required big, bold designs to fill and animate them. The windows were small, to aid defence, and the dimness of the light they admitted encouraged the use of reflective gold leaf on screens and ceilings. Practical considerations apart, the artistic ebullience of the age matched the hubris and megalomania of its great leaders, Oda Nobunaga and Hideyoshi Toyotomi, low-born men who rose to the height of wealth and power. After centuries of spirituality, nuance and restraint, Japanese art exploded in a blaze of colour and ornament, 'a procession as with torches against the sober grey mist that lay behind' in the words of one historian.

Momoyama motifs, even where they were used in temples, were generally secular: flowers, landscapes, birds, animals (lions, tigers, dragons) and human figures of sages and children, painted in thick, bright pigments on gold foil. The greatest works were produced by a hereditary school of painters headed by Kanō Eitoku (1543–90) who decorated the *shoin* style rooms of Nobunaga's (long-gone) Azuchi castle, and whose work survives in several Kyoto temples. During the **Edo period** (1600–1868), the Kanō school flourished as official painters to the great Tokugawa Ieyasu and the succeeding shoguns. Kanō Tanyū, Eitoku's greatest heir, supervized the painting of the pines in Kyoto's Nijō castle.

By the mid-17th century, contact with foreign countries was effectively outlawed; the Momoyama and early Edo years were the last time for two centuries when foreign styles and subjects could work their influence on Japanese art. In the 1590s, Hideyoshi's brutal campaigns in Korea produced much continental loot, and the simple, rustic work of Korean potters was prized for use in the tea ceremony. Until the banning of Christianity, European goods and learning were extremely fashionable. The huge galleons, flouncing costumes, bright hair and big noses of Westerners (called *nanban* or 'southern barbarians') became popular subjects. Japanese artists were exposed to perspective painting and began, for the first time, to experiment with oils, although it was centuries before these techniques were widely adopted.

The most dazzling figure of the early 17th century, Hon'ami Kōetsu (1558–1637), established his own artistic colony outside Kyoto, where painters, potters, paper-makers and lacquerers lived and worked communally. Kōetsu was a superb craftsman and tea master, as well as an artist. Everyday objects, such as a case for writing instruments, were turned into works of art, by treating the curving exterior as a single plane surface and wrapping the design around it. During the same period, men like Tawaraya Sōtatsu (d.1643) of the Rimpa school created evocative landscapes by dropping ink onto wet paper to create blurred, cloudy, watery outlines. Unlike the aristocratic Kanō artists, both men came from the rising urban merchant class, which became increasingly important as a source of patronage and which had its heyday during the exuberant period known as **Genroku** (1688–1704). Ōgata Kōrin (1658–1716) is the great name from this time, an outrageous extrovert whose bold, vigorous compositions of waves and flowers are strikingly modern. Kōrin was also a great perpetrator of artistic 'happenings'. Once he presented a friend with a giant rice dumpling. When it was sliced open, hundreds of tiny live crabs scuttled out, each one decorated on its back with a minute gold-lacquered landscape.

By the Genroku period, the art of the Kyoto aristocrats and the Edo samurai had become stagnant and mannered. All the most interesting art (as well as drama and literature) was being produced in the 'floating world' of the cities of Edo (Tokyo) and Ōsaka, dominated by merchants and an increasingly literate population of craftsmen and shopkeepers. Improved woodblock techniques allowed artist-printers to produce large cheap editions of illustrated prints, often combining text and pictures. The subjects of these *ukiyo-e* ('floating world pictures') reflected the urban, earthy, often frankly erotic concerns of the Edo townsman: street scenes of local festivals and bustling crowds; and portraits of *kabuki* actors and famous courtesans, the pop stars of the age. Earlier print-makers like Suzuki Harunobu (flourished 1765–70) and Kitagawa Utamaro (1754–1806) produced elegant, gently humorous renderings of *geisha* and their patrons. During the 18th century *ukiyo-e* became increasingly grotesque and satirical. Even the world famous Katsushika Hokusai (1760–1849) created several albums of *manga* (cartoons) and euphemistically entitled *shunga* or 'spring pictures'—rollicking albums of pornography featuring grimacing couples with gargantuan genitalia. His delicate, visionary landscapes of Mt Fuji, like *The Great Wave,* are the most famous Japanese pictures in the world. Andō Hiroshige (1797–1858) explored the Edo townsman's fascination with travel in the series *Fifty-three Stations of the Tōkaidō*, showing famous spots on the road between Kyoto and Edo.

The Modern Period 1868–

With the opening up of the country after the Meiji Restoration of 1868, Japan was swamped by a wave of Western influences which threatened for a while to extinguish native traditions altogether. Woodblock artists produced charming impressions of the new brick quarters of Tokyo and the foreigners who were increasingly to be seen in and around them, and during the Sino-Japanese (1894) and Russo-Japanese (1904) wars they served as war correspondents dispatching vivid, if nationalistic, depictions of Japanese valour back to the public at home. Bright Western dyes replaced the delicate shades of the early masters, and perspective was employed, sometimes uneasily. Young artists studied abroad in Europe. The best of them, like Kuroda Seiki (1866–1924) achieved an intelligent synthesis of Western technique and Japanese subject matter and sensibility; many more produced only lifeless pastiches, and *yōga*, as Western-style painting was called, yielded few masterpieces. A new genre, contrastingly called *nihonga* (Japanese pictures), emerged in the early 20th century. Despite Western pigments and perspective, the work of painters like Kobayashi Kōkei (1883–1967) and Higashiyama Kaii (born 1908) retains a distinctively oriental feel, in plangent, misty landscapes of pine, snow and mountain. But it's a minor genre and attracts little attention outside Japan.

20th-century Japanese art still seems to be uneasily poised between native and Western traditions, neither fully assimilated or at ease with the other. There are several great names: Noguchi Isamu (1904–88), the half-American sculptor; and the woodblock artist Munakata Shikō (1905–77), whose unique, primitive black and white images might have come from any age. The successes of the Folk Arts Movement, lead by the potters Hamada Shōji (1894–1978) and the Englishman Bernard Leach (1887–1979), gave crafts (particularly ceramics) an impetus and popularity which they retain to this day. In recent years, Japanese designers like Ishioka Eiko, Issey Miyake, Kawakubo Rei and Yamamoto Yōji have brought Japanese simplicity to international cat-walks and advertising. But culturally, Japan is at a stage it has been through many times before: a transitional period in which powerful foreign influences are being digested and assimilated and where fully fledged movements of any significance are difficult to identify.

Architecture

Shrine Architecture

The earliest Shinto shrines were not buildings, but natural features: boulders, ancient trees, even the mountains themselves. At festival times, the deities would be summoned from their natural abode to temporary, probably portable, structures where prayers and offerings could be presented directly. These developed into permanent shrine buildings.

Buddhism brought with it an ancient architectural tradition that greatly influenced Shinto; no shrine which still stands today can have been untouched by it. The oldest, and probably the purest, shrine styles are Sumiyoshi (named after the Sumiyoshi shrine in downtown Ōsaka), and Shimmei and Taisha, exemplified by Ise Jingū in Kansai, and Izumo Taisha on the Japan Sea coast, respectively. Principal features of the different styles are as follows:

Shimmei

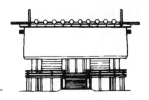

Crisp, straight lines, with almost no use of paint, inlay, carving or other decoration. Steps lead under an entrance which is beneath the eaves, on the long side of the building, parallel to the roof ridge. The floor is raised on posts which are driven directly into the earth; the roof is often thatched. Cylindrical billets of wood (*katsuogi*) lie along the roof ridge, and forked finials (*chigi*) project upwards. Shimmei shrines are thought to have been based on ancient storehouses.

Taisha

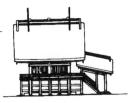

With its curving roof and metal ornaments, Izumo Taisha shows more of the Buddhist influence. The entrance, up steps and via a covered porch, is through the gable end. The posts rest on stone foundations. Roof billets are smaller and fewer than the Shimmei style; the finials do not project up from the bargeboards, but are attached to the roof as separate structures. The Taisha style was based on early palace buildings.

Sumiyoshi

Similar to the Taisha style, but with straight eaves, and without the covered entrance porch. While Ise and Izumo are plain, Sumiyoshi Jinja is painted in white and red.

The influence of Buddhism produced over the years the following styles:

Nagare

This is the most common of all shrine types, and examples can be seen all over the country. It resembles the Shimmei style, minus billets and finials, and with the eave on one side sweeping outwards over the entrance and steps to provide a sheltered area for worshippers.

Kasuga

The second most popular style is named after the ancient Kasuga Shrine in Nara. It resembles the Sumiyoshi shrine (painted, entrance under gable, billets and finials), but on a smaller scale and with the addition of a wide protective roof over the gable entrance.

Hachiman

In some shrines, a sheltered oratory (*haiden*) where worshippers could offer prayers was built separately from the main hall (*honden*), the residence of the deity. In shrines dedicated to the god of war, Hachiman, a Kasuga-style *honden* and *haiden* were built so close together that their front and back eaves touched, and they effectively became one structure. In the **Gongen style**, a second roof ridge was built at a right angle to the two roofs of a Hachiman structure. The area beneath it is a corridor linking the main hall and oratory.

In the Momoyama and Edo periods (late 16th to late 19th century), shrines became increasingly ornate and elaborate. Tiles came to replace the traditional thatch and cypress shingles, the supporting struts beneath the curved hip and gable roofs were carved into shapes of humans and beasts, and the outer surfaces were painted, gilded and studded with metal ornaments. This reached its gaudy climax in the Tōshō-gū Shrine to the Tokugawa shoguns, in Nikkō.

Visiting a Shrine

Shinto worship is a casual and ill-defined business with no distinction between the faithful and the infidel. The chances are that you will be invited to pay your respects at one some-time during your visit to Japan.

Shrine architecture, like Japanese society, is much concerned with the division between inner and outer, and the delimitation of areas of greater and lesser sanctity. The entrance to every shrine is marked by a *torii*, a symbolic gateway consisting, at its simplest, of a pair of uprights topped with a single horizontal bar. These can be made of wood, stone, concrete or metal, painted or unpainted. There may be a series of *torii* one after another, each marking a deeper level of sanctity. These are sometimes flanked by **guardians**, frequently a pair of *koma inu* (Korean dogs), dragons, archers, or—in the case of an Inari shrine—foxes. *Shimenawa*, twisted ropes of straw, often very thick, are another sacred marker. They're hung around sacred trees or boulders, or from the beams of *torii*. *Gohei* are zig-zags of paper, a bit like stylized thunderbolts, which adorn shrines and signify the pres-ence of the *kami* (deities). Often these, and the round mirrors seen inside the shrine buildings, are the closest thing to a representa-tion of the deity. Unlike Buddhism, the gods of Shinto are very seldom pictured in statues or paintings.

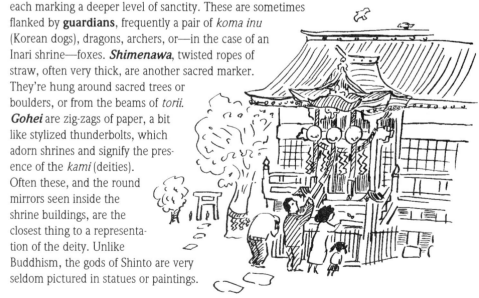

Inside the shrine, perhaps at the end of a wooded path, will be a courtyard of blank **white gravel**, another symbol of purity. Here is found a *chōzuya* (ablution basin) where worshippers cleanse themselves before proceeding. Rinse each hand with water poured from one of the ladles provided. Then ladle water into your hand and rinse it around your mouth, before spitting it out. Finally fill the scoop for the last time, and tip it backwards so that purifying water runs back over the long handle which you have been holding. Water—from hands, ladle or mouth—mustn't be allowed to fall back into the basin, but only onto the surrounding gravel. Don't worry if you get this wrong—many Japanese don't know the proper way to do it either.

At the edges of the courtyard there are likely to be **shrine shops** selling information booklets (ask for one in English), and dedicated to bringing various kinds of good luck (safe childbirth, success in exams, safety from traffic accidents). At the edges of this area may also be wide racks hung with *ema* or votive plaques: tablets of wood bearing a picture on one side (usually of an animal or legendary scene), and with a blank reverse on which worshippers write their prayers and requests. You can buy these from the shop for about ¥500. Even if you don't want to leave a prayer, they make attractive souvenirs. Other lesser shrine buildings may include a **stage** for the performance of sacred dances, and a **storehouse** for the *mikoshi* portable shrine.

At the far side of the courtyard will be the entrance to the shrine proper. Generally no one but the priests is allowed into the inner sanctum where the *kami* lurk. What visitors see is an outer **oratory** where prayers and offerings are made. The usual way of paying respects is as follows. Stand in front of the large slatted cashbox and throw in a small coin. Ring the bell by shaking the thick rope—this attracts the attention of the deity. Make two deep bows and two claps, then stand with eyes closed and hands clasped muttering your prayer. Conclude with two more bows. For an account of Shinto and its deities, *see* pp.90–94).

Temple Architecture

Buddhism came to Japan with a long-established architectural tradition which distinguished itself from native styles by the use of tile on roofs and floors, painted surfaces, and clay wattle and daub walls, rather than planks. Central to the earliest temples was a reliquary where fragments of the Buddha's body were stored. In India, this was a stupa, a dome of earth and stone with a spire on top; in China and Japan, it developed into the **pagoda** (*tō*), a roofed tower of three or five storeys, built around a huge central pillar beneath which relics were buried in a sacred vessel.

As the historical Buddha yielded in importance to other deities, the focus of worship moved from the pagoda to the **golden hall** (*kondō*), where statues were displayed. In Hōryū-ji, near Nara, the country's oldest pagoda and *kondō* (*c.* 710) stand side-by-side, on an equal footing. Forty years later, when Tōdai-ji temple was built, two pagodas (neither of which survives) were raised in front of the main precinct, but by now they were marginal, supporting structures, rather than centres of sanctity and worship. The halls of this period, like Tōshōdai-ji and Yakushi-ji in western Nara, are Chinese in inspiration: big, stately buildings with massive hipped roofs of tile, arranged symmetrically on a north–south axis.

During the **Heian period** (794–1185), new currents in Buddhist thought produced new temple styles. In particular, the cult of Amida, the Buddha of the Western Paradise, gave rise to the **Paradise hall**, the finest of which is the Phoenix Hall of the Byōdō-in in Uji, near Kyoto. The deity was enshrined in a hall representing the 'Pure Land' where all devout souls hope to travel when they die. The interior walls were painted with murals of thronging heavenly scenes, and the halls were often surrounded by ponds; worshippers sat on the far side, or even on a floating raft, and adored Amida across the 'Western Ocean'. Two other sects, Tendai and Shingon, built their headquarters at the top of mountains (Hiei and Kōya), which necessarily broke up the symmetry of the compounds. Being remote from centres of craftsmanship and manufacture, the architects of these halls depended more on natural materials: thus, shingles of cypress wood and wooden boards replaced ceramic tiles on the roofs and floors.

The sect that gave architectural impetus to the **Kamakura period** (1185–1333) was **Zen**, introduced from China in the 12th and 13th centuries. Zen emphasized discipline and regimentation, in the design of the monks' environment as much as in their daily routine. Seven principal halls were prescribed, the most important of them arranged in a straight line from south to north: main gate (*san-mon*), Buddha hall (*butsu-den*), lecture hall (*hattō*). Also within the compound, at points to either side, were the dormitory (*sōdō*), kitchen (*kuin*), latrine (*tōsu*) and bath house (*yokushitsu*)—Zen discipline encompassed everyday activities like sleeping, eating and bathing. In the bigger temples, like Daitoku-ji and Nanzen-ji in Kyoto, small sub-temples grew up around the edges of the formal main compound. These were often strikingly informal in character, converted villas or houses with rambling and irregular paths and gardens.

The new sect brought with it from Sung China a number of new architectural details: even today Zen temples look distinctively foreign and exotic. Each of the main halls is set on a raised stone base, and has a stone floor, often made up of diagonally arranged flags. The posts are set into the floor on stone plinths, and the doors swing open (rather than slide) on wooden hinges. Light is admitted to the interior through open-work transoms above the doors, and through the distinctive arched or cusped windows.

In the **Muromachi period** (1333–1573), these ornamental details were combined in the pleasure pavilions, later converted into temples, which two of the Ashikaga shoguns built for themselves on the margins of Kyoto. The Golden Pavilion (Kinkaku-ji, 1398) has the ground floor of an aristocratic villa (veranda and removable shutters), the middle floor of a Japanese-style Buddha hall (sliding wooden doors), and the top floor of a Zen chapel (cusped windows and swinging doors). The Silver Pavilion (Ginkaku-ji, 1484) does the same with two storeys.

The warlords who brought peace to the country during the **Momoyama period** (1573–1600) were great patrons of the arts, especially Toyotomi Hideyoshi, who built two lavish castles in Kyoto. After his death they were dismantled and distributed among the temples: the Chinese Gate in Daitoku-ji and the *shoin* villa of Nishi Hongan-ji are examples. The best of the Momoyama style had passed by the mid-17th century, but the rich detailing which characterized it—curved eaves, brightly painted woodwork, elaborate carving— was employed in diluted form throughout the Edo period (1600–1868). Registration at a

Buddhist temple became compulsory for all the shogun's subjects, and pilgrimages became popular as a means of circumventing the restrictions on travel. As a result, temple halls became very large, capable of holding huge congregations, with bright, attention-grabbing paintings and big, exaggerated statues. Kyoto's Kiyomizu-dera and Zenkō-ji in Nagano were ancient temples rebuilt in this manner.

Secular Architecture

The life of the Heian aristocracy, intimately chronicled in Lady Murasaki's *Tale of Genji*, revolved around the sprawling residential pleasure complexes where they lived, entertained and conducted their wistful love affairs. The *shinden* style, as it's known, survives only in bastardized reconstructions, like the Kyoto Imperial Palace and Heian Shrine, as well as in numerous narrative picture scrolls (*emakimono*) illustrating the writings of women like Murasaki. A 'sleeping hall' (*shinden*) faced, to the south, a large pond with bridges, islands and piers where dragon-shaped pleasure boats were moored. The master of the house lived in the *shinden*; covered corridors extended on either side, linking it with satellite halls and pavilions where wives, children and mistresses resided with their own retinues of servants and guards. Walls were flimsy and removable; the wooden-floored interior was partitioned off by hanging curtains, bamboo blinds and painted screens. The entire complex was surrounded by tile-roofed earthen walls.

By the late 16th century, the *shinden* had developed into a distinctive new style called *shoin*, literally 'writing hall'. The elements of the *shoin* room developed out of the study rooms of abbots in Zen monasteries, and were later adopted by secular scholars and leaders as a mark of their learning, wealth and piety. The classic *shoin* room, like those from Toyotomi Hideyoshi's palace (now reassembled in Kyoto's Nishi Hongan-ji temple) contains certain recurring elements. It is carpeted entirely with *tatami* mats, which had by now become the standard floor covering, and has a coffered ceiling. *Fusuma* (sliding screens, often elaborately painted) divide rooms from one another; on the outside of the building are thinner paper screens (*shōji*), protected from the elements by heavier sliding panels. Parts of the room may be raised a few centimetres above the rest, and at the back lies an alcove called a *tokonoma* where a hanging scroll, an incense burner and a flower arrangement are often set. In the same wall are staggered shelves (*chigaidana*) for books or ornaments, and on the adjacent wall is a long, narrow desk (*tsukeshoin*), built into the wall, perhaps below a window overlooking a garden or view. Opposite this are a set of double doors (*chōdaigamae*), ornamented with brightly coloured tassles. These last four— alcove, shelves, desk and doors—are the defining elements of the *shoin* style, used in the most elegant inns and restaurants even today.

The finest examples of *shoin* architecture—in Kyoto's Nishi Hongan-ji temple and Nijō Castle—are prodigies of ornamental excess, with screens, ceilings and even nail covers lavishly painted and gilded for the glorification of the generals who commissioned them. Around the same time, though, the *sukiya* style, altogether quieter and more refined, was being developed by the much older families of the Kyoto aristocracy. *Sukiya* means 'abode of refinement' and was influenced by the austere aesthetics of the tea ceremony. An intimate, rustic atmosphere was cultivated, by the use of irregularity and gentle understatement. Posts were left unplaned, with some of their bark still adhering, paintings (on gentle, natural themes) were simple and unpretentious, and the few adornments were unobtrusive and witty—symmetrical openwork carving on the transoms between rooms, door handles in the shape of plants or musical instruments. Katsura Detached Villa near Kyoto is the finest example of the style.

With the rise of the military class from the 12th century onward, a distinctive style of warrior architecture began to emerge. **Castles** are the most obvious manifestation of this (*see* the description of Himeji Castle on p.429 for design features), but during peacetime the feudal lords and their samurai lived in stout dwellings outside the inner citadel. The **buke yashiki** (samurai houses) of the Edo period (1600–1868) often had defensive features (massive gates, thick walls and secret rooms for bodyguards or eavesdroppers), but above all they embodied the minute social distinctions on which the shogunate was based. Certain rooms were reserved only for those of a given rank or above; strict sumptuary laws forbade the use of lavish decoration by merchants and other members of the lower classes.

The Japanese Arts

The Floating World

Ukiyo, 'floating world', is one of those unique terms which seems to provide the key to an entire culture, but which remains tantalizingly resistant to translation or straightforward definition. Even in Japanese the word is ambiguous. In the Heian period, *ukiyo* meant 'sorrowful world'—the human vale of tears and impermanence for which faith in the Buddha was the only escape and remedy. During the decadent Genroku era, the first element, *uki*, came to be written with the character that means 'floating'. The floating world of the brilliant cities of Edo (later Tokyo) and Ōsaka seemed as different as could be from the sorrowful one of the ancient Buddhist monks. Money, sex and style were its currency; at its heart were the licensed pleasure quarters where samurai, merchants, craftsmen, artists, poets and apprentices could escape the stifling social codes of the feudal state to eat, drink, dress up, watch plays and street shows, and enjoy the attentions of *geisha*, courtesans and prostitutes.

But something of the old Buddhist melancholy remained: for all the gaiety and life of the theatres and brothels, the floating world was haunted by a consciousness of its own artifice and evanescence. The cherry blossoms in a woodblock print (*ukiyo-e*, 'floating world picture') of a famous *geisha* are celebrated for their beauty but serve also as a *memento mori*: like them, her beauty will wither and die. The love affairs between courtesans and their admirers, celebrated in novels and poems, and in the plays of the *kabuki* and *bunraku* (puppet) theatres, cannot survive outside the boundaries of the pleasure quarters and inevitably end in suicide or tragedy. The prints and plays are still admired and performed, but much of the art of the floating world—its literature, for instance—has dated less well. The essence of the era lay in fashions of dress and behaviour. Books, plays and pictures might record but could never capture it. 'Edo culture', wrote Edward Seidensticker, 'was better than anything it left to posterity.'

The cities which fostered the floating world have changed beyond recognition, but the aesthetic which developed there is still in evidence. There are *geisha* in Tokyo's Ginza, Kyoto's Gion, and old cities like Kanazawa, but they are fewer, older and more expensive than ever. Their place has been taken by bar hostesses who—instead of playing the *koto* or performing classical dances—pour drinks, squeeze knees and sing karaoke. Prostitution was outlawed in 1957, but survives in the 'bath houses' and 'massage parlours' where an extraordinary menu of activities, from the conventional to the bizarre, are purveyed under a range of ingenious euphemisms. Above all, there's a contradictory innocence about it all, and a poignant sense of escapism. The same salaryman who pays hundreds of pounds to manacle teenage girls in an S&M parlour might be seen, an hour later, weeping senti-mental tears as he wails folk songs in a karaoke bar. The next morning, he will cram himself into the early train, spend the day bowing to his superiors, and dine with his wife and family with no sense of incongruity whatsoever.

Geisha

Geisha—true *geisha* anyway—are not prostitutes. A man might have an affair with his *geisha* just as he might with his piano teacher, but it would be many expensive evenings and presents before that stage was reached, and even then the relationship would be closer to that of patron and protégé than client and call girl. The word means 'art person': *geisha* are highly-trained performers whose principal function is to create a lively, civilized atmosphere at the kind of male gatherings which, these days, can only be afforded by the very rich or well-connected.

The numbers of practising *geisha* are on the decline, as much thanks to the demands of modern compulsory education as to cheap alternatives like bar hostesses. The apprentice *geisha* is called a *maiko*. Traditional training begins as young as seven, when the trainee becomes attached to a *geisha* house where she may also live. Over the years, she studies classical dancing, the playing of traditional instruments like the *shamisen*, and the arts of the kimono, the tea ceremony, flower arranging and calligraphy. *Geisha* are also expert conversationalists: jokes, teasing banter, and the performance of little skits are as much a part of the job as more formal accomplishments and the serving of food and drink.

Hiring *geisha* is a costly business, and several intermediaries take their cut of the fee paid by the client. The entertainment itself generally takes place in a high class Japanese restaurant or 'tea house'. Even money is not enough in itself; indeed, without an introduc-tion, and usually some knowledge of Japanese, the casual visitor is unlikely ever to encounter *geisha*, except as fleeting presences in the early evening streets of Ginza or Gion. Travel companies sometimes advertise night-time tours including an hour or two at a 'geisha party'. Be assured: if it's that easy, then it can't be the real thing.

Sumo

With its colossal wrestlers, medieval costumes and barking ritual, sumo, at first glance, looks impenetrably alien and remote, but turns out to be one of the most appealing and accessible of Japanese spectator events. The fights themselves are intense bursts of energy seldom more than a couple of minutes long—so it's impossible to become bored with any one bout. The stamping, glaring stand-offs which precede each one are bravura dramas of bluff and psychological warfare. Anyone can enjoy sumo, and, even if baseball wins bigger audiences these days, it is still very much the *Kokugi*—National Accomplishment.

Like *nō* drama, its origins are religious. Wrestling matches were performed on festival days for the entertainment of the Shinto gods, and today the sport is a repository of ancient details and superstitions. The sumo ring, the *dohyō*, is a platform of clay and straw, blessed by a priest, which would once have stood in a shrine or temple. Until quite recently, all *dohyō* had pillars at their four corners, like a *nō* stage, but wrestlers kept injuring themselves on them. Now, the shrine-style roof hovers above, supported harmlessly from the ceiling. The ritualized bowing, touching of the earth, clapping and stamping which the wrestlers carry out when they enter the ring, honour the gods and scare away evil spirits. The handfuls of salt which they hurl about are also a traditional means of purification. Women, being impure beings, are strictly forbidden from entering the ring, and the sport, administered by the ultra-conservative Japan Sumo Association, remains a chauvinistically male preserve. (The top wrestlers, national sex symbols and celebrities in their own right, have an impractical habit of marrying exquisitely tiny models and actresses.)

The wrestlers (*rikishi*) live and train in hierarchically organized 'stables', administered by retired champions. Like *geisha* and *kabuki* actors, they begin their apprenticeships young, cooking, cleaning and skivvying for their seniors (the apprentice's duties are rumoured to include wiping the buttocks of colleagues too bulky to perform their own ablutions), and bulking themselves out on high-protein foods, including a famous stew called *chanko nabe*. Mature *rikishi* look extraordinary, like members of an entirely different race. The average weight is around 300 pounds, and the mightiest are half as big again. But not all of them are gross: victory requires agility and strength as well as bulk, and a relatively slimline *rikishi* can often overcome a much larger adversary. The fighting names they adopt on entering the profession contain delicate references to flowers, trees and mountains.

The tournaments, called *basho*, last 15 days, and are held six times a year. If your visit coincides with one, you will know about it: every TV, radio and newspaper is seemingly tuned to the comprehensive coverage which continues late into the night with post-match highlights and analysis. The day's bouts are preceded by a great deal of ritual, as the contenders parade around the ring in their ceremonial aprons. The rules themselves are very simple. On the clay floor of the *dohyō* is a ring of thick rope, similar to the *shime-nawa* sacred ropes seen in Shinto shrines. The wrestlers face one another across it, glaring and stamping through several false starts designed to disconcert their opponent and demonstrate their 'fighting spirit'. Finally, in an atmosphere of rising tension, the kimono-clad referee gives the signal, and the *rikishi* hurl themselves at one another. The wrestler who forces his opponent out of the rope ring, or causes him to touch the ground with any part of his body other than the soles of his feet, is the winner. There are dozens of different techniques for achieving this, from sheer bulldozing force to picking up the opponent by his waist band and hurling him bodily out of the ring.

At the end of each day, the complicated rankings are revised. Excitement gathers towards the end of the *basho* as the leading fighters struggle to move up the ranks to qualify as champions: *ozeki* or, highest of all, *yokozuna*—grand champions, who wear sacred white ropes around their waists. For information on tournaments and tickets *see* 'Sport', p.000.

Tea

Unlike the Chinese and Indian varieties drunk in the West (called *kocha* in Japan), the leaves of Japanese tea are not fermented, and remain their natural colour: a rich green. Infused with hot water, green tea comes out yellow, and foreigners sometimes find the pale, urinous colour off-putting. But the delicate taste is easy to acquire, and the sharing of tea is one of the basics of Japanese hospitality. Every *ryokan* room, corporate conference table and Japanese home has its small ceramic teapot and handleless cups (always in sets of three or five—the number four, *shi*, is homonymous with the taboo word for death). The hot water is added and the tea brewed for a few moments before pouring. It is drunk without any milk, lemon or sweetener. There are many different grades and varieties; the general word for green tea is habitually prefixed with the honorific: *o-cha*, 'esteemed tea'.

It was introduced from China and popularized in the 12th century by Zen monks who used it as a medicine and a stimulant during long periods of meditation (a few cups can deliver a surprisingly strong caffeine kick; insomniacs should avoid it before bedtime). From these religious beginnings developed a unique rite, called in Japanese *chadō*, 'The Way of Tea', and commonly referred to in English as the tea ceremony. In the 15th and 16th centuries, it became formalized under the patronage of the Ashikaga shoguns, great connoisseurs of *nō* drama, Chinese Sung pottery, Zen Buddhism, pavilion architecture and gardens. *Chadō* combines elements of all these in a secular act of communion very hard to describe. Like much Japanese art, it is about the cultivation of mood and tranquil emotion. The preparation and serving of the tea, according to a strict sequence of prescribed actions, fosters an atmosphere of harmony and heightened aesthetic appreciation—of the tea, the company, the setting and the ineffable order of things.

Famous tea masters, like the 16th-century samurai Sen-no-Rikyū, commanded the respect and reverence accorded to the greatest painters and poets. Even today, there are schools of tea run by the descendants of great practitioners where students can spend years studying the practice and philosophy of the Way. There are varying degrees of formality—the most authentic tea ceremonies are inaccessible to casual visitors since they are, by definition, private gatherings of a few hand-picked initiates. Hotels, tourist shops and temples, as well as the big schools of tea, like Ura Senke in Kyoto, sometimes put on tea ceremony demonstrations open to the public which capture the outer form of the ritual, even if the inner resonances are lost.

A full-blown tea ceremony lasts several hours and includes a formal *kaiseki* meal followed by sweets and 'thick' tea. This is followed by a break during which the guests enjoy the garden, then a drink of informal 'thin' tea, and a light dry sweet or biscuit. It takes place in a purpose-built tea house, often part of a villa or garden complex, expressing through its architecture the tea ceremony's ideals of simplicity and rustic beauty.

Less rigorous versions can be held in any *tatami*-matted room. The guests kneel in front of the host, and eat a small sticky sweet while he or she attends to the cooking implements: an iron kettle (ideally heated over a charcoal fire), a bamboo water ladle, a wooden or ceramic tea caddy, a bamboo scoop for measuring out the tea, a large tea bowl and a bamboo whisk. All of these objects are handmade; the finest tea bowls are priceless artworks handed down from one generation of tea masters to the next. Even the simple bamboo objects are made and treated with great care and respect—every year there are special ceremonies, when piles of exhausted tea whisks are burned in front of altars and ritually 'thanked' for the service they have provided.

The tea used in the tea ceremony is powdered; when a small amount of water is added and whisked, it bubbles up into a thick, dark green froth. The host places the bowl in front of the guest who carefully picks it up, and rotates it clockwise a few inches. This is to avoid drinking out of the 'front' of the bowl, a gesture of modesty. The tea has a refreshing, slightly bitter taste; it is drunk by raising the bowl up to the face, in two or three slow sips. When the bowl is empty, the guest cradles it for a few moments, admiring its beauty and perhaps offering a few learned words of appreciation, before replacing it in front of the host. Host and guest bow deeply to one another, the bowl is retrieved, and the same routine is performed for the next guest.

Performing Arts

Nō and Kyōgen

Nō has been performed continuously since the 14th century, making it the world's oldest theatrical form. Little has been added to the repertory in the last 450 years, and the stage, masks, costumes and acting conventions were established in their present form before the time of Shakespeare. Of all the Japanese forms, *nō* (pronounced more like English 'nor' than 'no'; frequently written as 'noh') retains the most obvious links to the religious rituals from which most world drama originally sprang. It's performed on a special cypress stage, polished to a slippery shine using only the natural oils of the wood. The stage is 5.8m square; at each corner is a pillar. The use of plain wood, white gravel which surrounds the stage, and the shrine-style roof, all suggest the Shinto architecture from which it is derived. The stage is undecorated, apart from the painting of a gnarled pine tree on the back wall. Earthenware jars, carefully placed beneath the stage, amplify the noise of the actors' dancing feet.

A covered corridor lined with three real pine trees leads off from rear stage right, along which the actors and musicians enter and exit. First to appear, in formal, undecorated kimono, are the chorus and musicians. The latter sit at the back and consist of a flautist and two or three percussionists playing drums of various sizes and tones. The music serves as an emotional and atmospheric accompaniment to the songs and dances, its pace and volume increasing at climactic moments. The musicians are also responsible for the yelping cries ('Hyioow!') which contribute so much to the strangeness of a *nō* performance. The chorus usually numbers six and sits at stage left. They comment on the action and, as in the Greek theatre, relate events which take place offstage, or before the opening of the play.

Nō performers are all male, and are categorized according to the kind of part each actor plays. The first character to appear on stage is generally a type called the *waki*. *Waki* never wear masks and play the supporting, passive role—the priest, warrior or traveller to whom the central mystery of the story will eventually be revealed. The principal character is called the *shite* (pronounced 'sh'teh'). He (or she, although female roles are always taken by men) may not be what he first appears—a peasant who turns out to be a ghost, for instance, or a demon in the shape of a court lady. If the *shite* is a woman, an elderly person, a court noble, or a non-human ghost or monster, he will wear one of the beautiful masks for which *nō* has become famous. The third main group comprises the *kyōgen* actors. Not every *nō* play features *kyōgen*, but they sometimes take supporting roles as peasants or retainers. Their most important function is to summarize, in simple language, the events of a play during its interval. *Kyōgen* is also the name of a separate dramatic genre: homely, satirical comedies about venal priests, drunken lords, dim-witted samurai and their rascally retainers, originally performed as light relief during a lengthy *nō* programme. *Kyōgen* is as light and accessible as *nō* is profound and demanding, and these days it is increasingly performed in its own right.

All the actors wear elaborate formal costumes of the finest brocade. The sumptuousness of the kimono usually indicates the importance of the character, although costume, like everything else, is stylized—even peasants and fishermen wear clothes of beauty and quality. *Kyōgen* actors are identifiable by their yellow *tabi*—cotton slippers with a separate compartment for the big toe, like mittens for feet. Especially striking are the trousers worn by samurai characters, with extra long legs which trail behind them as they walk.

Nō plays are simple in the extreme, and their stories, such as they are, can be summarized in a few lines. There are various different types of play, but the typical 'plot' goes like this: a traveller (the *waki*—often a priest, warrior or imperial envoy) encounters the *shite*, who may be young or old, male or female, great or humble. The *shite*, however, is disguising his true form. In the second act of the play, this will be revealed in a climactic dance. Then, after pious concluding remarks, the actors, chorus and musicians slowly process off stage. There are five different types of play, labelled according to the nature of the *shite* character: 'god plays' which are generally upbeat and celebratory, 'warrior plays', in which the *shite* is often a member of the warring Taira or Minamoto clans, 'woman plays', 'madman plays' and 'devil plays'.

The language is highly poetic and allusive—even a Japanese spectator will often use an annotated script to follow the densest speeches. Without some knowledge of the plot (or good Japanese), it would be very difficult to work out, from simply watching the actors, what is going on. Realistic portrayal of action is irrelevant to a *nō* actor. In fact, it is considered vulgar and a distraction from the real purpose of the form—the cultivation of *yūgen*, an untranslatable concept meaning something like 'mysterious profundity'.

Restraint is everything. *Nō* solves the central question of the theatre—how to portray real lives and emotions in an essentially non-realistic environment—by withdrawing utterly from any attempt at naturalism. Movement is slow and stately; the passage of an actor across the stage might indicate a journey of thousands of miles. Props are simple and few—chief among them is the actor's fan which can stand for anything from a sword to chopsticks. (In one play, a dying lady is represented by a folded robe at the front of the stage.) In such an austere, understated atmosphere, tiny gestures can stand for deep and powerful emotions—a mother's delight at finding her long-lost son might be suggested by nothing more than the tilt of a mask; a hand brushing the face represents tears of grief.

Getting the Most out of *Nō*

A fine *nō* performance can be a hauntingly transcendent experience, a piece of living history, mysterious far beyond the sum of its parts. To first timers with unrealistic expectations, however, it can also be gibberish—a fiasco of atonal wailing and tuneless twanging, like a two-hour-long Monty Python sketch. Certainly, it's the least accessible of the traditional performing arts, and you have to approach it in the right frame of mind. Don't come expecting anything as mundane as action, plot or character. Leave the children at home.

Try to get hold of an English version of the play. Several of these are available, including classic translations by Arthur Waley and Donald Keene, but the most comprehensive is probably *Japanese Nō Dramas*, translated by Royall Tyler (Penguin Classics). If the play you're planning to see isn't in one of these, consult *A Guide to Nō* by P G O'Neill (Hinoki Shoten) which contains character lists and plot summaries of all the plays still in the repertoire. *Nō* theatres often hand out photocopies of these to foreign members of the audience.

Kabuki

Kabuki is the exact opposite of *nō*. Where one form whispers, the other yodels. If a grieving father in a *nō* play laments the murder of his son by brushing a sleeve against his downward tilted mask, his *kabuki* counterpart will wail, sing and perform a stamping dance, before metamorphosing into a dragon to avenge his child's death. *Kabuki* is noisy, camp and over-the-top, and, for newcomers to Japanese drama, it's the ideal place to start.

Kabuki's louche beginnings were in the early 1600s, when a woman named Okuni led a troupe of female dancers in performances of *kabuki odori* (frolicsome dances) on the banks of Kyoto's Kamo River. The shows were associated with lewdness and prostitution, and the authorities intervened to ban women from taking part. They were replaced by handsome young boys, but the problem of prostitution did not go away. Eventually the rules were changed again—today *kabuki* parts are played by adult men.

The plays became popular as part of the merchant's culture which grew up in 17th- and 18th-century Edo (Tokyo), and incorporated all the elements closest to the Edo townsman's heart: lavish and stylish costumes, beautiful women (even if they were men), and epic tales of love, betrayal, gallantry, war, ghosts and death, set in the feudal present as well as the heroic past. It was very much an actors' theatre—the big *kabuki* players were the pop and movie stars of their day, portrayed in their famous roles by woodblock print artists, and famously fond of improvization and banter with the audience. Even today, actors wink effortlessly in and out of character, and plays written centuries ago are spiced up with sly references to contemporary politics, scandals, sport, TV and pop music.

The *kabuki* stage is big, and closer to the Western proscenium style than the platform employed by *nō*. Its most striking feature is the *hanamichi* (flower path), a long catwalk linking the front of the stage with the back of the auditorium; along it, principal characters make important entrances and exits. The stage floor conceals complicated apparatus for the stunts and *coups de theatre* in which *kabuki* revels: trap doors through which characters leap or vanish; revolving panels for quick changes of scenery; ropes and pulleys for flying a character across the stage. Music is played live, but the players are usually semi-concealed behind wooden slats. The music is more exuberant and noisy than *nō*, but still far from melodic, with much use of drums and clackers to point up spectacular moments.

Kabuki actors serve long apprenticeships, being born or adopted into long-standing acting families which have dominated the art since the Edo period. As in *nō*, actors specialize in certain kinds of role, the most specialized of all being the *onnagata*, female impersonators, whose exquisite dress, movement and high-pitched voices render them more feminine than any real woman ever was. They wear thick white make-up, like *geisha*; other actors are painted to indicate their character, with red suggesting evil. *Aragoto* is the rough, gruff, bombastic style of acting used to portray heroes and warriors. These actors sometimes have stripy make-up, a bit like that in the Peking Opera; at key moments they freeze in dramatic grimaces, and turn their faces to the lights. Aficionados demonstrate their connoisseurship at these moments by shouting aloud the name of the actor's family.

Bunraku

The traditional puppet theatre of Japan (also called *ningyō jōruri*) is as far as could be from the Punch and Judy shows and twitchy marionettes of the West. Wandering puppeteers were known in Japan in the 11th century, but it was during the 17th century that *bunraku* achieved huge popularity, largely thanks to a playwright named Chikamatsu Monzaemon whose 130 plays are the core of the modern repertoire. The subjects and style of *bunraku* are quite different from those of *nō*: Chikamatsu developed the genre known as *sewa-mono*, 'talk of the town plays' about recognizable Edo-era types (*geisha*, apprentices, merchants, samurai) and the tragic conflicts that arose between feudal duty (*giri*) and human feeling (*ninjō*). The archetypal *bunraku* plot traces the course of an ill-fated love affair, and its pathetic, and usually fatal, consequences. Chikamatsu's most famous play, *Sonezaki Shinjū*, was one of 20 he wrote on the subject of love suicides, often based on contemporary real-life tragedies. *Bunraku* became a forum for propagation of the latest gossip and scandal, often thinly fictionalized with Chinese or historical settings.

The *bunraku* stage is wide, and on two levels. On the lower, rear stage stand the puppeteers, three for each puppet. All are plainly visible throughout the performance—the great thrill of the best *bunraku* is the way in which one's attention is tugged away from the work of the puppeteers by the delicate and realistic movement of the puppets. One assistant operates the left arm and hand, another controls the legs and feet. Both are masked and dressed in black. The master puppeteer moves the face, eyes, mouth and right arm; he wears a plain formal kimono, and is unmasked.

The puppets are works of art in themselves, hand-made by a dwindling number of specialist craftsmen. They are about two-thirds life size, realistically clothed in miniature Edo-period costumes, similar to those used in *kabuki*. The narration and the voices for all the different characters, including women, are performed by a chanter (*tayū*), who sits at stage right alongside a *shamisen* player. His is the most important and exhausting role of all; a long play might involve several different narrators, substituted through a revolving door in the side of the stage.

Religion

Visitors often find the subject of religion in Japan difficult to get to grips with. By Western standards, it is riven with contradictions and surprises. Few countries, on the face of it, appear so relentlessly committed to the secular virtues of technological progress and materialism; yet every new bank or factory building is blessed by a priest, and frequently has a miniature shrine on its roof. The typical young Japanese professes no strong religious beliefs; but he or she would never dream of visiting a temple or shrine without faithfully going through the rituals of cleansing, clapping, bowing and making offerings. 107 million Japanese claim affiliation to a Shinto organization, 96 million to a Buddhist one; yet the total population is only 124 million. Plainly, religious life in Japan is organized along very different lines from those of the Christian West.

The most important religions of Japan are Shinto, indigenous and unique to Japan, and Buddhism, the great religion of Asia, founded in India in the 5th century BC. Shinto deities are worshipped at buildings called *jinja* or *jingū* (*-gū* or *-sha* at the end of a word); this book follows the standard practice of translating these words as 'shrine', in contrast to the Buddhist *tera* (*-dera* or *-ji* or *-in*) which is always given as 'temple'.

Perhaps the greatest historical difference between Japanese and European religion is the tolerance with which Shinto and Buddhism have always regarded one another. For centuries, rival groups of Japanese carved one another up in ruinous civil wars, but these were almost never fought for sectarian reasons, and it is still common to find shrines and temples standing side by side within the same precincts. As statistics show, most Japanese regard themselves as both Shinto and Buddhist, at different times and places. In general, Buddhist ritual is used to mark the solemn, transcendent occasions such as funerals, Shinto for auspicious events like weddings or festivals.

Shinto

The survival of Shinto as a living faith is remarkable; it's rather as if the Classical or Celtic deities were still being revered in modern Greece and Britain, alongside the Christian God and his saints. Historically, in fact, there have been many kinds of Shinto; one of the reasons for its survival is undoubtedly its adaptable, multi-valenced nature. Over the years,

Shinto has been many different things to different Japanese, and it is unfortunate that it is known in the West almost exclusively for its last incarnation: State Shinto, a sentimental, nationalistic brand of emperor worship invented in the Meiji period and exploited during the 1930s by the fascists and totalitarians of the Pacific War.

Early Shinto was vague and inchoate; the word itself didn't exist until after the 6th century when the introduction of Buddhism made it necessary to distinguish between the traditional 'Way of the Gods' (*Shintō*) and the imported 'Way of Buddha' (*Butsudō*). It began as the religion of a nation of rice farmers. Fertility rites, both human and agricultural, have always been important elements in Shinto worship, and many of the most important *matsuri* (festivals) are essentially prayers for the success of the crop offered at crucial moments of the rice-growing cycle. The earliest deities were thus the sun, which nourishes the crop, the storm, which can ruin it, and natural features like mountains, rivers and lakes, which collect and supply the water essential for irrigation. Worship seems also to have been offered to natural features which were not necessarily useful or fearful, but simply impressive. The earliest shrines were not buildings at all, but natural objects like rocks or trees, which were marked with sacred symbols. Even today it's common in the older shrines to see particularly ancient cedars or boulders girt with a rope or paper streamers indicating the presence of a *kami*, a Shinto deity. This delicate appreciation of natural beauty for its own sake is a constant thread in Japanese art and aesthetics of all periods.

If a fertility cult based on nature worship is the first element in Shinto, then reverence for ancestors, a common strand in much Asian religion, is the second. The two fused naturally enough in Shinto's most controversial aspect, the cult surrounding the emperor and his family. The imperial family, after all, started out as one of a number of clans whose wealth and power depended on their success as rice farmers. As the most successful of the bunch, they were able to dominate and rule over their peers; and it was only natural that they should legitimize their power by setting up their forebears, not just as honoured conquerors and administrators, but as children of the gods. The earliest surviving Japanese book, the *Kojiki*, was compiled in 712 with this very purpose in mind: the genealogy of the 8th-century emperors is traced back to the sun goddess and beyond, to the legendary founders and begetters of the islands of Japan.

These three kinds of worship—of nature, ancestors and the emperor—have formed the basis of Shinto. Beyond this, though, it's difficult to make definite statements about Shinto belief. It possesses no scripture (the *Kojiki* and similar collections are legends, not dogma) and no commandments, code of ethics, or system of philosophical speculation. Shinto answers none of the abstract questions posed by the great world faiths. It's difficult in fact to call it a religion at all.

Instead, Shinto asserts the existence of many thousands of *kami*, a word usually translated as 'god' which literally means 'superior'—those removed from or above humanity, but not necessarily transcending it. *Kami* range from Amaterasu Ōmikami, the sun goddess, ancestor of the imperial family, and principal deity of the pantheon, down to the nameless spirits who inhabit rocks, trees and wayside shrines. These *kami* possess power over different areas of life, and can be propitiated or angered by the practice, or omission, of certain ritual acts. It is in the observance of these rituals, rather than in any abstract beliefs about the nature of the deities or of existence, that Shinto endures.

Outstanding among these rituals are those concerned with purification: the contrast between clean and unclean is as strong in Shinto as the dualism of good and evil, innocence and guilt, in other religions. Certain states of impurity are offensive to the gods, and much ritual concerns itself with the elimination or avoidance of pollution. Physical grubbiness was only part of the story: among the things that made the original *kami* squeamish were sex, menstruation and childbirth—in early times, separate buildings were constructed away from human habitation where affected individuals (principally women, of course) would confine themselves for the period of their pollution. Illness, injury and death were also great taboos. One of the reasons why the imperial capitals shifted around so much before the 8th century was that entire palaces had to be moved and rebuilt after the death of an old emperor. In Heian times, even the death of a cat within the precincts of the imperial enclosure was the cause of much troublesome purifying and exorcizing.

Vestigial traces of this urge to cleanliness can be seen throughout modern Japanese society. Every shrine and temple contains in its courtyard a font where worshippers wash their hands and rinse out their mouths, and at some Shinto services the (white-clad) priest will wave a wand of paper streamers over worshippers—an act of cleansing, rather than blessing. When sumo wrestlers toss salt over their shoulders before a bout, they are performing a purification ritual; piles of salt can often be seen on household altars and shrines. Even the white gloves worn by taxi drivers, and the Japanese love of hot baths and spas undoubtedly owes something to this deep-rooted preoccupation.

Actual historical figures can become *kami*—Heian-period statesman and scholar Sugawara Michizane is worshipped in shrines across Japan as Tenjin-sama, god of learning, principally by high school students hoping for success in their university entrance exams. With more recently deceased figures, it can be difficult to distinguish between worship and reverence. The great 19th-century Emperor Meiji is enshrined as a *kami* in Tokyo's Meiji Shrine, but how much this has in common with the ancient shrine to the sun goddess at Ise, for instance, is open to question. The traditional belief in the ruling emperor as a living god was renounced by Emperor Hirohito in 1945; nonetheless, some Japanese still regard him as a *kami* in the literal sense—one symbolically 'above' his subjects and nation.

Shinto worship is loose and open ended. Its most obvious and enjoyable manifestations are in *matsuri* (festivals) which vary from a small fair at a village shrine to spectacular three-day extravaganzas of dance, music and drunkenness which dominate an entire city, and attract visitors from all over the country. *Matsuri* are big tourist attractions, but the entertainment they offer—parades of floats, dances, traditional drama, stunts involving fire, contests of strength, feasts and boozing—were originally intended for the entertainment of the *kami*. At a typical *matsuri*, the priests, after carefully purifying themselves, use prayers, offerings and sacred music to summon the *kami*, who is then paraded around the neighbourhood in an ornate portable shrine called a *mikoshi*, carried on the back of chanting, and often extremely drunk, local men. *Matsuri* vary in scale and spectacle, but they are always joyful, earthy, raucous occasions which the gods are intended to enjoy as much as the participants. Having fêted and entertained the *kami*, it is hoped that they will bring luck and prosperity to the people and their crops over the next year.

There are no mandatory services, fasts, or days of Shinto obligation. On request, after payment of a fixed 'donation', shrines will perform rituals of blessing or purification, often accompanied by sacred dances, for worshippers with a particular prayer or wish (good luck in education, child-bearing, marriage, etc.). Most babies are still presented, a few weeks after their birth, at their parents' shrine; and the *shichi-go-san* ('seven-five-three') festival is a popular event held in November when children of those ages dress up and accompany their families to the shrine. Other than that, Shinto observation is simply a matter of purification and prayer at individual shrines, as often or as seldom as an individual wishes.

'A person is Shinto in the same way that he is born Japanese', wrote Ian Buruma in *A Japanese Mirror*. 'It is a collection of forms and ceremonies that give form to a way of life. It is a celebration, not a belief. There is no such thing as a Shintoist, for there is no such thing as Shintoism.'

Notable Deities

Amaterasu Ōmikami

The prime deity of the Shinto pantheon, she is the goddess of the sun and light, born out of the left eye of her father, Izanagi. She taught her earthly subjects to plant rice and weave but was so incensed by the unruly behaviour of her brother, the storm god Susano-o, that she hid herself away in a cave, and plunged the earth into darkness. The other gods gathered to discuss the problem, which they solved with a trick. A female *kami* performed an obscene dance which caused great amusement, and tempted Amaterasu to peep out of her cave to see what all the fuss was about. She was pulled out into the open, the cave blocked off, and light returned to the world. Her grandson's great-grandson was Jimmu, the legendary first ruler of Japan; all subsequent emperors have claimed descent from her. Amaterasu is worshipped in different shrines all over Japan. The great shrine of Ise is the oldest Shinto site in the country.

Hachiman

The Emperor Ōjin (legendary dates 201–312), deified as the god of war, and worshipped alongside his mother, the Empress Jingū.

Inari

The most widely worshipped god in Japan, a popular name for the rice or food deity, and the patron of wealth and commercial enterprises. Inari shrines vary from the huge Fushimi Taisha in south Kyoto to countless local shrines in gardens, temples and at roadsides. They're recognizable from their tunnels of closely built red *torii* gates, and the sinister-looking statues of foxes, the messengers of the god.

The Seven Lucky Gods

The *Shichi Fuku-nin* are a popular, but obscure, collection of folk deities apparently derived from Hindu, Chinese and native traditions, representing the blessings of longevity, wealth, virtue, contentment, popularity and wisdom. The father and son team, Ebisu and

Daikoku, are the most commonly represented. The former carries a fishing rod and a fat *tai* (sea bream), the latter a mallet and a pair of bulging rice bags. The others are the goddess Benten and the gods Fukurokuju, Bishamon, Jurōjin, and Hotei.

Tenjin-sama

Sugawara no Michizane was a 9th-century scholar and statesman unjustly framed by jealous enemies and exiled to Kyūshū. After his death, evil portents were witnessed in the capital. In order to appease his angry spirit he was posthumously awarded high office, and a cult developed around his memory. As the patron of intellectual endeavours, he's fervently worshipped by students and schoolchildren facing examinations who throng his many temples, including Dazaifu Tenman-gū in Kyūshū. The plum blossom is his flower, and the ox his messenger.

Tōshō-gū

Tōshō-gū is the deification of Tokugawa Ieyasu, first and greatest of the Tokugawa shoguns who united Japan in the early 17th century. His main shrine is the gaudily magnificent Nikkō Tōshō-gū, north of Tokyo. Others are found in castle towns, where the Tokugawa family wielded influence.

Buddhism

The religion founded by the Indian Prince, Siddhartha Gautama, posthumously known as the Buddha or Enlightened One, is the greatest of the many outside influences that have worked on Japan, and few areas of Japanese culture remain untouched by it. Japan's most magnificent buildings, its finest statues, its greatest philosophy and its most plangent poems have been created by men who were either Buddhist priests themselves, or whose view of the world was shaped profoundly by its gentle and melancholy tenets. It is difficult to come to an understanding of Japanese culture without some knowledge of Buddhist history and iconography.

After its genesis in the 5th century BC, Buddhism spread outwards from India and divided into two branches. Hinayana ('Lesser Vehicle') Buddhism is the faith still practised in South and Southeast Asia, emphasizing monasticism and an individual quest for personal salvation according to the teachings of the historical Buddha. The Buddhism practised in Japan is known as Mahayana ('Greater Vehicle'). It was a thousand years old by the time the first Buddhist images were shipped over from Korea in the 6th century AD, and on its long journey through Central Asia, China and Korea, it had acquired doctrines, superstitions and iconography undreamed of by its Indian founders. Over the centuries, and during the long periods of isolation from the rest of the world, the sects took on native Japanese characteristics, incorporating traditional Shinto beliefs and deities; new sects broke away and developed their own teachings to form a panoply of faiths and deities quite as varied as the denominations of European Christianity.

Deities

The Buddhist hierarchy is a complicated one, as a glance at a mandala—a beautiful picture diagram of the heavenly pantheon, with buddhas in the middle, human saints at the edges—will demonstrate. Local variations, inconsistent use of Sanskrit and Japanese terms, and the countless exceptions to every rule, make the task of deciphering Buddhist art a baffling one. The following should help enlighten you as to which of the Enlightened Ones you are looking at. The first term given is Japanese; it is followed by the phrase most commonly used in English, often a transliteration of the Sanskrit. The use of the male or female pronoun, by the way, is a misleading convention; apart from Shaka, heavenly beings are effectively sexless.

Nyorai (Buddhas)

Originally there was only one Buddha—**Shaka** (or Sakyamuni in Sanskrit), also known as the Historical Buddha, or Prince Gautama Siddhartha, the name he bore during his earthly life between about 563 and 483 BC. Shaka was an Indian prince who abandoned his powers and privileges for the life of a wandering holy man. After years of fruitless austerities, he achieved enlightenment while meditating under a linden tree. In a flash, he grasped that the cause of suffering is ignorant desire, and that it can be eliminated only by adherence to the Eightfold Path: right understanding, right thought, right speech, right conduct, right livelihood, right effort, right mindfulness, and right concentration. By following the Path, an individual hopes to achieve freedom from the endless cycle of rebirth—the state known as Nirvana. The stupas and pagodas associated with Buddhist temples were originally reliquaries enshrining ashes, a tooth, or a fragment of bone of the Historical Buddha.

Dainichi Nyorai ('Great Light'; also known as the Cosmic or Universal Buddha; in Sanskrit, Mahavairocana or Roshana) is the supreme Buddhist deity, the Nyorai of ultimate reality, who embraces, and is manifested in, all things. The Shinto sun goddess, Amaterasu Ōmikami, is identified with Dainichi; even Shaka is but an aspect of him.

Amida (Amitabha) is one of the most popular Nyorai, and in the Heian period (794–1185) a number of sects emerged based on his worship. He is a merciful and accessible being, ruler of a western paradise called the Pure Land, into which he welcomes all souls who sincerely call on him with the simple formula *Namu Amida Butsu* ('Save me, Amida Buddha').

Yakushi Nyorai (Bhaisajyaguru) is the Buddha of Healing, recognizable in sculpture for the jar of medicine which he often holds out in his left hand.

Bosatsu (Bodhisattvas)

The Bosatsu are beings of great spiritual merit who have attained the self-knowledge necessary for enlightenment, but who choose to defer it in order to save other beings. They're widely worshipped and represented in art, and are often depicted flanking the Nyorai in triptychs.

Kannon Bosatsu (Avalokitesvara) is one of the most popular of all Buddhist deities, honoured all over the country as the Goddess of Mercy. Tokyo's Sensō-ji (Asakusa

Kannon) and Kyoto's Sanjūsangen-dō temples are dedicated to her, and there is a famous pilgrimage of the 33 Kannon temples in the Kansai area. With her gentle, feminine nature, Kannon has often been likened to the Virgin Mary. During the religious persecutions of the early 17th century, Japanese Christians used to worship images of 'Maria Kannon', with a cross concealed underneath or on the back. Other manifestations of the deity include *Jūichimen* (Eleven-faced) Kannon (the supernumerary faces are on the top of the main head), *Senju* (Thousand-armed) Kannon whose limbs grasp and save floundering souls, and *Bato* (Horse) Kannon whose miniature steed peeps out from the deity's crown. Kannon is an aspect of Amida Nyorai, whom she often accompanies.

Jizō Bosatsu (Ksitigarbha) is another profoundly merciful being, usually represented as a wandering monk with tonsure and staff. He is the patron of travellers and children. As the former, his image is often found along roadsides; as the latter, statues of him are often adorned with red bibs and childish toys, like windmills. These are offerings left by the parents of *mizu-ko*, miscarried or aborted children whom Jizō guides and protects from demons in the grim Buddhist limbo.

Miroku Bosatsu (Maitreya) is the 'Buddha of the Future'. Five thousand years after the enlightenment of Shaka, he will descend from heaven and bring all beings to enlightenment. Miroku has several manifestations. Two of the most beautiful are the early, probably Korean, statues in Nara's Hōryū-ji and Kyoto's Kōryū-ji, showing a young, slim youth seated in meditation.

Other Deities

Fudō Myō-ō was one of a group of deities (the Myō-ō or Vidyaraja in Sanskrit) absorbed into the Buddhist pantheon from Indian Hindu mythology. He is depicted as a ferocious demon, seated amid flickering flames, with a long pony-tail, snarling fangs and skin of red or blue. In his right hand is a sword, in his left a lasso. With these he ensnares and punishes evil, and terrifies the good into renewed discipline.

Ni-ō (Guardian Kings) are the half-naked musclemen often found in pairs in the main gate of a Buddhist temple. They wear fierce expressions, and serve to protect the sacred precincts from evil influence. One has his mouth open, the other closed. They are said to be pronouncing the letters ah and un, the alpha and omega of the Sanskrit alphabet.

Emma-ō is the King of Hell, the fearful judge who weighs the souls of the departed and dispatches them to paradise or damnation. He sits cross legged, wearing a crown bearing the character for king; the style of his robes indicates his Chinese origins. He is sometimes accompanied by lesser scribes of hell who record the deeds of the living with scrolls and ink brushes.

The Shi-Tennō (Four Heavenly Kings) guard the four cardinal points. They're usually sculpted in the armour of central Asian warriors, with fierce expressions, stomping comically grotesque demons beneath their feet. Bishamonten, one of the most popular, is also one of the Seven Lucky Gods of Shinto folk religion. He guards the north, and is depicted with a pagoda in his hand.

Business Culture

In Nagasaki, I was pleased to see that business was at a low ebb.
The Japanese should stay away from business.

Rudyard Kipling

Of all the activities which bring foreigners to Japan, none is as fraught with prejudice and disinformation as the world of business. The subject unites a range of foreign anxieties about Japan: an alien language, impenetrable rules of politeness and etiquette and, above all, dazzling and world-beating success, equalling or outstripping that of the West. You only have to glance at the shelves of an English-language book shop in Tokyo for one symptom of this confusion: the countless advice books and 'How to...' guides to business with the Japanese, new ones published every month, as indistinguishable and repetitive as sex manuals. They're like sex manuals in other ways too: they contradict one another; they make something naturally appear fraught and complicated; and they're dedicated to creating problems to which, suspiciously, they are also the solution.

There is no magic formula for doing successful business in Japan, any more than for Britain, America or Europe, and the search for one is a wild goose chase. Markets and consumers differ, management styles and work habits vary, but business anywhere is about adaptability, and what is good practice in London and New York will never be unacceptable in Tokyo. The recipe may alter, but the basic ingredients are the same.

What follows is a general introduction to ways of thinking about business in Japan. Ninety per cent of good advice is a statement of the obvious. One of the 'How to...' guides recommends staying in as smart a hotel as you can afford, since this will inspire respect and confidence in your Japanese clients and customers—although it's hard to think of any country in the world where this wouldn't be the case. Another warns against the dangers of blowing your nose in business meetings (excuse yourself and go to the toilet, or make do with a series of sniffs). But, come to think of it, noisily relieving oneself of nasal mucus would be an uncool move in formal settings all over the world. The lesson is: trust in your instincts. Care, patience and sincerity are the secret of doing successful business in Japan—and they are no secret, because they apply to successful business all over the world. Demonstrate these qualities, and it really won't matter how you hold your chopsticks.

Zaibatsu and *Keiretsu*

The Japanese economic 'miracle', which transformed a defeated country into the second largest economy in the world, was, of course, not miraculous at all. Industrial power was nothing new to Japan, and the foundations of many of the country's most distinctive institutions were laid long before the US Occupation and the huge injections of American aid which got the economy back on its feet in the 1950s. Japan was becoming an industrial power as early as 1905 when the Imperial Navy destroyed the Russian Baltic Fleet in the Straits of Tsushima. By 1915, almost half of the Japanese workforce was employed in industry, which organized itself into the notorious *zaibatsu* collectives whose successor corporations, the *keiretsu*, remain such a distinctive feature of Japanese business today.

The *zaibatsu* developed from the policies of the 19th-century Meiji government which, having established key industries, passed them on, at ridiculously cheap prices, to a small group of privately owned family companies. After the war, they re-emerged as the *keiretsu*, looser but increasingly massive agglomerations of financial, commercial and manufacturing power, each grouped around a major bank. Between them the six groups—MItsubishi, Mitsui, Sumitoma, Fuyo, Sanwa and Gai-ichi Kangyo embrace a total of 650 companies, employing 5 per cent of the Japanese workforce, and netting 17 per cent of the nation's profits.

The strength and influence of these institutions on all aspects of life is enormous, and Japan's economic history would have been utterly different without them. Structurally, they function not through outright ownership of one company by another, but through a dense web of cross-shareholdings. About a fifth of any one company's equity will typically be distributed among fellow members of the combine, while it in turn owns a proportion of their shares; their presidents may well be on its board of directors, and vice versa. This produces an elaborate and irregular structure resembling (in Peter Tasker's words) 'complex molecules, each component binding with several others'.

The arrangement is based firmly on the values of loyalty and group consciousness visible throughout Japanese society. The *keiretsu* function as giant industrial department stores, providing member companies with all the services they require, and conveniently reducing the need to shop elsewhere. Thus, having secured loans from the Mitsubishi Bank and purchased land through Mitsubishi Real Estate, the Mitsubishi *keiretsu* member will hire Mitsubishi Construction to build its new factory with materials from Mitsubishi Metal and Asahi Glass (a Mitsubishi company). Machinery, lifts and air-conditioning will come from Mitsubishi Heavy Industries and Mitsubishi Electric, and trucks from Mitsubishi Motors. The whole lot will be covered by Tokyo Fire and Marine Insurance, the finished products will be sold through the Mitsubishi Corporation trading company and, at the factory's launch party, guests will drink Kirin beer, and soft drinks bottled by Chukyo Coca Cola Bottling—all of them companies under the Mitsubishi umbrella.

The members of a *keiretsu* are under few formal obligations to one another, but transactions like those described above usually make sense for all concerned. Fellow companies can share resources in finance, research, marketing and personnel. It's not a completely closed shop, of course, but it is common for *keiretsu* members to favour one another, even though outside companies can offer better term. Cost, in other words, isn't always the bottom line when a company has the future of its relationships within the *keiretsu* to take into account. To the Japanese mind, this is loyalty, but also common sense. To foreign critics, it's an NTB, a Non-Tariff Barrier to free trade. Recently several analysts have predicted the gradual dissolution of the combines under the eroding forces of international competition. But for the time being, at least, they are a fact of business life.

The character of the collectives is probably the single most important difference between Japanese and foreign markets. An inclination to operate in mutually supportive groups permeates all levels of Japanese business. Even if you're not dealing with one of the big six combines, the chances are that you'll encounter elements of this arrangement, which may affect the way you do business. Does the company you are pitching to already have a relationship with an existing supplier in a *keiretsu* or similar association? If so, this must be taken into account when presenting new proposals. Even if the answer is no, the principles behind the *keiretsu* are the principles by which Japanese customers will judge you and your business: loyalty, a preference for long-term relationships over quick and easy profits, sensitivity about the effects of any action on others (on a personal, as well as company, level). Awareness of these values will add greatly to your prospects for success.

Getting Started in Japan

Clichés and misconceptions work both ways; however mistaken the Western view of Japan, the Japanese have some clunking prejudices of their own. A European or American stereotype of the Tokyo businessman might include the following impressions: hardworking, devoted to the company, protocol-bound, sexist, soulless and inscrutable, tends to copy the ideas of others. The equivalent Japanese picture of the Westerner might go like this: creative and energetic, but impatient, opportunistic and concerned only with the short-term; incapable of understanding Japan and its unique culture; enviably 'free' from social constraint, but correspondingly irresponsible, unreliable and, potentially, untrustworthy. Not every Japanese will hold these individual opinions but they may underpin dealings, and it is in your interests to counteract them as early as possible.

Your biggest initial disadvantage is very simple. Japanese society is structured around membership of (often fiercely competing) groups which exist at all levels—from the family, through the individual's school and university, to the company, the *keiretsu*, and finally the Japanese nation itself. As a foreigner, you exist outside the outermost of these concentric and overlapping rings, and you are different from those inside. This, to the Japanese mind, is not a value judgement, but a statement of immutable fact. Outsiders *can* be allowed to enter into relationships with those on the inside. But this is a slow and gradual process, not to be undertaken without long reflection and consultation. The trick in dealing with a Japanese company, therefore, is to minimize your 'outsideness'. This doesn't mean trying to act like a Japanese; it means observing the Japanese business virtues, and offering as little disruption as possible to the established way of doing things.

Preparation

Thorough preparation before you go to Japan isn't just an optional extra, it's the basis of any successful visit. The cost of travel alone makes it essential that as much as possible of your itinerary is organized before you get on the plane.

The most valuable commodity you can take with you from home is a good set of **introductions**. Japan is absolutely not the sort of country where you can breeze into town, make a few calls and watch the meetings materialize in your diary. How you secure these contacts will depend on the nature of your business: for some it will be necessary to hire an agent in Tokyo. Others should contact the organizations listed below, especially JETRO and (in Britain) the Department of Trade and Industry. Your first meetings in Tokyo should be with your country's Chamber of Commerce, and the commercial department of its embassy. Don't forget that many Japanese companies have European and American offices: acquaintance with a member of staff at one of these may stand you in good stead when you get to Japan. Try to remember the names and titles of Japanese acquaintances when you encounter their colleagues in Japan. Don't be shy of a little name-dropping, or underestimate its power to break the ice.

Equally important is mental preparation. Some people take to Japan better than others, and a few, it must be admitted, react negatively. More than in Europe or America, selecting **appropriate personnel** to send to Japan is an important decision which will bear directly on the success of your mission.

It's difficult to generalize usefully about the type of person who will respond well to Japan, except to say that the most valuable quality is adaptability. In the age of multinational corporations and international business schools, styles are becoming homogenized—for every Japanese manager who speaks through an interpreter and says no when he means yes, you'll come across a fluent English-speaker educated in Europe or America. Half the trick (as in all communication) is to judge who you are talking to, and engage them in the appropriate tone. If in doubt, err on the side of caution. Japan is a conservative country where the quieter virtues of patience, deference to seniors and attention to detail are still primary. What in the West passes for grit and determination can easily seem in Japan like American insensitivity or European arrogance. No one ever won a contract in Japan by bullying; no one ever lost one by being over formal or courteous.

Business is war in Tokyo as much as anywhere else, but campaigns are fought slowly and strategically, and a combative, gung-ho approach to negotiation will not bring success. Patience, coupled with persistence, is the most important abstract quality a Japan-bound businessperson can possess. In practice this means a willingness to sit out a decision-making process much longer and more drawn out than is common in the West, through seemingly endless meetings whose only function may be to repeat what has already been stated and give the participants an opportunity to get to know one another better. Straightforwardness is always a good thing but 'straight-talking', as the expression is commonly understood, is inappropriate.

Harmony, an appearance of outward concord and good feeling, is to be preserved at all times. This doesn't mean that dissatisfaction and disagreement can never be expressed, only that they must be phrased indirectly in such a way as to preclude personal blame and ignominy. Thus 'I am surprised' comes to mean 'I'm disappointed'; 'that's interesting' all too often means 'that's difficult'; and 'that's difficult' means 'it's absolutely impossible'. Indirectness of this sort is used by everyone from time to time, but in Japan it is a way of life. Some people find it exasperating and hypocritical; to others, it's a challenge. On your team you want the second sort, not the first.

Also desirable in your salespeople or negotiators is good standing within the company, and thorough grounding in the field of business under discussion. Loyalty to the organization is still an esteemed Japanese virtue. One of the first questions new arrivals are asked is how long they have been with the company, and a seasoned and long-serving manager will fare better than a recent recruit.

The Language Barrier

You'll hear contradictory things about the usefulness of Japanese in international business. Some claim it's essential: so many of the codes and distinctions of Japanese society are embodied in its language that it's impossible to penetrate the culture without it. Others complain that confident use of Japanese can be a barrier to communication, that it provokes mistrust in Japanese clients who enjoy the opaque cloak of their language.

Neither view is adequate. Unquestionably, a command of spoken and written Japanese is a tremendous advantage to anyone doing business in Japan. But it is not the most important skill, and the considerations discussed above (personality, standing within the company, experience in the field) should take precedence. A good firm can succeed in Japan with no Japanese speakers at all, and fluency in the language will never bring success to an inherently undesirable business proposition.

Still, it is dangerous (and discourteous) to assume that the other side will automatically speak good English. All Japanese have studied some English, but many are more comfortable with the written than the spoken word and, for this reason, faxes are often a safer way of communicating than phones. Even if the Japanese contact speaks good English, important details (prices and orders, dates and times of meetings) should be confirmed in simple language by fax.

In conversation, speak clearly and evenly (which doesn't mean loudly and slowly). Avoid baby-talk and never omit particles, conjunctions or auxiliaries in the interests of supposed clarity ('You, me—we go meeting?'). Be literal-minded. In many ways, Japanese is a very logical language compared to English; usages likely to get you into trouble include colourful metaphors and idioms ('If you go out on a limb, it'll raise the stakes—but it's your funeral'), double negatives ('I don't dislike what you're saying') and negative questions. In answer to the question, 'Don't you want to buy my marmalade?', a Japanese will answer 'Yes', meaning, 'Yes, you're right, I don't want your marmalade,' or 'No', meaning 'No, you're wrong. I want your marmalade'.

If interpreters are required, it is the responsibility of the sellers to provide them. Japanese companies will often detail one of their own staff to interpret for you in situations like this, but it's wiser and politer to hire your own, despite the expense. When it gets to the stage of drawing up contracts and product specifications, professional translators and lawyers should be engaged.

Mastering a few simple phrases of Japanese (*see* p.509–12) and using them at the beginning of a meeting is a gesture that will be appreciated, however awkward it makes you feel.

Sex and Race

Women are active in all areas of Japanese business—but not at all levels. In some fields—the leisure industries, for instance, especially areas like fashion and design—the differentials are less obvious, but surveys routinely show that female employees start lower down the company than their male contemporaries, have poorer prospects for promotion, earn less for the same work and occupy only a tiny fraction of the top posts. In the long term, international competition will bring about change, for the simple reason that sex discrimination halves the number of talented employees which a company has to draw upon. By the standards of Europe and America, though, the Japanese businesswoman's situation is dismal.

Most Japanese understand that the situation is different abroad, and it would be a remarkably old-fashioned and unworldly busimessman who received more than a superficial surprise at encountering an opposite number in a skirt. If the best person for the job is a woman, then that is that. Part of her suitability, however, will be a discreet awareness of what her gender means to those she's dealing with. All over the world there are men who feel uncomfortable with confident and powerful women; Japan contains more than most. For the foreign businesswoman who ends up facing one, the challenge is to understand his behaviour, and act in such a way as to command his respect, as well as putting him at ease. This can be difficult and ultimately depends on making snap judgements about the people you find yourself with. There may be occasions when it would appear more seemly for a woman to decline an invitation (to a hostess bar, for instance), and leave it to her male colleagues. On the other hand, a bit of noisy carousing with the lads may be just what's needed to break the ice. Either way, there is no point in becoming paranoid; an alert set of antennae is necessary, nothing more.

Race, however, is a different matter. Non-white foreign workers are well-established in Japan, including Iranians, South Americans, Afro-Caribbeans and other Asians. Certainly, they face prejudice in work, education and social situations; life is harder for them than for white-skinned *gaijin*. But in many ways business transcends these prejudices. In China, for instance, despite a history of war and enmity, Japan is the biggest foreign investor, a major export market for many of its former enemies in the Asia Pacific region. The broad picture proves that whatever the superficial state of relations between the Japanese and other races, if the product price, service and quality are good enough, money will flow. Racism exists in Japan as elsewhere, but it should not be seen as a barrier to successful business.

Meetings in Japan

Like face-to-face meetings everywhere, your formal dealings with Japanese businesses have two functions: to communicate clearly and pointedly the message you are trying to get across; and to cultivate the personal bond, to build up ease, trust and intimacy between the participants. All meetings will contain an element of both, but in Japan—and especially in the early stages—expect the emphasis to be firmly on the latter. However innovative your product, however incisive your presentation, there's little hope of a quick decision after the first meeting. You should go into it with this in mind: you are not expecting a deal, you are building up a relationship.

Relationships are based on trust, respect and—a key word—harmony: a sense that the parties understand and empathize with one another and, despite cultural differences and communication difficulties, are making efforts to move in the same direction. This is the intangible, magical quality which you are trying to achieve, but it depends on much more than a few points of etiquette. Meeting Japanese clients is not like taking a driving test (one mistake, and you fail). If you suspect you have made a gaffe, apologize, make a joke of it, and carry on (apology is a way of life in Japan; your hosts will do it incessantly, and on the flimsiest of pretexts).

For every meeting (as well as supporting documents, texts and summaries of presentations, etc.) you will need a good supply of **business cards**, with English on one side and a Japanese translation on the other. They should indicate clearly your rank within the company. You can order them from a specialist printer before you go, through big hotels in Japan, and sometimes even from your airline. Keep a supply of them in a pocket.

Arrive on time, and be confident that you have spaced your meetings so that you will not need to leave early, or hurry your presentation, in order to make it to your next appointment. Allow more time than you expect: Japanese meetings can be interminable, with lots of recapitulations and ruminative silences. Use of a translator will add dramatically to the time it takes to deliver your pitch.

Introductions are important and not to be skipped over. Once you have been led to the meeting room, address yourself to the most senior person. Don't try to bow—foreigners never really get it right, and a deep nod does just as well. Instead shake hands (your host may find this a little uncomfortable, so no bone-crunchers), give your name and say 'How d'you do?', 'Nice to meet you', or *Hajime mashite* (Ha-jee-meh mash-teh). Present your business card (held in both hands if they are free, and with the writing facing your host), and receive his. The general rule, not worth worrying about too much, is that you should offer your card first if you are the seller, or junior in rank or age.

Don't put the card away. Scrutinize it politely, repeat the name, and then place it on the table. When you take your leave, put the collected cards away in a briefcase or wallet. Never fold them up or stick them casually into a back pocket. Once you're outside, it's a good idea to jot notes and aides-memoires on the back (Mr Fuji likes golf, Miss Watanabe studied in LA, etc.) to facilitate small talk at the next meeting, but don't do this in the meeting. A business card is the proxy of its owner: treat them with respect.

Follow your hosts' lead on what to do next. Sometimes everyone in the room will swap cards with everyone else (this takes ages); sometimes one side will each present their cards once to the senior member of the other side. It's common to line up the cards on the table to correspond with the seating order of the team facing you—that way you can see at a glance who is sitting where, and whom you are addressing. The most important thing you should have gathered by now is who is senior to whom. This can be a tricky one because, if the boss doesn't speak good English or is the strong and silent type, then the person doing most of the talking may be quite junior. If anyone present does not proffer a card then they are probably a secretarial, non-executive type. Be polite, but don't devote them too much of your attention. Cards, of course, are only exchanged at a first meeting, but bring a person's card along every time you think you're likely to meet him or her.

Next comes coffee or tea (if it's Japanese green tea, don't add sugar or milk), and small talk. Don't feel that you have to do any selling at this point. Small talk can be very small indeed and, after a few first-time meetings, you will be thoroughly acquainted with the standard questions: when did you arrive, how is your hotel, is this your first time in Japan, do you like Japanese food, what is your impression of Japan? Insight and profundity is not expected here, but if you have just visited an interesting temple or eaten an interesting meal, then do say so. Japanese often assume complete ignorance on the part of foreigners; being able to discourse knowledgeably on the temple you've just visited will surprise and impress.

Gift-giving generally marks a significant stage in the relationship between two companies and isn't usually necessary at a first meeting—but a corporate memento, or a picture book about your country or region would be a nice token.

When the time comes to deliver your presentation and talk business, speak clearly and steadily (which doesn't mean slowing to half speed). Remember that low price in itself will not be enough to win over your potential customers: you must offer them strong additional incentives to overcome their reluctance to switch from an existing supplier and to engage an outside, foreign company. Quality must be emphasized and re-emphasized; so must reliability, and the capacity to meet delivery times unfailingly. Talk also about service, the ability to support your product with spare parts, overhaul, even accessories like Japanese-language manuals. Demonstrate to your audience that you are aware of these issues and have thought about them. Many sales of good products have been lost because the service and back-up details have been neglected.

Visual aids like overhead projections are helpful in breaching the language barrier. Remember that you will be judged by your efficiency and organization, and that general information is as important as the hard sell. Remember also, especially in the early stages, that your Japanese opposite numbers are trying to build up a general impression of the feel of your organization, and its compatibility with their own. Make your sales pitch forcefully, but don't omit background remarks on the nature of your operation, its history, subsidiaries, etc. Always begin a presentation by introducing yourself, describing your role in the company, and emphasizing your years of service or experience within your field.

Try to make all claims modestly. Japanese respect pride in the company, but displays of personal arrogance or over-confidence will go down badly. In the same way, you should always receive a professional compliment by passing the credit on to your team or company.

Don't be rattled if your audience fails to react, avoids eye contact or sits in silence during or after your presentation. Nods and smiles of encouragement are not the Japanese style, and you shouldn't play it for laughs, as you might back home. The time for amusement will come later; be sober, restrained and politely direct.

After Hours

After hours socializing is a crucial part of any business relationship and, if your initial contact is successful, you are certain to be entertained by your Japanese associates sooner or later. Where you are taken will depend on the nature of the business and the state of the relationship: if you are invited out in the evening, then you can expect eating and drinking, possibly in at least two different venues which could be Japanese, Western, or anything in between. Anything involving golf, hostesses or *geisha* is an especially profound honour, simply because of the gargantuan sums of money involved.

This is the time to relax, and to cultivate getting on well with everyone. The contrast between your hosts' office and after-hours demeanour may amaze you. Singing, teasing, tearful declarations of affection and loyalty, and extreme drunkenness are routine. Go with the flow, and take every chance to show what a good egg you are: if the party ends up at a *karaoke* bar, and if it has songs in English, then (horrible though it is) you must stand up and warble. Tipsiness, at the very least, is routine: if you don't drink alcohol, accept one glass for the toast and nurse it all night. This kind of drinking can be particularly debilitating when combined with jet lag: if you want to stop drinking then leave a full glass. An empty or half-empty one is an invitation to your neighbour to refill it (you should perform this service for him or her too).

The only rules are to enjoy yourself and to think *harmony*. Beware of the temptation to talk only about yourself. Trenchant debates on controversial topics don't generally go down well in Japan so, unless you have something anodyne to say, avoid subjects like the Imperial Family, trade disputes, Japanese politics, the war, sexism or racism, at least until you know your hosts better.

The Decision-making Process

With any important proposal, it is rare for a decision to materialize quickly after the initial meeting. The famous Japanese method of consensus decision-making is called *nemawashi*, a horticultural term meaning 'digging around the roots'. Briefly, a decision is established from the middle up, not imposed from the top down. All parties who might be affected by dealings with your company are required to add their seal and comments to a consultation document which is then submitted to senior management. Several drafts may travel up and down before the executive with the final say feels in a position to make a decision, a process which may take weeks or months.

In the meantime, you may be left completely in the dark. If you find yourself faxed or telephoned with tough questions or requests for further information, then the signs are good: this means that the man with responsibility for compiling the consultation document is doing his job, and responding to queries from his own colleagues. Expedite the process by responding promptly, however tiresome or pointless these requests may seem.

If you hear nothing, then it may mean that the answer is no. Alternatively, the consensus-building process may be simply ticking along quietly behind the scenes, based on the comprehensive information which you have already furnished. Make a habit of keeping in touch with your contacts even if you have to invent pretexts to do so: fax them to thank them for their time and invite them to contact you for more information; dispatch 'updates' and news of 'new developments' relating to your products or services; send greetings cards at Christmas or New Year.

The advantage of the *nemawashi* process is that by the time a decision is made and a final agreement reached, all the parties are so familiar with the proposal that they are already moving at full speed. This can catch foreign companies out: late delivery is one of the worst sins of Japanese business, so you need to remain alert and capable of delivering the basis of your proposal long after it was originally made. A Japanese customer may test a new supplier's efficiency and 'sincerity' with a small order as a preliminary to large-scale business; it would be a mistake to be dismissive of a disappointing order, or to give it a low priority.

Negotiation

The most important quality in dealing with Japanese companies, it must be emphasized again and again, is patience. Few successful deals materialize on the basis of introductory meetings and a few faxes, and the blow-by-blow negotiations towards the conclusion of an agreement are certainly the most challenging and difficult part of any business deal.

The biggest hurdle may be divining whether your Japanese counterparts are, in fact, interested in a deal at all. The word for 'yes' (*hai*), famously, does not always mean yes but something more like 'I understand'. The word for 'no' (*iie*) is used reluctantly (in everyday conversation, dissent is more usually expressed by the word *chigaimasu*, literally 'it is otherwise'). It would be almost inconceivable for a Japanese businessman facing a potential client to inform him, even in the most polite terms, that his proposition was of no interest. For those unused to the signs, this can be very frustrating indeed.

The most obvious sign may be silence. Persistent evasiveness, late or non-existent replies to queries, or vague promises to get in touch in the future may all be ways of saying no. Don't assume that further meetings are necessarily a positive sign; if you find yourself facing junior employees with no power or inclination to commit one way or another, this, too, may be a way of letting you down gently. The best way to pose a direct question is to reverse it so that your interlocutor is able to disappoint you by answering 'yes'. If the query 'Is this arrangement "difficult" for you?' provokes the response *hai*, then *hai*, you can be pretty sure, means *hai*.

Even if it is simply details which are being quibbled over, you must be conscious of the importance of face. Solutions to differences must be resolved in a way that lets both sides appear—at least superficially—to have come out on top. Typically, this might involve offering a discount as a gesture of 'sincerity' during final negotiations. The best business deals, like the best Japanese baseball games, are those that end in a draw.

Help and Further Reading

The best approach to dealing with Japan depends, of course, on the nature and scale of your business; the best advice will always be individual. Luckily, there are several sources of generous information and aid, much of it free.

The **Japan External Trade Organization (JETRO)** was originally established by the Ministry of International Trade and Industry (MITI) to promote Japanese trade overseas. By the 1980s, however, Japan's trade surplus had become so embarrassingly large that its function was virtually reversed. JETRO now has 80 international offices dedicated principally to helping foreign companies export their own products into Japan, and establishing links between Japanese and foreign businesses.

Approaches to JETRO should be made in writing, explaining the nature of the business and the information being sought, as far in advance as possible of the planned trip to Japan. JETRO libraries contain information and reports on different market sectors. One of its most valuable resources is its Business Support Centres, in Tokyo, Nagoya, Ōsaka and Kōbe, containing specialist advisers, libraries, and free office space. Not everyone is considered eligible for these; applications must be made well in advance.

JETRO London, Japan Trade Centre, 6th Floor, Leconfield House, Curzon Street, London W1Y 7FB, UK, ✆ 0171 493 7226.

JETRO New York, 44th Floor, McGraw-Hill Building, 1221 Avenue of the Americas, New York, NY 10020–1079, USA, ✆ 212 997 0400.

JETRO Los Angeles, 725 S. Figueroa Street, Suite 1890, Los Angeles, CA 90017, USA,✆ 213 624 8855.

JETRO Toronto, Suite 700, Britannica House, 151 Bloor Street West, Toronto, Ontario M55 1T7, Canada, ✆ 416 962 5055.

JETRO Sydney, Level 19, Gateway 1, Macquarie Place, Sydney, New South Wales 2000, Australia, ✆ 02 241 1181.

The British Government's **Department of Trade and Industry (DTI)** has a full-time Japan Desk. General information about markets, the economy and useful contacts in Japan is available free. Individual businesses can get advice from desk officials or from several export promoters on secondment to the DTI from the private sector. More detailed or specific reports on markets and companies can be commissioned from embassy staff at less than commercial rates.

DTI Japan Desk, Kingsgate House, 66–74 Victoria Street, London SW1, ✆ 0171 215 4269.

Dodwell Market Research Consultants publish *Industrial Groupings in Japan* annually, providing comprehensive listings and statistics on the cross-holdings of Japanese companies, invaluable in navigating the *keiretsu* conglomerates.

Doing Business in Japan by Jonathan Rice (BBC Books) is a calm, sensible and readable overview by an experienced consultant, with chapters on the work ethic, joint ventures and negotiation.

Hokkaidō

Hokkaidō

Soya Straits
Cape Soya
Rebun Island
Wakkanai
Rishiri Island
RISHIRI-REBUN-SAROBETSU NATIONAL PARK

Nayoro
Mombetsu

HOKKAIDO

Rumoi
Sōunkyō Onsen
Asahikawa Kamikawa
Asahidake Onsen
Kuro-dake
Takikawa
Tenninkyō Onsen
Asahi-dake
Ishikari-dake
Nukabira Onsen
L. Nukabira
NAT L
Furano Tokachi-dake
DAISETSUZAN NATIONAL PARK
Me-Ak

Otaru
Iwamizawa
KUSHI N A

Sapporo
SHIKOTSU-TŌYA NATIONAL PARK
Yubari
Chitose Kūkō
Obihiro

Yōtei-zan
L. Shikotsu
Shikotsu-ko Onsen
Tōya-ko Onsen
Tōya Shōwa-Shin-zan
Tarumae-dake
Tōya Usu-zan
Shiraoi
Noboribetsu Onsen
Noboribetsu
Tomakomai

Uchiura Bay
Muroran

Samani

Esashi
Hakodate

Tsugaru Straits

Shimokita Peninsula

N

Land over 500 metres

80 km
50 miles

Aomori

110

Despite its active volcanoes, boiling lakes, weird algae, ferocious bears, Cold War tensions and winter ice floes, there's something reassuringly familiar about the landscapes of Hokkaidō. The mountain ranges are rolling and gradual; the plains are

Sea of Okhotsk

SHIRETOKO NATIONAL PARK — Shiretoko-dake
Shiretoko Peninsula — Iō-zan — Kamuiwakka Falls
Rausu-dake — Rausu
Abashiri
Kunashiri Island
Utoro
Shari
Bihoro
Kawayu Onsen
ssharo — Kawayu
L.Mashū
L PARK — Teshikaga
O-Akan-dake
Akan
Kohan
Nemuro
Shibetsu
RUSSIA
Kurile Islands
SHITSUGEN AL PARK
Kushiro

broad and unblighted by urban development. There are sheep and cows in the fields and prairies of yellow wheat. Hokkaidō's half dozen large towns are modern and low-rise, and their neatness is emphasized by the grid layout of streets which several of them adopt. The biggest single difference from the rest of the country is the weather. Geologically and climatically, Hokkaidō belongs to southern Siberia rather than northern Japan, and arriving by air from Honshū you notice the difference as soon as you get off the plane. Winter, especially in the mountainous national parks, is long and harsh; but while the rest of the country is sweating under cloudy skies and hot summer drizzle, Hokkaidō is mild, crisp and comfortable. No rainy season also means less air-conditioning, and none of the acrid recycled fug which Honshū's office buildings pump out into the streets during the summer months. To Japanese visitors, the island has an appealingly unexplored, frontier atmosphere. There are tour coaches, of course, but the northern reaches of the island also attract independent travellers—cyclists, bikers and youth hostellers, many of them young, plenty of them English-speaking, some of the friendliest and most approachable Japanese you will meet.

Hokkaidō, then, is clean, sparsely populated, laid-back—and completely unrepresentative of Japan. Apart from a few Ainu museums, there are no historical relics more than 130 years old—no ancient architecture, no traditional crafts, no legendary heroes. To visit only Hokkaidō would be to waste your journey half-way across the world. But for city-weary expatriates or travellers with time on their hands, Hokkaidō is a beautiful, refreshing and mysterious island.

The Ainu

'I am in the lonely Aino land...'

Isabella Bird, 23 August 1878

By the late 19th century, when Westerners first began to arrive in Japan in significant numbers, the wishful idea of the country as a fairy land of misty mountains and kimono-clad elves was already insupportable. 'The Japanese people are simply a mode of style, an exquisite fancy of art,' Oscar Wilde had written. But foreigners who actually visited the mysterious East found a country frantic with social and industrial modernization, well on the way to becoming a Westernized military empire. Ports like Yokohama were a pageant of foreign influences, with European-style buildings, railways, pidgin English and natives dressed in European styles. The Victorian mind, nourished by the imperial subjugation of 'lesser' races and by Darwinian ideas of evolutionary progress, yearned for something simpler, older, more 'authentic'. 'I long to get away into the real Japan,' wrote Isabella Bird after her first day in Yokohama. She, and various other explorers, missionaries, botanists and amateur anthropologists found what they were looking for in Hokkaidō, then called Ezo, and in its ancient aboriginal inhabitants, the Ainu.

The origins of the Ainu will probably never be fully understood. Until inter-marriage diluted the gene pool, pure blood Ainu were visibly different from the Japanese majority, with lighter skin, hairier bodies and more pronounced eyebrows. Their ancestors have been identified, variously, as Polynesians from the South Pacific, Aryans from Central Asia and the Neolithic Jōmon people, who were supplanted in the south and west by immigrants from Korea and China. Traditional Ainu culture had none of the metal-forging or rice-growing skills which these Asian settlers brought with them. The Ainu lived by hunting deer and bear, fishing for river salmon, and gathering and cultivating millet, grasses and edible bulbs. The territories they inhabited—formerly northeastern Honshū, the Kurile Islands and Sakhalin, as well as Hokkaidō—were cold, but rich. Stores of preserved meat and fish were taken in for the winter freeze, and when there was a surplus this was bartered with neighbouring Ainu and visiting Japanese traders.

Related hunter-gatherer tribes seem to have migrated into Hokkaidō from Sakhalin and Siberia at various times, but the Ainu were never nomadic. Small loosely organized settlements of a few families (called *kotan* in the Ainu language) were established close to the salmon breeding grounds. The layout and architecture of these villages can be seen in several tourist *kotan* reconstructed throughout Hokkaidō. Storerooms built on stilts and log cages for captured bears formed the outbuildings; the families themselves lived communally in houses of matting and thatch lashed to poles, with a central hearth and a 'god window' through which Ainu deities entered and exited.

Victorian Christians like Isabella Bird were very rude about Ainu spiritual beliefs ('There cannot be anything more vague or destitute of cohesion...') but these were more sophisticated than she gave credit for. Like that of many hunting people, Ainu religion was animistic: everything, even inanimate objects like tools and houses, was held to contain an essence of one of the *kamui* (gods) which fled back to the land of the gods when it died or was broken. Thus, at Ainu funerals, food, cooking utensils, sometimes an entire house, would be broken or burned so that their spirits might accompany the soul of the dead Ainu into the next world. The *kamui* themselves were worshipped in different forms, the most important being the animals, especially the bear, which the Ainu depended on for survival. Skulls of hunted animals—turtles, foxes, owls, deer and bears—were stuffed with streamers of wood shavings and mounted on poles in the Ainu *kotan*. Here the most

 important rites were conducted, including the *iyomante* bear ceremony in which a young bear is released and ritually killed with arrows; his soul returns to the land of *kamui* carrying with it thanks and petitions for future good hunting. Other religious objects include *mokuhei*, wands with curling bouquets of wood shavings whittled from their tops; and *inau*, ceremo-

nial spatulas about 20cm long, serving no practical purpose, but beautifully carved with images of houses, boats, whales, bears and dogs. Although the Ainu language has no written form, a colourful oral literature existed in the form of *yukar* epic songs of gods and heroes, which were passed down the generations and recorded by Japanese researchers in the 1930s.

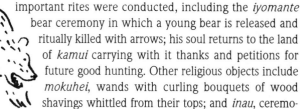

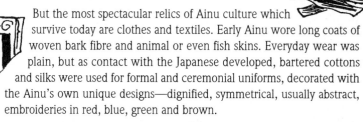 But the most spectacular relics of Ainu culture which survive today are clothes and textiles. Early Ainu wore long coats of woven bark fibre and animal or even fish skins. Everyday wear was plain, but as contact with the Japanese developed, bartered cottons and silks were used for formal and ceremonial uniforms, decorated with the Ainu's own unique designs—dignified, symmetrical, usually abstract, embroideries in red, blue, green and brown.

Because they had no written language, and because there was virtually no academic interest in them until the Meiji period, vast swathes of Ainu history have been lost forever. A handful of references and the names of a couple of chieftains crop up in Japanese records. In 658 the Japanese general Abe no Hirafu conducted a successful campaign against the Ainu of northern Honshū; Ainu warriors thereafter served in Nara, and the objects they took back home with them have been dug up in Hokkaidō. The term *shōgun*, short for *sei-i-tai-shōgun* (great-barbarian-quelling-generalissimo) was first awarded to the general who in 795 forced an Ainu retreat into the northern reaches of Tōhoku. Among the defeated were a number of Japanese settlers who sided with the Ainu in order to maintain their independence from the Kyoto government. There was also conflict with the mysterious 'Okhotsk people'—a loose conglomeration of sea-going tribes who traded on the sea of Okhotsk and made inroads into northern Hokkaidō between the 6th and 13th centuries.

This period seems to have been the Ainu's golden age. Society became stratified, with hereditary military chieftains living apart from the common people in fortified stockades.

Trade was established with the Japanese; objects like silks and lacquered bowls took on the status of treasures, and possession of them was a mark of wealth. Japanese settlers continued to live in southern Hokkaidō, and from the 15th century the coexistence of the two peoples was a source of frequent conflict. In 1456 an Ainu was murdered by a settler in a quarrel over a knife, which escalated into a full-blown revolt. A chieftain called Koshamain succeeded in taking several castles, but in 1457 he was killed by a member of the Japanese Matsumae family who thereafter became lords of Hokkaidō.

Five revolts flared in the first 40 years of the 16th century, but the Matsumae had no intention of relinquishing their monopoly in the rich Hokkaidō fur trade. Taxes and controls on freedom of trade and movement were imposed upon the natives. The ancient hunting and fishing stocks became depleted, and Ainu-occupied lands were awarded to Japanese officials. Finally, in 1668 the Ainu hero Shakushain led a huge revolt, bloodily suppressed in 1672. The Ainu military class ceased to exist, and the growth of trade brought Ainu and Japanese into closer contact, diluting the native culture. Epics record that the Ainu gods and heroes left the land in anger at the weakness of the people.

The next 200 years were relatively peaceful, but the gods never returned. After the Meiji Restoration, the government embarked on the full-scale colonization and agricultural development of Hokkaidō. Wildlife was hunted intensively; forests and underbrush where the natives used to forage were cleared. The new settlers brought diseases and *sake* with them, and the Ainu, accustomed to neither, succumbed in large numbers.

In an attempt to wean them off their hunter-gatherer way of life, awards of farmland were made. To the Ainu, the land was theirs anyway; the small plots remained uncultivated or were rented to Japanese farmers. A farming economy brought inequalities of wealth, further weakening the unity of the people. Ainu children, educated compulsorily in Japanese schools, were denied the chance to learn their own language.

These were the people—'the hairy Ainos,' as she called them—with whom Isabella Bird lived for a week in August 1878, and whom she made famous in *Unbeaten Tracks in Japan*. The Japanese she met were incredulous at her interest. 'Treat Ainos politely!' they exclaimed, 'They're just dogs, not men.' She herself was touched and saddened. 'They have no history,' she wrote, 'their traditions are scarcely worthy the name, they claim descent from a dog, their houses and persons swarm with vermin, they are sunk in the grossest ignorance, they have no letters or any numbers above a thousand, they are clothed in the bark of trees and the untanned skins of beasts, they worship the bear, the sun, the moon, fire, water, and I know not what, they are uncivilizable and altogether irreclaimable savages, yet they are attractive, and in some ways fascinating, and I hope I shall never forget the music of their low, sweet voices, the soft light of their mild, brown eyes, and the wonderful sweetness of their smile.'

The Ainu Today

By the 1940s, Ainu culture was comatose, but today—against expectations—it can't be said to have died completely. Revival would be too strong a word; for many Japanese of Ainu descent, the label is nothing more than a nuisance, a focus for discrimination in marriage and employment. The new generation know little of the old traditions—even if young Ainu wanted to hunt for bear, there is almost nowhere left for them to do it. The Ainu language is spoken fluently by a handful of old people in their 80s. A full dictionary is in preparation, but once the spoken language is dead it will be an uphill struggle to re-establish it. The population, however, has remained constant since the Meiji era, at about 17–18,000, although virtually none of these are pure blood. Poor employment opportunities have undoubtedly driven many Ainu descendants to assimilation in mainland Honshū, but they have been replenished by intermarriage and adoption. There are Ainu organizations, and Ainu delegations were active in the United Nations Year of Indigenous People in 1993. The following year, an Ainu leader named Kayano Shigeru was elected to the Japanese Diet. In effect, though, the only Ainu who support themselves in anything approaching a traditional way are in the tourist villages described in this chapter: performing dances, singing songs, carving tacky ornaments. It gives one a funny feeling watching these performances, surrounded by laughing crowds of Japanese. But the Ainu are still a few steps away from the fate predicted for them by Isabella Bird, 'that vast tomb of conquered and unknown races which has opened to receive so many before them.'

A Word About Bears

Hokkaidō, in popular myth at least, is Bear Utopia. The *Ezo Higuma* (Hokkaidō Brown Bear) is a distinct sub-species, bigger and potentially much grumpier than the timid black bears which survive in mountainous areas of Honshū: adult males can grow to a height of 2m and weigh 300kg. If the stories of hikers and staff in the youth hostels are to be believed, the island's overrun with them, and you can scarcely step off the main road without bumping into a fuzzy nine-footer and her cubs, tucking into a picnic. There are even tales of hungry bears strolling into empty farmhouses, opening the kitchen door, and helping themselves to the contents of the fridge.

Beneath the light-heartedness, there's a genuine nervousness here. Hostel staff may discourage you from doing a particular hike (or even pretend that no such path exists) for fear that you will end up lining some ursine stomach. How seriously this should be taken is hard to gauge. One local said that he had lived in Rausu for 30 years and never laid eyes on a bear or met anyone else who'd seen one. Less than one per cent of the average bear's diet consists of other mammals; there are occasional attacks by bears who are surprised, or mothers nursing cubs, but of the thousands of walkers who visit Hokkaidō, the majority return, unmauled, to their homes. It would be sad to end up as the exception, of course, but given that they are just as scared of you as you are of them, bear danger is not difficult to avoid. In Utoro, the souvenir shops sell jars of bear meat in yellow cans. Even in Hokkaidō, this is the closest you are likely to get to the real thing.

⚠ Avoid surprises by giving bears advance warning of your presence. Talk, sing, hang a bell from your belt and make a noise.

⚠ If you do encounter a bear, don't panic. Move calmly and steadily away, avoiding any sudden movements and noises that could startle the animal.

⚠ Never approach bear cubs even if you cannot see their parents. Never come between a mother bear and her young.

⚠ When camping, be careful in storing food and disposing of rubbish which may attract hungry bears by its smell. Put food in a bag a good distance from your camp, ideally suspended from the branch of a tree. Bury or dispose of rubbish a long way from your camp.

⚠ In known bear areas it may be unwise to hike alone.

Getting Around

Hokkaidō is the one area of Japan where **driving** (by car, motorbike or cycle) is unquestionably the easiest way of getting around. Roads are straight and fast, and traffic is light. Railway lines are sparse, local bus services sometimes infrequent, distances are large and fares are correspondingly expensive. It's quite possible to circumnavigate Hokkaidō by public transport, but in the remoter areas you may need to supplement it with **hitch-hiking** which is easy, fun and safe.

Accommodation

Japanese **youth hostels** can be extremely dreary and irritating places, but Hokkaidō has the best in the country: comfortable buildings in beautiful settings run (most important of all) by young and enthusiastic volunteers. Rates are cheap, food is often excellent, and in mountain and national park areas they are essential for picking up information about trail and weather conditions. Many hostel 'masters' are experienced climbers and mountaineers, and often hold daily briefings where maps are handed out and hiking companions can be found—even if you're not actually staying for the night, it's often worth popping in to see what you can pick up. The atmosphere of communal jollity which pervades some of these places can get a bit wearing—but it beats the grim authoritarianism found in so many Honshū hostels.

The popularity of Hokkaidō among cyclists and bikers has fostered a network of **baikā hausu** (biker houses)—absolutely basic, frill-free accommodation, often consisting of no more than a rectangle of tatami matting in a communal room with or without showers, kitchens or hot water. Look for the signs by the roadside, ask around among fellow bikers or enquire at tourist information offices. Expect to pay ¥1000 or so a night.

Climate

Hokkaidō is colder and drier than the rest of Japan. There is no humid rainy season, but from the middle of November until the end of March the temperatures start dropping below zero, and from the end of December until February they seldom rise above it.

Bear all this in mind when packing; bring multiple layers of clothing and, if necessary, gloves and warm hats. Sensible footwear is probably the single most important item. In mid-winter, even in Sapporo, tarmac streets become treacherous with ice and compacted snow—you will need thick socks and strong, warm shoes with a thick rubber tread.

Hakodate

In fine weather, Hakodate's setting—a steep hill jutting out on a narrow spit into the Straits of Tsugaru—is dreamily beautiful. For much of the year, though, this impression is obliterated by snow, rain and Siberian winds. Until this century, the town was a remote maritime outpost, a desolate and unpopular one inhabited by whalers, fishermen and traders in bear, seal and otter skins from the northern interior.

Nowadays, the Seikan rail tunnel and a small airport have opened up Hakodate, and the port has developed a smart and rather sophisticated centre, with museums, modern restaurants and numerous Western-style Meiji-era buildings, popular with Japanese visitors. You don't come to Hokkaidō for its cities, but this is still the most atmospheric and historic town on the island. Everyone who enters or departs Hokkaidō by rail must pass through here: Hakodate is a pleasant and undemanding place to break a long journey.

History

Hakodate's brief brush with history came in the mid-19th century and the dying days of the Tokugawa shogunate. In 1853, US Commodore Perry forced a meeting with shogunal officials and demanded trade concessions which were reluctantly granted in 1858. Hakodate, along with Yokohama and Nagasaki, was named as one of the first 'Treaty Ports' where foreign merchants could conduct trade within strict geographical limits. Britain, Russia and the United States all had consulates here, and the diplomatic records list in detail the dramas and frustrations experienced by foreign diplomats. In fact, residents of Hakodate, the most remote and insignificant of the concessions, suffered more in the way of frustration than drama. The weather was grim, life in the port was uneventful, and communications with Edo (Tokyo) were impossibly slow and unreliable. In 1878 the Victorian traveller Isabella Bird visited Hakodate. She recorded her impressions in *Unbeaten Tracks in Japan*:

> *A rocky head like Gibraltar, a cold-blooded-looking grey town, straggling up a deep hillside, a few coniferae, a great many junks, a few steamers and vessels of foreign rig at anchor, a number of sampans, riding the rough water easily, seen in flashes between gusts of rain and spin drift, were all I saw, but somehow it pleased me from its breezy, northern look.*

The one serious challenge to Hakodate's chilly docility came in 1868 when the town became the site of the Shogun's last stand. The final remnants of the shogunal navy had been driven north by the forces supporting the restoration of the Emperor Meiji. After defeats in Kyoto, Tokyo and Tōhoku, they retreated to Hokkaidō where an independent republic was declared. The following year, the Restoration army successfully besieged them in the five-sided Goryōkaku fortress.

JAL and ANA **fly** from Tokyo's Haneda airport; a round trip costs about ¥40,000 and takes 1hr 15mins. By **train**—a combination of *shinkansen* and limited express—it takes between 7 and 8hrs, and costs ¥18,000 one way.

Visitors to Hakodate will pass through two principal areas: the run-down, rather coarse area around the station, with its modern hotels and a lively morning market; and northwest of here, **Motomachi**, a sloping network of streets between the port and the peak of Mt Hakodate, where the museums and old Western-style houses are found. For hot spring lovers, there's also **Yunokawa Onsen**, a spa resort in the eastern suburbs.

A simple **tram** system links the main points of interest. The **tourist information centre** is next to the station.

Motomachi

Tram no.5 runs from Jūjigai, a large three-way junction, to Hakodate dokku-mae (Hakodate Docks). Above, to its west, are the slopes of Motomachi; below, to the east, is the waterfront.

Upper Motomachi

Starting from Jūjigai tram stop, the logical way to start is with a survey of the whole city from the top of **Hakodate-yama** (Mt Hakodate)—although you may want to save this for evening and enjoy the spectacle of the town at night. The ropeway station is signposted in English, a 5-minute walk west of the tram stop. The view from the top (335m) is indeed stunning: to the south, the blue Tsugaru Straits and the far mountains of the Shimokita Peninsula; to the east and west, the arching coastline of southern Hokkaidō; to the north, Hakodate spread out like a map and, far beyond, the Fuji-like volcano, Komaga-take. But the trip is not cheap (¥1130 one way), and you should eat before going up: the restaurants and souvenir shops in the observation station are overpriced and commercialized.

Descending to the town again, you will see a Christian church with green copper roofs, **Haristos Orthodox Church**, built for the Russians who were active in the trade between Hokkaidō and Siberia. The original, built in 1859, was even older than Tokyo's Nikolai-dō Greek church (1874), but it was rebuilt after a fire. The small interior has a wooden altar and icons.

The curious-looking modern church next door is Episcopalian; below is **Motomachi Roman Catholic Church** with nothing especially interesting inside, apart from a poignant plaque commemorating a French missionary who, along with 143,000 others, perished in the great Tokyo earthquake of 1923.

A few hundred metres north of here, on the road which runs just below the Russian church, is the **Old Prefectural Meeting Hall**, a reminder of just how odd Meiji architecture can be. It was rebuilt in 1910 after a devastating fire and restored in 1982 in pastel blue and lemon yellow, which accentuate the skinny wooden pillars with their carved capitals. It's a very Japanized 'Western-style' building with jutting verandas, fussy skylights and carved wooden columns in a flimsy, Disneyland parody of European opulence.

Just below is **Motomachi Kōen**, a park with a small information hut, and below that is the **Old British Consulate**, a solid and uninteresting building containing doll tableaux of scenes from the uneventful lives of early foreigners. Those with a craving for tartan souvenirs or a plate of roast beef can find them in the small shop and restaurant inside.

Lower Motomachi

The main street of Motomachi has a number of Meiji-period buildings, including **Kanemori Haberdasher's Shop** (1880), but the most interesting display is inside an old bank building just before Suehiro-chō tram stop on the harbour side. The **Hakodate City Museum of Northern Peoples** is the most modern and attractive museum of its kind, assembled from the collections of a number of ethnologists who studied not only the Ainu, but other Eastern Siberian races like the Nivkhi and Uilta of Sakhalin, and the Koryak and Itelmen of the Kamchatka Peninsula. The museum presents fascinating evidence of the internal trade that was conducted between these people across the Sea of Okhotsk, including an exquisite Chinese silk robe acquired by an Ainu chieftain from one of the Sakhalin tribes, who had bought it in turn from Chinese traders of the Ching dynasty. The Santan trade, as it was called, flourished during Japan's Tokugawa period; it has been described as a Northern Silk Route. In return for their bear, seal and marten furs, the Siberian tribesmen took home silks, ornaments and metal goods which found their way to the far shores of the Sea of Okhotsk. Also displayed here are many religious, musical and everyday objects as well as reproductions of *Ainu-e*, 'Ainu pictures', by a Japanese artist who lived in Hokkaidō during the last years of the Tokugawa period, just before Meiji economic measures snuffed out the traditional way of life forever.

Goryōkaku (Five-sided Fort)

Tram no.2 or 5 to Goryōkaku-koen-mae, then 10 minutes' walk northeast, or bus no.5, 6, 7, 12, 27 or 59. The fort is right below an ugly but distinctive concrete tower with a doughnut-shaped observation deck.

This star-shaped, five-pointed, Western-style fortress was built in the 19th century as a precaution against marauding Russian warships, but it saw action only once, in the dying days of the Bōshin War, the short-lived civil war that accompanied the Meiji Restoration and the defeat of the Tokugawa shogun. In December 1868, eight warships of the shogunal navy, along with the remnants of its defeated army, docked in Hakodate under the command of the Tokugawa admiral, Enomoto Takeaki. In January 1869 Enomoto declared Ezo, as Hokkaidō was then called, an independent republic, and even gained recognition by the British and French squadrons stationed in Hakodate.

The Republic of Ezo lasted five months. In June, Enomoto and his men holed up in Goryōkaku, after a mass landing by the imperial forces who bombarded the defenders from their own fort, Shiryōkaku, a few miles to the north. A week later the Tokugawa men surrendered, marking the end of the last resistance to imperial rule.

Today, the fortress is little more than a large park, with a small **museum** containing cannon balls and blood-stained uniforms from the siege. **Goryōkaku Tower**, next door, is expensive and commercial but it does offer the only good view of the fort's peculiar shape. The **history display** on the ground floor is excellent and free with brief accounts (in English) of the history of Hokkaidō from the 6th century.

Shopping

There's a lively market beginning at 5am every morning except Sunday in the streets behind the station. Many of the warehouses around the dock area below Motomachi have been redeveloped into restaurants, beer halls, shops and malls. Try the **History Plaza** in the old Kanemori Warehouses, which is a pleasant, though not especially economical, place to shop.

Hakodate's single most famous product is its **butter cookies**, manufactured for a hundred years in a **Trappistine Convent** a few miles out of town, and sold in the market and in souvenir shops. To visit the convent itself, built amid gardens in 1898, take bus no.10 or 19 to Yunokawa Danchi Kitaguchi stop, or no.59 to Torapisu chinu-shita.

(℗ 0138–)   Where to Stay

The **Kokusai (International) Hotel**, ℗ 23 5151 (*moderate to expensive*) is the grandest place and is close to the station, as are the cheaper business hotels **Acqua Garden**, ℗ 23 2200 (*inexpensive*) and **Kikuya**, ℗ 26 1144 (*inexpensive*). **Pension Hakodatemura**, ℗ 22 8105 (*cheap*) is right in the centre of Motomachi, near Suehiro-chō. **Hakodate Youth Guest House**, ℗ 26 7892, is a youth hostel 10 minutes from Hakodate-yama ropeway station.

(℗ 0138–)   Eating Out

Some of the old brick warehouses around the harbour beneath Motomachi have been converted into smart shopping centres and entertainment complexes. Here you can find *inexpensive* European food and beer halls (which also serve food). **Chat Noir** is one of these, on Union Square Meijikan.

Daimon-dōri, the main road running away from the station, has plenty of noodle and rice restaurants with plastic models in the window for easy ordering, as well as *sushi* restaurants serving freshly caught seafood. **Sushi-gin**, on Daimon-dōri, is the most famous and one of the most *expensive*. **Renga-tei**, ℗ 23 3091, just south of Daimon, is a *moderately*-priced fish restaurant famous for grills and stews.

Shikotsu-Tōya National Park

Between Uchiura Bay and Sapporo, bounded by an expressway to the south and Chitose Airport to the east, is a mountainous, volcano-studded lake district, Hokkaidō's most accessible, and consequently most commercialized, national park. Tour buses seem to swarm the resorts for most of the year. Apart from the astonishing Shōwa Shin-zan (New Mountain of the Shōwa Period) and the excellent Ainu museum at Shiraoi, it can be passed through quickly in favour of the remoter parks of the interior.

Getting Around

The region is well-served by public transport. **Bus** connections link most of the resorts listed below to one another, and to Sapporo and Hakodate. The Hakodate to Sapporo **JR line** passes through Tōya (for Lake Tōya), Noboribetsu, Shiraoi, and Tomakomai and Chitose Airport (the last two both connected to Lake Shikotsu).

Tōya-ko (Lake Tōya)

*The resort town, called **Tōya-ko Onsen**, is on the south shore of the lake, 15 minutes by bus from JR Tōya station which is close to the coast. The bus station is a couple of streets up from the lake. Just below it is the cabin of the local tourist association.*

Tōya-ko itself is a beautiful doughnut-shaped caldera lake with a large rugged island at its dead centre, like a green pupil in a watery eye. On the far northern side, you can see the crisp volcanic cone of **Yotei-zan**, scored down its slope with deep grooves.

The usual lake-side attractions are available: boats to hire (from motor launches to swan-shaped paddle boats), fishing, camping and 90-minute pleasure cruises (the boats visit the main island, **Nakano-shima**, as well as two smaller ones, **Benten-jima** and **Kannon-jima**, which have small Shinto and Buddhist shrines respectively). There's no serious hiking to speak of, but a road circles the lake for walking, cycling or driving.

The top floors of the **bus station** contain the **Volcano Science Museum** (*open 9–5, adm ¥400*), two chaotically laid-out floors detailing the recent activities of **Usu-zan**, the sandy-coloured peak to the southeast of the town. It first became active in 1663; on 7 August 1977, 32 years since the last eruption (*see* below), a seismic jolt was felt at 3am and, when the inhabitants of Tōya-ko Onsen rose the next morning, a huge plume of smoke, illuminated by flashes of lightning, was towering over the resort. Dust and pumice rained down for 17 days, and Tōyako Onsen was evacuated. Three people died, two were wounded, and 382 houses were destroyed. The exhibition contains a wrecked piano and a fleet of written-off cars which were crushed by falling boulders or buried in ash. The upper floor contains a (somewhat repetitive) display of pumice from sister volcanoes around the world, and the 'Experience Room', showing news footage of the eruption with a thundering 16-speaker soundtrack.

Shōwa Shin-zan (New Mountain of the Age of Shōwa)

Regular buses from Tōya-ko bus station.

In the last years of the Second World War, the inhabitants of Fukaba hamlet, 2km south of Lake Tōya, suffered, in the words of the *Guide Book to Shōwa Shin-zan*, 'a series of severe earthquakes, remarkable topographical deformation, paroxysmal eruption and protrusion of a mass of juvenile magma.' In other words, an erupting volcano suddenly grew out of the ground beneath their feet, changing forever the landscape of their home. It was named after the reigning emperor, and today you can visit and stand beneath its steaming slopes. Shōwa Shin-zan is what geologists call a 'parasitic' volcano, an off-shoot of the mightier Usu-zan from whose eastern foot it bulges. The first rumblings of the impending drama were literal ones: between December and June of 1943 and 1944, localized and extremely shallow earthquakes were felt, accompanied by cracks in the earth and a gentle upheaval of the ground. In June the upheaval became extraordinary; the ground rose by up to a metre and a half a day reaching 50m at its summit. At the end of the month, mud and steam began spitting weakly out of the top. In early July a village 2km away was scattered with a covering of ash. By the autumn, there were seven separate craters, regularly pluming forth clouds of glowing particles which floated towards Lake Tōya and wasted the intervening crops and forests. Finally, beginning in October 1944, red-hot lava was observed gathering in a pyramid shape on the surface of the heaving mass. When it stopped growing, in September the following year, the new mountain was 405m above sea level.

The effects of this upheaval were drastic. Towns as far as 50km away were coated with ash (a roof 2.5km from the cone, accumulated 20cm of the stuff) and 340,000 square metres of fields and forest land were ruined. The land around the Fukaba hamlet rose by 150m—one day the view was all trees, the next you could see all the way to the Pacific Ocean. Railway lines had to be re-laid, and a river reversed its course and threatened a village of 2000 people with inundation.

The new volcano was a cause of concern to more than just the baffled farmers in Fukaba. The wartime authorities, too, developed a strange, superstitious paranoia about the upstart mountain. 1944 and 1945 were the darkest days of Japan's war; to the flailing and beleaguered government, the imagery of Shōwa Shin-zan (fire, ashes, the trembling of the ground beneath one's feet) must have seemed like a premonition of all their worst fears. An information blackout was imposed, on the grounds that widespread news of the volcano might 'create anxiousness and unrest among the people'. Signs were erected warning the populace against 'conjecture and rumours', and locals were forbidden to discuss the matter. Eventually, military police occupied the hamlet, ostensibly to protect and assist the villagers during the emergency; actually, their role was to stop anyone who might spread news of the eruption from leaving.

In July 1944 the Americans recaptured Saipan, putting Tokyo within range of their heavy bombers. The military approached the local headmen with the extraordinary request that they 'cover up' the glowing mountain to prevent US planes from using it as a navigation beacon. In July 1945 the nearby port of Muroran was indeed pounded with incendiaries. In August 1945 the war ended, a few days after the bombing of Hiroshima and Nagasaki. Within a month, after just 20 months of active life, Shōwa Shin-zan too became extinct.

But the story of Shōwa Shin-zan went on. Its hero was Mimatsu Masao, the 57-year-old post-master of nearby Sobetsu village. Mimatsu was something of an amateur vulcanologist himself. He grew to love the new mountain, and the records which he made of its birth and growth represent the first ever scientific account of such an event. Mimatsu had almost no resources or instruments at his disposal; his methods were beautifully simple. Every day, from the very first movements of the earth, he made detailed observations and careful drawings from a number of fixed points. Each new bulge and fumarole was painstakingly marked on simple black and white drawings which are displayed in the **Mimatsu Masao Memorial Hall** (near the entrance to the car park and tourist precincts), along with other Mimatsu memorabilia, some of it in English. He suspended horizontal wires between upright poles; these corresponded to contour lines, so that the upward progress of Shin-zan could be accurately charted. The resulting layered drawing was presented at the International Conference of Vulcanology in Oslo in 1948 and named the 'Mimatsu Diagram', in honour of its assiduous inventor.

With the end of military censorship, news of the miraculous new mountain quickly spread. Tourists descended like locusts and carried pieces of it away as souvenirs; speculators came to stake claims on the rich mineral deposits newly exposed to the air. Mimatsu's beautiful mountain was disintegrating before his eyes. He raised money and bought the land containing it off the grateful farmers. But the property lines had been distorted by the buckled earth; the squabbles were only just beginning. Souvenir shops set up to cater for the gawping tourists quarrelled with one another—in 1969 Mimatsu had one stall torn down by the Health and Welfare Ministry. There were rumours that he'd been offered ¥300 million by a businessman who wanted to exploit the tourist potential, but he held out until his death at the age of 89.

Today, ownership of Shin-zan has passed to Mimatsu Saburō, Masao's son-in-law, an affable chap who is often in the museum and who speaks a bit of English. Despite the old man's efforts, the area round the car park is a carnival of dull, overpriced tourist shops. But the volcano dwarfs them all, a weird sight, like a vast mound of smoking builder's sand.

Since the 1977 eruption, **Usu-zan** (Mt Usu) has been off limits to climbers, but the cable car (¥1350 return) is back in service and begins at the foot of Shōwa Shin-zan. Smoke still billows from ducts in its side, and at the top you can see the silver stumps of trees killed in the big blow-out. The view from the top is one of the loveliest in Hokkaidō. Not only can you look down on Shin-zan, you can also see rivers, a lake, plains, mountain ranges, two active volcanoes (and half a dozen dormant ones), gleaming ports and the great silver bay stretching out before you.

(✆ 01427–)   *Where to Stay*

Tōya Park Hotel Tensho, ✆ 5 2445 (*expensive*) is the best of the various big *ryokan* in Tōya-ko Onsen. Smaller and cosier are the **Hokkai Hotel**, ✆ 5 2325 (*moderate*), the **Green Hotel**, ✆ 5 3030 (*inexpensive*), and the **Ryokan Yoshinoya**, ✆ 5 2073 (*inexpensive*).

    The **Shōwa Shin-zan Youth Hostel**, ✆ 5 2283 (*cheap*), is 8 minutes by bus from Tōya-ko Onsen. Get off at the Tōzan-guchi stop.

Noboribetsu Onsen

*Buses from Sapporo, Chitose Airport, Tomakomai, Muroran and Tōya-ko go directly to Noboribetsu Onsen resort. The trains stop at Noboribetsu town, 13 minutes from the hot springs by local bus. The **Tourist Association** has an office just north of the bus station, on the same side of the road.*

Nupuripetsu, 'White muddy river', as **Noboribetsu** was originally called in Ainu, is one of the most famous hot springs in Japan. The sulphurous waters were first exploited in 1858 by a local official who built a wooden bath house over one of the springs. Later Takimoto Kinzo founded an inn here; the biggest hotel in town still bears his name.

Whatever charm Noboribetsu once possessed has been smothered under layers of vulgarity and commercial kitsch. Even the town's biggest attraction—a hearty mixed *onsen* in the old Takimoto hotel—lost all its character when the wooden baths were rebuilt in marble and steel, the sexes were segregated, and the friendly staff became cool and supercilious. There is a boiling lake, and an impressive nature walk past seething mud pools, but the other tourist attractions are feeble and, in the case of the bear pits, repulsive.

Jigoku-dani (Hell Valley) is at the north end of town, beyond the Dai-ichi Takimoto-kan hotel and guarded by two giant models of cartoon demons. Half a dozen paths criss-cross the area; they are well marked with sign-post maps and it's difficult to get lost.

The most popular walk leads, via wooden duck boards, into the heart of the 'hells'—burping, steaming basins of geothermally heated water and mud. Beyond here an attractive path leads to a sinister lake called **Oyu-numa** (Hot Water Lake). This is the engine behind Noboribetsu Onsen; every day 3000 tons of mineral-rich water pump out of here, through Jigoku-dani, and finally to the Pacific, heavily depleted by the town's many bath houses. The lake is 1km in circumference, 22m deep, and steams eerily. Its surface is 50°C, but the bottom is 130°, quite enough to soft boil anyone unlucky—or desperate—enough to fall in. Suicides are not unknown, and the water is strictly off-limits to tourists, although boats are allowed on from time to time to rake the bottom for its valuable sulphur deposits. The still-active volcano behind Oyu-numa is **Hiyori-san**, meaning Weather Mountain—profuse smoke is said to presage storms.

Kuma-yama (Bear Mountain) is reached by cable car from a station to the west of the main road (¥2300). The disparate attractions at the top don't justify the entrance fee. There's a mildly interesting reconstructed Ainu village with displays of dance and Ainu crafts, and a dull bear museum. The main attraction—two grim concrete bear pits, crowded by cooing tourists—is pitiful and distressing.

(© 0143–)   **Where to Stay**

Noboribetsu has many modern resort *ryokan* catering to Japanese coach parties, and it will seldom be difficult to find lodging: enquire at the Tourist Association. Inns with their own hot baths are more costly than those without. It is cheaper to stay in one of the latter and visit one of the many public baths in the town.

Dai-ichi Takimoto-kan, *©* 84 2111 (*expensive*), is a famous old establishment founded by the Mr Takimoto who pioneered Noboribetsu Onsen. Its mixed baths have been segregated and sanitized and service these days is rather haughty. The **Takimoto Inn** is a small, Western-style annexe. **Noboribetsu Grand Hotel,** *©* 84 3430 (*expensive*), is a rival to the Takimoto-kan with supposedly even bigger baths and a similar atmosphere of plastic swank.

Ryokan Hanaya, *©* 84 2521 (*moderate*), is a former Welcome Inn in a nice wooden building which has unfortunately upped its prices.

Akashiya-sō, *©* 84 2616, and **Kanefuku** are the two **youth hostels,** both *cheap.* The former is bigger, a bit closer to the centre of town, a little more expensive and has its own hot bath.

Eating Out

For lunch there are several inexpensive restaurants of the plastic-models-in-the-window type along the main street. The best food is likely to be served in your hotel, *ryokan* or youth hostel, but if you want to get out, the side alleys contain a few drinking and eating places which are open in the evening. None is particularly distinguished—just look for the red lanterns. Like most hot spring resorts, Noboribetsu also has a sprinkling of hostess bars and places of male entertainment. You will know if you wander into one of these; just remember that they can be as shockingly expensive in Hokkaidō as in Tokyo.

Shiraoi

Shiraoi has only one tourist attraction worth getting off the train for, the **Ainu Poroto Kotan** (Ainu Pond Village) with its excellent museum, **Ainu Minzoku Hakubutsukan** (*both open April–Oct 8–5; Nov–Mar 8.30–4.30; adm ¥515*). To reach it, take the footbridge to the rear exit of Shiraoi station and turn right; there are signposts along the road.

The village is entered through an arcade of identical souvenir shops but inside commercialism is minimal. *Chise* (Ainu huts) have been reconstructed between a lakeside and attractive woodland. Contemporary Ainu in traditional costumes adorn the grounds and, when enough visitors have assembled, there is a show: an Ainu elder delivers a droll monologue (in Japanese) in one of the huts; and songs and dances are performed on an open air stage to the peculiar accompaniment of the *mukkuri,* Ainu-style Jew's harp.

The *chise* contain costumes, lacquerware, ceremonial wands, zig-zag mats, smoking hearths and soot-darkened log rafters. Inside one of them are illustrations of the tattoos worn by both sexes—diamonds, triangles, rings and checks carved on the hand and arm, and a thick, moustache-like band around the women's lips. The smaller houses elevated on stilts are for the dry storage of food; the log cages are for bear cubs.

The exhibits in the **museum,** a large modern building modelled after a *chise,* aren't as gorgeous as those in Hakodate or Sapporo, but they're informative and educational, with excellent English labels, and there are a number of good bilingual books in the shop. The various aspects of Ainu life are treated in turn: one case contains stuffed examples of the animals which represented Ainu gods; another displays hunting and fishing tools and techniques; a third shows the various styles of *chise* built in different regions of Hokkaidō. One of the most interesting displays concerns the Ainu's Siberian cousins, hunter-gatherer tribes like the Uilta and Nivkhi, who used to inhabit Sakhalin and the Kurile islands (as far north as the Kamchatka Peninsula), and whose descendants survive in small numbers all over Eastern Siberia.

Shikotsu-ko (Lake Shikotsu)

Two hundred and sixty people—suicides and unlucky fishermen—have drowned in Lake Shikotsu since 1930, and 90 per cent of them are still at the bottom, 360m down. This is Japan's second deepest lake—the Ainu used to say that the god who was building it dug too deep and connected it with the sea, which also explains why it never freezes in winter. Despite its high body count, Shikotsu-ko is one of the most appealing and unspoiled lakes in Hokkaidō: an attractive resort town with cheap accommodation, piercingly blue waters and a ring of dramatic, and very climbable, mountains.

Shikotsu-kohan (Shikotsu Lakeside), on the mouth of the Chitose River on the east shore of the lake, is a pleasant town with a little block of picturesque shops and inns, and a quiet wooded park along the waterfront, well away from the bus terminal and mercifully unmarred by loudspeakers and piped classical music.

Getting There and Around

The **bus station** connects with Tomakomai (on the JR line), Sapporo and Chitose and its airport, but services are infrequent and you should double check onward connections. Nearby is the **Visitors' Centre** with guide maps in English.

Getting around is a bit tricky without your own car. The lake is 41km in circumference, the attractions are spaced widely around it, and there are no buses. The youth hostel has a **minibus** which drops hikers off at the trailheads and Koke no Dōmon—non-hostellers could probably get a lift too, if they asked nicely. The hostel also rents **bicycles**, although they are ¥200 cheaper (¥1000 a day) at the Shikotsu Lakeside National Vacation Village across the river to the south.

The pier offers **sightseeing cruises** and **rental boats**, but these look dull and there are no islands.

Around the Lake

Travelling clockwise, the first place of interest is 15km from Shikotsu-kohan: **Koke no Dōmon**, a long gulley between high rocky walls smothered in velvety moss. There's a pretty, 50m **waterfall** at Bifue, on the western shores of the lake, and from the north shore a road leads to the tiny, lucent **Lake Okotampe**. A few kilometres to the east are two open-air hot springs, **Marukoma** and **Ito Onsen**, formed where thermal water gushes out into the chilly lake.

Hiking

The closest mountain is **Morappu-yama** (507m), on the left as you face the lake from Shikotsu-kohan. There's a ski run and resort, and roads all the way up. **Monbetsu-dake** (886m) is on the other side of the town, to the north. A road winds up through a quiet forest, and you could climb it, enjoy the view and be back in town in the space of two hours. Unfortunately, you need permission to ascend: the telecommunications station at the top periodically emits microwaves. Ask at the Visitors' Centre.

The most popular hike is up **Tarumae-dake** (1038m), southwest of the town, and immediately recognizable from all over the lake area. It's an active volcano (the last eruption was in 1955); the peak resembles a plate with a badly burned pork pie in the middle. Irregular buses (enquire at the Visitors' Centre) carry climbers from the town to the seventh station, from where it's a half hour climb to the summit across spectacular volcanic rock. **Fuppushi-dake** (1103m), in front of Tarumae-dake, is off-limits because of bears.

On the northern side of the lake, a trail leads from the Poropinai campsite up **Eniwa-dake** (1320m). It takes about four hours to reach the summit; the views over the cliffs to the lake and town below are stunning.

(✆ 0123–)   ***Where to Stay***

There are half a dozen impersonal-looking resort *ryokan*: the **Shikotsu-ko Kankō Hotel**, ✆ 25 2211 (*moderate*) is the most central.

The little shopping quarter, hung with lanterns and colourful signs, contains some very good cheap lodgings, aimed at young people and climbers. The **Mizūmi**, ✆ 25 2722, **Kogetsu-sō**, ✆ 25 2726, and **Shikotsu-sō**, ✆ 25 2718, are simple guest houses (all *inexpensive*). The **Log Bear**, ✆ 25 2738 (*cheap*), is a log hut with a single dormitory sleeping half a dozen people. It has friendly owners and a coffee shop downstairs.

For climbers and hikers, the most useful place in town (as well as the cheapest) is the **youth hostel**, ✆ 25 2311, which hires bikes, gives lifts, and briefs hostellers on the best walks and current weather and path conditions.

Sapporo

Sapporo is a lively city and its pleasures are hearty and physical: beer, noodles and lamb hot pot; strolls along the broad parks and avenues; the winter Snow Festival; a racy entertainment district. The conventional tourist sights—apart from an excellent Ainu museum—are dull, but communications are such that almost everyone visiting Hokkaidō will pass through here. An afternoon and, ideally, a night here will be well spent.

History

By the late 19th century, territorial incursions by prowling Russian ships presented the Meiji government with a choice: either exploit the island of Ezo (as Hokkaidō was then called) or risk losing it to the tsar. In 1870 the *Kaitakushi* (Commission for Colonization) was established, with responsibility for the whole region. Ezo was renamed Hokkaidō ('Region of the Northern Sea') and Sapporo (from the Ainu *Sari-poro-betsu*, 'a river which runs along a plain filled with reeds') was chosen as its headquarters.

Central government invested heavily in the frontier region. In 1880 it was honoured with the country's third ever railway line (only the ones in Tokyo and Ōsaka preceded it), built by an American engineer. Foreign advice was also sought out on the *Kaitakushi's* primary task, the development of agriculture, and the commission engaged 63 Europeans and Americans, worthy but unexciting men who have nonetheless achieved a kind of cult status as the founders of modern Sapporo: numerous statues and paintings of these dreary stalwarts adorn the city's parks and municipal facilities.

The most celebrated of them all is the epically mediocre Dr William S. Clark, who spent a year in Sapporo in 1876 setting up what was to become Hokkaidō University. Inexplicably, Clark's parting words to his pupils—'Boys, be ambitious!'—are considered deeply profound and have become an unofficial civic motto, engraved on a thousand tourist brochures and on the minds of Sapporo school children.

The *Kaitakushi* was abolished in 1882, but the American influence survives in the city's oldest buildings and in the grid layout of the streets (Sapporo avoided heavy bombing during the war). In 1950 the annual Snow Festival was held for the first time; in 1972 Sapporo hosted the Winter Olympics. Today, 1.6 million people live in the city, the fifth largest in Japan.

Getting There

There is so little difference in price between air and rail fares, and such a large difference in time, that—unless you have a Japan Rail Pass—it is far easier to fly to Sapporo.

by air

Chitose Airport (an hour's drive from Sapporo station by airport bus or 30mins by limited express train) connects with 12 Japanese cities. There are 30 flights a day to and from Tokyo alone; the standard one-way journey takes 1hr 25mins and costs ¥23,850. Internationally, Chitose connects with Hong Kong, Korea, Saipan and Guam. Carriers in Sapporo include:

Japan Airlines, ✆ (domestic) 011 231 0231, ✆ (international) 011 231 4411.

Japan Air Systems, ✆ (domestic only) 011 222 8111.

All Nippon Airways, ✆ (domestic) 011 231 5131, ✆ (international) 011 281 1212.

In the winter several companies offer bargain ski-package plans including flights to Hokkaidō and accommodation. Ask a travel agent like NTA (Nihon Ryokō).

by rail

The quickest way to get to Sapporo by rail is by a combination of *shinkansen* (to Morioka) and express (to Aomori and from there to Sapporo by the tunnel). It takes about 9hrs in total and costs ¥21,270. A sleeper service departs from Tokyo's Ueno station, and takes 16hrs.

Orientation

Sapporo is built on a mercifully simple grid, making it one of the few cities in Japan where you can find addresses on your own.

Ōdōri Kōen is the name of a long broad park running east to west in the centre of the city. Parallel streets north and south of here are numbered according to their relative direction from this park: North (in Japanese *Kita*) Ōdōri, North 1st Street (Kita ichi-jō), North 2nd Street (Kita ni-jō), North 3rd Street (Kita san-jō), etc; South (*Minami*) Ōdōri, South 1st Street, South 2nd Street, etc.

The north–south avenues work on a similar system except that avenue zero is a canal to the east of the station. Almost all the sightseeing spots are west of here and are prefixed accordingly: West 1st Avenue (Nishi it-chōme), West 2nd Avenue (Nishi ni-chōme), etc.

For simplicity's sake, addresses in this chapter are abbreviated. 'N5 W4' represents the junction of North 5th Street (Kita go-jō) and West 4th Avenue (Nishi yon-chōme), i.e. the crossing directly in front of the station. When referring to buildings or premises, the address given is the junction to the *southeast* of the block.

Getting Around

The regularity of Sapporo's streets and the compactness of the town centre makes **walking** the easiest way of getting about. There are **tram**, **bus** and **subway** lines but they are chiefly useful to commuters from the suburbs. The green **Nanboku-sen** (South–North Line) usefully links Sapporo station, Ōdōri, Susukino entertainment area and Nakajima Kōen (Nakajima Park, location of a number of hotels) by subway.

Car Hire

For onward travel to other parts of Hokkaidō the following companies hire cars:

Budget, S1 W4, ✆ 011 241 0543.

Nippon, N7 W4, ✆ 011 717 0919.

Nissan, N7 W4, ✆ 011 717 4123.

Tourist Information

The information counter in the station has limited material in English. Consult instead the charming staff at the **Sapporo International Communication Plaza**, N1 W3, opposite the Clock Tower. This combined library, information centre and advice counter has bound files containing booklets on the whole island and is worth visiting even if you plan to leave Sapporo itself on the next train. There's a board with ads and notices of interest to foreigners; all the material can be photo-copied for a small fee.

There's a branch of **Maruzen book shop** on South 1st Street (S1 W2) where you can buy English books including *Sapporo Handbook*, a run of the mill sightseeing and restaurant guide by a local foreign resident, Howard N. Tarnoff.

Festivals

The **Sapporo Yuki Matsuri** (Snow Festival) in early February is the one time of the year when Sapporo is worth a visit in its own right. One thousand troops from the Japanese 'Self-Defence Forces' (*Jieitai*) spend 20 days carving vast sculptures—of cartoon characters, mythical heroes, iconic buildings and rock stars—out of vast blocks of ice in Ōdōri Park. Nearly two million people visit the city during the week. It's advisable to come a few days before the official opening, visit the statues early, and then spend the festival itself enjoying the carnival atmosphere and non-stop entertainment. Advance reservations for accommodation are essential.

Batchelor Kinenkan (Memorial Museum)

N3 W8. Open May–Sept, 9–4; Oct, 9–3; closed Mon and Nov–April; adm ¥400.

The most interesting attraction in Sapporo, worth visiting even if you only have a few hours to kill between trains, is just inside the **botanical gardens**, two blocks south and four blocks west of the station plaza. It's administered by the Hokkaidō University Faculty of Agriculture in memory of Rev John Batchelor, a 19th-century British minister who spent half a lifetime researching the aboriginals of Hokkaidō and eastern Siberia, and published the definitive English work on the subject, *The Ainu of Japan*. The small one-room exhibition is a well-chosen showcase of the Reverend's huge collection of Ainu artifacts: its English labelling and superb condition make this one of the best and most accessible Ainu museums in Japan.

The first case on the left contains models of *chise*, the rush and reed houses of the kind which are reconstructed in the Ainu tourist villages; in the middle of the room is the sacred hearth, abode of the Goddess of fire, the mediator between men and humans, and one of the prime deities of the Ainu pantheon; on top of the left-hand display case sits a long, dug-out canoe.

The rest of the cases are filled with beautiful and pristine examples of cooking utensils, hunting, fishing and farming tools, weapons, musical instruments and religious items. Ainu ingenuity with all kinds of wood (evident, in debased form, in the carvings and ornaments sold in contemporary souvenir shops) is beautifully demonstrated here. As well as plain, unvarnished trays, bowls and paddles, there are ladles and porridge bowls fashioned from strips of bark, which is also spun into fibre for bags and coats, and sewn onto clothes in wriggling designs. Cotton, spun on the mainland, is dyed with traditional Ainu patterns. There is a coat and some boots stitched entirely out of cured salmon skin (complete with fins), and a lovely winter garment made of the pelts of puffins from the Kurile Islands.

Most interesting of all are the objects in the big case facing the door—religious items from the *iyomante* bear ceremony, most sacred of the Ainu rituals. A framed print by a Japanese artist illustrates the scene: a specially bred cub is shot with arrows then ritually gutted and cooked. The altar consists of poles wrapped around with geometrically patterned rush mats and topped with bear skulls, stuffed and festooned with curly wood shavings. A similar, smaller altar is devoted to the worship of the owl.

Other Sights

Tours of Sapporo's day time sights—only worthwhile for those with time on their hands—generally begin at the **Tokeidai** (Clock Tower) at N1 W2, a forgettable building based on the architecture of (guess where?) William Clark's Massachusetts State Agricultural College. The American-made clock has been wound every three days since 1933 by the faithful Mr Kiyoshi, in case you were wondering. Inside is a small, missable history museum. Those with a craving for more Meiji-period architecture might follow the crowds of Japanese tourists to the **Old Hokkaidō Government Building** (N3 W6) or the **Hokkaidō University** campus (N8 W7).

Ōdōri Kōen, immediately south of the Clock Tower, is the park that hosts the spectacular February Snow Festival, and it is a decent enough place to bask on a warm day. Anyone with ¥600 burning a hole in their pocket can ascend the 147m **TV Tower** for sweeping views of the surrounding area.

(✆ 011–)	*Where to Stay*

expensive

Hotel Alpha Sapporo, ✆ 221 2333 (S1 W5), a block south of Ōdōri Park, is the best hotel in Sapporo with noted restaurants.

moderate

Tōkyū Hotel, ✆ 231 5611 (N4 W4), is the local branch of the excellent city hotel chain; it is situated one block from the station.

Washington Hotel I, ✆ 251 3211 (N4 W4), and **Washington Hotel II**, ✆ 222 3311 (N5 W6), are both convenient for the station. Number II is newer and a bit more expensive.

inexpensive

Tōkyū Inn, ✆ 531 0109 (S4 W7), a few blocks west of Susukino is an unfussy chain business hotel, convenient for night life. The adjacent Plaza 109 contains numerous restaurants.

Nakamuraya Ryokan, ✆ 241 2111 (N3 W7), near the botanical gardens, is a member of the Japanese Inn Group; it has traditional rooms in a modern building.

cheap

International Inn Nada, ✆ 551 5882 (S5 W9), is within walking distance of Susukino. It offers plain, Japanese-style rooms for about ¥3500; meals are extra. English is spoken.

Sapporo House Youth Hostel, ✆ 726 4235 (N6 W6), is a 7-minute walk northwest of the station. It is basic, but very handy for the station.

In keeping with its blokey, down-to-earth character, Sapporo's edible specialities are simple and hearty. **Sapporo Ramen** (Chinese noodles) have a thicker sauce than that used in other parts of Japan, but their most obvious distinction is the seafood with which they're frequently served. The most famous noodle venue is **Ramen Yokochō** (Ramen Alley) which runs north–south through the block numbered S5 W2. It's expensive, though, and you could easily find yourself paying up to ¥2000 a bowl. Try somewhere in the station or Ōdōri area, like **Ajino Sanpei** in the Daimaru Fuji Building (S1 W3).

The other attraction is the **Sapporo Biiru-en** (Beer Garden, N6 E9), a handsome collection of brick buildings dating from 1891 which used to be the Sapporo Brewery. A **Beer Museum** (*open June–Aug, 8.30–4.40; Sept–May, 9–3.40*) contains displays on the history and processes behind the famous Sapporo brew, but the main attraction is the several restaurants and beer halls which occupy the main body of the old factory. Here you can drink lots of exceptionally fresh beer and sample Hokkaidō's 'national dish', a lamb barbecue called *Jingisukan* (Genghis Khan) after its supposed origins on the Mongolian steppes. For ¥3000 you can eat as much as you like (a single course costs less) of the lamb slices, beansprouts, cabbage and carrots. It's tasteless, fat-laden swill, but the atmosphere is lively, and the brick setting, with its old Heath Robinson-like brewing tanks, is fun.

Fuji Soba, S3 W4, is an old-fashioned shop which sells hand-made *soba* buckwheat noodles.

Kurumaya, S4 W5, situated in the basement of Plaza 109 Building, is a popular *yakitori* bar.

Sushizen, S7 W4, is a small and moderately priced *sushi* bar selling excellent fresh fish.

Yoyotei, S4 W4, on the 5th floor of the Matsuoka Building is a better than average 'Genghis Khan' restaurant/beer hall.

Nightlife

Susukino, comprising the blocks southwest of the subway station of the same name, is one of the most frank and famous examples of what are discreetly labelled 'pleasure quarters'. Bars, coffee shops, restaurants, karaoke dens and nightclubs of a conventional nature are plentiful, but the lurid neon signs and loitering barkers outside every other doorway indicate the presence of 'soaplands' offering more specialized services. Susukino is reputed to have some of the most imaginative and exotic soaplands in Japan—establishments where the ladies dress as schoolgirls, nurses, air stewardesses, cheerleaders, Edo-period courtesans and South Sea islanders. As in all such districts, the chances of being deliberately conned are low: just check what the entrance, cover and drinks charges are *before* you commit yourself to paying them.

AL's Bar, S7 W2, in the basement of the Hosui Building is a friendly American-style bar run by two English-speaking brothers.

Casa Marcos, S6 W4, on the 9th floor of the Jasmac Building is a glittering cabaret club staffed by glamorous Filipino transvestites. Charges include drinks and are based on a 90 minute period.

Exing, S4 W3, on the 8th floor of Green Building No. 3 is a huge but conventional disco, popular with Sapporo foreigners.

Mugishutei, S9 W5, in the basement of the Onda Building is a comprehensively stocked bar with 250 brands of beer from 30 countries, and a young, student-age clientele. It is popular with foreigners.

Susukino Reien, S4 W3, on the 8th floor of Green Building No. 2, is a bizarre restaurant bar on a funereal theme, decorated with mummies and gravestones.

Northern Hokkaidō

Wakkanai

A few miles from Cape Sōya, the northernmost tip of mainland Japan, is Wakkanai, a grey, chilly port with a fishy smell and signs in Cyrillic advertising second-hand car dealerships—a reminder of the closeness of the Russian island of Sakhalin, just 60km away. There is nothing here to linger over; for travellers it's the gateway to the twin islands of Rebun and Rishiri with their bleak-lovely scenery and extensive hiking trails.

Getting There

Even as the crow flies, it's 260km from Sapporo to Wakkanai, through a bleak interior of hills and flat salt-marshes. There are two direct **trains** every day, taking just under 6hrs either way, but to save daylight take the service departing Sapporo nightly at 10pm. You can take your chances in a regular seat, or pay extra for a **sleeper** (advance reservation necessary; the sleeper supplement is *not* included in the Japan Rail Pass, although the basic fare for a seat is). At around ¥7400, this is no more expensive than the cost of a middling business hotel, although it's cramped, even by Japanese standards. Wakkanai Airport has a daily **flight** or two to Chitose Airport and Tokyo, depending on the season.

From Wakkanai JR station, turn right then right again to reach the **ferry terminal**. Departures to each of the islands vary between one a day (in Jan and Feb) to four a day (in June, July and Aug). The sailing to Rebun-tō takes about 1¼hrs and costs ¥3710 for an adult foot passenger; Rishiri-tō is 15mins and ¥400 nearer. Between Rebun and Rishiri the ferry takes 40mins and costs ¥1240.

(© 0162–)   *Where to Stay*

Wakkanai has 80 hotels, *ryokan* and *minshuku* for unlucky travellers who get stranded here overnight. Try the **Minshuku Omote**, © 23 2924—it's no palace but it's cheap and dead opposite the ferry terminal; or the

Wakkanai Sun Hotel, © 22 5311 (*moderate*), next to the station. **Moshiripa Youth Hostel**, © 24 0180, is also cheap and conveniently central. If all else fails, ask at the ferry terminal **information desk**; stop here anyway to pick up a guide map (in Japanese only, but still useful) of the island(s) you plan to visit.

Rebun-tō (Rebun Island)

With mild, rippling hills and little salt-encrusted villages, Rebun-tō looks like a Scottish island as you approach it from the sea. A coastal road runs along the east and north sides and, for much of the way, a flanking avenue of grey stones separates it from the sea wall. Here stand wooden shacks draped with nets where local fishermen and their wives mend their tackle, dry out wreaths of seaweed and gut their catch. On the other side of the road stand their houses, also wooden, with brightly coloured roofs weighted down with stones against the gales.

Getting Around

In shape, Rebun-tō resembles a tall isosceles triangle, with its sharp point to the south, and its short northern side scooped out to form a curving bay. The ferries dock at **Kafuka** near the bottom of the eastern side; accommodation is concentrated around here, and in **Funadomari**, at the northeastern tip. The long west coast has no road; this is where the wildest scenery is found, and where the famous Eight-hour Hiking Course runs. At its north end is Sukoton Misaki (Cape Sukoton).

Six **buses** a day run between Kafuka ferry terminal and points up the east coast, round to Sukoton Misaki. Minshuku Ohōtsuku (right from the ferry terminal, a few houses down) rents **bicycles**; Mitsui Kankō Hotel has a **car hire** service.

Hiking

Serious walkers take the **Hachijikan Haikingu Cōsu** (Eight-hour Hiking Course) from Sukoton Misaki to Momo-iwa (Peach Rock). Bring good shoes, warm and waterproof clothing (the weather can change suddenly), food and something to drink. There are plenty of other less taxing trails available, including the **Yonjikan Cōsu** (Four-hour Course) which follows the longer route for a third of the way. In fact, both times allow for a very slow pace: the chances are you'll do the eight-hour course in seven, and the four-hour hike in three and a half.

Starting at Sukoton (the name, written in *katakana*, is an old Ainu word of unknown meaning), look beyond the small Todo-shima island towards the north: on a clear day you'll see the hulking shape of Russian **Karafuto** or **Sakhalin**. Start walking down the road until a signposted right-hand turn. The trail runs up and down the grassy ridges of the cliffs, passing a number of fishing hamlets on the way. At Nishi-Uedomari, the four-hour course turns inland and towards the north; the last stretch, along a macadamized road, ends at a bus stop where you can catch a lift back to Kafuka. The eight-hour course, however, continues south all the way down the coast. Parts of it are steep, or cross slippery rocks; care is required, and it would be unwise to attempt the full course alone.

Other trails include ones to the island's highest peak, Rebun-dake (490m), from either Nairo or Kitōsu on the east coast (around three and a half hours there and back).

(𝄞 01638–)   ***Where to Stay***

There are plenty of places to stay on Rebun but youth hostels and camp-sites often close in the winter and spring.

In **Kafuka**, convenient for the ferry, the biggest hotel is the **Mitsui Kankō Hotel**, 𝄞 6 1717 (*moderate to expensive*). It looks out onto the waterfront.

Minshuku Hokkaidō, 𝄞 6 2137 (*inexpensive*), is known for its excellent sea food. **Pension Ūnii**, 𝄞 6 1541 (*moderate*), has comfortable Western-style rooms. Both are a few hundred metres inland; ask for directions at the port.

Funadomari, at the northeast corner of the island, is another small port, prettier than Kafuka and located near the small airfield. Try **Minshuku Yūnagi**, 𝄞 7 2127 (*inexpensive*).

Hikers are well-advised to stay in one of three **youth hostels** which all offer maps, briefings, and organized hiking groups. On Hokkaidō these tend to be relentlessly, even fanatically, cheerful places: fun is compulsory, 16 hours a day, and those who prefer keeping themselves to themselves will find their smiles wearing thin. In **Momoiwa Youth Hostel**, the grinning doesn't stop from the moment you are picked up from the ferry until lights out. Communal fun (hard to wriggle out of even for non-Japanese speakers) includes songs, sketches and incomprehensible folk dancing. You have been warned.

Rebun Youth Hostel, 𝄞 6 1608 (*cheap*), is a 10-minute drive from Kafuka port.

Momoiwa Youth Hostel, 𝄞 6 1390 (*cheap*), is situated on a beautiful stretch of coast surrounded by unusually shaped crags—Neko-iwa (Cat-shaped rock), Jizō-iwa (Jizō Bosatsu-shaped rock) and Momo-iwa (Peach-shaped rock). There are lovely sunsets.

Funadomari Youth Hostel, 𝄞 7 2717, is *cheap.*

There's a **camping ground** at the north end of the island, by Kushu-ko lake, a few miles from Funadomari.

Rishiri-tō (Rishiri Island)

Where Rebun is long and low, Rishiri-tō is round and tall, a gently sloping volcano elegantly breaking the surface of the ocean. The single peak (nicknamed, as all cone-shaped mountains inevitably are, Rishiri Fuji) is 1721m high and dominates the island.

Getting There and Around

The ferry from Wakkanai docks at **Oshidomari** like most of the services from Rebun-tō. However, one or two boats a day go from Kafuka to **Kutsugata**, Rishiri-tō's second port, on the western side of the island.

The ferry terminal building contains an **information desk** with detailed maps showing hiking trails and contours—ask them to write out the names of the main landmarks in English. Ask here about **rental bicycles** and **cars**. Kameya Rentakā, ✆ 01638 4 2252, hires vehicles and runs a taxi service. Infrequent **buses** circle the island; they are more frequent in peak season.

Hiking

Three trails climb to the summit of **Rishiri Fuji**, from Oshidomari, Kutsugata and from a smaller town called Oniwaki, on the southeast coast of the island. In each case a road leads to the trailhead at about 300m or 400m; all three routes take seven or eight hours, there and back. The climbing isn't particularly difficult, but it's steep, cold and windy at the top so the usual preparations are essential—warm clothes, gloves, decent footwear, food and drink, an early start. Inform someone of your plans.

From Oshidomari, there are a number of easier trails. All of them lead from a campsite at the end of a new macadamized road, which is also the trailhead for the Rishiri Fuji path. The gentlest of all leads to **Pon-yama** (440m), a foothill of the main mountain with a fine view of the port below. The walk, through pine and silver birch forest, takes about half an hour from the campsite. Just below Pon-yama, another path leads down to **Hime-numa** (lake); from here you can descend to the coast road and back into Oshidomari, a circuit of three or four hours.

(✆ 01638–) *Where to Stay*

Oshidomari

Kitaguni Grand Hotel, ✆ 2 1362 (*moderate–expensive*).

Rishiri Marine Hotel, ✆ 22 1337 (*moderate*), is a bit cheaper than the Grand and more convenient, overlooking the harbour.

Pension Misaki, ✆ 2 1659 (*cheap*), has simple Japanese-style rooms with a view over the harbour.

Guriin Hiro Youth Hostel, ✆ 2 2507 (*cheap*), is on the western edge of town, 15 minutes from the ferry.

Kutsugata

Hotel Rishiri, ✆ 4 2001, is a *moderate* hotel, with an inexpensive people's lodge (*kokuminshuku-sha*) attached.

Eastern Hokkaidō

At Cape Sōya the Asian **Nihon-kai** (Sea of Japan) gives way to the Siberian **Ohōtsu-kai** (Sea of Okhotsk), a bleak coastline of salt marshes, winter ice floes and occasional memorials to the ships, Russian and Japanese, which have gone down in these desolate seas. At Sōya itself there's a monument to an even more bitter catastrophe: the Korean airliner shot down by a Soviet fighter in 1983.

The coastal road runs for almost 600km, and for three-quarters of them there is almost nothing worth stopping for. At **Abashiri**, where the railway finally meets the coast, the biggest attraction is a famous prison and the related **high-security prison museum**. Together with **Shari**, further along the coast, it serves as the northern gate to the inland **Akan National Park**. More adventurous and remote, though, is the **Shiretoko National Park** to the northeast, pointing like a finger into the Sea of Okhotsk and towards the Russian Kurile Islands.

Shiretoko Hantō (Shiretoko Peninsula)

The peninsula is a spiny ridge of steep mountains which taper into the sea at Cape Shiretoko. You could get the flavour of it in a night and two days, but to enjoy the activities available properly—climbing mountains, taking cruises, bathing in hot waterfalls— you'll need three days or more. Note that many of the tourist facilities described here go into hibernation over the winter months.

Getting There and Around

The gateways to Shiretoko are Abashiri and Shari, in themselves unremarkable towns. Both can be reached by **train** from Sapporo and southern Hokkaidō (change at Asahikawa if necessary), and there are car hire offices close to the station. The JR Senmo Main Line also connects with Kushiro, for adventurous types coming from the seldom visited south.

The southern part of the peninsula proper is served by an efficient main road which runs along the coast and crosses the peninsula about half way up, linking the main town **Utoro** with the village of **Rausu**. North of here, minor roads, rough in parts, continue on but peter out 15km from the tip which is accessible only by boat or hiking.

The terrain of Shiretoko is too steep for all but the most fanatical cyclists, but this is certainly a place where a **car** or **motorbike** would make travelling much easier; hire in Abashiri. Another reliable option is to **hitch-hike** with the friendly Japanese outdoors-types who drive through Shiretoko at all times of the year.

Infrequent **buses** link Shari, Rausu and Utoro, from where there are also connections to the Five Lakes and the hot waterfall. Check timetables in advance and plan ahead to make the most of these services.

Sightseeing boats run from Utoro along the rocky west coast between April and October. There are two cruises: the shorter one goes only half way up the peninsula and takes 90mins; the longer trip goes all the way to the cape and takes 3hrs 45mins.

Touring Shiretoko Hantō

The **Shiretoko Hakubutsukan** (*open 9–5; adm ¥200*), an interesting little museum 15 minutes' walk west of **Shari** station, gives a taster of what to expect on the peninsula, with geological models of volcanoes, relics of the Ainu and the even older prehistoric

Jōmon people, and a large display of animals and birds, including seals, foxes, bears, eagles and enormous marine turtles.

From Shari, the well-made road runs high above the cliffs, commanding views of the waterfalls which plunge into the sea below. **Utoro**, the peninsula's main town, is dramatically situated on a harbour sheltered by vast rocky upthrusts, but this doesn't save the town from dreariness. There's an **information hut** by the **bus terminal**, and plenty of hotels and *minshuku*, many of them supplied with hot spring water. But you'd be better off staying at the next stop, **Iwaobetsu**, with its youth hostel and old spa hotel which even non-residents can use (*see* 'Where to Stay'). Just before here, the main road swings right through the Shiretoko Pass to **Rausu**. There's even less to say about this fishing town than about Utoro; students of the strange may want to try **sea lion meat** which is served in a couple of restaurants here.

The main tour trail carries on north, however, past Iwaobetsu and through a thickening forest; cars and buses frequently have to stop for the fearless orange foxes which stand in the middle of the carriageway, eyeballing tourists. The first of the major sights, and the most hyped, is the **Shiretoko Go-ko** (Five Lakes), a pretty nature trail around a series of marshy ponds, above which the peaks of Mt Rausu glower impressively. A trail map is available, with detailed accounts of the varied flora and fauna for the botanically ignorant—look out for the tree trunks clawed by brown bears. The walk takes about an hour, and on weekends and holidays you can expect to share the paths with several coach loads of garrulous pensioners.

Press on to Shiretoko's most fascinating natural attraction, **Kamuiwakka-no-taki** (Kamuiwakka Falls), a geothermally heated cascade that steams in the cold and flows hot into the sea. There's room for cars at the bottom, and stands selling food and *awaji*—straw sandals bound tightly round your feet, a worthwhile purchase for those without wellingtons or rubber-soled sandals. You ascend the falls through the water itself, over rocks dyed green by subterranean minerals. It's a slippery and, in parts, uncomfortable climb: apart from being alarmingly warm, the water is acidic and stings open cuts and grazes.

After half an hour's scramble, you come to the first of the **rock pools**, a natural *rotenburo* (open air hot spring), with a plunging view of the sea below. There are several levels, but the climb gets trickier (and the water hotter) the higher you go. There's barely room to climb, let alone change, so wear bathing suits under trousers or skirts—or come early enough to have the place to yourself. There's another set of *rotenburo* 50 minutes up the trail which leads from Kamuiwakka to Iō-zan mountain.

Hiking

The source of all wisdom is the **Iwaobetsu Youth Hostel** which has nightly briefings on weather and conditions and organizes group hikes up the more difficult peaks. Try to drop in here for a word with the master even if you're not actually staying here.

The most popular of the hard hikes is to **Rausu-dake** (1661m), the peninsula's highest peak. The trail begins behind the Hotel Chinohate which is reached by a gravel road from

Iwaobetsu bus stop; it takes 4hrs to go up, of which the last two are a clamber over rocks, and 3hrs down.

From the summit, a path leads across a ridge to the next mountain along, **Iō-zan** (Sulphur Mountain, 1563m). You could make a round trip of it, by descending from here to the Kamuiwakka Falls for a rejuvenating dip in the hot pools. To climb Iō-zan from Kamuiwakka (the trail begins a few metres beyond the bridge) would take about 8hrs, there and back. These are all tough hikes up cold, windy mountains.

Easier is the walk down to **Rausu-ko** (Lake Rausu) from **Shiretoko-tōge** (Shiretoko Pass), half way along the main road as it cuts across the peninsula.

Where to Stay

Iwaobetsu is just a bus stop. There are no shops, banks or amenities other than the two establishments listed below. But they are two of the best, in one of the most attractive parts of the peninsula.

Hotel Chinohate, ℭ 01522 4 2331 (*moderate*), is reached from Iwaobetsu bus stop by a long gravel road. It is an old-style hotel with *tatami* rooms, and its own *rotenburo*. This can be used by non-residents, for a fee. The hotel is closed in winter. **Shiretoko Iwaobetsu Youth Hostel**, ℭ 01522 4 2311 (*cheap*), is opposite the bus stop. It is closed Nov–May. This is the nerve centre of hiking in Shiretoko, with excellent food and rental bikes available.

Utoro

Shiretoko Grand Hotel, ℭ 01522 4 2021 (*moderate*), is an old *onsen* hotel. **Shiretoko Youth Hostel**, ℭ 01522 4 2034 (*cheap*), is closed Nov–April. It enjoys a central location, but no food is served.

Rausu

Rausu Youth Hostel, ℭ 01538 7 2145 (*cheap*), is a basic hostel on the seafront.

The Kurile Islands (Chishima)

In theory, the Pacific War, which climaxed in August 1945 with the atomic bombings of Hiroshima and Nagasaki and the Red Army's invasion of northern Japan, has never ended. No peace treaty was ever signed with the Soviet Union or any of its successor states. The reasons for this state of affairs lie a few miles off the coast of eastern Hokkaidō and, even in poor conditions, you can see them quite clearly.

The **Kuriles** (called the Northern Territories by the Japanese, or *Chishima*, 'the Thousand Islands') are a necklace of 30 or so islands, many of them no more than seaweed-strewn outcrops of rock, which stretch between Hokkaidō and the Russian peninsula of Kamchatka. Japan claimed the southern Kuriles in 1855, and in 1875 the whole chain was ceded to the shogunate by the tsar. But after the end of the war in 1945, the Soviet forces refused to withdraw. The Japanese inhabitants were deported, Russians were imported in their place, and all communication across the narrow Nemuro Straits was forbidden.

In the 1960s, when Japan's recovery seemed to have put sufficient distance between it and memories of the war, successive prime ministers began to press, always unsuccessfully, for the return of the southern four islands: Kunashiri and Etorofu, and the smaller Shikotan and Habomai. The 'Northern Territories problem' became an obsessive concern of Japanese foreign policy, and a focus for nationalist grievance. The blaring black loud-speaker vans driven by demonstrating ultra-nationalists often sport flags bearing a map of the disputed region. Even conventional Japanese maps include them as part of Japanese territory, even though no towns or geographical features are marked, and very few Japanese have ever set foot there.

The islands themselves are desolate: rock, seaweed and bleak, beautiful Siberian flora and fauna. The infra-structure is chronically underdeveloped: there are no hotels, no civilian airport and all journeys to the mainland have to be made by sea, via the Russian island of Sakhalin. The inhabitants, many of them the children of Russians 'settled' in the Far East by Stalin, make an unsteady living as fishermen and in canning factories. But Russia tenaciously holds on to the islands, for understandable reasons.

The Kuriles are potentially rich in several ways. For a start, they are believed to contain rich mineral resources and oil which, with improved communications, could make a rich frontier out of the region. Secondly, they are strategically crucial to Russia's defence of its eastern flank. With control of the Kuriles, the Sea of Okhotsk becomes a private Russian lake. Throughout the Cold War, large garrisons were stationed there, mere kilometres from Japan's northern shores. The Soviet navy and airforce had bases all over Sakhalin and Kamchatka, although present strengths are harder to determine. When the Korean Airliner was shot down between Sakhalin and Hokkaidō in 1983, the attacking planes came from this region, and there are still occasional spats between Russian gunboats and Japanese fishermen who have strayed just a little too close. Various initiatives have been attempted to resolve the dispute but, even with the end of communism, a settlement is still a long way away.

In the present state of uncertainty, it would be virtually unthinkable for a leader in Moscow to be seen to cede Russian territory, although the promise of Japanese aid and investment is a tempting carrot. Tokyo, too, has locked itself into an attitude of uncompromising insistence on unconditional return of the islands. The ultimate Japanese nightmare of columns of Soviet troops advancing on lonely Hokkaidō has receded. But it will be a long time before visitors can do more than stand on the shore, stare across, and wonder.

Akan National Park

Based around three lakes, this is the least interesting of Hokkaidō's major national parks, with a scarcity of hiking trails and an abundance of identical souvenir shops selling identical 'Ainu' carvings. It's slick, expensive and superficial—ideally suited to the Japanese tour parties who whizz through on their coaches. Regular bus links make it possible to see all there is to see of Kussharo-ko and Mashū-ko in half a day, ending up in Akan for the evening Ainu show which is tacky but entertaining.

The main points of access to the park are **Kushiro** to the south, and **Abashiri** and **Shari** to the north.

The JR **trains** between Shari and Kushiro stop at **Kawayu station** (a bus ride from Lake Kussharo and Lake Mashū), and **Teshikaga** (for Lake Akan). **Bihoro**, on the JR line south of Abashiri, also has bus connections with all the lake areas.

The most useful **bus** services are as follows (frequency depends on the season—check timetables):

From **Bihoro**, stopping at Wakoto Onsen and Kawayu Onsen, both on Lake Kussharo. Continuing on to Lake Mashū, before stopping at Teshikaga and terminating in Akan Kohan on Lake Akan.

A second service begins in **Kushiro** and stops in Teshikaga, reaching Kawayu Onsen, by Lake Kussharo, in about 2hrs 25mins.

Many buses are air-conditioned, with a taped tour commentary, but they can be treated just like scheduled services: get off when you like, pay for the journey so far, and hop on the next one that comes along.

Kussharo-ko (Lake Kussharo)

Kawayu station is an unmanned halt by a cluster of inns and coffee shops, overlooked by a smoking mountain peak. **Kawayu Onsen**, where the bus terminal, information office, and most of the hotels and amenities are located, is 3km away. The bus stop is just in front of the station; there are six services a day until about 5.30pm, and the journey takes 10 minutes.

So long as the smell of sulphur doesn't turn you off, the town is pleasant enough, with open beds of steaming volcanic gravel among the woods and roads. The **bus terminal** is behind a veil of trees; walk south to the traffic lights, turn left in front of the post office, and a few hundred metres on the left is the helpful **tourist information hut**.

The source of the rotten egg smells is **Iō-zan** (Sulphur Mountain), the peak visible from the station, accessible either by bus or by a 1-hour walk from Kawayu Onsen. There's an obnoxious souvenir mall in the car park near the summit, but even this can't snuff out the mystery and menace of the place. Much of the weirdness comes from the clashing natural colours: the pinkish rock, green foliage, white smoke and the canary yellow of the sulphur crystals which have formed around the lips of the fumaroles which puncture the mountain side. Below the summit (which you can approach, but not reach) two gulleys are constantly shrouded in billows of pungent smoke.

Every morning between 10 June and 10 September, local volunteers lead hikers across the meadows and up to Iō-zan. Meet in front of the Kawayu Onsen post office at 5.30am.

Lake Kussharo itself is a few miles further down the road; buses stop briefly at several points along its east and south shores. It's no Loch Ness (though this hasn't stopped some feeble-minded local tourism *apparatchik* inventing a lake monster—'Kusshie'—to go with the lake), and there is little here to linger for. The first stop, **Nibushi**, has a friendly *minshuku.* **Sunayu** is a heavily touristed beach with restaurants, souvenir shops and boats for hire. Kitsch enthusiasts can pay to don Ainu garb and be photographed amid a tableau of stuffed bear, deer and foxes. The name of this beach means 'hot water sand'; sure enough, a hole dug here fills up with naturally warm water. The last stop of any interest is **Wakoto Hantō**, a jutting spit of land formed when a small volcano (now extinct) emerged from the lake and joined itself to the mainland. There's a campsite, and a gentle nature trail with two small and exceedingly hot *rotenburo* on the water's edge.

Mashū-ko (Lake Mashū)

This perfect caldera lake is reached from Kawayu by a road which sometimes closes in winter. It hairpins drastically as you reach the top, and the bus pauses at two observation points. Below, almost always shrouded by tufts of low mist, is the second clearest lake in the world, after Russia's Lake Baikal. It still looks like the mouth of a volcano, with steeply sloping sides and a maximum depth of 211m. In the middle is a tiny fortress-like island: Kamuishu, the abode of Ainu gods.

Akan-ko (Lake Akan)

Akan Kohan (Akan Lakeside) is the only town in the National Park worth spending the night in. The main attraction is revealed at sundown when a loud-speaker van cruises the streets, shattering the mountain calm with announcements in Japanese and a hideous recording of what sounds like a Jew's harp. It's advertising nightly performances (in season) at the **Ainu Kotan** (Ainu Village), the remnants of what used to be one of the island's biggest Ainu communities. There are 200 individuals of Ainu descent living here in 36 families, almost all of them of mixed blood. Their *kotan* is actually less of a village and more of a shopping arcade—two dozen near-identical souvenir shops and a couple of noodle stands—although many proprietors also live above their businesses. Most of the merchandise is cheerful tat: carved foxes, eagles, phallus-headed Shinto deities and bears hugging whisky bottles. Genuine traditional objects—like the streamers of wood shavings used in the old religious ceremonies—are hard to come by because they don't have mass appeal. Don't expect much. Of authentic Ainu culture there is little trace left here.

At the top end of the street, though, is the **Ainu Chise**, a lovely thatched hall where the performances (*adm ¥1000*) take place. The dancers themselves are beautifully dressed in ankle-length cotton robes and small round hats for the women, and a knee-length coat and leggings for the single man. He does a sword dance; the other performances are lively and light-hearted, accompanied by clapping, singing or by the twanging *mukkuri* (Jew's harp), a bamboo object held in the mouth and vibrated by jerking a piece of attached string back and forth to produce a throbbing, almost electronic sound. Even though the language is incomprehensible, the dances are plainly inspired by nature: the women whoop and flap their coats like birds; an old lady gives a humorous impersonation of a horse or cow. Authentic or not, they are interesting and entertaining. Next door to the theatre hall is a small **museum** room with open hearth, blackened beams and displays of clothing, swords, bows and whittled sticks.

The **tourist information centre** is over a little square to the right of the bus terminal.

Where to Stay

Kawayu Spa has plenty of resort *ryokan*, but the more interesting places are out of town, along the shores of Lake Kussharo. The **Misono Hotel**, ✆ 01548 3 2511 (*expensive*) and **Wagaya Minshuku**, ✆ 01548 3 2989 (*cheap*) are both central, the former smart and pricey, the latter informal and reasonable. If you miss the last bus into town from the station, **Hotel Park Way**, 01548 3 2616 (*inexpensive*), is a simple and unpretentious Japanese-style place with its own *rotenburo*.

Nibushi no Sato, ✆ 01548 3 2294 (*cheap*), is a *minshuku* with a friendly, English-speaking proprietor on the lakeside, close to town. At the next bus stop, Sunayu, there is a **campsite**, and **Pension Pipirio**, ✆ 01548 4 2201 (*inexpensive*). Wakoto has another **campsite** and a number of grotty *minshuku*; **Sanko Onsen**, ✆ 01548 4 2140 (*cheap*), is one of the better ones.

In **Akan Kohan** there is a row of ugly modern hotels along the lakefront; the **Hotel Ichikawa**, ✆ 0154 67 2011 (*moderate*), is less impersonal than most; in the middle of the range is the **Akan Park Inn**, ✆ 0154 67 3211 (*inexpensive*); *minshuku* include **Rakuten**, ✆ 0154 67 2003 (*cheap*). **Akan Angel Youth Hostel**, ✆ 0154 67 2309, offers a free shuttle service to and from the station, and discount coupons on the Ainu show and souvenir shops.

Central Hokkaidō

Daisetsu-zan National Park

Japan's biggest national park is also one of the country's few near wilderness areas, a sparsely inhabited cluster of contour lines at the centre of the map, where two of Japan's longest rivers, the Ishikari and the Tokachi, rise from their sources. At its heart are a cluster of peaks, not particularly high (the biggest, Asahi-dake, is 2290m), but spread over a wide enough area to allow continuous hiking expeditions of a week long. On the right paths, at the right time of year, you could still walk for hours without meeting anyone, but there are enough chair-lifts and buses to make the brilliant views accessible to the less energetic. The little-visited, southern part of the park is even emptier and can only be fully explored by driving or hitch-hiking.

Getting There and Around

Most visitors approach Daisetsu-zan from the north or west.

For the northern part of the park, **Asahikawa**, the main transport hub for central Hokkaidō, will be your point of transit. From here, roads and railways lead to **Kamikawa**, and the buses go on to **Sōunkyō Onsen** where lifts and paths lead into the mountains.

For the western approach you can also start from **Asahikawa**, where buses depart for **Tenninkyō** and **Asahi-dake** which both have trail heads and (from Asahidake) a mountain lift. **Furano**, to the south of Asahikawa, has access to **Shirogane Onsen** and **Tokachi-dake** where the westernmost paths to the interior begin.

You could also begin in the south by travelling to the town of **Obihiro** which has a train link with Sapporo. From there you could take a bus to **Nukabira Onsen**. Little-used mountain trails begin here, and you can drive or hitch-hike (there are no buses) up highways 273 and 39 to **Sōunkyō Onsen** where civilization begins again.

By **train**, Kamikawa and Furano are the closest you can get to the national park.

Buses go to most of the places described below, except between Sōunkyō Onsen and Nukabira. Services vary with the season; assume that they are infrequent and start early to avoid unnecessary hanging around. **Driving** is the easiest option; **hitch-hiking** is also a good way of getting around, although in parts of the park traffic is thin.

Asahikawa

Asahikawa is a dull, flat city with road and rail connections to every part of Hokkaidō. The **bus** situation is confusing because several companies offer services from different bus stops. Facing the train station, and a little to the right as you exit it, is the office of the Dōhoku Bus company which serves **Kamikawa** and **Sōunkyō Onsen**. Just round the corner from here the Asahikawa Denkikido company departs for **Asahi-dake** and **Tenninkyō**. For buses to other cities, check with the station **tourist information desk**.

There's an **Ainu Kinenkan** (Memorial Hall) on the outskirts of Asahikawa (inconveniently distant from the station; take a taxi) with a good collection of relics in a thatched *chise* hut: photographs of long-departed Ainu chieftains, intricately carved arrows, figures fashioned out of ribbons of wood shavings, as well as the usual taxidermy.

Sōunkyō Onsen

Bus or train to Kamikawa, then bus. The Visitors' Centre has guide maps.

This small cluster of car parks and hot spring hotels is in a thrilling setting, at the bottom of a deep gorge surrounded by raw cliffs. This is the gorge of the Ishikari River, the second longest in Japan, and the road from Kamikawa continues past the town to a dam very near its source. Along the way are spectacular rock formations which are one of the town's attractions. In the absence of a car, you could take a taxi to the car park/souvenir centre at Ōbako and walk or cycle back on a hired bike (the hire shop has another branch in Sōunkyō Onsen). **Ōbako** (Big Box), is named after the point where the river makes a narrow passageway past an angular cliff face, planed into geometric lines by the elements; its counterpart, **Kobako** (Little Box) is further on. All the way along there are waterfalls and fantastic crystalline formations with fanciful nicknames like Princess Rock and Candlestick Rock. The path is heavily protected from above by wire mesh, and there's evidence of rock falls and mud slides all the way along.

Back in the town itself there's not much to do other than rise above it. There's a small museum with examples of the local fauna stuffed or pinned behind glass cases, but the main point of coming here is the **ropeway station** next door. Cable cars go half way up in about 8 minutes, then a chair lift (15 minutes) connects to the upper slopes of **Kuro-dake** (Black Mountain); paths also go all the way up. The view is epic, especially at sunset and during the autumn, and in winter there is skiing. From here you can start on any number of mountain hikes.

Asahidake Onsen

By bus from Asahikawa.

Asahidake is even smaller than Sōunkyō, but the view from the top of the mountain is, if anything, more dramatic. The **ropeway** carries you to a plateau on the 1800m level of the 2290m **Asahi-dake** mountain. There's a restaurant by the uppermost cable car station, and a pleasant 40-minute walk around a small caldera lake for those who can't face the climb to the summit—about 3 hours there and back. The mountainside is spectacularly beautiful: in summer it's a field of white alpine flowers, in winter, flaming autumn colours. Below, the other Daisetsu-zan mountains recede to the horizon. There's a big notice with the usual warnings about bears, and even if you don't bump into one of these (the chances are thousands to one against), you'll certainly see the dauntless little **red foxes** (*kita kitsune*) and perhaps the *nakiusagi* or **crying rabbit**, a mouse-like Siberian rodent. At the highest point of the short trail, two sulphurous vents belch fumes; nearby there's a Peace Bell and a simple mountain hut, one of many dotted all over the mountains for the use of benighted climbers.

Tenninkyō Onsen is an even smaller and less-touristed version of Sōunkyō, with the same towering, geometrically chiselled cliffs, and a waterfall said to resemble angel's wings, the meaning of its name. The buses go on here after dropping passengers off at Asahidake; the two villages are on different forks of the same road. A **hiking path** links the two, not steep, but passing through dense and sometimes marshy mixed forest. The walk takes about 2hrs, and just before Tenninkyō it descends steeply and dramatically into the gorge—tricky in wet weather.

Hiking

A great web of trails criss-crosses the Daisetsuzan National Park, linking Sōunkyō, Aizankei, Asahidake, Tenninkyō and Nukabira Onsens. In theory it would be possible to spend several days out there, hopping from peak to peak and sleeping in the simple mountain huts which are maintained during the climbing season.

Long-range treks such as these require careful planning and preparation, specialized maps, equipment and stores, and a professional appraisal of weather and trail conditions. A detailed account is beyond the scope of this guide, but *Hiking in Japan* by Paul Hunt (Kodansha) contains a good section on Daisetsuzan; pick this up in a big city book shop before you leave. The Visitors' Centres and Park Rangers' offices in trailhead towns like Sōunkyō can give you the best, up-to-the-minute advice, though not necessarily in English.

For this, and for much else, consult the staff of the local youth hostel who often organize, and even lead, groups of hikers up the more difficult trails.

Where to Stay

Charges in the grander *ryokan* often increase in the peak season.

Sōunkyō Onsen

Sōunkaku Grand Hotel, ✆ 01658 5 3111 (*expensive*), has its own *rotenburo* open air bath. **Minshuku Kitagawa,** ✆ 01658 5 3515, is *inexpensive*. **Ginsenkaku Youth Hostel,** ✆ 01658 5 3003, is *cheap*.

Asahidake

Ezo Matsu-sō, ✆ 0166 97 2321 (*moderate*), is a big resort hotel. The shop in the lobby has a good selection of hiking maps. **Daisetsuzan Shirakaba-sō,** ✆ 0166 97 2246 (*cheap*), is an excellent hostel with its own *onsen*. It can be booked through the Welcome Inn service.

Tenninkyō

Tenninkaku, ✆ 0166 97 2111, is a *moderate* and pleasant *ryokan*. **Hotel Shikishima-sō,** ✆ 0166 97 214, is *inexpensive* to *expensive*. There is no youth hostel.

Asahikawa

Asahikawa has plenty of business and city hotels for those whose connections prevent them staying somewhere more interesting. Enquire at the station information desk, or try the **New Hokkai Hotel,** ✆ 0166 24 3111 (*moderate*), the **Asahikawa Terminal Hotel,** ✆ 0166 24 0111 (*inexpensive*), or the **Asahikawa Youth Hostel,** ✆ 0166 61 2751 (*cheap*).

Eating Out

Asahikawa has the usual selection of Japanese and Western-style restaurants around the station, but in the village and at the trailheads you are limited to a few noodle restaurants, most of which close early in the evening. Eat at your lodgings, or buy a picnic.

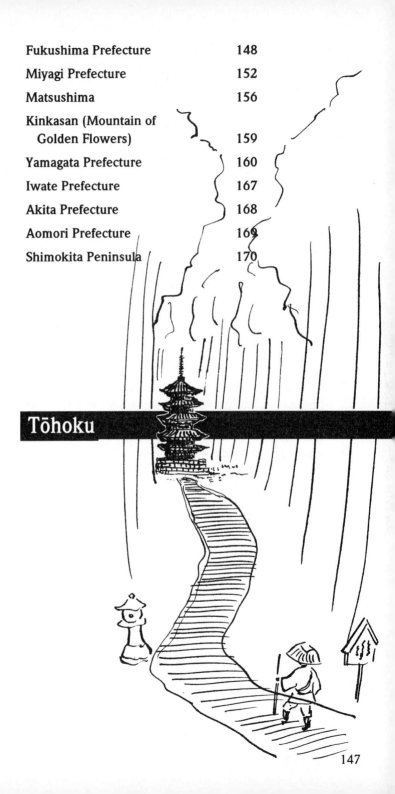

Tōhoku

Here I am, in the second year of Genroku, suddenly taking it into my head to make a long journey to the far northern provinces. I might as well be going to the ends of the earth.

Matsuo Bashō, *The Narrow Road to the Deep North*, 1689

Since the famous *haiku* poet Bashō made his lonely pilgrimage in 1689, plenty has changed in Tōhoku, the collective term for the six prefectures at the northern end of Honshū island. Today Tōhoku has its fair share of post-war drabness—faceless modern cities, concrete expressways and industry. The *shinkansen* from Tokyo penetrates as far north as Morioka, and what took Bashō five months on foot in 1689 could now be done inside a week, even on public transport. (Around the tricentenary of the poet's journey, in 1989, travel companies started offering 'Bashō Tours' of the famous route, in high-speed, air-conditioned buses.) But for all the superficial signs of modernity, Tōhoku has resisted homogenization far better than other parts of the country. In part, this is due to its mountainous terrain and harsh, snowy winters, which make much of it satisfyingly inaccessible even today. For modern Japanese, it's a remote, magical, faintly melancholy place, of thick dialects and quaint conservatism, a symbol of the rural homeland that, for city dwellers, is no more than a nostalgic folk memory.

For foreigners, especially those with limited time, it may not be a natural first choice. The conventional reasons for coming to Japan—the grandest temples and shrines, the finest museums, and the liveliest cities—are all south of here. Tōhoku's charm is in its atmosphere and natural beauty, which unfold slowly in hot springs, mountain pilgrimages, volcanic lakes and small, ambling towns and villages with subtle local folk crafts. It's also a repository of those surreal oddities unimaginatively ironed out in more respectable parts of the country: the blind witches of Osore-zan, mouth of the Buddhist underworld; the pyjama-wearing mountain holy men of Dewa, the noodle-slurping contests of Morioka. Wrap up warm, plan your trains in advance (better still, hire a car), don't expect a lot of English speakers, pack a copy of Bashō and remember the concluding words of his gentle book: 'As we turn the corners of the narrow road to the deep north, we may soar with exhilaration, or we may fall flat on our faces, doubled up by the suffering in our hearts.'

Fukushima Prefecture: Aizu-Wakamatsu

Aizu-Wakamatsu is a medium-sized country town with a reconstructed castle, a preserved samurai manor house, a small garden and various interesting remnants of the feudal era (it escaped bombing during the war). Its greatest claim to fame, however, is based on a more recent historical cult, one of those blithe celebrations of fanaticism which still give mild reason to worry about contemporary Japan.

The castle was built here in 1384 by the Aizu family, and passed through the hands of several clans before being entrusted in 1644 to the powerful Matsudaira, stalwart allies of the Tokugawa shoguns. The ninth lord, Katamori, was a son of the shogun, adopted by the Matsudaira at the age of 18, and in the 1860s he led an army of Aizu samurai to save Kyoto from an anti-Tokugawa rebellion. Their adversaries in this battle were the Chōshū clan of western Japan, who by 1868 had won the struggle to restore the lapsed powers of the Meiji Emperor. The shogunal forces held out in a series of straggling battles, the so-called Bōshin War, and in 1868 the Matsudaira and their *daimyō* (lord) were defeated after a long siege of Aizu. Katamori himself survived defeat to become a priest at the Tokugawas' Nikkō mausoleum. But it was during this famous last stand that the legend of the *Byakkotai*, 'White Tigers', was born.

Getting There and Around

JR **trains** of various speeds connect with Aizu-Wakamatsu—from Koriyama (on the *shinkansen* and regular JR line from Tokyo) and Niigata.

The principal places of interest are Iimori Hill, the Samurai Mansion, and the *Sake History Museum* (you could add the castle, although it's a modern concrete reconstruction). They're quite widely scattered and **walking** will prove tiring. Combine it instead with the loop line **buses** which serve most of the sites. **Bicycles** can be hired near the station.

Tourist Information

There's a **tourist information** booth near Aizu-Wakamatsu station which has an English map guide. English-speaking **Goodwill Guides** are based in the castle, Tsuruga-jō; you can call them on ✆ 0242 29 1151.

Iimori-yama (Iimori Hill)

In the final battle for Aizu-Wakamatsu, young locals of both sexes organized themselves into cadres of volunteers and fought for their lord against the invading Restoration forces. Among them was the *Byakkotai*, the 'League of the White Tigers', who suffered heavy losses in fighting just outside the town. The 20 survivors escaped by crawling along a drainage ditch up to this small hill. Peering down, they saw smoke apparently billowing from the castle. Believing that the battle was lost, the youths committed suicide on the spot by cutting their own throats and by ritual disembowelment. One alone was saved from bleeding to death and survived to learn the humiliating truth that the *Byakkotai* had died completely in vain. The castle was not in danger at all (the surrender didn't come for weeks and it was food shortages that caused it, not flames). The smoke that the White Tigers had seen came from small house fires below the castle.

Of course heroic suicides, even (especially) pointless ones, occupy an elevated place in Japanese history and art to the present day, and the dead volunteers quickly became legends. But two things make the White Tiger incident peculiarly pointless and unappealing. The first is that the man in whose name the *Byakkotai* died, their *daimyō* Matsudaira Katamori, showed no such reverence for samurai ethics, as his subsequent career showed: at the fag end of the feudal era, the boys' deaths were, as much as anything, a naively old-fashioned reaction to events. The second is the White Tigers' age: they were none of them more than 17 years old, former students at a famous school of samurai ethics.

Rather than being sheepish or regretful about this massacre of innocents, the town of Aizu celebrates the event with a barely concealed cheerfulness. From tragic symbols of wrong-headed fanaticism, the *Byakkotai* are transformed into icons of cutesiness. The souvenir shops on the steps up the hill overflow with *Byakkotai* souvenirs. There are White Tiger mugs, banners, fans, curtains, pictures, lanterns, swords and cushions, all bearing cartoons of dinky little samurai, their fringes flopping over their head bands, looking deliciously determined as they wield their toy swords. More worrying are illustrated accounts of the sad tale intended to inspire the young successor to the White Tigers. They don't, needless to say, dwell much on the nastier details of *seppuku*: cartoon characters with their guts spilling out might distract from the moral lesson being inculcated here. The character of that morality is perhaps indicated by two monuments erected by foreign admirers of the *Byakkotai* close to their graves. The first, a block of black granite bearing a black Nazi cross, was donated by the German military attaché in 1938. Beyond it, a Roman eagle stands atop a marble column from the ruins of Pompeii. The Italian inscription is dated 1928 and is translated thus: 'Rome, the birthplace of civilization, sends this Fascist Party symbol with an ancient column, symbol of undying greatness, to honour the young warriors of the *Byakkotai*'. The monuments were removed during the American Occupation, but resurfaced during the 1950s.

For those short of puff, the long flight of steps has been supplemented by an escalator for which you must pay. The *Byakkotai* themselves rest in a kind of secular shrine, reached through a pair of pillars to the left of the stairs. A row of rectangular stones bears the names of the boys. Visitors offer money, incense and even prayers at this dubious chapel.

Lower down are a couple of jumbled old museums, the **Byakkotai Kinen-kan**, a memorial museum (*open April–Nov, 8–5; Dec–Mar, 8.30–4.30; adm ¥400*), and the **Byakkotai Denshō-shigakkan**, a historical museum (*open 8–5; adm ¥300*), both containing photos of distinguished Aizuites, plus weapons and bric-a-brac from the period of the Bōshin War.

Also on Iimori-yama is the **Sazae-dō** (*open 8–sunset; adm ¥250*), an ingenious building, unique in Japanese architecture. The name, meaning 'Hall of the Spiral Shell', is explained when you go inside. It is 60m high and appears to be a kind of Buddhist fun house, with a covered slide sloping around the outside. This is actually a steep walkway which spirals up the building and then down again on a quite separate track. Thus, in passing through one never revisits the same spot; the sensation is of being inside Dr Who's Tardis, with an impossible amount of space squeezed inside a small structure—like the shell of the *sazae* shellfish (*Turbo cornutus*). The Sazae-dō was built in 1796 as a representation of the pilgrimage of the 33 Kannon temples in the Kansai area. Within are 33 statues of Kannon *bosatsu*. In passing up the Sazae-dō and down again, one is considered to have symbolically completed the entire pilgrimage.

Buke Yashiki (Samurai Mansion)

The road from Iimori-yama passes close to the **Oyaku-en** or Physic Garden (*open 8–5; in winter 8.30–4.30; adm ¥300*), an attractive stroll garden, the private resort of the Matsudaira *daimyō*, built around a pond with an island tea house. Three hundred different herbs are grown here; remedies made from them are sold in the souvenir shop.

Signposts point the way to the **Buke Yashiki** (*open 8.30–5; Dec–Mar, 9–4.30; adm ¥800*), a few minutes' walk to the south. This former estate of Saigō Tanomo, chief retainer of Matsudaira Katamori, burned during the Bōshin Wars, but has been beautifully reconstructed out of traditional materials.

At the ticket booth you are handed an English guide map. Trace your way through the square gate (where a drummer beats a welcome) to the **Karo-yashiki**, the residence of the Saigō chieftain. It contains a total of 13 rooms: servants and guards lived here, as well as the chief retainer and his family. The **Onari-no-ma** was the principal guest room; a detached section just off it was reserved for the visits of the Matsudaira *daimyō* alone. At the back is a small annex on stilts, below which, from the outside, you can see a sand-filled cart on rails. This was the *kawaya*, a lavatory for the exclusive use of the visiting lord. As the English sign explains: 'The cart was filled with sand in order to separate the excretions for health advisors to examine'. As in all feudal houses, the layout embodies the social distinctions of the time: a room for everyone, and everyone in their room. There is a **tea room** (*cha-shitsu*), and separate rooms reserved for official messengers, guards, chief maidservant, lesser maidservants, married retainers, unmarried retainers, grandmother and daughters, wife, younger sons, eldest son, and finally the chief retainer himself. The **Tsugi-no-ma** was the family living room. Here, on 23 August 1868, while Saigō was holed up in Tsuruga Castle, his wife and daughters, aged two to 13 years old, killed themselves to prevent being captured as hostages. One 16-year-old daughter, Taeko, lingered on to be dispatched by one of the victorious soldiers.

Beyond the impressive **rice mill** (a huge hydraulic wheel powers 16 rice-pounding columns) is a black and white *kura* store house containing a museum which details the migration of the Aizu clan after their defeat. A large **kitchen** contains equipment for catering to the large numbers of people connected with the house.

Outside the main residence is a *jinya*, or magistrate's house, moved here from Nakahata, a nearby village. As well as overpriced restaurants and souvenir shops, there's also a **sericulturalist's house** where silk worms were raised, a museum of lacquerware (a characteristic craft of the area), and a shop selling the produce of another local industry: household Buddhist altars.

Tsuruga-jō (Tsuruga Castle)

Open 8.30–5; adm ¥310.

The old park, moat and outer stone foundations of this once great fortress are originals, but the keep is a 1960s reconstruction: if you've already seen a Japanese castle, there's no particular reason to visit here. More worthwhile is the nearby **Fukushima Kenritsu**

Hakubutsukan, Fukushima Prefectural Museum (*open 9.30–5; adm ¥450*), a well laid-out survey of the life and times of the area, including its well-documented prehistory. North of the castle is the **Aizu Shuzō Rekishi-kan**, *Sake* History Museum (*open 8.30–5, 9.30–4.30 in winter; adm ¥300*), devoted to the art of the *toji* or *sake* brewer. 'They love rice deeply and brew *sake* tenderly like they raise their own children,' the pamphlet explains, and the museum amply demonstrates the complexity of the traditional nine-stage brewing process. The rice is first polished (three or four times more than rice for eating), then washed, soaked and steamed into a mash which is seeded with mould spores. After lengthy admixtures and filtrations, *sake* and (from the dregs) *shōchū* is squeezed out and pasteurised. After your tour you will be served free samples in the museum shop, which is decorated with signed photographs of *sake*-tippling celebrities. Novelty brews on sale include *Oni-goroshi*, 'Demon-killer' (for ¥2500 a bottle) and a *sake* made from melted Antarctic icebergs.

Where to Stay

The usual business hotels cluster round the station: try the *inexpensive* **Green Hotel**, ✆ 0242 24 5181. **Tagoto Ryokan**, ✆ 0242 24 9182, is recommended for its home cooking, served around a smoking hearth (*inexpensive*). The *cheap* **Aizu no Sato Youth Hostel**, ✆ 0241 27 2054, is actually closer to Shiokawa station, a few minutes north of Aizu Wakamatsu.

Eating Out

Aizu-Wakamatsu's two most famous restaurants, both serving traditional country cooking in antique premises, are close by one another between the station and the castle. Ask any taxi driver for **Takino**, which specializes in *wappa-meshi*: fragrant herb rice served in a wooden box and topped with vegetables, fish or poultry. **Ebiya**, two blocks north, serves *unagi*, delicious broiled eel. Both are *moderate*.

Miyagi Prefecture: Sendai

With a population of 910,000, Sendai is Japan's twelfth largest city, and the unofficial capital of Tōhoku. In the 17th century, a famous feudal *daimyō* named Date Masamune (1567–1636), the 'One-eyed Dragon', ruled from Sendai castle. A great diplomat and a patron of the arts and Christianity, he left impressive monuments, many of them destroyed by incendiary bombing in 1945. There's nothing especially thrilling to do here, but half a day can be pleasantly spent visiting the museums and the ruined hill-top castle.

Getting There

Sendai is a key stop on the Tōhoku *shinkansen*. From Tokyo station it takes 2hrs and costs just over ¥10,000; there are cheaper regular services, but they take between 4½ and 6hrs. Cross-country lines also link the city with Niigata and the Japan Sea.

The **bus** is almost half the price of the *shinkansen* but takes 5hrs (7½hrs for the night bus). It leaves from the Yaesu-guchi side of Tokyo station; ask at the tourist information centre for up-to-date departure times and details of how to make the necessary reservation.

Getting Around and Tourist Information

The station is at the east end of the town centre and most of the sights are in the west, across the Hirose River. A tangle of pedestrian overpasses traverses the station plaza; **Aoba-dōri** is the main east–west drag, location of banks, department stores and hotels. Keep walking west along it and you will eventually cross the **Ōhashi** (Big Bridge); the City Museum and castle hill are a bit further along, on the left.

Getting from here to the other sights is a bit of a problem, however. **Buses** serve all of them but they link only with the station, not with one another. Unless you're prepared to bus back to the terminal and then bus out again, you'll either have to **walk** (long distances) or take **taxis**. Sendai is, therefore, the kind of place where you might profit by taking an organized **bus tour**. The **subway** line is only of use to commuters.

The city **tourist information centre** is on the second floor of the station, at the back. Pick up an English map and pamphlets, and a useful sheet showing the destinations of the various buses and their points of departure from the station plaza.

The **Sendai International Centre** (Kokusai Sentā, ✆ 022 265 2211), opposite the City Museum, has a library, work room and information centre with a wide range of materials in English about Sendai and Japan.

Sendai City Museum (Shiritsu Hakubutsukan)

Open 9–4.45; adm ¥400. Bus from stand number 9 to Hakubutsukan-mae.

Thanks to good labelling and an informative English pamphlet, a turn round this smart museum greatly enhances a visit to the somewhat vague traces of Aoba Castle. After an account of the pre- and early history of the area, the second room contains relics of Sendai under the Date clan, including some extremely gruesome paintings of the rice famines which occurred at intervals during the Edo period. A ghastly exhibit, entitled 'Picture to Prevent the Murder of Newly Born Children', matches any Catholic imagery in its vision of sin and punishment. It consists of two halves. In the lower section, a pregnant woman writhes on a bed while various blood-spattered attendants perform an abortion; fragments of childish limbs lie in a basket below. In the upper half is a dream-bubble connected by a snake-like thread to the woman's ear. Four ghostly babies wielding clubs lurch towards her; behind them is a rabble of demons drawing a terrible fiery engine.

There are further displays on Aoba Castle (including a scale model), modern Sendai, and a small gallery of Date clan arms and armour. The most interesting room tells the story of **Hasekura Tsunenaga**, a local samurai who undertook one of the most heroic and ultimately pointless voyages in Japanese history. In 1613 Date Masamune dispatched

Hasekura on an extraordinary mission. He was to travel to Europe and personally deliver letters to the King of Spain and the Pope requesting more missionaries to be sent to Japan. Masamune's motives for this are obscure. He had come under the influence of a Spanish missionary, Luis Sotelo, and may have been moved by genuine religious feeling; equally, the pragmatic *daimyō* may have had his eye on future trade with Europe and Mexico. On 15 September, the small Spanish galleon *San Juan Baptista* sailed from the Ojika Peninsula. After traversing Mexico by land, and an eight-month crossing of the Atlantic, the mission presented itself before Philip III. On 17 February 1615, Hasekura was baptized Don Felipe Francisco Hasekura. Nine months later he was received by Pope Paul V and declared a citizen of the city of Rome. Trade talks with the Spanish were unsuccessful and Hasekura headed for home, after dropping Sotelo off in the Philippines. In 1620, seven years after beginning his journey around the world, he arrived back in Japan.

To his dismay, Hasekura was told that the situation had changed utterly. Not long after his departure, Shogun Tokugawa Hidetada (whose father, Ieyasu, had approved of the expedition) had outlawed Christianity and severed foreign relations. Date Masamune, above all a pragmatist, had lost all interest in the new faith. Hasekura refused to apostatize, but died in 1622, a disappointed man. Father Sotelo arrived back in the same year, and was immediately arrested. In 1624 he was burned alive in Nagasaki.

Aoba-yama (Green Leaves Hill)

This small hill, 132m high, is a natural fortress, with steep slopes to the west, the Hirose River to the east and north, and the Tatsu-no-kuchi (Devil's Mouth) Ravine to the south. Date Masamune finished his castle here in 1602, and it remained the clan headquarters until 1875 when the most important buildings were dismantled by order of the Meiji Government. The old Ōte-mon gate house burned in a 1945 air raid. Walls and a few monuments remain, but to get any sense of its past scale you need to look at the display in the City Museum.

The site of the castle, **Aoba-jō**, is reached by a steep road above the museum, and then a set of steps through a gun metal *torii* gateway. There's a bronze statue of Masamune surveying his domain, and an eagle on a plinth commemorating the Sino-Japanese war; the modern **Gokoku Shrine** is also dedicated to the war dead. The only original remnant—apart from the outer walls, entrenched deep in the side of the hill—is a **corner turret** (*sumi-yagura*). The **Aoba Castle Exhibition Hall** has craft demonstrations and a computer graphic display about the former keep, but it's basically a souvenir shop, and you may well share the sentiments of Doi Bansui (1871–1952) whose poem, *Moon Over The Ruined Castle*, is engraved on a nearby stone:

> *At cherry blossom parties in this keep*
> *Old pine trees caught the new light of the moon*
> *And cast it glittering on the sake cup:*
> *How can such brilliance have passed so soon?*

Ōsaki Hachiman Jinja

Open 9.30–4.30; adm free. Bus from stand number 10 in front of the station to Hachiman Jinja-mae.

This ancient shrine, Sendai's sole National Treasure, is positioned in the northwest of the city. From the City Museum area the only convenient option is a taxi. From the road you approach down a long gravel avenue lined with pines, cedars and lanterns. The earliest shrine was founded in 1100 by the Minamoto clan and moved here from its original site. The present buildings were raised by Date Masamune in 1607 and are strikingly well-preserved. Instead of the usual vermilion, the beams and woodwork are painted a lustrous black, and decorated, in typical Momoyama style, with carved dragons, phoenixes, elephants (looking more like sabre-toothed tigers), roosters and intricate foliage. Each face of the *hijiki* (elbow) joints beneath the eaves has been painted a different colour, and there is elaborate gilt metalwork on the doors, railings and beams. Dedicated to the god of war, Hachiman, a deification of the historical 3rd-century Emperor Ōjin, the shrine is one of the earliest surviving examples of the attractive *gongen* style of architecture: two parallel halls, inner and outer, are joined by a third roof which bisects them at a right angle.

Zuihō-den

Any bus from station stand 11 or 12 to Ōtamaya-bashi or Zuihō-den iriguchi.

Sendai suffered grimly from American bombing in 1945 (on 10 July alone, 124 B-29s dropped 912 tons of bombs); among the casualties was this old mausoleum of the Date lords in the grounds of the Zuihō-ji Zen temple. The hill on which it is situated is pleasant enough, but the mausoleum buildings are reconstructions, in the old Momoyama style, finished in 1979.

(✆ 022–)   ***Where to Stay***

The most convenient joint in town is the **Sendai Hotel**, ✆ 225 5171, opposite the station. Single rooms (there are Japanese suites as well as Western) begin in the *moderate* category and rise to the *expensive*. The nearby, *moderate* **Hotel Metropolitan Sendai**, ✆ 268 2525, is also handy and has a swimming pool and gym.

Aoba-dōri, the main avenue leading from the station plaza over the river to the museum and castle, has banks and shops and a couple of good city hotels, both *moderate*: the **Tōkyū Hotel**, ✆ 262 2411, and the **Washington Hotel**, ✆ 222 2111, with its two annexes.

For *inexpensive* business hotels, try the **Fuji Hotel**, ✆ 262 8711, south of Aoba-dōri, just before the Tōkyū Hotel; the **Hokke Club**, ✆ 224 3121, on Higashi Gobanchō-dōri; or the central **Hotel Universe**, ✆ 261 7711, on Higashi Ichibanchō-dōri.

The **Miyako Hotel**, ✆ 222 4647, is a centrally situated *ryokan* with a *moderate* room rate, including two meals. **Japanese Inn Aisaki**, ✆ 264 0700, a member of the Japanese Inn Group, is *inexpensive*, verging on the *cheap*, and has Western-style rooms as well as Japanese. It was founded in 1868, but the present building is concrete; it is a 12-minute walk from Sendai station.

The **Chitose Youth Hostel**, ℂ 222 6329 is about 20 minutes' walk north of the station, the opposite direction from the castle and sights.

Matsushima

The islands are situated in a bay about three miles wide in every direction and open to the sea through a narrow mouth on the southeast side. Tall islands point to the sky and level ones prostrate themselves before the surges of water. Islands are piled above islands, and islands are joined to islands, so that they look exactly like parents caressing their children or walking with them arm in arm. The pines are of the freshest green, and their branches are curved in exquisite lines, bent by the wind constantly blowing through them. Indeed, the beauty of the entire scene can only be compared to the most divinely endowed of female countenances, for who else could have created such beauty but the great god of nature himself? My pen strove in vain to equal this superb creation of divine artifice.

Matsuo Bashō, *The Narrow Road to the Deep North*, 1689
translated by Yuasa Nobuyuki

Bashō's famous description immortalized Matsushima, and sealed its fate. As one of Japan's official Three Most Beautiful Views, the famous bay suffers from the worst depredations of mass tourism, and a seeming absence of any town planning or building restrictions. The islands are still there (patched up in places with witlessly applied cement), but the shore of the most beautiful spot in the whole country of Japan is like every other tacky tourist town: concrete-walled buildings, rampant advertising hoardings, a thatch of power lines and even a smoking power station. Flocks of snap-happy tourists complete the degradation. Apart from the grand feudal temple of Zuigan-ji, an afternoon here would be far more pleasurably spent reading a translation of *The Narrow Road to the Deep North*. Image, in the case of Matsushima, infinitely surpasses reality.

Matsuo Bashō was born into a samurai family in 1644 and spent most of his life in Edo, where he became the leading poet of his age; today there is no Japanese who hasn't heard of him, or who can't recite a few of his most famous *haiku*, the tiny, delicate poems which Bashō established as the most famous of all Japanese forms.

He wrote a number of short accounts of his travels, but his most famous journey began on 27 March 1689. Its purpose was vague—he wasn't making a pilgrimage to any particular place, the usual excuse for a journey at a time when travel was strictly controlled, and even visits to the next-door province had to be sanctioned by the shogunate. Instead, he called on friends and fellow poets, and visited famous spots, most of which survive, more or less unchanged, even today. In Bashō's time the mountainous country, with few roads and few people, was about as dangerous as you could get. *Oku*, the word conventionally translated as 'the Deep North', means something more like 'the Back of Beyond'.

Above all, travel was an excuse to write poetry. *The Narrow Road* is studded with *haiku*, three-line poems of five, seven and five syllables. With so few words at his or her disposal, it's impossible for the *haiku* poet to tell a story or convey character. Instead, the aim is to catch a passing moment—of personal emotion, seasonal beauty, or a moment experienced at a particular place—and freeze it in words. The form suits Japanese, with its propensity for word plays and ambiguous homonyms, but it's notoriously difficult to translate and all too often ends up reading like captions to someone's holiday photos. There seem to be few happy *haiku*—the over-whelming emotion is one of sadness at the passing of time and beauty and the imminence of death. This, and the melancholy landscape through which he passed, suited Bashō's personality down to the ground. He was an endearingly gloomy sort of chap, never happier than when the rain was falling, his feet were hurting, and everything was going wrong.

Getting There

The JR Senseki Line **trains** go from Sendai direct to Matsushima Kaigan station in 40 minutes, but the classic route is to travel by rail to Shiogama (there's an attractive shrine nearby) and from there catch a **sightseeing boat** (about ¥1400 one way) across the bay to the town.

Shiogama Jinja (Salt Cauldron Shrine)

The shrine is about ten minutes' walk from both Shiogama and Hon-Shiogama stations. A flight of over 200 steps leads up to it, through a grey *torii* gateway flanked by a pair of huge lanterns.

Since ancient times this has been one of the most important shrines in Tōhoku. The first reference to it is in a chronicle of 820, by which time it was already well-established: the record states that the shrine was awarded 10,000 bales of rice by the imperial court and exempted from taxes. You can see at once why it was built here. On a clear day the view from the top stretches for miles out to sea, and it is as the patrons of sailors and fishermen (as well as expectant mothers) that the deities of Shiogama have principally been worshipped. Various votive offerings scattered about the grounds indicate the shrine's historical prestige: there's an **iron lantern** dated 1185, a tall copper one from 1807, and a stone **sundial** of 1792. The main shrine buildings date from 1704.

The nearby **museum** (*open 9–4.45; adm ¥200*) contains assorted relics of the old whaling and fishing industries and an upper floor display about salt extraction, including a crown and a windmill modelled entirely out of salt crystals.

Matsushima Bay

Shiogama Harbour is closest to Hon-Shiogama station on the JR Senseki Line, and from here the sightseeing boats cross the bay. In *The Narrow Road to the Deep North*, Bashō was so awe-struck by its beauty that he was left *haiku*-less. But a poem (probably apocryphal) does survive which eloquently dramatizes the inadequacy of mere words in the face of this marvel. It is the simplest *haiku* ever written:

> *Matsushima ya*
> *Ah, ah, Matsushima ya*
> *Matsushima ya*

which means exactly what you'd expect, *ya* being equivalent to 'Lo!' or '!'.

The islands *are* pretty, with their tiny caves, elegant natural bridges and fanciful poetic names—'Helmet Island', 'Bell Island', 'Hōrai Island' (named after the mythical abode of the gods). The problem is the hundreds of others crammed onto the boat, all gasping their admiration, and the incessant squeaking of the taped commentary.

There's a sightseeing **information booth** just in front of the jetty. To the right is a medium-sized islet connected to the shore by an arched vermilion bridge. On it is an attractive hall called the **Godai-dō**, built by Date Masamune in 1609, but it is opened only once every 33 years. Ask around if you are here in 2006 or 2039. Further away, to the left as you disembark, is **Ōshima** (Big Island), an ancient meditation spot, also served by a bridge, with Buddhist deities carved into the rock walls of the grottoes.

Closer at hand, left and a little behind the information booth, is the **Kanran-tei** (*open 8.30–5; adm ¥200*), a small tea house, presented by the great Toyotomi Hideyoshi, and assembled here so that Date Masamune and his guests could contemplate the waves while taking their tea. An attached **Matsushima Museum** contains Date relics including armour and a feudal toilet seat.

Zuigan-ji

Open 8 to between 3.30 and 5, depending on the season; adm ¥500.

The halls and courtyards of Zuigan-ji have a distinctly secular, almost martial, feel to them, closer to that of a fortified palace than a Buddhist temple. It was founded in 828 by the famous priest Ennin and known, in its early years, as Matsushima-dera. Four hundred years later it had fallen into decline. It was revived by the Zen sect under the name Enpuku-ji, and completely rebuilt by Date Masamune in 1609 from which period most of the present treasures date.

The temple is at the centre of Matsushima in a wooded glen, walled with steep cliffs. At one time six sub-temples stood on either side of the main avenue. To its right is a winding approach past a rock face, cut with caves and carved with worn reliefs in the shape of stupas and memorial tablets. The main compound is entered by the **Onari-mon** gate; opposite is the **Onari-genkan**, a formal entrance at the end of a zig-zagging corridor reserved for imperial and shogunal visitors. The warrior origins of this temple are most obvious in this courtyard, with its formidable walls, sturdy buildings forming an unbroken barrier on three sides, and watchtower. Two famous apricot trees—one pink, one white— are themselves war booty, brought back by Masamune from the bloody Korean invasion of 1593 and transplanted here.

The **Hon-dō** (Main Hall) has interior castle features, like the famous 'nightingale floorboards' which squeak to give away the presence of intruders, and hidden compartments for bodyguards.

The great beams of cedar and zelkova were transported from Mt Kumano, near Ōsaka. You enter the Hon-dō at the southeast corner and proceed clockwise along a magnificent wide corridor which fronts the most important rooms. All are richly decorated with Momoyama-period screen paintings of Chinese legends, trees, mountains, birds and wild animals—although a torch would help to cut through the sometimes dim illumination. First on the right is the **Taka-no-ma** (Hawk Room), with a famous self-congratulatory picture of hawks (representing the Date samurai) glaring hungrily down on herons and rabbits (the little people). The **Kujaku-no-ma** (Peacock Room) is the temple's spiritual centre: services are held on the plain wooden floor, and at the back is the altar room.

The temple's kitchens and living quarters are closed to the public, but in front of them is the **Seiryū-den**, now a **treasure house** containing art and religious objects, much of it endowed by the Date lords. There's a lifelike statue of the seated Masamune in full armour which clearly shows his wasted right eye, and a pair of candlesticks in Venetian glass, a gift from the Pope, brought back from Rome by the ill-fated Hasekura Tsunenaga.

Kinkasan (Mountain of Golden Flowers)

For the kind of unravaged beauty which once inspired Bashō, pass quickly through Matsushima for Kinkasan Island, an old gold mining settlement with an ancient shrine, varied walks, deer, monkeys and sea gulls, and mercifully little else.

Getting There

Ferries to Kinkasan are infrequent even in high season, and you should check departure times in advance in Sendai or Matsushima. Take the JR Senseki Line to Ishinomaki. You can take a boat from there (1hr 55mins) or catch a bus down the scenic Ojika Peninsula to Ayukawa, from where the ferry takes just half an hour.

The Island

The ferry terminal on the island has sketch maps in Japanese showing the roads and principal paths, but it's only 24km in circumference and easy to find your way around. The solitary harbour is on the west side. A rough road heads south about half way around the island, serving the lighthouse on the east (Pacific) side. There are a few *minshuku* along here, and the crumbling Kankō Hotel, abandoned in 1985.

To the north (left as you get off the ferry), the road climbs to the **Koganeyama Jinja**, a shrine founded in 749 by Emperor Shōmu who built Nara's Tōdai-ji temple. Shōmu needed gold for the temple's Great Buddha; when it was found here, he raised the shrine in gratitude to the local deities. It is still associated with gold and prosperity, and in the shrine resthouse you will see framed designs of Chinese characters, shrine gates and other patterns, formed with coins. Jingling strings of coins hang from the shrine buildings, and there are statues of Ebisu and Daikoku, the popular gods of wealth and business. The present main hall dates from the Edo period. Set among lantern-strewn, deer-grazed grounds, with tall pillars and copper roofs outlined against the steep wooded hillside behind, it's a mild and relaxing spot, satisfyingly secluded and informal.

Behind the shrine, to the right of the buildings, a rough path leads to the 445m summit of the island where the inner shrine, a simple wooden structure called **Owadatsumi Jinja**, stands, commanding superb views of the sea and coastline. It's only a couple of kilometres, but quite a climb: allow 45 minutes to get to the top. With an early start, you could climb down to the far side of the island which is virtually unvisited. There's a famous formation of flat coastal rocks here called the **Senjō-jiki**—'One Thousand *Tatami* Mats'.

Where to Stay

There are numerous little *minshuku* on the island (**Shiokaze** is a particularly friendly one), and the shrine has more luxurious accommodation for pilgrims (unfortunately the youth hostel has shut). However, a lot of places close during the off-season, and may get booked up at busy times. Make a booking before you arrive (from Sendai or Matsushima tourist offices) or enquire early at the ferry terminal.

There are a couple of rather poor tourist restaurants by the ferry terminal: you'd be better off dining in your *minshuku*.

Yamagata Prefecture

Dewa San-zan (The Three Mountains of Dewa)

The interior of Yamagata Prefecture is tricky to get to and slow to travel around, but, with its sacred mountain pilgrimage, mysterious holy men and desiccated mummies, it is one of the most intriguing areas of Tōhoku. You could visit the principal site on a day trip, but that would be a waste of all the time it takes to get there. Allow three days to absorb the atmosphere: visit the shrines, walk the pilgrimage, stay a couple of nights in a temple inn.

The *Yamabushi* and the Holy Mountains of Dewa

> *Forbidden to betray*
> *The secrets of Mt Yudono*
> *I drench my sleeves*
> *In a flood of reticent tears*
>
> Matsuo Bashō, *The Narrow Road to the Deep North*

> *The aim of the* yamabushi *is to take the spirit of the mountain into themselves. They live on the mountain, eat the mountain plants, breathe its air, drink its water, become one with it. They go to all the shrines of all the gods who live on the mountains and worship at each one. So the gods are content and ensure the peace and prosperity of Japan.*
>
> A *yamabushi* holy man, quoted by Lesley Downer in
> *On the Narrow Road to the Deep North*

The *yamabushi*—conch-honking, pantaloon-wearing holy men of the mountain—are a living relic of the old fusion of Buddhist and Shinto theology, effectively abolished by the 19th-century reformers of the Meiji Restoration. It's hard to tell how seriously the ascetic rites are practised today, but this remote mountain corner of Tōhoku is full of their traces and traditions and, at certain times of the year, their latter-day practitioners, dressed like characters from a Monty Python sketch, in straw sandals and blue-check pyjamas. Many of them, certainly, are weekend *yamabushi* who change back into salarymen on the bullet train journey home on Sunday night. In some ways the modern sect resembles Freemasonry, plus mountain-climbing; many of the rites are still as secret as when Bashō wrote the poem quoted above.

The *yamabushi* (the name means 'those who incline towards the mountains') are more correctly known as *Shugenja*, practitioners of *Shugendō*, a branch of Japanese religion associated with both the Shingon and Tendai sects of Buddhism, which seeks to combine their teachings with the native superstitions of Shinto. Its origins are murky, but *yamabushi* legend has it that the founder of the movement was an imperial prince named Nojo, nicknamed Hachiko ('Bee Child'), on account of his unfortunate facial resemblance to the winged insect. A famous picture of him, widely reproduced in museums and pamphlets about the area, shows him to be indeed an ugly, malevolent-looking chap with creased, swarthy skin, staring eyes and an evil smile.

Hachiko's father was Emperor Sushun, and he was born at a turbulent time in Japan's early history when the evangelists of Buddhism, newly introduced from the continent, were engaged in a power struggle with the proponents of Shinto. When his father was assassinated, Hachiko wisely fled the capital and made the dangerous sea journey north by the Japan Sea. Near Sado Island, his boat struck rocks and began to sink. Just off present-day Tsuruoka he was rescued by eight mysterious maidens and was able to land. Led inland by a mysterious black crow with three legs (images of this creature crop up frequently in the area) he came to Mt Haguro (which means 'Black Wings') and had a vision. The spirit of the mountain was, he learned, a *gongen* or avatar of the Buddha. In the Year of the Horse he founded a temple/shrine there (simultaneously Buddhist and Shintoist). In the Year of the Rabbit he did the same on Mt Gassan. And in the Year of the Cow he 'opened' Mt Yudono, the innermost and holiest of all.

Whatever the truth of this story, by the 9th century the area had become the centre of a syncretic mountain cult which was attracting ascetics from all over Japan. Kōbō Daishi and Dengyō Daishi, saintly founders of the Shingon and Tendai sects respectively, are said to have visited. During the troubled years of the 15th century, the pilgrimage around the three peaks became very popular. By 1745, around 38,000 worshippers a year were doing it and, at its height, there were 350 pilgrim temples on and around Mt Haguro. 'There are hundreds of houses where the priests practise religious rites with absolute severity,' said Bashō, declining to go into any detail about what those rites actually involved. 'Indeed the whole mountain is rich in miraculous inspiration and sacred awe. Its glory will never perish as long as man continues to live on the earth.'

Its glory took a tumble, nonetheless, in the late 19th century when the Meiji government, in its efforts to bolster its own authority and diminish that of the vanquished shogun, initiated a 'purification' programme of Shinto shrines, seeking to cleanse them of 'foreign' Buddhist influence. The monks and Buddha halls were removed from the mountains, although their influence clearly survives.

Yamabushi are immediately recognizable by their surreal uniforms. They wear checked blue and white tunics over white leggings and undergarments, and carry staves. On their heads they wear tiny black hats, like felt margarine tubs, held in place with a black cord, but their most characteristic accessory is the large conch horn (emitting a low mournful note) with which they signal to one another across the mountains, and which is attached to a rich orange and white harness. Asceticism is—or was—the key to their worship. Worshippers would undergo long, lonely sojourns in the mountains, living in caves on a diet of mountain vegetables, and performing austerities like meditating under icy waterfalls. The principal *yamabushi* festival—and the one worth timing your visit to see—is elemental: after a five-day march through the area, a spectacular fire festival is held on Haguro-san on 31 August; a similar event takes place on 31 December.

Despite its secrecy, aspects of Shugendō are accessible to outsiders. Japanese speakers 'with strong hearts' might be interested in five-day courses run from Yudono-san shrine in July and August. The fee includes accommodation, mountain treks, meditation, etc. Ring for details on ✆ 0235 54 6131. Not for casual gawpers.

Getting There and Around

Getting around the Mountains of Dewa isn't easy, and information is hard to come by in English. If you ever find yourself stuck, ring the free Japan Travel Phone, ✆ 0120 222800, and ask them to help you out.

There are two gateways to the region: Yamagata, the pleasant but unexciting prefectural capital, and Tsuruoka, a small town near the Japan Sea coast. **Buses** run between the two along route 112 which passes close to Yudono-san Jinja and Dainichi-bō and Chūren-ji, the temples containing the Buddhas. The traditional pilgrimage, however, begins at Haguro-san, which can only be reached via Tsuruoka. Note that services on mountain roads (the one to Haguro-san, for instance) may be curtailed during the snowy season. With such intermittent public transport, an organized coach tour might be a good idea: no English is spoken, but they fit a lot into a short time. Enquire at the tourist information centre in Yamagata for up-to-date details.

Haguro-san (Black Wings Mountain)

The Dewa pilgrimage begins at Haguro, the most accessible of the three peaks; travellers with limited time could get a taste of the area by coming on a day trip from Tsuruoka.

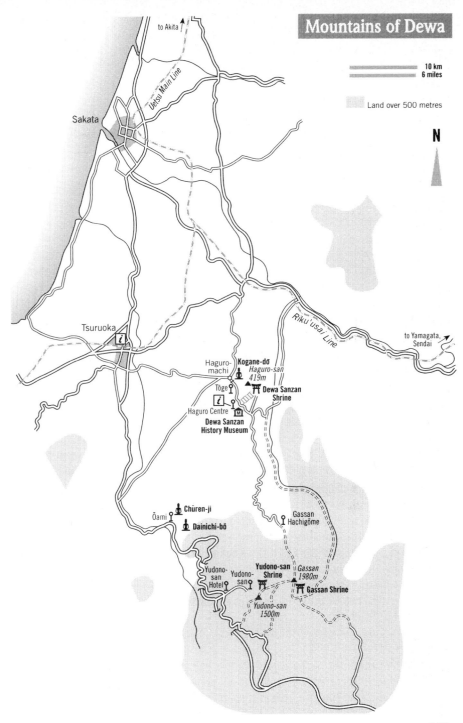

10 km
6 miles

Land over 500 metres

N

to Akita

Uetsu Main Line

Sakata

Tsuruoka

i

Riku'usai Line

to Yamagata,
Sendai

Haguro-
machi

Kogane-dō
Haguro-san
419m

Dewa Sanzan
Shrine

Tōge

i

Haguro Centre

M

Dewa Sanzan
History Museum

Ōami

Chūren-ji

Dainichi-bō

Gassan
Hachigōme

Yudono-
san
Hotel

Yudono-
san

Yudono-
san

Yudono-san
Shrine

Gassan
1980m

Yudono-san
1500m

Gassan Shrine

163

The road climbs steadily into the mountains and through the middle of a great red *torii* gateway, the official threshold of the sacred area. If you've been to Miyajima, near Hiroshima, you'll recognize the shape of this *torii*: each of the vertical uprights is flanked at 90° by two smaller gate-like forms, a style associated with the syncretic Shinto-Buddhism practised here until the Meiji Restoration.

Soon after, the bus enters the town of Haguro which stretches along the highway for several kilometres. **Haguro Sentā** is the central bus stop; there are restaurants here, and a tourist office where you can book accommodation in one of the temple *shukubō*.

The walk up the mountain begins near the bus stop. Beyond a small grey *torii* is a fading red building combining Buddhist and Shinto elements. Climb down a set of steps, past four small shrines and over an arching bridge across a stream where former pilgrims would purify themselves before entering the holy mountain.

The path bends through an ancient cedar forest. A few hundred metres along you will see a particularly huge and venerable tree ringed with ropes and white zig-zags (marking the presence of the *kami* or Shinto deity). This is **Ojii-chan sugi** (Grandpa Cedar). Until a few years ago Grandpa had a mate, Grandma Cedar, but he was widowed during a typhoon. Just beyond here, standing like a man-made version of the trees around it, is a 600-year-old **five-storey pagoda**, a National Treasure.

2446 steps ascend to the top of the mountain, and the ascent takes about an hour. It's possible to cheat and take a bus up the back toll road, but the walk is well worth the effort (you could compromise by taking the bus up and walking down). There's a refreshment stall half way up; the intriguing little paths off to the side lead to the graves of priests.

The hundreds of houses seen by Bashō, which made the summit of Haguro-san a holy city to rival that of Kansai's Kōya-san or Mt Hiei, were severely thinned out during the Buddhist persecutions of the Meiji period. The halls that remain are all technically Shinto, but carry the unmistakable characteristics of a syncretic establishment. While the priests' dress and the *torii* gates are Shinto, the architecture of the halls is Buddhist, with curving gables and ornate carvings beneath the eaves of elephants, tigers, lions, plants and flowers.

The first significant building you come across is the **Sai-kan**, a purification hall and refectory for pilgrims which still serves vegetarian cuisine at certain times of the day. During the winter, Gassan and Yudono-san are closed by snow so, for admirably practical reasons, the deities of all three mountains are enshrined in the **Gassai-den**, the big, tripartite worship hall at the top. In front of it sits **Kagami Ike** (Mirror Pond). In the days when women were forbidden to enter the sacred precincts, their male relatives would stop before this pond and throw into it offerings of hand mirrors which were believed to reflect their prayers. The nearby **museum** contains examples of these, dragged out of the ooze, and dating back centuries.

Gassan (Moon Mountain)

Infrequent buses to the eighth station, the start of the walk, go from Haguro (50mins). There are buses to the ski area from Yamagata (1hr 20mins) and Tsuruoka (1hr 10mins). Gassan is open from 1 July–10 Oct.

In Bashō's time, pilgrims had to walk more than 20km from Haguro to Gassan. Nowadays, all but the most fanatical *yamabushi* take the bus as far as it goes and start at the eighth station. From here it will take from two to two and a half hours depending on your pace.

You begin by walking over wooden planks across a marshy green plateau, the **Midagahara**, rich in foxgloves, thistles and Alpine plants, a very European landscape. Tiny shrines and Jizō statues punctuate the path. Skiers come to the area in winter and even in August there's often a residue of snow. After an hour you come to a resthouse by a pond selling soft drinks at an exorbitant ¥350. Outside are thousands of neatly packaged cans which are helicoptered off the mountain at the end of the season.

The path is seldom steep, but it is rocky. Just before the summit (1980m) you climb a set of steps to a cluster of buildings. Before entering the shrine, every pilgrim must be purified, and that includes you.

Hand over ¥300 and receive a paper fortune (carry it in your wallet or purse for good luck), and a second piece of paper in the shape of a person. Bow your head while the priest (still standing in his booth) chants a short prayer and shakes a bough of white paper streamers over your head. Then take the anthropomorphic paper, rub it over your shoulders, and drop it into one of the water troughs to either side.

Now you can continue up the steps to the small shrine, protected from the elements by metre-thick dry-stone walls. The view on a clear day appears infinite, but just as often a chilly mist surrounds the place. Set into the walls are offertory boxes with metal versions of the paper purification streamers (*gohei*) which were just shaken over your head. The inner shrine (built to withstand tons of snow rather than for beauty) contains a mirror, candles and offerings of food, *sake* and money. There are mirrors on its roof as well, and stylized swords, symbols of the *kami* (god), lean against the walls bearing written prayers and the names of those offering them. You may see your fellow pilgrims participating in other rituals here, prayers for the sick or needy.

Yudono-san (Bath Tub Mountain)

Buses from Tsuruoka (1hr) or Yamagata (1hr 40mins) to Yudono-san Hotel, or walk from Gassan as described below.

The innermost of the Three Holy Mountains is next door to Gassan and can be reached on foot in another two hours. From Gassan Jinja you descend along an undulating ridge called an *uma no senaka*, 'horse's back'. The path curves around a peak and descends to cross a stream after which there's a resthouse, looked after by an old man who's been living alone here every summer for 50 years. Soft drinks are sold, but try instead his *yakutō*, a delicious medicinal tea, brewed to his own recipe out of mountain grasses.

After this the path becomes difficult, as you have to negotiate six sets of iron steps descending almost vertically down a rocky gully. Good shoes are essential, although the *yamabushi* you'll meet here still do the walk in the traditional straw sandals.

Finally you reach **Yudono-san Jinja**, mysteriously concealed behind walls. Take off your shoes and socks, leave them in the little resthouse, receive your purification (¥*300*), cast your paper man on the waters, and take the doorway on the right. At the end of a walled path is the final surprise. The *kami* of Yudono-san resides not in a building or even a tree, but in a huge, rust-coloured rock, bathed in hot mineral water from an underground spring. Your fellow pilgrims each bow three times, make an offering, and then paddle through the very hot water which dribbles down. Coins thrown into it have become petrified by the rich mineral content. There's something very impressive about the whole thing: numinous and alien at the same time. When Bashō visited Yudono-san, he was forbidden from describing what he saw; today's visitors are strictly forbidden from photographing the inside of the shrine.

Twenty minutes' walk down the hill are the car park, visitors' centre and restaurants. If you haven't walked from Gassan, this is where you'll arrive. Buses from here go to Tsuruoka and Yamagata.

Dainichi-bō and Chūren-ji

Both are off the main route 112 between Tsuruoka and Yudono-san. If using the infrequent buses, disembark at Ōami bus stop.

These two rather ordinary little country temples have a macabre distinction, as the one-time homes and now the tombs of Shugendō sect monks who became 'Buddhas in their own bodies', in other words *mira,* or mummies. The specimen in Dainichi-bō sits slumped behind glass, a couple of electric candles flickering in front of him. Most of him is covered in rich orange robes from which jut grey, shrivelled limbs and a tiny shrunken head with a grimacing mouth.

Mummification is a lengthy process, and the chap displayed here, an Edo-period monk, started the task young. The grim trick was to come as close to death as possible before actually expiring so that when the big sleep finally came it made little physical difference. Aspirant mummies would shut themselves up in caves, meditating deeply and subsisting on the simplest diet—nuts, acorns, grasses and water. In the final stages even this was cut down. Having starved themselves to a near skeleton, they were buried alive with a breathing straw. Only when this had stopped moving were they dug up again: the result you see before you. Self-mummification was outlawed in the 19th century, but the temples sometimes have copies of an English-language booklet, *How to Become a Buddha in Your Own Body,* for overseas visitors who may want to try it at home.

(✆ 0235–)   ***Where to Stay and Eating Out***

There are pilgrim lodgings (the nicest of them are *shukubō,* temples in their own right) in **Haguro Town** (also known as Tōge) and below **Yudono-san**, plus a few hotels and *minshuku.* **Tsuruoka** is a dull little town but a convenient place to stay for an early start on train or bus the next day.

Ask at the information counter by the bus stop, knock on a few doors, or try **Sankō-in**, ✆ 62 2302, run by a family of friendly *yamabushi.* If you're lucky, you'll be asked to sit in on one of their services. Bed and two meals costs about ¥6000, and they'll make up a packed lunch for hikers.

On the summit of **Haguro-san** is the **Sai-kan** pilgrim lodge, ✆ 62 2355. The inexpensive **Sanhojo**, ✆ 54 6131, can be found by the visitors' centre at the bottom of **Yudono-san**.

There are tourist restaurants serving lunch by the bus terminals, but in the evening dine in your *shukubō*—many of these serve unique local Buddhist cuisine.

Iwate Prefecture

With its thick regional dialect and mountainous, unproductive land, Iwate is the poorest of Japan's prefectures, a byword for yokel naivety and backwardness. For those with time to wander, there are acres of rugged empty mountains dotted with hot springs.

The Tōhoku *shinkansen* puts the area within easy reach of Tokyo, as far as the prefectural capital **Morioka**. Change at Ichinoseki for **Hiraizumi**, a little town which, for a hundred years, was a gleaming capital of power and culture to rival Kyoto. It was founded by the 'Northern Fujiwara', a Tōhoku clan who claimed descent from the great family of emperors and ministers who dominated the Heian period. In 1094 Fujiwara Kiyohira established his capital here in conscious emulation of Kyoto, with a geometrical grid of avenues and lavish temples. The greatest of these, **Chūson-ji**, survives today. Its sumptuous **Konjiki-dō** (Golden Hall), the burial place of the mummified Northern Fujiwara lords, rivals Kyoto's Byōdō-in, and is even better preserved. Another, **Mōtsū-ji** (founded, like Chūson-ji, in the 9th century by the great monk Ennin) was restored by the second lord, Motohira, although only the garden and foundations are to be seen today.

Hiraizumi was a marvel. It is said to have been stories of Chūson-ji, rather than the palaces of Kyoto, which inspired Marco Polo's accounts of 'Zipangu' with its palaces paved, roofed and walled with pure gold. But the glorious blossoming was short-lived. At the end of the 12th century, the southern Kyoto Fujiwara were supplanted by the warrior family of Minamoto no Yoritomo. He was supported by his brother, Yoshitsune, a folk hero who spent much of his early life hiding from enemies in the remote city of Hiraizumi. Having secured his victory, Yoritomo became jealous of his charismatic brother, who was forced to flee to his old stamping grounds in Tōhoku. The third Fujiwara, Hidehira, gave him sanctuary, but Yoshitsune was betrayed by Hidehira's son, and forced to commit suicide to evade capture. This treachery did the boy no good. Within a few months he, too, had been hunted down and killed, his family disinherited, and his beautiful city put to the torch.

Tōno (*change from the JR Tōhoku line or* shinkansen *at Hanamaki or Shin-Hanamaki respectively*) is an old town, rather spoiled these days, famous for a collection of grim old folk tales recorded by an amateur folklorist in 1910. It still preserves several old *magariya*, big L-shaped farmhouses with thatched roofs. The **Chiba House**, a few kilometres from the town centre, is one of the grandest. Another, the **Minshuku Magariya**, ✆ 01986 2 4564, takes guests for a moderate rate.

Morioka isn't bad as prefectural capitals go, but there's no reason to make a special trip here. There's a ruined castle, a couple of unexciting museums and a district of old craft shops selling the city's most famous product, *nambu tetsubin*, handsome, primitive-looking black kettles and other ironware. If you're passing through (Morioka is the northern terminus of the Tōhoku *shinkansen*), your best bet would be to take a taxi or bus to the **Hashimoto Art Museum**, an eccentric collection amassed by a dead painter which includes iron tea kettles, dolls, ceramics, furniture, a reconstructed rural farmhouse and Mr Hashimoto's own, rather impressive oil paintings.

Morioka's most memorable tradition is culinary: a mode of competitive noodle-eating called *wanko soba*. The strands of buckwheat *soba* are eaten from tiny dishes, each bearing just a few strands which are plopped down in front of diners by the waitresses. The idea is to tip each dish straight into your mouth and to down it in one—no chopsticks, no chewing. As soon as one dish is empty, the waitress replaces it with another one; you keep track of how many you've swallowed with matchsticks provided for the purpose on each table. Anyone who pauses or regurgitates is disqualified. Finish more than a hundred dishes and you'll be rewarded with a commemorative certificate. **Azuma-ya** is the most famous *wanko soba* restaurant, with a branch in the station as well as the main establishment near the ruins of the old castle, 15 minutes' walk from the station.

Akita Prefecture

Iwate's mirror image on the western, Japan Sea coast of Tōhoku, Akita is similarly rustic and mountainous. **Akita City** isn't worth getting off the train for, but **Kakunodate**, to the east (50 minutes by express train) is a lovely town of cherry trees and original Edo-period **samurai houses**. About half a dozen are open to the public; several others can be viewed from outside as you walk or cycle around this compact town. The **Aoyagi** and **Ishiguro** family houses are the most impressive. Kakunodate is also famous for *kabazaiku*, wooden items coated in a veneer of cherry bark, one of the most attractive folk crafts of Japan.

Deep in the interior of Akita are two mountain lakes linked by myth. The larger in area is **Lake Towada** on the northern border of Akita and Aomori prefectures. The other is **Lake Tazawa** (just northeast of Kakunodate), Japan's deepest: the sides of this extinct volcano plunge down from the shore to a maximum depth of 423m.

An amusing legend explains why, in the heart of Japan's cold north, this freshwater lake never freezes over. Lake Towada, the story goes, was formed after an unfortunate accident involving one Hachirō Tarō, a young local man who suffered a terrible thirst after eating a fish. For 33 days he gulped down water, and became so bloated that he was transformed into a water dragon. After damming up a stream to form the lake, he was driven away by a sorcerer and fled to a lagoon called Hachirō-gata, north of Akita City.

Another metamorphosis was meanwhile taking place at Lake Tazawa. A beautiful local girl called Takko Hime (her statue stands on the shores of the lake) was told by a voice that if she drank from a particular spring she would be granted

eternal youth. She obeyed and—gulp—found herself, too, changed into a reptile and took up residence in the lake. Takko Hime was as gorgeous a dragon as she had been a human, and pretty soon attracted the attention of the two local personalities: the sorcerer of Lake Towada and good old Hachirō Tarō of Hachirō-gata lagoon. The two battled it out and Hachirō won his dragon queen. During each of the equinoxes, he journeys from his lagoon to Takko Hime's lake to enjoy his bride. At the coldest time of the year it is their scaly passion which stops the waters from freezing over.

Both lakes have lost some of their charm recently as mass tourism has brought resort hotels, pleasure boats and, in the case of Towada-ko, skiing. Towada also has some pretty, gentle walks or bike rides down the **Oirase Valley**. Remote **hot springs**, in simple wooden inns high in the mountains, offer complete escape. Ask (in Kakunodate, Hirosaki or Aomori) about **Sukayu Onsen**, north of Lake Towada, and **Tsurunoyu Onsen**, east of Lake Tazawa.

Aomori Prefecture

As the northernmost of Japan's prefectures (the island of Hokkaidō is a -dō, 'territory', not a -ken, 'prefecture'), Aomori's attractions are rustic and offbeat. The capital, **Aomori City**, has nothing to recommend it (though if you're stuck between trains there's a good museum dedicated to the modern woodblock artist, Munakata Shikō), but **Hirosaki**, to the south, is a student town with a well-preserved samurai quarter. The prefecture's unique attraction, though, is the mysterious mountain called **Osore-zan** (Mt Terror) on the **Shimokita Peninsula**: the mouth of the Buddhist hell, the gathering place of ghosts and shamanesses.

Hirosaki

A lively student town, overlooked by a beautiful, conical volcano, Hirosaki is proudest of all of its famous apples which were introduced by American agriculturalists in the 19th century, and which are seen every few hundred metres on posters, in the names of coffee shops and department stores, and in big shiny pyramids in greengrocers' shops.

The principal tourist attractions are close to the **castle** (Hirosaki-jō), a few kilometres west and a little bit north of the station, with a small, three-storey keep (built in 1600, rebuilt after a fire in 1810) in generous and attractive gardens. To the north is a beautiful quarter of antique **samurai houses** (*buke yashiki*) with especially deep, thickly thatched eaves for warding off the heavy winter snow falls. The small **Shiritsu Hakubutsukan**, at the south end of the park, is the city museum which has a small collection of prehistoric pieces; over the road is the **Fujita Kinen Teien** (Fujita Memorial Garden) which incorporates the cone of Mt Iwasaki as a stirring piece of 'borrowed scenery'. Hirosaki has its own **Neputa Matsuri** festival from 1–7 August, a smaller, more refined version of the one in the city of Aomori. The festival floats, made of dyed wax-resist paper over a wooden frame, are displayed in the **Neputa Mura**, along with local crafts. There's all year entertainment at **Yamauta**, a restaurant of local delicacies, a few minutes' walk from the station, which presents nightly performances of **Tsugaru-jamisen**, an appealing and accessible style of folk music which originated on the bleak Tsugaru peninsula, north of Hirosaki. Jangling *shamisens* play a banjo-like accompaniment to the powerful female singers—it could hardly be further from the plangent twanging of traditional Japanese music.

Shimokita Peninsula

This remote axe-shaped peninsula is the northernmost point of the island of Honshū, and its main attraction—the volcano named Mt Terror, believed to be the mouth of the Buddhist underworld—confirms this impression of being at the end of the earth. Trains and buses are few and slow, and the gaps between them long. There isn't a lot to do while you're waiting for them.

Getting There and Around

The jumping off point for **rail** access is Noheiji, an otherwise insignificant town where travellers from Aomori (to the west) and Morioka (to the south) change from the JR Tōhoku Main Line onto the JR Ominato Line. This leads up the handle of the peninsula's 'axe' to the dreary town of Mutsu, the hub for exploration of the area. Confusion arises because of the various names given to the town's transport termini. Mutsu's principal railway station is called **Shimokita**, last but one on the JR Ominato Line.

Buses also travel into Shimokita from Aomori and Noheiji, finishing up at the **Mutsu Bus Terminal**. From here buses go to Osore-zan and the other parts of the peninsula. But the terminal is some way from the main station. Closer is the station called **Tanabu**, joined to Shimokita station by a small local branch line.

All services are infrequent and prone to seasonal variations. Enquire about departure times and plot journeys well in advance to avoid unnecessary hanging around.

A **car** would be very useful in this part of Tōhoku. You could hire one in Aomori (ask at the tourist information office) and take a **car ferry** to Wakinosawa on the southwest tip of Shimokita.

Osore-zan (Mt Terror)

Together in the Sai-no-Kawara are assembled
Children of tender age in multitude—
Infants but two or three years old,
Infants of four or five, infants of less than ten:
And the voice of longing for their parents,
Is never as the voice of the crying of children in this world,
But a crying so pitiful to hear
That the sound of it would pierce through flesh and bone.
And sorrowful indeed the task which they perform—
Gathering the stones of the bed of the river,
Therewith to heap the tower of prayers.

Saying prayers for the happiness of father, they heap the first tower;
Saying prayers for the happiness of mother, they heap the second
tower;
But ever as the sun begins to sink below the horizon,
Then do the Oni, the demons of the hells, appear...

From *The Legend of the Sai-no-Kawara*

The bus from Mutsu makes one stop at Kiyomizu Spring, where all the passengers disembark for a taste of its famous pure water. As the road climbs higher you will notice two things: small groups of stone Jizō statues at the side of the forest road; and an increasingly pervasive smell of rotten eggs.

Finally the road levels out as you enter the crater of Osore-zan, and an eerie landscape comes into view. The dense forest which has overshadowed the road fades first to scrub and then to bare dusty rock. You are at the centre of a wide caldera, a volcanic crater formed millennia ago by huge explosions, and ringed by dormant grey volcanoes. Dominating it is a lake, an intense greeny-blue. Yellow sulphur crystals form on the rocks around the steaming vents. Above, dust and arid rock; below, invisible heat, violent and unpredictable rumblings. It's easy to see how Osore-zan acquired its reputation as a ghostly place, a gateway between the living and the dead.

The lake still bears the name **Usori**, an Ainu word which was phonetically altered to fit the Japanese pronunciation of the word 'terror' or 'dread': as a holy site and place of communion with the dead it predates Buddhism—and even Shinto—to the time of the Ainu or before. The practice of shamanism (communication with higher powers through a divinely appointed medium) was recorded in the earliest Chinese descriptions of Japan, and survives today with the *itako* of Tōhoku. Twice a year, from 20–24 July and 9–10 October, these old, usually blind, women gather at Osore-zan for a shamanesses' reunion. Thousands of Japanese from all over the country converge on the mountain to exchange messages with dead relatives, and the spectacle at these times is extraordinary: like the witches' scene from *Macbeth*, filmed by Kurosawa, with dozens of hags instead of the usual three.

In the 9th century, the priest Ennin visited the mountain and founded the Entsū-ji Bodai-ji temple; thereafter, the ancient beliefs were absorbed and reinterpreted in the light of Buddhist eschatology. Osore-zan's religious significance derives from one of the most pitiful of Buddhist teachings—that concerning the fate of dead children in the Sai-no-Kawara, 'Dry Bed of the River of Souls'. This is Buddhism's River Styx (marking the boundary between heaven and hell) but also its limbo: according to traditional beliefs, not found outside Japan, this is where children and 'water children' (miscarried or aborted babies) come when they die. Unable to enter heaven, they remain on the dry river bed in great distress, as described in the hymn above. They build up little cairns of stones as a penance, but sadistic demons knock them over with their clubs, and torment the souls with memories of earthly happiness. The saving figure in all this is **Jizō bosatsu**, the *bodhisattva* of children and travellers whose image was seen alongside the road. Jizō drives away the demons with his staff, and shelters the children beneath his long robes. He helps them build up the stone towers again, and guides them on the long road to Paradise.

Elements of this story are found all over Osore-zan. The bus deposits you in front of **Entsū-ji** temple. Before it is the lake, behind it a grey vista of cindery volcanic hillocks, dotted all around with tiny cairns. They represent the towers built in the underworld, and you will see bereaved parents here, adding stones to the piles to help their dead children along. Hence, also, the many statues of Jizō and the pathetic offerings of sweets, toys and plastic windmills set before them. The straw sandals are for Jizō himself, to protect his feet as he walks backwards and forwards across the sharp rocks.

Other Sights

The **Hotokegaura** coast, the blade of Shimokita's axe head, is famous for remote fishing villages and spectacular cliff formations. You can view these from the **boats** which travel between **Sai** and **Wakinosawa**, where there is a colony of wild monkeys, claimed to be the northernmost in the world. There are simple **hot springs** at **Shimofuro** (on the north coast) and **Yagen** (inland, in a gorge at the north foot of Osore-zan).

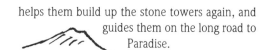

(℗ *0175–*)   *Where to Stay*

Mutsu has various simple *minshuku* at *inexpensive* prices including two meals. **Ueno**, ℗ 22 3640, and **Nakatake**, ℗ 22 4754, are close to the bus terminal; the information counter will make a reservation for you.

Yagen Onsen has more choice and quality. **Hotel New Yagen**, ℗ 34 3311, and **Yagen Kankō Hotel** are both in the *moderate* price category, including two meals and wonderful hot spring baths.

There is a **youth hostel**, ℗ 44 2341, at Wakinosawa.

Tokyo

There's no point apologizing for Tokyo: it's teeming, ugly, expensive but also, in Edward Seidensticker's words, 'the world's most consistently interesting city'. The 23 wards of the city proper are home to 7,976,000 people; add on the satellite cities and commuter towns of the contingent urban sprawl and the total for Greater Tokyo comes to 30 million, almost a quarter of the entire population. Tokyo has the world's biggest station, the most expensive property prices and the kitschest and most bizarre architecture. If crowds and excess and 24-hour city fever excite you, then it's the ultimate urban experience.

If they don't, then it's still not to be written off. There's another side to Tokyo, seldom discovered by tourists, but much appreciated by those who live here. Underlying the superficial chaos, there's a deep calm, almost an innocence to Tokyo. Trains and subways run like clockwork. Neighbourhoods are tidy. Street crime is negligible. Visually an urban hell, Tokyo, by any international standard, is law-abiding, harmonious and safe. The novelist Angela Carter lived here in the 1970s. 'Tokyo ought not to be a happy city,' she wrote, 'no pavements; noise; few public places to sit down; occasional malodorous belches from sewage vents even in the best areas.' But it 'somehow contrives to be an exceedingly pleasant place in which to live.' The title of Carter's essay is *Tokyo Pastoral*.

If it still gives you a headache, there's no point grinning and bearing it. You might as well accept the city on its own terms, and try to pack as much as possible into a short time before escaping to the more relaxing areas a train ride away. Of these, there's no shortage: from Nikkō, opulent burial place of the great shogun, Tokugawa Ieyasu, to the hot springs and lakes of Hakone and the Mt Fuji region, and the medieval town of Kamakura, a mini-Kyoto of temples, shrines and rural walks.

History

Few cities are so blindly and wilfully committed to the present (present profit, present convenience); but few are so earnestly and sentimentally attached to their own past.

Edward Seidensticker, *Low City, High City*

Tokyo's past is a struggle to get to grips with, even for long-term residents. The obvious historic sights are fragmentary and so frequently recycled (gardens on the grounds of old temples, palaces on the sites of castles, ancient shrines rebuilt in ferro-concrete) that it's hard to put them into a chronological perspective, to develop a clear picture of what led to what. The obvious reason—Tokyo's notorious accident proneness—isn't the only one. It's difficult to find a period of 50 years (the present post-war era may be the longest) when Tokyo hasn't been wiped clean by one calamity or another—fire, earthquake, flood, plague or war. But even allowing for acts of God, it's always been a restless and protean city. If the B-29s had stayed away, and the Great Earthquake had never struck, Tokyo, one suspects, would be none the less jumbled and chaotic.

The Founding of Edo

For seven of its eight centuries Tokyo has been called Edo, 'River Mouth', the name given by a junior member of the Taira clan to the spot where he built a fortified house in the 12th century. It was little more than a marshy fishing village until 1457 when a junior lord named Ōta Dōkan established a military presence here, training conscripts in a walled fortress. By 1486 Ōta's success had become a cause of anxiety to his masters; after taking sides in a factional dispute he was assassinated, and for the next century Edo was overshadowed by the castle at Odawara to the south.

In 1590 Odawara fell to Toyotomi Hideyoshi, the second of the three great warlords who between them brought about the unification of modern Japan. Hideyoshi offered the newly pacified eastern domain to his general, Tokugawa Ieyasu, who, to the surprise and dismay of his advisers, accepted it. Hideyoshi feared his cunning ally; at the time, this seemed like a transparent attempt to shunt him sideways, out of the Japanese heartland and out of harm's way.

But patience was Ieyasu's great virtue, and the distance and isolation worked in his favour. While Hideyoshi embarked on his ruinous invasions of Korea, Ieyasu stayed quietly put, draining and fortifying little Edo, and strategically doling out land to his supporters. When Hideyoshi died, the Tokugawa forces swooped, and in 1600 decisively defeated their rival lords at the Battle of Sekigahara. The mopping up operations lasted another 15 years, by which time Edo was firmly established as the *de facto* capital of the new Japan.

The High City

Personal conquest was not enough for Ieyasu; the great challenge was to pass on the fruits of victory to his heirs. This he achieved by a radical reorganization of the social structure, based on Confucian theory, which remained theoretically in place until 1868.

The Tokugawa state was essentially a military dictatorship: at the top of the social scale were the samurai, presided over by the shogun and his 270 regional *daimyō* (feudal lords) who divided up administration of the country between them. *En masse* the *daimyō* were more than a match for any individual shogun, and Ieyasu quickly instituted a complicated set of protocols designed to neutralize their power and freedom of action. He needed his lords to be kept busy and broke, and this he achieved by a system known as *sankin kōtai*, 'alternate attendance'. For roughly six months of the year, *daimyō* resided in their home fiefs, gathering taxes and keeping an eye on things; for the rest of the time they were required to live in Edo where their wives and children remained all year round, as pampered hostages.

The effect of these rules was dramatic, as the roads to and from the capital became crowded with *daimyō* and their retainers processing backwards and forwards on their annual pilgrimages to the shogun. Each one had to maintain an expensive Edo household, commensurate with his wealth and status. All lords were not equal; Ieyasu distinguished carefully between the *fudai daimyō* (dependent lords), whose families had fought along-side him at Sekigahara, and the *tozama daimyō* (outer lords) whom he had defeated. The innermost parts of the castle compound, clustered around the shogun's own citadel were reserved for the *fudai daimyō*; the outer lords dwelt outside, between the next ring of moats and fortifications. Pitched against one another in their struggle for the shogun's favour, the *daimyō*—as Ieyasu intended—strove to create ever more opulent and expen-sive mansions in the extravagant Momoyama style (which survives today in Kyoto temples like Nishi Hongan-ji). Surrounded by gleaming moats, with the towers of Edo Castle at the centre of the fortress hill, the *Yamanote* (High City) was a marvel, an architectural embod-iment of the tough new order which Ieyasu and his heirs had brought to Japan.

The Great Fire of 1657

The first great disaster came in January 1657. It became known as the *Furisode* (Long Sleeves) Fire, and ghostly tales and portents were associated with it. On 16 January 1655, a young woman named Okiku had died of a broken heart after falling in love with a myste-rious young man. She was buried in her long-sleeved kimono at the Honmyō-ji temple in Hongō. A year later—to the day—another girl named Ohana died in mysterious circum-stances shortly after receiving the gift of a purple long-sleeved kimono. When the priests of the temple found themselves conducting a third funeral—another young woman, another strange illness, another purple *furisode*—on the same day in 1657, they realized that something was very wrong. Solemn services were held two days later to placate the souls of the young women and whatever evil force was cutting them down.

Tokyo winters are dry; for 80 days there had been no rain and the wooden city was as parched as tinder. Every night the bells were rung as a warning against fire. The cere-monies began at Honmyō-ji on the afternoon of 18 January. Priests chanted the Lotus Sutra and, at the climax of the recitation, cast a long-sleeved purple kimono onto the sacred fire. The wind caught it and blew it up onto the temple roof, igniting the thatch, and the houses all around.

Fire tore uncontrollably through the crowded city; by the time it had burned itself out three-quarters of Edo—including 500 *daimyō* mansions, 800 samurai residences, and 350 temples and shrines—was reduced to cinders. Over 108,000 people died, a quarter of the population, including 20,000 who perished in a single spot when a city gate was locked against their flight. After three days the flames died down; the next morning it snowed.

The Low City

Less lavish and minus its central keep, the High City was rebuilt within a few years. Individual Tokugawas came and went, but, ensconced in its mansions and citadels, protected from intrigue by formidable networks of spies and informers, the institution of the shogunate ruled unchallenged for the next 200 years. It was an arid and paranoid regime, paralysed by hierarchy and conservatism, committed only to the perpetuation of its own power. The interesting and lively things in Edo culture were happening on the other side of the moats, among the teeming wooden dwellings between the castle and the Sumida River. This was *shitamachi*, the 'Low City'—low in the social as well as the geographical sense. *Shitamachi* occupied the flat, marshy reclaimed land in the east of the city, and it sprung up as the home of the *chōnin*, the townspeople who moved to Edo from the commercial cities of the west. Artisans and merchants stood on the lowest rungs of the Tokugawa social ladder, but they made up half the Edo population: 600,000 people crammed into 16 per cent of the city's area, more than three times as crowded as the most densely inhabited area of modern Tokyo. In this atmosphere, the stuffy hierarchies and minuscule social distinctions of the High City plainly could not hold. From about 1700, the Low City developed its own unique urban culture—as much an attitude to life and a sense of style as a formal aesthetic instinct of the kind expressed in literature and pictures.

The main streets of the Low City were lively and rather grand. Here were the homes of the merchants who, although socially despised, were among the wealthiest men in the city. They also functioned as shops, with open frontages where customers could step up to inspect and purchase goods, and warehouses, with fireproof earthen walls painted in black and white, and tile roofs. Most of the population lived in wooden dwellings, some elegant, but many—the *nagaya*, or 'long houses', which filled the alleys behind the main streets—comfortless slums, with a single bare room, and shared sanitation. 'Fires and fights are the flowers of Edo,' went the saying: in such teeming conditions, both must have flourished. As the city got back on its feet after the Long Sleeves Fire, new rules about the width of avenues and compulsory fire breaks in the centre of each block were quickly forgotten. Between 1603 and 1868 there were 100 major blazes. Firemen, organized into fiercely competitive local brigades, each with its own banners and livery, were the heroes of the city. The life expectancy of the average *shitamachi* building was no more than 20 years.

The other defining feature of the city in its early days was its gender ratio. Edo was an immigrant city and the immigrants, by and large, were men who left their families behind in their home towns. For several generations there was no more than one female Edoite for every three males. This imbalance accentuated the importance of what were, in any case, key areas in every Japanese city: the 'streets of flower and willow' (as the brothel areas were called), and above all Yoshiwara, the biggest and most celebrated of them all.

The Yoshiwara, the Nightless City, has been romanticized beyond all reason. It was, in many ways, a disgusting institution based upon child prostitution, sexual slavery and government-sponsored exploitation. During its heyday though, the area just north of Asakusa's Sensō-ji temple was the most exciting and creative in the city, much more than just a place for bought sex. The most famous *oiran* (courtesans) and *geisha* of Yoshiwara were paragons of fashion and sophistication, skilled dancers, story-tellers and players of the *shamisen.* Poets and print-makers idolized them as passionately as any *kabuki* actors; indeed the most popular Edo plays were often love stories about doomed affairs between *oiran* and their merchant or samurai suitors. It was a place subject to different rules from those that governed everyday life, where style rather than rank was the mark of status, and townsmen and soldiers could mingle if not on equal, then at least on intimate terms.

The Shogunate Goes to the Dogs

By the 1720s the population had grown to 1.3 million. Until London got ahead in the mid-19th century, Edo was the largest city in the world. It was a phenomenal place: a seething, expanding—frequently burning—urban sprawl pinned forcibly in place by the still, oppressive force of the shogunate at its centre. Ieyasu's system of ministers, bureaucrats and spies worked so well that within a few generations it ran itself. Like the emperors before them, the ruling shoguns became largely symbolic figures, dependent on the advice and consent of the inner cabinet: a fortunate arrangement, since individually the Tokugawas were weak and ineffectual and, in at least one case, barking mad.

Tokugawa Tsunayoshi, the fifth in his line, was a cultured and gifted ruler who took an active part in government, but he is known irrevocably to history as *Inu Kubō*, the Dog Shogun. Unable to father an heir, he was convinced by his overbearing mother that he was being punished for crimes committed in a previous life. By way of atonement, Tsunayoshi instituted a national policy of kindness to animals, with ferocious penalties for those who ignored it. He had been born in the Year of the Dog, and canine welfare was given the highest priority. Shogunal kennels were erected on Tsunayoshi's estates; their occupants were conveyed in covered palanquins with guards of honour. All canine deaths had to be reported to the authorities who were obliged to investigate them thoroughly for any evidence of foul play. Numerous dog-killers were executed or exiled, and in 1686 an Akita man was put to death for the murder of a swallow. The policy failed to achieve its objective. Tsunayoshi had no heir, and was succeeded on his death in 1609 by a nephew whose first act was to repeal all pro-animal legislation.

By the 19th century, worsening economic conditions were undermining the shogunate and breaking up the old feudal distinctions. Merchants grew richer, samurai poorer. The latter frequently adopted the sons of the former in return for money or liberation from debts. The arrival off Edo Bay of the American Commodore Perry in 1853 was only the catalyst for a reaction that had been slowly taking place for more than half a century.

The Birth of Tokyo

In 1868 the last of the shoguns abdicated and Emperor Meiji moved his court from the Kyoto Imperial Palace to the site of the vacated Tokugawa castle. In the brief civil war that accompanied the Meiji Restoration, the city—renamed Tokyo, 'Eastern Capital'—had been largely undamaged, but the social, intellectual and industrial revolution which took place over the next 50 years was to leave it profoundly altered, if not unrecognizable.

Tokyo did not just modernize, it Westernized: foreign clothes, foreign-style buildings and a few foreigners themselves transformed the superficial look of the streets and people. Most significant of all, perhaps, were the new forms of transportation which the new age brought. Palanquins gave way to *jinrikisha*, then horse carriages, then automobiles. The construction of railway termini brought new life to old areas, and marginalized others. The canals, arteries of the old city, were gradually filled in or built over. 'Venice would not be Venice if its canals were filled in', wrote Edward Seidensticker. 'Tokyo, with so many of its canals turned into freeways, is not Edo.'

The Great Kantō Earthquake

By 1923 Japan was a military empire with lands stretching from Taiwan, through Korea and Manchuria, to the southern part of Sakhalin Island. Tokyo, with a population of just under two million, was still largely built of wood, but had all the trappings of a bustling modern city: multi-storey buildings, asphalted roads, oil-powered industrial centres. The First World War in Europe had stimulated Japan's growing industrial production. In Hibiya, the ultra-modern Imperial Hotel had just been built by the American architect, Frank Lloyd Wright.

On 1 September 1923, one minute from noon, a huge earthquake struck Yokohama, and 45 seconds later the tremors reached Tokyo. All over town braziers were cooking lunch for the occupants of the wooden houses. When the multiple shocks had subsided, thousands of fires erupted spontaneously. There was no time for rescue work to get underway; anyone trapped beneath the rubble was done for. But even those who scrambled out of the wreckage were not safe as the flames joined hands across the city. The fires in Nihonbashi burned so fiercely that buildings on the far side of the Sumida River ignited spontaneously from the heat. In Hongō, to the north, 40,000 people took shelter on a vacant 20 acre plot of waste ground. Fire devoured all the buildings up to its edge, and the vacuum of air between these walls of heat sucked the flames in burning cyclones which incinerated all but a few hundred refugees. Elsewhere the fires turned the roads into giant fly-papers: fleeing crowds became mired in the sticky asphalt and asphyxiated where they lay. At Yokosuka, an oil tank ruptured and vomited burning oil into the sea where hundreds had taken refuge. Those who jumped into ponds and lakes were boiled alive. In the hysterical aftermath of the disaster, there were vile atrocities. Four thousand innocent victims—left-wingers, 'unpatriotic' elements and, above all, Koreans—were lynched by rampaging groups of zealots. The death toll from the earthquake and fire was 140,000.

Recovery and War

Once the initial shock had worn off, the city quickly recovered. By 1930 there were few traces of the destruction of less than a decade before, but at least one vital change had taken place. The Low City which had borne, as usual, the worst sufferings of the earthquake became depopulated as thousands of its inhabitants, weary of *shitamachi*'s constant misfortunes, relocated in the new suburbs that were mushrooming in the west of the city.

The inter-war years were lively ones when the districts of the capital took on much of the shape and relative importance which they have today. Tokyo had its jazz age, and it had its financial collapse as well, in 1927. Old-style drinking places yielded in popularity to cafés and dance halls. For the first time, baseball began to rival sumo as the national sport. But as nationalism tightened its grip, a mood of dour solemnity and growing xenophobia gathered in the city. Cigarette brands and popular performers who had adopted foreign names were constrained to change them to Japanese, and even architecture, like the *kabuki* theatre in Ginza, took on an oppressive, totalitarian character. In the months after Pearl Harbour, parks and gardens were converted into anti-aircraft gun emplacements. By the end of 1944 American forces had got close enough to the Japanese mainland to mount sustained raids on Tokyo. The worst of these were on the night of 9–10 March when as many as 80,000 people died in the space of a few hours, three-quarters of the city's entire civilian casualties. Winds fanned the incendiary bombs and two-fifths of the city was destroyed, with most damage, naturally, in the Low City.

The Post-War Period

By winter 1945, Tokyo was an occupied city: flattened, starving and brimming with American and Allied servicemen and administrators. The black market flourished; so did prostitution. In 1950, salvation came in the form of the Korean War. As off-shore supplier and victualler to the anti-Communist forces, Japan started to become prosperous again. In 1964 the Tokyo Olympics unleashed a frenzy of optimistic construction and national self-awareness: streets were widened, subways and monorails opened, and Shibuya was transformed by the athletes' village and the bold gymnasia designed by Tange Kenzō. In the late seventies and early eighties, opposition to the Japanese-American Security Treaty and the new Narita Airport fused in a noisy student protest movement: there were violent demonstrations, battles with police and a handful of deaths.

Within a few years, though, settled conformity had returned to Japan. The streets of Tokyo reflected the swelling economy as taller and grander and more expensive buildings rose in the booming sub-centres. For a few years, at the height of the bubble economy in the late 1980s, Tokyo might just have been the richest city in the history of the world. Its land area was said, in real estate terms, to be worth as much as the whole of the United States. With billions of yen of excess capital, company expense accounts swelled, employees' bonuses multiplied and Tokyoites found new and ever more absurd ways of spending money: £1,000 a head hostess bars, gold-leaf *sushi*, mink lavatory covers. The bursting of the bubble in the early 1990s gave corporations and politicians a nasty shock, but compared to the recession-blighted cities of Britain and North America, Tokyo still looks and feels like a city very much on the up.

Getting to Tokyo from the Airports

Tokyo, as you'd expect, is accessible by plane, coach or train from almost everywhere in Japan. Just one place, seemingly, lacks decent connections with the capital: its international airport.

Haneda, Tokyo's old airport, is close to the city, but only domestic airlines and a handful of international carriers still use it. Simply take the **monorail** to Hamamatsuchō station to the south of central Tokyo, and then pick up a subway, overland train or taxi.

Narita, where almost all international travellers find themselves arriving, is a different story. Your mode of transport will depend on where you are travelling to/from within Tokyo, and on the amount of time and money you have available. The **arrival lobby** of Narita Airport has ticket counters for the various buses and trains.

by taxi

You can forget this, unless someone else is paying. It takes about 1½ to 2hrs depending on traffic, and during the day costs around ¥18,000.

by rail

Tokyo station is the main station in the west side of the city.

The JR **Narita Express** (N'EX) travels non-stop between Narita Airport station and Tokyo station in 53mins, and costs about ¥2890 depending on the season. The N'EX also goes to **Shinjuku** and (infrequently) **Ikebukuro** stations, 74 and 87mins respectively, for ¥3050. Airport-bound expresses get booked up, especially in peak season. You should buy an advance reservation at a JR ticketing counter (found in most stations) or a travel agent.

The **Airport Narita** rapid train is a slower JR service which stops at Shinbashi station in Tokyo and various others along the way. It takes 1hr 20mins between Tokyo station and the airport and costs ¥1260.

The **Keisei** line is a private service between the airport and Keisei Ueno station, just south of Ueno Park. The **Skyliner Express** takes about an hour and costs ¥1740; the **limited express** (tokkyū) takes only 10mins longer, but at ¥940 is the cheapest form of public transport to and from Narita. For information, call ✆ 03 3831 0131.

by bus

The most convenient means of transport, especially if you have heavy luggage to heave around, is the **Limousine Bus** service which shuttles between the airport and a number of key locations and big downtown hotels. Even if you're not booked in at one of these, you can have yourself dropped off at the one nearest to where you're staying and take a short taxi or subway ride from there. On the return journey out to the airport, a useful trick is to make your way to the **Tokyo City Air Terminal** (TCAT; Suitengūmae subway station on the Hanzōmon line) where the Japanese airlines (and a few foreign carriers) have check-in counters. From here you can take a bus direct to the airport, unencumbered by your luggage.

The bus to and from TCAT takes between 70 and 90mins, depending on traffic, and costs ¥2500. Tokyo station is another 10mins or so, and an extra ¥100. To Shinjuku station and the hotels in the Shinjuku area, it takes about two hours in total, and the fare is ¥2700. For information, call ✆ 03 3665 7232.

Getting Around

Tokyo is a vast city, but it has one of the cheapest, safest, cleanest and most reliable urban transportation networks in the world. Compared to the grimy urinals which pass for subways in some countries, it is a joy to use; the speed and efficiency of the system makes Tokyo seem smaller than London or New York.

orientation

A good idea of Tokyo's general layout can be had by looking at the **Tourist Map of Tokyo**, provided free by the tourist information centre.

Roughly in the centre is the empty green blob of the **Imperial Palace**. Just to the east of here is a dense conglomeration of office buildings and department stores and hotels, centering around **Tokyo station**. Many railway lines converge here, but the most useful for tourists is the **Yamanote line** which girds the city in an irregular oval loop, intersected by ten criss-crossing subway lines. This is Tokyo's most important railway, and its 29 stations enclose and include most of the places you will want to see while you are here.

The Yamanote line isn't a perfect circle, but its most important stations can be approximately counted off as the points of a clock:

At 3 o'clock is **Tokyo station**, adjacent to the **Imperial Palace** and districts like **Ginza** (famous for cafés and department stores) and **Yūrakuchō** (location of the tourist information centre).

At 4 o'clock is **Hamamatsuchō,** where the monorail departs to and from **Haneda**, the domestic airport.

At 6 o'clock is **Shinagawa**, a convenient station for trains to Yokohama and the cities immediately south of Tokyo.

At 8 and 9 o'clock are **Shibuya** and **Harajuku**, centres of night-time entertainment and youth culture, and disembarkation points for **Yoyogi Park** and the **Meiji Shrine**.

At 10 o'clock the mighty city-within-a-city, **Shinjuku**, is home to the febrile **Kabukichō** red-light district, and a dense concentration of skyscrapers. At 11 o'clock is **Ikebukuro**, a smaller and less interesting version of Shinjuku.

At about 2 o'clock is **Ueno**, a historic area with a museum-filled park.

Yamanote means 'High City'; the area bounded by the Yamanote line still corresponds more or less to the land settled by the Tokugawa shoguns and their feudal servants (*see* 'History'). The 'Low City' or *shitamachi* still exists, in the districts to the east of Tokyo station around the Sumida River; the most interesting and accessible area, **Asakusa**, is directly east of Ueno.

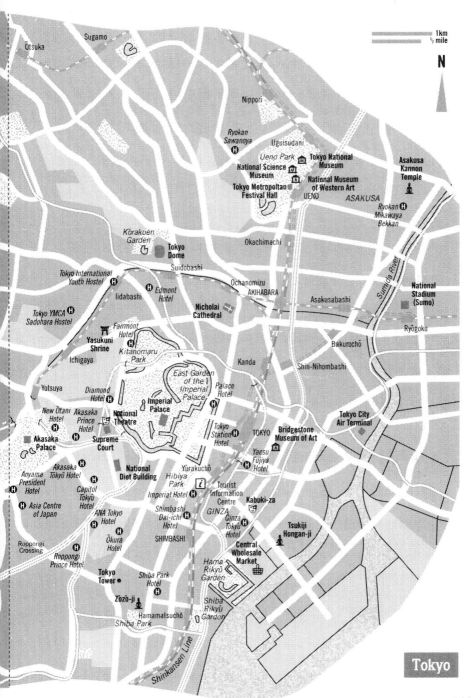

Ōtsuka

Sugamo

1km
½ mile

N

Nippori

*Ryokan
Sawanoya* ⊕

Uguisudani

Ueno Park
**Tokyo National
Museum**
National Science
Museum
**National Museum
of Western Art**
Tokyo Metropolitan
Festival Hall
UENO

**Asakusa
Kannon
Temple**

ASAKUSA

Ryokan ⊕
*Mikawaya
Bekkan*

*Kōrakuen
Garden*

**Tokyo
Dome**

Okachimachi

Suidobashi

Sumida River

Tokyo International
Youth Hostel ⊕

⊕ *Edmont
Hotel*
Iidabashi

Ochanomizu
AKIHABARA

Asakusabashi

**National
Stadium
(Sumo)**

Tokyo YMCA ⊕
Sadohara Hostel

*Fairmont
Hotel*
**Yasukuni
Shrine**
Ichigaya

**Nicholai
Cathedral**

Bakurochō

Ryōgoku

*Kitanomaru
Park*

Kanda

Shin-Nihombashi

Yotsuya

*Diamond
Hotel*

*East Garden
of the
Imperial
Palace*

*Palace
Hotel*

New Ōtani ⊕ *Akasaka
Hotel Prince
Hotel*
**National
Theatre**

**Imperial
Palace**

*Tokyo
Station
Hotel*

TOKYO

**Tokyo City
Air Terminal**

**Akasaka
Palace**

⊕ **Supreme
Court**

**Bridgestone
Museum of Art**

*Yaesu
Fujiya
Hotel* ⊕

Akasaka ⊕
Aoyama *Tōkyū Hotel*
President ⊕
Hotel
*Capitol
Tōkyū
Hotel*

**National
Diet Building**

Yūrakuchō
*Hibiya
Park*
Imperial Hotel ⊕

ℹ Tourist
Information
Centre

Kabuki-za

⊕ **Asia Centre
of Japan**

*ANA Tokyo
Hotel*

*Shimbashi
Dai-ichi
Hotel* ⊕

GINZA

*Ginza
Tōkyū
Hotel*

*Tsukiji
Hongan-ji*

Roppongi
Crossing

*Roppongi
Prince Hotel*

*Ōkura
Hotel*

SHIMBASHI

**Central
Wholesale
Market**

**Tokyo
Tower** ●

*Shiba Park
Hotel*

*Hama
Rikyū
Garden*

Zōjō-ji ⊥

*Shiba
Rikyū
Garden*

Hamamatsuchō
Shiba Park

Shinkansen Line

Tokyo

183

The usual rules about finding your way around in a city without addresses apply (*see* 'Practical A–Z', p.14).

by bus

The Tokyo bus network is complicated, vulnerable to traffic jams, and, unlike the JR lines and subways, little help is available in English. It's a matter of trial and error; visitors with limited time who are interested in just the main sights will be better off using the trains.

Various private companies operate buses in Tokyo but the most comprehensive system is the **Tō-basu** (City Bus) service. Most of these charge a flat rate fare of about ¥180, regardless of the length of journey. Drop coins or insert a ¥1000 bill into the fare box by the driver as you enter; change is dispensed automatically. Books of multiple tickets, called *kaisū ken*, can be purchased from the driver or from bus terminals at a slight saving over individual tickets.

A recorded voice announces destinations in advance. Tell your destination to the driver or a passenger, and someone will see you off at the right place.

The following is a small selection of useful routes. The tourist information centre doesn't usually have English bus maps, but local ward offices may be able to help.

Tō [東] 01 runs between the south exit of Shibuya station (i.e. not the Hachikō exit) and Shinbashi station, along Roppongi-dōri—an area poorly served by trains.

Tō [東] 03 runs between Shinjuku station east exit (*higashi guchi*), along the south moat of the Imperial Palace, through Hibiya and Yūrakuchō, to wind up finally in Harumi Wharf on Tokyo Bay.

Higashi [東] 42 goes from the Yaesu exit (to the east) of Tokyo station up along the Sumida River, near to Asakusa.

by subway

Tokyo's first subway opened between Ueno and Asakusa in 1927. Today there are ten lines forming a dense interconnecting grid penetrating far into the suburbs. A map of the subway system is printed on the inside back cover of this book.

Fares start at ¥140. Exact fares are shown on the wall maps above the ticket machines in each station, but these have very little English on them. Ask a passer-by or pay at the manned window. Failing that, it's acceptable to buy the minimum ticket and pay the difference at the other end. Just present the ticket at your destination, offer the inspector a handful of change, and let him fish out the excess.

Several subway stations, especially those which unite a number of lines, are labyrinths of underground pedestrian tunnels. There are good bilingual maps every few yards, but allow time for getting lost if your journey includes a change in one of these stations.

by train

The Yamanote is only one of dozens of JR and private lines which connect central Tokyo with its dormitory suburbs. Buy tickets in the same way as on the subway.

After the Yamanote, the most useful service is the **Chūō line**, which cuts through the centre of Tokyo north of the Imperial Palace, joining Shinjuku (and the suburbs to the west), Ochanomizu and Tokyo. For information, call ℂ 03 3423 0111.

car hire

With such good trains, you'd be mad to attempt driving within Tokyo. However, the following agencies have branches all over the city, and English-speaking staff.

Nippon Rent-A-Car: ℂ 03 3485 7196.

Nissan Rent-A-Car: ℂ 03 3587 4123.

Orix Rent-A-Car: ℂ 03 3779 0543.

For motorcycle hire, try the following (in Japanese only):

S.C.S.: ℂ 03 3827 5432.

55 (*Gogo*) Miles: ℂ 03 3487 9655.

tours

Several package companies offer morning, afternoon, evening or all day **coach tours** in English to spots in Tokyo, as well as day trips outside the city—pick up their ubiquitous brochures at the tourist information centre or your hotel. They're a superficial and expensive way of doing what, with a little more time and for much less money, you could easily organize yourself. Tours promising 'geisha parties' and the like are tacky fakes.

Japan Gray Line: ℂ 03 3433 5745.

Japan Amenity Travel: ℂ 0120 00 1417.

Japan Travel Bureau: ℂ 03 3276 7777.

Hato Bus: ℂ 03 3435 6081.

Mr Oka Nobuō conducts highly-praised personal guided tours of the *shitamachi* area. Contact him directly on ℂ 0422 51 7673.

Tourist Information

The Japan National Tourist Organization's **tourist information centre** (open Mon–Fri 9–5, Sat 9–12 noon, ℂ 3502 1461) is on the west side of the railway tracks, 100m south of Yūrakuchō station. Here you can pick up endless English pamphlets, maps, fact sheets, timetables, price lists and events calendars for Tokyo and the rest of the country, make reservations at establishments in the Economical Inn Group and arrange a **Home Visit**. From outside the city you can call them free on the **Japan Travel Phone** number, ℂ 0120 222800.

There's another information centre in Terminal One of **Narita Airport** (open Mon–Fri 9–8, Sat 9–12 noon, ℂ 0476 32 8711).

Teletourist Service is a recording of current events in and around Tokyo, ℂ 03 3503 2911.

Nippon Travel Agency (Nihon Ryokō)

Foreign Tourist Department, 3rd Floor, Shinbashi Ekimae Building No.1, 2–20–15 Shinbashi, Minato-ku, Tokyo 105, ✆ 03 3572 8744, ✉ 03 3572 8766.

Japan Travel Bureau (Nihon Kōtsu Kōsha)

1–6–4 Marunouchi, Chiyoda-ku, Tokyo 100, ✆ 03 3276 7777.

maps and media

The tourist information centre's free **Tourist Map of Tokyo** is perfectly adequate for sightseeing purposes, with an overall view of the city, area close-ups, a subway map and a transit diagram on the back. It wears out quickly; pick up a fresh copy when you pass by. *Tokyo: A Bilingual Atlas*, available from English-language book shops, is full of clear maps of the whole metropolitan area on many different scales.

Numberless city **magazines** and tour companions, many of them little more than advertising supplements, are available. Only one is worth spending money on: *Tokyo Journal*, an excellent monthly magazine which combines comprehensive listings of art, theatre, music, film, restaurants, nightlife and festivals with the wittiest and most irreverent English-language journalism in Japan.

Japan's **English-language newspapers** are all published in Tokyo, and the *International Herald Tribune*, *Asian Wall Street Journal* and *Financial Times* print Japan editions, available in book shops and news stands at large stations. Other foreign newspapers can be bought—at great expense—at big book shops like Maruzen and Kinokuniya.

The American Center (Exit A3 of Shiba Kōen subway station) and the British Council (Iidabashi subway or JR station) have **libraries** of English books relating to their respective countries. For books on Japan, try the Japan Foundation Library by Kojimachi subway station.

Tokyo Itineraries

Tokyo, like all capital cities, is an aberration. To come away with anything like a rounded picture of Japan, make sure that you spend at least half of your holiday outside it. What you see during your time here will naturally depend on personal interests. The following suggestions may help you establish priorities:

If you spend just 24 hours in Tokyo, go to Asakusa and (if you have time) Ueno in the day, and Shinjuku in the evening.

It makes a big difference to an experience of any city to know someone who lives there, and the people of Tokyo are kind and enthusiastic guides. As early as possible go to the tourist information centre to arrange a Home Visit (two days' notice is usually enough).

A very full but interesting day can be spent by visiting the Tsukiji Fish Market at 5am, having a *sushi* breakfast and then walking round Hama Rikyū garden. In the afternoon, you can either walk up to Ginza, or travel by boat from Hama Rikyū to Asakusa on the Sumida River.

Try to visit Yoyogi Park on a Sunday when the street performers are out.

Kitanomaru Park and Ueno Park each possess several museums, useful in bad weather. Remember that almost all museums close on Mondays, except when Monday is a national holiday, in which case they close the following day.

Festivals

The best Tokyo *matsuri* are living dramas of Edo history. *Tokyo Journal* has a festivals section, and the tourist information centre publishes a comprehensive pamphlet called *Calendar Events* which lists happenings big and small, inside and outside the city.

January

1–3	**New Year celebrations (*Hatsumōde*)** take place at shrines and temples all over town. The Meiji Shrine and Asakusa's Sensō-ji temple attract the biggest crowds.
2	The Palace grounds are open and the Imperial Family waves at the crowds from behind bullet-proof glass.
6	**Dezomeshiki**. This is a throwback to the Edo period when the guilds of firemen were the most heroic and dashing men in the city. Present-day firefighters in period dress perform cunning stunts on top of ladders in Harumi, a dock island on Tokyo Bay.
Early–mid-month	A fifteen-day **sumo tournament** (*sumō bashō*) takes place at the National Stadium in Ryōgoku.

February

3	**Setsubun**. Local worthies and members of the public mark the New Year (according to the old calendar) by throwing beans at temples and shrines like Asakusa's Sensō-ji.

March

18	**Asakusa Kannon Jigenhoyoe.** The Goddess of Mercy is honoured at Sensō-ji temple. There are parades, traditional dancing and huge crowds.

April

Early	Performances of ***gagaku*** (ancient court music) take place in the Imperial Palace. Seats are available to the public; enquire at the tourist information centre well in advance.
Early–mid-month	**Cherry Blossom Viewing** takes place all over Tokyo, but especially in Ueno Park, Shinjuku Gyōen garden, Yasukuni Shrine, Chidorigafuchi Park and Hama Rikyū garden.
21– 23	Yasukuni Shrine has a **Spring Festival**.

May

Mid-month	**Kanda Matsuri** is held at Kanda Myōjin Shrine. This is one of the great Edo townsmen's festivals held in full only on even-numbered years, in alternation with the Sannō Matsuri. Three *hōren* (palanquins) and 76 *mikoshi* (portable shrines) are paraded through the streets from dawn until late into the night by extremely drunk men in *happi* coats.
Mid-month	Tokyo's biggest and most popular festival, the **Sanja Matsuri**, takes place at the Asakusa Shrine. A hundred portable shrines fill the streets; in the shrine itself, there are performances of weird and ancient music and dance.
Mid-month	A fifteen-day **sumo tournament** is held at the Ryōgoku National Stadium.

June

Second Sunday	**Torigoe Jinja Taisai**. The largest portable shrine in Tokyo, the *Sen-gan Mikoshi*, is paraded through the streets (Kuramae subway station).
10–16	The **Sannō Matsuri** alternates with the Kanda matsuri, being held in its full form only on odd-numbered years—an arrangement decreed after violent clashes between celebrants of the rival festivals. Held at the hilltop Hie Shrine. At its climax, mounted samurai accompany an ox-drawn carriage in a magnificent procession through the streets.
Late	Displays of **irises** at the Meiji Shrine.

July

9–10	**Hozuki Ichi**. Wind chimes and plants are sold at the Asakusa Sensō-ji temple on a day when Kannon is believed to bring blessings of happiness.
13–16	**Mitama matsuri**. Music, dance and *nō* are performed at the Yasukuni Shrine.
Late	There are firework displays (*hanabi*) over the Sumida River near Ryōgoku. Both banks of the river become packed very early on; the alternative to the crowds is to purchase an expensive place on one of the sightseeing boats on the water (enquire at the tourist information centre).

August

Early	**Takigi Nō**. Torchlit *nō* performances take place at the Hie Shrine in Akasaka.
Late	**Asakusa Samba Carnival**. A bizarre modern innovation: Asakusa's inhabitants adopt the accoutrements of a Latin-American carnival (parades of ladies in sequinned bikinis, etc.).

September

Mid-month	A fifteen-day **sumo tournament** is held at the Ryōgoku National Stadium.

October

Early	Performances of **gagaku** in the Imperial Palace. Seats available to the public; enquire at the tourist information centre.
Mid-month –early Nov	**Chrysanthemum displays** can be seen at Asakusa Sensō-ji temple, Yasukuni Shrine, Hibiya Park and Shinjuku Gyōen garden.
17–19	Yasukuni Shrine has its **Autumn Festival**.
18	Offering of chrysanthemums and **dancing** at Asakusa Sensō-ji.

November

On the Zodiacal Days of the Cock	A traditional festival of courtesans and *geisha* of the Edo entertainment quarters, held at Otori Shrine near the old Yoshiwara district (check with the tourist information centre for dates and how to get there).

December

23	The Emperor waves at the crowds in the Imperial Palace on his birthday.

Central Tokyo

The Imperial Palace (Kōkyo)

The best place to view the Imperial Palace is from above, from the upper storeys of one of the many high-rise office buildings that line the avenues of the adjacent government and business districts. There, even more starkly than on a map, the strangeness of the city's structure becomes clear. Apart from the roofs of the Emperor's residence and the Imperial Household Agency in its southeast corner, there is nothing palatial about the *Kōkyo* whatsoever, certainly not in the sense of Versailles or Buckingham Palace or even the palaces of Kyoto. It's a park, a shaggy forest of mixed trees with ponds and a few faint tracks visible in between. There used to be a nine-hole golf course there, built in the 1920s by the then Crown Prince Hirohito (he caught the bug on a visit to Britain). But years later—so the story goes—the biologist Emperor spotted a rare flower growing there, and decreed that the links should be allowed to return to their natural state. All around the palace grounds, pressing up against its moats like hungry predators, are the money palaces of Marunouchi and Kasumigaseki. This is the most expensive real estate in the world; the 130 acres, as every tour guide will tell you, are worth as much as the entire state of California.

The comparison is meaningless: this land, the green yolk at the centre of Tokyo's grey egg, can never be sold, developed or—by most people—even walked upon. It's tempting to see in this expensive nothingness an image of its inhabitant. Stripped of responsibility, divinity and power, the Japanese Emperor has survived, like the Imperial Palace, by doing precisely nothing. It is a space, not a place, just as he (to his subjects) is a symbol of state, not a human personality. But, like him, the palace grounds wield a symbolic influence far beyond their functional insignificance. Like a magnet, they transmit an invisible field that ripples through the city around them. From the imperial centre a whorl of moats and canals, partially filled in but still obvious on the map, spiral outwards to link up with the Sumida River. At a further remove is the circling Yamanote loop line. Aircraft flight paths, subway lines and expressways are all carefully routed to avoid encroaching above, below or upon the palace grounds. For years, building regulations forbade any structure which might be said to 'look down' upon the emperor.

Parts of the palace gardens are open to the public. In good weather the park is lovely; there are trees and plants to be enjoyed and history to be traced, and the whole thing can be adequately seen in a morning or an afternoon. But the Palace is interesting above all as a symbol, and one which provides clues to many aspects of Japanese culture and thought. 'One of the two most powerful cities of modernity,' wrote Roland Barthes in *Empire of Signs*, 'is built around an opaque ring of walls, streams, roofs and trees whose own centre is no more than an evaporated notion, subsisting here, not in order to irradiate power, but to give the entire urban movement the support of its central emptiness'.

History

All great capitals have their founding legends and Tokyo's is more bizarre than most. Ōta Dōkan, the 15th-century *daimyō* who unified the Kantō area, was sent here by Benten, the goddess who is worshipped on the island of Enoshima near Kamakura. As he was passing the mouth of present-day Tokyo Bay, a fish leaped from the waters and flopped onto the land at the foot of an adjacent hill. The fish was the kind called *konoshiro*; the words *kono shiro*, rendered in different Chinese characters, mean 'this castle'. Following the goddess's hint, Ōta constructed a fortification on the site in 1457, and it was passed down through the families who succeeded him. But it was as the seat of the shoguns and the capital of the Tokugawa state that Edo Castle achieved its greatest flowering.

Construction work began after Ieyasu's victory at the Battle of Sekigahara in 1600, as feudal lords, desperate for his favour, vied to outdo one another in the lavishness of their contributions and the number of workmen they committed to the project. Apart from the castle keep itself, the shogun's engineers set themselves the task of constructing a series of canals, serving both as waterways and fortifications, beginning at the Sumida River and its docks, and curling in on themselves in a tightening spiral to form the inner moat of the palace itself. Contemporary observers compared Edo with Venice, and many place names, like Sotobori-dōri (Outer Moat Avenue) commemorate these waterways. These days they're easier, and more rewarding, to find on the map than *in situ*—most have degenerated into malodorous drainage ditches, capped in many cases by concrete expressways which follow their course.

Reeds and sand had to be distributed over the swampy soil before foundations could be laid, and stones for the castle walls were ferried from the Izu Peninsula in 3000 ships. From the sea they were hauled by men and oxen, on carpets of slippery seaweed. Ships sank, walls collapsed and the retainers of rival *daimyō* feuded. But, by its completion in

1640, forty years after Ieyasu had made Edo his headquarters, the castle complex was a wonder. With boat-laden canals criss-crossed with bridges, waterside warehouses, smooth granite walls, fortified gates and guard towers, imperial and aristocratic residences, government offices and military barracks, it was a city within a city, the greatest castle Japan would ever see, and the centre of power and intrigue in the newly unified nation. At its heart was the keep, one of the biggest in the world: 40m above ground, and 84m above sea level, five storeys of sombre black tiles and plaster with a gleaming copper roof topped at its finials with *shachihoko*, dragon-like carp believed to ward off fire.

In fewer than 20 years it had burned to the ground. When the great blaze of 1657 swept Edo, a flaming whirlwind blew in the windows and quickly devoured the keep's wooden skeleton, igniting the gunpowder stores in the castle towers. Within two years the lesser buildings had been renewed, but Japan was by now at peace and, as a symbolic fist clenched above the city, the keep itself was unnecessary; apart from its stone foundation, it was never rebuilt.

By the Meiji Restoration, fires had done for most of the other buildings too. When the Emperor made the bold decision to site his palace here, in the very heartland of the defeated enemy, the Nishinomaru (Western Citadel) was chosen as the spot. The celebrated wooden buildings were praised by visitors, but they burned with the rest of the city during the air raids of 1945.

Visiting the Imperial Palace and Gardens

The palace grounds are divided into several areas with varying opening hours and degrees of accessibility.

Imperial Plaza (Kōkyo-mae Hiroba)

This is a public space, with free and unlimited access to all, except on special occasions. It is the most relaxed part of the imperial gardens, which isn't to say that it's comfortable or inviting: a roughly rectangular grid of lawns (on which you can at least sit, unlike those in the more popular Hibiya Park to the south) divided by broad gravel avenues and a busy road, **Uchibori-dōri**, which runs down the middle. In the winter, the unsheltered space is knifed by the wind; in summer, the gravel reflects the sun into a shimmering heat haze. It's a liminal place, a kind of annex to the palace, neither wholly imperial nor indisputably public. The Plaza serves as the official disaster evacuation zone for the Marunouchi business district. It's also the closest thing Tokyo has to a place of public assembly: demonstrations and open-air meetings are from time to time held here, and it's common to see the black vans of the *Uyoku*, the right-wing political groups, blaring their nationalist messages on the street in front of the moat. The most notorious incident occurred in 1952, just after the end of the American Occupation. A May Day assembly in Hibiya Park occupied the Plaza, and a frenzied battle broke out with police. Cars were overturned and burned, tear gas was fired, hundreds of police and civilians were injured, and two demonstrators were killed by police gunfire.

A turn around the Plaza is still something of a national institution for Japanese visitors. Whatever the weather, ant-like columns of uniformed schoolchildren troop backwards and forwards to have their photographs taken in front of **Nijū-bashi**, a double-arched iron bridge of 19th-century German design which, curiously, has become a sentimental symbol of the Japanese nation. Before 1945, young conscripts would come here to be photographed with their families before going off to war. Immediately after the surrender, ultra-nationalists chose the palace gates and bridges as the place to commit ritual suicide. The statue of the mounted warrior by the **rest house** in the southeast corner is **Kusunoki Masahige**, a 14th-century samurai, and a paragon of imperial loyalty.

Just beyond Nijū-bashi, and out of bounds, is the Fushimi turret, one of the few surviving Edo-period structures, apart from the walls. The **Sakashita-mon** gate, in the north part of the Plaza, is one of the main entrances into the palace. From the police box here, you can glimpse the roofs of the imperial residence and Household Agency.

Nishinomaru (Western Citadel)

The **Nishinomaru** is the private domain of the Imperial Family and Imperial Household Agency whose residences and offices it contains. Without an official invitation, it has always been difficult to enter this area: the cynical view has it that those commoners who have made it inside—the Empress Michiko and her daughter-in-law Princess Masako, for instance—are never seen again. However the Imperial Household Agency does run a little-known **group tour** of selected areas of the grounds and palace. Apart from the thrill of actually getting inside, there isn't much to get excited about. The original palace built for Emperor Meiji was burned by American bombers in 1945 and the oldest palace building dates from 1964. A new home for the Emperor and Empress was finished (for a controversial ¥5 billion) in 1993, and illustrated the problems of contemporary imperial taste: how to combine the simplicity and plainness of traditional Japanese structures with the opulence expected of international heads of state. The results—at least according to the official picture book released by the Agency—are bland in the extreme.

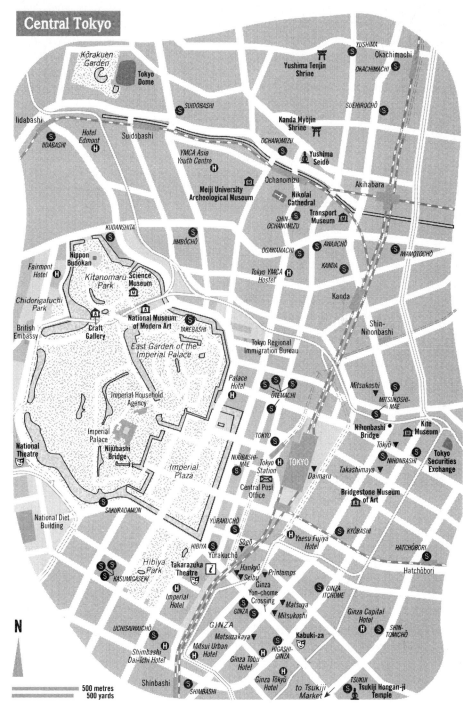

Central Tokyo

Kôrakuen Garden

Tokyo Dome

YUSHIMA

Okachimachi

Yushima Tenjin Shrine

OKACHIMACHI

SUIDOBASHI

SUEHIROCHÔ

Iidabashi

Hotel Edmont

Suidôbashi

Kanda Myôjin Shrine

IIDABASHI

YMCA Asia Youth Centre

OCHANOMIZU

Yushima Seidô

Meiji University Archeological Museum

Ochanomizu

Akihabara

Nikolai Cathedral

KUDANSHITA

Transport Museum

SHIN OCHANOMIZU

JIMBÔCHÔ

Nippon Budôkan

Fairmont Hotel

Kitanomaru Park

Science Museum

OGAWAMACHI

AWAJICHÔ

IWAMOTOCHÔ

KANDA

Chidorigafuchi Park

Tokyo YMCA Hostel

Kanda

British Embassy

Craft Gallery

National Museum of Modern Art

TAKEBASHI

Shin-Nihonbashi

East Garden of the Imperial Palace

Tokyo Regional Immigration Bureau

Imperial Household Agency

Palace Hotel

ÔTEMACHI

Mitsukoshi

MITSUKOSHI-MAE

National Theatre

Imperial Palace

Nijûbashi Bridge

TOKYO

Nihonbashi Bridge

Kite Museum

Tôkyû ▼

Imperial Plaza

NIJÛBASHI-MAE

Tokyo Station

TOKYO

NIHONBASHI

Tokyo Securities Exchange

Takashimaya ▼

Daimaru

Central Post Office

Bridgestone Museum of Art

National Diet Building

SAKURADAMON

YÛRAKUCHÔ

KYÔBASHI

HIBIYA

Sôgô

Yûrakuchô

Yaesu Fujiya Hotel

HATCHÔBORI

Hibiya Park

Takarazuka Theatre

Hatchôbori

KASUMIGASEKI

Hankyû ▼ Seibu

Printemps

Ginza Yon-chome Crossing

GINZA ITCHÔME

UCHISAIWAICHÔ

Imperial Hotel

Matsuya

Ginza Capital Hotel

GINZA

Mitsukoshi

SHIN-TOMICHÔ

GINZA

Matsuzakaya ▼

Kabuki-za

Shimbashi Dai-ichi Hotel

Mitsui Urban Hotel

HIGASHI-GINZA

Ginza Tôbu Hotel

N

Shinbashi

SHIMBASHI

Ginza Tôkyû Hotel

to Tsukiji Market

TSUKIJI

Tsukiji Hongan-ji Temple

500 metres
500 yards

*For those set on going, the guided tour lasts 90mins and is in Japanese only; admission is likely to be granted only reluctantly to non-Japanese speakers unless accompanied by a Japanese friend. Securing a place requires a phone call to the Visitors' Office (Sankan-gakari) of the **Imperial Household Agency**, ✆ 03 3213 1111 ext. 485, which will issue a permit to be picked up at least a day before the appointed time. At the time of writing, tours are conducted on weekdays and begin at either 10am or 1.30pm at the Kikyō-mon gate (one down from the Ōte-mon) on the east (Marunouchi) side of the moat. The tourist information centre has up-to-date information and may even make an appointment for you.*

The public are also allowed into the Inner Palace on 2 January and 23 December to pay their New Year and birthday respects to the Emperor. He can be seen with his family waving at the loyal crowd behind a sheet of bullet-proof glass, installed after an alarming incident when an over-excited subject hurled a steel *pachinko* ball at his sovereign.

Higashi Gyōen (East Garden)

The East Garden is the former site of Edo castle, the shogun's seat, and contains relics of the old keep, attractive gardens and good views of the city. You can enter or leave by three of the old palace gates: the **Ōte-mon** (the main entrance, near Ōtemachi subway station), the **Hirakawa-mon** (opposite the Mainichi newspaper building and near Takebashi subway station); and the **Kitahanebashi-mon** (which leads into Kitanomaru Park). (*Open 9–4 exc. Mon and Fri, but open when those days fall on a national holiday; closed 25 Dec–5 Jan; adm free—pick up a token at the admission booth which you surrender at the exit; last adm 3pm.*)

The most common entry to the East Garden is through the **Ōte-mon**, a 1967 reconstruction of the main gate of the shogun's castle, originally built over 420,000 man days by Date Masamune, the powerful *daimyō* of Sendai. Inside, you pass several buildings, modern and traditional: on the right, the new **Shōwa Memorial Hall**, currently under construction, and a couple of **rest houses**; on the left, the **Cabinet Library**, the headquarters of the imperial palace police division, and then a long, low wooden building in Edo style—the **Hyakunin-bansho** (Hundred-man Guardhouse).

The right-hand path just beyond here leads you to a stretch of the old **Hakuchō-bori** (Swan Moat), at the foot of an impressive section of walled rampart, constructed without mortar out of smoothly finished cyclopean blocks. The area in front of these is the old **Nino-maru** (Second Citadel), containing a stroll garden, with a pond and tea house, designed in the mid-17th century by the master landscaper Kobori Enshū. A steep path, just north of the Swan Moat, is called the **Shiomi-zaka** (Tide-Viewing Slope): from here you can see the buildings of Hibiya which was, in the early Edo period, a coastal inlet and port, before land reclamation drove back the waters of Tokyo Bay.

The slope leads up to the **Hon-maru** (Inner Citadel); you can also get there by returning to the Hundred-man Guardhouse and taking the left-hand turn. Following this route and keeping to the left you come, in the southernmost corner of the garden, to the **Fujimi Yagura** (Mt Fuji-Viewing Turret) which may once have lived up to its name, before the days of photo-chemical smog. When the decision was made after the great fire not to rebuild the main keep, this became the primary defensive point of the castle; finished in 1659, the three-storey building suggests in miniature something of the original architecture of the citadel.

At the north end of the Hon-maru, the huge stone pedestal is all that remains of the keep itself which, though splendid, was only intended for occupation as a last resort, and remained largely empty for its brief life. The residential and administrative base of the shogun and his court lay between here and the Fujimi Turret. At the south end were the halls used for state and ceremonial occasions including the **Ōhiroma** (Hall of a Thousand Mats), where distinguished petitioners, including the factor of the Dutch trading post in Nagasaki, were received in audience by the shogun. Twice a month all of the feudal lords serving their six-month stint in Edo also assembled in these chambers.

The second group of buildings contained the shogun's personal offices, and behind them were the inner chambers where no men, apart from doctors and a few guards, were allowed to trespass. This was the shogun's seraglio, a centre of profound intrigue, ruled over by his wife and the 500 to 1000 maidservants and concubines who served beneath her. In the 19th century, politicking in the inner chambers got particularly out of hand, despite the extraordinary precautions that were taken to avoid corruption—even at the most intimate moments between the shogun and his partners, at least two other ladies remained in discreet attendance to ensure that the concubine of the moment didn't abuse her power by asking for political favours.

The bizarre octagonal structure in the northeast corner, decorated with abstract mosaics, is the **Tōgaku-dō**, a private concert hall built in 1968 for the then Empress.

North of the Palace

Kitahane-bashi (the name means 'Northern Drawbridge', although the modern structure no longer lifts up and down) connects the East Gardens with **Kitanomaru Kōen** (North Citadel Park), a former territory of the Imperial Palace which was given to the nation on the Shōwa Emperor's 60th birthday in 1969.

In the south part of the park are four museums, although they don't measure up to those in Ueno Park to the northeast of the city. On the right, and before the Shutō expressway which makes a rare incursion into the Palace grounds, are the **National Archives** (Kokuritsu Kōbunsho-kan), of little use to anyone who can't read Japanese, and the **Tokyo National Museum of Modern Art** (Kokuritsu Kindai Bijutsukan, *adm ¥400 for permanent collection only*), which has a permanent display of paintings, prints and sculpture post-1868, and a space for visiting exhibitions. Of more interest is its satellite museum, the **Crafts Gallery** (Kōgei-kan), housed in a Meiji-period brick building, five minutes' walk west of the National Museum. The pottery, textiles, lacquerware and carvings on display here are a tribute to the subsidies and support which the Japanese government has given to its traditional industries. The select collection includes work by Living (and Deceased) National Treasures. Look out for Arakawa Toyozō's ceramics, and the beautiful raw silk kimono by Shimura Fukumi. The building, complete with chandeliers, used to be the headquarters of the Imperial Guard, who had the run of Kitanomaru Park after the Meiji Restoration. In 1878, in an event almost unprecedented in Japanese military history and symptomatic of the social turmoil caused by the Restoration, 200 privates mutinied against their officers, resentful at the division of rewards after the suppression of Saigō Takamori's Seinan rebellion. After attempting to petition the Emperor, they were defeated and 49 of them executed.

The **Science Museum** (Kagaku Gijutsu-kan) is north of the others, and crowded with uniformed high school students at whom the beeping, button-pressing displays seem primarily to be aimed. At the north end of the park is a squat building with a gleaming octagonal roof topped with a gold mushroom: the 14,000-seat **Nippon Budō-kan** (Japan Martial Arts Hall), familiar to rock stars the world over as the venue for many of Tokyo's most lavish concerts. It was built for the 1964 Olympics, but achieved its greatest fame two years later when the Beatles sold out for five nights here. Profits were a hundred million yen; the 8000 police deployed to protect the Fab Four from their fans cost another ninety million.

The **Tayasu-mon** (Tayasu Gate) at the northern end of the park is one of the oldest and most impressive portals in the castle grounds, built sometime in the 1620s, with two gates: a wide inner one to allow a mass of defenders to exit easily; and a narrow outer gate to impede the progress of attackers. The two stand at ninety degrees to one another, and between them is a square courtyard surrounded by turrets and high walls. Even if enemies did penetrate the first gate, they would be assailed by arrows and rocks as they wheeled round to face the second, sturdier portal. The inner courtyard is called the *masugata*, after the *masu*, a square wooden drinking cup whose shape it shares.

Yasukuni Jinja (Yasukuni Shrine)

The lantern originally stood in the grounds of **Yasukuni Jinja** (Shrine for the Repose of the Nation), the area's controversial main attraction, entrance opposite the Tayasu-mon. This was founded in 1869 as the *shōkon-sha*, the 'shrine to which the spirits of the dead are invited'. Specifically, it enshrined the souls of those who had perished in the civil wars of the Meiji Restoration, and since then it has become a kind of Valhalla for all who have died in the service of the nation or—more controversially—the Emperor. Among the glorious dead honoured here are victims of the Boxer Rebellion, three Englishmen who died in the naval battle of Tsushima during the Russo-Japanese War, and the fallen of the Pacific War, including the wartime Prime Minister Tōjō Hideki and eight others hanged by the military tribunals as Class A war criminals. It is the resort of right-wing extremists (the ultra nationalist assassins of at least one prime minister made solemn vows here before carrying out their crime); but it is also the closest thing in the popular imagination to a national Cenotaph or Tomb of the Unknown Soldier. Every year there is a tremendous fuss when members of the Cabinet are invited to pay their respects here. If they accept, they are accused by the left of violating the constitution which separates government and religion; if they decline they are noisily denounced by the right. Recently ministers have fudged the issue by attending the services but stating that they were doing so only as 'private individuals', not as members of the government.

For all this, the shrine is a pleasant place and a famous and beautiful cherry blossom-viewing spot with a number of different varieties primed to go off at various times over the April season. A 15m tall bronze **Ōtorii** (Great Gate) marks the entrance to a long, cherry-planted avenue, with the formidable shrine sanctuary (built in the Ise style, with jutting 'horns' at the finials) at the far end. There's a stage in front; at the **Mitama matsuri** (festival) from 13–16 July, traditional dances and candle-lit *nō* plays are performed on it.

East of the Palace

Hibiya, at the southeast corner of the palace, between Kasumigaseki and Ginza, was a tidal inlet in the early days of Edo—the name comes from a kind of oyster trap which was set on the mud flats by fishermen. After the land had been reclaimed *daimyō* built their houses here. Today, it's a quarter of banks, theatres, concert halls and hotels, busy and purposeful during the day, rather still and empty in the evenings.

Hibiya Kōen (Hibiya Park) was laid out in 1903 on the site of a parade ground where the emperor used to review the troops. It was the city's first Western-style park. By day it is respectable, with a popular fountain plaza, a library and meeting hall. But quite early on it gained a night-time reputation, which it retains today, as a meeting place for couples who don't have the price of a love hotel, and the Peeping Toms who come in their wake.

On Hibiya-dōri, the avenue which runs along its east side, are the **Imperial Hotel** and the **Takarazuka Theatre**, described later on. Just south of them, until its demolition in 1941, was the famous **Rokumei-kan** (Deer Cry Pavilion), which lends its name to that part of the Meiji period (the 1880s) when the craze for things Western was at its height. It was designed by Josiah Conder, the most famous of several British architects who more than compensated for their mediocre talents by simply being in the right country at the right time. Ochanomizu's Nikolai Cathedral and the Mitsui Club in Mita are the only designs of his to survive, but photographs and prints show the Rokumei-kan to have been more elaborate and pretentious than either.

It was built in brick on two storeys in an eclectic, vaguely Italian style with a high arcade of arched pillars along the front, and a Gallic tiled roof. Inside were 15,000 square feet of residential suites for visiting guests, a ballroom, and chambers for music, billiards, reading and cards. At the time of its completion in 1883, Japanese foreign relations laboured resentfully under humiliatingly unequal trade treaties. Shows of lavish modernity were part of the policy of convincing the West that Japan was just as civilized and enlightened as the next country; the Rokumei-kan, in other words, was a shameless act of international social climbing.

The Rokumei-kan era was intense but short-lived. For a while bustles, ballroom dancing lessons and charity bazaars were *de rigueur* among the wives of aristocrats, academics, politicians and diplomats. But the snobbery and naivety of Rokumei-kan diplomacy were transparent, and within a few years a reaction set in. The Prime Minister, Itō Hirobumi, was caught out in an affair with a married noblewoman; shortly before, he had been waltzing at a fancy dress ball attired as a Venetian prince. The two may not have been connected but, in the public mind at least, enough was enough. High jinks at the Rokumei-kan petered out of their own accord, and after an earthquake in 1893 the building remained in a state of semi-dilapidation until its demolition.

Yūrakuchō and Marunouchi

Ever since General MacArthur established his Occupation HQ in the present day Dai-Ichi Insurance building round the corner, **Yūrakuchō** has been at the heart of foreign life in Tokyo. Any exploration of the city should begin at the excellent **tourist information centre**, a few metres south of the west exit of Yūrakuchō station. Plenty of other international institutions are clustered in the blocks opposite, including the **American Express** office, the **American Pharmacy**, stocking foreign drugs, cosmetics and magazines, and the Foreign Correspondents' Club of Japan. Yūrakuchō means 'The Place Where Pleasure Can Be Had', and in the 1950s it was notorious for another kind of service available to visiting foreigners: the *pan-pan* girls, described by Fosco Maraini as 'painted harridans, with huge heels and misshapen legs, who shout, smoke, spit, chew gum, and call out "Hey, Johnnie!" at passers-by.' The *pan-pan* are less visible now, but parts of Yūrakuchō still have an agreeably raffish atmosphere, especially the underpasses beneath the railway tracks where tiny stalls serve cheap *yakitori* as the trains roll overhead.

Marunouchi means 'Within the Citadel', and *daimyō* built their houses here from the earliest years of the 17th century. By the late 19th century it had stagnated. 'Marunouchi was a place of darkness and silence, of loneliness and danger,' wrote the poet Takahama Kyoshi, 'the abode of foxes and badgers. Here and there were weed-grown hillocks from aristocratic gardens. The murder of Ōtsuya [a young local girl] was much talked about in those days.'

The area was called Mitsubishigahara, 'the Mitsubishi wasteland', after the family company which had bought the area for a knock-down price when no other buyer could be found. Mitsubishi commissioned Josiah Conder (he of the Rokumei-kan) to build their headquarters here, and slowly a crossroads of brick offices, 'Londontown' (Itchō Rondon), formed. In 1914 a student of Conder built Tokyo station which survives—minus its bombed domes and upper stories—to give some idea of **Itchō Rondon**'s original appearance. At the time, everyone considered Mitsubishi to have made a stupid purchase; now, of course, Marunouchi is the corporate capital of Japan, and the most desirable business address in the country. Useful buildings in the heart of the district here include the credit card agent in the **Shin Marunouchi Biru** (New Marunouchi Building) on the west side of the station plaza, and the 24-hour, 365-days-a-year **Central Post Office** on its south side.

Ginza

Few urban districts in the world—Broadway, perhaps, or the Champs Elysées—have had such a hold on the national imagination as Ginza. Fifty-one popular songs, at the last count, contain the word *Ginza* in their titles. There are 500 regional Ginzas in towns throughout Japan, and countless Ginza Bars, Ginza Clubs and Ginza Shopping Centres. Ginza has become a brand name and an advertising slogan, a by-word for the most sophisticated shops, the most urbane cafés, and the most exorbitant property prices. Shifting exchange rates frequently prove such generalizations wrong, but it used to be said that if one took a ¥10,000 note, folded it as tightly as possible, and dropped it on the pavement at Ginza Crossing, it would not be enough to purchase the land it rested upon.

Ginza is also synonymous, of course, with Westernization and with the renewal and affluence that, until recently at least, were associated with the products of the West. It began to acquire this status in 1872 when the country's first railway line was opened between Yokohama and Shinbashi. Ginza, a few blocks to the north, found itself the natural disembarkation point for foreign goods, foreign ideas and foreign nationals as they arrived in Tokyo from the port. A few months earlier, a fire had destroyed the old wooden Ginza and the opportunity was taken to carry the new principle of Civilization and Enlightenment into bold practice. A British architect was hired and the quarter was rebuilt in expensive imitation of a Western city. Within a couple of years, two-storey brick houses with balconies flanked the main thoroughfares which were lined with trees, gas lamps and— another first—pavements. 'Bricktown', as it was called, drew crowds of sightseers, including woodblock artists whose prints show lively scenes of horse-drawn carriages and big-nosed foreigners strolling beneath the cherry trees and colonnades. But few Japanese, in the early days at least, were willing to live there. The houses harboured bugs and were damp and badly ventilated; rumours persisted that their inhabitants were prone to horrible diseases. Squatters and street entertainers with performing animals moved in, and the trees on the boulevards withered and died.

With generous subsidies the municipal authorities lured businesses back, and by the turn of the century Ginza was established as the place to buy Western-style suits, hats and other exotic goods like watches and spectacles. Newspaper offices, another foreign innovation, moved their offices here, and a *geisha* quarter was established by Shinbashi station.

Tram tracks (electrified in 1903) were laid down the main street, and horse-drawn omnibuses were seen earlier here than anywhere else in the city. Many of Japan's most famous department stores and venerable family businesses were established in Ginza at this time. The famous clock tower which still stands outside the Wakō store on Ginza Yon-chōme appeared there in 1894.

It was also the place where the social fashions which spread through Japan in the early 20th century were most visible. Ginza was the habitat of the *moga* (modern girl or *gāru*) with her bobbed hair, gloves and earrings, and the *mobo* (modern boys) who hung out in cafés, milk bars, beer halls or ballrooms where, for one and a half yen, they could hire a 'taxi partner' to teach them the steps of the unaccustomed new dances. The street fashions were French in inspiration; the most famous cafés were the Plantain, the Lion, the Paulista, and the Colombin, with its 8m model of the Eiffel Tower. A new word was coined to describe the favoured activity of these spangled exotics: *Gimbura*, combining the first syllable of Ginza with the first syllable of *burabura*, meaning to loll or loiter or idle. While flappers were flapping in New York and London, their counterparts in Tokyo were loafing in Ginza.

The earthquake and fire of 1923 destroyed the crumbling remains of the old Bricktown, and between the world wars Ginza acquired a high-rise character, with the new multi-storey shops like Wakō, Mitsukoshi and Matsuya. The shortage of foreign goods during the war put a dampener on the district's traditional activities, but it suffered less from the bombing than many areas, and was reborn in the American Occupation, benefiting from the proximity of General MacArthur's HQ round the corner in Hibiya. Along with Akasaka, Ginza is one of the few places left in Tokyo where you just might see *geisha*, stepping in and out of taxis between the tea houses.

A Loaf through Ginza

The *burabura* approach is still the best one to take in Ginza. A stroll from the **tourist information centre** to the **Kabuki-za theatre** (try to time your walk to coincide with a performance there) can take anything from half an hour to a whole day, and even if the centres of youth fashion have shifted west to Shibuya and Shinjuku, Ginza still has a flourishing streetlife with Tokyo's most magisterial shops, some striking architectural oddities, and the smelliest drains in central Tokyo: despite their colossal expensiveness the streets have never been properly plumbed, and waste is still disposed of through open sewers.

Turning right outside the tourist information centre and passing under the railway tracks (bullet trains pass overhead, as well as the more conventional JR trains) you remain technically in Yūrakuchō until the fly-over of the expressway. But the **Mullion Building**, between the railway and the road, is spiritually part of Ginza, with an exterior of vertical pieces of glass, and equally gleaming shops. Herein is a complex of banks, cinemas, subways, and a stunning, gravity-defying central atrium which ascends the full 12 storeys, dividing the **Hankyū** and **Seibu department stores**. At the front of the edifice, beneath the Japanized versions of American film posters, is a large innocuous-looking clock which every hour bursts into an animated display of electronic chiming. Ask for *Marion no tokei*, 'the Mullion clock'—it makes a useful Ginza rendezvous point.

Beyond the expressway, on the south side of the road, is the **Sony Building**, with its façade of 74 rectangular TV screens, a huge electronic canvas periodically reprogrammed with abstract designs by video artists. Inside are hands-on displays of the latest Sony gizmos like High-Definition TV and laser discs. **Jena** (*Iena*) book shop, a few metres along, has a cramped but diverse selection of English titles.

Ginza's most eminent institutions are concentrated around **Ginza Yon-chōme Crossing** where Harumi-dōri, the west–east street along which you have been walking, meets the north–south Chūo-dōri. On the southwest corner is the **San'ai Building**, a cylindrical sandwich of neon lights and glass-walled shops and cafés. Just behind here, on Chūo-dōri, is **Kyūkyodō**, a 300-year-old vendor of products made from *washi* Japanese paper. Upstairs are brushes and other paraphernalia associated with calligraphy.

Opposite the San'ai Building, on the northwest corner of the crossing is **Wakō**, a pricey department store which began life as a street stall, opened by an enterprising clockmaker's apprentice in the late 19th century, when gentlemen's watches were a badge of Civilization and Enlightenment. North of it, on Chūo-dōri, is the Tokyo branch of the **Mikimoto** pearl business whose patriarch invented the cultured pearl in 1893. On the east side of Chūo-dōri are three vast department stores: in ascending order of prestige, **Matsuya** (to the north), **Matsuzakaya** (to the south) and **Mitsukoshi** (on the corner).

The original **Kabuki-za** (Kabuki Theatre), 250m east of Mitsukoshi, couldn't have been more different from the present building. It was finished in 1889; surviving prints and photographs show what looks like an unusually attractive European-style structure, with columns, arches and large sculpted pediments. *Kabuki* had always been considered a rather vulgar, low city form, but in the posh new theatre *shitamachi* townspeople and high city toffs sat side by side. Then, in 1925, it was rebuilt in an ornate, bristling Momoyama style: the curved arches and heavy tile roofs were reproduced in modern materials which endow the building with a rather sinister, overbearing atmosphere, unpleasantly appropriate to the authoritarian political regimes which grew to dominate Japan between the wars (*see* p.244 for details of tickets and times).

Nihonbashi

Before 1868, Nihonbashi was at the heart of *shitamachi*, the 'low city', where, in popular imagery, the salt-of-the-earth townspeople of Edo lived in rowdy contrast to the stuffy shogunal types over the moat. It was always the richest area of *shitamachi*, home—by virtue of the docks that once existed just to the south here—to the big shipping and retail businesses. Today, the area is indisputably high city, with flagship department stores and big financial institutions, but these days it has a rather dowdy, neglected atmosphere as if the rest of Tokyo has forgotten that it is there. Of the Edo period nothing remains, although there are a few Meiji buildings and some interesting, long-established shops.

Ginza becomes Nihonbashi just north of the expressway. Chūō-dōri, the main north–south street leading up from the Ginza crossing, is probably the closest Tokyo gets to the airy boulevards of European cities, and the further north you go, the more civic and respectable it becomes. There are occasional wacky touches: a giant paint pot with a brush sticking out on top of a building, and, a few blocks further north on the left-hand turning into Yaesu-dōri, a beautiful bronze giraffe, contoured in gold and wearing a gold crown; **Mon Coffee**, the café just above it, is a stylish place to watch the world going by.

In the middle of Yaesu-dōri is a memorial, in Japanese and Dutch, to Jan Joosten, a ship-wrecked Dutch sailor of the early 17th century who settled in Edo, and lent his name—characteristically mangled first to Yayosu, then Yaesu—to the area on this side of Tokyo station, the east exit of which is the *Yaesu-guchi*.

On the other side of Chūō-dōri is the **Bridgestone Bijutsukan** (*open 10–6; closed Mon*), an art museum which offers a superb short history of European painting and sculpture. The collection, owned by the tyre company, is small and select, with hardly a duff item and many masterpieces, beautifully presented. It begins with Greek and Roman statuary and a superb Egyptian corner, but the majority of the pieces are Impressionist or later: typically overripe Renoirs and Monets, a Cézanne of Mont St Victoire, an attractive faun by Rodin, paintings by Modigliani and Derain, some outstanding Picassos. Interesting too are the period works by Japanese artists, like Okada Saburosuke's 1907 *Portrait of a Lady*, a perfect example of the 'Japonesque' style that represented the only real attempt to meld foreign and native approaches to painting. The oriental elements—a *taiko* drum, a kimono, a gold screen—are clichés, mere decorative fancies. The other Japanese painters represented seldom ascend above pastiche: a Japanese Renoir, a Japanese Picasso, a Japanese Chagall.

Chūō-dōri continues, past **Maruzen** book shop and the **Takashimaya** and **Tōkyū** department stores (Takashimaya's lift attendants have the snappiest livery in Tokyo: mustard yellow suits and black straw hats), until it reaches the feature which gave Nihonbashi its name: 'The Bridge of Japan' which marked the meeting point of the five highways linking the capital and the provinces, including the great Tōkaidō between Edo and imperial Kyoto. All roads led to Nihonbashi, and all distances were measured from the marker in its middle. It burned and collapsed at regular intervals (on one occasion 1200 people who were escaping from a fire went down with it), and in 1911 was rebuilt in its present form: an elegant construction of low arches, paved in granite, guarded by four lions and four unicorns. The bridge should be a point of pride and a much-needed breathing space between buildings; instead it is dirty, seedy and in perpetual twilight. In 1962, in the rush for modernization before the Tokyo Olympics, an expressway was built right over the top of it, and the once lively Nihonbashi River was transformed into a subterranean canal.

Turning right just after Tōkyū department store you will come, on your left, to the Taimeiken Building with a restaurant of the same name on the ground floor. On the fifth floor is the **Kite Museum** (Tako no Hakubutsukan), an eccentric little place founded by the late Shingo Motegi, a kite enthusiast of international repute. The total collection numbers 3000; ten per cent are on display here, including kites in the form of birds, insects, warriors, demons and squid.

Mitsukoshi department store (closed on Mondays), on the north side of Nihonbashi bridge, went through numerous transformations from the Mitsui dry goods store founded in the 17th century. Mitsukoshi was the first of the merchant retailers to turn itself into a department store in the modern sense. From 1908 to 1914 it occupied a Western-style building inspired by London's Harrods. It was the first shop to display its goods in glass cases, rather than bringing them out of storage at the customer's request; it also installed Japan's first escalators in 1914. The present Mitsukoshi went up in 1935. The two great lions guarding the main entrance are imitations of those in Trafalgar Square, but the façade still has a decorative, distinctly oriental air about it.

You couldn't say the same for the building to the northwest, the old **Bank of Japan**, completed in 1896 on the site of the old gold mint, and next to **Tokiwa-bashi**, Tokyo's oldest stone bridge which is also still there. Its architect was Tatsuno Kingo who later designed Tokyo station, and its cobbled courtyard, solid columns and green bronze dome make it one of the most elegant and refreshing Meiji-era buildings in Tokyo.

North Tokyo

Between the Imperial Palace and Ueno Park is an interesting and subtle area, little frequented by tourists, with some of the most tranquil inner city escapes in the metropolis. This has long been a centre of scholarship in Tokyo: the Tokyo University (Tōdai) main campus is in Hongō just a few minutes' walk from the Yushima Tenjin, one of several important shrines and temples.

Akihabara (The Field of Autumn Leaves) is one of several places in Tokyo that are straight out of science fiction. It assumed importance in the Meiji period as a freight yard, and a market selling combs and accessories, and later bicycles, sprang up beneath the railway tracks. After 1945 it was the point at which army surplus goods entered Tokyo from the Chiba peninsula, and chief among these were radios, a prestige item in the post-war years. Technology students from the nearby universities set up their own stalls selling home-made gadgets, and Akihabara developed into the beeping, buzzing, whirring, electronic amusement arcade that exists today. In 1991, the turnover in these few blocks was ten trillion yen, fully 10 per cent of the national total in domestic electrical goods. Everything—from fridges and washing machines to pocket-sized computers and trans-lating machines—can be bought here, and bargained for. 'At Akihabara,' wrote Edward Seidensticker, 'and we who do not know must take the statement on faith, the electroni-cally sophisticated person can find anything that has been invented.'

For all its technological sophistication, the atmosphere of the black market still lingers around Akihabara: most of the traders are small and specialized, and you can tell at a glance what kind of goods they sell. Almost everything can be tried out in the shop. In recent years, Akihabara is said to have lost its competitive edge in goods like cameras to the discount chain stores in places like Shibuya and Shinjuku, and committed bargain hunters should shop around. In any case the crippling exchange rate neutralizes a lot of yen reductions: Japanese goods may actually be cheaper back home, or in Hong Kong. Balance any savings against the inconvenience of adapter plugs and instructions and war-ranties in Japanese (although international brands like Sony and Toshiba can be serviced and repaired anywhere). Above all, Akihabara is a fun place to shop, even if you don't buy: gizmos and innovations go on sale here before anywhere else in the world (*see* p.231).

Nikorai-dō (Nikolai Cathedral)

Open Tues–Sat, 1–4; donation expected.

This small cathedral, the headquarters of the Orthodox Church in Japan, is one of the most peaceful, calming and un-Japanese places in Tokyo. Officially called the Cathedral of the Holy Resurrection of Our Lord, it's popularly named after its founder, St Nikolai Kassatkin (1836–1912), who first travelled to Hakodate as chaplain to the Russian consulate in 1861. It was built between 1884 and 1891 from a design by the ubiquitous British architect Josiah Conder, and suffered badly during the Great Earthquake when the dome collapsed and the interiors were gutted by fire. The dome was lowered to avoid a repeat disaster; today, squatting beyond a high embankment wall, the building is certainly no beauty. But its Byzantine appearance and green copper roofs are unique in Tokyo and an Ochanomizu trademark; there's even a coffee shop by the station with its own version of the onion dome.

The interior is surprisingly small, but the cool, echoic darkness is stunning after the noise and smog of Tokyo. Candles flicker on metal spikes before the languid icons—buy one in lieu of an entrance fee.

Yushima Seidō (Confucian Temple)

On the right, 100m north of Ochanomizu JR station east exit. Open 9.30–5; adm free.

Buddhism and Shinto (frequently the two were indistinguishable) remained the popular religions of Japan during the Edo period, but it was Confucianism—or rather a Japanese inflection of the teachings of the Chinese sages—which provided the ideological base for the Tokugawa state, and a code of ethics which is still discernible in Japanese society today. Just as Buddhism, with its concentric ranking of lesser *bosatsu* around a supreme deity, suited the centralizing policies of the early emperors, so the Confucian virtues of obedience, loyalty to elders and rulers, and sublimation of individual impulses in the interests of the group, were vigorously promoted and idealized by the shoguns. Scholarship, for a long time, meant only Confucian learning, and the centre of its practice and propagation was in present-day Ochanomizu.

One of Tokugawa Ieyasu's sons built a Confucian academy in Ueno in the 1630s, which was moved to this site in 1691 by the fervent Confucianist, Tsunayoshi, the fifth shogun. Promising sons of the samurai completed their military educations with study of the Chinese classics; the senior academicians were among the Tokugawas' closest and most esteemed advisers, and twice a year the shogun and his lords gathered here for lectures and ceremonies. What remained of the old complex burned utterly after the 1923 earthquake, and the present buildings, dating from 1935, include the **Nyūtoku-mon**, a black wooden gate with a green roof, and the concrete **Taisei-den** (Hall of Accomplishment) where Confucius and his followers are enshrined.

Kanda Myōjin Shrine

Ochanomizu contains institutions at the poles of Edo culture: on one block, the Confucianism of Yushima Seidō, the cold disciplinarian faith of the High City; over the road, the boisterous Shinto of the **Kanda Myōjin**, the Edo townsman's shrine whose bi-annual festival held on 9–15 May (odd-numbered years only) is one of the biggest and noisiest in the city.

The shrine was founded in 730 and was long associated with Taira no Masakado, a 10th-century lord who rebelled against the Kyoto court and declared himself Emperor. He was killed in battle, but his headless body was seen haunting Edo until he was enshrined, originally in Ōtemachi. In 1616 Tokugawa Ieyasu, no lover of emperors himself, moved him to Kanda and declared him guardian deity of the entire city. When the Emperor Meiji elected to worship there, however, the presence of this rebellious god was considered inappropriate. The shrine priests were prevailed upon to transfer his numen to a lesser shrine, and substitute that of an uncontroversial deity.

A copper *torii* gate behind the Seidō leads to the main shrine buildings, rebuilt attractively enough in concrete, with elegantly jutting tile roofs. Alongside them is the **Mikoshi-den**, the hall containing the ornate portable shrines paraded through the streets at festival time. The biggest is called **Sengan Mikoshi**, 'The Shrine Weighing 1000 *Kan*'—just under four tons. It's an exaggeration, but not by very much. During the festivities 400 porters in *happi* coats, often very drunk, are required to bear it through the neighbourhood.

Yushima Tenjin

Yushima subway station (Chiyoda Line); at the north end of Hongō-dōri, 800m from Kanda Myōjin.

Ten minutes' walk from the main campus of Tokyo University, this is Tokyo's principal shrine to Sugawara no Michizane, the 9th-century courtier deified as Tenjin, god of scholarship. These days he is worshipped principally as the god of passing exams (which isn't, of course, the same thing at all). During the entrance exam season, the precincts are crowded with candidates making supplications to the deity and buying the talismans (exam-passing amulets, even exam-passing pens and pencils) sold in the shrine shop. Wooden votive plaques festoon the grounds bearing detailed instructions to the deity on universities applied for and grades required. Late February and early March is also the season of the *ume* (plum) blossom, Tenjin's flower whose five-petalled crest adorns the 19th-century buildings.

Ueno

Compared to other districts of Tokyo, Ueno has a complicated and mixed atmosphere, and no one tribe holds sway. Ladies with Gucci handbags stroll beneath the trees at the northern end of the park, *en route* to piano recitals at the Festival Hall or exhibitions at the cluster of civic museums. At the southern entrance, the steps are crowded with homeless vagrants, pavement artists and Iranians dealing in counterfeit phone cards and expensive, illegal drugs. For a week or so in April, the park becomes the most densely peopled spot in Japan, as tens of thousands gather for liquid picnics beneath the cherry blossoms. Ueno feels like a remnant of an earlier Tokyo, less self-conscious and squeakily affluent. The young are not so obviously dominant; older people feel comfortable here too.

History

Originally a headland jutting out into the sea, Ueno, by the time of the Tokugawa shoguns, was a feudal estate owned by Tōdō Takatora, the engineer of Edo castle. In 1624 the second shogun had a temple built on the hill and installed the monk Tenkai, a confidant of Tokugawa Ieyasu, who developed it into a huge complex of 36 sub-temples and 36 lesser halls. The temple's name was Tōeizan (Hiei-zan in the East) Kan'ei-ji, and its function was similar to that of the great Enryaku-ji on Kyoto's Mt Hiei: to protect the shogun and his city from the unlucky northeast direction, the source of plague, fire and evil spirits.

The temple flourished, despite being outside the city limits, and a thriving quarter of restaurants, workshops and brothels grew up around it. In 1868, however, Kan'ei-ji became one of the few significant casualties of the generally bloodless Meiji Restoration. As well as being commandingly situated on a hill, the temple grounds contained the tombs of six shoguns, and a band of about 2000 Tokugawa loyalists, rejecting the surrender which had been agreed by their leaders, holed up here and dispatched patrols into the city. On 4 July the imperial forces on adjacent high land in Hongō mounted an artillery attack on the resisters. Many of the shells fell short, and fires were started. The remaining buildings were finished off in hand-to-hand fighting after the imperial troops breached the temple's main Black Gate. Three hundred men died and the ancient halls and temples were almost completely destroyed.

The land was due to be used for a medical school, but one Dr Bauduin, a Dutch adviser to the government, persuaded the authorities to create a park instead (a statue of the far-sighted doctor stands even today). For a while it became a popular spot for horse racing on a track which ran around the Shinobazu Pond. In 1882 the National Museum was opened, along with Tokyo Zoo, and a series of public-spirited concert halls, libraries and galleries. The pond was drained and, along with much of the park, given over to agriculture during the war, but it was restored during the Occupation. It was too late, though, for many of the zoo animals: as wartime food shortages became graver, they had to be put down. Those too big for bullets or poison, like the elephants, starved to death.

Ever since its station opened in 1883, Ueno has been the point of entry into the capital from the northern provinces. During the post-war period, poor farmers flocked to Tokyo in their thousands to start new lives in the city. Many of them never got further than Ueno which was for a couple of years a refugee camp for the homeless, a melancholy role which it hasn't entirely shaken off today.

Ameyoko (Candy or America Alley)

Hard left outside the Park Exit of Ueno station is the main relic of post-war hardship, a narrow alley of shops and stalls running beneath the tracks as far down as Okachimachi station, the next stop down on the Yamanote line. An apocryphal story tells of a Tokyo judge who, in the days of the tightest post-war rationing, refused to compromise himself by eating anything which had been obtained on the black market. He starved to death, along with dozens of others every day. Ameyoko, conveniently positioned on a busy corner out of sight of the local police boxes, was the solution to this dilemma. In the weeks after the war, farmers with sacks of contraband rice mingled with Tokyo people selling off the contents of their homes for cash or barter.

The second element of Ameyoko means 'alley' and the first is a pun. 'Ame' is Japanese for candy, and as life began to return to normal, it was this simple luxury that the market specialized in. Later, during the Korean war, GI surplus goods like jeans, watches, pens and belts appeared, and the name was painlessly adapted to reflect the change—from *ame* (sweets) to the first syllable of *Amer*ican.

After half a decade of turning a blind eye, the authorities legalized the market in 1950. It's still cheap, and shopping here is a salty contrast to the hushed atmosphere of Tokyo department stores. Stall keepers bellow their prices; shoppers bargain and jostle. Despite the superficial chaos of the tiny shops, it runs smoothly—lubricated, no doubt, by the discreet ministrations of the local *yakuza* gang syndicates.

Ueno Park

Shinobazu Pond, the wartime vegetable garden, is periodically threatened with plans to drain it and turn it into something else (a car park or a baseball stadium). You may utter a grateful prayer to Benten, the Shinto goddess enshrined on the **Benten-jima** island in the middle, that this has never been allowed to happen.

At the southeast corner is the **Shitamachi Museum**, Shitamachi Fūzoku Shiryokan (*open 9.30–4.40, closed Mon; adm ¥200*), with faithful reproductions of a range of typical low city houses (merchant's house, poor tenement, coppersmith's workshop, etc.) from the period before the Great Earthquake of 1923. English labelling is adequate, and you can enter the rooms and handle the everyday objects arranged inside. On the second floor is a children's area with Meiji- and Edo-era toys, plus rotating exhibitions of clothing, tools and festival objects.

Just above **Keisei-Ueno station** (shuttles depart from here for Narita Airport) is a set of broad steps leading into the heart of the park. As a foreigner, the chances are that you will be accosted by young Iranians intent on selling you something illegal. A further set of steps on the right leads up to the park's most famous landmark and rendezvous point: a bronze statue of **Saigō Takamori**, the heroic Satsuma samurai who turned villain in 1877 by taking up arms against the Emperor whom he had fought so hard to restore eight years before. The shameful circumstances of Saigō's demise (he committed suicide in a cave, trapped there by attacking imperial troops) are reflected in the style of the charming statue, which was cast in 1893. Instead of a heroic martial pose, he is portrayed in clogs and informal kimono, casually walking his lap dog.

To the west of Saigō and his podium, a gravel avenue leads deeper into the park. On the east side is the **Kiyomizu Kannon-dō**, built in imitation of Kiyomizu temple in Kyoto and, a little further on, the original **Kuro-mon** (Black Gate) which once marked the entrance to the Kan'ei-ji complex, and still bears bullet holes from the siege of 1868.

Three shrines stand to the east, between the path and the Shinobazu Pond, from south to north: a shrine to the rice deity, Inari, reached, as usual, through a tunnel of orange *torii* gates and guarded by sleek fox statues; the **Gojōten**, dedicated to Tenjin, god of learning; and the Tōshō-gū which begins at the stone **Ōtorii** (Great Gate) and is reached by a long approach of stone and bronze lanterns.

The **Tōshō-gū** (*adm ¥200*), dedicated to the first Tokugawa shogun, Ieyasu, is one of the oldest in the park, founded in 1627 with a main hall dating from 1651. It was established by Kan'ei-ji's first abbot, Tenkai, who played an important role in Ieyasu's deification. The statues were donated by *daimyō* from all over Japan; the most ornate, closest to the shrine's outer wall, were the gift of junior branches of the Tokugawa family. These days, the delicate woodwork and opulently painted interiors are in a terrible state: the drapes are smoke-stained, the statues are mottled, and the shrine drum has a hole in its skin. Most shocking of all are the four famous lions by the master of Edo screen painting, Kanō Tanyū, worn to invisibility in places.

As you exit, notice the open-work depictions of the ascending and descending dragons on the **Kara-mon** (Chinese Gate), carved by the famous Hidari ('Lefty') Jingoro, who was also responsible for the famous 'sleeping cat' in Nikkō. The fabulous beasts are so realistically executed that in bygone days, of course, they used to slip off their gate at midnight and drink in the Shinobazu Pond; crowds of dragon-spotters used to gather from time to time to observe their movements.

The **Five-Storey Pagoda** (Gojū no tō) over the wall on the north side of the approach to Tōshō-gū is one of the few surviving relics of Kan'ei-ji, dating from 1647. To inspect it at close quarters you have to enter the **zoo** (famous for its pandas) whose entrance is a little further on to the north.

The northeast acres of the park are dominated by a number of public halls of culture, including the largest of Japan's national museums and the **Tokyo Metropolitan Festival Hall** (Tokyo Bunka Kaikan), opposite Ueno JR station, which hosts frequent musical events, including concerts by foreign artists. Next door, south of the **National Science Museum**, is the **National Museum of Western Art**, not as *bijou* as the Bridgestone in Nihonbashi, but with a big collection of Rodins and French Impressionist and Post-Impressionist paintings. The building is based on an old design by Le Corbusier.

Tokyo National Museum (Kokuritsu Hakubutsukan)

9–4.30; adm ¥400 plus extra fee for special exhibitions.

In terms of the size of its collection (90,874) and its number of visitors (three quarters of a million annually) the **Tokyo National Museum** is the most important in Japan, although it's hardly the most beautiful or the best laid out. From the front, the three buildings compose a neat history of Japanese architectural tastes in the 20th century. On the left-hand side is the oldest wing, the **Hyōkeikan**, built in 1908, a languid European-style building with a green copper dome; in the middle is the **Honkan** (1937), the museum's main gallery, in a bristling neo-traditional style, half Greek and half Chinese temple; on the right is the **Tōyōkan** (1968), modelled after a temple hall, but constructed out of undisguised grey concrete.

Hyōkeikan

This houses vivid archaeological finds of the prehistoric periods (up to about AD 600), plus later excavations from cemeteries and cremation grounds. An unusually imaginative display on the ground floor demonstrates how the eponymous designs were applied to the pottery of the early Jōmon (Rope Pattern) period; there are perfect examples too of later Jōmon vessels, inlaid with ridges of clay which flow over their surfaces in irregular swirls and zig-zags, protruding above the lip to produce the famous 'flaming' pottery. The rear wing of the ground floor contains a small display of objects associated with the indigenous Ainu people of northern Japan, although anyone who has visited the Ainu museums of Hokkaidō will have seen far better examples of the wooden clubs, fur coats and geometric designs appliqued onto cotton.

The upstairs rooms contain finds from the *kofun* (tumuli) erected over the bodies of powerful chieftains in the 3rd to 6th centuries. The human and animal figures found there are among the most accessible objects of Japanese art, especially the *haniwa*, witty clay renderings of courtiers, warriors, houses and pets which took the place of human retainers who, at one time, were dispatched into the next world along with their master. Creepier and more stylized are the *dogū*, squat figures with elaborate head dresses and swollen limbs, identified by at least one writer as space-suit-wearing extraterrestrials.

Honkan

The **Honkan** contains the main body of the collection, two floors and 25 rooms of rotating exhibits, mapping a chronological course through all the main genres of Japanese art. Clear labelling and a good English map make it easy to find your way around here. Although there are many masterpieces, the vast size of the collection makes it difficult to say which will be on display at any one time.

The ground floor houses sculpture, metal work, arms and armour, textiles and ceramics. As well as many religious statues, there is a near-contemporary portrait of the 12th-century shogun, Minamoto no Yoritomo, in the striking style shared by paintings of the same period: an expressive, naturalistic face (in Yoritomo's case the look is one of wary cunning), combined with symmetrical and abstract treatment of his billowing formal robes. The next two rooms contain metal objects—Buddhist ritual bells and wands, and some cast metal kettles which display the painstaking attention to detail so prized in the tea cult. One, said to have been used by the 16th-century master, Furuta Oribe, was cast so as to boil with a melodious warble. Its decoration is subtle and stands out faintly on the purposely rough, rustic surface: horses gallop before the vague forms of hills; the lid handle is a dragon and rings on either side are in the form of fabulous beasts.

Beyond the display of arms and armour is a long room devoted to textiles: *nō* and *kabuki* costumes, and scarcely less lavish examples of aristocratic dress and uniform. By the 17th century, Japan had its own silk industry and no longer needed to rely on imported textiles. A native idiom developed, drawing on the traditions of the past but adapting the conventions of painting and craft, and making use of what little imported material was available in Japan during the secluded Edo period. Outstanding among the exhibits is a *kosode* (short-sleeved robe) made for a courtesan during the early 19th century, with a striking design of a hawk and a dragon dramatically embroidered on black velvet (a very exotic fabric) and using gold foil.

Upstairs are paintings, prints, calligraphy and lacquerware and, again, the range defies brief summary. As well as the exquisite hand scrolls created by courtiers, there are admonitory depictions of the horrors of hell, like the famous *Hungry Ghosts Waiting to Feast on Faeces*, as graphic as its title. In the 15th century, monk artists painted ink landscapes to accompany poems, inspired by Chinese works of the Yuan and Ming dynasties: Shūbun's *Reading in the Bamboo Studio* shows a tiny figure, perched in a hut on a jutting crag, a kind of symbol of the monk philosopher, contemplating the void from his precarious earthly perch. Look out also for the penetrating, haggardly realistic portrait of the Zen master Ikkyū by Bokusai.

The use of monochrome brush strokes to create elliptical, almost abstract landscapes gives many of the greatest Japanese paintings a very modern, or rather timeless, atmosphere. *Pine Forest* by Hasehawa Tōhaku, on two six-fold screens, is a superb example. Eighty-five per cent of their area is left blank, but the space between the smudged, erect pines breathes with the mistiness of dawn light.

Tōyōkan

The **Tōyōkan** houses art objects from other Asian countries, but it has been closed recently for long-term refurbishment, as has the **Hōryū-ji Hōmotsuden** which used to display one of the greatest collections of ancient Japanese art: the treasures of Hōryū-ji temple, near Nara, founded by the 7th-century Prince Shotoku, father of Japanese Buddhism. The objects were displayed for only one day a week in the old building; because of their fragility, it was closed in case of rain or damp. A new building will allow them to be displayed more freely; unfortunately it will not be open until 1999.

West Tokyo

Shinjuku

Don't miss Shinjuku: if you spend only one night in Tokyo, try to spend it here. The other *sakariba* (roughly 'lively places')—Shibuya, Ginza, Roppongi, Ueno—are cities within a city. Shinjuku is better described as a metropolis within a megalopolis, a place of extremes, and the area which epitomizes the most dramatic features of modern Tokyo: teeming crowds (above and below ground), an epic railway station, visionary high-rise architecture, multiple department stores and a maze of neon-lit snuggeries devoted to *mizu shōbai*, the 'water trade' of drinking, entertainment and sex. On a Friday evening, Shinjuku station's east exit plaza, beneath the giant TV screen of Studio Alta, has to be one of the most exciting places in the world.

History

Shinjuku's associations with the pleasure industries go back a long way. It began life as an equestrian post station (the name means 'new lodging') founded in 1698 by five Asakusa brothel owners. Naturally, the refreshments on offer extended to more than just the horses, and in 1620 the stews were closed down for 50 years after a scandal involving a retainer of the shogun. For centuries after, Shinjuku was an insalubrious and unfashionable area, unfondly known as the anus of Tokyo on account of the queues of night-soil trucks which would form in the evenings, carting the city's waste out to the farms in the west. But it was spared the worst devastation of the 1923 earthquake, and slowly prospered on the backs of the refugees from the gutted districts of the Low City.

Like Shibuya and Ikebukuro, Shinjuku made its biggest fortune as the playground of commuters, who caroused and dallied in large numbers before returning to the western suburbs from Shinjuku station. The first national railway line was built here in 1885. Tram lines and private railways followed, and by 1928 it had become the busiest station in Japan; today, it is the biggest in the world. Twenty lines converge here, dispatching three million passengers every day. The metal clippers which the inspectors still use to punch tickets are said to wear out every three days.

Incineration in May 1945 proved little more than a minor inconvenience. The station was rebuilt and quickly established itself as the centre of Tokyo's black economy—the Ryūgū (Dragon Palace) Market was the biggest in the country. Japan's first strip show, The Birth of Venus, was held in the now defunct Teitoza theatre, and the banning of prostitution in 1958 caused barely a pause: the former *toruko* (Turkish baths) renamed themselves 'soaplands', and carried on as before. There was another clamp-down in 1985, but the *mizu shōbai*, controlled by the *yakuza* and tolerated by the police, remains cheerfully visible.

In the two decades after the war Shinjuku became known as the hangout of students, journalists, writers and radical intellectuals, a reputation which still clings to parts of the area. In October 1968, student rioters, in emulation of their counterparts in Paris, began tearing up the paving stones and hurling them at policemen (the stones that remained were efficiently removed by the authorities and replaced by asphalt in the course of a single night).

Until the seventies, all the action had taken place on the innermost east side of the station. West of the tracks was a very different kind of water trade: a tract of grey reservoirs which were moved out west in 1965, suddenly releasing an expanse of untouched real estate. The first skyscraper, the then impressive Keiō Plaza Hotel, went up in 1971; since then it has been dwarfed by a battery of rivals, and several plots still remain vacant. In 1992 Shinjuku's transformation was completed by the opening of the new City Hall in a complex of extraordinary post-modern towers designed by Tange Kenzō. The remote suburban satellite is now the centre of Tokyo's government; Ginza/Marunouchi, the old centre, finds itself in the astonishing position of slipping to the margins. In little more than a hundred years, Tokyo's anus has become its heart.

Exploring Shinjuku

There are two mutually distinct areas. **West (Nishi) Shinjuku** is the skyscraper zone, a cool, impassive area of thrillingly tall hotels and office buildings which regularly disappear into the mist on cloudy days; the Odakyū and Keiō department stores are also on this side. Smaller shops, cinemas and street life are in **East (Higashi) Shinjuku**, as well as the pleasant **Shinjuku Gyōen** (Park), and **Kabukichō**, Japan's most famous red light district, which also contains numberless restaurants and bars offering innocent entertainment.

Shinjuku station is a unique cultural experience in itself, especially at rush hour and last thing at night. One writer suggested that 'you can find out more about the horrors and pleasures of modern Japanese life by spending ten gawping minutes in Shinjuku station than by reading a dozen industry textbooks.' Whether or not this is an exaggeration, for most people, ten minutes is quite enough. Long-term residents regularly get lost; if the constant buffeting crowds don't get you, then the profuse and mutually contradictory signposts will. The best advice is to get out, stay out and then take your bearings from the detailed enlargement of Shinjuku on the back of the tourist information centre's free Tokyo map. The west exit (*nishi guchi*) is closest to the skyscrapers, the east exit (*higashi guchi*) to Kabukichō, but even if you find yourself at the north or south exits, it's an easy matter to sidle round the station at street level. The second character in the Japanese word for exit, *guchi*, also means 'mouth': chewed up and spat out is how you will feel.

The smart way to avoid this bedlam is to take the Marunouchi or Shinjuku lines to the subway station called **Shinjuku san-chōme**, 500m to the east of the main overland tracks. This is linked to an underground promenade (called 'Subnade' in Japanese English) which runs directly beneath the main street all the way to the station. Detailed maps, labelled in English, show exactly where you are in relation to the surface, and the stair exits for all the main landmarks are clearly indicated.

The most popular rendezvous points in Shinjuku are below the giant video screen of the **Studio Alta department store** (on the north side of the plaza by the east exit) and—less crowded, and with a bit more intellectual cachet—the **Kinokuniya** book shop, two blocks to the east.

West (Nishi) Shinjuku

The Escher-like convolutions of West Shinjuku continue even outside the station proper, with a subterranean walkway and multi-level roads making it difficult to know where exactly ground level is. **Chūō-dōri** (Central Avenue) is the road you want, a broad highway cutting through the centre of the skyscraper district.

The view from this approach will be familiar to aficionados (they do exist) of late-night Japanese monster films: the 'scrapers of Shinjuku are regularly trashed by Godzilla and his many adversaries. Individually, few of them are architectural works of art, and the combined effect is curiously unreal. Like many of the imported accoutrements of the West, there's something rather undigested about them, a self-consciousness that is difficult to put your finger on, as if one were viewing a display of skyscrapers, rather than the things themselves.

One at least—the newest, although not for long—is a wonder. The **Tokyo City Hall** by the grand-daddy of contemporary Japanese architects, Tange Kenzō, shows up most of its neighbours for the overgrown cigarette lighters they are. It is a fitting monument to the mighty but bizarre city over which it presides: dignified but never pompous, dynamic without being busy, witty but not corny. The wonderful check texture of the exterior— glass and contrasting shades of stone—is surprisingly warm, like an expensive tweed. Around 13,300 people, including the Governor of Tokyo, work in the linked complex of offices and (at the front) Metropolitan Assembly Hall. The tallest towers are both 243m high and contain 48 floors, and if they look familiar, they are: despite its relentlessly secular function, the hall is modelled on Notre Dame in Paris. The joke seems to have worked in a touching and unexpected way. Like the French capital, the City Hall has achieved a reputation among young Japanese as a place for romance. On clear evenings the twin **observation decks** on the 45th floor of each tower are busy with moony young couples enjoying one another's company, and the view.

Of course, the best view of the architecture is from outside the building itself, ideally in one of the flanking skyscrapers. The **Keiō Plaza Hotel** faces it (no one will mind you sneaking up if you do it discreetly); the handsome, triangular **Sumitomo Building**, to the northeast, has four floors of observatory restaurants—try the Café Bar on the 51st.

Nestling alongside all this magnificence, near the west exit of the station, is an alleyway of scruffy shopfronts and overhead wires possessing the rather sonorous Japanese name *Shomben Yokochō*: 'Piss Alley'. It may not have a fragrant aroma, but it's a lively place for tasty, and extremely cheap, *yakitori* and noodles, served in packed, noisy little restaurants.

East (Higashi) Shinjuku

Kabukichō

Kabukichō has countless bars, abundant cinemas, some great restaurants (especially Thai), but the commodity which animates it and gives it its character is unquestionably sex. Kabukichō is to sex what Tokyo's department stores are to shopping. It comes in all kinds of shapes and sizes, and most tastes and budgets are catered for. There are Kabukichōs in many Japanese cities, but Shinjuku's must be the most varied and densely-packed of them all. A survey revealed, in the southern quarter alone, 37 porn stores, 21 massage parlours, 21 nude shows, 17 'soaplands', 15 love hotels, 13 peep shows, 4 porn cinemas, 4 private video houses, a couple of strip theatres and two 'no-pants' coffee shops (the waitresses eschew underwear; the floors are mirrors)—all in the space of a few hundred metres.

By a crashing irony, Kabukichō (Kabuki Town) was christened and organized in its present form in an attempt to bring a touch of class and high culture to Shinjuku. Before the war it had been a characterless residential area. In its aftermath, a local notable named Suzuki pioneered a scheme to erect a *kabuki* theatre here, the centrepiece of an expensive project of reconstruction and gentrification. But the money ran out just as the water trade, which had always had a shadowy presence in the area, flowed in. By that time the name had stuck. Legal crackdowns—in 1958 and, most recently, in the so-called 'St Valentine's

Day Massacre' of February 1985—have never put more than a temporary lid on its exuberant activities.

The best tactic, on a first visit anyway, is just to amble around and enjoy the unique, sinister-innocent atmosphere. Despite the superficial sleaze, Kabukichō is notoriously safe compared to equivalent quarters in other big cities — look at the crowds of high school age kids all around you. It would be hard to get into trouble, even if you did elect to sample some of the attractions on offer—the biggest risk would be running up a huge bill which you couldn't pay and couldn't argue with.

Kabukichō, in its broadest definition, consists of the blocks north of the avenue, Yasukuni-dōri, between Seibu-Shinjuku station to the west and the small Hanazono Shrine to the east. To the northwest is **Shinjuku Plaza**, a scrappy square surrounded by multi-screen cinemas, some of them respectable. Just round the southwest corner, behind Shinjuku Joy Cinema 1, is **Virtual Theatre** where, for ¥1200, you are strapped into a 'body-sonic' chair which bucks and rattles in synch with a variety of 3-D action films.

Next to the shrine a honeycomb of tiny drinking and eating cells, known as the **Gōruden Gai** (Golden Block), has a particular reputation as the intellectuals' hangout. **Shinjuku ni-chōme** (in the blocks east of Shinjuku san-chōme subway station, a 10-minute walk from Kabukichō proper) is a lively area of gay bars and clubs, popular with customers of all orientations, and the abode of the famous *okama-san*, 'honourable transvestites'.

Shibuya and Harajuku

At first glance, **Shibuya**, western Tokyo's second great pleasure district, has little to distinguish it from its bigger brother Shinjuku, three stops up the Yamanote line: both were once outlying, semi-rural neighbourhoods; both contain baffling conglomerations of railway lines and department stores, and numberless hidey holes for drinking, eating and sex. But the ingredients combine in very different proportions, and the atmospheres of the two districts are distinct. Shibuya is teen city—trendy and 'cute'—where Shinjuku is raffish and seedy. In Shibuya, fashion replaces sex. The character swaggering down the sidewalks is less likely to be a *yakuza* touting for a peep show, than a 15-year-old high school student in baseball cap and vintage $1000 Levi's. Young Japanese generally appear to foreigners to be younger than they are, but the immaculately dressed midnight crowds giggling, tottering and vomiting on the slopes of Shibuya look very young indeed.

Shibuya, and the areas immediately to the north and west of it, have more daytime attractions than Shinjuku: near **Harajuku station** is **Meiji Jingū**, Tokyo's biggest shrine, and the adjacent **Yoyogi Park**, which at weekends and national holidays becomes an open-air circus of musicians, teen fashion victims and street performers. Omotesandō-dōri, built as the shrine avenue, is more grown-up, an elegant boulevard of cafés and designer shops.

Shibuya

Shibuya station isn't as crowded as Shinjuku and for students of Tokyo streetlife there is only one important exit: **Hachikō Plaza**, on the west side of the station, near the JR tracks.

Hachikō (the name has been variously translated as 'Little Number Eight', 'Lord Eight' or, ingeniously, 'Octavius') was a very ordinary Akita dog whose sad little story has made him the most famous pet in Japan. He belonged to one Ueda Eisaburō, a professor at Tokyo University. Every day he would accompany his master to Shibuya station in the morning, and return to meet him off his regular train in the evening. One day in 1925 he found himself waiting for a very long time. Old Professor Ueda had died—but how could this be explained to little Hachikō? The family gave him away to friends in Asakusa, but every afternoon the faithful hound would cross Tokyo to wait in his accustomed spot for the master who never came home. Within a few years, Hachikō's dumb loyalty had made him a national institution. In 1934 he posed for a sculptor and a bronze statue was unveiled in front of the station. When he *was* reunited with his master a year later, his mortal remains were elaborately buried, minus his pelt which was stuffed and preserved in the National Science Museum. Hachikō's loyalty was tested to the limits during the war when he was melted down for gun metal, but the little chap has since been reinstated and remains Tokyo's most famous meeting spot.

Like many cult figures, however, Hachikō's reputation has been tarnished in recent years by revisionist historians. In his book, *Tokyo Rising*, Edward Seidensticker blasphemously suggests an alternative interpretation of the story. According to some eye witnesses, Hachikō didn't conduct his vigil in the evenings, but loitered around the station all day. His new owners, it seems, mistreated him, and once his reputation was established, there were rich pickings of food to be had from sentimental passers-by. The tale, Seidensticker suggests, is not one of trust and loyalty, but greed and cunning. Needless to say, this remains a deeply unpopular view. Japanese people of a certain age tend to adopt a very sad, wounded expression when they are told this version of the story.

The dog has now become such a popular rendezvous spot that it is often impossible to find the person you are supposed to be meeting there. Wait instead by the Hachikō *kōban* (police box) on the right-hand side as you exit the station; or by the Hachikō Wall, a ghastly relief of ceramic Hachikōs, which stands on the same side.

Exploring Shibuya

Five big roads, and several million people a day, converge on the crossing in front of Hachikō Plaza; when the lights change and the pedestrians stream across in a dozen different directions, the scene is exhilarating. Standing on the edge of the road with Hachikō and the station behind you, a large department store called **109** is visible to your left. The road to the left of this is **Dōgen-zaka**, named after a famous 13th-century highwayman, Owada Dōgen, who preyed on travellers through what was then a dim and isolated valley. At the top of the slope on the right is an extraordinary enclave: a village, clustered round several narrow alleys, of love hotels. Neon signs hum below mirrored, one-way windows; room charges—by the night or the hour—are discreetly displayed outside the covered entrances, and couples stroll around them in the evenings unselfconsciously looking for available rooms. At weekends, when the rates double, they are very often booked out.

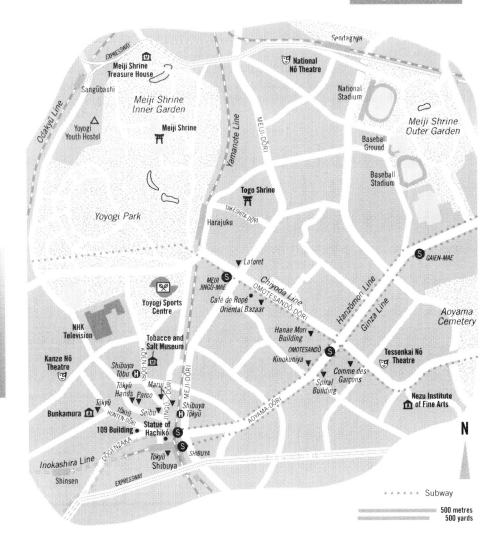

This air of lively innocence pervades the whole district. There are, no doubt, *yakuza* operating on the streets of Shibuya, but far more visible in their competition for the money and loyalties of its citizens are the huge department store and railway corporations which have effectively carved up the main highways between them. The road to the right of 109, **Tōkyū Honten-dōri**, leads up to the **Tōkyū department store**, the huge transport and retail conglomerate that first laid claim to the area. There aren't many activities in Shibuya that Tōkyū doesn't have a stake in. Attached to the store is the **Bunkamura** (Culture Village), a multi-level complex of cafés, restaurants, cinemas and a gallery which displays some of the best visiting exhibitions (largely of Western art) in the city, as well as the 2000-seater Orchard Hall, home of the Tokyo Philharmonic Orchestra, and the smaller Theatre Cocoon. The original Tōkyū store is in the station complex, above the terminus of one of the many Tōkyū commuter lines. To the east of the station (the other side from Hachikō) is another arts centre, the **Tōkyū Bunka Kaikan** (Culture Hall); the **Tōkyū Inn** hotel is a little to the north, beneath the railway tracks. Even 109 is another of Tōkyū's masks, the name a pun on the Japanese readings of the numbers 10 (*tō*) and 9 (*kyū*).

The competition begins in **Jingū-dōri**, the avenue leading north, dead opposite Hachikō. A few metres up on the left-hand side, joined across a side road by a bridge, are the trendy **Seibu** department store and its **Annex**, owned by the poet millionaire Tsutsumi Seiji. Opposite, and dowdy in comparison, are the **Marui** stores.

A left turn just after the Seibu Annex takes you to another big crossroads and—well, well, well—another department store, among the most exciting in Shibuya: **Parco**, a fantasy land of boutiques and designer concessions and an off-shoot of the Seibu corporation. Plainly, no self-respecting Shibuya *depāto* could make do with just one shop; Parco has three, all of them adjacent. It needs them, for lurking just up the road (turn left—i.e. west—at Parco) is an enemy stronghold: **Tōkyū Hands**, eight fascinating floors of household hardware, DIY materials and craft paraphernalia.

Continuing north over the crossroads in front of Parco, you enter **Kōen-dōri** which leads up to **Yoyogi Park**. On the second block on the right, opposite the Tōbu Hotel, is the **Tobacco and Salt Museum** (*open 10–6; adm ¥100*), a surprisingly interesting exhibition of artefacts relating to these former government monopolies. Apart from 2000 tobacco packets from around the world, there are biographies of famous smokers and displays relating the history of the weed, which was introduced into Japan at the turn of the 16th century. In the early days, pipes were smoked in much the same way as tea was drunk, with much solemnity and formal ritual. The floors devoted to salt are, as you might expect, less entertaining. No smoking, by the way, on the 2nd or 4th floors.

Harajuku

Harajuku station is one up from Shibuya and two down from Shinjuku on the Yamanote line. It has two exits; the Yoyogi Park one, at the south end, becomes impossibly congested at weekends.

Yoyogi Park

The scene in Yoyogi Park on a holiday or Sunday afternoon has almost become a Tokyo cliché. Spaced at intervals on the wide avenue are bands of Japanese youths dressing and behaving in a way that Western prejudice holds to be anathema to the polite Japanese. Spiky punks gob into their microphones, brilliantined Elvis impersonators croon, and the whole street, closed to traffic, quakes beneath the sound of over-amplified guitars. Ever since the 1964 Olympic Village, which brought a flavour of hip cosmopolitanism to the area, was dismantled to create this park, it has been the assembly point of the Tokyo *zoku*.

The word means 'breed' or 'tribe', and *zoku*-spotting has been a popular activity for newspapers and magazines ever since the first 'modern girls' were identified 80 years ago on the streets of Ginza. There are the *takenoko zoku* (bamboo shoot tribe), named after the Harajuku shop which sells the tribe's uniform (baggy, androgynous trousers and smocks); and the more notorious *bōsōzoku* (speed tribe) who roar around in ferocious leathers on unthinkably expensive imported motorbikes, frightening old ladies. In the late 1980s many of the performances had real charm, with mime artists, *butō* dancers, folk and classical musicians—Japanese and foreign— sharing space with the inevitable rock'n'roll imitators and brutish thrash metal bands. On a recent visit, only the last were in evidence. But it may just have been an off day; change, after all, is in the nature of the place.

Yoyogi National Stadium

Two stadia, one large and one small, are mounted on a stone-flagged emplacement reached from Harajuku station by a network of spidery overpasses. Both were built for the 1964 Olympics, and both were designed by the Grand Old Man of Japanese architecture, Tange Kenzō. Great aluminium skins are swathed over a helix-shaped steel frame: the main stadium looks like the bit of a huge screw emerging from out of the earth. Look inside and up: the apex of the second, smaller gymnasium is a prodigy of swirling, geometric curves.

Meiji Jingū (Meiji Shrine)

For the two emperors who succeeded Emperor Meiji, no shrine has been dedicated. Taishō died mad in 1926, after only 14 years on the throne; Shōwa's long reign is too irrevocably associated with the Pacific War for any memorial to be other than controversial. But Meiji, or Mutsuhito as he was known during his 44-year reign, had presided over a revolution and, however much one might deplore aspects of it, no one could wish for, or even imagine, a return to the old days of the Tokugawa shoguns. Meiji died on 29 July 1912, an event as traumatic as the death of Queen Victoria a decade before. At his funeral, on the night of 13 September, the whole city fell silent as eight white oxen drew the Emperor's body to the station for transportation and burial in Kyoto. Within a matter of days, preparations had begun for his deification. **Meiji Jingū** was formally dedicated in November 1920.

The entrance to the shrine grounds is just to the right of Yoyogi Park, down a long gravel avenue marked by two 12m high *torii* gates of unvarnished Taiwanese cypress, the biggest of their kind in Japan. The Emperor commandeered this land from the lords of Ii, and often spent time here. The June irises which bloom in the **Inner Garden** (*adm ¥300*) were the favourite flowers of his consort, Empress Shōken, and remain the shrine's most famous seasonal attraction. The shrine itself is a plain, rather blank set of buildings, impressive from the air but, from the ground, striking mainly for the green copper of the roofs, stained brown by fume-poisoned rain.

Behind the shrine buildings the grounds become overgrown and meadow-like; even at weekends they're rarely as crowded as Yoyogi Park. At the north end is the **Hōmotsu-den** (Treasure Museum, *open 9–4.30; adm ¥200*), built in 1921 in concrete emulation of the log cabin style of the Shōsō-in in Nara. As a man, Meiji is a distant and inscrutable figure; the personal objects on display here do not bring him any closer. A famous portrait by an Italian artist shows an intelligent-looking man with wispy hair and beard. Empress Shōken was a chinless lady who devoted herself to good causes like the Red Cross. Meiji reintroduced medieval formal court dress for ceremonial occasions, but is pictured with his wife in Western attire. Many of the exhibits here exemplify the schizophrenic tastes of the time—like the modern horse carriages topped with ornate traditional phoenixes, or the Emperor's dress uniform, a combination of Prussian twill and Japanese brocade.

East of Harajuku station, on the opposite side from the shrine and park, is **Takeshita-dōri** (Takeshita Avenue), shopping street of preference for the Harajuku *zoku*, and the closest thing Tokyo has to a Carnaby Street: a self-conscious higgledy-piggledy arrangement of cafés, record stores and boutiques, selling youthful fashions and trash accessories.

Omotesandō

This broad road (literally the 'avenue in front'—it was laid out as the formal approach to the Meiji Shrine) is one of the most elegant quarters of Tokyo, a place for café-hopping and boulevarding after a lazy afternoon spent in Yoyogi Park.

Three hundred metres down from Harajuku on the north side is the **Laforet department store** and, in a side street behind it, the **Ōta Memorial Museum of Art** (*open 10.30–5.30, closed Mon and from 26th to the end of each month; adm ¥500 or ¥800 for special exhibitions*), an attractive and intelligently curated museum displaying a small, scholarly selection of the 12,000 *ukiyo-e* (woodblock prints) collected by an insurance tycoon. Artists represented include Utamaro, Hokusai, Hiroshige and Kiyochika, as well as dozens of others less well known internationally.

Beyond the next main intersection on the south side of the avenue is **Café de Ropé**, a classic Omotesandō rendezvous and haunt of beautiful people. Just east of it is the souvenir shop **Oriental Bazaar**.

Omotesandō crossing is marked by a big *torii* gateway. Southwest of here, down Aoyama-dōri, are **Anderson's Bakery** (opposite the prominent Fuji Bank), where Omotesandō ex-pats buy their bagels and patisseries, and (on the opposite side) the deluxe **Kinokuniya** supermarket. A quiet side road beyond here leads up to **Las Chicas**, with café, restaurant, bar, gallery and hair salon in a beautifully designed multi-purpose building.

Kottō-dōri begins opposite Kinokuniya and leads down to Roppongi-dōri. Along it are expensive shops selling art pottery, and the **Blue Note**, off-shoot of New York's famous jazz club. At the Roppongi-dōri end there's a good little map shop, with stock from all over the world.

Back at the crossing, Omotesandō continues southeast, past designer shops and cafés of chrome and frosted glass: impersonal, expensive and cool. Designers **Issey Miyake** and **Comme des Garçons** both have shops here. The glittering minimalist interiors of **Yokku Mokku** do for coffee and cakes what the designers do for clothes. Opposite is the trendy **Tessenkai Nō Institute** in a squat concrete building.

Keep going down and you come to another intersection. On the south corner, behind a wall, is the excellent **Nezu Institute of Fine Arts** (*open 9.30–4.30, closed Mon; adm ¥1000*), an eclectic complex of galleries situated in a beautiful old garden. It was founded in 1940 and houses painting, calligraphy, sculpture, ceramics, textiles, lacquer and wood- and metal-work, including some of the most famous individual pieces of Japanese art, like the famous Shinto painting of the Nachi Waterfall. (The exhibits, however, are rotated so there is no guarantee of seeing the National Treasures on any one visit.) Some of the finest and most accessible objects are Chinese: some stone Buddha heads with pigments still thick on their faces, and amazing bronzes from the Shang dynasty—furious-looking, 3000-year-old cauldrons studded with spikes, knobs and ridges, bristling with arrogant energy. Paths dip around a hilly garden filled with statues, stone pagodas and reproductions of famous art objects including, in the courtyard, the delicate 8th-century lantern from the front of Nara's Tōdai-ji temple.

South Tokyo

Tsukiji

A few minutes' walk from genteel Ginza, Tsukiji's main attraction—a huge, raucous, early-morning fish market—could hardly be more different in terms of atmosphere. The nearby Shiba and Hama Rikyū gardens are tranquil, inner city escapes: from the latter you can take a boat trip up the Sumida-gawa, Tokyo's historic, if grimy, main river.

History

Tsukiji means 'built land': like so much of Tokyo's coast it is polder, reclaimed in the 17th century using ashes from the great Long Sleeves Fire of 1657. Some interesting characters have lived here over the years, including Maeno Ryōtaku, an 18th-century physician who, despite the restrictions placed by the shogunate on foreign books, taught himself Dutch and translated into Japanese an influential book on anatomy. At his home in Tsukiji he assembled a clique of young specialists in what was then known as *rangaku*, 'Dutch studies' (the Dutch being the only nation allowed trading rights by the Tokugawa regime). An admirer of Maeno, Fukuzawa Yukichi, set up his own school in the area in 1858; it grew into Keiō, one of Japan's most prestigious private universities. Fukuzawa, remembered as a pioneer of enlightened Westernization, is commemorated on the ¥10,000 note.

The foreign trade treaties of the same period brought numbers of foreigners to Tokyo, and in the earliest years of the Meiji period, a special walled settlement was built for them in

Tsukiji. The American Legation moved here, but the experiment was not a success. Most foreigners chose to live in Yokohama and the hundred or so who remained in Tsukiji were mostly Chinese merchants and missionaries. The New Shimabara red-light district, thoughtfully established by the government for the convenience of the foreign gentlemen, closed within a few years. When the settlement was destroyed by the 1923 earthquake, no one felt the need to rebuild it.

Central Wholesale Market (Chūō Oroshiuri Ichiba)

The optimum time to arrive is about 5am, before the subway opens. Tell your taxi driver to go to **Tsukiji ichiba**. *On busy mornings the streets round about will be congested; get out and ask for the* **Sei-mon** *(Main Gate) which is opposite the offices of the* Asahi Shimbun *newspaper.*

To someone who has never been to Tsukiji market, the idea of getting up at four in the morning to view buckets of dead fish may not be immediately appealing. It would be a pity to surrender to this disinclination. Tsukiji has as much in common with your local fish-monger as the Shinjuku terminus has with a country railway station. It's one of Tokyo's most unusual and exciting outings: vast, noisy and chaotic, and teeming with some of the strangest and most grotesque forms of life in Tokyo, human as well as icthyoid.

The market was moved here in 1935 from its centuries-old site in Nihonbashi. Fruit and vegetables are also sold here, but the principal attraction, to buyers and tourists alike, is marine produce, for which Tsukiji serves as supplier to the whole of eastern Japan. The statistics are staggering: 704,169 tons of fish were sold here in 1992, worth $5.9 billion (two and a half thousand tons—21 million dollars' worth—every working day), and fruit and veg add another billion dollars a year. Nine immense refrigerators have a combined capacity of 30,000 tons; there is parking space for 5000 vehicles, and the stalls get through 200 tons of ice daily.

The action starts early and continues through mid-morning, but the sooner you turn up the more there is to see. Walk straight through the main gate towards the large building directly in front of you. Inside are 1600 wholesalers' stalls arranged in avenues in a great quarter circle. For now, walk straight through to a set of concrete buildings on the far side. The fish have been arriving all night and from 5am they are auctioned in big rooms inside these annexes.

Freshwater fish go under the metaphorical hammer first, from about 5am, then live fish at 5.20, and crustaceans at 5.40. For three-quarters of an hour there's something interesting going on in almost every room, but the highlight is the tuna auction scheduled at 5.30am. Deep-frozen, and with their tails chopped off, the tuna, each as big as a man, lie in steaming rows, like long aluminium bombs or pods from outer space. Yellow labels detail their weight and country of origin (as far away as Nigeria). The buyers prod and tap them (prime cuts, for the best sashimi, cost ¥25,000 a kilo), and a siren signals the beginning of the auction, a baffling drama of high-speed chanted prices and cryptic nods, hand-signals and gesticulations from the assembled brokers.

After the auctions, the fish are transported into the giant covered market building you passed through earlier. Watch your step in here: all the rules of Japanese courtesy and caution are discarded in this outer ring of Fish Hell. The two hazards of Tsukiji are the slippery floors (dress practically in trousers and flat, rubber-soled shoes) and the constant traffic of blaring, chugging, fuming vehicles: fork-lift trucks bearing pallets of twitching crustaceans; convoys of wagons distributing freshly-powdered ice; and bizarre, primitive scooters, like motorized planks. Even more varied is the produce: from familiar cod, mackerel and sardines, through squid and octopus wriggling vigorously in tanks and buckets, to sea slugs, giant clams and polychrome beauties from the China Sea. It's a tribute to the strict hygiene controls enforced here that, after 60 years filled with fish carcasses, the market buildings really don't smell that bad.

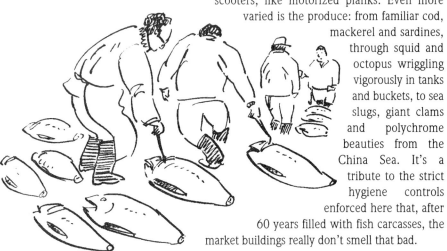

Breakfast in Tsukiji

For those who have an appetite this early in the morning, Tsukiji is the place to eat the freshest sushi in Japan. Between the market and Tsukiji Hongan-ji is the area called the **Jogai Ichiba** (Outer Market) with hundreds of little restaurants, shops and workshops supplying Tsukiji and its employees. Naturally, the fish sold is of the highest quality, although it's not always as cheap as you'd expect. The following open early:

Daiwa Zushi is a tiny shop in front of the big market area inside the market precincts, open from 5.30am; **Tatsuzushi** is just inside the northeast entrance of the market (not the main entrance), and opens at 7am. Both sell individual pieces of sushi for around ¥300–400, or courses from ¥2000.

Just outside the northeast entrance, over the bridge and to the left, is **Tsukiji Sushisei**, an extremely popular bar founded in the Edo period which attracts long queues at lunchtime. Individual pieces from just ¥150; it opens at 8am. Even cheaper is **Segawa Sushiten**, a stall situated just before Tsukiji Hongan-ji on the corner of Shin Ōhashi-dōri and Harumi-dōri, which sells only *maguro* (tuna) and also does take-aways, five pieces for ¥500.

If raw fish seems a bit ambitious at this time in the morning, try the 24-hour noodles at **Uogashi Ramen**, one block before Tsukiji Sushisei. The Outer Market has plenty of coffee shops doing breakfast sets of toast and coffee from around 7am.

Hama Rikyū (Beach Palace)

Between Tsukiji and Hamamatsuchō railway station to the south are two attractive water-front gardens, remnants of the private parks and hunting grounds of the shoguns and their lords. **Hama Rikyū** later became a palace for imperial receptions, and VIPs like the former US President General Ulysses Grant were put up here. It was filled with gun emplacements during the war and bombed to ruin, but today it's an attractive stroll garden based around a brine pond which swells with the tides of the Sumida River estuary, and has barnacle-encrusted rocks around its margins. The **Naka-jima (Central Island) teahouse,** reached by a zig-zagging wooden bridge, is a 1945 restoration of a surviving Edo-period building. The duck pond is still used by private shooting parties: turf-covered hides are dotted around the fenced-off perimeter.

Shiba Rikyū is smaller, less popular, and in some ways more striking, especially when viewed from the monorail linking Hamamatsuchō station with Haneda Airport to the south. The *shinkansen* tracks have encroached upon it, but the contrast between the still, green garden and the shimmering steel multi-storeys around it is dramatic.

Shiba Park Area

North of Hamamatsuchō station, a road leads west to **Daimon**, the gate of the once great Zōjō-ji. Down a side street to the south of here is the private **Tolman Collection** of contemporary Japanese prints, run for the last 20 years by a talkative American couple. Thirty artists sell their work here, among them the American Clifton Karhu, famous for his boldly coloured scenes of Kyoto, and the octogenarian Shinoda Toko. Prices go up to ¥10 million, but you can pick up a print for ¥5000 or a book of Karhu postcards for ¥1480. Anyone with an intelligent interest is welcomed; call ✆ 03 3434 1300 for precise directions.

Shiba Kōen, beyond the Daimon, is the site of one of the most overused photographs of Japan: the stately eaves of **Zōjō-ji** and, behind, looming above it like a headless Godzilla, the vermilion girders of Tokyo Tower. The caption for this picture is usually something like 'Tokyo: city of contrasts', but in fact the contrast is not what you'd expect. The tower opened in 1958; the hall went up 16 years later, replacing the temporary structure erected on the fire-bombed ashes of the old Zōjō-ji.

The park, now little more than a collection of golf greens and hotels, with a few Buddha halls in between, was once the greatest temple complex in Tokyo, covering 660,000 square metres, with 48 sub-temples, 150 schools and 3000 priests and novices, plus their servants and the pilgrims who made their way here along the Tōkaidō highway from Kyoto. **Zōjō-ji** was founded in 1393 by the Jōdō sect and became the chief burial place for the Tokugawa family. Today, what remains is rather a jumble and only the 21m high **Sanmon** gate (1612) is of any antiquity.

Tokyo Tower

Kamiyachō or Daimon subway stations. Open 9am–7 or 9pm depending on season; adm ¥800 main observatory; ¥1400 includes upper observatory.

According to its pamphlet, this is 'the world's tallest self-supporting iron tower'—333m high, although the highest that tourists can go is the upper observation deck at 250m. Eight TV and four radio stations broadcast their signals from Tokyo Tower, although its primary purpose may simply have been, as Edward Seidensticker suggests, to be higher than the Eiffel Tower, which it mimics slavishly. Tokyoites certainly seem to love it dearly and almost any organized tour of the city will end up here. Crammed into the lift with a horde of over-excited schoolchildren, ¥1400 lighter in pocket, the tower is best appreciated for what it is: a Japanese folly, and a monument to urban kitsch. Solicitous stewards and stewardesses, wearing the Tokyo Tower livery (dark green suits with cream lapels), give the impression of being in a holiday camp, a vertical Butlins. At the low levels are the Tokyo Tower Aquarium, the Tokyo Tower Wax Museum, and the Tokyo Tower Holographic Mystery Zone. At 150m the lower of the two observatories is a bazaar of overpriced snacks, offensive souvenirs and Tokyo Tower tat (kitsch lovers on a budget should look out for the set of five Tokyo Tower fridge magnets, just ¥500). The only half-decent reason for wasting your time and money here is the view. Visibility is rarely good enough to see more than a few kilometres, but there is always something horribly compelling about the sprawl of Tokyo seen from the air.

Shitamachi (The Low City)

For years the decline of *shitamachi* (pronounced 'sh'tamachi') has been the great theme of writers on Tokyo, and no history of the city is complete without a nostalgic lament for the 'Low City', a lost paradise of folk culture, obliterated by earthquakes and bombs, and by the relentless march of Japan's modernization. *Shitamachi* was the home of the *Edokko* (Children of Edo): the merchants, traders, artisans, fishermen, cooks, entertainers, prostitutes, apprentices and housewives who formed the mass of the Edo population at a time when it was the biggest city in the world. The *Edokko* were Tokyo's Cockneys: raucous, fun-loving rascals with an eye for the main chance, and a tearful fondness for sentimental love stories and old tales; chirpy under-dogs, contemptuous of their pompous masters in the ruling military class, but fiercely proud and insular, with a conservative suspicion of novelty and change. *Kabuki* was their drama, in the days before it became respectable and artistically regarded. Woodblock prints and scandal sheets, produced in bulk out of tiny workshops, were their reading. Yoshiwara, the licensed brothel quarter which so many print artists commemorated, was their recreation. Edo culture, the popular entertainment of the *shitamachi* townsman, is one of the great artistic achievements of the feudal period. 'Asakusa people are old-fashioned', wrote the novelist Kawabata Yasunari in the early part of our own century. 'They look after others and others look after them, they care for people and have a sense of duty, all of them, the dealers and hawkers at the top to the tramps and beggars at the bottom...the toughs in Shibuya and Shinjuku are a newer sort than the ones we have here. They don't have a tradition, but Asakusa does.'

Asakusa of the myriads flings everything forth in the raw. All manner of desire dances there naked. All classes and all races mix into one great flow, limitless, bottomless, not distinguishing day from night. Asakusa is alive. The masses edge forward. Asakusa of the masses, melting down old forms to be cast into new ones.

Soeta Azembō, quoted in Edward Seidensticker's *Tokyo Rising*

From the mid-19th century until the Pacific War, Asakusa was the capital of *shitamachi*, and the liveliest of Tokyo's *sakariba*, 'lively places'. Contemporary chroniclers, like the one quoted above, describe it in almost mystical terms, but its attractions were simple and earthy: large crowds, a big temple in a park, and entertainments spanning every degree of respectability and taste. In 1920 the novelist Tanizaki Jun'ichiro, later to win the Nobel Prize for Literature, enumerated the attractions of Asakusa: 'old theatre, new theatre, moving pictures, things Western, things Japanese, Douglas Fairbanks, Onoe Matsunosuke [the Japanese Fairbanks of the day], ball riding, equestrian acrobatics, *Naniwa* ballads, girlie theatre music, merry-go-rounds, Hana Yashiki funfair; the Twelve Storeys Tower; air-gun shooting, prostitution, Japanese food, Chinese food, Western food, *Rairaiken* restaurant, wonton, noodles, oysters, rice, horse meat, snapping turtles and eels.' These days Asakusa's temple and old shops make it an essential day out on any holiday in Tokyo, but the fun does tend to peter out after sunset. When the temple grounds empty and the shopping alley is boarded up, the streets become empty and echoic. The films in the cinemas are second-run; the old-style monologists attract small audiences. You can still get eels and snapping turtles at interesting old restaurants, but seldom after 8pm. All the other twenty-four-hour attractions of Tanizaki's list have moved west, and Asakusa has entered its old age.

History

Asakusa's existence is a paradox: it became the heart of Edo by virtue of its isolation, beyond the pale of the old city walls. The Sensō-ji temple, with its ancient statue of Kannon, has been a centre of pilgrimage since the 7th century, positioned on the main road to the north by an important crossing point on the Sumida River. In 1657, the shogunate took advantage of a disastrous fire to expel from the city the prostitutes of the Yoshiwara pleasure quarter who were held to be injurious to public morals. The site chosen for their new home was well out of harm's way, among deserted paddy fields to the north of the old temple. Asakusa soon became a handy refuelling stop for thirsty townsmen on their way to, or from, the delights of Yoshiwara. In 1841, a similar decree forced the *kabuki* theatres, also held to be hot beds of licentiousness, to up sticks and move to Asakusa. The district now had the most popular temple in the city, as well as a virtual monopoly on the two great traditional recreations of the Edo townsman: plays and tarts. There was no looking back.

Tanizaki's list gives some idea of Asakusa's variety, but it represents only a fraction of the circus acts, story tellers and freak shows which encamped there in the temple grounds in a permanent, informal funfair. There were tea shops, stalls selling cosmetics and combs, quack doctors, wild animals and performing monkeys, magicians and fortune tellers, acrobats and jesters, and oddities like a spider man, a woman who smoked a pipe through her navel, and a man who ate and drank through a hole in his stomach. Notorious were the proprietresses of the 'archery stands' which provided flimsy cover for much simpler sport in the tents at the back, and provoked the anger of the licensed ladies of Yoshiwara. Westerners who witnessed the fun in the early Meiji period noticed a new attraction: life-size papier-mâché puppets of foreigners, with livid red hair and staring blue eyes.

Asakusa reached its peak of excitement in 1890 with the opening of a 60m tower, the highest in all Japan, containing art galleries, exotic shops filled with international goods, and an observatory reached via the country's first lift (perhaps rightly, this was considered dangerous and closed after two months). The edifice, octagonal in shape and built of red brick, was called the Ryōunkaku (Cloud-Surpassing Pavilion), but everyone knew it as the Jūnikai (The Twelve Storeys). Nearby was the Panorama-kan, which contained life-size models of soldiers against panoramic backgrounds of painted battle scenes. In 1903 the first cinema, the Denki-kan (Electric Hall), opened amid great scandal. Asakusa youths, it seems, were taking advantage of the darkness to do what couples have traditionally done in the back rows of cinemas all over the world. Strict rules were introduced, segregating the sexes and insisting that the usherettes should, at all times, wear underwear. In the days of silent cinema, the picture houses employed flamboyant performers known as *benshi* who, like the narrators in the *bunraku* puppet theatre, declaimed all the parts as well as narrating the story in alternating couplets of five and seven syllables. Realistic touches were added, like the burning of incense during funeral scenes. When the talkies arrived, the *benshi* went on strike in a vain attempt to save their unique profession.

In 1917 Asakusa theatres began to put on 'opera', although the word encompassed a wide range of forms from *The Magic Flute* to musical frivolities like *The Women's Army Is Off For The Front*, a kind of Carry-On-Up-The-Trenches set in Europe during the First World War. Performers attracted claques of fierce partisans called *peragoro*, 'opera ruffians', who would cheer and applaud passionately for their favourite singer, then beat up the fans of her rivals after the show. After the earthquake (which toppled the top two floors of the Twelve Storeys cloud-scraper, but left the temple unharmed), opera yielded in popularity to live cabaret in the style of the Parisian Folies-Bergère. This, like the movies, attracted fierce moral scrutiny. The dancing soubrettes were not allowed to kick in the direction of the audience or wriggle their hips (*swaying* only was allowed); their costumes had to cover their breasts and upper bodies, and below the waist the top 10cm of thigh must be concealed by fabric which could not be flesh-coloured. Troupes were regularly summoned to the police station to have the length of their drawers measured by frowning officers.

In 1927 the first subway line ran between Asakusa and Ueno (today's Ginza line), but the district lacked an overland railway station and this contributed to its decline in favour of Ginza, Shibuya and Shinjuku. The war put on hold the pleasures which Asakusa specialized in, and in 1945 the great temple was finally razed by American bombs. Afterwards, the ponds of the park were filled in. Having slipped from opera to cabarets, the new staple of the Asakusa theatres was strip shows. These days even these are dwindling, and no new popular entertainment is there to take their place.

Asakusa has its own **tourist information centre** (opposite the famous Kaminari-mon gate, a few minutes from the subway stations) with English-speaking helpers, pamphlets on the *shitamachi* area, and a touch screen video guide which will print out information sheets on individual places and events.

Sensō-ji (Asakusa Kannon)

As with all of modern-day *shitamachi*, the pleasures of Sensō-ji are in its atmosphere. Most of the buildings are concrete; few are more than 40 years old. But this is a living temple: the human circus of shoppers, worshippers and fun-seekers is as vigorous as any in the country.

Archaeological remains on the site of Sensō-ji—better known as Asakusa Kannon—go back to the Nara period, but traditional history is much more precise. On the morning of 18 March AD 628 two fishermen, Hinokuma Takenari and his brother Hamanari, found a tiny gold statue in their net which was enshrined by their lord in a temporary sanctuary. Twenty years later, the 5cm image was sealed inside an altar where it is said still to remain, a survivor of the temple's destruction by fire bombs in 1945. No human has laid eyes on it since that time, although a copy was created for public display.

Begin at the famous **Kaminari-mon** (Thunder Gate), site of a million tourist photos, a huge red portal crowded with people, flanked on either side by two snarling deities. On the right is Fūjin, God of Wind, his garments flapping about his body. On the left is Raijin, God of Thunder: in his hands he clutches gold dumb-bells with which he beats a halo of *taiko* drums. The huge red lantern beneath the gate bears the characters for 'Thunder Gate'; a dragon is carved in wood on its base.

The street beyond here is called **Nakamise** (Inner Shops). There are no freak shows anymore, but by day, and especially during festivals, the human traffic jam that develops here still suggests the atmosphere of Asakusa during its glory days. This is one of the best places in Tokyo for buying souvenirs. In the tiny, crammed shops which line the pedestrian arcade there is plenty of tat, but also old establishments producing hand-made goods by traditional techniques—swords, seaweed crackers, lucky cats, paper balloons (*see* pp.229–32 for shopping guide).

The Main Compound

At the end of Nakamise is the two-storey **Hōzō-mon** (Treasure Storing Gate) containing the temple's sutra library, 5428 volumes of it. Beyond lies the courtyard, with the **Hondō** (Main Hall) ahead.

Savour the scene from this end. The Hondō, rebuilt in 1958, is nothing special close-up, but from a distance, with its steeply raked roof and milling crowds of worshippers, visible through a haze of incense smoke, it's a stirring sight. Visitors waft the smoke over their heads and hands as a rite of purification; the temple stalls sell talismans, postcards and fortunes. Inside the Hall is the Gokūden, a gold plated inner shrine which contains (we must take it on trust) the original Kannon statue of 628. Aizen Myō-ō and Fudō Myō-ō, two of the Fierce Kings, are enshrined to the left and right. On the ceiling are modern paintings of soppy, lily-toting angels and a dragon; the walls bear impressive Edo-period votive paintings of bloodthirsty scenes from Japanese literature.

The shrine to the right and rear is **Asakusa Jinja**, a good illustration of the symbiotic relationship between Shinto and Buddhism. While the temple contains the Buddhist Kannon, the shrine deifies the two fishermen who hauled her out of the waters of the river, along with their lord who installed her in the first temple building. The pleasingly weathered building survived the bombs and dates back to 1649. The famous Sanja Matsuri festival in May centres on this shrine. Behind it, there is the smaller **Hikan Inari** shrine to the rice deity. It was established in 1854 by a local fireman as a thanksgiving for his wife's recovery from illness. At the back, a little house on stilts contains hundreds of clay figurines of foxes, messengers of Inari.

West of the main Kannon Hall, a five-storey pagoda is visible over an enclosed wall. These are the precincts of the **Denbō-in**, the abbot's residence, but gaining admittance is not straightforward. Ask at the Temple Office on the west side. You may be lucky and get in that day, but the chances are you'll have to return for a later appointment. Inside is the **pagoda**, rebuilt in 1973 (it looks it), and a fine 17th-century garden by the landscape artist Kobori Enshū.

South of the Denbō-in compound a road runs west, and a gate leads into the small **Chingō-dō temple**, dedicated to the *tanuki* (racoons) who once inhabited the grounds of Senso-ji. The grounds contain numerous statues of these comical, plaintive-looking creatures, famed for their round bellies and their unfeasibly large testicles—apart from this indelicate feature they could have been designed by an oriental Beatrix Potter. On the other side is a black statue of Jizō *bosatsu* being supplicated by tiny children in red bonnets, and surrounded by offerings of milk, pop and sweets.

Kappabashi

Seven hundred metres west of the temple, a road called Kappabashi-dōri runs north to south, lined with shops devoted to kitchen and restaurant supplies. For tourists, this is the place to buy a unique Japanese souvenir: the glistening plastic food models displayed in restaurant windows. Surreal favourites are the forks levitating above a bowl, suspended only by a thin strand of noodles or spaghetti. The Asakusa tourist information centre has a useful map of the street detailing the products sold in each shop.

A Note about Directions

In the listings which follow, every effort has been made to provide clear, accurate directions which the reader can follow on the ground. This an almost impossible task: the streets have no names; the building numbers are not consecutive; the signs are in Japanese; landmarks (noodle shops, car parks, petrol stations, etc.) are regularly torn down and converted into something completely different.

If the directions to some of these establishments appear infuriatingly vague, it's not for want of trying. Even if they appear precise, don't take them for granted. The best one can ever do in Tokyo is to aim the reader at roughly the right area. After that, a few simple urban survival skills are required (*see* 'Practical A–Z', p.14).

Shopping

art

Haguro-dō, ✆ 03 3815 0431, opposite Yushima Tenjin shrine, displays and sells *nikuhitsu*, paintings of the Edo period.

Ōya Shobō, ✆ 03 3291 0062, is near the junction of Yasukuni-dōri and Ochanomizu-dōri. It sells woodblock prints and illustrated books, old and new.

Tokyo Ochanomizu Kottōkan, ✆ 03 3295 7110, is an antique hall containing a dozen different dealers.

Tolman Collection, ✆ 03 3434 1300, by Daimon subway station, is a private gallery of contemporary Japanese prints run by a larger than life American couple.

books

Maruzen in Nihonbashi (a few minutes from exit B3 of the subway station or the Yaesu exit of Tokyo station) is biggest and best of the Tokyo bookstores. It has a good crafts floor as well as foreign books on the 2nd and 4th floors.

The **Yaesu Book Centre** is a few minutes south of Tokyo station. It often has sales of cheap and attractive reproduction antique maps.

South of here, in Ginza (within walking distance of the tourist information centre) is **Jena** which stocks a lot of glossy foreign magazines and art books.

Kinokuniya (5 minutes from Shinjuku station east exit), a useful meeting place, has foreign books on the 6th floor. There's another branch in Shibuya in the Tōkyū Plaza, beyond the bus terminal at the west exit of the station.

Kanda-Jinbōchō is the traditional bookselling quarter of Tokyo. In the old days there were tales of foreigners picking up uncut first editions of *Ulysses* for a few yen: the shop keepers couldn't read the titles. These days they know exactly what they're doing; prices aren't cheap, but it's still a fascinating place to browse.

Kitazawa, by the B1 exit of Jinbōchō subway station, would be a fine English-language bookshop in any city, selling antiquarian works of literature and travel, and modern editions of literature, the humanities and social sciences. A 15-minute walk east down Yasukuni-dōri and on the same side of the road (the south) is

Charles E. Tuttle with a large stock of paperbacks on Japan. Just beyond here is **Sanseidō** with a large general selection.

clothes, jewellery and accessories

The department stores are the best places for scouting out traditional Japanese dress, like kimono. Even if you eventually buy elsewhere, it's worth visiting one of them to get an idea of the available fabrics and prices.

Hayashi Kimono, ✆ 03 3591 9826, in the International Arcade, near Yūrakuchō station, has a range of second-hand kimono, and long experience of dealing with foreign customers.

Grand Back, ✆ 03 3478 6942, is Japan's equivalent of 'High and Mighty', a chain, with branches in several Japanese cities, specializing in large sizes. A lifesaver for the businessman whose shoe bag has been mislaid by the airline. It is on Aoyama-dōri, east of Gaien-mae subway station.

Mikimoto, ✆ 03 3535 4611, is the Tokyo saleroom for the exquisite cultured pearls, invented and cultivated in Toba, near Nagoya.

crafts and ceramics

Again, the department stores are the best place to get your bearings. **Maruzen**, in Nihonbashi (*see* 'books'), has a good crafts floor.

On the north side of Roppongi-dōri, towards Roppongi, are two shops selling excellent souvenirs. **Saga Toen**, on the northeast corner of Nishi-Azabu crossing, has a small but broad selection of remarkably inexpensive ceramics from all over Japan. **Washikobo**, further east on the same side, sells dolls, wallets and books made from traditional paper, as well as plain sheets in various colours.

Taketori Monogatari, ✆ 03 3954 3395, facing the Yamanote line tracks north of Mejiro station, specializes in Japanese dolls for festivals like Girls' Day on 3 March, and also sells Western-style dolls. It is expensive.

department stores

Most of the items you may want to take home from Japan can be bought in department stores, plus a good many that you never dreamed of. They're not always the cheapest places to shop (look out for the sales in June–July and Jan–Feb), but for choice, convenience and service, they're unrivalled. Ask about tax free discounts for tourists. Every sizeable station in Tokyo has at least one *depāto*; the following are the most famous:

Ginza, the birthplace and spiritual home of the Japanese department store (*see* pp.198–201), boasts **Wako**, ✆ 03 3562 2111; **Mitsukoshi**, ✆ 03 3562 1171; **Hankyū**, ✆ 03 3575 2233; and **Matsuya**, ✆ 03 3567 1211.

Shibuya is the *depāto* battleground, with the Seibu and Tōkyū chains competing for customers on adjacent blocks (*see* pp.214–17): **Seibu**, ✆ 03 3462 0111; **Tōkyū**, ✆ 03 3477 3111; **Tōkyū Hands**, ✆ 03 3476 5461; **Parco**, ✆ 03 3464 5111.

Harajuku and **Omotesandō** have **Laforet,** ✆ 03 3475 0411, with boutiques and accessory stores in the heart of Harajuku, next to Meiji-jingū-mae subway station; the **Hanae Mori Building,** designed by Tange Kenzō, isn't technically a department store but contains a number of classy, independent designer fashion shops.

Go to **Shinjuku** (see pp.210–14) for **Isetan,** ✆ 03 3352 1111.

Ikebukuro offers **Seibu** and **Parco,** ✆ 03 3981 0111.

electronics and music

Akihabara is still the most spectacular and varied place to buy electronics in Japan. The main stores are west of the station. Biggest and most convenient for foreigners is the **Laox** (Japanese pronounce it *Raokkusu*) chain with eight stores (*open seven days a week, 10–7*): there's a main store, two **conpyūtā-kan** (computer buildings; number 2 sells second-hand machines) and satellite shops specializing in audio, musical instruments, and computer games. Just northwest of the station, on the station side of Chūō-dōri, is the **Duty Free-kan,** which specializes in goods adapted for export to the overseas market. Staff here speak English, but are sometimes surprisingly ignorant about their stock. If you have a particular item in mind, shop around and don't take no for an answer: the gizmo of your desire almost certainly *is* here, if you have the energy to track it down.

Recently a number of discount chains have sprung up, claiming to rival Akihabara in price, if not in choice:

Dynamic Audio, ✆ 03 3478 5881, is an alternative to the Akihabara stores, with bargains in used stereo equipment. The nearest subway is Meiji-jingū-mae.

Wave (*Ueibu*), west of Almond, on the south side of Roppongi-dōri, is the shopping equivalent of a Roppongi nightclub: every kind of pop music available on tape, CD, video, laser disc and DAT. On the 4th floor is classical music, plus expensive interior design novelties, like an inflatable upright version of Munch's *The Scream* for ¥6000.

food

For an overview of Japanese comestibles, the department store food halls (always in the basement), once again, are the most accessible. Matsuya in Ginza has a particularly graphic fish section.

Musashiya, ✆ 03 3821 1687, specializes in that quintessential, but acquired, Japanese taste, *tōfu*—red pepper *tōfu,* ginger *tōfu, tōfu* croquette, to name but a few. In an old *shitamachi* area between Nippori (Yamanote line) and Sendagi (Chiyoda subway line) stations.

markets

Tsukiji's Central Wholesale Market (for fish) and Ueno's **Ameyoko** (an old black market site) are attractions in themselves (see pp.221–2 and 206). *Tokyo Journal* lists irregular and one-off flea markets and sales.

The **Nakamise**, the long avenue leading up to Asakusa's Sensō-ji temple, is lined with shops selling dolls, swords, fans, kimono, Japanese snacks and other useful souvenirs. **Bairin**, on the left-hand side of the first block, sells nuts and crackers with various flavourings—sesame seeds, seaweed, beans and pistachios. A little further on is **Kazusaya**: kimonos and accessories, *yukata* (cotton kimonos) from about ¥3000, and *noren*, the short cotton curtains, blazoned with calligraphy or designs, which hang down from the doors of traditional shops and restaurants. The third shop on the left of the second block sells eels and prawns, pickled. On the left-hand side of the third block are **Bunsendō** (decorative fans and paper products) and **Kaneso** (cutlery and kitchenware). About half way down on the right-hand side is an ivory-carver's shop—predictably expensive given the world-wide hunting ban. From old ivory are carved shoe horns, cigarette holders, tiny figures of priests, pilgrims, gods and skeletons. A pair of chopsticks costs ¥17,000, a chopstick rest only a little less. The second to last shop on the right is **Sukeroku**, a tiny room filled with miniature dolls of Edo types, expensive and cutesy. On the far side of the same block is an appealing shop called **Fujiya** which specializes in *tenugui*, cotton hand towels with designs from traditional sources like *kabuki* and *ukiyo-e*.

Oriental Bazaar, ✆ 03 3400 3933, is an unashamedly touristy shop with a conveniently wide selection of souvenirs for those in a hurry. It is fine for small items, but if you're investing in anything expensive, then shop around. It's on the south side of Omotesandō-dōri slightly nearer Meiji-jingū-mae than Omotesandō subway station.

International Arcade, beneath the railway tracks behind the Imperial Hotel, contains stalls selling clothes, craft souvenirs and electronic novelties like computer dictionaries and translating machines. Fun and touristy.

American Pharmacy, ✆ 03 3271 4034, sells US brand-name drugs, cosmetics and magazines. Behind the Yūrakuchō Denki Building, near the American Express offices in Yūrakuchō.

Kiddyland, ✆ 03 3409 3431, on the south side of Omotesandō-dōri, east of Meiji-jingū-mae subway station, is a mind-boggling seven storeys of toys with samples for test-play.

Where to Stay

Having spent 13 or more hours in a plane and schlepped your way into town from Narita Airport, the last thing you'll want to worry about is finding somewhere to stay for the night: Tokyo is one place where you'd be well advised to make a booking before you arrive, at least for the first night or two. Reserve especially early for late spring and late autumn. In February thousands of students converge on Tokyo to take university entrance exams, and cheaper accommodation gets booked up.

Hotels in Tokyo are expensive: you get less for your money, and in a less convenient position, than anywhere else in the country. Having said that, Tokyo's deluxe hotels are no more expensive than their counterparts all over the world. Standards of service, if a little impersonal, are uniformly high.

Those with business to do and tourists on generous budgets will want to stay in one of the central areas: Ginza, the Tokyo station area, Akasaka or the districts around the palace moat. Shinjuku has fine hotels and is well connected with the rest of the city, but its station is a horror: unless you can afford to take taxis, this will add to your journey times. Shinagawa, on the southern reaches of the Yamanote line, is also a bit out of the way. Visitors on a tighter budget and those whose main interest is sightseeing should consider one of the quieter, older, more outlying areas like Ueno or Asakusa.

Almost every kind of accommodation in Tokyo, even down to the lowliest hostel, will have someone who speaks English.

(✆ 03–)   *Japanese-style*

Tokyo has disappointingly few Japanese-style inns, and no world-class ones; those that survive tend to be modest establishments in the older districts, full of history and atmosphere, but remote from the business and nightlife areas. If you plan to splash out on an expensive *ryokan* then save your money until you are out of Tokyo.

moderate

Hotel Happu Kaku, ✆ 3982 1181, is a little out of things in Ikebukuro (3min walk south of the east exit; ring for exact directions) and built in uninspiring concrete, but it has both Western- and Japanese-style rooms. Rooms without their own bath fall into the *inexpensive* category. Breakfast and dinner are extra.

inexpensive

Ryokan Mikawaya Bekkan, ✆ 3843 2345, is one of the best deals in town, recommended even if you can afford better. It's a simple, elegant, unfussy wooden *ryokan*, with its own tiny garden, tucked away in a quiet street right next to the Asakusa Kannon temple, Sensō-ji. A small dining room serves breakfast (Japanese or Western) and Japanese dinner. A *tatami* room for one person (without meals) begins at ¥5700. To get there, walk up the Nakamise shopping street in front of the temple; take the second road from the end on the left—not the one that runs beneath the wall of Denbō-in, but the one before that. The *ryokan* is a few metres down on the left.

Kikuya Ryokan, also in Asakusa, is ¥1000 cheaper, but less convenient and in a concrete building, ✆ 3841 6404/4051.

Ryokan Sansuisō, ✆ 3441 7475, is a plain wooden inn in Gotanda, an unusual place for tourists, although not inconvenient: it's three stops from Shibuya, five from Shinjuku, and only half an hour from distant Ueno by the JR Yamanote line. 5 minutes from Gotanda station; ring for directions.

cheap

Ryokan Sawanoya, ✆ 3822 2251, is an exceptionally friendly place, popular with foreign tourists, and run by the one-time president of the Japanese Inn Group. It's in Nezu, an old *shitamachi* district near Ueno, inconvenient for downtown but possessing its own eccentric attractions like a clock museum and an old neighbourhood shrine (free guide brochures available). Nezu subway station is nearest; ring for directions.

(✆ *03–*)
Western-style
luxury

The **Imperial**, ✆ 3504 1111, opposite Hibiya Park, is the city's most famous and historic hotel, although it's lost a lot of its atmosphere since the old Frank Lloyd Wright building (which survived the Great Earthquake) was replaced by a predictable shiny edifice in 1968. The Imperial Suite must be the single most expensive room in Japan: ¥800,000.

The **New Ōtani Hotel**, ✆ 3265 1111, near the Akasaka Palace (Nagatachō subway station), is Tokyo's biggest, the venue for top level international conferences. It has beautiful gardens.

Hotel Ōkura, ✆ 3582 0111, south of the Imperial Palace, is the most expensive and prestigious Tokyo hotel, the address to impress, the place for top-level business, receptions and the swankiest weddings. The nearest subway station is Toranomon, but if you can afford to stay here then you can afford to take a taxi.

The **Tokyo Hilton**, ✆ 3344 5111, and the **Century Hyatt**, ✆ 3349 0111, are both grand, meticulous, and slightly cheaper than the above, but lose out in terms of convenience by their position in Shinjuku (unless that is where you want to be).

expensive

The Tōkyū chain has three fine hotels in central Tokyo. In descending order of expense:

The flagship **Capitol Tōkyū Hotel**, ✆ 3581 4511, is close by Kokkai-gijidō-mae subway station, between Hie Shrine and the Diet Building. It has a plush atmosphere, comfortable rooms and good secretarial and translation facilities.

A few hundred metres away is its little brother, the **Akasaka Tōkyū**, ✆ 3580 2311, on top of Akasaka Mitsuke subway station, another glamorous city hotel with its own arcade of elite shops.

On the other side of town, just round the corner from the Kabuki-za theatre and Higashi Ginza subway station, is the refurbished **Ginza Tōkyū Hotel**, ✆ 3541 2411, an elegantly glitzy hotel in a useful position.

ANA Hotel Tokyo, ✆ 3505 1111, is in Ark Hills, a huge gleaming agglomeration of apartments, offices and a concert hall, just east of Roppongi.

More convenient for the dedicated nightlife animal is the **Roppongi Prince**, ✆ 3587 1111, a bizarre creation built by the architect Kurokawa Kishō around a central swimming pool with transparent sides like a goldfish bowl. From the poolside area you can see the door of everyone's room; even the lifts are glass. A voyeur's dream, low on privacy, but high on humour, favoured by visiting rock bands who appreciate its proximity to the bright lights, and its stern ways with trespassing groupies and autograph hunters.

Keiō Plaza Intercontinental Hotel, ✆ 3344 0111, was Shinjuku's first skyscraper, and purveys all the usual comforts, with fine views of Tange Kenzō's splendid City Hall opposite.

moderate

The **Tokyo Station Hotel**, ✆ 3231 2511, is as convenient as its name suggests and, if the rooms are nothing special, it does have atmospheric bars overlooking Marunouchi, and is housed inside the old Meiji-period station building.

The **Yaesu Fujiya Hotel**, ✆ 3273 2111, is at the other (east) side of Tokyo station, past the Yaesu Book Centre: an efficient, modern business hotel.

The **Hotel Kokusai Kankō**, ✆ 3215 3281, is a similarly workman-like place, on the same side, nearer the station.

Ginza Capital Hotel, ✆ 3543 8211, is a business hotel with a nearby annex, and small cheap rooms, near Tsukiji or Shintōmichō subway stations.

Shinjuku Washington Hotel, ✆ 3343 3111, 8 minutes' walk from Shinjuku station, has a dehumanizing façade—hundreds of equally-spaced, identical portholes—but the rates are good, the restaurants numerous and the service warm.

The **Fairmont Hotel**, ✆ 3262 1151, near Chidorigafuchi Park on the northwest bank of the Imperial Palace moat, has one of the loveliest settings in Tokyo, especially during the spring cherry blossoms.

inexpensive

Shinjuku Park Hotel, ✆ 3356 0241, is a very good deal at the top end of *inexpensive* (verging on *moderate*). It is a cosy city hotel, south of Shinjuku station, overlooking Shinjuku Gyōen park.

Asia Centre of Japan, ✆ 3402 6111, is a plain, clean business hotel near Nogizaka and Aoyama Itchōme subway stations.

Japan YWCA Hostel, ✆ 3264 0661, and the **Tokyo YWCA Sadohara Hostel**, ✆ 3268 4451, both offer frill-free accommodation within walking distance of Ichigaya station. The former receives women only; the latter accepts couples. **YMCA Asia Youth Centre**, ✆ 3233 0631, near Jinbōchō and Suidōbashi subway stations, takes both sexes.

Suigetsu Hotel, ✆ 3822 4611, close to Nezu subway station or 15 minutes from Ueno JR station on the west side of the park (near Ueno Zoo) is a foreigner-friendly hotel, with attached *ryokan*, near old Ueno.

cheap

Kimi Ryokan, ✆ 3971 3766, is Tokyo's best backpackers' hang out, with a famous notice board of news about jobs and travel; it's well worth consulting even if you don't actually stay here.

Tokyo has two principal youth hostels, both of which get booked up and have a (loosely enforced) three night maximum per guest. **Tokyo International Youth Hostel**, ✆ 3235 1107, is near Iidabashi station. **Yoyogi Youth Hostel**, ✆ 3467 9163, is the part of the old Olympic Village near Sangūbashi station. Guests at this one are expected to be International YHA members.

Gaijin houses

Occupying the lowest step of the accommodation ladder is the Tokyo *gaijin* house, so called because no Japanese would be so unhygienic as to live there. The best of them offer extremely cheap accommodation (usually by the week or month, rather than the day) and a friendly, communal life with self-catering kitchen facilities. The worst are prodigies of squalor and inconvenience (some of the horror stories you hear—dishes unwashed for a year, dead monkeys in the bathroom—are exaggerations, but *some* are true). Most are just cheap and messy. While many people are grateful for them for a short while, no one is ever sorry to leave.

The following looked all right at the time, but no promises. A fuller list can be had from the tourist information centre. Remember that *gaijin* houses generally cater for long-term visitors to Tokyo, renting by the week or month. Daily terms may not be available at all and the best (i.e. least vile) often have waiting lists.

Tokyo English Centre, ✆ 3360 4781, is near Higashi Nakano station on the Chūō line, west of Shinjuku.

Friendship House, ✆ 3327 3179, has various locations including Higashi Kōenji on the Marunouchi subway line, and Ōimachi in south Tokyo.

Tokyo House, ✆ 3391 5577, is in Ogikubo.

Marui House, ✆ 3962 4979, is at least close to a major Yamanote line station (Ikebukuro).

---

love hotels

Friday and Saturday nights are the busiest for love hotels when rates double and rooms book out. At other times, they are a rather economical—if bizarre—form of one-off accommodation, as long as you don't mind a late check-in and early check-out. Rooms are rented by the hour during the day and evening, but from about 10pm nightly rates apply. These are generally no more than the cost of a single room in a business hotel, with the advantage that you pay by the room, not per person. In theory, the whole family could bed down in a room costing ¥10,000.

Love hotels are identifiable by their gaudy neon signs, opaque windows and discreet entrances screened from full view of the street. Once you can recognize them, you'll start spotting them everywhere, especially in quiet back streets near major stations and nightlife areas. Shinjuku's Kabukichō has a large number, as you'd expect; Dōgenzaka, near Shibuya, has an extraordinary love hotel village set back from the road. For straightforward budget accommodation, you'll want the plainest and cheapest possible. Couples with something more adventurous in mind might want to visit one of the many 'themed' love hotels, including the following:

Rosa Rossa, in Dōgenzaka, features boudoirs in the style of a 19th-century French brothel.

In **P&A Plaza**, ✆ 3780 5211, also in Dōgenzaka, the top rooms contain miniature swimming pools with transparent walls.

Hotel Alpha Inn, ✆ 3583 3655, in Higashi Azabu, caters for athletes of a different inclination: 26 S&M zones fully equipped with riding horses, uniforms and a fearsome collection of whips and leather goods.

Hotel Japan, ✆ 3461 1303, in the Maruyamachō district of Shibuya, has rooms with tanning beds, karaoke machines, and built-in ceiling planetariums.

Eating Out

Tokyo is rich in good restaurants and dining out is one of the city's great pleasures, for the huge number of foreign and ethnic restaurants, as well as native dishes. The key word in contemporary Japanese cooking is *mukokuseki* (meaning 'no nationality' or 'eclectic') and refers to the interesting twists which Japanese-born, foreign-trained chefs give to imported recipes. Like cars, buildings and fashion, European and Asian-style food in Tokyo rarely turns out to be quite the same as the model which inspired it.

Most of the establishments classed here as *expensive* and *moderate* are one-offs for holiday treats and special occasions; excluded are the numberless chain restaurants and anonymous local noodle bars and *yakitori* shops which provide thoroughly decent, modest nourishment at much cheaper prices. Remember that even the flashiest restaurants usually do inexpensive lunchtime sets for a fraction of their evening tariffs (on which the following listings are based). To save money, treat lunch as the main meal of the day, and fill up on something cheaper and simpler in the evening.

Tokyo Journal has good restaurant reviews. Rick Kennedy's book, *Good Tokyo Restaurants* (Kodansha International), lives up to its title.

(✆ *03–*)   ***Japanese***

expensive

Aotsuyu, ✆ 3205 1638, on the edge of the Golden Gai, a teeming block of tiny restaurants to the east of Kabukichō (Shinjuku station or Shinjuku-sanchōme subway station), serves grilled fish, *tempura* and the finest *sashimi* à la carte or in a set course.

Botan, ✆ 3251 0577, in Kanda, between the Transport Museum and Awajichō or Ogawamachi subway stations, was founded a century ago by a man who once worked in a button factory, hence its name. It's a simple, comfortably old-fashioned place specializing in chicken *nabe* (stew) cooked at the table on a charcoal brazier.

Fukuzushi, ✆ 3402 4116, is behind the Roppongi Roi Building: from Roppongi subway station, take the main road to the left of Almond, it's a few minutes' walk on the right. This is a flamboyant and trendy *sushi* restaurant in a tiny bamboo garden which stays open until 11pm.

Jiro, ✆ 3535 3600, in the basement of the office opposite the Sony Building in Ginza, has the most expensive, meticulously prepared and highly praised *sushi* in Tokyo.

Kakiden, ✆ 3352 5121, is just south of My City, the department store on top of Shinjuku station. It is an elegant, innovative restaurant serving *kaiseki*, the delicate, bitty *haute cuisine* of Kyoto. At about ¥6000 the 'mini-*kaiseki*' course is not exorbitant.

Yama no Chaya, ✆ 3581 0656, by the Hie Shrine, Akasaka-Mitsuke subway station, is a simple, exquisite and extremely pricey (well over £100 a head) teahouse restaurant serving a delicate sea food course based around *unagi* (eel).

Yūsan, ✆ 3237 8363, is north of Yama no Chaya, a relaxed and unstuffy *kaiseki* restaurant, near the Akasaka Prince Hotel.

moderate

Body and Soul, ✆ 5466 1877, is a *mukokuseki* ('no nationality') restaurant in which the Japanese influence still remains strong: Chinese, Cambodian and Korean dishes, light but fiery, plus native dishes like fried noodles.

Robata, ✆ 3591 1905, below the railway tracks, just south of the tourist information centre in Yūrakuchō, serves superb farmhouse cooking in an atmospherically dingy wooden building, frequented by poets and other bohemians.

Tomoegata, ✆ 3631 6729, specializes in *chanko nabe*, the high-protein wonder food which makes sumo wrestlers look the way they do. It's two blocks south of Ryōgoku in the heart of *shitamachi*, not far from the National Sumo Stadium.

inexpensive

Kaotan Ramen, ✆ 3475 6337, on the right, coming down the Aoyama Cemetery hill from Nogizaka subway station, is a deliriously popular *ramen* shack which is open until 5am.

Komagata Dojō, ✆ 3842 4001, is on the west side of Edo-dōri avenue, three blocks south of Asakusa station on the Asakusa line. It is an old Edo-style restaurant specializing in *dojō* (loach), stewed (*dojō nabe*) or in an omelette (*yanagawa*).

Kujiraya, ✆ 3461 9145, on Shibuya's Tōkyū Honten-dōri, just past the 109 Building, is the more famous, more conveniently positioned, but less interesting of

Tokyo's two whale restaurants. Dishes like *kujira sukiyaki* are in the *moderate* price category, but there are cheaper sets, especially at lunchtime.

Maisen, ✆ 3470 0071, near Omotesandō subway station (ring for precise directions), is a big, bustling restaurant devoted to *tonkatsu*, crispy battered pork cutlets, with a variety of accompaniments.

Nanaki, ✆ 3496 2878, third on the right from the overhead tracks as you walk west from Ebisu JR station, is an esteemed, but very affordable, shack serving *soba* (buckwheat noodles).

Negishi, ✆ 3232 8020, northwest of the cinema-filled square in Shinjuku's Kabukichō, near the tracks of the Seibu Shinjuku line, is a cheap and cheerful diner serving beef and vegetable stew.

Sweet Paozu, ✆ 3295 4084, on Suzuran-dōri, parallel and to the south of Yasukuni-dōri, in the heart of the Jinbōchō book selling district, is an authentic Chinese *gyōza* (dumpling) shop, more than 60 years old and utterly without frills. It closes at 8pm.

Taruichi, ✆ 3208 9772/3, is one of Tokyo's two *kujira* (whale) restaurants, and the more lively by far. The menu consists of a cross-sectional diagram of a whale with arrows pointing to the various different cuts which range from whale steak (the most expensive, almost like rich beef) to whale penis (the cheapest, served in thin slices, very chewy). The cheerful proprietor, Mr Sato Takashi, is a whale-meat evangelist, and a passionate believer in the humanitarian benefits of killing and eating as many whales as possible. The minke whales swim around in a tank at the front of the restaurant—you decide which one you want, and harpoon your own (only joking). Taruichi is near Shinjuku station, but takes a little finding. From the central east exit, walk out into the plaza so you are facing the giant video screen of Studio Alta. Take the road just to the left of here, and continue down it across the next main road, Yasukuni-dōri, between a games arcade on the left and the Daiwa bank on the right. The restaurant is on the 5th floor of a rather dingy building a few metres down on the left.

Yabu Soba, ✆ 3251 0287, is in Kanda between the Transportation Museum and the Tokyo Green Hotel Awajichō (Awajichō or Ogawamachi subway stations). It is the mother restaurant of another famous Tokyo chain, this time specializing in *soba* noodles served in a traditional atmosphere.

(✆ *03–*)   **Foreign**

expensive

Aux Sept Bonheurs, ✆ 3498 8144, off Aoyama-dōri, behind the Kinokuniya supermarket block, is a serious, painstaking Chinese restaurant serving Shanghai-style Schezuan dishes, in a series of small, beautifully presented courses.

Buone Buono, ✆ 3566 4031, on the 2nd floor of Nishi-Ginza department store opposite the Sony Building in Ginza, is at the very low end of expensive, especially at lunchtime. It is a crisp, unfussy Italian restaurant overlooking busy Ginza.

Granata, ✆ 3582 3241, next to TBS TV, north of Akasaka subway station, is a bit pricier: a popular, informal Italian restaurant with its own built-in pavement café.

1066, ✆ 3719 9059, is tucked away near Meguro station on the Yamanote Line (ring for precise directions): a British restaurant with roasts, puddings, dozens of British ales, and live folk music on the first and third Wednesday of each month.

L'Orangerie de Paris, ✆ 3407 7461, in the striking Hanae Mori building near Omotesandō station, is one of Tokyo's best French restaurants—and in a great position on Omotesandō-dōri, the closest Tokyo has to a continental boulevard.

moderate

Angkor Wat, ✆ 3370 3019, is a bit off the beaten track (between Yoyogi and Minami-Shinjuku stations), but serves sweet, spicy Cambodian dishes in a noisy, fast-moving atmosphere.

Ban-Thai, ✆ 3207 0068, in the Dai-ichi Metro Building, next to the Shinjuku Prince Hotel, in the southwest corner of Kabukichō, is one of Tokyo's oldest and most popular Thai restaurants; reservations are recommended.

Brasserie Bernard, ✆ 3405 7877, is next to the Ibis Hotel on Gaien-Higashi-dōri, the road that leads north opposite Almond coffee shop near Roppongi subway station: an unpretentious French restaurant serving beefy stews, black puddings etc. in a hearty provincial style.

La Playa, ✆ 5379 0820, on the 3rd floor off an alleyway near Shinjuku San-chōme subway station, is a small shadowy Spanish restaurant run by an eccentric Japanese *señor*. There is no menu: tell him how much you want to spend and see what comes.

Las Chicas, ✆ 3407 6865, at the end of a sidestreet west of the Kinokuniya supermarket (Omotesandō subway station), is the best outdoor café in Tokyo, with an eclectic European menu, and good *café au lait* in French-style bowls. There is more formal, expensive food inside, as well as a bar, art gallery and hair salon.

Le Mange-Tout, ✆ 3268 5911, nearest stations Kagurazaka or Ichigaya, though neither are particularly near (ring for directions), is a Tokyo secret that's becoming increasingly well known: a studenty and very inexpensive French restaurant serving good portions.

Mugyodon, ✆ 3586 6478, is a few minutes south of Akasaka subway station. It serves unglamorous but wholesome Korean food (hotter and more garlicky than Japanese) in an otherwise forbiddingly expensive part of town.

inexpensive

The most atmospheric cheap food in Tokyo is to be had in the nameless, phone-less, unreservable *yakitori* stands under the railway tracks just south of the tourist information centre in Yūrakuchō. Service is fast and noisy, tables and chairs are tin and wobbly, and if they ask you to shove up and make room for another party, there's no arguing. Still, as the smoke wafts off the grills, and the trains rattle overhead, it's irresistible: a flavour of Tokyo during the 1950s.

Bindi, ✆ 3409 7114, in Nishi Azabu, on an alley off Roppongi-dōri, opposite the Fuji Film building, is a trendy but informal Indian.

Chao! Bamboo, ✆ 5466 4787, is on the alley behind Café de Ropé on the west side of Omotesandō-dōri, near Harajuku, and serves cheap, eclectic southeast Asian dishes at open-air tables.

Ganga Palace, ✆ 3796 4477, off Gaien-Higashi-dōri, between Nogizaka and Roppongi subway stations, is dramatically decorated (fountains, columns) and moderately expensive if you pile on the dishes, but substantial Indian curries can be had for under ¥2000. When the food stops at 11pm, the place turns into a trendy bar, open until 5am.

Ichioku, ✆ 3405 9891, near the Defence Agency (Bōeichō), Roppongi subway station, is a classic *mukokuseki* ('no nationality') restaurant, although the attributed influence is Balinese. The *gyōza* (traditional Chinese and Japanese meat dumplings) filled with mozzarella are celebrated.

Ninnikuya, ✆ 3446 5887 (call for directions from Ebisu station on the JR Yamanote and Hibiya subway lines), is another original, a restaurant whose menu is based entirely around garlic (the name means 'Garlic Shop'); it gets very busy and bookings are recommended.

Pas à Pas, ✆ 3357 7888, is on a sidestreet to the east of the main road between Yotsuya san-chōme and Akebonobashi subway stations. It is a simple, cosy, tiny French restaurant, the best value of its kind in town.

Sushi Tochigi-ya, ✆ 3291 9426, a minute from Ochanomizu station, serves dirt cheap *sushi* until 1am.

Tompo, ✆ 3405 9944, just off Meiji-dōri, east of Harajuku station, specializes in cheap Chinese stir-fry.

Zuien Bekkan, ✆ 3351 3511, on Shinjuku-dōri, a couple of blocks east of Shinjuku-gyōenmae subway station, is another cheap, rowdy Chinese: snapping turtle soup, sea slug in soy sauce, and the usual staples.

cheap

When maximum bulk at minimum cost is your priority, try the following:

Shakey's Pizza has branches in Harajuku, Shibuya, Ikebukuro, Shinjuku, Ginza and various lesser places where, between 11am and 2pm (except Sun), you can eat as much pizza, potatoes and spaghetti as you like for ¥600.

Takeya, ✆ 3836 3679, on the 6th floor of the Beklitas Building, a minute from the Shinobazu exit of Ueno station, has a similar deal for *shabu-shabu* and *sukiyaki* (plus extras). Men ¥2000, women ¥1800.

Tokaien, ✆ 3200 2924, is 3 minutes from Shinjuku station east exit. It is a Korean barbecue restaurant with an all-you-can-eat menu for ¥2500.

Branches of **Macdonalds**, **Kentucky Fried Chicken** and **Subway Sandwich** can be found all over Tokyo.

Nightlife

After-dark fashions in Tokyo change by the week, so the publishers take no responsibility for social embarrassment suffered by anyone using the following guide—for up-to-date fashion victimology, try the Nightlife section of *Tokyo Journal* or ask on the street. To dispense with confusing directions, phone numbers only are given for the more obscurely located places—most of them should have someone who speaks English.

Roppongi

During office hours, Roppongi crossing is an untidy crevasse of record shops, cheap cafés and fast food joints, pervaded by the migraine hum of the overhead expressway. But when the lights come on, above all at weekends, it's transformed into a neon carnival, the traditional party place of Tokyo's expatriate tribes. Icy European models, bullet-headed marines, Brazilian cocktail waiters, beer-chugging city bankers, Israeli street traders and Iranian bricklayers swarm the all-night bars, restaurants and clubs, along with the ubiquitous blue-suited salarymen and armies of Japanese girls in ferociously slinky, 'body-conscious' dresses. The diversity of the mix means that, however hard it tries, Roppongi is still nothing like Paris or L.A. But foreign influence definitely shows in the design of its bars and restaurants: compared to the more traditional entertainment districts, there are plenty of places on ground level with big windows that allow you to form some idea of what's inside before blundering in. Roppongi is open, tolerant and accessible and, wherever you end up, you will never be far from an English menu.

Almond, a nasty pink coffee shop on the southwest corner of Roppongi crossing, is Tokyo's second most famous meeting place, after Shibuya's Hachikō. Nightlife is mostly concentrated in the streets behind it, to the south.

Gas Panic, ✆ 3405 0633, and **Gas Panic Club**, 3402 7054, are the archetypal hang-outs of young *gaijin*, with a grungy and unpredictable adolescent atmosphere. For a more mature (some would say staid) atmosphere, try the **Lexington Queen**, ✆ 3401 1661, a Tokyo institution, the first stop for visiting showbiz royalty (preferential treatment given to models).

Immediately to the left of Almond as you face it, a busy road leads towards Tokyo Tower. Two hundred metres down it, on the right, is the **Roi Building** (pronounced 'Roa'), another useful rendezvous point. Just before it, a road leads right to a cluster of American restaurants: **Spago's**, **Tony Roma's** and the ubiquitous **Hard Rock Café**. The nearby **Charleston** is an inexpensive bar restaurant serving pizza and snacks at open air tables. Next door is **Salsa Cariba**, an enthusiastic, unpretentious Latin American bar, full of real Latin Americans. Signs forbid dancing; everyone ignores them.

Misterio, ✆ 5474 4366, is a men-only gay bar with kitsch decor and weekend strip 'performances'.

Café Mogambo, ✆ 3403 4833, is a friendly African bar.

Baccara Live, ✆ 3746 3693, has live ambient jazz at weekends.

Salsa Sudada, ✆ 3405 1967, has Latin music.

Nishi-Azabu

A 15-minute walk from the nearest subway station, Nishi-Azabu is isolated enough to avoid the worst of the Roppongi crowds.

Hobson's, a blue and yellow ice cream parlour on the southwest corner of Nishi-Azabu crossing is the rendezvous.

Acaraje, ✆ 3401 0973, is a Brazilian bar serving powerful cocktails.

Club Jamaica, ✆ 3407 8844, is a self-consciously cool reggae bar.

Live Stock, ✆ 5485 1277, has rock'n'roll from the 60s and 70s with live bands.

J Men's Tokyo, ✆ 3409 7607, features male foreigners who strip and twirl for excitable Japanese women (and men). Innocent hysteria. Reservations required.

Shibuya and Omotesandō

The multi-storey buildings around Shibuya station are a honeycomb of restaurants, bars and clubs catering for Japanese students. Omotesandō has more sophisticated, cosmopolitan clubs.

Bar Dark Side, ✆ 3476 2193, is a sleek, matt black cocktail bar on the 5th floor of the Brither Building, a few minutes' walk from Shibuya station.

DJ Bar Inkstick, ✆ 3496 0782, is an elegant, well-established music venue formerly in Roppongi.

Blue Note Tokyo, ✆ 3407 5781, is an offshoot of the famous New York jazz club with world class visiting acts. Consult *Tokyo Journal* for the current programme.

Shinjuku

Kabukichō is the sex capital of Tokyo with some of the most eye-popping shows, bars and theatres in Asia, but there is plenty of good entertainment of a conventional nature. Shinjuku ni-chōme is famous as the stomping ground of the *okama-san*—Tokyo's transsexuals and transvestites.

DX Kabukichō, ✆ 3232 9946 (Japanese only spoken), has a commercialized live sex show well used to gawping foreigners. Look out for the discount coupons in free English language papers like the *Tour Companion*.

Tokyo is a popular and lucrative stop for theatre companies from all over the world—avant-garde experimentalists, as well as Andrew Lloyd Webber—but the following list focuses on uniquely Japanese forms. *Tokyo Journal* and English-language papers like *The Japan Times* contain comprehensive monthly listings of drama (Western and Japanese), dance, ballet, opera and musicals.

The Ticket Pia booking agency has an English-language line, ✆ 5237 9999.

National Theatre (Kokuritsu Gekijō), ✆ 3265 7411, features alternating programmes of *bunraku* and *kabuki*, with English programmes and earphone commentaries. Nagatachō and Kojimachi subway stations.

Takarazuka Theatre, ✆ 3591 1711, near the Imperial Hotel and Hibiya subway station, is the home of the Takarazuka girls, a unique and extraordinary Japanese phenomenon. Young women, intensively trained for years at a special school, play male and female roles in achingly sentimental pastiches of Hollywood musicals.

Kabuki-za, ✆ 3541 3131, the bristling 'Japanese Gothic' palace on the edge of Ginza, is the best place to sample traditional Japanese theatre. The programmes have English plot summaries, and earphone receivers with a simultaneous English commentary can be hired. A full *kabuki* programme lasts most of the day, but at Kabuki-za, you can pay to see just one act, from ¥2500. The nearest subway station is Higashi Ginza.

National Nō Theatre (Kokuritsu Nōgakudō), ✆ 3423 1331, is a beautiful theatre near Sendagaya station. Check the press for performance times.

Kanze Nō Theatre (Kanze Nōgakudō), ✆ 3469 5241, is near Shibuya JR station.

Tessenkai Nō Institute, ✆ 3401 2285, is a fashionable theatre in a modern concrete building, popular with a young audience. It is near Omotesandō station.

Kantō

Kantō is Japan's biggest plain, and in a country so lacking in broad, unmountainous areas, it was bound to become a centre of population and power. Tokyo emerged as the dominant city relatively late, when the first great Tokugawa shogun, Ieyasu, made it his capital. Before then, Kantō had been ruled from Odawara, now a very ordinary town, and from the medieval capital, Kamakura, a mini-Kyoto of temples, shrines and rural walks. The opulent mausolea of the Tokugawa at Nikkō are the area's other great architectural treasures, and the encircling mountains contain national parks, hot springs, and the serene form of Mt Fuji, Japan's highest and most beautiful mountain.

Nikkō

Nikkō Tōshō-gū, the great mausoleum shrine of the Tokugawas, was to Japan's shoguns what the Pyramids were to the Egyptian Pharaohs: a symptom of megalomania and paranoia, a bid for immortality, and an important element in the national economy. Twentieth-century criticism has generally written off the Liquorice Allsort colours and minuscule carving as a fiasco of vulgarity and excess. Even Isabella Bird (who loved them, like most Victorian visitors) sounds a little overwhelmed when she writes that 'to pass from court to court is to pass from splendour to splendour; one is almost glad to feel that this is the last, and that the strain on one's capacity for admiration is nearly over.' 'Never say *kekkō* until you've seen Nikkō,' goes the Japanese proverb (c.f. 'See Naples and die'): *kekkō* means magnificent, but also full up, sated with overeating. As pure architecture, there are many finer and more profound Japanese buildings; but as a relic of its time, and of the frightening men who ruled Japan for 250 years, Nikkō is unsurpassed. It's also a perfect day trip from Tokyo: quick, convenient, with plenty to see and do in either fine or rainy weather.

History

With its seething streams and rumbling mountains, Nikkō has always been seen as an abode of gods, and places of worship were well established here long before the time of the Tokugawas. In 767 a priest called Shōdō Shōnin saw four strangely coloured clouds floating over a local mountain. He climbed it and founded the first of several temples, enshrining an image of thousand-armed Kannon, and calling it the Monastery of the Four Dragons.

Fifteen years later he founded the shrine of Futara-san, also pronounced Nikō-san, both names consisting of the characters meaning Two Unruly Mountains, in reference to the storms and eruptions which issued from Mt Nantai and Mt Shirane. In the 9th century, the great Buddhist divine Kōbō Daishi visited the area and, by marginally altering the pronunciation, re-christened it Nikkō-san, meaning 'Mountain of the Sun's Brightness'. Overnight, the storms retreated and the volcanoes became dormant. (As recently as the 18th century, the cave where the Daishi performed his exorcism was visited by priests intent on maintaining the supernatural weather control.)

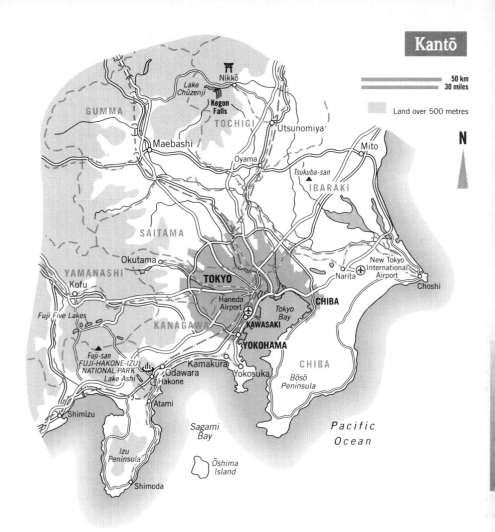

50 km
30 miles

Land over 500 metres

N

So Nikkō was already an ancient religious centre when, in 1616, the first Tokugawa Shogun, Ieyasu, died at his retirement home south of Tokyo, and the preparations began to deify him. The site was chosen with great deliberation: Nikkō was northeast of the city of Edo, the unlucky direction from which the spirit of the dead shogun would, it was believed, protect his capital. By 1617 a mausoleum had been prepared, and Ieyasu's ashes were carried there in state from his temporary burial place near Shizuoka. At the internment, Ieyasu was declared *Tōshō Dai-gongen*, 'Eastern Illuminating Great Avatar'. In the complicated theology of Ryōbu Shinto (Syncretic Shinto-Buddhism), he was both a Shinto god, the protector of the nation, and an aspect of Yakushi Nyorai, the Buddha of Healing.

Between 1634 and 1636 the mausoleum was entirely rebuilt by Ieyasu's grandson, the third shogun, Iemitsu; only the stone *torii* gate and the sacred washbasin remain from the original edifice. The intervening period had seen great advances in construction techniques and technology, and no expense was spared in making Nikkō the most dazzling, intricate and ostentatiously expensive shrine in the land. Painters like Kanō Tanyū supplied designs which were sculpted into carvings of unsurpassed delicacy and complexity by craftsmen such as Hidari Jingorō, famous for his left-handedness. 1,690,000 man days went into the carpentry alone; 23,000 days were spent applying gold leaf, and the transportation of materials accounted for another 2,830,000 days: 4.5 million (12,300 man *years*) altogether.

Iemitsu had two purposes in mind, both of them political: to glorify the memory of his grandfather (and thus bolster his own prestige and legitimacy); and to further impoverish the feudal lords who were expected to maintain teams of craftsmen on the construction site at their own expense, and whose voluntary 'offerings' (it would be a foolish *daimyō* who withheld) kept the whole thing afloat.

When Iemitsu died in 1651 and was deified as *Taiyūin*, the whole process began again as his mausoleum was constructed alongside his grandfather's. By now, Nikkō was firmly established as the spiritual heart of the shogunate. Every year, an imperial envoy travelled here to confirm the Tokugawas in their authority. During the Meiji Restoration, troops loyal to the shogun holed up here; and the whole place was set to become a battle ground until they were talked down at the last minute. It survived, but the reforms of the new government outlawed syncretism; many of the Buddhist accoutrements of the shrine buildings had to be removed or destroyed.

Getting There

The quickest way from Tokyo to Nikkō, and the cheapest for non-rail pass holders, is by the Tōbu line from Tōbu-Asakusa station. The trains range from the *kaisoku* rapid train (2hrs and ¥1260) to the limited express (1hr 40mins and ¥2530).

Even the *shinkansen* can't do better than this: it takes up to 2hrs with a change onto a regular train at Utsunomiya (¥5130 with a reservation). The local JR train from Ueno takes about 2hrs 20mins and costs ¥2470; both are free with a Japan Rail Pass.

Various bus companies run all-inclusive one- or two-day tours to Nikkō from Tokyo. Ask a tourist information centre for details.

Getting Around

The shrines and temple buildings are easily negotiable on foot, but the walk from the station to the shrine area takes 20mins uphill. Frequent buses leave the JR and Tōbu stations for Shin-kyō bridge (5mins), then the Chūzenji Onsen (40mins; ¥1050) and Yumoto Onsen (1hr 10mins; ¥1600) areas.

Tourist Information

There are information desks in Tōbu Nikkō station, and half way up the main road leading to the Shin-kyō bridge, on the left.

April

2   **Gohan-Shiki**. This rice eating ceremony takes place in the Sanbutsu-dō of Rinnō-ji temple.

May

17   **Ennen-no-Mai**. An ancient longevity dance is performed in front of Rinnō-ji's Sanbutsu-dō. In the evening a holy fire is kindled.

17–18   **Grand Spring Festival of the Tōshō-gū Shrine**. A procession of 1000 people dressed in Edo period costume is followed by a parade of *omikoshi* (portable shrines), containing the spirits of Tokugawa Ieyasu and his illustrious predecessors, Toyotomi Hideyoshi and Minamoto Yoritomo. There are sacred music recitals and horse-back archery.

July

31   **Tohai Matsuri**. Pilgrims pay a fee to climb Nantai-san from Chugushi
(–7 Aug)   Shrine, after being purified in the waters of Lake Chūzenji and dressed in white. The end of the 8km walk coincides with sunrise.

October

17   **Autumn Festival of Tōshō-gū Shrine**. Similar to the spring festival.

Touring the Nikkō Shrines and Temples

The Road to Tōshō-gū

The main road from Nikkō station crosses the Daiyagawa River on a modern concrete bridge, but a few metres upstream is the **Shin-kyō** (Sacred Bridge), a vermilion arch, 27m long, originally built in 1636 for the exclusive use of the shogun and his envoys, and rebuilt in 1907 after a fire.

When Shōdō Shōnin first visited Nikkō in the 8th century he was stopped short at this river. Finding no way to cross, he was praying on his knees when an immense supernatural being appeared on the opposite bank, wearing black and blue robes, with a string of skulls hanging around his neck. In his right hand, he clutched two green and blue snakes which he flung towards the priest; instantly they formed a long bridge across the chasm, 'like a rainbow floating among the hills'. Shōdō crossed gratefully; as soon as he had reached the other side both snake bridge and skull god disappeared without a trace.

From here, there are various ways to walk up to the shrines. The most convenient and picturesque is up the avenue opposite the Shin-kyō (a narrower set of steps begins opposite the road bridge) which climbs the slopes of the cryptomeria forest. Keep going up and to the left until you find yourself at the bottom of a wide straight avenue lined with more trees: this is the **Omotesan-dō**, the principal approach to the shrine. Like main roads all over the region, the trees on this approach were planted by a lord of the Matsudaira family who, it is said, was unable to afford the costly bronze lanterns which the Tokugawas expected from their *daimyō*. The planting took 20 years; 13,000 of the original trees still survive, strung along 40km of road.

Rinnō-ji

To the east of the Omotesan-dō is Rinnō-ji, the present name of the temple first established by Shōdō Shōnin in 767, which administered the Tōshō-gū complex until 1868. Its chief abbot used always to be a prince of the imperial blood, but with the Meiji Restoration and the disestablishment of Buddhism, it lost many of its privileges. Its small **museum** contains scrolls, furniture and ritual objects brought here by its rich abbots (who usually dwelt in Edo, visiting the temple three times a year). Behind it is the **Shōyō-en**, a pleasant stroll garden crowding steeply around a long narrow pond. The **Sanbutsu-dō** (Hall of the Three Buddhas) is a rather bare space dating from the 19th century and containing images of Amida Nyorai, and two effigies of Kannon—Horse-headed Kannon in the middle, and Thousand-armed Kannon on the left. The **Sorin-tō** (1644) is a rarity: a 'zero-storey' pagoda, consisting only of the tall metal spire which surmounts the top of the three- and five-storey type.

On the Omotesan-dō

At the top of the avenue is **Ichi no Torii**, an unusual stone gateway, also the gift of a *daimyō*, and hewn in 1618 from his own quarries in Fukuoka. The **five-storey pagoda** on the left dates from 1818 and looks even more youthful than that. The 12 animals of the zodiac are carved between the eave supports on the bottom storey; the tile ends bear the Tokugawa trefoil crest.

At the top of more steps is the **Ni-ō-mon**, traditionally a feature of Buddhist temples rather than Shinto shrines, which points to the syncretic nature of the worship here. Take a good look at the gate: it provides the first taster of what is to come. The Ni-ō guardians on either side are overwhelmed by the profuse coloured carvings which sprout from every inch of available wood: tuberous chrysanthemums bulge from the eight pillars, petal-eared elephants guard the inside of the gate, and on the ends of the gate are two terrifying, iridescent *baku*, legendary monsters resembling a cross between a lion and a dragon, who are said to devour dreams. To continue beyond here you must pay ¥1250. If you find the Ni-ō-mon hard to swallow, then be warned: from now on you can expect more of the same, but even gaudier.

Entering the Precincts

Having bought your ticket, you find yourself on a path leading through a courtyard. The buildings are set back from it in beds of large pebbles lined with mottled bronze statues. Immediately opposite and to the right, as you pass through the gate, are three **store houses** arranged on a zig-zag, with mild sloping roofs and walls which are stylized versions of the ancient *azekura* (log-cabin) style of interlocking logs. The third store house, furthest to the north as you enter, has carvings of an elephant attributed to the famous sculptor Hidari 'Lefty' Jingorō: look at the joints of the hind legs which bend the wrong way.

Facing these on the left-hand side of the path is the **Shinkyū-sha** (Sacred Stable), home to the ceremonial sacred horse, a beautiful creature presented to the shrine by the government of New Zealand. It is the only building in the precincts to be unpainted, apart from flowers under the beams, and a famous sequence of carvings depicting **monkeys**, including the See-No-Evil, Speak-No-Evil, Hear-No-Evil trio. For all its cartoonish extravagance, the buildings of Nikkō lack explicit humour. The three wise monkeys typify the comic, knockabout strain in Edo culture, although it's hard not to see them also as a dry comment on the totalitarian policies of the Tokugawa dictatorship, when everyone was a spy or a potential informer. The **Suiban-sha** (Sacred Washbasin), a bit further on, is in a distinctly Chinese style, characterized most obviously by the gables of its canopied roof with their flattened central arches trailing to the eaves. The pillars and water basin are granite and the latter is so perfectly set that the water, from a spring on a nearby hill, bubbles evenly over each side.

A final flight of steps leads to a still higher level with more bronze lanterns, a small **sutra repository** and a **drum tower**. Two of the largest lanterns here were gifts from Holland, unique among European nations in maintaining a trade link with Japan throughout the Edo period. The lanterns occupy pride of place near Ieyasu's tomb, but only foreigners would have got away with the tactless error that they contain: the Tokugawa crest as it appears on the lantern is upside down.

The building on the left, the **Honchi-dō**, is actually part of Rinnō-ji temple, and an additional ¥50 entrance fee is charged. The roof and interiors were destroyed by fire in 1961 and the famous 'Crying Dragon' painted on the ceiling is a reproduction. It earns its nickname from a curious attribute of the hall's construction. If a block is struck at a point directly below the painting's head, a high shrill echo can be clearly heard. Bossy priests lead regular parties of visitors to demonstrate this gimmick.

The Inner Shrine Precincts

The gate leading from this area into the shrine proper, the **Yōmei-mon**, is the climax of Nikkō's extraordinary style, its apex or nadir depending on your point of view. Its name means 'Sun Blaze Gate', and some visitors won't want to spend too long staring at it. Like the Ni-ō-mon, it houses two traditional guardians, this time the courtly archers who are to shrines what the muscular Ni-ō guardians are to temples. But once again form and function are eclipsed by the frenzy of ornamentation. The carving is relentless; there is virtually no unadorned surface on the entire gate. Above the white carved pillars are a row of white lion-like creatures; above these are scenes depicting famous sages— studying, making music, playing board games. A quadruple layer of supporting struts, covered in lacquer and gold leaf, is topped by a balustrade decorated with scenes of children dancing and playing with cards and hobby horses. It took two years to build this edifice, an estimated 55,970 man hours. The designers were so pleased with themselves that they incorporated a deliberate flaw, intended to avert the gods' envy at the perfection of what they had created: the far pillar on the left of the doorway has its geometrical pattern the wrong way up; it is called the **Mayoke no hashira** (Evil-Averting Pillar).

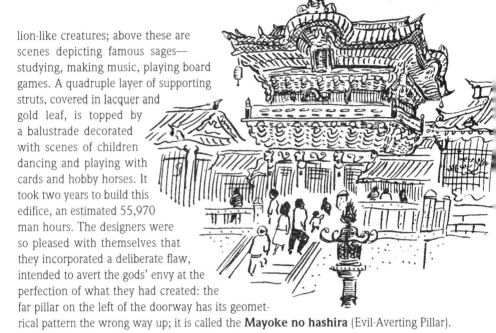

The **Kara-mon** (Chinese Gate) in the next courtyard is, in many ways, more satisfying; in comparison with it, the Yōmei-mon looks top-heavy and excessive. The milky paint lends it a (relative) austerity, highlighting the interesting details, like the ascending and descending dragons—unpainted—on the white pillar. Beyond here is the shrine itself, consisting of two halls, the outer **Haiden** (Oratory) and **Honden** (Main Hall), linked by a stone-flagged corridor. Paintings of dragons decorate the individual panels of the coffered ceiling in turquoise, green and blue. The Honden still has its original paintwork. The age-muted tones are relaxing and easy on the eye, an example of what softening effects time can work on the Nikkō style, when it is allowed to have its way.

The Grave of Ieyasu

Go out of the Haiden the way you came and exit by the **Sakashita-mon** gate in the eastern side. Above it is another famous carving by 'Lefty' Jingorō, of a **sleeping cat** (*nemuri no neko*) around which aficionados of the cute gather to cluck and giggle. More than 200 stone steps lead up from here to the actual burial site of Ieyasu—a bronze urn standing behind a small worship hall.

Futara-san Jinja (Shrine of the Three Unruly Mountains)

Returning to the five-storey pagoda outside the front gate of the Tōshō-gū, take a left turn (as you face the Ni-ō-mon) down a long, straight, narrow avenue; the shrine is at the end.

This was the original Nikkō shrine, founded in 782 by Shōdō Shōnin after an encounter with the mountain deities on the slopes of Nantai-zan. The **Oratory** contains votive plaques bearing pictures of mountain deer, foxes and hawks, and there's a pleasant garden (*adm ¥200*) containing a well, a store room for portable shrines and a stand of cryptomerias girt with aprons of sacred streamers. The most famous object in the grounds is the **bakemono tōrō**, a lantern fashioned in 1292 in the shape of a demon which was said to come to life and terrorize the locals. One day a brave man struck it a blow on the head with his sword; the scar is still visible on the lantern's top today.

Taiyūin-byō

This is the temple built for the builder of the Tōshō-gū, Tokugawa Iemitsu, grandson and spiritual heir of Ieyasu. He died in 1653 and the shrine was finished two years later. It's quieter—in every sense—than the older temple. Decorative and structural refinement balance out the blind pursuit of gorgeousness, and the shrine is small enough to absorb the atmosphere of the great forest around it. But it also gives an impression of half-heartedness. Japan in the mid-17th century was a different country from the one which fostered the great buildings of the Momoyama period. The construction of Tōshō-gū had trained and supported a generation of artist-craftsmen; but Taiyūin-byō had no equivalent of Hidari Jingorō. The woodwork of the two buildings shows the difference between the sculptures of an artist and the carvings of an artisan.

The individual structures and layout of Taiyūin-byō correspond closely to those of the grand-daddy temple. There is a **Ni-ō-mon** gate, and just beyond it on the left a **treasure house** with a painting of a dragon on the ceiling, by the 18th-century painter Kanō Yasunobu. The second gate is the more interesting: on its outside are Idaten and Bishamonten, two of the Guardian Kings; inside are Raijin and Fūjin, gods of (respectively) thunder (see the thunderbolt and ring of drums) and storm (the squeezed sack of wind).

The **Yasha-mon** (Demon Gate), beyond the small **drum** and **bell towers**, corresponds to the Yōmei-mon of Tōshō-gū, but with less encrustation and more breathing space for the demons which guard its corners. Beyond the final **Kara-mon** (Chinese Gate) are the joined **Haiden** (Oratory) and **Honden** (Main Hall). The inside is lovely—muted greys, greens and blues on big plain panels of gold leaf. Much of the outer surface is coated in black lacquer, which imparts an appropriately forbidding, authoritarian feel. Nonetheless, the gleaming gilt and candy colours manage, even more so than the bigger shrine, to make it look like a house of sweets.

Tōshō-gū Hōmotsu-kan (Toshogu Treasure Hall)

Open 8.30–5 (4pm off season); adm ¥500.

The **Treasure Hall** (a modern building situated in woods, on the road leading south of Taiyū-in and Futara-san Jinja) contains a small collection of objects associated with the Tokugawas, including armour worn by Ieyasu at the Battle of Sekigahara, musical instruments, and a fascinating arrangement of concentric, free-moving bronze bands representing the orbits of the planets, presented by a vassal in 1669. There's also an excellent 1:20 scale model of the Tōshō-gū which enables one to appreciate the structural beauty of the complex without the distractions of its outrageous detailing.

Chūzenji-ko (Lake Chūzenji)

West of Nikkō, the hairpin main road leads to this 11.5sq km lake, dramatically situated at the foot of Mt Nantai, and created centuries ago when the valley was blocked by lava flow from the volcano. The small hot spring town has all the usual features of Japanese lake resorts—boats, souvenir shops and tourist restaurants—but it's worth the trip to see the **Kegon Falls**, a 100m cascade formed by the outflow of the Daiya River from the lake. A lift, descending to a glass-windowed observation room, has been ingeniously plumbed into the cliff behind. **Chūzen-ji** temple, on the east shore of the lake, contains a strange 5.5m image, said to have been carved from a living tree trunk by the pioneer of the Nikkō area, Saint Shōdo. On the northern strand is **Futara Jinja** (sometimes called **Chūgushi Jinja**) where the pilgrims begin their torch-lit summer climb to the top of Nantai-san.

Hiking and Hot Springs

Walks of all levels begin and end in the Nikkō area. In theory, it would be possible to climb from Nantai-san (2484m) to Nyoho-san (2464m) to Akanagi-san (2010m), ascending each of the summits in turn on trails which link Chūzenji Onsen and Kirifuri Kōgen plateau (north of Nikkō town; accessible from there by bus). To attempt this you'd need mountaineering experience, the proper equipment and maps, and advance consultation with the Nikkō National Park Office regarding trail safety and weather conditions.

Less strenuous **walks from Nikkō** include a circular ascent of Nakimushi-yama (1104m) beginning near the Nikkō tourist information centre and descending to the road near the Tōshō-gū Shrine. Buses and hiking trails link Nikkō, the Kirifuri no Taki (Mist Falling Waterfalls) and the Kirifuri Kōgen (Plateau); by switching from one to the other, you can walk for as long or as little as you want.

From **Chūzenji-ko** the choice is even wider: try to get hold of a pamphlet called *Nikkō Yumoto-Chūzenji Area Hiking Guide* published by the Nikkō National Park. Trails go all the way around the lake (circumference 21km), and there are gentle walks to a small lake called Sainoko (to the west), and a hill called Hangetsu-san (to the south) which offers a spectacular view of the lake and mountains above.

North of Chūzenji is Yumoto Onsen, another hot spring resort on a smaller lake. It is 25min by bus, and the walk between the two lakes takes about 3hrs over the Senjogahara plateau, once a lake, now a marsh which is drying imperceptibly into a forest. In June, July and August it's especially striking, illuminated with summer flowers.

Oku Nikkō (Deep Nikkō)

Beyond Yumoto are even remoter *onsen*, few of them possessing more than a single inn. **Marunuma** is 40mins by bus from Yumoto. If you carry on to Kamata, you can change to another bus for **Oze-numa**, a highland lake famous for its summer Alpine flowers. The truly intrepid hot water enthusiast could hike from Marunuma to the *onsen* of the **Oku-kinu** area, which really is the back of beyond. To **Kaniyu** takes about 4hrs; more walking (no buses, or even roads, in these parts) will connect you with **Hatchōnoyu** and **Meotobuchi** from where a few buses a day can whisk you back to civilization.

(☎ 0288–) **Where to Stay**

Lodgings in Nikkō sometimes hike up their prices in the peak season (spring, autumn, summer weekends and national holidays). To book accommodation in the remote *onsens* of Oku Nikkō and Oku-kinu, consult the tourist information centre in Nikkō or Tokyo.

moderate

Nikkō Kanaya Hotel, ☎ 54 0001, is the best Western-style hotel in Nikkō. It is 120 years old, and very reasonably priced (although high season rates apply).

Nikkō Prince Hotel, ☎ 55 0661, is a luxurious Western-style chain hotel on the northeast shore of Lake Chūzenji. No single rooms are available; twin rooms begin at ¥22,000.

Chūzenji Hotel, ☎ 55 0333, is a big tourist *ryokan* overlooking Lake Chūzenji.

Namma Hotel, ☎ 62 2111, is in Yumoto, the secluded *onsen* to the north of Lake Chūzenji.

inexpensive

Tātoru In, ☎ 53 3168, is a friendly wooden inn with plenty of information on the surrounding area; the proprietor will usually pick you up if you ring from Nikkō station. The cheapest single rooms without a bath begin at ¥4000; breakfast and dinner are served.

Rojingu Hausu Sanbo, ☎ 53 0082, is a little pension built in the style of a mountain chalet, with Western-style and Japanese rooms. Ring to be picked up from the station.

cheap

Nikkō Daiyagawa Youth Hostel, ☎ 54 1974, or alternatively the plain **Nikkō Youth Hostel**, ☎ 54 1013.

Eating Out

There are plenty of restaurants, but not much choice. Most people make do with one of the many noodle or rice places on the road from the station, and by the souvenir shops around the shrine. These are adequate but nothing special: for something a bit more interesting, try the restaurant of the **Kanaya Hotel** (Japanese and Western dishes, *moderate to expensive*), on the station side of Shinkyō bridge.

We dyned this day at a towne called Camacra, which in tymes past (500 years since) was the greatest cittie of Japon...divers pagodas very sumptuose...I never did see such pleasant walkes amongst pyne and spruce trees as are about these pagodas, espetially 5 of them more renowned than the rest.

The Diary of Richard Cocks, 1616

Kamakura, for over a century the official capital of Japan, has been completely by-passed by the last 600 years of history, greatly to its advantage. Since the advent of the railways, it has been rediscovered by Tokyoites as a swimming and surfing resort (although the beaches are nothing special) and it can become irritatingly crowded. But, with 65 temples and 19 shrines, it's a worthy second best for culture seekers who can't make it down to Kyoto—and cheaper too, with average temple admission around ¥250, compared to Kyoto's ¥500.

History

For a city which lends its name to a historical epoch (1192–1333), Kamakura is today a very modest, parochial little town. History picked it up, dropped it, and quickly forgot all about it. Compared to Kyoto and Nara, former capitals in the heartland of the Japanese state, Kamakura's period of glory looks, in retrospect, like a bit of a fluke.

The town became great in the 12th century, as a consequence of the civil wars between the Taira and Minamoto families. In 1063, a Minamoto general had established at Kamakura a shrine to Hachiman, god of war. The town was sheltered by mountains on three sides and, on the fourth, by the sea—when the legendary Minamoto Yoritomo embarked on his campaign against the Taira in 1180, it was a natural headquarters. He set up a *bakufu*, or camp office, the name that came to be applied to the military administra-tions which ruled Japan right up until 1868.

After defeating the Taira at the Battle of Dan no Ura in 1185, Yoritomo quit the heady, intrigue-laden atmosphere of the Kyoto court for the bracing sea air and martial discipline of Kamakura. In 1192 he was declared shogun, and set about constructing a city suitable for the effective ruler of Japan. Not that Kamakura lacked intrigues of its own; the decades after Dan no Ura were rife with plots and betrayals which were to snuff out the Minamoto line within a generation of Yoritomo's death. Chief among these was the pursuit and persecution of the shogun's doomed younger brother, Yoshitsune.

Yoshitsune is an archetypal figure in Japanese history, a cross between Robin Hood and King Arthur, and the inspiration for countless legends, plays and poems. A brilliant and charismatic general, Yoshitsune had been instrumental in the defeat of the Taira, but his popularity made his brother jealous. The conflict came to a head in 1185, when Yoritomo, convinced that Yoshitsune was plotting against him, refused to let him enter Kamakura. Shortly after, he condemned him to death. There began the famous saga of pursuit and betrayal, the innocent Yoshitsune and his faithful sidekick Benkei fleeing further and

Kita-Kamakura Station

Engaku-ji

Meigetsu-in

Jōchi-ji

Yokosuka Line

Ten'en Hiking Trail

Hyakuhachi Yagura (Cave)

Kakuon-ji

Kenchō-ji

Ennō-ji

Tsurugaoka Hachiman Shrine

Zuisen-ji

Kamakura Shrine

Zeniarai Benten Shrine

Genpei-ike Pond

Steps

Kokuhōkan

Jufuku-ji

Sugimoto-dera

City Hall

Kamakura Tourist Information Centre

Kamakura Station

Myōhon-ji

Kamakura Daibutsu

Hase-dera

Enoden Line

Myōhō-ji

Hase

N

500 metres
500 yards

further into the northern wilderness, with the evil henchmen of Yoritomo on their trail. In 1189, they finally cornered him in a fortress in northeast Tōhoku. Yoshitsune committed suicide with his entire entourage, including his wife and children. According to some accounts, however, he escaped to Hokkaidō where, until the 19th century, he was worshipped as a god by the Ainu people. Another legend has him sailing to China where he took on a new identity: Genghis Khan.

The bloodshed was by no means over. The evil Yoritomo died after a riding accident in 1199, and the reins of power were taken over by his formidable wife, Masako, the Ama (Nun) Shogun. Under Masako, real power in the *bakufu* passed to her powerful family, the Hōjō, who ruled as regents (*shikken*) under the nominal authority of a puppet shogun. During the course of the power struggle, all Yoritomo's heirs died, including one son murdered on the orders of his own grandfather.

But Kamakura flourished under the Hōjō, largely as a result of the able newcomers who were drawn to the new centre of government. From Kyoto came scholars and administrators, disillusioned with the stagnant atmosphere of the court; and bonzes, returning from study in China, who brought back with them new approaches to Buddhist philosophy and worship. It was an age of great vigour and innovation in Buddhist thought, and of boisterous conflict. The Jōdō, Shinshū, Nichiren and Zen sects all took root in Japan during the Kamakura period. The austere disciplines of the latter found especial favour among the samurai warriors who began to coalesce as a distinct class with its own culture and code of ethics. It also found patrons among the Hōjō regents, men such as Tokiyori and Tokimune, the fifth and sixth of their line respectively, who endowed temples like Kenchō-ji and Engaku-ji, and appointed Chinese monks as their abbots. Kamakura period sculpture— vigorous, realistic, often comically grotesque—flourished in this refined but martial atmosphere and represents, along with the surviving temples (Zen, as well as those of the Nichiren sect in the east), the principal attraction of Kamakura to the modern visitor.

A century after Yoritomo, the population of Kamakura exceeded one million. Apart from Zen, Kamakura is dominated, in the east at least, by the temples of the Nichiren sect, founded by a 13th-century priest of the same name, who earned lengthy periods in exile (and, on one occasion, near execution) for his outspoken attacks on other sects and the rulers who tolerated them. Nichiren's greatest coup was to predict accurately the attempted invasion of Japan by the Mongol armies of Kubla Khan in 1274 and 1281. The only thing he got wrong was the prediction that the Mongols would be victorious if Japan didn't convert *en masse* to Nichiren's personal sect—they were repelled on both occasions by typhoons (the original *kamikaze*, or divine wind). But the effort of defence left the Hōjō family exhausted, and indebted to its samurai. In 1333, the ambitious Emperor Go-Daigo took advantage of the Hōjō Regent's unpopularity to rebel against him. The generals dispatched against him switched sides; Kamakura burned, and the Hōjō family was toppled in a tumultuous siege. The last Regent and his retainers took their own lives in a mountain cave. After 148 years, Kamakura's period of pre-eminence was at an end; the new Ashikaga shoguns established their dynasty in Kyoto.

Kamakura was rebuilt, and rebuilt again after sieges and fires in 1455 and 1526, but it never regained its former strategic or dynastic importance. By the 16th century, it was eclipsed by Odawara as the foremost town of the eastern provinces, and in the 17th century by Edo, later Tokyo. The Tōkaidō, the great arterial highway between Edo and Kyoto, bypassed Kamakura, marginalizing it still further. It wasn't until the opening of the Yokosuka railway line in 1889 that it regained a modest prosperity as a commuter town and holiday resort for booming Tokyo.

Getting There

The JR Yokosuka line is the quickest and cheapest way to Kamakura from Tokyo. **Trains** take just under an hour and cost ¥930 from platforms 1, 2 or 3 of Tokyo station (also stopping at Shinbashi, Shinagawa and Yokohama).

The **Kamakura Enoshima Furii Kippu** (free pass) lasts two days and allows unlimited free travel on JR lines to and from Kamakura and on the Enoden lines down to Enoshima island. It costs ¥1890, so it's only a saving if you do more than the straightforward return journey.

Getting Around

Walking is a pleasant way to see Kamakura, but the sights are scattered. There are a couple of **bicycle hire** shops near the station.

Buses go from the east exit of Kamakura station.

Orientation

Kita (North) Kamakura, site of several peaceful temples, is one stop before the main.Kamakura station as you arrive from Tokyo. From the latter, **Hachiman-gū** shrine is an easy walk along the broad north–south **Wakamiya-ōji** avenue which bisects the town. **West Kamakura** contains the famous **Daibutsu** (Great Buddha); to the **east** are smaller rustic temples and shrines. **Enoshima** is a resort island to the southwest, reached by bus or railway.

Tourist Information

There's a **tourist information bureau** by the station. Get the English-language picture map called simply *Kamakura*. On Wakamiya-ōji, opposite the station, is a large book shop with an English-language section selling guides and tour magazines, including *Exploring Kamakura* by Michael Cooper, a comprehensive and sympathetic guide by a long-term foreign resident.

Festivals

August

7–9   **Lantern festival** at Hachiman-gū shrine.

September

14–16   **Tsurugaoka Hachiman-gū Matsuri**. Costume parades, dancing and merrymaking. Arrive early on the 16th to get a good seat for the spectacular **yabusame** (mounted archery) competition.

18   **Mekake Gyōretsu**. At the small Gongorō Shrine, a procession of masked characters is led by an old man dressed up as a pregnant woman. His presence is supposed to ensure fertility and easy childbirth.

21–22   **Takigi Nō**. Old *nō* plays are performed by torchlight at the Kamakura-gū shrine.

West Kamakura

Hase-dera (Hase Temple)

Hase station on the Enoden line from Kamakura station; or take bus 2 from the station to the stop called Hase Kannon. Open 7–5.40; adm ¥200; Treasure House closes at 4.30; adm ¥100.

Hase-dera's gold and vermilion halls look rather fine from a distance, but close up they are disappointingly modern. Only the temple bell, cast in 1264, is of any great age, and even that post-dates the original temple by more than half a millennium. Pilgrims come from all over Japan to pray to the large and legendary statue of Kannon Bosatsu, but the best reason to climb the steps of Hase-dera, especially on a clear evening, is to enjoy the view from the observation platform of the town below, and the Pacific Ocean beyond.

History

The temple, and the neighbourhood which has grown up at its feet, is named after a remote mountain village in the Nara area. In 721, a monk called Tokudō discovered a massive camphor tree there, and from it commissioned two huge statues of Kannon, the popular Buddhist deity of mercy. The image carved from the lower trunk was installed in a local temple, the original Hase-dera, where it can be seen today. The larger statue, hewn from the upper half of the tree, was carried to the sea and set afloat, to drift at the whim of the gods. On 18 June 736 it was washed ashore on the Miura Peninsula. Despite 15 years bobbing in the Pacific, the light that shone from it was said to be as bright as the sun. The priests and officers who had sculpted it were summoned from Nara and it was enshrined in its present spot, for many years called the Shin (New) Hase temple.

The Temple Grounds

The little hall on the left, just inside the front gate, is dedicated to Daikoku, the round-bellied folk god of riches. Half-way up the hill is the **Jizō-dō**, containing thousands of windmills, tiny **Jizō bosatsu** in pink bibs, and toy images of Godzilla and Mickey Mouse. Mizuko (Water Child) Jizō, the protector of the unbaptized in the Buddhist Limbo, is worshipped here; the gifts have been left by the mothers of miscarried or aborted babies.

The biggest of the buildings at the top of the stairs is the **Kannon-dō**, where the miraculous floating Kannon is displayed. In comparison with the flickering candlelight of most old temples, the modern hall is rather antiseptic, more like an art gallery than a place of worship, but the statue can at least be examined in detail. At 9.18m it is said to be the largest wooden sculpture in Japan. With broad shoulders, short legs, long arms and ten supernumerary faces attached to its head (thus the name *jūichimen*—eleven-headed—Kannon), the statue has a solid, cool, muscular mien with little sign of the infinite mercy and tenderness which it was intended to express.

To the left of the hall is a **Hōmotsu-kan** (Treasure House, *adm ¥100*), containing scrolls telling the story of the temple's foundation, plus seals, coins and paintings, and the Hase-dera bell, cast in 1264. To the right is the **Amida-dō** containing a seated 13th-century statue of Amida Nyorai. It was donated by Minamoto Yoritomo himself as the superstitious antidote to a mid-life crisis. A man's 42nd year was considered unlucky; endowing the *yakuyoke* (good luck) Amida was an attempt to win over the favour of the deity to neutralize the perils of this dangerous time. The walls are stacked with Mizuko Jizō and other Buddhist statuary; admire in particular the black **Emma-ō**, King of Hell, on the left, with his gleaming white teeth.

At the far end of the temple's lower precincts (turn right as you come in by the main gate) is the **Benten Kutsu**, a claustrophobic catacomb carved with gold-leaf images of Benten, Indian goddess of eloquence, music, health and learning.

Kōtoku-in Daibutsu (The Great Buddha of Kotoku Temple)

Take bus number 2 to Daibutsu-mae stop, about 1km north of Hase Kannon. Open 7–5; adm ¥150 (¥20 extra to enter the statue).

> *But that which I did more admire than all the rest was a mighty idoll of bras, called by them Dibotes, and standeth in a vallie betwixt 2 mountaynes, the howse being quite rotten away, it being set up 480 years past. The idoll is made siting cros legged and yet in my opinion it is above 20 yardes hie and above 12 yardes from knee to knee...I doe esteem it to be bigger then that at Roads, which was taken for 1 of the 7 wonders of the world...In fine, it is a wonderfull thinge.*
>
> *The Diary of Richard Cocks, 1616*

If Captain Cocks returned to Kamakura today, there is not much that would be familiar to him. But the 'Dibotes' (Cocks' attempt at *Daibutsu*, Great Buddha) is barely changed, still sitting in its valley with the hills behind, still exposed to the elements (*roza*, the term used in Japanese, means 'seated in the dew'), still one of the wonders of Japan. Cocks' dates and statistics are as ropy as his spelling, but his excitement is easy to understand.

The origins of the colossus are rather obscure. It was created in the mid-13th century through the efforts of Inada no Tsubone, a courtier of the late Shogun Yoritomo, who toured the country raising funds with the help of a priest named Jōkō. Beginning in 1238, a large wooden statue was carved and a special hall raised around it in the grounds of Kōtoku-in, an important regional temple since the 8th century. The project took five years to complete, but after another five years a terrific storm tore down both Daibutsu and temple, and in 1248 fundraising had to begin all over again.

This time the sculptor worked in bronze. His name was Ono Gorōemon, but nothing more is known of him. Understandably, given the scale of the project, there were several false starts, but the bronze Daibutsu, the very same image which we see today, was finally inaugurated on 17 August 1252.

The Daibutsu's 'howse' was again destroyed by storms in 1335 and 1368; on both occasions it was rebuilt around the intact statue. Then, in 1495, a tidal wave inundated the valley and smashed the temple. Intermittent attempts to rehouse the Daibutsu came to nothing, and for 500 years it has been in the open air. In 1923, the Great Kantō Earthquake made it wobble alarmingly; its foundation has since been reconstructed to allow it to swivel freely on its base. Paradoxically, the lack of a wooden shelter may be the secret of the statue's survival: although lashed by sea and storms, the Daibutsu has never been harmed by fire, the only element capable of seriously damaging its metal bulk.

The Statue

The Great Buddha has become a tourist brochure cliché, but most photographs succeed in making it look rather weathered and gormless without capturing any of its size and majesty. The deity represented is Amida, Buddha of the Western Paradise, whose worship was popularized during the early Kamakura period by the Jōdo and Shin sects. Cocks in his eagerness exaggerates its size: excluding the base, Amida is actually 11.31m high, and 9m from knee to knee, making it smaller than the Daibutsu of Nara's Tōdai-ji. Being out in the open, it is sometimes hard to get a sense of scale: depending on where you are standing, it can appear looming, but it is essentially an intimate and personal figure, best appreciated from close up. Its beauty lies in its proportions. The danger of such a tall statue is that, like Tōdai-ji's, it will appear distant and indifferent (one of Amida's characteristics is his personal mercy and accessibility to all men, even the lowliest). The Kamakura sculptor compensates for this by making the head and shoulders massive compared to the lower body. From a distance it can look hunched and top heavy but, to the worshipper kneeling just in front, the statue's height cancels out its mass, and the limbs slip into proportion.

Historically, the statue is said to show a Greek influence transmitted, at many removes, along the Silk Road which linked East Asia with the Mediterranean. The long earlobes (hanging 'like dried fruit on a tropical tree' in Mishima's phrase), curly moustache, and snail-like curls of hair (there are 656 of them) are conventional; but the statue's nose is unusually full and curved, and the eyebrows and lids are sharply-defined and symmetrical, as are the draped robes. The whole figure has a neat, calm and disciplined air.

For ¥20 you can descend into the hollow interior where the construction technique can be examined. The bronze was cast vertically in separate layers—the joins between each one are visible even from the outside—and then filed smooth after it had cooled. The scars and cracks accumulated through its 750-year history can be clearly seen inside, especially round the head. In 1960, it was strengthened for the first time with plastic.

Zeniarai Benten (Money-Washing Benten)

5 minutes by taxi or a 25-minute walk (intermittently signposted) from the west side of Kamakura station.

Tucked away in a cramped gulley, enclosed on all sides by cliffs and trees, this is one of the liveliest and most entertaining folk shrines in Japan. It was founded, so the story goes, by Minamoto Yoritomo who, in 1185, had a premonitory dream that his dynasty would prosper if he built a shrine by a certain mountain spring. 1185 was the Year of the Snake, one of the twelve animals of the Oriental zodiac. Moreover, the dream occurred at the hour of the Snake, on the day of the Snake, in the Snake's month—so it was obvious to all that it had been inspired by the folk goddess Benten whose messenger is a white serpent.

At the entrance, a path leads through a narrow tunnel in the cliff, then another tunnel formed by close-set red *torii* gates. Inside is a jumble of higgledy-piggledy buildings in wood and corrugated iron with trees growing through their roofs, more *torii*, and dozens of stalls selling food, charms and fortunes. Jammed between are sanctuaries, altars and a number of grottoes where the natural spring bubbles up.

The spring has a remarkable property which adds a whole new dimension to the expression 'money laundering': believe it or not, any coins washed in its waters will double in value. Quite how this works in practice is not explained. The money, you gather, mustn't be hoarded, but spent normally; somehow twice its value will return to the owner. To take advantage of this unique service, push through the crowds to the main grotto which is hung with garlands of folded paper cranes. The efficacious water flows along a runnel, and wicker baskets are provided in which to rinse your lucre without the risk of it being swept away. Ardent money worshippers can even be seen washing bank notes and drying them on the incense burners outside. The magic is most effective, apparently, on *Mi no Hi*, the zodiacal days of the Snake; at these times the shrine grounds are crammed. Look out for offerings of eggs—these are the favourite food of Benten's snakes, just as fried *tōfu* is that of Inari-sama's foxes.

Central Kamakura

Tsurugaoka Hachiman-gū (Tsurugaoka Hachiman Shrine)

A 10-minute walk from Kamakura station.

Hachiman-gū isn't the oldest or most magnificent shrine in Japan, but few others are so central to the town in which they stand, or so saturated in its history and myths, many of them dramatic or bloody. With its legendary trees and heroic boulders, walking round Hachiman-gū is like strolling through a stage set—more than one *nō* or *kabuki* play, and regular TV samurai dramas, feature scenes set in its precincts.

History

The first Hachiman-gū was founded in 1063 by Yoritomo's great-great-great-grandfather, Minamoto Yoriyoshi, at a spot near the beach. The enshrined deity, Hachiman, is worshipped as the god of war, but the Kamakura shrine became important as the private chapel of the Minamoto family. When Yoritomo established his headquarters here in 1180, one of his first acts was to move it from the shore to its present elevated location on Crane Hill (Tsurugaoka).

A year later Yoritomo's wife, the redoubtable Masako, became pregnant, and a long avenue was constructed from the sea to the shrine, an offering for the safe delivery of the heir, Yoriie. The road, **Wakamiya-ōji** (Avenue of the Young Prince), is still Kamakura's main street; at its north end, in front of the shrine, is **Danzakura**, a central belt of cherry blossom trees, clogged with blossom watchers during the spring season.

The shrine grounds themselves begin on the far side of a semi-circular arched bridge (usually closed—you have to walk to the side of it) which was built in 1182, after rice fields which originally occupied this area were converted at Yoritomo's order into a pair of ponds linked by a narrow channel. The ponds embody a complicated numerological pun, designed as a kind of curse on the Minamoto family's great enemies, the Taira clan. In the right-hand pond there are three islands, and in the left pond four. But the words for three and four, *san* and *shi*, can also be written with different characters meaning, respectively, *prosperity* (that of the Minamoto, also called Genji) and *death* (willed upon the Taira, or Heike). By combining the abbreviated forms of these names, the pond takes its name: **Genpei Ike**. Lotuses cluster thickly on the water, and on one of the right-hand islands is a small shrine to Benten, goddess of beauty.

Beyond the bridge, the avenue opens out into a broad gravel yard with administrative buildings, paths heading in several directions and a broad flight of stone steps at the far end, leading up to the main halls. At the left-hand side stand stacked barrels of *sake* and soy sauce, offered by brewers; there are even cases of beer, for deities with more modern tastes. In the centre of the gravel expanse is a **Dancing Platform**, scene of a famous incident in medieval history, commemorated every year in the spring festival. During his campaign of persecution against his half-brother, Yoshitsune, Minamoto Yoritomo arrested the man's mistress, a famous Kyoto dancer called Shizuka Gozen, who had already saved her lover from one attempt to kill him. After repeated refusals, Shizuka was finally forced by Yoritomo to perform for him on this stage. Instead of a demure classical dance, she improvised a defiant protest song of love for Yoshitsune in full view of the shogun and his court. Yoritomo was furious; the woman's life was spared through the intervention of his wife, Masako, but when Shizuka later gave birth to Yoshitsune's baby son, the child was immediately taken down to the seashore and put to death.

At the bottom right of the steps is the **Wakamiya** (Junior Shrine), dedicated to Emperor Nintoku, son of the god Hachiman. The path to the right leads to an area of the precincts quiet even on busy days: the **Shirahata**, which means 'White Flag', but it is actually matt black, strikingly detailed in gold, white and pink. Within are enshrined Yoritomo and his second son Sanetomo, the third Minamoto shogun whose demise is described below. On the path leading up here, you will see on your right two hefty boulders known as **Benkei's Balls**. Benkei, the Friar Tuck to Yoshitsune's Robin Hood (*see* p.343), was famed for his amazing strength. In between adventures, he loved to play with these mighty rocks, tossing them around as if they were a child's balloons.

Back in the main plaza, to the left of the ascending stairs, is a huge gingko tree, 30m tall, 6.8m in circumference, draped in sacred *shimenawa* ropes and *gohei* paper ribbons. This tree is claimed (there is some doubt) to be over a thousand years old, and to be the place where Minamoto Sanetomo died in 1219. The younger of Yoritomo's surviving sons, Sanetomo had become the third shogun after the assassination of his elder brother, Yoriie, in 1204. In 1219 he was descending the steps after a ceremony of thanksgiving at the shrine when a man leapt out and mortally wounded him with a dagger. The assassin, quickly caught and executed, was the young Kugyō, only son of Yoriie, who had been living in the shrine as a priest, biding his time to avenge his father's murder.

The **Hongū** (Main Hall) was rebuilt in 1828 in the style known as Hachiman—two halls, one at the front and one behind, are built separately, but so close together that their roofs touch leaving no gap in between. If you pay ¥200 you can enter the little **Hōmotsu-den** (Treasure House, *open 9–4*) which contains portable shrines, a few maps and statues and some feudal armour. It's nothing special but does enable you to get a better look at the hall's architecture. Offertory dances are often performed in the **Haiden** (Oratory); hang around long enough, particularly at weekends, and there's a good chance you'll see one.

Kokuhōkan (National Treasure Hall)

Open 9–4; adm ¥150.

This concrete museum (on the east side of the shrine grounds, between the Genpei pond and the Shirahata) was built after the Great Kantō Earthquake to preserve the most valuable temple treasures in one disaster-proof building. As a result, it contains one of the best small collections of Kamakura art, especially sculpture. The exhibits are rotated every few weeks, but you're bound to see at least some of the Gods of Hell from Ennō-ji temple—the moral accountants, who keep track of a mortal's every action and report it to the King of Hell. There's the bestial Kisotsu, a club-wielding, loin-cloth-wearing demon of low IQ, but high savagery, who acts as jailer to the damned; and Shokō-ō, a lesser King of Hell. All are carved with relish in the realistic but humorous style characteristic of this kind of Kamakura sculpture: knotted brows and taut muscles, dramatic gesticulations of hand and arms, beady lumps of marble inserted disconcertingly into the eye sockets. One or two of the statues date from the earlier Heian period and the contrast is clear—they are stiffer, more formal and archaic-looking. There are also some fine portraits of regents and priests (including Eisai, the founder of Zen, with his extraordinary flat-topped head) in billowing, balloon-like robes; and a famous nude statue of a creamy-skinned Benten strumming on a (now missing) *shamisen*, coyly wrapped up in a dull robe. The Taima Mandala (not often displayed) is the best of the museum's painting collection, which also contains assorted scrolls, ceramics and some excellent examples of Kamakura-bori (woodwork), from the days before it became a tourist gimmick.

Kamakura-gū (Kamakura Shrine)

Bus 4 to Daitonomiya stop. Treasure House open 9–4.30; adm ¥300.

This modern shrine, founded and built in 1869 on the orders of the Emperor Meiji, is of no great intrinsic interest, but the story behind it is illuminating, both of medieval politics and those of the modern age. It is dedicated to Prince Morinaga, a son of Go-Daigo, the emperor whose stubborn resistance brought an end to the rule of the Hōjō regents. Denied the throne by Hōjō Takatoki, the prince became a monk on the mountain temple of Hiei-zan, near Kyoto. When Takatoki took up arms against his father a few years later, Morinaga organized the bonzes into an army, and was rewarded after Go-Daigo's victory with the title of shogun. This aroused the jealousy of the Ashikaga family, who slandered Morinaga and turned his father against him. He was imprisoned in a cave which can still be seen at the back of Kamakura-gū (the site was then occupied by a temple). In 1335, at the age of 27, he was executed, and buried on Richikō-zan, a nearby hill. During the early Meiji period, when loyalty to emperors was being vigorously promoted by the new government, the unlucky Morinaga was rediscovered. In 1873, Emperor Meiji paid a visit to the shrine of his tragic forebear. Relics of his trip constitute the main exhibits in the small and uninteresting museum.

Kakuon-ji

Tours at 9, 10, 11, 1 and 3; closed in August and 20 Dec–7 Jan; adm ¥300.

On the west side of Kamakura-gū, a slow, sleepy lane runs up to this temple at the head of the valley. The gates and yard have recently been refurbished, but a remote, unworldly atmosphere still prevails. There are strict rules for those who join the five daily tours (numbers limited; arrive early to avoid disappointment): no photos, no video cameras. This is a religious institution, first and last. Visitors, it is being made clear, are admitted only as a favour.

The monk guide's commentary is in Japanese only and the tour is brief. The **Yakushi-dō** contains statues of Yakushi Nyorai, Buddha of Healing, his two supporters and the Twelve Generals. In the **Jizō-dō** is a mysterious carving of Jizō Bosatsu, which always turns black no matter how many times it is painted. It is said to have been scorched irrevocably when it entered the flames of hell to save sinners; appropriately, the image has become venerated by local firemen who flock to see it at the annual festival on 10 August.

East Kamakura

Zuisen-ji (Temple of the Abundant Spring)

Open 9–5; adm ¥100.

Another remote rural temple at the end of a long lane, Zuisen-ji was founded in 1327 by Musō Kokushi, the priest and poet who invented the meditation garden and created such masterpieces as the Saihō-ji moss garden in Kyoto. The one he built here, consisting of a heart-shaped pond and austere expanse of sand in front of a cliff, was considered one of the finest of its type. But today it is in a sorry state: the water stagnant, the gravel overgrown with nettles. Musō focused the garden around a dramatic cave in the cliff where he would meditate, looking out onto his creation through a specially hewn window. Despite its disrepair, the grounds of the temple are wide and thickly forested, with the Buddha Halls, mostly of recent construction, nestling among the trees.

Sugimoto-dera (Temple under the Cryptomeria)

Bus 3 to Sugimoto Kannon stop. Open 8.30–4.30; adm ¥100.

This is a charming temple, probably the oldest foundation in Kamakura, with the atmosphere of a little country chapel. It was founded in 734 by Empress Kōmyō, wife of Shōmu, the emperor who built Nara's Tōdai-ji, and it has long been visited by worshippers of Kannon, goddess of mercy. Steep ancient-looking steps climb high above the road through the trees; the top flight is so troughed and mossy that it has had to be placed off-limits, and a new set built off and around to the left. The pilgrims have left their mark in other ways. The rafters of the thatched hall are blackened with incense smoke, pasted with decades of pilgrims' name stickers, and garlanded with origami cranes and *ema*, votive pictures left as offerings. Graves outside, and memorial tablets ranked like chessmen inside the hall, commemorate the fallen of the 12th-century Minamoto-Taira war.

The three images worshipped are statues of Jūichimen (Eleven-faced) Kannon: the first carved by Gyōki, the founding priest, the second and third by the priests Ennin and Genshin, in the 9th and 10th centuries respectively. On 23 November 1189 a fire destroyed the hall, but the three famous images survived after cleverly sheltering themselves beneath a huge cryptomeria tree, hence the temple's name: Sugimoto, 'beneath the cryptomeria'. The oldest Kannon is also known as **Geba (Get-Off-Your-Horse) Kannon** on account of its power to throw riders who had the temerity to enter the temple grounds without dismounting first.

North Kamakura

After the Daibutsu and Hachiman-gū areas, North (Kita) Kamakura is recommended as the most accessible and interesting quarter of the town. Kita Kamakura station, one stop from the main terminus on the JR Yokosuka line, still has the sleepy, rural atmosphere of the temples, principally of the Zen sect, which cluster around it.

Engaku-ji (Temple of Perfect Enlightenment)

Next door to Kita Kamakura station. Open 8–4.30; adm ¥200.

Engaku-ji was built in 1282 by the 6th Regent, Hōjō Tokimune, as a place of prayer and consolation for the souls of those who had died in the unsuccessful Mongol invasion the year before. Its first abbot was a Chinese priest called Sogen Mugaku (posthumously canonized as Bukkō Kokushi) who settled in Japan after Kubla Khan's forces had pillaged his own country. The story goes that the Mongols stormed Sogen's monastery, massacring all who stood in their way. At the heart of the temple they found the priest himself, in deep meditation, indifferent to the prospect of death and the carnage all around. Strangely impressed, they let him alone, and Sogen was able to escape to Kamakura.

A flock of white birds led Sogen to the site of the temple (a lake to the south, amputated from the main precincts by the railway line, still bears the name White Heron Pond). Engaku-ji conforms nominally to the canons of Chinese Zen architecture (a prescribed sequence of buildings on a south–north axis), but its position, in a narrow climbing valley, actually throws them attractively askew—the true orientation is more like southwest–northeast, and the paths between the buildings and sub-temples are narrow leafy alleys, rather than the austere formal avenues of the conventional Zen precinct.

Passing through the great **San-mon** (Main Gate), last rebuilt in the 1780s, you'll see on the right a flight of steps leading to a famous antique bell, 2.5m high and cast in 1301 on the orders of the then Regent. Souls who have been reprieved from death by the King of Hell are said to be guided back to the land of the living by the bell's plangent sound. Behind it there's a small shrine with a good view of Kamakura, and especially Tōkei-ji temple, nestling among the trees below.

Back on the valley floor, the path goes by the modern **Butsu-den** (Buddha Hall), rebuilt in 1964 after fires in 1284, 1526 and the Great Earthquake of 1923, to name only the most spectacular disasters. To the left is a rectangular turtle pond sarcastically christened **Myōkō-ike** (Pond of Sacred Fragrance), which began life as a monastic sewage tank.

Several of the sub-temples which lead off the main path after this are closed to casual visitors, but just after the pond a path to the left leads up to a gate which you should make a point of peering through. The building you will see is the **Shari-den**, a reliquary supposed to contain a tooth of the Buddha, and constructed in 1285 in the Chinese Sung style (the Hōjō regents were great admirers of Sung and sent their own architects to study Chinese techniques). It's considered one of the finest structures of its type, identical, on a smaller scale, to the very first hall of Engaku-ji which burned down in 1558.

A bit further up, again on the left, is a small hall situated in a pleasant courtyard where cups of green tea are dispensed (for a fee). This is the **Butsunichi-an**, dedicated to the memory of Hōjō Tokimune who was buried here in 1284; the interior contains statues of the 6th Regent, along with his son, Sadatoki, and grandson, Takatoki, the last of his line. On the other side of the path a cave is set into the rock, behind cedars. During the temple's inauguration in 1282, Priest Sogen was delivering a sermon when a herd of white deer issued mysteriously from this opening and listened to him with rapt attention. Finally, at the far end of the valley, is **Ōbai-in** (Temple of the Yellow Plum Blossom): a small Kannon shrine hard up against the bamboo-curtained walls of the valley.

Tōkei-ji

Open 8.30–5; adm ¥50.

This compact, quiet little temple is famous principally because of its nicknames: Enkiri-dera (Temple of Divorce) and Kakekomi-dera (Temple of Fleeing). It was founded as a nunnery in 1285 by the widow of Hōjō Tokimune, and quickly became famous for the sanctuary it offered to abused and unhappy wives. Fugitives could live in the temple as lay helpers for three years. During that time, no man could claim them back, and at the end of the period (later reduced to two years) they were officially released from vows of marriage (this at a time when divorce was simple for husbands, but very difficult for wives). The custom was respected until the Meiji period but, in the early years of this century, the last abbess died and Tōkei-ji became a monastery.

The huddle of temple buildings is best appreciated from the bell tower of Engaku-ji (*see* above). On the ground they are nothing remarkable, although the modern **Treasure House** (*open 10–5; adm ¥300*), beautifully built of pale unvarnished wood, contains some interesting pieces, including a Portuguese box inlaid with a Latin inscription, a 15th-century incense burner in *maki-e* lacquer, showing a famous scene from the *Tale of Genji*, and some Heian-era sculptures. The paths continue to the extensive cemetery at the back: numerous graves of famous abbots and royalty, set in niches carved in the rock face, and reached by worn stone steps canopied by maples and cryptomerias.

Kenchō-ji

Open 9–4.30; adm ¥200.

Kenchō-ji was founded in 1253 by the 5th Regent, Hōjō Tokiyori. Among the great Zen temples of Kamakura, it was ranked first; it is still one of the most impressive temples in the Kantō region. Where Engaku-ji is irregular, secretive and mysterious, Kenchō-ji (built on largely flat ground) is formal, stately and public. Fires in the 14th and 15th centuries reduced the former complex of 49 sub-temples to its present size. Nonetheless, this a big, grand temple: if it wasn't for the parked cars allowed to clutter the precincts and the usual knot of buses in the car park, it would be magnificent.

It shares with Engaku-ji the standard Zen layout. The first, small gate (**So-mon**) dates from 1783 and was moved to this spot only 50 years ago. The plaque hanging from it, however, is as old as the temple and bears characters painted by Emperor Go-Fukakusa, who reigned during the Kenchō era (1249–56) from which the temple takes its name. The **San-mon** (Main Gate) was rebuilt in 1754 and nicknamed the Tanuki-mon (Racoon Dog Gate) after a *tanuki* who metamorphosed into a man and worked alongside the carpenters. To the right of the gate is the **temple bell** (Bonshō), a National Treasure cast in 1255 and bearing an inscription by the founding abbot, Rankei Dōryū, a Chinese priest who arrived in Japan in 1246 and soon found favour with Tokiyori. The **monastic quarters** beyond the bell tower are out of bounds to the public.

Dōryū is said to have brought with him the seeds which germinated into the great **juniper trees** which stand beyond the San-mon. This would make them nearly 750 years old, not difficult to believe given their epic size. The **Butsu-den** (Buddha Hall), immediately facing the juniper trees, along with the **Kara-mon** (Chinese Gate) further along the path, was built as part of the Zōzō-ji temple complex in southern Tokyo. It was moved here in 1647, thus sparing it the many disasters that struck its mother temple. Instead of the usual *tatami*, the interior is floored in bare stone, giving it a chilly sepulchral feel characteristic of Zen halls. The uneven lay of the flagstones and the worn paint on the elaborate open-work carving add to the dusty, antique atmosphere. Unfortunately, the external proportions of the building are ruined by an ungainly modern shed tacked onto the back.

The central image in the Butsu-den is a hollow Jizō Bosatsu supposed to contain, in its turn, a smaller Jizō statue with which a miraculous tale is associated. A man called Saita was unjustly convicted of a capital crime. Led out to the execution ground, he secreted in his topknot this same tiny statue. When the executioner brought down his sword, for some reason it would not bite into the man's neck. The second time he tried it, the blade was shivered into pieces. The shaken constables let him go and the lucky Mr Saita was a free man.

The **Hattō** (Hall of Law) is an uninteresting building dating from 1814. The **Hōjō** (Abbot's Quarters), also called the Ryūō-den (Hall of the Dragon King), is reached through the old Zōzō-ji Chinese Gate. Around the back is a garden attributed to the great 15th-century Zen master, Musō: rather muddy and dilapidated these days, and marred by telegraph wires which sweep disagreeably low over the trees.

The Ten'en Hiking Course

Traversing the hills to the north of Kamakura, this extensive hiking trail takes from one and a half to two hours to complete in full, or less if you join it half way. It runs from Zuisen-ji in the east to Kenchō-ji in the northwest. The compromise starting point is the path beginning 200m before Kakuon-ji temple; from there proceed east or west. Worth looking out for are the **yagura** or ancient burial caves carved into the cliffs along the way.

The Enoden private railway line runs south and west from Kamakura JR station along a grubby strand of grey sand to **Enoshima**, a small island revered since ancient times as the abode of Shinto gods, especially Benten, a Hindu goddess associated with music, eloquence, islands and the sea. The terrain is steep and wooded, the island itself somewhat commercialized, hellishly crowded on warm weekends and holidays, but with pleasant walks, many small shrines, and views of the sea and—occasionally—Mt Fuji.

At **Inamuragaseki** (Inamura Point) a famous incident occurred which marked the end of the Hōjō family's regency and the eclipse of Kamakura as Japan's first city. The Emperor Go-Daigo, an unusually able and cunning monarch, was plotting against the 9th Regent, Hōjō Takatoki. Armies were dispatched against him, but their generals, Ashikaga Takauji and Nitta Yoshisada, quickly recognized the advantages to be gained from siding with the Emperor and they switched sides. In 1333, Nitta returned to Kamakura with his army, this time with the aim of capturing the city and deposing his erstwhile lord.

But they were halted at the narrow Gokuraku-ji Pass, where inconclusive fighting went on for several days. Finally, Nitta mounted the cliffs at Inamuragaseki and, praying to the gods, hurled his precious golden sword into the sea below. Like the Red Sea withdrawing for the fleeing Israelites, the waters of the Pacific shrank back, allowing the Emperor's troops free access and an easy victory over the doomed Hōjō. Today the peninsula is a park with rambling paths and commanding views of the countryside all around.

Another local incident occurred a bit further down the line at a spot now marked by a temple, **Ryūkō-ji.** It concerns Nichiren, the Martin Luther and Ian Paisley of his age, prophet of the Mongol invasions, who aggravated the Hōjō rulers by his outspoken denunciations of other Buddhist sects. In 1271, after numerous exiles and final warnings, he was sentenced to death. On 12 September he was led to a spot, just to the left of the present temple's front gate, where he offered his final prayers. As the sword descended, a bolt of lightning fell from the sky and shattered it in the executioner's hands. The sentence was commuted to another period of exile, and Nichiren was packed off to Sado Island, the Siberia of medieval Japan, where he spent a further two years.

The temple was built by Nichiren's followers in 1337. It's a pleasant enough place, thick with pigeons and a jumble of buildings in heterogeneous styles, few of them old (the finest is probably the five-storey pagoda at the back, dating from 1910). The liveliest time is the annual festival from 11–13 September.

(✆ 0467–)   **Where to Stay**

Because of its proximity to Tokyo, Kamakura doesn't have a wide range of hotels; many people stay in the capital and treat it as a day trip.

expensive

Kamakura Park Hotel, ✆ 25 5121, near Hase station on the Enoden Line (or 7 minutes by taxi from Kamakura JR station) is probably the best Western-style hotel, but it has been closed for refurbishment so check in advance.

Hotel Tsurugaoka Kaikan, ✆ 24 1111, is a resort *ryokan* conveniently situated on Wakamiya-ōji, close to the station and the central sights.

Kaihin-sō Kamakura, ✆ 22 0960, is a fancy *ryokan* near Yigashima station.

inexpensive

B.B. House Lady's Inn, ✆ 25 5859, as its name suggests, is a women-only establishment, a 2-minute walk from Hase station on the Enoden Line.

cheap

Kamakura Kagetsuen Youth Hostel, ✆ 25 1238, is near Hase station on the Enoden Line. For a slightly higher tariff you can stay in private rooms in an attached *ryokan.*

(✆ *0467–*)   ***Eating Out***

As an ancient monastic capital, Kamakura is one of the best places in Japan to try *shōjin ryōri,* the Buddhist vegetarian cuisine based on delicate combinations of herbs and *tōfū* bean curd. The most authentic (and reasonable) *shōjin ryōri* experience—in a temple refectory—takes a bit of arranging, and advance notice must be given. Ask the tourist information office in Tokyo or Kamakura a week or so in advance, or try calling (in Japanese) **Chōjū-ji,** ✆ 22 2147, a small temple in Kita Kamakura. **Monzen,** ✆ 25 1121, and **Hachinoki,** ✆ 22 8719, near the entrances of Engaku-ji and Kenchō-ji respectively, are commercial *shōjin ryōri* restaurants, both *moderate to expensive.*

Downtown Kamakura contains the usual wide choice of foreign and Japanese eating, including fast food chains. On the right-hand side of Wakamiya-dōri, as you walk up between the second and third of the big *torii* gateways, is **Asabane-ya,** ✆ 22 1222, which specializes in inexpensive to moderate *unagi*—broiled eel. Opposite the station at Zushi, a beach resort one stop east of Kamakura, is **Gin-no-To,** an unusual nouvelle restaurant combining French cooking with *kaiseki ryōri,* the classic Japanese *haute cuisine.*

Hakone

The air vibrated with the rush of a hundred torrents, and whenever the eye could pierce the undergrowth it saw a headlong stream breaking itself on a boulder. Up at the hotel we had left the grey chill of a November day and cold that numbed the fingers; down in the gorge we found the climate of Bengal with real steam thrown in. Green bamboo pipes led the hot water to a score of bathing houses in whose verandas Japanese in blue and white dressing-gowns lounged and smoked.

Rudyard Kipling, *From Sea to Sea,* 1908

If Hakone was anywhere else in Japan it would be considered rather a stale hot spring resort, crowded and commercialized as Kipling noted as early as 1908. But the area's proximity to Tokyo makes it an inevitable destination for anyone with a limited amount of time, and Hakone has plenty going for it, in the right weather: open air baths, dramatic mountain railways, a pair of interesting museums and fine views of Mt Fuji. It's always been a popular area with foreigners: 19th-century ex-pats treated it as a hill station, and several Western-style hotels sprang up to cater for them, including the legendary Fujiya at Miyanoshita. A local rail pass makes it a cheap place to get around if you're staying four days (although three, frankly, is enough). Enjoy Hakone for what it is, but treat it as an introduction to the pleasures of hot springs, not as the last word.

Getting There

From Tokyo, the launch pad into Hakone is **Odawara**, a bullet train stop on the JR Tōkaidō *shinkansen*. At Odawara station you can transfer onto the Hakone Tōzan railway to Hakone Yumoto and stations beyond. Buses also go there, and to Moto-Hakone. The only direct route from Tokyo to Hakone departs from Shinjuku station and terminates at Hakone-en on the shore of Lake Ashi.

From the west, the gateways are **Mishima** and **Atami**, both *shinkansen* stops, from which buses connect with the main Hakone centres.

Getting Around and Orientation

The Hakone Tōzan **railway** runs from Odawara up through the dramatic gorge which culminates in Gōra. Some trains go all the way through; others terminate at Hakone Yumoto, where you must change for the next stage of the journey.

Buses (times and frequencies vary with the season) are plentiful throughout the area, and **boats** shuttle along the eastern shore of Lake Ashi (Moto Hakone, Hakone-en and Tōgendai are the principal ports of call). Mountain **tramways** and **cable cars** connect Gōra with Tōgendai (via Sōun-zan mountain, and several stops along the way), and Hakone-en with Komaga-take mountain.

Ask for exact directions to Hakone and you will draw a blank. It's not a single town but a mountain region containing a number of small towns, several of them containing the element *Hakone* in their names.

From the tourist's point of view, Hakone can be thought of as a body of mountains with a lake on the west and a gorge on the east side. The lake is **Lake Ashi** (Ashinoko) and along its eastern shore are a number of pleasure resorts, including **Moto Hakone**, the area's biggest town. The gorge contains hot springs, museums and little resort towns joined by the dramatic Hakone Tōzan railway. The lake and the gorge are joined at their northern extremity (by a cable car and tramway) and at the south end (by road).

Along the Hakone Mountain Railway

Hakone Yumoto, the gateway to the Hakone area, is a tacky little town but, unless yours is a through train from Odawara, you will have to change here onto the Hakone Tōzan railway. Buses depart here for all destinations in Hakone.

Hakone Yumoto's **Sōun-ji** temple is historic but uninteresting, a once great complex built by a local *daimyō*, and used as a headquarters by the great 16th-century general Toyotomi Hideyoshi. **Shōgen-ji** is prettier, and has a legendary association with Jūrō and Gorō Soga, a pair of 12th-century brothers, whose fatal vengeance for their father's murder forms the subject of numerous plays and epics. **Tonosawa**, the next station up, is quieter and prettier, with cheaper accommodation. The 17th-century **Amida-ji** temple sits 2km up on the slopes of the mountain.

At the next stop, **Ōhiradai**, the train stops and reverses to negotiate the hairpin bend and continue on its way to **Miyanoshita**, the principal resort in the area. Apart from the transportation arrangements, little enough has changed since 1891 when *Murray's Handbook* recommended it for 'the purity of the air, the excellence of the hotels, the numerous pretty walks both short and long, the plentiful supply of "chairs" and of specially large and comfortable *kagos* [palanquins] for those who prefer being carried, and the delicious hot baths, which, containing but faint traces of salt and soda, may be used without medical advice.' The Victorian Hakone experience can still be enjoyed in the wonderful old wooden **Fujiya Hotel**—treat yourself to a night here if you can possibly afford it. Behind it, a path climbs **Sengen-yama** (804m), a 1hr ascent with good views of the whole area. (You can descend by a different route to Kowakidani, past the **Chisuji falls**.) The nearby village of **Dogashima** has a waterfall and hot springs in a dramatic enclosed gorge; you can walk it from Miyanoshita in about 10min or take a private cable car or tram operated by the two inns there.

Kowakidani, the next stop along, is an unpleasantly modern development with big, concrete hotels and tacky amusement arcades. **Chōkoku no Mori**, literally 'Forest of Sculpture', but translated as **The Hakone Open-Air Museum** (*open 9–5; Nov–Feb, 9–4; adm ¥1500*) is one of the area's most unusual attractions, and has its own railway stop. Founded in 1969, its 70,000 square metres of landscaped park contain galleries, gardens, cafés, shops and hundreds of sculptures—originals and reproductions—by artists including Rodin, Brancusi, Giacometti, de Kooning, Modigliani, Miro and Noguchi. Henry Moore has his own corner, and various Japanese sculptors are represented. All the sculptures are cheerfully scattered around the grounds with little sense of unity or purpose. Some of the juxtapositions are bizarre: Picasso is approached via a garden containing a clutch of repro Michelangelos.

The Picasso exhibit, housed in its own pavilion, is the highlight of the museum and almost justifies the price of admission on its own. It's an eccentric collection which above all demonstrates the artist's versatility. There are lithographs, some pieces in stained glass, and a couple of superb canvases, including the jokily sinister *Nature Morte au Chat* (1962), showing a grinning, skew-eyed cat eyeing a helpless lobster, and the beautiful pastel *Femme au chapeau bleu* from 1923. Picasso's talents as a sculptor are well demonstrated in the large collection of ceramics, a gallery of faces and forms on blocks, jugs, tiles and plates. Admire the big, elegant *Head of Jacqueline*, and the highly suggestive plate of ham and sausage. Only Picasso could make a fry-up erotic.

The Hakone Tōzan line ends at **Gōra**, where a steep tramway carries passengers up to **Sōunzan**, the trail head for the walk up to **Mt Sōun** (1137m). From Sōunzan station a cable car descends all the way down to **Tōgendai** on Lake Ashi, but get off at **Kōen-ue** tram stop, a couple of stops up from Gōra, to visit the **Hakone Bijutsukan** (Art Museum, *open 9–4; closed Thu; adm ¥800*), a three storey Chinese-style building in a beautiful landscaped moss garden planted with maples. It was established in 1952 by Okada Mokichi, founder of the World Church of Messianity, a Shinto-based cult which emphasizes the importance of works of art in achieving spiritual well-being. The collection is based mainly around medieval ceramics, some of them rather dun and inaccessible, but there's a great room of flaming Jōmon prehistoric jars with spiky ridges, and some beautiful *haniwa* burial figurines, including an unusual one of a rabbit. From the second floor window you can see across the valley to the giant character *dai* ([print kanji]), carved out of the hillside vegetation, and illuminated with torches once a year for the August Daimonji Festival.

Sengokuhara, to the northwest of Gōra, along Route 138 (buses go there), is a quiet little *onsen* town off the main tourist route. Its affluence is advertised by the presence of several golf courses, some expensive restaurants, and a private **Porsche Museum** (*open 9–5; admission a sporty ¥2000*).

South Shore of Lake Ashi

This is the alternative gateway to Hakone for those coming from the direction of Mishima and the west. The town which is most usually referred to as Hakone lies on a cove on the southeast edge of **Lake Ashi**, but it has a confusing number of bus stops, all prefixed by the name *Hakone*.

As you approach from the west, **Hakone-machi** is the first one to be announced. Get off here for **Hakone Sekisho**, the site of the old Hakone Barrier, a strategic checkpoint which monitored all traffic towards and away from Edo (Tokyo) on the old Tōkaidō highway. It was established in 1619 and abolished at the Meiji Restoration, but a replica has been rebuilt, complete with mannequins in period costume (*open 9–4.30; Dec–Feb 9–4, adm ¥200*). There is a small museum, the **Hakone Sekisho Shiryōkan**, 200m down the road.

The barrier was built in 1619 on the orders of the second Tokugawa shogun, Hidetada, to enforce the strict rules on freedom of movement which the Tokugawas imposed on all sections of society. Detecting smugglers was only part of the job of the barrier officials. At Hakone, the most sensitive contraband was *deonna, irideppo*—'women going out, and guns going in'. The latter might be used by plotters against the shogunate; the former were wives and daughters of feudal lords who were required to stay in Edo as hostages, a guarantee of their husbands' loyalty and cooperation. Penalties for dodging the checkpoint were grave: 'Persons who have passed over the mountains to avoid the barrier will be crucified there,' declares an old statute, displayed in the museum, which also contains grim photos showing the severed heads of transgressors. 'Persons who have guided these violators will also be crucified. Any women accompanying these violators will become slaves. Their heads will be shaved and they will be given to anyone who wants them.' The uncompromising ruthlessness seems to have paid off: from the early 16th century to the last third of the 19th, no significant *daimyō* insurrection took place.

The actual barrier was dismantled in 1869, and the present reconstruction isn't quite authentic. Contemporary illustrations show that the customs house, a long building beside a square wooden gate, was actually part of a larger corral complex, an immigration zone with a gate at both ends, where large numbers of people, animals and goods could be detained and searched. Only particularly suspicious or high-ranking travellers would be taken inside the customs house where the officials had their offices. Waxworks show a noblewoman being frisked by a female customs officer; the well outside was used to wash off make-up, fake scars, etc. The museum contains old maps, passports and devil masks, hung up in the examination rooms to intimidate suspects, plus some nasty spiked polearms called sleeve-catchers, used to tangle up the clothes of anyone who tried to slip through unauthorized.

Just north of the barrier, there's a pleasant little wooded promontory, the site of a former Imperial Detached Palace, built at the suggestion of the Emperor Meiji's physician, a German named Bülz, who was a great believer in the medicinal properties of hot springs. The present building is an uninteresting reconstruction, but several quiet paths ramble around it.

Beyond here, further along an elegant avenue of cryptomerias, is the bus terminus called **Moto-Hakone**, a place of tourist inns and restaurants, and the transportation hub for connections to the rest of the area. Around the shoreline of the lake is **Hakone Shrine**, its entrance marked by a red *torii* gateway in the waters of the lake. The shrine was originally founded in 757 and served until the Meiji Restoration as a headquarters of the local *yamabushi*, mountain-worshipping ascetics of the mystical Shugendō sect.

Lake Ashi Area

On a clear day, Lake Ashi reflects the cone of Mt Fuji, but such conditions are all too rare in these foggy parts, and the calm of the lake's surface is more typically broken by the pleasure boats that link the various resorts along its perimeter. At **Hakone-en**, there's an aquarium, and a ropeway up to just below the summit of Komaga-take (1327m); **Tōgendai** is the western terminus of the ropeway–tram link which crosses the mountains to Gōra, and the museums and railway on the other side.

There are paddle, rowing and motor boats too, and a gilt monstrosity called the *Victoria* which cruises the lake, broadcasting inanities through a loud speaker.

The Tōkaidō Highway

Between Moto-Hakone and Hakone Yumoto the quickest bus runs along a fast elevated highway. Far more interesting, for those with time to spare, are the restored sections of the **Tōkaidō**, the great post road which linked the imperial capital of Kyoto with the shogun's city, Edo, in the east. For much of its length, stone flags have been laid under the cryptomerias, especially at the Moto-Hakone end. You can catch buses in both directions from the stops along the way, when you're tired of walking. **Amazake no Chaya** is a famous tea house named after the drink it specializes in: *amazake*, a sweet, milky *sake*. At **Hatajuku**, a few kilometres further east, are a museum, **Yosegi Kaikan** (*open 9–5; adm free*) and shops displaying *yosegi-zaiku*, one of Japan's most striking and unusual wood crafts, and a fine souvenir. It's made by applying a geometric mosaic of tiny squares of wood onto the flat surfaces of boxes and trays.

At the Hakone Yumoto end of the road, by the bus stop called Oku-Yumoto, is the **Tenzan Notenburo**, ✆ 0460 5 7446 (*open daily 9am–11pm*), a modern but enticing outdoor hot spring complex which offers, amongst other delights, ingenious massage machines and a steam room inside a cave in the hillside (on the men's side only—the women have a less interesting Scandinavian-style sauna, though part of one of their pools is in a cave).

(✆ *0460–*)   ***Where to Stay***

luxury

Naraya Ryokan, ✆ 2 2411, is in Miyanoshita. From ¥30,000 upwards (including two meals), this is the finest and most expensive Japanese-style accommodation in Hakone. Most rooms have their own bath; there's also a communal marble *onsen* bath, dating, like most of the inn, from the Meiji period.

expensive

Fujiya Hotel, ✆ 2 2211, in Miyanoshita is the classic Hakone hotel, a Meiji institution that lives up to its reputation for eccentric elegance: rambling wings overlooking gardens, French food, a private golf course. Rates vary enormously according to the season and day of the week.

Taisei-kan, ✆ 2 2281, and **Yamatoya**, ✆ 2 2261, are traditional *ryokan* in Dōgashima, the hot spring in the steep gorge. The former is concrete and ferries guests from Miyanoshita via a private cable car; the latter is wooden and has its own tramway.

inexpensive

Fuji Hakone Guest House, ✆ 4 6577, has clean, modest *tatami* rooms in Sengokuhara, one minute from the bus stop called Senkyoro-mae (an announcement is made in English just before the stop), with a hot spring bath, self-catering kitchen and optional breakfast.

Moto-Hakone Guest House, ✆ 3 7880, is the sister establishment of the above in Moto-Hakone. Get off the bus at the stop called Ashinoko-en; from there it's a one-minute walk.

Aibii Sukēa (Ivy Square), ✆ 4 6776, is a pension with Western-style rooms in Moto-Hakone.

(✆ *0460–*)

Eating Out

Like all *onsen* resorts, the convention in Hakone is to eat at your inn. Some of the best food in the area can be had in the resort's classic hotels. The **Fujiya Hotel**, ✆ 2 2211, in Miyanoshita has a fine French restaurant; the **Kowaki-en**, ✆ 2 4111, in Kowaki-dani has two villas in its sprawling gardens where *kaiseki ryōri* banquets are served in the summer. Both accept bookings from non-residents and are well used to foreigners; both are *expensive*.

There are many unaffiliated restaurants clustering round the transport terminals and tourist spots, and finding lunch is never a problem. The cheaper places tend to close in the early evening, and close altogether out of season.

Fuji-san (Mt Fuji)

Even the rampant industrialization of post-war Japan hasn't been able to snuff out the magic of Mt Fuji, which must still rate as one of the world's most beautiful mountains. From the Tōkaidō *shinkansen* line, from Hakone's Lake Ashi, even (when pollution is light) from tall buildings in Tokyo—no matter how many postcards you've seen—the sight of the pristine cone, dusted for most of the year with snow, and lightly scored with the fissures and crevasses of ancient eruptions, is unfailingly moving and impressive.

Not surprisingly, people often want to get closer, but two misconceptions need to be cleared up from the start. First, the mountain is not nearly so beautiful close up as it is from afar. The upper slopes are strewn with grey volcanic scree which not only looks less than pretty, but is also uncomfortably loose and sharp. Second, climbing Fuji is never a solitary experience: during the open season, from 1 July to 26 August, 400,000 people ascend the trails, and on weekend nights, they seem to form an unbroken queue all the way up the mountain. It's physically demanding, too: the climb from the fifth station takes eight or nine hours up and down and isn't to be undertaken without preparation. Even in summer, temperatures frequently drop below freezing. 'Only a fool would miss the chance to climb Mt Fuji,' runs the well-worn saying. 'Only a fool would do it twice'.

Climbing Mt Fuji

There are various trails up Fuji, but several of them are suitable only for organized groups of experienced climbers. Each of the trails is punctuated by ten 'stations', which usually have rest houses and refreshment facilities.

The most popular starting point is the town of **Kawaguchiko**, a resort town on the edge of Lake Kawaguchi, one of the so-called Fuji Five Lakes. Frequent buses run from Tokyo's Hamamatsuchō and Shinjuku stations. On Sundays and national holidays between March and November, there is a twice-daily local train direct from Shinjuku; otherwise you have to take the JR Chūō line from Shinjuku, and then change at Ōtsuki onto the private Fuji Kyūkō line. The conventional method of ascent from Kawaguchiko is to take a bus (1 April–11 Nov) to the fifth station where the road ends, and walk from there. The climb takes about 5 hours, the descent about 3.

Gotemba, a small city west of Hakone, is reached from Shinjuku station, changing at Matsuda, or directly from Tokyo station. The Gotemba-guchi trail is long: 45 minutes by bus to the fifth station, then 8 hours up and 3 hours down.

Mishima, which can be reached by *shinkansen* from Tokyo, is the starting point for the southernmost trail. A 2-hour bus ride takes you to the Fujinomiya/Mishima fifth station. From there, it's about 4¼ hours up and 3¼ down.

In the open season, Mt Fuji is active twenty-four hours a day. Dawn is one of the busiest times, for the beauty of the sunrise and because the panoramic views are least likely at that time to be obscured by cloud. To reach the summit just before dawn, leave your departure quite late (the sun rises around 4.30am in the summer). Alternatively, you could climb during the day, and spend the night in one of the many mountain huts, offering exorbitantly priced noodles and lodgings, at regular intervals along the trails.

It's important to give some thought to clothing and equipment. If it's T-shirts and shorts weather in Kawaguchiko, it could still be a screaming blizzard on the summit, so try to dress in layers which you can put on or discard as necessary: gloves, a warm hat, and four layers including a good warm coat is the minimum. Strong boots are essential. If you're climbing at night, bring a torch. Carry your own snacks, water and soft drinks if you want to avoid paying inflated prices on the mountain.

Chūbu—Central Honshū

Chūbu, the mountainous bulge in the middle of Honshū, falls into three broad areas. The southern Pacific coast is industrialized and generally uninteresting, with the exception of Nagoya and the nearby town of Inuyama. The centre is dominated by the Japan Alps, 'discovered' as a mountaineering venue by a 19th-century English clergyman, and one of the country's most popular centres of mountaineering and winter sports. Old castle towns like Takayama and Matsumoto retain traces of the feudal past; and the steep-sided valleys contain well-preserved post towns and villages. Finally, there's the northern, Japan Sea side, perhaps the most interesting of all, with the great temple town of Nagano, Kanazawa, Japan's most interesting small city, and the remote exile of Sado Island and the Noto Peninsula. It's a rugged, adventurous territory, suited to those who like the outdoors and don't mind making their own discoveries off the well-posted routes.

Niigata and Sado Island

An industrialized prefectural capital on the northern Japan Sea coast, Niigata is an uninteresting city, but a useful one, especially for travellers from northeast Asia. International flights from Niigata airport fly to Vladivostok, Khabarovsk and Seoul, and ferries sail to Vladivostok, as well as to Hokkaidō and nearby Sado Island.

Getting There and Around

The *shinkansen* from Tokyo's Ueno station takes from 1hr 50mins to 2hrs 20mins and costs ¥10,080, including reservation. A good deal is the Seibu Bus, departing six times a day from Ikebukuro station, taking about 5hrs, and costing ¥5150.

From Kyoto there are several trains, including a sleeper; the slowest express takes 8hrs 40mins and costs ¥9270, without reservation or sleeper.

Niigata is the principal gateway to **Sado**, although there are also crossings from **Naoetsu** (120km down the coast) to **Ogi** on southwest Sado.

From **Niigata**, the quickest way in is the **plane** (25mins, ¥7210 one way) to Sado airport, near Ryōtsu. The **hydrofoil** takes an hour and costs from ¥5130. Regular **ferry** crossings take 2½hrs and cost upwards of ¥1780, depending on the season.

Sado-ga-Shima (Sado Island) is famous in Japanese history for two things: gold and exile. Plenty of inconvenient prisoners—including the 13th-century Emperor Nintoku, the turbulent Buddhist fundamentalist, Nichiren, and the *nō* playwright, Zeami—have spent mandatory extended vacations here. Until the 19th century, less posh prisoners were forced to work as slave labourers in the notoriously inhumane gold mines, now exhausted, except as tourist attractions. These days, the island is best known as the home of the internationally famous **Kōdo Drummers**, loincloth-clad masters of the traditional *taiko* drums, who have toured to great acclaim all over the world. Kōdo has its own village near the southwest corner of the island. Every August, percussion groups from all over the world converge on the nearby town of Ogi for the annual **Earth Celebration** drumming

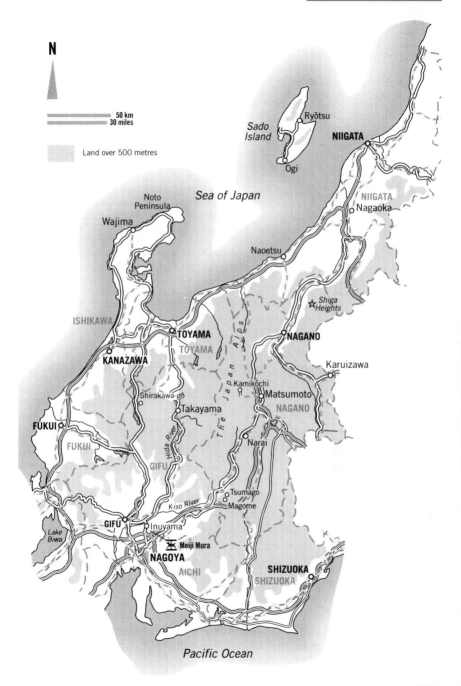

N

50 km
30 miles

Land over 500 metres

Sado
Island
Ryōtsu
NIIGATA
Ogi

Noto
Peninsula
Sea of Japan
NIIGATA
Nagaoka
Wajima

Naoetsu

Shiga
Heights

ISHIKAWA
TOYAMA
TOYAMA
NAGANO

KANAZAWA
Karuizawa

Kamikōchi
Shirakawa-gō
Matsumoto
Takayama
NAGANO

FUKUI
FUKUI
Narai

Hida River

GIFU

Tsumago
Magome
Kiso River

GIFU
Inuyama
Lake
Biwa
Meiji Mura
NAGOYA
SHIZUOKA
AICHI
SHIZUOKA

Pacific Ocean

festival, a unique event which you should make efforts to see (book months in advance, unless you're prepared to sleep on the beach).

Apart from this, Sado's attractions are simple: tiny fishing villages in isolated rocky coves, strange zoomorphic rock formations, rustic local temples and shrines, and little festivals of dance and music—several take place somewhere on the island every week of the year. The **Sado Gold Mine** is open as a museum, with tableaux demonstrating the short, wretched lives led by the slaves. Buses are slow and infrequent; the best way round the island is by bike or car (hire both in Ryōtsu).

The Japan Alps

Mountains have always played a central part in Japanese religion, both as deities and as the sites of retreat, meditation and ritual austerities, but until the late 19th century they were never climbed for pleasure. In 1896, an English missionary named Walter Weston compared the Hida Range, straddling Gifu, Tōyama and Nagano prefectures, to the European Alps. The name stuck, and the Japanese hiking craze was born—today there are many times more regular hikers than baptized Christians. Weston was awarded the Order of the Sacred Treasure (Fourth Class); in Kamikōchi he is honoured by a small shrine, in the manner of a Shinto god; a festival is held in his honour on the first Sunday in June.

Matsumoto, under 3hrs from Tokyo's Shinjuku station by limited express train, is the main city of the Alpine region. **Matsumoto Castle** (*open 8.30–5; adm ¥500*) is one of the oldest and most celebrated in the country, with a keep dating from 1597, and walls and moat from 1504. The moat is so wide that the castle appears like an island in a pond. It's a complex and elegant building, with striking black timber, white plaster and grey roofs. As well as the main keep, there's a secondary citadel, a turret and a one-storey structure, strategically unnecessary, constructed for the purpose of moon-viewing parties. All but the last have hidden floors: the main keep, for instance, appears to have five storeys, but actually possesses six separate floors, a tactic designed to mislead an attacking enemy into underestimating its strength and resources. The hidden fifth floor is the most impressive, designed for use during wartime as the commanding general's campaign nerve centre. Here the immense roof beams and supports are exposed to view; nestling among them is a tiny shrine dedicated to the castle's guardian deity.

The castle has the full range of defensive measures, including holes for marksmen (the rectangular ones were used by archers, the square ones by musketeers), and *ishi-otoshi*—chutes, built into the lowest storey, through which rocks, oil and sewage could be poured onto attackers scaling the walls. The second floor of the keep houses an exhibition on the development of firearms in Japan (they were introduced by Portuguese sailors in the 16th century and enthusiastically copied). An attached **museum** (*admission included in the* *ticket for the castle*) contains a routine display of prehistoric pots, armour, guns, stuffed animals and—the only highlight—an unusual collection of native and imported clocks.

Kamikōchi

This mountain resort and hiking base is in a spectacular position, perched alongside a clean, fast flowing river, beneath an epic panorama of plunging granite mountains. From Matsumoto you travel for 30min on the private Dentetsu railway to Shin-Shimashima (*¥670*), then take a bus (*1hr 20mins, ¥2000*) along a spectacular road through rock tunnels and above plummeting gorges and dammed up lakes (the bus runs only during the climbing season, from late April to early November). Four peaks of 2900m or more are visible from the resort, and—with adequate preparation—all can be climbed within a few hours. For the serious hiker, zig-zagging trails link up with more far-flung mountains of the national park. With Kamikōchi as a base, you could spend anything from a few hours to several days exploring the Alps. Manned mountain huts are maintained throughout the season, but naturally you should take professional local advice before attempting anything ambitious—the Visitor Centre (✆ *0263 95 2032*) and Park Ranger's Office (✆ *0263 95 2606*) keep up-to-date information on trail and weather conditions. For the less sturdy of thigh, Kamikōchi also has several lovely gentle walks along the forested river valley.

There are two catches. Unsurprisingly, the place becomes suffocatingly crowded for most of the open season. Late September and October, when the autumn colours are out, is probably the best time to come but even then be prepared to share the lower reaches of the valley with several thousand others. Second, it's expensive. Kamikōchi businesses take full advantage of their captive customers; everything from apples to accommodation is marked up and, absurdly, there is no youth hostel. The Kamikōchi Imperial Hotel (✆ *0263 95 2001*), a branch of the famous Tokyo institution, offers the glitziest accommodation. For cheaper rooms, make a booking through the Matsumoto City Tourist Information Centre. Do this before you get on the bus to avoid being stranded with nowhere to stay.

Nagano

Apart from the many pilgrims to Zenkō-ji, the ancient and awe-inspiring temple around which it grew up, Nagano has been untroubled by the great movements of Japanese history. In feudal times it was a post town on the road to the remote Japan Sea coast, and during the mid-16th century, the area to the south, Kawanakajima, was the scene of intense fighting between rival lords. The Pacific War left it largely undamaged, indeed the biggest changes to Nagano will come over the next few years as the city internationalizes in preparation for the Winter Olympics in 1998. The economic benefits for the region are obvious, but furious rows have taken place between environmentalists and developers concerning the construction of sports and resort facilities in the virgin mountains of Nagano prefecture.

Practical Information

From Tokyo's Ueno station, the limited express **trains** take 2hrs 40mins and cost ¥6580. The night **bus** from Tokyo station takes 6hrs 35mins and costs ¥5400.

The usual conveniences are found around **Nagano station** which is at the south-east end of town. Naganoites are very proud of this structure which is in the shape of Zenkō-ji's main hall. A hundred metres down the road that leads away from the main plaza opposite the station, a right turn takes you onto Chūō-dōri. This straight road leads 2km north to the precincts of Zenkō-ji and the museums in Jōyama Park. Buses and taxis are available at the station.

Zenkō-ji

Bus from the station, taxi or walk to Dai-mon (Great Gate).

Outside the heartland of Nara and Kyoto, Zenkō-ji is one of the biggest and most impressive temples in Japan. The surviving main hall, although less than 300 years old, is a perfect example of Edo-period architecture. The long pilgrim's avenue, still trodden by eight million visitors a year, has old shops and stalls, inns and sub-temples offering traditional overnight accommodation. Amid the echoes and incense smoke in the **Main Hall**, and in the famous black tunnel beneath the holy of holies, is a palpably spiritual atmosphere, unmarred by the commercialism and superficiality of other big temples. One of the reasons for its popularity is its unusual form of administration. The temple is not exclusively affiliated to one sect, but rather administrated alternately by an abbot and abbess of the Tendai and Jōdo sects respectively.

History

Zenkō-ji traces its history back to India and the 6th century BC, when a rich man, whose daughter had been saved from an epidemic, commissioned a gold statue which was sculpted by the Buddha himself. A thousand years later it had found its way to Korea, and in 552 AD it was presented to the Emperor of Japan by a Korean king. A hall was built for it by the Soga, an aristocratic family close to the Emperor, but others among his advisers resented the new religion, and attempts were made to destroy the temple and the image within it. As the statue was impervious to fire and blows, the best that could be done was to drop it into the waters of the Naniwa Canal, near present-day Ōsaka, where it remained for many years. One day, in the 7th century, a poor man named Honda Yoshimitsu (also called Zenkō) was passing by when the image called out to him. He carried it back with him to Nagano. News of the statue's miraculous properties reached Emperor Kōgyoku (642–644), and it was he who endowed Zenkō-ji, and who commanded that the image should be hidden away and never viewed again.

Touring Zenkō-ji

Starting at the point called **Dai-mon**, walk north towards the precincts along the last tree-lined stretch of Chūō-dōri, past shops selling staffs and rosaries and household altars, and old pilgrim lodgings like the Fujiya Ryokan. Sub-temples line the approach to the **Niō-mon** (Guardian Gate), a copper-roofed reconstruction of 1918, 13.6m high, containing two early 20th-century statues of the Guardian Kings. On the right are small temples, several of which offer accommodation to travellers; on the left is **Daihongan**, a nunnery of the Jōdo sect, whose abbess is one of the joint administrators of the temple. The silver chrysanthemums on the roof of the main hall indicate her second distinction: she is traditionally also an imperial princess. The **Hōmotsu-kan** (Treasure House) has accumulated treasures bequeathed to it over the years by successive incumbents: lacquer bowls and writing sets, giant rosaries and a vivid series of illustrations of souls in torment. Behind the Hōmotsu-kan is a small worship hall with a beautiful narrative scroll telling the story of Zenkō-ji's construction and the adventures of the marvellous statue. The big fountain in the front courtyard contains a statue of Mizuko Jizō, the protector of aborted and stillborn children.

Inside the Niō-mon is the **Nakamise**, a row of stalls selling pilgrims' staffs, hats and rosaries, incense, offerings, toys and local specialities like dried *soba* noodles. Two of the most popular souvenirs are wicker models of pigeons mounted on wheels, and small towels bearing the picture of an old woman chasing a cow. Crowds of birds inhabit the shrine courtyard which, in pigeon terms, is to Japan what Trafalgar Square is to Britain.

The towels illustrate a legend about an impious old woman who once lived nearby. One day, while she was drying out a valuable piece of cloth, a black cow appeared out of nowhere and ran away with it impaled on her horns. The hag pursued it, but lost the trail at dusk near to Zenkō-ji. Taking shelter for the night, she was visited in a dream by Kannon who told her that the cow had been a divine messenger intended to lead her to the temple, and to Buddha. When the harridan awoke, she was a changed character. On her return to the village she found her piece of cloth neatly folded on the local altar of Kannon.

The next gate is the impressive **San-mon** (Mountain Gate), 20m and two storeys high, rebuilt in 1750 with two massive roofs of cypress shingles. Just before this, on the left, is the second of the major sub-temples whose abbot, along with the Daihongan abbess, governs the temple. **Daikanjin** is reached via a bridge across a small pond. Inside is a pretty courtyard, a noted garden, and another treasure house, including a medieval scroll of *The Tale of Genji*.

It's the scene on the far side of the San-mon that you have come for, though. At the centre of the great courtyard, milling with crowds of people, is a huge covered metal cauldron filled with incense sticks. The smoke billows through the mouth of a metal lion on its lid and the lion's mouth drools with tar. To the left is an elegant 18th-century **Kyōzo** (Sutra Repository); to the right and towards the back is a **Shoro** (Bell Tower) containing a bell forged in 1667. But the building which dominates is the **Hon-dō** (Main Hall), rebuilt in 1707 in a style typical of the Edo period, with elaborate hip-and-gable roofs, and a huge worship area—1766 square metres, capable of holding a congregation of thousands.

The gables face you as you enter the courtyard by the San-mon gate. At first glance there appear to be two storeys: actually, the lower one is a pent roof, with no separate floor of its own. The woodwork of the gables is decorated with inlaid gold; there is a reversed swastika, an ancient Buddhist symbol, under the apex. It is 28m high, and the hall is 23m wide by 52m deep. The white curtains draped in front of the entrance bear purple chrysanthemums, indicating the imperial connections of Zenkō-ji's abbesses.

One of the most interesting characters associated with the temple is to be found just outside its main entrance, to the right of the steps. This weathered old statue, wearing a red bonnet and rubbed smooth by the hands of millions of pilgrims, is **Binzuru**, one of the 16 *rakan*, human disciples of the historical Buddha, who was expelled from their number for human frailty—an excessive fondness for alcohol, or for women, depending on the story. Barred from the inner precincts of the temple, he sits instead on the outside, healing anyone who rubs him on the portion of his body corresponding to their afflicted part.

Entering the hall proper under the great porch takes you into the **Gejin** (Outer Sanctuary), the outermost of several sacred areas (you can still wear your shoes). The volume of space is enormous; the whispering echo of feet and prayers produces an impression closer to that of a mosque or cathedral than most Japanese temples. Counters by the entrance sell talismans and postcards; a raised platform supports the painted festival drums. To the back, behind a wire mesh, is the **Chūjin** (Middle Sanctuary), an expanse of *tatami* in front of the main altar. Gold lamps hang from the ceiling; its coffers are decorated with red chrysanthemums. In front of this is the **Naijin** (Inner Sanctum); at the back and to the right you can see statues of Honda Zenkō, the pious founder, with his wife and son. In front of them is a mirror, suggesting that they are worshipped as Shinto *kami* rather than Buddhist deities. The holy of holies, however, is never displayed. No human has laid eyes on it since the 7th century when the statue retrieved from Naniwa Canal by Honda was hidden away at the order of Emperor Kyōgoku. An exact replica was made, but even this is now considered so sacred that it is displayed only once every seven years in Zenkō-ji's most important festival. The next one will be in April 1999.

The most famous of the pilgrim attractions of Zenkō-ji is *kaidan meguri*, 'circling the ordination platform', an allegorical search for the 'key to paradise' which is concealed, in pitch darkness, in a tunnel beneath the innermost altar. It's a spine-tingling experience which everyone of a non-claustrophobic disposition should try. After buying a ticket, you enter the Inner Sanctum, and follow the crowds down a narrow set of steps into a low, dark corridor, which bends in a circle under the Nainaijin (Inner Inner Sanctum). It's utterly, eerily dark; you can't see your own nose, and you'll find that your fellow pilgrims tend to stop giggling and fall rather quiet at this point. Feel your way along the smooth wooden walls and grope for the key to paradise—all who touch it are said to be guaranteed rebirth after death. It's really there, and reasonably easy to find: chances are you'll hear the paradise-seekers ahead of you rattling it as you approach. Clue: it's towards the end of the passage, on the right-hand wall, and feels less like a key than a lock.

The secret image is enshrined directly above this spot. The closest you get, apart from during the seven-yearly festival, is a replica of the replica enshrined in the **Chūrei-den**, a modern pink pagoda behind the main hall, built as a monument to the war dead. As well as ancient shell cases, mess tins and other relics of Japan's wars since 1868, it has good views of the main hall and its elaborate roofs.

Nagano Prefectural Shinano Art Museum and Higashiyama Kaii Gallery
Open 9–5pm; adm ¥300.

A single ticket covers both these small museums in Jōyama Park, east of Zenkō-ji. **The Prefectural Museum** contains a rag-bag of works by local artists, but the **Higashiyama**

Kaii Gallery is well worth the admission: a rotating selection from 700 works by the foremost practitioner of *Nihonga*, modern traditional Japanese painting. At their weakest, these simple images of the Japanese countryside and coastline, horses and the unpeopled streets of northern European cities are childish, almost cute; at their best, they possess a luminous beauty and mysticism.

(✆ 0262–)   *Where to Stay*

Japanese-style accommodation tends to be near Zenkō-ji; to be close to the station you'll need to stay in a city or business hotel.

moderate

Fujiya Ryokan, ✆ 32 1241, is a comfortable old *ryokan* very close to Zenkō-ji.

Mankatei, ✆ 32 2326, is a *ryokan* near Jōyama Park, just east of the temple.

Nagano Grand Hotel Kozumaya, ✆ 35 1231, provides *ryokan* accommodation opposite Zenkō-ji's Daihongan sub-temple.

Nagano Washington Hotel, ✆ 28 5111, is a smart chain business hotel, a few blocks north of the station.

cheap

The most interesting accommodation is to be had in the *shukubō* (temple lodgings) operated by the Zenkō-ji sub-temples. They get heavily booked up at holiday times. Enquire at the tourist association office by the station, or call central reservations on ✆ 34 3591. *Shukubō* cost between ¥6000 and ¥9000 per person per night including meals and are operated just like *ryokan*, except that your fellow guests are likely to be pilgrims who will rise at dawn for the temple services. **Kyōju-in**, ✆ 0262 32 2768, is a youth hostel *shukubō*, with youth hostel facilities and prices.

Eating Out

As in most temple towns, the best and most unique food in Nagano is to be had in the *shukubō* (temple inns) which line the approach to Zenkō-ji. If you're staying at one of these, your dinner and breakfast will be included in the price. If not, ask at the tourist information centre which of the temples serves lunches (or call in Japanese, ✆ 0262 34 3591). Usually they require a couple of days' notice.

For casual snacks and non-monastic food, Nagano has plenty of chain restaurants, noodle shops and bars. Those around the station are nondescript and open until late; the more interesting, traditional places towards Zenkō-ji tend to close early.

Kiso Valley

Between Matsumoto and Nagoya the JR Chūō main line runs alongside the Kiso River, along the course of the Nakasendō, an ancient mountain post road from Tokyo to Kyoto. Three of the old villages, where Edo-era travellers would stop for rest and fresh horses, have resisted the forces of modernization and, since the 1960s, made a conscious effort to preserve their 19th-century atmosphere. They resemble, and have frequently been used as, film sets—no vending machines, no concrete, no overhead wires. Actually, this lends them rather a dead and artificial air. But if daintily preserved old towns are to your liking, this is the place to find them. An hour or two is enough to look at one of them. The walk between Tsumago and Magome is delightful, and makes an overnight stay worthwhile.

Getting There

The three villages are Narai, Tsumago and Magome. From Tokyo, you should travel from Shinjuku station to Shiojiri and change there onto the Chūō line. **Narai** has its own station 25mins from Shiojiri, but only non-express trains stop there. For the other two, take a limited express from Shiojiri to Nakatsugawa. From there, 17 buses a day make the half-hour journey to **Magome**. **Tsumago** is a further half hour's bus journey, or a pleasant walk, away.

Around the Kiso Valley Villages

The buildings in these villages are narrow and long. Households were taxed according to the frontage of their house, so a wide façade indicates the home of a rich man. **Narai**, the least prettified and self-conscious (and consequently least crowded) of the three, has one such in the **Nakamura House** (*open 9–4.30; adm ¥150*), formerly owned by a rich merchant. Notice the crude stone relief of an embracing couple at the crook in the road: it's a *dōsojin*, an ancient charm associated with fertility, of a type once found all over the region.

Magome was the birthplace of the writer Shimazaki Toson (1872–1943), whose novels draw their inspiration from the changes that encroached on his simple home in the early 20th century. His books make a good introduction to this area—several are translated into English, including *The Broken Commandment*, about a member of the untouchable *eta* underclass. The **Toson Memorial Hall** (*open 8–5; adm ¥300*) contains photographs, manuscripts and relics of his life.

The **3-hour walk** from Magome to Tsumago is one of the best reasons for visiting the Kiso Valley. From April to June and September to November, a luggage carrying service is oper-ated by the tourist information offices in both towns, so that you can arrive by bus in Magome, walk on to Tsumago, and pick up your bags to stay the night there. The trail passes woods and waterfalls along the course of the old Nakasendō post road to the Magome Pass; shortly after it is the site of an old checkpoint which controlled the trans-portation of timber. Lumber from the Kiso area was highly prized and unauthorized tree-felling was punishable by mutilation or death.

Tsumago is the most perfect of the Kiso villages, with fine views of the surrounding green hills. **Terashita** is the picturesque area beneath the small Zen temple, **Kōtoku-ji**. The single most interesting building is the **Kyōdokan Okuya**, a local history museum in the former *waki-honjin*, a *sake* shop which also served as an official residence for officers of the shogunate when they passed along the Nakasendō. It was rebuilt in 1877, after the strict sumptuary laws had been lifted, and makes full use of the previously proscribed Kiso cypress. The Emperor Meiji once stayed here, and the sacred lavatory built for his use (with support handles in the shape of a Shinto *torii* gate) is a point of great pride. At the far north end of the village, before the bus terminal, is the **Gokosatsu-ba**, an official government noticeboard setting out the rules and penalties for various misdeeds, including the practice of Christianity.

(✆ 0264-) **Where to Stay**

Minshuku are generally *inexpensive*, including two meals.

In **Magome**, try **Shimoizutsu-ya**, ✆ 59 2039, **Tajima-ya**, ✆ 59 2048, or **Shiroki-ya**, ✆ 59 2035.

In **Tsumago**, try **Minshuku Daikichi**, ✆ 57 2595 or the moderate **Fujioto Ryokan**, ✆ 57 3009.

Nagoya

'Somebody stole the blueprint of hell,' wrote Angela Carter in 1974, 'and, with it, they built Nagoya.' Twenty years later, Japan's fourth city (third, if you count Yokohama as part of Tokyo) may not be many people's favourite, but no one could describe it as diabolical. The air has been cleaned up, smart new hotels, department stores and public buildings have gone up, and downtown Nagoya nowadays has rather a dapper, businesslike air to it. The city isn't worth a visit in itself, but it's a good place to recharge for the next phase of travelling, gather information, and enjoy good food, flash hotels and lively nightlife.

Getting There

Nagoya is the principal transport hub for the eastern Kansai and western Chūbū regions. The **Tōkaidō Shinkansen** takes 2hrs from Tokyo (¥*10,380*) and 1hr from Shin-Ōsaka (¥*6060*). Limited express trains connect directly with Ise, Inuyama, Takayama, Kanazawa, Matsumoto and Nagano.

The express **bus** (less than half the price of the *shinkansen*) takes 6hrs from Tokyo and 3½ from Ōsaka. Nagoya **airport** receives domestic flights from all over Japan, and a few international ones too.

Getting Around

There's a city tourist information centre in Nagoya's large and confusing station, but your first stop should be at the outstanding **International Centre** (Kokusai Sentā), ✆ 052 581 5678, a few hundred metres down Sakura-dōri, the avenue running west–east from the front of the station. It even has its own subway stop, called *Kokusai Sentā* on the red (Sakura-dōri) line. Here English-speaking volunteers will ply you with maps, pamphlets, up-to-date information about the whole region, and advice on organizing Home Visits.

Nagoya has three worthwhile tourist attractions. **Nagoya-jō** (*Shiyakushō subway station or bus from Nagoya station; open 9.30–4.30; adm ¥400*), was one of the greatest and best-preserved castles in Japan until 1945 when, along with much of the city, it was reduced to ashes by incendiary bombs. It was ordered in 1610 by the first Tokugawa shogun, Ieyasu, and its scale and opulence reflected his Pharaonic temperament. Rebuilt in concrete at a cost of ¥600 million, the five-storey keep, topped by golden *shachihoko* (fish-dragons supposed to repel fire), is one of the most impressive reconstructions in Japan.

For an idea of how the castle's former inhabitants might have lived, visit the magnificent **Tokugawa Bijutsukan,** Tokugawa Art Museum (*bus from green bus stop number 7 at Nagoya station terminal, get off at Shindeki stop, and walk 3mins; open 10–5; adm ¥1000*). Housed in the grounds of a 17th-century samurai house, it contains the superb art collection of the Owari family, a branch of the Tokugawa clan. Many of the objects on display were centuries old at the time they were inherited from Tokugawa Ieyasu himself. The prize item is a 12th-century set of illuminated scrolls of *The Tale of Genji,* rarely displayed except in photographs and reproductions. There are also thousands of pieces of armour, some superb centuries-old swords, treasures associated with the tea ceremony, and everyday items in the gold-sprinkled lacquer called *maki-e.*

Atsuta Jingū (*overland train to Atsuta or Jingū-mae stations*) is the city's principal shrine, second in national importance only to Ise, because it contains the sacred sword that forms part of the imperial regalia. The buildings, reconstructed after the war, are roofed in copper, stained these days by atmospheric sulphur; the precincts are pleasant enough, but lack the numinousness of Ise and Izumo. There's a treasure house (*adm ¥500*) containing swords offered to the deity, and a fascinating collection of early dance masks with bulging eyes and bizarre beak-like snouts.

(✆ *052–*)   ***Where to Stay***

expensive

Nagoya Hilton, ✆ 212 1111 and **Century Hyatt Nagoya,** ✆ 571 0111, are the usual international standards, the latter close to the station, the former a few minutes by taxi. The equally deluxe **Nagoya Tōkyū Hotel,** ✆ 251 2411, is close to Sakae subway station.

moderate

Meitetsu Grand Hotel, ✆ 582 2211, is 2 minutes from Nagoya station.

inexpensive

Hotel Lions Plaza Nagoya, ✆ 264 1732, is a modest business hotel 3 minutes from Sakae station.

Ryokan Meiryu, ✆ 331 8686, is a budget travellers' place, a few minutes' walk from Kamiaezu station, and not far from the Tokugawa Museum.

(✆ *052–*)   ***Eating Out***

There's no particular reason to stay for dinner in Nagoya, but no shortage of places to eat if you do: at night, the main streets glow with the usual multi-storey restaurant buildings. Two recommendations, both *moderate–expensive*: **Torigin Honten**, ✆ 973 3000, two blocks east and one block north of Sakae subway station, serves Nagoya's famous chicken; **Sensui**, ✆ 586 3330, on the second block east of the main Nagoya station, serves delicious fish and duck stews.

Inuyama

Inuyama, a compact little city on the banks of the River Kiso, is a good place to stay the night after a day in Nagoya. The river near Inuyama is nicknamed the 'Nihon Rhine' for its wide, turbulent waters and high rocky banks. Various commercial boats traverse the rapids, a pleasant way of passing a fine day, but not so heart-racingly daring as the tourist brochures like to make out.

The Kiso River at Inuyama, along with the Nagara River in the bigger city of Gifu, 20km to the east, is famous for a unique sport called *ukai*—**cormorant fishing**. The technique was in use as early as the 7th century as a means of catching the delicious *ayu*, a prized river fish, which refuses the baited hook. Every summer evening (except for nights of the full moon or after rain), small wooden boats are poled out containing cormorants on cords, with rings around their long necks. The fishermen hold lighted torches over the front of their boats which lure the *ayu*, a kind of smelt, and other river fish like carp, close to the surface. The cormorants dive in and catch them in their beaks—but because of the rings round their necks, they cannot swallow, and instead release the fish into the boats. The spectacle of the little boats, flapping birds and flickering torches has become a famous tourist attraction, and larger

sightseeing boats moor alongside the fishermen carrying spectators.

The town's two main attractions are very close to the river and bridge. **Inuyama-jō**, visible from all over the bankside part of town, is the only privately owned castle in Japan, and one of the most attractive. It is tiny, little more than a big turret, and has a gentle appearance, with little of the bristling look of bigger castles like Himeji and Matsumoto. It was begun in 1601 (the early Azuchi-Momoyama style is seen in the rough, uncut stones around its base), and it was built on a hill as a genuinely defensive castle, not (unlike later keeps) as a symbol of feudal authority and control. The walk to the top, and the views of the surrounding river and country-side, are lovely.

Uraku-en (*open Mar–Nov 9–5; Dec–Feb 9–4; adm ¥800*) is one of the most beautiful and little-known gardens in Japan, a confectionery of hedges, bushes, moss and minutely graded pebbles and sand, laid out in 1618 by a younger brother of the ferocious warlord Oda Nobunaga.

Getting There

Travel from Nagoya to Inuyama on the private Meitetsu **railway**. There are two stations in town: Inuyama station is the biggest one, near the main road and with a **Sightseeing Information Centre**. But the smaller Inuyama-Yūen station is closer to the river and the sightseeing spots. Check in advance which of the two is nearest to your accommodation.

Tourist Information

Boat tours on the rapids of the 'Nihon Rhine' cost around ¥3400 per person.

Places on *ukai* spectator boats cost around ¥2500. They depart from the moorings near Inuyama Bridge, and the fishing takes place every night from 1 June–30 Sept.

Near Inuyama

A bus ride from Inuyama is **Meiji Mura** (*open Mar–Oct 9.30–5; Nov–Feb 9.30–4; adm ¥1240*), a unique theme park of Meiji architecture, the peculiar buildings—neither quite Western, nor wholly Japanese—which were all the rage in the last three decades of the 19th century. Few survived the depredations of the Second World War and the economic boom; to modern Japanese, they are fascinatingly exotic and attract crowds from all over the country. There are some nice buildings here—churches, theatres, banks—but archi-tecturally the highlight is Frank Lloyd Wright's famous **Imperial Hotel**, opened in Tokyo in 1923, the day before the Great Kantō Earthquake, which it sailed through unscathed.

South of Meiji Mura are two celebrated shrines, of a kind which was once common, but which fell victim to a Western censoriousness imported by the Japanese at the same time as their Victorian buildings. **Tagata Jinja** (*Tagata Jinja-mae station*) and **Ōgata Jinja** (*Gakudan station*) are devoted to Izanagi and Isanami, the legendary father and mother of the nation, whose frantic copulation peopled the newly-formed islands of Japan. The holy symbols representing the lusty duo could hardly be franker: Izanagi's Tagata Shrine is littered with representations of erect penises in wood, bronze and stone. Izanami's Ōgata Shrine contains collections of vulviform fissured rocks and trees. Every year in mid-March the giant prick of Tagata Jinja is paraded through the streets on the shoulders of local men to meet his mighty wife. Even if you're not around for the festival itself, pick up some picture postcards of the procession which are unimprovably surreal.

The Meitetsu Inuyama Hotel, ✆ 61 2211, is the best in town: *inexpensive* Western-style rooms and Japanese-style annexe.

Inuyama Youth Hostel, ✆ 61 1111, is a 20-minute walk from the nearest station.

Inuyama is a quiet town, and restaurants close early. Eat in your hotel or *ryokan*, or nose around the side streets near the station: there are a few little red lantern bars open all night.

Takayama

In a mountain basin, 573m above sea level, Takayama is one of the prettiest and most compact small cities in Japan, possessing all the charm of the Kiso Valley villages, without their rather twee, glass case atmosphere. The old Sannomachi quarter might have a few TV aerials and vending machines, but the narrow streets of wooden restaurants, *sake* breweries, merchant houses, old bridges and museums have the authentic tang of the Edo period, with the advantage of a living, bustling town all around them. A day and a night, with an early start at one of the riverside morning markets, is enough to take most of it in, with perhaps another morning to see the Folk Village outside town. On the winding roads south of Takayama are mountain villages of 100-year-old thatched A-frame houses, temples, museums and beautiful family inns.

History

Takayama has always had a reputation as a centre of skilled craftsmen and builders. As early as the 8th century, the region had a special deal with the central government in Nara whereby, instead of rice, it supplied artisans to work on the palaces and temples for a specified number of days a year. In 1585, a vassal of Hideyoshi Toyotomi named Kanamori defeated the resident *daimyō*, and ruled the area from the castle on Shiroyama hill. Just over a century later, though, his descendants were transferred to a northern province, and the rich timber, minerals and human resources of the Hida region were brought under the direct control of the Tokugawa shogun through his personal appointee.

Takayama Jinya

When the Tokugawa shogun assumed personal control of the Takayama area in 1692, he appointed an official called a *daikan* to supervise its administration, and a purpose-built local government office called a *jinya* was built for his use. Such buildings once existed all over Japan, and served as administration centres, collection points for taxes, magistrate's courts, and as police stations and fortified military headquarters in time of conflict. Takayama Jinya was rebuilt several times and, after the Meiji Restoration, it became the offices of the new local government. Now restored at a cost of ¥700 million, it is the only surviving example of an Edo-period government building.

The *daikan*'s job wasn't always a straightforward one. He was just a shogunal servant, after all, with no local ties or clan history with which to command respect, and the job—

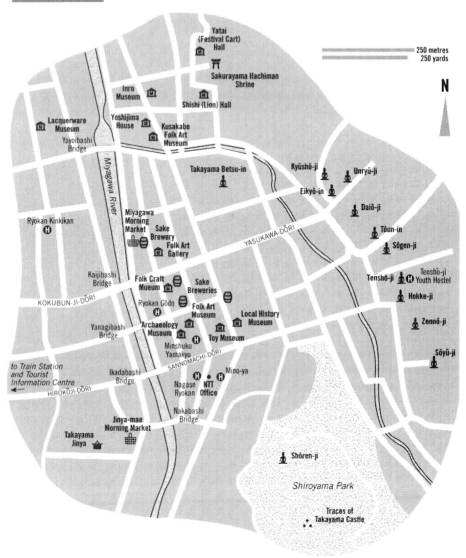

Yatai
(Festival Cart)
Hall

250 metres
250 yards

N

Sakurayama Hachiman
Shrine

Inro
Museum

Shishi (Lion) Hall

Lacquerware
Museum

Yoshijima
House

Kusakabe
Folk Art
Museum

Yayoibashi
Bridge

Miyagawa River

Takayama Betsu-in

Kyūshō-ji

Unryū-ji

Eikyō-in

Daiō-ji

Ryokan Kinkikan

Miyagawa
Morning
Market

Sake
Brewery

Tōun-in

YASUKAWA-DŌRI

Folk Art
Gallery

Sōgen-ji

Kaijibashi
Bridge

Folk Craft
Mueum

Sake
Breweries

Tenshō-ji

Tenshō-ji
Youth Hostei

KOKUBUN-JI-DŌRI

Ryokan Gōdo

Folk Art
Museum

Hokke-ji

Local History
Museum

Yanagibashi
Bridge

Archaeology
Museum

Toy Museum

Zennō-ji

Minshuku
Yamakyu

SANNOMACHI-DŌRI

Sōyū-ji

to Train Station
and Tourist
Information Centre

Ikadabashi
Bridge

Mino-ya

HIROKŌJI-DŌRI

Nagase
Ryokan

NTT
Office

Nakabashi
Bridge

Jinya-mae
Morning Market

Takayama
Jinya

Shōren-ji

Shiroyama Park

Traces of
Takayama Castle

taking people's rice away from them—was bound to provoke resentment. The bloodiest period of all came under a *daikan* called Ohara, who in 1771 put down an uprising of peasants who had burned down four merchant houses in a protest about taxes. One was executed and three were banished, but two years later another tax rise led to another riot. For quelling it, Ohara was rewarded with promotion to the senior rank of *gundai*. But in 1788, after another riot, it was decided that if two revolts could be put down to bad luck, three amounted to carelessness. Ohara was exiled for tyranny, and his chief officials executed. The story has inspired comic book accounts of the struggle of the heroic peasants which are on sale in the *jinya* shop.

The main entrance leads into the **Genkan-no-ma**, the highest status reception room in the *jinya* which only the *daikan* and his most important visitors were allowed to use. The wave-pattern wallpaper was also reserved for those of high rank: these are reproductions but original pieces are on display in the storehouse.

A wooden corridor runs along the slatted front of the building. Off it are rooms designated as the work places of officials and servants of various ranks: the *daikan*'s deputies, census takers, and the scribes who made fair copies of official documents. At the back is the **Hiroma**, a large formal room with *tokonoma* alcove, used for conferences. The **Shirasu** was an interrogation and torture chamber: officials sat on the *tatami* above, prisoners on the rough stones below. If these weren't uncomfortable enough, there was the *samedai kakaeishi*, a brilliantly simple instrument of pain consisting of square pieces of wood fastened together with their edges uppermost. Prisoners were forced to kneel on this so that the hard edges bit into their bones. Blocks placed on their laps increased the pressure. Stones are said to have been used for the floor because they were easy to keep clean. You'll also see here an Edo-period prison van: a big bamboo bird cage mounted like a palanquin for transporting captives.

One of the most important parts of the *jinya* was the **rice storehouse** where taxes were gathered. After a typical harvest, 15,000 60kg sacks would be held here for dispatch to the shogun.

Getting There

The most common way into Takayama by **rail** is from Nagoya to the south, which is on the main *shinkansen* artery, 2hrs from Tokyo and 45mins from Kyoto. Limited expresses on the JR Takayama Line take about 3hrs from Nagoya and 2hrs from Toyama in the north.

Sannomachi

The east bank of the Miyagawa River, at the bottom of Shiroyama (Castle Hill), is a preservation area with more than a dozen museums or exhibitions, all within 15 minutes' walk of one another, as well as several *sake* breweries, recognizable by the balls of cryptomeria fronds hanging out in front of them. These represent the traditional way of timing the brewing process. They were cut as the rice was mashed; when they became thoroughly brown, the *sake* was considered ready to drink. At certain times of the year, some breweries may open their doors to the public.

The following attractions are listed roughly from south to north:

The **Hida Minzoku Kōkō-kan** (Archaeology Museum, *open 7.30–6.30; adm ¥350*) was built in the late 17th century as a samurai house, and was later inhabited by the official doctor to the *daikan*. Its martial origins are suggested by one room with a booby-trapped ceiling which will collapse on the occupants when a rope is cut. The house's title is a bit of a misnomer: apart from its sturdy feudal architecture, it's notable mainly for the furnishings and *objets d'art* of its wealthy occupants; there's a small collection of prehistoric Jōmon period jars, daggers and phallic symbols.

On the street just south of here is an appealing shop called **Matsuoka** which specializes in *washi*, Japanese paper. As well as stationery, postcards and prints, they carry *ema*, literally 'picture horses', which are offered at temples and shrines all over Japan. In Takayama the custom is particularly strong: the paper *ema* sold in this shop, printed from a block first carved during the Edo period, can be seen all over the town, pasted onto the walls of homes and shops as a charm for good luck, good health and success in business.

The **Fujii Bijutsu Mingei-kan** (Folk Art Museum, *open 9–5; adm ¥300*) was rebuilt in glowing new wood just 20 years ago, and the exhibits are better displayed than those in the Archaeology Museum. The ground floor includes some big dishes of Imari porcelain from the Edo period, along with contemporary maps of known Japan. The first floor has dolls, textiles, tools and lion head masks.

Takayama-shi Kyōdo-kan (City Museum of Local History, *open Mar–Nov, 8.30–5; Dec–Feb, 9–4.30; adm ¥300*), is housed in a fine, big-beamed building formerly used as a *sake* brewery. The huge rice vats can still be seen along with exhibits concerning the guilds of firemen which at one time operated in every Japanese town. The Takayama firemen worked in fierce competition: their banners and sets of livery are displayed here. There's also a rather dull display of objects associated with the 17th-century *daimyō* family, the Kanamori.

The museum's **kura**, a white-walled fireproof storehouse where families kept their most valuable items, is today occupied by some prehistoric bits and pieces and several carvings by the priest-sculptor Enkū, a maverick wanderer whose rough, expressive work is unique in Japanese art.

During the 18th century, **Hirata Kinen-kan** (Hirata Memorial Hall) was a shop called Utsuboya, a supplier of two important commodities: wax candles, and pomade, crucial to the creation of samurai hair-dos. The two big *kura* storehouses at the back display wax making equipment, and exhibits on the history of illumination. The wax berries were dried and crushed, and their pulp squeezed, heated and pressed, the resulting gunge being refined in hot water. The left-hand *kura* features items relating to female beauty, including jars, pots and brushes used for tooth-black, an essential cosmetic for Edo-period ladies who considered the glitter of unpainted teeth disgusting. The right-hand room has good examples of the local Takayama lacquerware (*shunkei*), and bracken-motif ceramics. In the upstairs rooms are maps and early travel guides.

The **Hachiga Minzoku Bijutsukan** (Hachiga Folkloric Art Museum, *open 9–4; adm ¥300*) is another old family house with a standard collection of folk art and Edo-era antiques. The only specially interesting items are a collection of relics of the 'hidden' Christians who secretly maintained their faith after it was outlawed in the early 17th century. There is a statue of the Virgin disguised as Kannon, and crosses cunningly disguised in the geometric patterns on cups, on sword handles, or behind statues and beneath bowls.

The finest of the old houses, but also the most crowded on busy days, are **Kusukabe Mingei-kan** (Kusukabe Folk Art Hall, *open 9–5; adm ¥500*) and **Yoshijima-ke** (Yoshijima Family House, *open 9–5; closed Tuesdays; adm ¥300*). Both were rebuilt in the Meiji period when the strict sumptuary laws, which placed merchants at the bottom of the social scale and restricted the luxuriousness of their houses, had been repealed. As a consequence, they are built with unrestrained magnificence—huge beams support a soaring roof above an earthen floor where customers could enter and inspect merchandise. Inside are *tatami* rooms where business would be conducted, and where members of the family lived and slept. The smoking hearth was the focus of family life, especially during the winter; vents conducted the smoke upwards and partially heated the upper rooms.

The **Inro Bijutsu-kan** (Inro Museum, *open 9–4.30; closed Dec–Feb; adm ¥500*) contains a superb collection of *inro*, the lacquer boxes which Edo-era gentlemen used to carry on the belts of their kimono in place of pockets. The *inro* were attached by the use of a decorative toggle or *netsuke*. This collection is unusual in having many examples of witty pairs, the *netsuke* serving as the punchline to the design on the *inro*. Thus, for the *inro* inlaid with beautiful iridescent dragonflies, the *netsuke* is a hungry-looking frog. An *inro* design of swaying grasses is capped by a *netsuke* of a grasshopper. The craftsmanship, on the *netsuke* especially, is amazing: one tiny pod actually opens up to reveal two minuscule backgammon players hunched over a microscopic board. These are the consummation of the national love for small, shiny, ornate, highly-detailed objects, and represent some of the most uniquely Japanese art in the world.

The **Sakurayama Hachiman-gū** shrine, northeast of the Sannomachi area, is the town's principal shrine and, along with Hie Jinja on the other side of town, acts as host for two nationally famous annual festivals, the **Sannō Matsuri** on 14–15 April and the **Hachiman Matsuri** on 9–10 October. The reasons that these attract such crowds from all over the country are displayed in two exhibition halls. If you're not here for the spring or autumn festivals (they are certainly the liveliest times to visit Takayama, if you can get a hotel reservation), make a point of visiting them.

For centuries, the 12 Takayama neighbourhoods have sponsored elaborate floats (*yatai*) which are paraded through the streets for the duration of the festival. For most of the year these are kept in tall narrow *kura* storehouses of white painted clay, which you may spot as you wander round town. At any one time, however, 4 of the 12 floats are displayed in the **Takayama Yatai Kaikan** (Festival Float Exhibition Hall, *open 8.30–5; adm ¥600*), an attractive modern building in front of the shrine. Regular tours of the museum are conducted in English: ask at the ticket desk.

The *yatai* truly look like the carts of the gods: huge wedding cakes of iron, brass, paint, lacquer and gold, topped with a shrine-like roof, and drums, phoenixes or blossoms of golden zig-zags. They're the culmination of local craftsmanship and expertise, made without nails, and containing exotic ingredients like tassels woven from yaks' hair. Each of the 12 is different, and most have been much repaired over the centuries. Their exact ages are unknown, but the oldest seem to date back nearly 300 years. Built from scratch today, each one would cost about £2 million.

A *mikoshi*, a palanquin-style shrine, is also displayed in the hall, but it hasn't been used for 40 years—it weighs 2½ tons, and it's impossible these days to muster the team of 40 men necessary to carry it. The carts themselves are pulled along on wheels. Each also has a 'rainy-day' float, a small carriage with a banner bearing the name of the neighbourhood.

The most popular *yatai* are the ones with *karakuri ningyō*—ingenious mechanical puppets which perform cunning stunts on the tops of the carts. The Yatai Kaikan has a room with a continuous film of the two festivals which show these in action, but the place to go for a live display is the **Shishi Kaikan** (Lion Mask Exhibition Hall, *open 8.30–6.30; 8.30–5 in winter; adm ¥600*), just south of the Hachiman Shrine, which puts on a *karakuri* show every half hour or so. It's a hilarious and charming performance, like a kind of clockwork *kabuki*: the puppets (operated by levers from below, without strings) dance, walk up steps, abseil on ropes across the stage, vault on poles and perform spasmodic flips, jumps and costume changes. The secrets of their operation are passed down from father to son.

Hida Minzoku Mura (Hida Folk Village)

Regular buses from Takayama station make the journey in about 10 minutes. Open 8.30–5.

Attractively landscaped on a broad hillside a few kilometres outside Takayama, this outdoor museum of traditional architecture makes a good fine-weather antidote to museum overload. The houses and farm buildings, some of them 250 years old, were all lived in at one time, and several were brought here after the valleys in which they stood were slated for inundation as reservoirs. Most have thatch roofs, huge roof beams, earthen and *tatami* floors, and smoking hearths, which season and protect the wood from insects as well as creating an authentically fuggy atmosphere. Ancient rustic types sit around the fires, weaving baskets and chatting to visitors in dense dialects. The Nishioka and Wakayama houses are good examples of the A-frame, *gassho-zukuri* style still seen in some villages. The upper floors contain displays of materials used for silk worm cultivation.

(© *0577–*) **Where to Stay**

Takayama has some nice old *ryokan*. **Kinkikan**, © 32 3131, is noted for its great food, but little English is spoken. **Nagase Ryokan**, © 32 0068, is more famous and tends to get booked up. Both are *expensive*. The *inexpensive* **Minshuku Matsuyama**, © 32 1608, is close to the station. **Minshuku Hachibei**, © 35 2111, is near Hida Folk Village.

For a Western-style hotel, try the **Takayama Green Hotel**, © 33 5500, or the **Hida Hotel Plaza**, © 33 4600, which also has Western rooms, and is close to the station. Cheaper business hotels are much of a muchness: **New Alps Hotel**, © 0577 32 2888, **Business Inn Sansui**, © 32 4390, and **Takayama Central Hotel**, © 35 1881, are all close to the station.

Pension Ann Shirley, © 32 6606, is close to the castle park.

Takayama is a centre for *sansai ryōri*, a mountain cuisine making use of wild roots, grasses and vegetables. Most inns serve it as part of their evening meal. Failing that, **Suzaki**, ✆ 32 0023, is the best *sansai* restaurant, 250 years old, with five figure yen prices (reservations essential). It has a cheaper, less formal offshoot inside the same building, with *moderate* set meals. It is on the right, as you cross over the bridge from the Takayama Jinya and morning market.

If meat is what you crave, try **Hatoya**, ✆ 32 0255 for *moderately* priced hot pots such as *sukiyaki* and *shabu-shabu*. It's opposite the Kusukabe Mingeikan and Yoshijima house. **Ebisu Honten**, ✆ 32 0209, is an old shop serving *inexpensive soba* noodles, right in the centre of the old Sannomachi area, off Yasukawa-dōri.

Takayama's ubiquitous local speciality is *mitarashi dango*, chewy white blobs of pounded rice served on skewers, dipped in a nutty sauce and sold from streetcarts and stalls all over town for ¥100 a stick.

The Shōkawa Valley

In the mountains between Takayama and Kanazawa, highway 156 winds alongside the Shō River in a mountainous valley containing villages right out of the Hida Minzoku Mura. Many of the *gasshō-zukuri* houses here are family-run inns: book them through the tourist information offices in Takayama or Kanazawa. **Ainokura** is the most popular of a cluster of villages collectively known as **Gokayama**. To the south, **Shirakawa-gō** (the bus stop name is Ogi-machi) contains A-frame museums, an A-frame park and an A-frame temple. Many of the houses display materials related to silk-worm cultivation, for which the warm dark interiors of the house offered ideal conditions.

Kanazawa

Kanazawa is Chūbu's star attraction, one of the best preserved castle towns in Japan, with museums, old neighbourhoods and the finest stroll garden in the country. It was also one of the first Japanese cities to make conscious efforts at becoming foreigner friendly. The language courses run by the Society to Introduce Kanazawa to the World attract students from around the globe and, although there are plenty of *gaijin* around, few of them are tourists.

History

Kanazawa means 'Marsh of Gold' and, even if the stories about gold leaf floating up from the streams are exaggerated, the area has always been a source of exceptional wealth in the form of its rice crop. From the 12th century onwards, the Kaga region (which, together with Noto, forms the modern Ishikawa Prefecture of which Kanazawa is capital) was governed by the Togashi family who ruled from a fortress called Takao-jō. Then, during the turmoil of the civil wars of the 15th century, a remarkable revolution occurred. In 1488, the Togashi family were deposed, and their citadel captured, by a force of farmers

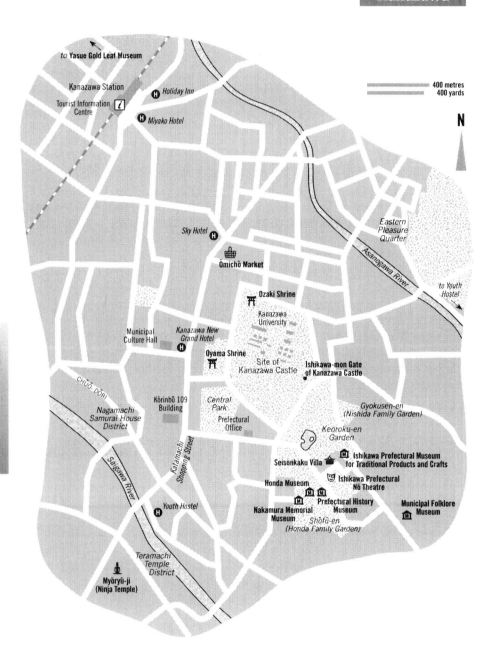

Kanazawa

to Yasue Gold Leaf Museum

Kanazawa Station

Tourist Information Centre

Holiday Inn

Miyako Hotel

400 metres
400 yards

N

Sky Hotel

Ōmichō Market

Eastern Pleasure Quarter

Asanogawa River

Ozaki Shrine

Kanazawa University

to Youth Hostel

Municipal Culture Hall

Kanazawa New Grand Hotel

Oyama Shrine

Site of Kanazawa Castle

Ishikawa-mon Gate of Kanazawa Castle

CHŪŌ-DŌRI

Nagamachi Samurai House District

Kōrinbō 109 Building

Central Park

Prefectural Office

Gyokusen-en (Nishida Family Garden)

Kenroku-en Garden

Katamachi Shopping Street

Saigawa River

Seisonkaku Villa

Honda Museum

Ishikawa Prefectural Museum for Traditional Products and Crafts

Ishikawa Prefectural Nō Theatre

Youth Hostel

Nakamura Memorial Museum

Prefectural History Museum

Shōfū-en (Honda Family Garden)

Municipal Folklore Museum

Teramachi Temple District

Myōryū-ji (Ninja Temple)

and monks of the Ikkō-shu (Single-Minded Sect), an off-shoot of Jōdo (Pure Land) Buddhism. The zealots were inspired by a radical saint named Rennyo, who had been driven out of Kyoto by rival sects. They founded a fortress temple on the site of present-day Kanazawa University, and for nearly a hundred years Kaga lived an independent existence as Japan's only theocratic state.

The century of the 'peasants' province' is still remembered today. Taxes were low; war, which was ravaging the rest of the country, was kept at bay. Government was administered on a decentralized basis, with communities organized around local temples. But national politics couldn't be ignored indefinitely. In 1580 the monks' fortress in Kanazawa was destroyed by the forces of Oda Nobunaga, first of the great warlords who united 16th-century Japan. In 1583, Maeda Toshiie was installed as *daimyō* (feudal lord). His heirs ruled for the next 285 years.

It was a great period for Kaga, and its principal city Kanazawa. Spared the destruction of the previous century, it quickly became the most productive region in Japan, yielding a million *koku* of rice (one *koku*, 180 litres, was reckoned as the amount of rice consumed by one person in a year). As the Tokugawa shoguns secured their control of Japan, the Maedas were able to direct their wealth away from military spending and into patronage of the arts and culture. Craftsmen from Edo (Tokyo) and Kyoto were recruited to create an urban culture rivalling that of both cities; the resulting lacquers, silks and ceramics were shipped all over the country. By the end of the Edo period, Kanazawa was the fourth largest city in Japan with a population of 120,000.

It lost its edge spectacularly after the Meiji Restoration, and opted out of the race to industrialize and internationalize during the late 19th and early 20th centuries. Today, Kanazawa is a small and out of the way city. In one way, this was its salvation: like Kyoto and Nara, Kanazawa was untouched by bombing during the Pacific War.

Getting There and Tourist Information

The cheapest **train** is the limited express from Tokyo's Ueno station, which reaches Kanazawa in a little over 6hrs, for just over ¥10,000. Pricier combinations of *shinkansen* and express can reduce it to about 4½hrs.

There are four **buses** a day from Tokyo's Ikebukuro and nine from Kyoto, taking 7½ and 4hrs respectively. Kanazawa's Komatsu airport is 55mins from town.

The **Kanazawa Tourist Association** has an office in the JR station. More useful and geared up to foreigners are the **Kanazawa International Exchange Foundation**, ✆ 0762 20 2522, near the Nagamachi samurai houses, and the **Society to Introduce Kanazawa to the World**, ✆ 0762 22 7332, in Honda-machi. Both are manned by good English speakers.

Site of Kanazawa-jō (Kanazawa Castle)

The central park now occupied by Kanazawa University was the strategic heart of the region. It was here that the monks of the Ikkō Sect built Oyama Gōbō, their temple-fortress, in the 1480s, and here on the Gōbō's ruins that Maeda Toshiie built his headquarters on his appointment to the fief in 1583. Fires were a way of life throughout its 300-year history. When the last big one burned down the keep in 1881, a time of anti-feudal feeling when many castles were being dismantled anyway, it was never rebuilt. Many of the walls and a few stretches of moat remain, however, and the grounds are a pleasant place for strolling, and a natural short cut from one side of town to another.

Two pre-feudal castle structures survive. The **Sanjū-ken Nagaya** (Long House of Thirty Bays) was a two-storey armoury, preserved today as the stacks of the university library. To the east, at the north corner of Kenroku-en garden, is the **Ishikawa-mon**, a complex of gates and turrets, itself the survivor of an 18th-century fire. It seems odd that such a resolutely stone edifice should be vulnerable to fire until you step underneath it and see the huge tree trunk which supports the main gate. It has an unusual roof of white tiles: they're actually made of lead and were intended to be melted down and turned into shot *in extremis.*

Oyama Jinja, the shrine on the west side of the castle, is interesting principally for its main gate, a unique and brilliant fusion of Shinto and European styles. The hand-rails and carvings are traditional, the red and blue stone is *tomuro* rock widely seen in Kenroku-en garden, but the pillared arches and stained glass in the upper window give the whole structure a hybrid, almost Mediterranean cast.

The shrine was built in 1873 on the site of the Maeda family's peace-time villa, the Kanaya Goten, and is dedicated to the first Maeda lord, Toshiie. Two years later, the gate was built with the collaboration of Dutch instructors from the Kanazawa medical school. Originally it doubled as a lighthouse, but high-rise developments have cut it off from sight of the sea.

Kenroku-en (Garden of the Six Qualities)

Open 7–6; 16 Oct–28 Feb, 8–4.30; the gate on the south corner, between Seison-kaku villa and Kanazawa Shrine, is open before sunrise; adm ¥300. Kenroku-en has lots of entrances. The description below begins at the garden's westernmost corner, a few metres down from the prefectural office (Kenchō).

Kenroku-en, like the Empire State Building and the Oxford Colleges, is one of those places in the world which attracts true obsessives—stroll garden fanatics who will happily spend a whole afternoon contemplating a particular turtle-shaped rock, or who can spout for hours about the significance of a patch of moss. According to Kenroku-en aficionados, at least eight hours is required for a cursory tour of the garden's rocks, while a superficial introduction to the best of the 11,800 trees can be squeezed into an hour and a half. One of the park's bridges is called 'Live-long Day Bridge'—this, it is said, is the amount of time that a true connoisseur can gaze at it before becoming restless. There is even a special 'Early Birds Society', the *Hayaoki-kai*, a fanatical band of elderly gentlemen who gather every morning at dawn to watch the sun rise over the beloved garden. In winter this is around seven o'clock, in summer it is closer to four.

Even if you spend only a couple of hours here (a full morning is the optimum time on a first visit, with refreshment breaks), you'd be well advised to follow their example. *Go to*

Kenroku-en as early as you can bear. Not only is it at its loveliest, but from 11am onwards the tranquillity of the garden is violated by a ceaseless procession of megaphone-toting guides, giggling schoolchildren, and cooing coach parties. The crowds tail off about an hour before closing time, but nothing beats an early start.

Kenroku-en wasn't created at a stroke, but developed over a century and a half as the accumulation of the taste and resources of several of the Maeda lords. It started off as an outer park of Kanazawa Castle, used to put up distinguished guests, and it wasn't until the 1670s that the fifth *daimyō*, Tsunanori, began to turn the high land around the guest villa into a formal stroll garden. Fires and cash shortages delayed the landscaping until its completion under the 13th lord, Nariyasu, in the early 19th century. Its name (literally 'Combined Six') refers to the six virtues possessed by a perfect garden: spaciousness, seclusion, artificiality, antiquity, abundant water and broad views. In 1872 it became a public park and until 1975, when the cost of upkeep became too much, admission was free.

Touring Kenroku-en

The admission price includes a pamphlet with a good scale map, labelled in English.

Entering by the westernmost entrance, you walk up a sloping path to a pond called **Hisago Ike** (Gourd Lake). The area around here is called Renchi-mon (after a gate just north of the pond), and represents the oldest bit of Kenroku-en. The lake, like many of the garden's features, is named after its fancied shape. **Higurashi no Hashi**, the bridge you're supposed to spend a whole day marvelling at, joins the path to the larger of two islands here. Its diamond-shaped blocks are cut from *tomuro*, a red and blue stone hewn from the nearby Mt Tomuro, and widely used in the garden, as well as in the castle walls and the graves of high-ranking feudal officers.

The lantern on the island was presented to Maeda Toshiie by Hideyoshi Toyotomi, who plundered it in the 1590s from Korea, along with much else. The **weeping cherry** above it is one of the great attractions of the April blossom-viewing season, when Kenroku-en is at its busiest (*entrance is free*). It takes eight days to blossom from its lower branches to its tips. The rocks of the **Midori Taki** (Green Waterfall) have been adjusted half a dozen times by different *daimyō*, searching for the perfect watery gurgle to accompany tea ceremonies in the **Yūgao-tei** (Moon Flower Pavilion) opposite. The essence of the ideal tea house was peasant simplicity, but there is something rather sophisticated about this one, with its broad veranda, complicated multiple roofs, and elaborate stone wash basins. The larger of these was reserved exclusively for the use of the *daimyō*; the smaller one, said to be a piece of fossilized bamboo from Thailand, was for his wife and children. A little modern tea house by the water's edge serves *matcha* (frothy green tea) and sweets.

A little higher up from the tea house is a **fountain**, Japan's first, constructed in 1861, and still operating on natural hydraulic principles with no mechanical assistance whatsoever. Water is piped in from mountains outside the city, and at one time supplied the castle as well as Kenroku-en. Its force depends on the pressure at the source; the jet is at its highest during the June rainy season.

To the right of the fountain, a path leads along the stream to **Kōmon-bashi** (Yellow Gate Bridge), carved from a single piece of *tomuro* rock. To its left, a particularly rampant rock formation has been christened **Shishi Iwa**—Chinese Dragon Rock.

The zoomorphic theme is continued at **Kasumi-ga-Ike** (Misty Lake), a big pond at the heart of the garden. The apparent island in the middle is actually a gargantuan turtle, with a rock for a head and a lantern for a tail, a traditional symbol of longevity. The flickering of shutters and clustering tourists will signal your proximity to **Kotoji Tōrō**, a lantern with one leg in the water and one on a rock, said to resemble the stringed *koto* instrument. This is the single most famous object in the garden, and a civic symbol. Nearby, you may find yourself menaced by a large tiger, poised to leap down on you and gobble you up. Don't panic: it's just **Tora Ishi**—Tiger Rock.

Clustered around the shore of Misty Lake are a number of gnarled and twisted pines, several of them suffering from typhoon damage, held up by a carpentry of scaffolds and supports as well as upright poles bound with plaited ropes. You'll see these on trees all over the city: in November they're unfurled like the ribbons around a maypole, and pegged into the ground at intervals around the trunk. They're called *yuki-tsuri* (snow umbrellas). The canopy they create keeps snow from settling where it could break the branches with its weight.

The lawns northeast of the lake provide a good view of the plain on which Kanazawa is built, and the Japan Sea beyond. To the southeast, the stream meanders around lawns and trees. The large copper statue represents Yamato Takeru, a 4th-century barbarian queller; it was erected in 1880 by supporters of a movement to invade Korea. To the south of here, the tongue of turf bounded by the stream contains several of the park's most famous trees, including an old pine standing on a gnarled base of its own roots, and the **kiku zakura** (chrysanthemum cherry), descended from a 12th-century clipping from the Kyoto Imperial Palace, which blooms a month later than the other cherries in a prismatic progress of red, green and pink. In the southeast corner, opposite the one by which you entered, is the maple-covered **Yamazaki Hill**, site of the Maeda *daimyō*'s ice house. Ice, cut in the depths of winter, was buried here beneath earth, straw and bushes. In the summer, express palanquins filled with it were sent as a gift to the shogun in Edo (Tokyo).

In the south corner are a number of interesting historical buildings, outside the borders of the park proper. The **Kenroku-en Jimushō** (park offices) are housed in a magnificent old samurai house, moved here in 1922, which used to belong to high-ranking retainers of the Maeda. The inside is off-limits, but you can nose round the mighty entrance porch. Look up at the high ceiling: it's still faintly stained with the blood of the victims of an ancient feud.

Kanazawa Jinja is a lovely vermilion shrine with a phoenix on its roof. Just after the big *torii* gate, to the right of a stone bridge, is a black stone believed to cure warts. The **Kinjō Reitaku**, to the west of the shrine, is a sacred well associated with Kanazawa's name, 'Gold Marsh'. Here, the story goes, a long-ago Kanazawa man was washing potatoes, when pieces of gold began to run off them onto his hands.

Seison-kaku

Entrance from the road on the southeast side of Kenroku-en. Open 8.30–4.30; adm ¥500.

This small, dazzling villa was built in 1863 for Shinryū-in, the Lady Dowager of the Maedas. On her husband's death in 1824, she had taken the tonsure. But the palace in which she lived out her last days couldn't have been less monastic. It demonstrates two things: the bold, unorthodox tastes of the Maeda family, in contrast with the austerity and understatement of Kyoto style; and the growing influence of Western imports even at this early stage, just five years after the arrival of Commodore Perry and his Black Ships.

There are crests on everything; the *tokonoma* alcoves are huge and sprinkled with gold. The wainscots of the *fusuma* sliding screens are decorated with playful motifs of turtles, butterflies and fish. The walls of the upstairs rooms are painted in purple, black, gold and ultramarine, and, instead of the usual paper, several of the *shōji* screens contain stained glass, imported from Holland.

Museums

The slopes and gardens south and east of the Kenroku-en used to contain the houses of high-ranking retainers of the Maeda clan. These days they're the home of half a dozen small museums, none of them especially outstanding in itself, but collectively offering a rich selection of local artefacts.

Just in front of the Seison-kaku, the **Ishikawa-kenritsu Dentō Sangyō Kōgeikan** (Ishikawa Prefectural Museum for Traditional Products and Crafts, *open 9–5; closed 3rd Thursday of month; adm ¥250*) is an essential stop for anyone planning to purchase local objects, and a handsome and informative museum in itself. Eighteen different products, from gold leaf to string, are exhibited in illuminating displays which demonstrate the manufacturing process step by step. There are three types of lacquerware: Wajima, a tough and durable lacquer from the nearby Noto peninsula, made with an underlayer of baked earth; Kanazawa, with a spareness and elegance suggesting Heian Kyoto; and the popular Yamanaka—simple, unpainted ware with distinctive grooves and lathe patterns produced on the turning wheel. Upstairs are beautiful displays of Kutani porcelain, famous for its deep overglazed colours. Unlike most craft museums, the price of the pieces is marked, and, although these examples are not for sale, it gives potential purchasers an idea of what to expect. Unfortunately, much Kutani ware is mass produced these days and individual potters with their own kilns are becoming rare and expensive. Anyone with a specialist interest should ask for an introduction at the International Exchange Foundation. Gold leaf manufacture is another industry almost unique to Kanazawa: 99 per cent of the nation's supply comes from here, and there is even a **Gold Leaf Museum** near the JR station.

A few metres south, and on the other side of the road, is the **Nōgaku Bunka Kaikan** (*Nō* Culture Hall), which stages regular performances of various traditional arts. If no show is in progress, visitors are usually welcome to enter for a close-up look at the polished wooden stage. (*Regular nō performances at 1pm on the first Sunday of every month.*)

The road running down the southwest side of Kenroku-en garden has two museums on it: the **Ishikawa-kenritsu Bijutsukan** (Prefectural Art Museum, *open 9.30–4.30; adm ¥350*), with a rotating collection of Maeda family treasures, including a famous incense burner in the shape of a life-size pheasant; and the **Prefectural History Museum** (*open 9–5; adm ¥250*), housed in a converted red brick barracks dating from 1910. Borrow the English-language pamphlet from the ticket desk to make the most of the routine displays. The best reasons for coming here are the regular visiting exhibitions and the 'Historical Experience Area' where visitors can dress up in suits of samurai armour and court kimono.

The area behind these two museums is called Honda-machi, after the samurai family who served throughout the Edo period as hereditary ministers and senior vassals to the Maeda clan. The Maeda estates were so rich that the Honda chief received 50,000 *koku* of rice a year—the largest stipend of any feudal retainer, enough to make him a *daimyō* in his own right in poorer parts of the country. The **Hanrō Honda Zōhinkan** (Honda Museum, *open 9–5; adm ¥500*), just behind the Prefectural Art Museum, is on the site of his old 300-room mansion, and houses the elegant family collection, administered by his present-day heirs. As well as opulent lacquerware, armour, medicine chests and household objects (many of them given to the family as the trousseaux of high-ranking Honda brides), there is a spectacular set of ceremonial 'fire-fighting' robes, gorgeous stylized versions of the felt uniforms worn by genuine firemen, embroidered with silk tortoises and dragons. The Hondas were also right-hand men of the Tokugawa shoguns, who granted them the right to use the *aoi*—the shogunal trefoil crest, which adorns many of the exhibits.

A flight of stairs behind the Prefectural History Museum leads down to the **Nakamura Kinen Bijutsukan** (Nakamura Art Museum, *open 9–4.30; adm ¥300*), another private collection, but the social and historical opposite of the haughty Hondas. This one was bequeathed by Nakamura Eishun, a wealthy local *sake* brewer, and includes Korean and Chinese ceramics, and Japanese paintings by Edo-period masters, exhibited in rotation. Look for the droll 16th-century calligraphy box, lacquered with the design of a big-nosed European merchant, and his equally ill-favoured parasol-bearer.

Nagamachi Samurai House District

The 109 Building, a gleaming complex of department stores and boutiques, stands on the west side of the street known as Kōrinbō, by Kanazawa's central junction. A couple of blocks behind it is a quarter called **Nagamachi** containing many of the city's best surviving **samurai houses**. Several of these are actually late 19th-century reproductions, but the best ones retain the traditional features: thick earthen walls topped with tiles, heavy defensive gates, elegant gardens and forbidding wooden mansions with slatted fronts. They tended to cluster along narrow streets around the outer edges of the central castle, and would have served as an outer defence in time of battle—invading enemies, milling through the labyrinthine alleys, would be vulnerable to attack by warriors hidden in these miniature fortresses.

From being the richest feudal retainers in the most powerful fief in the land, the Kanazawa samurai suffered a spectacular fall after the abolition of feudalism in 1868. Stranded without skills or purpose, and increasingly in debt to the low-caste merchants, they painfully tried to adapt to the new situation. Some, like the Nomura family, became farmers. For a short while their apple orchards were a success but, when large-scale production started up in Tōhoku, they were forced into selling off their large estate piecemeal. The last portion went to a rich businessman who replaced the house with one from a nearby village. The **Nomura House** (*open April–Sept, 8.30–5.30; Oct–Mar, 8.30–4.30; adm ¥400*) is today the only one regularly open to the public. Although no samurai lived in it as it is today, it's a pleasant rambling building. Escape from the irritating taped commentary to the upper tea room, which has a lovely view of the inner garden.

Another samurai residence open to the public, the **Terashima House**, is northeast of the castle grounds, not far from the Ume-no-hashi bridge.

Teramachi (Temple Town)

Temples, like samurai houses, were grouped together in the typical castle town, often at crucial points of entry into the city. The reasons for this too were defensive: attackers, it was reckoned, would be reluctant to burn and kill where there were priests and sacred images around.

Kanazawa has two temple districts: in the east on the far side of the Asanogawa River, and a larger one to the west of the Saigawa. The only temple worthy of note is in the latter: **Myōryū-ji**, better known as **Ninja-dera** (Ninja Temple, *open Mar–Nov, 9–4.30; Dec–Feb, 9–5.30; adm ¥500*). Founded by the Nichiren sect in 1643, it has probably never had anything to do with the famous *ninja* assassins, but it commanded a fine view of the area around Kanazawa and incorporates some ingenious defensive gimmicks in its labyrinthine interior.

Groups of visitors are shown round in guided groups of limited size, so it's necessary to make reservations on ℂ 0762 41 2877. Bookings can only be made in Japanese (ask the International Exchange Foundation to do this for you). The tours aren't translated either, although there's sometimes an English-speaking monk on hand to help out, and, after the lengthy introductory preamble, most of the tricks you'll be shown are self-explanatory. The main building is constructed to appear smaller than it actually is, with multiple mezzanines and hidden, windowless floors to confuse invaders, and there are dozens of secret doors, some of them opening onto two different passages, depending which way they are pulled. It's quite fun penetrating deeper and deeper into the belly of the building, but not as heart-stoppingly thrilling as the breathless monk guides seem to think.

Geisha District

Alongside Kanazawa's temples on the outskirts of the old town were the brothels and *geisha* houses of the pleasure district. The best surviving relics of this arrangement (common to many Edo-period cities, and the inspiration for much sniggering humour in the literature of the time) are in the **Higashiyama** area, on the northeast side of town. The old streets lined with wooden inns and tea houses are a beautiful place for a twilight stroll (in the early evening you might even glimpse one of the few surviving *geisha* who still meet their clients in this area). The restaurants round here are expensive, but the **Ochaya Shima** (*open 9–5; adm ¥200*) is open to the public. *Geisha*, of course, are quite respectable entertainers, by no means equivalent to prostitutes, but the rooms of this house have a deliciously illicit atmosphere, with brothelly red walls and a big door with a peep hole, where the *mama-san* could size up her prospective guests. On display are *geisha* accessories, such as combs, cosmetic jars, and musical instruments.

(✆ *0762–*)   *Where to Stay*

Kanazawa has some smart *moderate* city hotels. The choice is between a location close to the station, or one nearer to the castle and sights. In the latter category is the **Kanazawa Tōkyū Hotel**, ✆ 31 2411, on Korinbō, the main downtown shopping street. Opposite the station is the familiar **Holiday Inn Kanazawa**, ✆ 23 1111. In between the two is the brand new **Sky Hotel**, ✆ 33 2233. **The New Grand Hotel**, ✆ 33 1311, is close to Kenroku-en garden.

Chaya, ✆ 31 2225, is a luxurious *ryokan* near the station. **Murataya**, ✆ 63 0455, is an inexpensive wooden *ryokan* well used to foreign guests, and situated close to the sights on the way to the river and the Ninja temple.

Eating Out

Kanazawa's *Kaga ryōri* is a delicate, eclectic cuisine as distinctive as Kyoto's, which draws foodies from all over Japan. Its most famous dishes involve seafood, considered at its best in the winter months: *ama ebi* (sweet shrimp, eaten raw as *sashimi* or *sushi*), *tara* (cod) and *kani* (crab). *Kabura-zushi* is a winter *sushi* made of yellowtail and turnips, sandwiched in slabs of vinegared rice. *Jibu* is a thick, rich hot-pot, often made with duck. *Gori* is a tiny river fish, best in springtime.

Ōtomoro, ✆ (0762) 21 0305, is an *expensive* but impeccably traditional *Kaga-ryōri* restaurant. The proprietor claims descent from the chef to the Maeda lords (reservations required). It's on the opposite side of the road, and a block north, of the Kanazawa New Grand Hotel, on the way towards the station. The New Grand has a less atmospheric but equally classy restaurant in its basement called **Kincha-ryō**, ✆ (0762) 33 1311.

Daimyō Jaya, ✆ 0120 013488 (a freephone number), is less authentic, more touristy, but much *cheaper*—around ¥4000 for a set menu. It's a black and white, tiled building in the style of a samurai house, close to the Kanazawa Station Hotel.

The neon downtown areas north and south of Kōrinbō teem with the usual variety of inexpensive Japanese and international eating places, but for a more traditional atmosphere stroll south over Saigawa Ōhashi bridge towards the Teramachi district, where the Ninja Temple is also located. **Teraki-ya**, ✆ (0762) 42 2244, on the left-hand corner as you cross the bridge, is a fine *moderate* fish restaurant where you simply point at the specimens you want to eat.

Kyoto

Kyoto is one of the most beguiling ancient capitals in the world, but it is a beautiful city rather than a splendid one, and its charm takes some adjusting to. Here are no etched skylines, broad boulevards or monumental architecture. Kyoto's marvels are quiet and interior. The important things, like much else in Japan, are on the inside, hidden from public view: temples, shrines, palaces, villas, treasure houses, gardens. They are the finest of their kind anywhere. For anyone remotely interested in Japan's visual art and architecture, this is the place to start. The complaint that 'temples all look the same' doesn't stand up; the lesson of a few well-spent days in Kyoto is what contrasts of mood, style and setting Japanese art affords.

In 1994 Kyoto celebrated its 1200th birthday. For a good ten of those centuries visitors have been shaking their heads and promising one another that it wouldn't be there for much longer. The Japanese idea of *mono no aware*, nostalgia for the transience of things, was born in Kyoto and has flourished here ever since. It was invented by the courtiers of Heian-kyō (Capital of Peace and Tranquillity), as the city was originally called, and finds its fullest expression in *The Tale of Genji*, but the sentiment lives on in every contemporary discussion of the city, especially among foreigners. You should have seen it before the economic boom! You should have been there in the Occupation! You would have loved it before the War! In Kyoto it is axiomatic that Things Aren't What They Used To Be.

Don't be fooled. Things never have been what they used to be. They never will be. The image of a once perfect, now sullied Kyoto is a myth. Compared to the violence and unpredictability of earlier eras, the 20th century has been good to the city; there are better reasons than usual for believing in its survival for another 1200 years.

In the 10th century, priests and aristocrats got into quite a lather about the supposed imminence of *Mappō*, the End of the Law, a long period of decline and decadence which would culminate in the Buddhist Apocalypse. For decades it seemed as if they might be right, especially in the 15th century when feuding nobles torched the city during the Ōnin Wars. But Kyoto rebuilt itself, and came relatively unscathed through political reorganization under the Tokugawa shoguns and the transfer of *de facto* government to Edo (Tokyo). The next crisis was in the late 19th century when the Emperor moved out too, and when industry and Westernization were drastically altering the look of urban Japan. But the changes were absorbed and quickly became inseparable from the city's charm: when the streetcar system was torn up in the 1970s it was mourned by the same people whose grandparents fought so bitterly against its introduction 80 years before. It's a city that inspires deep love and loyalty: Kyoto's most recent brush with destiny came during the Pacific War when, against all logic, it was spared the incendiary bombs which devastated every other large Japanese city. The story goes that a Japan-educated art historian, Langdon Warner, talked the US War Secretary out of including it on the shortlist of targets for the atom bomb.

The newest threat is not war or apocalypse but development. In 1894 Kyoto celebrated its 1100th anniversary with the unveiling of the bold Heian Shrine. The 1200th birthday was marked in very different style: with the construction of the colossal new Kyoto Hotel and a thunderous new station development, both far exceeding previous height restrictions of 30m. Protesters foresee a nightmare escalation of skyrise construction which will overshadow the temples and block out forever Kyoto's mountain panorama. The city, they fear, will never be the same again.

History

From its foundation until the early 17th century, when **Shogun Tokugawa Ieyasu** moved the seat of administrative power to Edo, the history of Kyoto was the history of Japan (*see* pp.60–1). Political power might be bandied between emperors, courtiers and regents, wars and natural disasters might drive them from the city from time to time, but it was always Kyoto to which they returned. The Minamoto family tried to escape in 1185 by establishing their military headquarters (the *bakufu*, 'camp office') in the coastal town of Kamakura and appointing governors to keep a beady eye on Kyoto and its imperial occupants. It didn't work and, in the 1330s, the Kamakura rulers were toppled by a clever emperor whose schemes had been allowed to develop unchecked. Their successors, the Ashikaga shoguns, adored Kyoto and maintained its position as capital when it was burning about their ears. Always, power hovered over the Emperor's city, even if it rarely rested in one place for very long.

Kyoto's dominance of Japanese history is all the more remarkable when one remembers that, until 794, no capital had lasted for more than 75 years. In 784 Nara was abandoned by **Emperor Kammu** in an effort to escape the big Buddhist monasteries which had become greedy for a slice of power. A new palace was established at Nagaoka-kyō, a few miles southwest of present-day Kyoto, but the place gave everyone the creeps. There were murders and portents and court intrigues, and within a few years Kammu was scouting around for somewhere else to pitch his palace.

The choice of an auspicious site was a complicated business, made according to the strict rules of Sino-Japanese geomancy. *Feng shui*, as it's called in Chinese, conceives of the world as a system of energy flows uniting humans and nature, the animate and the inanimate. Any potential interruption of these 'dragon lines'—from a city, to an individual house or even a marriage bed—has to conform to their flow or risk misfortune to the place and its occupants. Kyoto's splendid position, like Nara before it (and like their common ancestor, the mighty capital of Tang China, Chang-an), is no accident.

The principles behind the city's location are best appreciated from perches like **Mt Hiei** or the platform of **Kiyomizu Temple**. It sits on a plain, sloping south towards Ōsaka and the sea, and bordered to the north, east and west by mountains—the back and arm-rests of a great geographical armchair supporting and protecting the emperor and his people. A river, the **Kamogawa**, flows south and west, and a mountain, Mt Hiei, deflects the evil forces which were believed to emanate from the northeast.

Internally, too, the new city followed Chinese models. Like Buddhist temples, it was constructed on a north–south axis. Just as the stars in the night sky revolve around Polaris, the great north star, so life in Heian-kyō (as Kyoto was then known) revolved around the Emperor's palace compound (*daidairi*) in the centre of the northern city. The streets were arranged in a five-by-four kilometre grid of intersecting avenues; one of these (on the site of the present day Senbon-dōri) was 85m wide and ran from the main gate in the south to the palace, dividing the city into an east and west district. Placed symmetrically on either side of this street were an east and a west market, east and west reception halls for visiting dignitaries and two temples which flanked the main southern gate.

The city has sprawled far beyond these limits, and the size and position of many of Heian-kyō's avenues and institutions have changed. But one of the attractions of Kyoto is how precisely the ancient avenues still frame the most modern developments. **Tō-ji**, the temple of the eastern district, survives on its original site today, and its reconstructed halls house statues carved during the lifetime of Emperor Kammu's son. The **Imperial Palace** has moved its position, but traces still remain of the great Heian pond garden which filled its southern stretches. Even when changes have been forced on Kyoto they have been made with the symbolism of its history firmly in mind. When the Tokugawas built **Nijō Castle** as a symbol of their power in Kyoto, they relished the fact that it had once been the site of a Fujiwara lord's villa, and before that the palace of Kammu himself.

Like Nara before it, Kyoto broke out of its neat frame and began to crawl east over the Kamo River. Communities naturally developed around temples, and these tended to cluster in the foothills at the edge of the city, especially **Higashiyama**, the Eastern Mountain. The western part of the city, prone in any case to flooding and poor drainage, atrophied and died. These days, the area west of Senbon-dōri is a dreary industrial zone with virtually no sites of cultural interest; before the Pacific War large parts of it were uninhabited marshland.

The grid pattern, though it survived, quickly became blurred about the edges. **Fires** made this inevitable: Kyoto was rebuilt virtually from scratch after huge conflagrations in 960 and 1180, and almost no original structures pre-date them. The greatest surviving Heian temple, **Byōdō-in**, is south of the city in Uji. **Kōryū-ji's Kōdō** is probably Kyoto's oldest hall, dating from 1165—**Sanjūsangen-dō** temple was originally constructed the year before but burned and was rebuilt a hundred years later.

Large-scale construction in Kyoto has come in phases, as successive rulers sought to establish their legitimacy. In the 13th century the ruling military class adopted the new Buddhist sect, **Zen**, and temple complexes like Tōfuku-ji and Nanzen-ji were founded, although much wealth and power was concentrated in the camp HQ, Kamakura. The

Ashikaga shoguns brought power back to Kyoto in the 14th century, although the many beautiful temples and gardens created at this time—including Saihō-ji and the Gold and Silver Pavilions—were overshadowed by the civil wars which convulsed Japan during the Muromachi period. The ten years between 1467 and 1477 were the most wretched of Kyoto's history. By the time the Ōnin Wars petered out—due more to sheer exhaustion than outright victory and defeat—200,000 buildings had been destroyed, Kyoto's population had dwindled from half a million to 40,000 and its *raison d'être*, the Emperor, was literally homeless, subsisting on noodle soup and flogging off furniture and even samples of the imperial handwriting. 'Today much of Kyoto lies in ruins', reported Francis Xavier in 1551. 'Many people have told us that it once had 18,000 houses, and it seems to me that this must have been true, to judge from the very large size of the city.'

Around this time, Japan's fortunes began to rise again under the great warlord **Oda Nobunaga** who began the slow job of uniting Japan. Nobunaga's talent, however, was war; the benefits he brought to the country as a whole were often at the expense of its capital. He razed the troublesome monasteries on Mt Hiei, burned the northern part of the city when it withheld its taxes, and only managed to build a Kyoto castle by stealing the heads of carved Buddhas to use as building stones. It was his low-born successor, **Toyotomi Hideyoshi**, who gave Kyoto the attention it deserved and lavished money on the biggest and most concerted restoration of the city in its history.

Hideyoshi's ambition and ebullience gleam through the magnificent structures which rose in the city during the Momoyama ('Peach Mountain') period, named after the hill in southern Kyoto where he built the second of his extravagant palace-castles. Both these structures were dismantled shortly after his death and their gates and halls distributed, piecemeal, to the temples of Kyoto, where they remain today as the most dramatically opulent buildings in the city. Momoyama architecture is recognizably 'Chinese' in appearance, with curved gable roofs and deep eaves sheltering elaborate carved and painted woodwork. Interiors are dimly lit and decorated with gorgeously colourful screen paintings applied to canvases of gold leaf. Later on, the ostentation of Momoyama art was taken to excess in the bristling vulgarity of buildings like the Tokugawa shogun's mausoleum at Nikkō. Under Hideyoshi, in buildings like the audience chambers of **Nishi Hongan-ji** or **Daigo-ji** temples, it struck its perfect note: assertive and confident, bold but never shrill.

Hideyoshi's lively extravagance found expression in other ways. He overturned the exclusive conventions of the tea ceremony by holding a giant tea party lasting ten days, to which all the tea lovers in Japan—*daimyō* (feudal lords) and peasants alike—were invited. Often these artistic diversions served a practical end, like the 52m Buddha (destroyed in an earthquake long ago) which he built in Higashiyama. Like Nobunaga he commandeered the materials of its construction; unlike his predecessor, they were not religious icons, but swords which were confiscated from the peasants and melted down. In 1591 Hideyoshi accomplished what Emperor Kammu had planned but never completed: 23km of city wall, a military necessity since the introduction of firearms by Portuguese sailors. Hideyoshi didn't follow the old plan in every respect though. The new fortification was not rectangular but irregular, reflecting the evolved shape of the contemporary city.

Kyoto didn't die under the Edo-based **Tokugawa shoguns**, but its character changed. The buildings wrought by Hideyoshi were demolished or dispersed by the new dynasty and the walls were left to crumble so that no sign remains of them today. Nijō Castle was the Tokugawas' main contribution to Kyoto's architecture, a lavish but little-used symbol of authority, a snub and veiled threat to the imperial house. Instead of being the centre of the empire, Kyoto became one terminal of the Tōkai-dō, the great arterial highway linking the emperor's capital with the shogun's power base in Edo. Kyoto was under the cultural influence, if not the authority, of the old court aristocracy, who built great melancholy stroll gardens for themselves at Katsura and Shūgaku-in, and dreamed of the halcyon Heian period. Edo, on the other hand, was the home of the warrior, as well as the ascendant merchant class who grew in importance as the population swelled and communications improved. This perceived distinction between the two cities survives today and the contrast—between the fey aristocrats and bonzes of Kyoto and the brusque warriors and rascally merchants of Edo—inspired much of the period's literature and drama.

Merchants thrived in Kyoto too; the richest endowed temples of their own, and financed civil engineering projects to alleviate the flooding of the Kamo River and link Kyoto and Ōsaka by canal. The leisure needs of this newly-moneyed class were provided for by pleasure quarters like the one at **Shimabara**, west of Nishi Hongan-ji temple, which was surrounded by its own wall, a city within a city. Crafts like weaving and ceramics became established too, and are still practised in the Nishijin and Kiyomizu areas respectively.

Commodore Perry always gets the credit for 'opening' up Japan and forcing the Meiji Restoration but, in fact, anti-shogunal feeling had been growing in Kyoto for decades. In the 1780s a samurai called Takayama Hikokuro had symbolically decapitated the statues of three Ashikaga shoguns and dumped them on the bed of the Kamo river. Ashikaga-bashing became a popular way of expressing indirect discontent with the ruling shogunal dynasty, and the plotters of the Restoration gathered their forces around the emboldened emperor. When the shogun was humiliatingly ordered to Kyoto to explain his dithering over Perry to Emperor Kōmei, it was the beginning of the end for the Tokugawas. In 1867 Kōmei's son, Meiji, received the shogun's resignation in the Great Audience Chamber of Nijō Castle. The following year, 1074 years after its birth, the Emperor left Kyoto for Edo (now renamed Tokyo) taking with him the status of capital city. Ironically, the triumph of Kyoto's Restoration forces spelt the end of the city's historic role.

Getting There

Almost everyone will arrive by **train**. The *shinkansen* takes 2hrs 40mins from Tokyo, 3hrs 35mins from Fukuoka (Hakata). **Tourist information** and major hotels and attractions are north of the station, beyond the Karasuma Exit.

Kyoto is served by **Kansai International Airport**. Connecting buses arrive and depart from **Avanti department store**, south of the station.

Orientation

Arriving in Kyoto by train is a shock from which many visitors never recover. This, they have been led to believe, is one of the most elegant cities in the world.

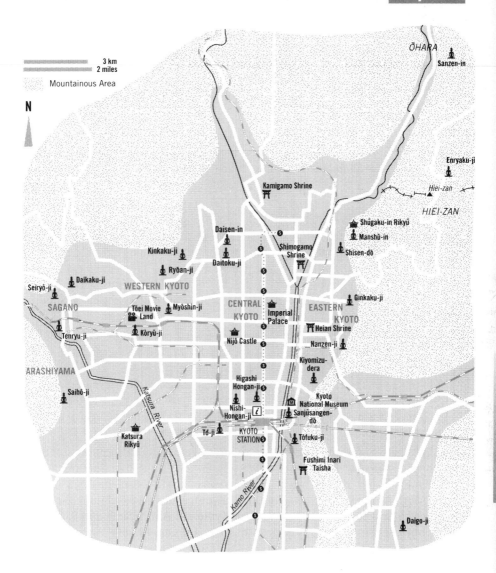

3 km
2 miles

Mountainous Area

ŌHARA
Sanzen-in

N

Enryaku-ji

Kamigamo Shrine

Hiei-zan

HIEI-ZAN

Shūgaku-in Rikyū

Daisen-in

Manshū-in

Kinkaku-ji

Shimogamo
Shrine

Shisen-dō

Daitoku-ji

Ryōan-ji

Daikaku-ji

Seiryō-ji

WESTERN KYOTO

Ginkaku-ji

SAGANO

Tōei Movie
Land

Myōshin-ji

CENTRAL
KYOTO

Imperial
Palace

EASTERN
KYOTO

Tenryu-ji

Kōryū-ji

Nijō Castle

Heian Shrine

Nanzen-ji

Kiyomizu-
dera

ARASHIYAMA

Saihō-ji

Katsura River

Higashi
Hongan-ji

Nishi-
Hongan-ji

Kyoto
National Museum

Sanjūsangen-
dō

Katsura
Rikyū

Tō-ji

KYOTO
STATION

Tōfuku-ji

Fushimi Inari
Taisha

Kamo River

Daigo-ji

When they finally fight their way out of the station (presently under noisy recon-struction), they are confronted, not with cherry blossoms and pagodas, but with a concrete plaza of jammed buses surmounted by the wretched Kyoto Tower, the stupidest civic monument in Japan. It doesn't even have the teeming ant-like quality of Tokyo's sub-cities. It looks like what it is—an abject failure of city plan-ning, a monument to petty cost-cutting and short-termism. At least nothing of

Orientation 315

particular value has been sacrificed to produce this mess—the southern quarter of the old capital was always one of its least savoury. But it does make one thing essential: get away from the station as soon as possible. Check into your *ryokan* or hotel, then escape quickly to a big temple or garden (**Kiyomizu** is ideal).

Ancient Heian-kyō's grid layout makes navigation simpler than in any other Japanese city—which isn't to say it's easy.

Nine numbered avenues, running east–west, formed the old city's lines of latitude. The northern boundary, **Ichijō-dōri** (First Avenue), is on the approximate level of today's Imperial Household Agency. The southern limit, **Kujō-dōri** (Ninth Avenue), runs just south of Tō-ji temple. All nine of these avenues exist today and, if you know your numbers, they are a useful indication of relative north–south position: thus **Shijō** (Fourth Avenue) station is north of **Gojō** (Fifth Avenue) and **Shichijō** (Seventh Avenue) stations, but south of **Sanjō** (Third Avenue) and **Nijō** (Second Avenue) Castle.

Unnumbered avenues form the north to south longitudes. The most important of these are **Imadegawa-dōri** (directly north of the station and above Kyoto's subway line) and **Kawaramachi-dōri** (parallel with the Kamo River). Major junctions are named after the avenues whose intersection they mark, and these compounds are often used for bus stops. So, for the teeming crossroads in front of Hankyū and Takashimaya department stores, you should get off at **Shijō-Kawaramachi**.

The bad news is that most of the places you want to visit were built outside this helpful grid. Big tourist attractions are well known and well sign-posted. For private addresses and smaller establishments the usual rules apply: ask for precise directions or a hand-drawn map with directions in Japanese which you can show to passers-by; collect business cards, match books and anything with a Japanese address on; allow plenty of time for getting lost and seeking directions; and carry a phone number in case you have to call and ask to be met.

This chapter is divided up as follows: **Central Kyoto**, with entertainment, conveniences and a few good temples and palaces; the few attractions of **Southeastern Kyoto**; **Eastern Kyoto**, the rich historical area on the far side of the Kamo River, enough for a holiday in itself; **Northeast Kyoto**, with a couple of rustic temples and an isolated imperial villa; **Western Kyoto** and **Arashiyama and Sagano**, really a series of separate, scattered attractions; and **Outer Kyoto**, describing the best of many day (or even half-day) trips possible from the city.

Getting Around
by bus

Since the demise of Kyoto's trams, buses have become the main form of transportation within the city. As the bedlam in front of the station demonstrates, they are numerous, and you can take them almost anywhere if you have time and don't mind the crowds and slowness. As well as **Kyoto Eki-mae** (in front of Kyoto

Station), there's a big bus station called **Kitaōji Bus Terminal**, on Kitaōji-dōri in the north central part of the city.

The standard fare is ¥200 and you feed your money into the driver's box as you alight. At bus and subway stations you can buy a **one-day unlimited pass** (*ichinichi jōshaken*) for the price of five or so journeys.

Both the International Community House and the tourist information centre maps carry colour-coded plans of selected bus routes. A more comprehensive map is available, but only the major stops are transliterated into Roman characters.

by subway

Kyoto's single subway line runs through Kyoto Station, beneath Karasuma-dōri and up to Kitayama station. Fares begin at ¥140; the one-day bus and subway pass can also be used.

by train

As well as the inter-city JR lines and private services linking Kyoto with the rest of Kansai, there are useful commuter trains connecting points within the city (main stops only listed):

JR Sagano Line	Kyoto–Nijō Castle–Uzumasa–Saga
Keifuku Arashiyama Line	Shijō–Ōmiya–Uzumasa–Saga
JR Nara Line	Inari–Uji–Nara
Keihan Main Line	Demachiyanagi–Marutamachi–Sanjō–Shijō– Gojō–Shichijō–Tōfuku-ji–Fushimi Inari–Ōsaka
Keihan Keishin Line	Keishin–Sanjō–Keage (near Nanzen-ji)– Hama-Ōtsu (Lake Biwa)
Eizan Line	Demachiyanagi–Shūgaku-in–Yaseyuen
JR Biwako Line	Kyoto–Ōtsu (Lake Biwa)

by taxi

Taxi drivers charge a bit less than their Tokyo counterparts, but are no more likely to speak English. **MK Taxis**, ℰ 075 721 2237/4141, has English-speaking drivers who—for a price—will act as guides to the city.

car hire

Mazda Rent-A-Car, ℰ 075 681 7779.

Nippon Rent-A-Car, ℰ 075 681 0311.

Both are near the south exit of Kyoto Station. Before hiring a car, enquire at the tourist information centre. They sometimes have English-language leaflets which entitle the bearer to big reductions (up to 20%). Note: driving in Kyoto is no fun.

bicycle hire

Rent-A-Cycle Yasumoto, ℰ 075 751 0595, near Sanjō-Keihan station.

Rent-A-Cycle Heian, ℰ 075 431 4522, west of the Palace.

Both of these hire firms, aimed at tourists, charge around ¥1000 a day. Much cheaper, at ¥100 per day, is **Green Flag,** ✆ 075 381 4991, with offices near Matsuo station and Nonomiya Shrine in Sagano. They can also arrange delivery and collection from elsewhere in Kyoto.

tours

Coach tours with English-speaking guides run daily except for New Year, and can include a trip to Nara as well as the big Kyoto sights. They're an expensive way of fitting a lot of superficial sightseeing into a short time: expect to pay ¥5000 plus for half a day and at least ¥10,000 for a full day. The two biggest companies are Kinki Nippon Travel Agency's **Kintetsu Gray Line Tours,** ✆ 075 691 0903, and JTB's **Sunrise Tours,** ✆ 075 241 1413. Many hotels and inns, large and small, act as agents for these companies and will make reservations for you.

Cheaper but, if anything, more irritating, are **Japanese-language tours** leaving from Kyoto Station. Enquire at the tourist information centre.

Tourist Information

The excellent **tourist information centre** (open Mon–Fri 9–5, Sat 9–12 noon; ✆ 075 371 5649) is underneath Kyoto Tower, a few metres up and on the west side of Karasuma-dōri, the main avenue stretching north directly in front of the station. The multi-lingual staff provide up-to-date maps, timetables, price lists, magazines, pamphlets and advice. They keep information on the rest of the country too. From outside Kyoto you can ring them free on the **Japan Travel Phone** line, ✆ 0120 444800.

Student **Goodwill Guides** can also be arranged from this office, an excellent free service which you should take advantage of, especially for sites like the Palaces and Nijō Jinya which can only be visited on a Japanese-language guided tour.

If you'll be in Kyoto for more than a week, pay a visit to **Kyoto International Community House** (open 9–9; adm free; ✆ 075 752 3010), near the approach road to Nanzen-ji, a few minutes southeast of Okazaki Park and the museums (buses 5, 27, 32 or 46 to Kaikan Bijutsukan mae; or Keihan Keishin Line train to Keage station). The material here is really aimed at longer-term residents, but the bulletin board advertises events open to all. There's a CNN TV link, an inexpensive French restaurant, and a library of foreign newspapers, travel guides and books on Japan.

The ICH also runs Japan's biggest **Home Visit** system, with 100 families who between them speak English, French, German, Chinese, Italian and Spanish. Make your application a couple of days in advance.

maps and media

English-language bookshops sell maps, but a perfectly adequate one of Kyoto and Nara is available free from the tourist information centre. Bigger and more comprehensive is the handsome map given away by the International Community House.

They're not supposed to give these to casual tourists, so you may have to exaggerate the time you're planning to stay.

The long-established monthly **Kansai Time Out** has features aimed at tourists and residents as well as comprehensive listings for theatre, cinema, music, TV, festivals, sport, meetings and exhibitions and hundreds of classified ads. There are countless English free sheets and events guides; best is the tourist information centre's **Monthly Information**, a newsletter listing festivals, markets, exhibitions, performances and special openings.

Kyoto Itineraries

You wouldn't waste your holiday in Japan if you spent every day of it in Kyoto and Nara. If your stay here is limited (likely if you have a rail pass from which to extract value), the following suggestions may help you divide up your time:

Day One—Eastern Kyoto

AM: Kiyomizu-dera and/or Sanjūsangen-dō (temples)
PM: Philosopher's Walk to Ginkaku-ji (canal and temples)

Bad weather alternative: Kyoto National Museum, Kawai Kanjirō's House (potter's traditional house), Museum of Traditional Industry (crafts).

Visit the tourist information centre and Imperial Household Agency to make reservations for special temples, palaces and Nijō Jinya.

Day Two—Northwest Kyoto

AM: Daitoku-ji (Zen temple compound)
PM: Ryōan-ji (Zen garden) or Kinkaku-ji (gold temple)

Bad weather: Kōryū-ji Treasure House (sculpture), Tōei Movie Land (theme park), Nishijin Textile Centre.

Day Three—South Kyoto and Uji

AM: Uji's Byōdō-in (temple)
PM: Fushimi Inari Taisha (hillside shrine)

Bad weather: Kyoto National Museum, Kawai Kanjirō's House.

Day Four—Central Kyoto

AM: Nijō-jō (castle)
PM: Nijō Jinya (ninja-style house)/Sentō Gosho (Retired Emperor's Palace).

For the Jinya and Sentō Gosho you must make a reservation. Both of these and Nijō Castle are good in wet weather.

Day Five—Western Kyoto

AM: Katsura Rikyū (Imperial Villa) and/or Saihō-ji (temple moss garden)
PM: Arashiyama and Sagano (pretty local neighbourhood)

Katsura and Saihō-ji require reservations; the latter is very expensive. You could spend a whole day in Arashiyama and Sagano.

Day Six—Northeast Kyoto

Early: Shūgaku-in Rikyū (Imperial Villa)
Rest of Day: Mt Hiei (scattered mountain temples)
Uncomfortable in bad weather. Shūgaku-in requires a reservation. Exploring Mt Hiei could fill a whole day.

Day Seven—Day trip to Ōhara

Festivals

Every week there are several festivals going on somewhere in Kyoto (see the tourist information centre's *Monthly Information* for a comprehensive list). Those given here are just the most famous *matsuri* which you might want to time your visit to coincide with. Bear in mind that big festivals always mean big crowds, and that accommodation, tours and everything else get booked up early at such times. Restricted temples and treasure houses are most likely to be open in the autumn, and most likely to be closed in the winter months.

January

1–3   Millions congregate at Fushimi Inari Shrine for **New Year** celebrations. Everything else is closed.

15   Edo period **archery** marathon at Sanjūsangen-dō temple.

21   **Hatsu Kōbō.** Lively festival, the first of the year, at Tō-ji temple, held in memory of the Buddhist saint Kūkai, posthumously known as Kōbō Daishi.

February

2–3   New Year according to the old calendar. Capers involving dancers in demon costumes, beans and fire (both to drive out the demons) go on at several shrines and temples. Check at the tourist information centre for times and places.

March

15   The anniversary of the **death of Shaka**, the historical Buddha. Numerous commemorative services and performances of religious drama. Giant torches are lit at Seiryō-ji in Sagano.

April

All month Geisha and their **maiko** apprentices perform **traditional Kyoto dance** at the Gion Kaikan theatre.

Mid-month Kyoto goes on a week-long drinking binge beneath the **cherry blossoms** which come out all over the city. Famous spots are the Heian Shrine, Imperial Park, Arashiyama, Maruyama Park and Philosopher's Walk.

May

15   **Aoi Matsuri** (Hollyhock Festival). Riders in Heian court costume process from the Imperial Palace to Shimogamo Jinja and Kamigamo Jinja, two ancient shrines in the north of the city, re-enacting a 6th century rite of thanks to the deities who saved Kyoto from a plague.

Third Sun   **Mifune Matsuri**. Musicians and actors perform on river boats at Arashiyama.

June

1–2   *Nō* plays performed by torchlight in the Heian Shrine.

July

All month   **Cormorant fishing** (Ukai) at Arashiyama and Uji. Trained cormorants dive for river fish from torch-lit boats.

14–17   **Gion Matsuri**. Kyoto's most important festival attracting millions of visitors, and featuring famous floats offered by the old merchant quarters. Music, lively costumes and carnival atmosphere.

August

All month   **Cormorant fishing** continues at Arashiyama and Uji.

Various days **Rokusai Nembutsu Odori**. Dances, noise and acrobatics to drive away demons throughout the month.

7–10   **Rokudō Pilgrimage**. Families welcome the spirits of the dead with lanterns and gongs in various temples near Kiyomizu-dera, an area where corpses used to be buried.

16   **Daimonji**. At the end of **Ō-bon**, the festival of the dead when families honour the visiting spirits of their ancestors, five huge bonfires are lit on the mountains surrounding the city. The most famous two form the character for great, *dai*. They can be seen simultaneously from tall buildings and hillsides in the north of the city.

September

Full moon   Moon-viewing ceremonies at Daikaku-ji and Uji.

October

22   **Jidai Matsuri** (Festival of the Ages). Thousands of people in historical costume parade from the Imperial Palace.
          Hi-matsuri (Fire Festival). Fiery torches are carried through the village of Kurama, to the north of Kyoto.

November

All month   Maple and ginkgo trees blaze into spectacular autumn colours all over the city, especially beautiful in Hōnen-in, Tōfuku-ji, Shūgaku-in Imperial Villa, Ōhara and Saihō-ji. Chrysanthemums in Nijō Castle.

First week	Several temples and halls which are usually closed admit members of the public.

December

1–26	**Kaomise *Kabuki*.** Annual *kabuki*-fest at the Minami-za theatre.
21	**Shimai Kōbō.** Last market of the year at Tō-ji temple, in honour of Kōbō Daishi.
31	**New Year's Eve** celebrations, include a fire ritual at Yasaka Shrine.

Visiting Temples and Villas

Admission fees and opening hours for Kyoto temples are fairly standard; only the exceptions to the general rules will be noted.

Try to start early. After 11am the famous temples become choked with crowds even off season. Buddhist monks rise at dawn and no one will mind a few discreet early visitors wandering around the grounds. However, halls and treasure houses, and anything involving admission fees and tickets, generally open between 8am and 9am and close between 4pm and 5pm. Many shut at 4pm during the winter months. Expect to be refused admission if you arrive less than half an hour before closing time. Kiyomizu-dera opens at 6am and closes at 6pm (occasionally even later), so it can be usefully fitted in at the beginning or end of a day's sightseeing. Dawn and dusk are in any case the best times to view this great temple.

Shinto shrines like Fushimi Inari Taisha and Heian Jingū never really close, although the Heian Jingū's garden does.

Certain smaller temples and sub-temples receive visitors for only a few days a year, usually in the autumn colours season at the beginning of November (the best time to visit Kyoto, if you can stand the crowds). In the pages that follow **Anraku-ji** and **Reikan-ji** on the Philosopher's Walk, **Kōdai-ji**, and the Abbot's Quarters of **Daitoku-ji** fall into this category. Several of the Daitoku-ji sub-temples not described in detail here also open only for that week, and if you're here in November you should certainly pay them a visit. Full and up-to-date details are always available from Kyoto tourist information centre.

Temple **entry fees** are between ¥300 and ¥500 unless otherwise stated; the November special openings generally cost ¥600. Only **Saihō-ji**, the Moss Temple, charges exorbitantly: ¥3000 per person (*see* pp.356–7).

Special Arrangements

Most of the places listed in this chapter can be freely visited without appointment but a few, among them some of the most worthwhile places in Japan, limit visitor numbers and require you to make a booking on a guided tour.

The procedures are quick and straightforward and no one should be discouraged by them: the limitations on numbers actually make these places a more pleasant experience by eliminating the human traffic jams which clog many temples. At busy times of year such as public holidays, August weekends and the cherry blossom and maple leaf viewing seasons, tours may become full in advance. Make your enquiries as early as possible and be prepared to offer alternative times and dates. Tokyo and Kyoto tourist information centres can help out with arrangements; so will the JNTO office in your home country, or a good agent like Nippon Travel Agency or JTB.

The Imperial Household Agency (Kunai Chō)

Subway to Imadegawa station. Inside Kyoto Imperial Park, just to the southeast; open Mon–Fri, 8.45–4, closed 12–1; ℂ 075 211 1215.

This should be one of your first stops on arrival in Kyoto. The Agency issues permits for the **Kyoto Imperial Palace**, **Retired Emperor's Palace** (both in Kyoto Imperial Park in the centre), the **Katsura Imperial Villa** (southwest) and the **Shūgaku-in Imperial Villa** (northeast). Bookings for the Imperial Palace can be made up to 20 minutes before the tour leaves. A tour of the Retired Emperor's Palace can usually be arranged on the morning of your proposed visit, and tours of the villas within a couple of days, but the Agency does not guarantee this and to be absolutely sure, you should make arrangements in advance. Outrageously, it is much easier for foreigners to see the palaces and villas than for Japanese, who often have to wait weeks for their applications to be processed.

One member of your party must put in a brief personal appearance at the office in Kyoto Imperial Park, and be prepared to list the full name, passport details and ages of everyone who wishes to be included—extras who turn up on spec at the last minute will not be admitted. For the Imperial Palace, children must be accompanied by an adult, which in Japan means over 20. In the other three, no one under 20 is allowed—though tall Westerners in their late teens probably won't be challenged. There is no admission fee to any of these places.

Your permit will usually be issued on the spot. Arrive promptly bringing it and your passports, which may be checked.

Tours are available at the following times:

Kyoto Imperial Palace (Gosho)—50min tour. Mon–Fri, and every Sat in May, Oct and Nov only: 10am and 2pm. During other months, every third Sat only: 10am. This is the only one of the imperial properties which sometimes offers tours in English. Ask when you make your application.

Retired Emperor's Palace (Sentō Gosho)—50min tour. Mon–Fri, and Sat only in May, Oct and Nov: 11am and 1.30pm.

Katsura Imperial Villa (Katsura Rikyū)—60min tour. Mon–Fri, and Sat only in May, Oct and Nov: 10am, 11am, 2pm and 3pm.

Shūgaku-in Imperial Villa (Shūgaku-in Rikyū)—60min tour. Mon–Fri, and Sat only in May, Oct and Nov: 9am, 10am, 11am, 1.30pm and 3pm.

Nishi Hongan-ji—tours of the *shoin* depart at various times between Mon and Sat. Reserve in English at the **Reception Office** (*Sanpaibu*), ✆ 075 371 5180, the modern block at the far left as you enter the Horikawa Avenue gate.

Nijō Jinya—45min tours at 10am, 11am, 2pm and 3pm every day. ✆ 075 841 0972. Phone in Japanese to make a reservation. The tourist information centre, a travel agent or your hotel can do this for you.

Saihō-ji—the tourist information centre issues a sheet showing exactly how to apply for this temple. From a post office purchase a return postcard (*ōfuku hagaki*) which is two-sided. On the 'send' side write the temple's address in the space below the blue stamp: Saihō-ji Temple, 56 Kamigaya-cho, Matsuo, Nishikyo-ku, Kyoto 615. On the 'return' side (bearing a green stamp) write on the left-hand side the address in Japan where you wish to receive your appointment card. On the right-hand side list the names of your party, their occupations and ages, and a choice of two or three possible dates. The 'return' postcard will be sent back to you with an explanation in Japanese and English. Turn up promptly on the specified date with this card and ¥3000 per person in cash.

Central Kyoto

Today's downtown Kyoto occupies the eastern half of Emperor Kammu's old capital, Heian-kyō. Not much of the imperial peace and tranquillity remains today, but the gridiron layout is obvious, and this area is still Kyoto's centre of power and leisure. The main rail and bus terminals, the single subway line, and the mass of its cinemas, hotels and department stores are located in a two and a half kilometre square north of the station and west of the Kamo River. Banks, local government offices, department stores, and useful businesses like travel agencies and airlines are all concentrated in the station area, and around the intersection of Shijō-dōri and Kawaramachi-dōri.

Equally abundant are heavy traffic, dense pollution and chaotic city planning. Few historical sites have survived the city's frequent levellings and the pressure to exploit this expensive land. With the exception of a few of the old wooden quarters, mostly around the canals near the Kamo River, this is the part of Kyoto most like every other Japanese city. Change your money here, stop by the Tourist Information Centre, and visit a few of the places listed below. After that, get out of the city centre to the east and west margins, where Kyoto is at its most distinctive and elegant.

Tō-ji (East Temple)

Bus 17 to Tō-ji, or 18 or 207 to Ōmiya.

Tō-ji's mighty five-storey pagoda used to be the first landmark glimpsed by travellers from the nearby port of Sakai, the symbol of arrival in Kyoto; nowadays it is overshadowed by the grotesque Kyoto Tower. The exhaust-singed quarter immediately southwest of the station is one of the least appealing in the city, but at the time of its founding it was key, marking the capital's southernmost boundary. Emperor Kammu decreed that there would be no temples within Heian-kyō itself (turbulent priests, after all, had been the main reason for quitting Nara), except for one on either side of the great southern gate, **Rashō-mon** (later the title of a novel by Akutagawa Ryūnosuke, filmed by Kurosawa). **Sai-ji** (West Temple) had burned down by 1233 and nothing of it survives. **Tō-ji**, its eastern twin, was luckier: in 823 it was entrusted to the care of Kūkai, the great founder of Shingon Buddhism (posthumously canonized as Kōbō Daishi).

Shingon, with its colourful pantheon of deities arrayed hierarchically around a divine central essence, was a useful doctrine for a ruler trying to establish his authority in a new, permanent capital. Tō-ji was awarded the title **Kyōō Gokoku-ji**, Temple-for-the-Transmission-of-the-Teachings-to-the-King-and-for-the-Protection-of-the-Nation. This special status, and the undying popularity of Kōbō Daishi, ensured rich patronage and survival as one of the finest repositories of Heian art.

The temple buildings are classically arranged on a north–south axis, although the most interesting are fenced off and entered via a ticket booth. (The rest of the wide grounds are open to all, and there is a big market here on the 21st of each month, the Daishi's traditional birthday.) The **Kon-dō** (Main Hall) is the biggest building in the temple. It was rebuilt around 1600 in stern majestic style, and has an interesting middle roof between the upper and lower eaves at the front. Within, a gold-covered statue of Yakushi Nyorai, Buddha of Healing, sits between Nikkō and Gakkō, *bosatsu* of the sun and moon. The statue is 3m tall but the great hall, flagged in diagonal stones, gives an impression of space and tranquil emptiness.

The single-roofed **Kōdō** (Lecture Hall) north of it is similar: from the outside, grand and rather haughty; inside, dim, voluminous and often very cold. The Lecture Hall, however, is transfigured and overwhelmed by its contents: an awe-inspiring, three-dimensional mandala, created through the arrangement of the temple's finest statues, many of them carved in the 9th century by Kōbō Daishi himself. Even without a precise knowledge of the identity and iconography of the 21 figures, the effect is profound and suggestive of the theological complexities of Esoteric Buddhism.

The statues form three distinct groups of five deities, with three guardians at both the east and west (right and left as the viewer faces them). In the middle of the central group, Dainichi Nyorai, source and essence of all things, sits in his royal crown, right hand clasping his left index finger in the sexual, 'All-Is-One' *mudra* (sacred hand gesture). Around him are four *nyorai* (Buddhas), including Amida at front left—all date from the Momoyama period.

The flanking groups follow the same pattern but these are original Heian period National Treasures. To your right are five *bosatsu*, earthly manifestations of the *nyorai*, their worldly status indicated by their crowns and jewellery. To the left, the show is stolen by a superb phalanx of the **Go Myō-ō** (Five Fearful Kings), many-armed, multi-headed bruisers, mounted on bulls or stomping wrong-doers beneath their feet, whose role is to intimidate evil and deliver the short, sharp shocks all mortals occasionally require. The mandala is protected at its corners by the Four Directional Guardians, the most handsome and familiar of which is **Bishamonten**, at back right, his miniature pagoda held high. Two of the finest statues are interpretations of Indian deities, standing between the pairs of

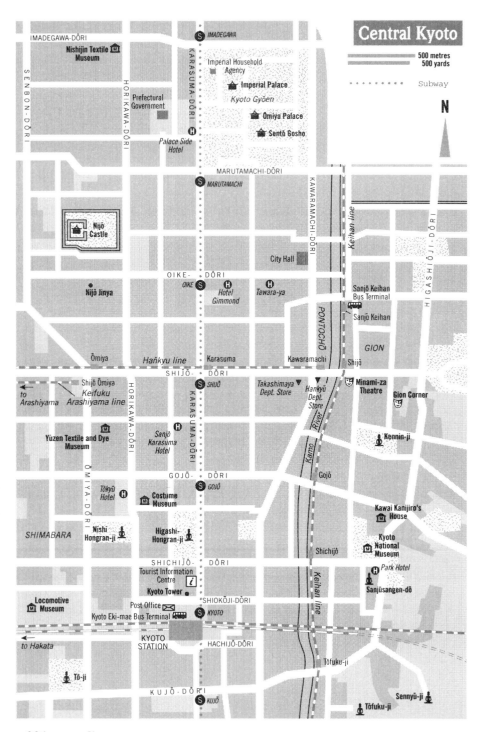

Guardians, one at either side: on the right **Bonten** (Brahma), four heads and four arms supported on a lotus borne by four geese; and **Taishakuten** (Indra) elegantly astride a Shetland-pony-sized elephant.

The **Treasure Hall** opens in the autumn for a special exhibition of its Tibetan art, as well as distressing examples of statues charred and mutilated in a recent fire. You may well see the restorers at work on them around the temple.

Just north of Tō-ji is the **Kanchi-in** sub-temple where frothy powder tea is served in an attached pavilion (say 'matcha' at the ticket booth and they will give you the more expensive ticket entitling you to this). The main hall contains a curiosity: five jowly **Kokūzō-bosatsu** statues from Tang China, their lotus leaves supported by a lion-dog, elephant, horse, peacock and garuda.

Nishi Hongan-ji (West Temple of the Primal Vow)

Buses 9 or 75.

Northwest of the station, off Horikawa-dōri, is another big temple, although stylistically and doctrinally it could hardly be more different from Tō-ji. **Nishi Hongan-ji** is a centre of Shin, one of the most popular Buddhist sects in Japan, a simple and accessible creed and the antithesis of Esoteric Shingon. Hongan-ji was founded in the late 13th century at the mausoleum of the sect's founder, Shinran Shōnin. For centuries, it was dogged by misfortune and persecutions, repeatedly burning to the ground to be rebuilt on half a dozen different sites. In 1591 it finally found a patron in the 16th-century warlord Toyotomi Hideyoshi, who donated the plot of land on which it now stands; the most notable of the present buildings were built over the next few years or moved here after his death from Hideyoshi's palaces.

Hongan-ji's abbots buckled down and did as they were told during the Edo period; consequently, it has survived virtually undisturbed as a matchless example of Momoyama architecture and decoration.

Note

Make sure you get the correct Hongan-ji. There's a **Higashi (East) Hongan-ji** too, offshoot of a 17th-century rift, and unmissably positioned on the main road in front of the station, two blocks up from the tourist information centre. The layout of the halls is virtually identical to the West temple, but the buildings here date from only 1895 when they were rebuilt after a fire. Such was the popular devotion inspired by the sect that female followers offered their hair to be plaited into great ropes used to haul building materials. One of these can still be seen, coiled in a glass case by the Amida-dō (Hall).

Touring Nishi Hongan-ji

The Amida Hall, Founder's Hall and courtyard are open to all from dawn until dusk, but the treasures can only be seen on a special tour. This is straightforward to arrange (*see* pp.323–4). No photography is allowed in the interiors. The temple **book shop**, to the immediate left of the main gate, sells an excellent glossy brochure with detailed information about Hongan-ji and the Shin sect.

The Shoin

The chambers and *shoin* (studies) of Nishi Hongan-ji contain all the traditional elements of Momoyama architecture, but compared to later examples of the style they are relaxed— pure heady opulence, unmotivated by the paranoia and obsession with hierarchy which pervades Nijō Castle. The temple's policy of limiting access has paid off: the condition of the wooden structures and, particularly, the colours of the paintings are outstanding. Look out also for the carved openwork transoms above the partitions; the panels of the coffered ceilings, each one hand-painted with an individual design, often humorous; and the ornate nail covers and sliding door handles.

The tour guide passes a gravel courtyard with a 17th-century *nō* **stage** to begin in the **Great Audience Hall**, a 203-mat room with the classic *shoin* arrangement of raised floor, staggered writing-shelf and *tokonoma* alcove, viewed from the main part of the room through a circular fan-shaped window. The paintings on the doors are by the great Kanō school, and illustrate the acts of good and evil Chinese emperors.

Next to it are small waiting rooms, each with a decorative motif. The **Chamber of Geese** follows the progress of these birds from the morning (right-hand side) to the evening (left); if you stand at the right-hand corner of the room and look up at the top left transom, the geese carved into it appear to be flying against a rising moon. The **Shiro Shoin** (White Study) is a jewel, with peacocks on fields of gold and unfathomably complicated carvings of birds and peonies. Opposite this room is the **Northern *Nō* Stage**, the oldest in the world, built in 1581 and set in black pebbles for enhanced acoustics.

The **Kokei Garden** is a curiosity: a dry gravel 'lake' with bridges and boulders but, remarkably, no pine trees. Instead, cycad palms lend the scene a spiky, un-Japanese air. Look at the ceiling panels in the corridor running alongside here: among the books, scrolls and scholarly appurtenances is a single cat, painted, your guide will explain, to protect the paper from mice.

The **Hiunkaku** (Pavilion of Floating Clouds), in the southwest corner of the temple grounds, came from Hideyoshi's Juraku-dai Castle and is ranked for its perfection alongside the Golden and Silver Pavilions; unfortunately it's closed to casual visitors. The **Kara-mon** (Chinese Gate), north of the main entrance in the temple's east side, is a typical Momoyama structure of curving roofs and rich woodwork.

Nijō-jō (Nijō Castle)

Buses 9, 12, 27, 50, 52, 61 or 67; or subway to Ōike subway station.

The buildings of **Nijō-jō** ('the most ornate, materialistic structures that a Japanese man ever raised for himself,' as Gouverneur Mosher called them) form one of the least typical and most fascinating castles in all Japan, more of a palace than a military installation, the ultimate expression of the aspirations and paranoias of the Tokugawa family. It was begun in 1602 by the first shogun, Ieyasu, soon after his victory at the battle of Sekigahara, and extended under his two successors until 1625.

Even its construction was laden with historical symbolism. Parts of Nijō-jō were recycled out of Fushimi Castle, the seat of Toyotomi Hideyoshi from whose son Ieyasu had recently seized power. He positioned them on the site of an old Ashikaga palace, hoping, justifiably as it turned out, that some of that dynasty's longevity would rub off on his own. The turrets looked insolently down on the Imperial Palace, just blocks away. In 1626 Emperor Go-Mizuno'o actually paid a visit there, an unprecedented act of submission. 'The castle is a symbol of...occupation by a group of outsiders,' wrote Mosher. 'Nothing could have less to do with Kyoto.'

Having made their point in stone and wood, the shoguns lost interest in Kyoto. Tokugawa Iemitsu, shogun number three, marched 300,000 men into the city in 1634 but, as the Edo police state established itself, blatant muscle-flexing became unnecessary. Several halls were dismantled, and Nijō-jō spent the next two centuries in political mothballs.

Then, in the crisis years of the late Edo period, a curious reversal took place. In 1863, with the foreign powers clamouring to be allowed in, the penultimate shogun, Iemochi, was summoned to Kyoto and instructed by the Emperor to resist all barbarian demands. His successor, Keiki, spent most of his beleaguered two-year rule in Nijō-jō, and the edict abolishing his office was promulgated from the Ōhiroma reception room. The very symbol of shogunal power was hijacked by the emperor; with satisfying irony, the Tokugawa dynasty came to a humiliating end in the very building designed to glorify it.

The Grounds

The main **East Gate** (Higashi Ōte-mon) is on Horikawa-dōri. Once inside, turn left then right to approach the **Chinese Gate** (Kara-mon), a preview of the decorative pageant within. The beautifully painted carvings (look especially for the tiger among the bamboo on the inside beam) will remind anyone who has been there of the Tokugawa mausoleum at Nikkō—both were crafted by the left-handed artist Jingoro, nicknamed *Hidari* ('Lefty'). But to appreciate fully the hyperbole of Nijō-jō, take a look at the baroque metal ovals set into the wood at regular intervals on this gate and throughout the palace. Eagles and chrysanthemums soar and bloom on them in copper and gold; they look like the shields of midget warriors. In fact, inasmuch as they have a practical function, they are nail covers, exaggerated beyond recognition.

In most Japanese castles it is the central defensive keep, the *Hon-maru*, which provides the focus of interest, and the outer buildings—the residences and administrative rooms occupied during peace time—which fall victim to fire and dismantling. Here the reverse happened. Nijō-jō's *Hon-maru* burned in 1750 and the site is occupied by a 19th-century replacement, brought from the Imperial Palace in 1893. It opens occasionally to the public, but the real attraction here is the **Ni-no-maru Palace** opposite the Chinese Gate.

Externally, the structure is unusual: five separate Momoyama-style buildings, joined by corridors at their corners, and staggered diagonally from southeast to northwest. Inside, the 33 *tatami* rooms compose a unique architectural map of the rigid social structure which the shogunate imposed upon the whole country. Everything was built on a grand scale, but the grandeur was carefully calibrated according to the rank of those for whom the room was intended, the outer block being for humble messengers, the fifth and inner room for the shogun alone.

The screen paintings, for example, were all done by members of the Kanō school, but different artists were assigned different chambers depending on the richness of their style. The carved transoms above the partitions sometimes depict different scenes on their twin sides: the more gorgeous one, with peacocks and thick gold leaf, faced into the room of higher rank. Above all, the buildings resonate (literally) with the Tokugawas' obsessive fear of assassination. Doors between the buildings can be unlocked only from the higher-ranking side; the 'nightingale floors' of the corridors sing squeakily when the slightest pressure is applied to them; and each of the five buildings has at its centre a concealed, windowless room where bodyguards lurked.

The first block, the **Tozamurai-no-ma** (Retainers' Room), was an administrative and reception area where low-ranking visitors were frisked and made to wait. The paintings are big, bold and symbolic: lions and leopards representing courage romp among the bamboos of moral rectitude. Here and elsewhere, many of the ceiling panels are damaged and crudely repainted: the vandalism occurred during the Meiji period when shoguns and their works were fair game.

Much the same style is seen in the adjacent **Shikidai-no-ma** (Reception Room) block where shogunal ministers carried out their business. The climax of opulence is in the central **Ōhiroma** (Grand Chamber), though this was not designed for the most honoured guests. Here the shogun received the outer circle of his *daimyō*, the feudal lords who had failed to back Ieyasu at the Battle of Sekigahara and whose loyalty might be in doubt: the intention was to awe and intimidate as much as to delight.

A tableau of mannequins dramatizes the magnificent scene. In the lower part of the room the shogunal ministers and visiting *daimyō* kneel opposite one another. Above, on the raised *tatami* mats, the shogun and a single page sit in front of a glorious *tokonoma* alcove, its shelf made from a single 5m plank of zelkova. To his left, a pair of bright red tassels advertise the presence, in the lightless room behind, of the shogun's bodyguards—tactfully kept out of the way, but no secret. The big chamber painted with pines and a hawk, on the other side of the Ōhiroma (viewed from the other side, on your return journey from the inner sanctum), was where these men armed themselves.

The **Kuro Shoin** (Black Study), where the *Fudai-daimyō* (inner lords) were received, is friendlier, quieter, more delicate in style; its painting of pines and herons on a golden beach by Kanō Naonobu is beautifully preserved, one of the finest in the palace. Sparest of all is the shogun's private apartment, the **Shiro Shoin** (White Study), accessible only to him and his female attendants. The partitions bear delicate ink paintings of misty Chinese scenes, and the hand-painted ceiling panels are of flowers, supplied as tribute by different *daimyō*. Even in use, the rooms would have been devoid of furniture, with tables supplied from the kitchen, and bedding carefully stowed.

Before leaving, glance at the **garden**, as sumptuous and expensive in its way as the palace. Its appearance has changed over the years and one theory holds that it was originally a huge dry garden, without water or even trees. The reason for this says a lot about the vulnerability of the Tokugawas even at the height of their splendour—the shogun, it seemed, didn't want to be reminded of the passing of the seasons.

Nijō Jinya

. One and a half blocks south of Nijō-jō.

It's hard to translate the word *jinya*—'encampment house' is something like it, although really they were unique institutions, products of the state apparatus during the Edo period. The Tokugawas' hegemony stood or fell by their handling of the *daimyō*, the feudal barons who governed the regions by proxy, and who were perpetually scrutinized for signs of over-ambition and revolt. Certain barons were permitted to build castles; the rest made do with smaller headquarters which developed in time into the fortified house known as the *jinya*. Another shogunal management technique was to keep the barons busy (and broke) with twice-yearly journeys between Edo and their regional seats. So commercial *jinya*, hired by the night, sprang up along the principle routes, where *daimyō* and their samurai could put up in the comfort—and security—to which they were accustomed. It's in this last category that **Nijō Jinya**, one of the most dastardly buildings in Japan, falls.

Touring Nijō Jinya

The house is privately owned and visitors must join the 40-minute tours which depart regularly (*see* p.324). The tourist information centre can also arrange student **Goodwill Guides**, and the *jinya* is a worthwhile place to take advantage of this free service—the tour commentary is extremely detailed and in Japanese only.

History

The *jinya's* first master, an intriguing character called Ogawa Hiraemon, had been a *daimyō* himself with a castle in Shikoku, but blew it all by backing the wrong side at the battle of Sekigahara in 1600. In Kyoto he re-established himself as a rice merchant and apothecary, and his aristocratic connections won him powerful customers who developed the habit of staying at his house—ideally positioned for both Nijō Castle and the Imperial Palace. Over the course of 30 years, Ogawa remodelled the place as a purpose-built *jinya*, cramming the tiny area with anti-espionage devices, unique decoration and brilliant defences against fire. It's tempting to see it as an early example of the Japanese genius for miniaturization—a capsule castle. At any rate, it survived incineration on numerous occasions, including the Great Fire of Temmei in 1788, and is still owned today by the 13th generation of Ogawas.

Inside the Jinya

Positioned in the heart of the capital city, Nijō Jinya was never designed to withstand full-frontal military assault. What Ogawa and his expensive clients feared most of all was stealth: the eavesdropping of spies, and the surprise attacks of *ninja* or disguised assassins. How real these threats were, and whether or not the ingenious snares were ever put to the test, we don't know: one of the interesting things about the *jinya* is that it probably says more about the atmosphere of paranoia fostered by the shogun, than about the actual dangers which *daimyō* faced.

The *jinya's* first line of defence is its unobtrusiveness. Even today, with a sign mounted outside for the tourists, it's easy to miss: a modest old merchant's house with sections of its walls constructed out of fireproof clay in the style of a *kura* store room. It's also misleadingly compact: there are actually three separate levels within, although the roofs suggest only one.

The tour proper begins in the **Ōzashiki** (Main Parlour), a 15-mat room where visiting *daimyō* could receive visitors, and the most lavish in the house. The floor of the shelf alcove here is a single 2m plank of maple, said to cost as much as the rest of the house put together; the screens are painted with a panorama of eastern Kyoto. The incense alcove to the left is inlaid with mother-of-pearl and also glass, an exotic commodity at the time; the porcelain nail covers would have struck Edo-period visitors as equally bold. But the room's most exciting feature is above your head: an opening in the ceiling, apparently just a skylight, which gives onto a sound-proofed hidden room where four bodyguards could lurk, listening in to their master's audiences below, ready to leap down on any aggressor.

By the garden south of this room, and at points throughout the house, hooks project beneath the eaves of the roof where wet mats were hung to repel the heat of neighbourhood fires. East of the **Ōzashiki** you will be shown a smaller room whose *tatami* could be lifted to uncover a miniature **nō stage**, complete with jars beneath the floorboards to absorb sound. Secret conferences may also have been held here: the screens contain an elaborate, sound-proofing combination of paper and wood, designed so that the shadow of any eavesdropper would be cast onto the partition.

On the north side of the house a small **garden** with a stone lantern is viewed from the **Kasuga-no-ma**, a 6-mat room with a painting alluding to the famous Kasuga Shrine in Nara where the Ogawa ancestors served. The garden pond represents Nara's Sarusawa pond, and valuables were submerged here in case of fire—the *jinya* had access to twelve wells and three ponds so that no part of the house need ever be without water. Each of the 24 rooms has at least three exits, many of them concealed. One such is found in the cupboard of the adjacent **tea room**; if that failed, defenders could hop through to the corridor outside, where the ceiling flips down to reveal a staircase to the second storey.

The upper floors of the *jinya* are even more cramped and shin-barking than the ground floor. The most interesting room is the novelty **Tomabune-no-ma** (Boat Room) which juts out over the former site of a large pond; its floor, now too weak to support visitors, is said to make a 'rowing sound' when stepped upon. There's another **tea room** with a raised floor, beneath which is a concealed hidey-hole. Various other chambers are reached via a narrow corridor made deliberately low and dingy to hamper swordsmen. At the eastern end, for attackers who made it that far, is an especially painful sequence of dirty tricks: two unguarded staircases, one of them leading only to a dead end, down which unwary pursuers would topple; and a series of removable floor-boards designed to trip enemies up before pitching them into the open pit below.

Kyoto Imperial Park (Kyoto Gyōen)

A few minutes' walk south of the east exit of Imadegawa subway station. Buses 51, 59, 201 and 203.

This large public park contains the **Kyoto Gosho** (Imperial Palace) and the **Sentō Gosho** (Retired Emperor's Palace). All the coach tours come here, but visitors who are short of time can confidently skip them in favour of the outlying Katsura and Shūgaku-in Imperial Villas. You will have to come to the park in any case, though: permits for all four places are dispensed by the **Imperial Household Agency** whose office is here. *See* 'Special Arrangements' (pp.323–4) for details of the tours and how to apply for them.

Imperial Palace (Gosho)

Visitors who come to the Imperial Palace expecting the Japanese equivalent of Versailles or the Forbidden City will be disappointed. Of all Kyoto's major attractions, this is the least vital: a series of impressively large, but listless, beige 19th-century buildings, set amid oceans of raked gravel. Since 1990 when Emperor Heisei discarded tradition to be enthroned not in Kyoto but in the Tokyo Imperial Palace, it's become little more than a museum. But even in its heyday, it was a self-contained private area closed to all but a few, and never intended to inspire public awe. The resemblances between these buildings and Shinto architecture, notably the Ise Shrine in Aichi Prefecture, are no coincidence. The buildings here embody not worldly power, but ceremonial authority, and above all the importance of ritual purity, expressed in the unvarnished natural materials and the empty courtyards of sere white stones. In the old days all forms of perceived uncleanliness—death or menstruation, for instance—were rigorously excluded from the palace grounds. No one bothers with such minutiae today, although you might detect a faint echo in the solemn entrance procedures and the exclusion of visitors from various areas of the palace.

History

The original Imperial Palace was west of the present site, part of a huge compound of ministries and pavilions accounting for one-fifth of the entire area of Heian-kyō. A permanent imperial home, to be used continually by successive emperors, was one of the cornerstones of Emperor Kammu's new city. But the place seemed ill-starred and fires and earthquakes eventually drove the emperors out altogether, back to the 'village palaces', temporary dwellings between which the itinerant court could move at its convenience. In 1331 one such village palace became the new permanent *gosho*, narrowly avoiding destruction in the civil wars of the 15th century. The present buildings are based on original designs, but the oldest of them were rebuilt in 1855.

Touring the Imperial Palace

The main gate of the palace, the **Kenrei-mon**, is in the south wall; only the Emperor may enter here. There is another gate for empresses or empress-dowagers, a second for imperial consorts, and the **Gishu-mon** for nobles. Visitors—even Prince Charles and Princess Diana—use the humblest entrance, the **Seisho-mon**, in the middle of the west side. Note the five parallel white lines which encircle the walls—an invariable sign of imperial status or patronage.

The tour passes by a number of tall porches where carriages and palanquins deposited their distinguished burdens, before wheeling to the left to pause between the thatched **Kenrei-mon** and a lower gate with tiled roof and vermilion columns, the **Jōmei-mon**. Rarely are tours allowed to pass through here, but take a look: this is the most important part of the palace. The enclosure, filled with raked gravel, was the venue for state ceremonies like the New Year Audience and religious services involving the emperor; architecturally, it echoes the pristine courtyards of the Ise Shrine. At the far side, built into the roofed corridor which surrounds the yard, is the **Shishin-den** (Pure Dragon Hall) where the thrones of the Emperor and Empress still stand, great inlaid platforms, with curtains and a canopy topped by phoenixes. The hall is 30m wide and 21m deep; its rippling roof is thatched with 40 layers of cypress bark, half a metre thick. In front is a broad staircase where nobles would stand, one step for each of the 18 ranks. To the east a cherry blossom, and to the west a mandarin tree, represent the Ministries of the Left and the Right.

The **Seiryō-den** (Pure Cool Hall) was the emperor's daily home in the Heian period and still contains chambers for the Empress and her maids, and a bedroom for the Emperor with a 20cm thick mattress of *tatami*. Later it became a ceremonial space: the rectangle of white marble in the corridor at the front was where prayers were offered to the imperial forebears at Ise. The **Kogosho** (Lesser Palace) belonged to the Crown Prince. The courtyard and garden in front of it were the venue for courtly entertainments like poetry-writing parties and *kemari* or 'kick ball', a Pythonesque game played by men in court costume with a sphere of deer- and horse-hide.

Retired Emperor's Palace (Sentō Gosho)

The **Sentō Gosho** was a product of the Japanese abdication system whereby emperors, while still young, could pass on the ceremonial responsibilities of state to their infant heirs. Early retired emperors sometimes wielded considerable influence as back-stage power brokers, a state of affairs which the newly-empowered Tokugawas were determined to avoid. They set about putting the imperial family in its place, first by marrying off one of their daughters to Emperor Go-Mizuno'o, and then by having him visit them in the ludicrously opulent Nijō Castle. A series of squabbles led to Go-Mizuno'o abdicating in favour of his half-Tokugawa daughter in 1629. For the shoguns it became essential to keep him busily occupied and out of harm's way.

The third shogun, Iemitsu, gave the plot known as the *Sentō Gosho* as a permanent home for the Retired Emperor and his consort. Originally it was divided into two by a wall running from east to west, the Emperor and his entourage living in the south, the Empress and her ladies in the north. But the palaces burned repeatedly and after the last blaze in 1854 the southern palace was not rebuilt. So the Sentō Gosho does not actually exist—the buildings that stand today in the northwest corner are the Empress's **Ōmiya Palace**, where an old Dowager lived until 1872. With the abolition of the abdication system in 1909, the supply of retired emperors dried up forever, and the buildings were remodelled in a Western style and used to accommodate visiting dignitaries, including the Prince of Wales in 1922.

 But it is the **garden** that visitors come here to see. Go-Mizuno'o was a cultured man and with his fat allowance from the shogun he was able to indulge his artistic interests to the full. He hired as his chief adviser Kobori Enshū, the outstanding landscape architect of his age. The garden has been changed and augmented by successive occupants, but the basic 17th-century plan remains the same. Two lakes, joined by a narrow channel, are circled and bridged by a network of carefully laid out paths in the manner of the classic stroll garden. This style, not so ladenly symbolic as the Zen dry garden, is artful nonetheless. The paths lead the walker through a series of carefully plotted viewing positions: vistas open up dramatically, framed by trees or the banks of artificial valleys, to direct attention to the terrain ahead or to give a new perspective on what has just been passed. The garden begins simply with the plain tree-fringed **North Pond** and gathers detail and artifice as one moves south. The two lakes are divided by a bridge between two lovely banks of maples; another, more ostentatious stone bridge reaches an island in the south lake. It zig-zags beneath a sheltering wisteria trellis, turning the stroller's gaze one way and then another. The most stylized and interesting area is around the southern lake which has a striking 'shore' of mango-sized pebbles, gifts from a *daimyō*, said to have been delivered individually wrapped in squares of silk.

Southeast Kyoto

Fushimi Inari Shrine

Train to Inari station (JR Nara Line) or Fushimi-Inari station (Keihan Oto Line); bus no.5 to Inari Taisha-mae.

The flat, smoky sprawl south of Kyoto Station is grim, but on its eastern side is Mt Inari, home of the photogenic **Fushimi Inari Taisha** and Kyoto's best urban escape. It's the chief shrine of what has become one of the most ubiquitous and popular of the Shinto cults—partly through the importance of its deity (Inari, God of Rice, and hence money and commercial prosperity), and also because of the inherent fascination of its symbols—the cute-sinister foxes, servants of Inari, which cluster the thousands of lesser shrines dotted over the mountainside.

The rice god has been worshipped here since the 8th century when the Hata, the local clan who donated the land for Heian-kyō, founded a shrine on the peak of Mt Inari. It was moved down to the present site in 816; the present **Sha-den** (Main Sanctuary) dates from a post-Ōnin War rebuilding as long ago as 1499, although it hardly looks it beneath its rich vermilion paint. The other structures in the precincts are a bit of a jumble: a big two-storey **gate**, a **stage** for shrine dancers, a **tea house** donated from his palace by Retired Emperor Go-Mizuno'o. The **Main Sanctuary** and **Worship Hall** are in the **nagare style**, with broad eaves sweeping out horizontally to shelter the worshipper. Elsewhere, and all over the mountain, you will encounter sub-shrines in every idiom imaginable: roofs curved and straight, in tile, copper and shingles, with and without *chigi*, those projecting 'horns' characteristic of early Shinto architecture.

But the shrine's most famous feature is to be found above these, on the paths leading up the slopes of the mountain. Clustered together, as close as they will stand, are thousands of red **torii** gates forming a series of low tunnels beneath which all climbers must pass. The *torii* are tax-deductible: those characters painted on them in black are not prayers or sacred texts, but the names of the companies which erected them (a supermarket, a swimming school), all hoping to win recession-proof divine favour.

Inari-san, the mountain behind the shrine, is one of the stillest places in Kyoto, especially lovely in the early morning. Tracks criss-cross the woods and bamboo thickets and you can amble for hours without taking the same path twice. Among the numberless miniature shrines stacked on top of one another you will find various deities represented, jumbled randomly among thickets of statuary—Kannon, for instance, and the fierce Buddhist king Fudō Myō-ō. But the mountain belongs to the foxes which, even within their basic pointy-eared, sharp-nosed design, take on an amazing variety of forms. Many of them are canine, but some are more like snakes, or even dragons. They can be seen grimacing, jumping, galloping or just sitting alertly to attention, like demonic grey-hounds, 'snickering weirdly at mankind' (Lafcadio Hearn).

The lanes leading up to the front gate of the shrine are notable for their pilgrim shops selling miniature *torii*, ceramic fox statuettes, and Fushimi *ningyō*—painted clay dolls sold as symbols of good luck. The pathetic-looking corpses on wooden skewers are another local speciality: broiled quails and sparrows.

Tōfuku-ji (Eastern Good Luck Temple)

Buses 202, 207 or 208.

This big Zen compound was founded in 1236 by an ambitious nobleman in emulation of the great Nara temples, **Tōdai-ji** and **Kōfuku-ji**, and christened by combining a character from each of their names. By the 14th century it rated alongside Daitoku-ji as one of the five great Zen temples of Kyoto, although the two can hardly compete today. **Tōfuku-ji** is justly famous for its matchless autumn colours which flare beautifully in November in a gorge of maples crossed by a wooden bridge. Otherwise the compound is sprawling and unkempt, with only one or two interesting buildings among the parked cars and empty paths.

The finest of these is the Kamakura-period **San-mon** gate, a National Treasure, although more immediate amusement is to be had from nosing round the long building to the west (i.e. left) of this as you walk in. This is the magnificent 14th-century **Tosu**, or lavatory block. You can still peer through the wooden slats and make out the rows of latrines which would originally have been partitioned into individual cubicles. Sadly, they appear to be unused these days—more than one has well-fertilized foliage protruding from within.

The **Hōjō** (Abbot's Quarters) dates only from the Meiji period, with unusual geometric gardens laid out in 1939. Cross the maple gorge by the **Tsūten-kyō** (Bridge to Heaven) to the **Kaisan-dō** (Founder's Hall) which has its own 17th-century garden: on one side mossy mounds, planted with shrubs and rocks; on the other, a chess board of squares raked into the gravel.

Sennyū-ji (Temple of the Bubbling Spring)

Buses 202, 207 or 208.

This little-visited temple was founded as a hermitage by the Buddhist saint Kōbō Daishi and rebuilt in 1218 on a spot where a miraculous spring appeared. Sixteen emperors are buried here, and the grounds have a regal air with broad quiet avenues and tall trees. The **Goza-sho** contains imperial apartments furnished in quasi-Western style with carpets, tables and chairs; beyond an expanse of gravel is the enclosed mausoleum containing the remains of the emperors, from the 13th-century Shijō to Kōmei, father of Emperor Meiji and the last of his line to live in Kyoto.

Just inside the main gate, on the left, is a small hall devoted to the **Yōkihi Kannon**, a Chinese image of a famous beauty and imperial consort of the Tang dynasty. This placid, rather cow-like sculpture receives the kind of attention commonly devoted to European images of the Virgin, with half a dozen different postcards and even Yōkihi paperweights on sale.

Eastern Kyoto

Sanjūsangen-dō (Hall of the Thirty-Three Bays)

Buses 206 and 208.

This extraordinary temple presents one of the most awe-inspiring sights in Kyoto. Ranged ten deep, in 100 diagonal rows, are 1000 gilt statues of the Buddhist deity of mercy **Kannon bosatsu**, all of them subtly different in the carving of their draped garments, in the arrangement of the ritual objects in their many hands, and in the texture of their ageing over 800 years.

Sanjūsangen-dō was founded in the 12th century by Go-Shirakawa, a brilliant and manipulative emperor who acceded at the age of 29, abdicated at 31 to take the tonsure, and died in his sixties after three decades of *de facto* rule as *Ho-o* or retired emperor-priest. Go-Shirakawa was born into the vacuum left by the decline of the Fujiwara, when the Taira and Minamoto clans played out the epic struggle that was to mark the end of the Heian Period. By keeping his allegiances cunningly flexible, he held on to power through a series of bloody wars and succeeded in wresting back some of the authority that had slipped away from the throne. Sanjūsangen-dō was the fruit of his friendship with the doomed Taira chief, Kiyomori. Eighty-five years after its foundation in 1164 it burned; the present building, and all but 156 of the statues, were replaced in 1266.

Its official name is Rengeō-in, Temple of the Lotus King, but everyone knows it as Sanjūsangen-dō, Hall of the Thirty Three *Ken*—the bays between the pillars in which the statues are arrayed. Their vast number, all of them facing in the same direction, gives the building unusual dimensions, only 16m deep, but 119m wide. Originally the outer wood-work would have been brightly painted; the dignified exterior gives little hint of the complex opulence within.

Sanjūsangen-dō was a response to the widespread belief in the coming of *Mappō*, the period of earthly decay which would herald the end of the world. To counteract its effects, seen in the civil wars of the late 12th century, priests and rulers placed their faith in sheer weight of numbers. Many new temples were built, monks spent lifetimes chanting the name of Amida Buddha, scribes repeatedly copied out sutras to be buried in special mounds. And in Sanjūsangen-dō the 1001 statues of Kannon were individually assembled out of wood, lacquer and gold leaf.

The arrangement and design of the statues are riddled with numerological conceits, best observed in the large seated central image. Like its companions, it represents **Jūichimen Senjū Kannon**, eleven-headed thousand-armed Kannon, a common manifestation of the deity who is also well known as a graceful feminine figure, the popular goddess of mercy. The eleven smaller faces are arranged around the crown of the head. Count the arms and you will find only 21 pairs: but these represent 1000, because every hand has the power to save 25 worlds (Buddhist arithmetic, it is true, leaves something to be desired). Each Kannon, what's more, can metamorphose into 33 different forms, depending on the needs of the supplicant. So the hall effectively contains 33,033 deities each capable of saving 1000 worlds—powerful allies, even in the age of *Mappō*.

There they wait like a Buddhist version of the US Cavalry, ready to sweep into action to save the world from the circling forces of darkness. The 42 visible hands pray or grip symbolic objects—a trident, a staff, statues of Amida, an axe, a wheel, a skull, a bell, a mirror, a lotus, a sword, a bow and arrow, a rosary, a flaming jewel. The sculptors, both at the original founding and the reconstruction, were all members of the family workshop which included Kōkei, Unkei and Tankei. Many of their works are signed, all are slightly different, and the game played by Japanese visitors is to search out a face resembling that of a loved one, often the recently deceased. More individually fascinating, however, are the **Nijūhachi bushū**, the 28 attendant deities, flanked by the gods of wind and thunder, which stand in front of the Kannons. These masterpieces of Kamakura vigour derive from Hindu deities. They include the winged, beaked birdman **Karuraō (Garuda)**; **Magoraō**, the five-eyed lute player; and **Basūnennin**, a deathly, emaciated old sage.

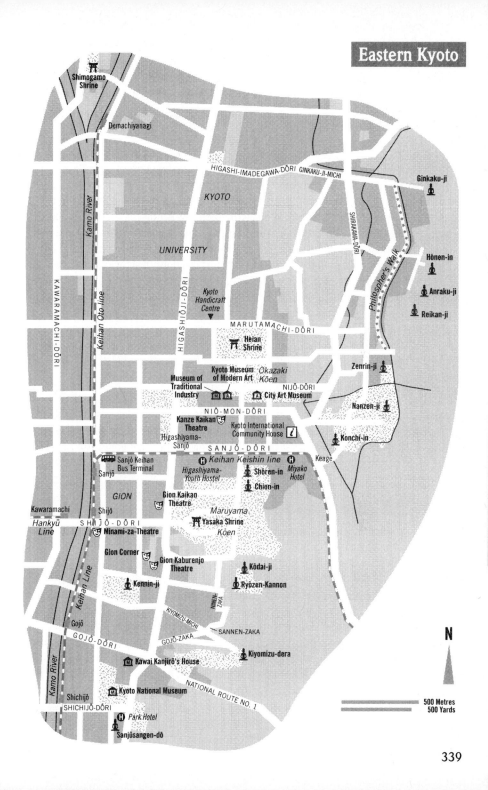

Eastern Kyoto

Shimogamo Shrine

Demachiyanagi

HIGASHI-IMADEGAWA-DŌRI GINKAKU-JI-MICHI

Ginkaku-ji

KYOTO

Kamo River

UNIVERSITY

Hōnen-in

Keihan Oto line

SHIRAKAWA-DŌRI

Anraku-ji

KAWARAMACHI-DŌRI

Kyoto Handicraft Centre ▼

Reikan-ji

HIGASHIŌJI-DŌRI

Philosopher's Walk

MARUTAMACHI-DŌRI

Heian Shrine

Kyoto Museum of Modern Art

Okazaki Kōen

Zenrin-ji

Museum of Traditional Industry

City Art Museum

NIJŌ-DŌRI

NIŌ-MON-DŌRI

Nanzen-ji

Kanze Kaikan Theatre

Kyoto International Community House

Higashiyama-Sanjō

SANJŌ-DŌRI

Konchi-in

Sanjō Keihan Bus Terminal

Keihan Keishin line

Keage

Sanjō

Higashiyama-Youth Hostel

Shōren-in

Miyako Hotel

Chion-in

GION

Gion Kaikan Theatre

Kawaramachi

Shijō

Maruyama

Hankyū Line

SHIJŌ-DŌRI

Minami-za-Theatre

Yasaka Shrine

Kōen

Gion Corner

Gion Kaburenjo Theatre

Kōdai-ji

Keihan Line

Kennin-ji

Ryōzen-Kannon

Gojō

KYOMIZU-MICHI

HINEN-ZAKA

SANNEN-ZAKA

GOJŌ-DŌRI

GOJŌ-ZAKA

Kiyomizu-dera

Kamo River

Kawai Kanjirō's House

NATIONAL ROUTE NO. 1

Shichijō

Kyoto National Museum

SHICHIJŌ-DŌRI

Park Hotel

Sanjūsangen-dō

N

500 Metres
500 Yards

Since 1606 an annual archery contest has been held at Sanjūsangen-dō, with contestants firing the 390ft width of the hall at a target for 24 hours non-stop. The record was set in 1686 when a 22 year old shot 13,053 arrows (544 an hour) and hit the target with 8,133 of them. These days a shorter exhibition match takes place on 15 January every year.

Kyoto National Museum (Kyoto Kokuritsu Hakubutsukan)

Opposite Sanjūsangen-dō. Open 9–4.30; closed Mon; adm ¥400.

Across the road from Sanjūsangen-dō, to the west of the junction of Shichijō-dōri and Higashiyama-dōri, this fine, compact museum provides a historical overview of Japanese art in all media, from the Jōmon to late Edo periods. It was established as the Imperial Museum in 1889 'for the purpose of collecting and protecting the cultural properties which had been kept in the old temples and shrines'. This, remember, was the mid-Meiji period when state-sponsored persecution of Buddhism was in full swing. It is true that many temples were selling off their works to foreign collections (mainly to compensate for the financial restrictions which were suddenly imposed on them), and the sturdy museum was much less vulnerable to the fires which every year carried off a few more master-pieces. Nonetheless, more than a whiff of coercion surrounds the circumstances in which the temples 'handed over' their treasures. Without them, though, the museum would be a shadow of its present glorious self. Temple and shrine loans compose only 16 per cent of the museum's holdings, but make up 80 per cent of its collection of National Treasures and Important Cultural Properties.

Sadly, the famous **French-style brick building** of 1895, itself an Important Cultural Property, is now used only for temporary exhibits. The main collection sits rather dingily in the concrete New Exhibition Hall, but it's compact and pleasingly negotiable. The first floor contains good prehistoric pieces, including a large clay coffin from a *kofun* burial mound, and ceramics, the best of them—including a winsome court lady with a Pekinese—imported from Tang China. The central rooms contain sculpture, ranging from the grotesque figure of Emma-ō, the king of Hell, to large-scale figures of Amida Buddha and Kannon, inscrutably aloof and inward-looking.

On the second floor are lacquerware and metalwork, and a selection of paintings, textiles and calligraphy which are replaced monthly in order to conserve them. The collection from which they are drawn is second only to that of the Tokyo National Museum in size and scope, and a few hours here, accompanied by one of the museum's inexpensive English catalogues, will give you a good grounding in painting of all periods. Among the most accessible are the ink paintings, many of them by monks. *Priest Hui Kuo Showing His Amputated Arm* by the 15th-century master Sesshū illustrates a famous Zen legend about a supplicant of the sect's founder, Bodhidharma, who proved his devotion by severing his limb; the scroll, with the ghostly, thickly outlined figure of the patriarch beneath the carefully hatched walls of the cave, combines horrid realism with the arche-typal qualities of an icon. Anonymous, but equally outstanding in their medium, are the hand scroll of the Hungry Ghosts, a poignant and curiously humorous admonition to penance; the lovely Hikone Screen depicting musicians, gō-players and stroller in a

17th-century pleasure quarter; and a stern likeness of Minamoto Yoritomo in stylized, almost abstract formal robes.

Kawai Kanjirō's House

Buses 202, 206 or 207 to Higashiyama Gojō. Open 10–5; closed 10–20 Aug, 24 Dec–7 Jan, and every Monday (except national holidays in which case closed the next day); adm ¥700.

On a quiet side street parallel to Higashiyama-dōri, on the second block south of the tumultuous National Route No. 1, is one of the most soothing spots in Kyoto, the preserved home and workshop of the leader of the Japanese *mingei* (folk crafts) movement, and one of his finest works of art. Kawai settled here in 1920 and in 1937 redesigned the house in a beautifully relaxed, hybrid style. The basic model is the traditional wooden rural cottage with floors of both wood and tatami. The furniture has the lovely rough elegance of *mingei*, but much of it is upright in the Western style—a fine line to be treading in the 1930s when foreign influences were vigorously discouraged. It's a relaxed, tactile place: you can browse through books and magazines on well-worn wooden chairs. At the back is Kawai's great multi-chambered 'climbing' kiln, deified as a Shinto god with a straw apron and paper zig-zags, but rendered unusable by anti-pollution laws. Arranged about the house are original pieces in bronze, wood and ceramics, many of them featuring a recurring motif: the mystical clenched hand with pointing index finger which obsessed Kawai in his later years.

Kiyomizu-dera (Pure Water Temple)

The traditional pilgrim's approach to Kiyomizu begins via Kiyomizu-michi or Gojō-zaka, two bustling alleys lined with souvenir, craft and ceramic shops. Ask a taxi driver for either of these by name or take buses 202, 206 or 207. Open 6–6.

A more dramatic approach to **Kiyomizu-dera** is by the little path which climbs the hill from the south side and suddenly reveals the temple buildings and the famous precipitous gallery across the gaping ravine, 'like being in a small boat on a calm sea and suddenly encountering a battleship under full steam' as Gouverneur Mosher wrote in the 1960s. In those days the path led 'through a small village, a quiet wood, a peaceful isolated graveyard'. The peace and isolation is today compromised by National Route No.1, but if you can put up with the fumes for a few minutes the detour is worthwhile. Starting at the Higashiyama-Gojō intersection, walk along the left-hand pavement of the National Route for 600 unpleasant metres. A lesser road leads up from here to the path for Kiyomizu. You know you are nearly there when you reach a small but elegant three-storey pagoda. The best view of Kiyomizu is from just in front of here, and a path leads down into the gorge, past restaurants and noodle shops, and up to the temple via the main stone stairs. The description of the precincts below follows the crowds from the main gate. Those coming from the back should simply read it in reverse order.

Kiyomizu-dera is to Kyoto what St Paul's is to London or Notre Dame to Paris: a religious institution that is also a national icon, a place famous for being famous, and known to people who have never been near it. Japanese visitors to Kyoto come here before anywhere else, and you too should make it a high priority. You could spend most of the day here, but the temple is close enough to the station for a taxi excursion between trains.

Many Kyoto temples are famous for just one hall or treasure: Kinkaku-ji's Gold Pavilion or Byōdō-in's Phoenix Hall. Kiyomizu has its postcard image too—the gravity-defying flying platform—but the temple's charm is pervasive, and there are no dull or disappointing parts. At first glance the precincts are a jumble, though a fascinating one. Steep, narrow streets crammed with noisy craft shops suddenly open out before a great red gate. Climbing through it, you encounter a three-storey pagoda, and an asymmetrical line of gates and halls overshadowed at the far end by the great roof of the main hall. From inside the latter, the reasons for the temple's informal arrangement become clear: the buildings occupy the ridge of a hill and below the main hall is a precipice over which it projects on wooden stilts. From this platform a huge tract of Kyoto can be seen, lapping at the feet of the surrounding mountains to west and east. Pilgrims have been climbing the hill to take in this scene since before Kyoto was founded. It is this spectacle, and the relationship it has fostered with the city below, that makes Kiyomizu such a special place.

History

The origins of Kiyomizu lie in the 8th century and a legendary meeting between two men: Enchin, a Nara priest, and the warrior Sakanoue Tamuramaro, the first man to receive the title of *sei-i-tai-shōgun*, 'great barbarian subduing generalissimo', for his victories over the Ainu aboriginals of the north. Enchin came to the remote mountain as a novice after dreaming of a golden stream—the 'pure water' of the temple's name, beneath which worshippers practise austerities to this day. There he encountered a mysterious old man meditating beneath a tree. The hermit persuaded Enchin to take his place for a while, and entrusted him with a log, and instructions that he should carve it into a statue of Kannon. The man, inevitably, was not what he seemed. He disappeared, heavenwards, leaving only his shoes at the top of the mountain. Plainly young Enchin was going to be waiting for a very long time.

Twenty years later he was still keeping his promise to the mountain deity, and wondering what to do with the log, when General Tamuramaro entered the picture. His wife was pregnant, and Enchin caught him in the act of killing a deer, the skin of which was thought to ensure safe delivery (Kiyomizu still has a nationwide reputation as an efficacious spot for the prayers of expectant mothers). The monk was horrified, and delivered an electrifying sermon on the evils of killing animals. The effect on Tamuramaro was remarkable. He became Enchin's patron and gave over his own house to be reconstructed on the mountainside as the first Kiyomizu Temple. The troublesome log was duly carved and installed as its principal image.

Enchin was a priest of the Hossō sect which, being based in Nara, was exempt from the destructive internal feuding of the later Kyoto temples. There were fires of course, but perched on its magic mountain the temple quickly became popular with the inhabitants of the new capital, and there were always eager benefactors willing to donate new halls and raise them from the ashes. In 1629 all but four burned down; the present buildings date largely from the second Tokugawa shogun's rebuilding of 1633, but they're believed to follow the old designs closely. By Kyoto standards, Kiyomizu's buildings, though distinguished, are young. They are only a part of its complex charm which, like a Shinto shrine, depends as much on nature as on architecture, and on the numinous beauty of the place itself.

The Precincts

The 1629 fire did its greatest damage in the east, and several of the buildings at the west end predate it. The red **Niō-mon** (Gate of the Two Kings) and its guardian deities are 15th century, and the bell in the facing **bell tower** was cast in 1478, making these the oldest features of the temple. The bell tower itself and the **Sai-mon** (West Gate) are about a hundred years younger: the carved animal heads and deeply curved Chinese gables are typical features of Momoyama architecture. Beyond the West Gate is the three-storey pagoda followed, in an irregular line, by the **Sutra Hall** and **Tamura-dō**, honouring the temple's heroic founder. The latter building was originally Kiyomizu's main hall, and it still contains statues of the *dramatis personae* of the founding myth: Enchin, the hermit-deity, Tamuramaro and Takako, the pregnant wife.

Just before the Main Hall, and swarming with schoolchildren on most days, are the curious *geta* **(clogs) and staff of Benkei**, the sidekick of the 12th-century warrior Minamoto Yoshitsune.

Countless legendary accounts of heroism and strength feature the heroic pair, who were finally hounded to their deaths by Minamoto Yoritomo, Yoshitsune's jealous older brother. In several ways they resemble Robin Hood and Friar Tuck. Just as in the English legend, the young warrior won the holy man's respect by defeating him in a staff fight on a bridge—the Gojō-bashi in Kyoto. In one version of the legend, Benkei was so confident of beating the young Yoshitsune that he braggingly swapped his wooden staff and clogs for ones made of iron, thus ensuring his own humiliation. The giant set displayed here, actually 19th-century reproductions donated by a grateful blacksmith who was cured of his blindness, commemorate the famous incident.

Kiyomizu's present **Hon-dō** (Main Hall) dates from 1633, but its unique structure bears the traces of centuries of growth and adaptation. The famous jutting platform, suspended above the ravine by five layers of interlocking wooden scaffolding, was not, of course, designed as an observation platform. It is actually a stage for shrine dancers—its wings can accommodate an orchestra—and the feat of engineering which enables it to hang suspended in mid-air was actually a brilliant piece of improvisation. When this became the site of the first worship hall, Kiyomizu was a remote and little-visited temple. Buddhism, too, was then a much more self-contained and inward-looking religion, centred upon the rites of a few priests and not requiring space for lay worshippers. When these started to arrive in large numbers there was only one direction in which to build from the crowded hillside—out, into space. Tales are told of worshippers who jumped off the edge to survive or break their necks, according to their faith or sinfulness.

Kiyomizu's eccentric development also shows in what many consider to be its finest feature—its immense shingle roof, best appreciated from the slope leading to the small shrine behind. The original roof structure—with its thick ridge and hipped ends—is still apparent, but has been augmented by the hip-and-gable projections which cover the orchestra wings. It's the interplay of these two elements—the great, massy, convex roof and the lighter, perpendicular, concave extensions—which gives the hall its restless energy.

Inside, the principal image of eleven-headed, thousand-armed Kannon is said to be the one carved by Enchin from Gyōei's log, and is so sacred that it is displayed only once every 33 years, even to the temple's priests. The visible statues include Jizō and Bishamonten, and the 28 disciples of Kannon, but more appealing are the big weather-beaten **ema** (votive plaques) which hang beneath the wide eaves. Several depict horses, three show early Edo period ships and are famous for the supposedly occidental faces among the sailors on deck. *In situ* they are hard to make out; reproductions can be seen in the nearby **pilgrims' shop**.

Other Buildings

The priests' lodgings and administrative headquarters of Kiyomizu are in a sub-temple called **Jōju-in** (Achievement Temple), closed to tourists for most of the year but worth seeking out during its brief open season in early November. Tucked away in the north part of the compound is a famous **pond garden**, unreliably attributed to the 17th-century master Kobori Enshū, which makes famous use of the 'borrowed scenery' of the Yuya Valley at its rear.

There are more fine views from the **Jishū-gongen**, an independent Shinto shrine within the Kiyomizu precincts, said to have been founded at the same time in 798. The buildings, with curved Momoyama-style gables, are pleasant enough, but the shrine's greatest pull is its self-proclaimed status as a 'Love Shrine'. Charms and amulets promise amorous success, and the yard in front contains two stones which are said to bring fortune in love to anyone who can walk between them with eyes closed.

The Eastern Halls

To the east of the main hall a set of wide stairs descends into the ravine, and a row of smaller halls stands above it, their backs against the hillside. The northernmost of these, and the smallest, is dedicated to Jizō, the *bosatsu* who protects travellers and children. Next to it the **Shaka-dō** honours the historical Buddha, and next to that is the hall of Amida Buddha (**Amida-dō**), an unusual example of a Jōdo sect hall in a Hossō sect temple. The hall next to it, **Oku-no-in** (Inner Temple), also raised up on piles and housing a statue of Kannon, is one of the most important in Kiyomizu, and the focus of much of its symbolism. This was the spot where Enchin first met the supernatural hermit. The golden spring of his dream, **Otowa-no-taki** (Sound of Feathers Waterfall), flows out of the mountain just below it, and behind the hall is another emblem of water and purity: an image of Kannon standing in a flowing basin which worshippers anoint as an act of devotion.

Gion

Centered upon Shijō-dōri, between the Kamo River to the west and Maruyama Park to the east, **Gion** is celebrated as the home of Kyoto's most famous **geisha**—or *geiko*, to use the local word. Kyoto *geiko* become older and fewer every year and, unless you have expensive connections, the innocent pleasures they provide (singing, dancing, joke-telling; *geisha* are not prostitutes, although they may become mistresses of their well-established clients) are beyond the reach of tourists. The few still left are most likely to be seen in the early evening when they walk or are driven to the tea houses where they perform their entertainments; or at the annual Miyako Odori dance season in April (it's said that these days non-*geiko* are recruited for these displays to swell numbers)—*see* p.320.

Other peak times for visiting Gion are the **cherry blossom season** in April, when Maruyama Park becomes a human carpet of drunken picnickers; **New Year's Eve**, when the entire city seems to converge on the Yasaka Shrine to light tapers of rope from a sacred fire; and 17 July when the city stops for the **Gion Matsuri** parade of ancient shrine floats. Gion also has Kyoto's greatest concentration of traditional shops; the best of these are listed in the 'Shopping' section.

Exploring Gion

Walking east from **Shijō station**, the first notable building is the **Minami-za** theatre on the right, a bristling tiled structure where the country's top *kabuki* actors perform their December *Kaomise* (Face-showing) season. Three hundred metres down, the road is crossed by Hanami-kōji, an attractive street of old **tea houses**, many of them fronted with the angled bamboo slats called 'dog-repellers'. To the south is **Gion Corner**, which presents a nightly show of traditional arts for tourists, and **Gion Kaburenjō** where the *geiko* perform their spring dance season. On the southeast corner of the Hanami-kōji crossing is **Ichiriki-tei**, an old and exclusive tea house and a prime *geiko*-spotting point.

Shijō-dōri ends at a T-junction opposite the heart of the district, the **Yasaka Jinja** (Yasaka Shrine, also known as **Gion Shrine**), and one of the liveliest spots in the city, especially on summer evenings when food and souvenir vendors erect stalls under the trees. The shrine is said to have been founded in the 7th century by Korean immigrants, and the surviving buildings show a strong Buddhist influence, diluted somewhat after the 19th-century Meiji Restoration when Shinto-Buddhist syncretism was discouraged. **Maruyama Kōen** (Maruyama Park) is just behind here, and northeast of it **Chion-in**, temple head-quarters of the Jōdo sect, a huge and rather overbearing place, with the biggest temple gate in Japan (the **San-mon**, dating from 1619), and a famous bell rung 108 times at midnight on New Year's Eve.

Walk north of Shijō-dōri where the streets parallel to it take on a sleazier and altogether more contemporary tone. **Shinbashi-dōri**, east of Hanami-kōji, is slick with hostess bars and love hotels; to the west, along the **Shirakawa canal**, are old houses and *ryokan*. **Shinmonzen-dōri**, the next east–west street up, is a good place to look for antiques and unusual souvenirs.

Heian Jingū (Heian Shrine)

Buses 5, 27, 32, 46, 202, 203, 204 or 206.

Due north of Maruyama Park is **Okazaki Kōen** (Okazaki Park), a worthy civic affair containing several museums of limited interest to first-time visitors. The **City Museum of Traditional Industry** (Dentō Sangyō Kaikan), in the southwest corner, is the most accessible, with displays and practical demonstrations of regional crafts. The **City Art Museum** (Shiritsu Bijutsukan) and the **Kyoto National Museum of Modern Art** (Kokuritsu Kindai Bijutsukan) both feature modern and contemporary Japanese work, but most visitors will pass by beneath the vast vermilion *torii* gate which straddles the road between them. This marks the approach to the **Heian Shrine**, raised in 1894 to mark Kyoto's 1100th birthday and boost civic morale in the decades after the departure of the Emperor.

The imperial connection is obvious in the profusion of chrysanthemum crests on walls, pillars and regalia. Two descendants of the sun goddess are worshipped here. As late as 1937, the last of the Kyoto-based sovereigns, Emperor Kōmei (1831–66), was enshrined here by the proponents of state Shinto. The principal deity, though, is Emperor Kammu, 50th ruler, who presided over the founding of Heian-kyō, as Kyoto was then called. The shrine was designed, after much consultation with archaeologists and ancient plans, in imitation of the Daigoku-den (Hall of State) of Heian-kyō's first Imperial Palace. The mimicry is imperfect, but this is still the best place to get an idea of what an early Heian building would have looked like in mint condition.

Once inside the **Oten-mon** gate, the structure will be familiar to anyone who has seen the present Imperial Palace or the Phoenix Hall at Byōdō-in temple in Uji. On the far side of a vast gravel courtyard is the Outer Sanctuary, 15m high and 30m wide. Two covered corridors sweep to either side, enclosing the rear half of the courtyard like arms, topped at their ends by bristling turrets. The initial shock, especially after the aged silvery wood of authentic Heian buildings, is one of colour: the pillars and outer woodwork are vermilion-orange, the walls brilliant white, and the roofs greeny-blue. They are roofed in tile which contributes to the Chinese look of the place, in contrast with the softer smooth textures of Japanese cypress shingles.

The scale of the buildings is all the more impressive when you realize that they are actually only two-thirds the size of the originals. This shows rather absurdly in the small terminal turrets, which would have been cramped anyway but which become, in this diminished replica, Munchkin-sized.

At the back of the Shrine is a five-acre garden, laid out in the Meiji period in a nostalgic style. The East Garden strives hardest after an antique effect: a roofed bridge with a central moon-viewing pavilion alludes to the Gold and Silver Pavilions of the 14th and 15th centuries; the famous stepping stones were taken from the piers of the old bridges built across the Kamo River in the 16th century. Still, the imprint of Westernization is unmistakable: this is more of a park than a garden, whose outstanding features are not rocks, bridges or gravel beds, but trees and plants—although it is no less attractive for that, and in the spring the blooming parasols of pink cherry blossom are idyllic.

Nanzen-ji

Bus no.5 to Eikan-dō.

Politically, Nanzen-ji was one of the most powerful and important of the Kyoto Zen temples and still serves as headquarters of the Rinzai branch sect. But fires and war have jumbled the compound's layout; today it lacks the cloistered, microcosmic appeal of Daitoku-ji, although for its great gate, screen paintings and an intriguing sub-temple it's still a worthwhile stop for those in the area.

The pine forest in which Nanzen-ji was raised was originally claimed by the Retired Emperor Kameyama as the site for a detached palace, after he fell out with the Kamakura shoguns. The place acquired a reputation for being jinxed, and when a priest of Tōfuku-ji successfully exorcized it in 1291, the Emperor was impressed enough to reward him with one of the imperial halls. Later Kameyama converted the entire palace into a temple, in emulation of Tōdai-ji in Nara, and personally carried earth used in its construction.

The monks of Mt Hiei set fire to the temple in 1393, and it was Hideyoshi Toyotomi who rebuilt it in the late 1500s after another bonfire during the Ōnin Wars. Nanzen-ji's greatest century was the 17th, when it gained its present **Hōjō** (Priests' Quarters), several sub-temples, a number of fine paintings, and its garden, attributed to Kobori Enshū.

The **San-mon**, rebuilt in 1626, is famous as the gate which, in the manner of a Zen paradox, leads from nowhere to nowhere. The paths pass around rather than through it; its presence is largely symbolic, but it is one of few such gates which visitors can pay to ascend. The view from the top is excellent, and the paintings of phoenixes, angels and tentacular waves on the ceilings and pillars of the worship hall are remarkable colourful and well-preserved, although irritatingly obscured by chicken wire. This was the legendary hiding place of Ishikawa Goemon, a popular outlaw who holed up here before being captured and boiled alive in a cooking pot.

The **Hōjō** (Priests' Quarters) is a chimera of two halls, both reconstructed here in 1611: the Seiryō-den from the old Imperial Palace and a smaller hall from Hideyoshi's Fushimi Castle. Their sliding doors contain fine paintings by the Kanō family, including a beautiful sequence of surly tigers and leopards prowling and sleeping in a bamboo forest.

There's a dry Zen garden by the Hōjō, although it's not as interesting as the one in **Konchi-in** (entrance to the right, just before the entrance to the Nanzen-ji compound), the most accessible of Nanzen-ji's sub-temples. It came to prominence under a powerful priest called Sūden, a henchman of Tokugawa Ieyasu and one of those who kept an eye on affairs in the emperor's city after the shogun moved the seat of government to Edo (Tokyo). After the ticket booth, signs lead you past tall hedges to the **Tōshō-gū** which he built in his boss's honour. The *gongen*-style shrine is schizophrenically decorated—to its rear are the gaudy colours and carvings suggestive of the head Tōshō-gū shrine at Nikkō; at the front, the worship area is a forbidding matt black. The shrine is thought to have been deliberately placed near the entry point into Kyoto of the Tōkai-dō, the great road from Edo—an effective warning to travellers that, however distant they felt themselves to be from the power of the shoguns, Big Brother was always watching them.

To the right-hand side of the shrine, a gate leads onto narrow stone steps and past a small chapel dedicated to Sūden. Opposite here is Konchi-in's own Priests' Quarters, and the **temple garden**, a subtle and cunning work of abstract art. A sea of raked gravel stretches in front of the temple veranda to a pair of rock islands, and beyond them to a thickly planted embankment. The right hand 'crane' island consists of solid upright stones and a tall upright regular pine; the left one is a 'turtle' shape with low, round stones, stumpy shrubs and a gnarled tree. The two are linked across the gravel by a long, flat rock in a pool of dark pebbles. The crane and tortoise have long been symbols of longevity, but in this arrangement they seem suggestive also of one of those oppositions of two archetypal principles—male and female, mind and spirit, yang and yin.

Philosopher's Walk (Tetsugaku no Michi)

Start from Nanzen-ji in the south or Ginkaku-ji to the north.

North of Nanzen-ji, the small **Shishigatani canal** curves between a pair of tree-lined paths, right up against the foothills of Higashiyama. In the early years of the century Nishida Kitarō, a professor at Kyoto University, used to take his morning constitutional here. Fifty years after the philosopher's death, his modest walk has become the most famous in the city, and a definite tweeness surrounds the perfumed tea rooms and craft shops which have sprung up here. Just above the canal, though, on the slopes of the mountain are three of the most secluded temples in Kyoto, and the walk ends just outside **Ginkaku-ji**, the eccentric and fascinating Temple of the Silver Pavilion.

The walk can be made in either direction, and takes a leisurely hour excluding breaks. Proceeding from south to north, the first of the temples, seldom open to the public, is **Reikan-ji** (Sacred Mirror Temple), a small imperial convent whose abbess is always a member of the old aristocracy (before 1868 she would have been a princess). The two simple buildings, one of them housing the eponymous mirror, are rarely open even when the grounds are, but the sloping garden is exquisite: raked gravel blends into sand and moss which merges in turn into a grove of flowering trees on the upper level.

A few yards up the same road, and smaller still, is **Anraku-ji**, a neat, secluded temple with something of the atmosphere of an English country churchyard. It belongs to the Jōdo sect, an off-shoot of Tendai Buddhism which gained a vast and rather unruly popularity during the time of the ex-emperor Go-Toba at the end of the 12th century.

In 1206 two priests of the sect, Anraku and Juren, were preaching in this area where they won two distinguished converts—the Emperor's favourite concubines, Pine Beetle and Bell Cricket, who were so impressed by the charismatic monks that they took the tonsure and never returned to the palace. Whether it was conversion, or something more like seduction, is a matter of legendary conjecture. Either way, the news that his mistresses had deserted him for a pair of upstart bonzes drove Go-Toba into a frenzy. He had both the monks arrested and, when they refused to recant, executed. Anraku was beheaded on the shore of the Kamo River. Miraculous purple clouds gathered over the spot and the monk's fearless tranquillity won many more converts to Jōdo—although the unhappy nun-concubines committed suicide.

By 1212, the Jōdo sect became acceptable once more, and the temple was founded in memory of the tragic events. A pile of boulders at a crossroads of paths just inside the temple points to the graves: to the right are formal stones marking the resting place of the priests; ahead, at the end of the path, the smaller memorials of Pine Beetle and Bell Cricket. The small **Main Hall** contains images of Amida Buddha, the Jōdo founder Hōnen and, to the right, statues of the monks and their ladies. Anraku-ji is open during the cherry blossom season, the beginning of November, and at odd times during the year.

Hōnen has his own temple, the **Hōnen-in**, beyond a dense bamboo wood a few strides north of here. The buildings can't generally be entered, but the grounds are open daily and in the maple-viewing season you will have to run the gauntlet of kimono-clad ladies and their tripod-laden husbands obsessively photographing one another beneath the beautiful trees. Despite a return to imperial favour at the end of his life, Hōnen's Jōdo sect was persecuted in Kyoto after his death. For years the image of Amida worshipped here sat naked on the hillside after zealots destroyed its chapel; the present arrangement is 17th century. Peer into the back of the **Main Hall** and notice the 25 *bosatsu*, represented not by statues but by 25 fresh flowers strewn on the polished floor in front of the weather-beaten Amida Buddha. By the main gate is another lovely curiosity: two raised rectangular beds of sand raked into the shapes of leaves, petals and patterns of water, depending on the season.

Ginkaku-ji (The Temple of the Silver Pavilion)

Buses 5 or 32.

Ginkaku-ji, with a little exaggeration, might be called the Nero's palace of Imperial Kyoto. Nero was Yoshimasa, not an emperor himself but a shogun, eighth of the Ashikaga dynasty which seized power in the 14th century. Japan during this period was remarkable in two respects: under the shoguns' patronage, the gentle arts—painting, gardening, drama, the tea ceremony and flower arrangement—achieved standards of sophistication unmatched since Heian times. Politically, anarchy—bordering on outright civil war—prevailed under a government which had shed all pretence of authority. Fires and floods, earthquakes, plagues and famines fanned persistent riots and petty rebellions, and for ten years between 1467 and 1477 the wretched Ōnin Wars razed large sections of the capital.

It was in this atmosphere, with bodies unburied in the charred streets, that Yoshimasa made his plans for the Temple of the Silver Pavilion. He built it as a retirement villa, in emulation of the Golden Pavilion erected on the other side of the city by his grandfather Yoshimitsu, the third shogun. The landscape artist Sōami designed the grounds; the finest craftsmen and materials were requisitioned—although the silver leaf covering for the principal hall, which gives the temple its popular name, was never actually applied. When Yoshimasa died in 1490, the complex became a Zen monastery known as Jishō-ji and was used, at various times, as an army camp and battle ground; intermittent restorations, notably in the 17th century, prevented the gardens melting completely into the hillside.

The Grounds

The hedonistic origins of Ginkaku-ji—pleasure villa turned Zen monastery—are obvious even before you are inside the grounds. Instead of the monumental portal and north–south avenue of approach common in purpose-built temples, a modest tiled gate opens onto a sandy lane bound with hedges and a bamboo fence. Round a corner and past a miniature grove of trees and sand, the garden is glimpsed, just, through the arched window of a **Chinese gate**. The intention is to tease visitors: by depriving them of a panoramic view until the very last moment, Yoshimasa played with his guests and whetted their sophisticated appetites.

Three distinct elements make up the view within the grounds proper, and your judgement of the temple will depend on whether you find their juxtaposition daringly bold or simply inappropriate. The **garden** itself is based around the **Brocade Mirror Pond** studded with a large number of carefully positioned rocks bearing poetic names. Stone bridges link the small islands, and the westernmost channel culminates in the **Sengetsusen** (Moon Washing Fountain), a waterfall prized for the delicacy with which its ripples disperse the reflection of the moon.

The main body of buildings is to the left of the visitors' entrance. The only original one here is the **Tōgū-dō** (special permission required to enter), beyond the Main Hall and joined to it by a roofed corridor. Here Yoshimasa lived, and here he installed the simple **Dōjin-sai**, a prototypical tea ceremony room, the first one ever built to the now standard size of four and a half mats. The shogun's play-house, the **Silver Pavilion** (Ginkaku) itself, stands next to the pond, a dreamy, fine-boned, unobtrusive building that makes even Kinkaku-ji (the Golden Pavilion) look coarse by comparison. Architecturally it's a hybrid, with a villa-style ground floor of screens and moveable walls, and an upper storey with swing doors and bell-shaped Chinese windows. The notched corners of the lower roof and the surmounting phoenix add a touch of tasteful flamboyance. Significantly, Yoshimasa had it facing to the east, away from the charred city of which he had washed his hands.

But the temple's dominant and most controversial feature is not its buildings or greenery. Beyond a bamboo barricade, between the Ginkaku and the Tōgū-dō, are two weird **sand mounds**, one a decapitated cone, Mt Fuji-style, the second a flat irregular blob said to model the shape of a famous Chinese lake. The material used to fashion them is much finer than the gravel found in classic Zen gardens: the edges and curves of each mound are as sharp as if they had been planed out of wood, or freshly tipped from the jelly mould. They appeared at some point during the Edo period: nobody knows who put them there, or why, although there's no shortage of theories. The 'lake' is said to have been created to enhance moon-viewing parties—the light sand would naturally reflect the moonlight thus illuminating the rest of the garden. The Fuji mound might have originated in the piles of sand which the temple gardeners kept in reserve to replenish the paths. Whatever the original intention, the sandcastles have become their own justification—bizarre, almost grotesque, but essential. You would never add features like this to an existing garden. But this one would be completely different— and not half so intriguing—without them.

Bus no.5, 北 5 or 65 or the private Eizan Line to Ichijōji station will drop you in the general vicinity of Shisen-dō and Manshū-in. From there a short journey in a taxi would save time.

The stretch of foothills between Ginkaku-ji and the Shūgaku-in Imperial Villa has a sleepy small town atmosphere. It doesn't have the calculated picturesqueness of Arashiyama or the Philosopher's Walk, but it's not on the tour bus trail either, and there will always be fewer crowds here than in the more famous temples of the city.

Public transport in this area isn't especially good and it's easy to lose your way among the vague, bendy lanes that amble up the hillside.

Shisen-dō (Hall of the Poets)

The palpable melancholy that surrounds Kyoto's hillside retreats must have something to do with the fact that so many of the men who built them were failures—forgotten princes, unpopular shoguns, retired emperors gelded of all real power. The founder of **Shisen-dō** was no exception. Nominally a temple, Shisen-dō was actually an exquisite private hermitage created by Ishikawa Jōzan, an ally of Tokugawa Ieyasu, who fell out with his boss over the siege of Ōsaka in 1615. He was exiled to Kyoto where he devoted many years to the care of his ailing mother. He built Shisen-dō in 1636 and lived there, as a poet and full-time dilettante, until his death in 1672 at the age of 89.

The villa shares the exquisite idleness of Katsura and Shūgaku-in, but on a much smaller and more intimate scale. The deliberately modest 'rustic' entrance opens onto a little stone path which minces through a bamboo grove to a second small gate. The twists and turns in the path create an impression of exaggerated distance from the everyday world outside. The villa itself is small, and painted beneath its ceiling are images of the eponymous **Shisen**, 36 famous poets of China and Japan. The **garden** is the villa's main attraction and falls into two parts. The lower section, a stroll garden with paths of fine white sand, is pretty enough. But the best view is from the veranda. Beyond a conventional gravel 'sea', are 'mountains', not of stone, but azalea bushes, clipped into smooth orbs, and blending skilfully into the forested mountains behind. The effect is very different from a Zen-style stone and gravel garden—cosier, more emotional, in keeping with the secular, dandified atmosphere of the whole villa.

Manshū-in

This is a mercifully isolated temple, well off the tourist beat, but all of its features are better exemplified elsewhere, especially in the Katsura Imperial Villa with which it is contemporaneous. It was originally founded in the 8th century on the top of Mt Hiei, and after several changes of scene, the monks constructed the present buildings here at the beginning of the Edo period (early 17th century). Prince Yoshihisa, for a while the adopted son of Tokugawa Ieyasu, was dispatched here when the shogun no longer needed him; the temple has ever since enjoyed *monzeki* (imperial temple) status. The **Daishoin** (Large

Study) shares the ornate decoration and foppish detailing (sliding door grips in the shapes of gourds, fans, etc.) of Katsura. The more interesting **Koshoin** (Small Study) is unfortunately closed to visitors.

Shūgaku-in Rikyū (Shūgaku-in Imperial Villa)

The biggest of the imperial villa complexes, **Shūgaku-in**, outshines even Kiyomizu in the splendour of its setting: built around an artificial lake, with sweeping views of the city below and the foothills of Mt Hiei above. A big proportion of the 70-acre site consists of **paddy fields** which are leased out and farmed privately even today. Compared to the refined literariness of Katsura Rikyū, Shūgaku-in has a gentler, more authentic air which you may prefer. The two palaces were built by men in the same predicament—imperial figureheads robbed of power by the ruthless Tokugawa shoguns. But where Katsura's designers turned inwards (self-consciously filtering and reshaping nature according to a fixed set of aesthetic principles), in Shūgaku-in the viewer is thrust outwards into a natural world which is allowed to speak for itself. Frail, uncomplicated buildings, open to the breezes and to boundless views, gave an illusion of space and dominion to an emperor whose authority was a charade, and whose movements and freedom were sharply controlled by the very men who posed as his servants.

History

The genius behind Shūgaku-in was Retired Emperor Go-Mizuno'o, a thorn in the side of shogun Tokugawa Hidetada whose daughter, nonetheless, he was pressured into marrying. When this reluctant union produced a son, Go-Mizuno'o's Tokugawa brother-in-law tried to force him to resign in the child's favour. But the boy died, and the Emperor held out until 1629 when he abdicated in favour of his daughter. Relations with the shoguns thawed and Go-Mizuno'o was allowed to begin two big building projects. Sentō Gosho (Retired Emperor's Palace) was his city address; Shūgaku-in was his country cottage. He visited it more than 70 times between its completion in the 1650s and his death in 1680.

For 200 years thereafter its customary state was tangled neglect. From time to time emperors took a passing interest, and there was a big spring clean in 1824 when many of the present buildings were erected. The Emperor Meiji took over in 1883, and the grounds have been immaculately tended ever since.

Touring Shūgaku-in Imperial Villa

Reservations for the regular tours (conducted in Japanese only) should be made in advance at the Kunai Chō *(Imperial Household Agency), see pp.323–4.*

Shūgaku-in was built as a pleasure park, and was never intended to house the Retired Emperor for more than a short visit. Its buildings are frail and less playful and innovative than those at Katsura, but look out all the same for the storm shutters which fold away into a discreet case, and the paper screens which, instead of sliding horizontally, hinge upwards to create an awning. Notice, too, a small but important distinction as you are admitted to the villa grounds: you enter by a door in a gate, not by the gate itself, which is opened only for emperors and distinguished guests.

The Lower Villa

This sheltered grove served as a reception area, and is built around the **Jugetsu-kan**, an 1824 reconstruction of Go-Mizuno'o's original. Three of the *tatami* in the biggest room are raised, and beside them is a *tokonoma* (alcove) and shelves, and another smaller narrow alcove. This was where the Emperor sat; the extra space was designed to hold his beloved *biwa* (lute). On the little island in the pond is a famous **lantern** called, for its shape, 'kimono sleeve' or, more puzzlingly, 'alligator mouth'.

The Middle Villa

At the back gate, the comforting enclosure of the Lower Villa gives way to a sudden expanse of mountains, paddy fields and stern gravel paths—these used to be simple tracks through the rice, later primped up by the Meiji emperor. The path forks and your party is led to the right into the **Middle Villa** through a series of gates. The last of these has the thick tiles and gables of a temple gate, which it is. This villa was built later than the other two for Princess Ake, Go-Mizuno'o's eighth daughter; the **Rakushi-ken**, with its tile and shingle roof, was her residence and survives from 1668. In 1680 she became a nun and the small temple next door, **Rinkyu-ji**, was built for her. The most interesting structure is the **Kyaku-den**, once the dressing room of Go-Mizuno'o's empress, rebuilt in Shūgaku-in after her death. The doors bear beautiful paintings of floats from the Gion Festival and a famous family of crafty-looking carp. The fish, it is said, were so lifelike that they used to escape from the wall during the night and play in the pond. A later artist solved the problem by painting a net over them, but the carp have already chewed holes in it.

The Upper Villa

 Returning to the junction of paths, the alternative fork leads through the paddy fields past a huge **hedge** which crowds thickly around the track. This huge buttress of vegetation is one of the garden's glories. It contains 40 different kinds of shrub which flower in season; enormous razor-sharp scythes are specially forged to keep them trimmed.

The hedge was planted to cover the stone dam beneath, but it also serves to conceal the view of the lake until the visitor has reached the highest point. It's a breathtaking view and the symbolism, given Go-Mizuno'o's historical circumstances, is poignant. Since the earliest rulers, the ceremony of climbing a mountain and viewing the land from on high had been an important expression of kingly authority. This garden creates an illusion of the same power. On the horizon, seamlessly incorporated into the composition as 'borrowed scenery', are the mountains, the abodes of the gods. Below is the pond with its islands, landing stages and pleasure pavilions—the domain of the emperor and his courtiers. On the lower slopes come the farmers in their rice fields, and in the plain is the city of Kyoto lapping, these days, at the very gates of this one-time retreat.

The pavilion at this high point is called **Rin'un-tei** (Pavilion in the Clouds). At the front is a porch called the **Senshi-dai** (Poem-Washing Platform) where the Emperor sat painting and writing. Around the pond are waterfalls and lanterns, and **tea huts** designed by Go-Mizuno'o, some of them decorated with name plaques in his own hand. The pond's islets are linked by bridges, the most striking of which is the **Chitose-bashi** (Bridge of Eternity), a splendid Chinese-style structure with two roofed platforms and a gilt phoenix on the top. The story behind it says a lot about the surveillance under which the emperors lived. It was donated during the renovations of 1824 by a regional governor, much to the annoyance of the shogun who reacted paranoiacally to any perceived liaison between his nobles and the imperial house. The bridge was allowed to remain; its donor was ordered to disembowel himself.

Katsura Rikyū (Katsura Imperial Villa)

A permit must be obtained from the Imperial Household Agency (see p.323–4). Travel by train to Katsura station (Hankyū Line), or by bus 33 (a 30-minute journey; buses infrequent).

Three miles west of Kyoto Station, on the far bank of the Katsura River, lies an outstanding product of Kyoto imperial taste and Edo military money. Its creator was Prince Toshihito, another of those potentially troublesome aristocrat-aesthetes who were richly pensioned off in the early decades of the Tokugawa regime. He was an emperor's younger brother and had been adopted by Toyotomi Hideyoshi, only to be discarded a few years later when one of the general's concubines bore him a son. The consolation prize, awarded by the Tokugawa shogun, was the Katsura plot and permission to build a villa here. Work on the park began in 1615 and was continued by Toshihito's son, Toshitada—also a cultivated man, and also in the pocket of the shoguns (his wife was a daughter of the Maedas, one of the richest and most favoured of the *daimyō* families).

The earliest villa buildings were raised in the 1620s, at the same time as Nijō Castle; the contrast between the two expresses the aesthetic paradox of the age. While *arriviste* generals were raising sumptuous palaces, the true aristocrats—with no power to flaunt and nobody to cow or impress—took for their inspiration the humblest of models: the simplicity and poverty of the rural farmer.

Katsura is an oriental Arcadia, an aristocrat's idealization of the Chinese and Japanese countryside, replete with learned allusions to myth, famous places, classical poetry, and the vernacular literature of the Heian court such as *The Tale of Genji*. Architecturally, the villas here fostered a new type of building: the *sukiya* style, combining the lightness and fresh simplicity of the tea house with the traditional elements (desk, alcove, staggered shelves) of the *shoin* study.

The Katsura buildings depart in almost every respect from the orthodoxies enshrined so portentously in Nijō Castle. Instead of coloured tigers on gold leaf, the alcoves and partitions bear graceful ink sketches, or crisp and unusual wallpaper designs; in contrast with the baroque metalwork of Nijō Castle, the door pulls and nail covers are slim and unobtrusive, fashioned in the shape of hats, pine needles, etc. The sliding doors in many of the rooms can be removed altogether, opening the traditionally enclosed tea room completely to the garden. The pillars are frequently no more than rough, unplaned logs, further blurring the distinction between inside and outside, building and garden. The *sukiya* style is plain where the old *shoin* were gorgeous; light and witty where they were dense and oppressive. It was the classic response of aristocracy to the usurpation of its mannerisms by the *nouveaux riches*. As soon as the soldier shoguns could afford to build and live like emperors, the rules of imperial taste were changed again. The Tokugawas built their gaudy castle only to discover that it had just stopped being fashionable.

The grounds themselves were also innovative, combining the glittering other-worldliness of the Heian Paradise style with the sophisticated rusticity and minute detailing of the tea garden. This is one of the very earliest stroll gardens, and the path which visitors follow around the pond is famous for embodying the principle of *shin-gyō-so* (formal–semi-formal–informal). At different points the path is composed in three different combinations: smooth, geometrically cut slabs (formal); coarse, randomly-spaced stepping stones (informal); or a crazy paving of cut and natural rocks (semi-formal). The lumpy informal arrangement is often employed very deliberately: for visitors in kimono and wooden clogs, these stretches would be tricky to negotiate. Forced to keep their eyes on the ground, they would look up a few moments later to find a new vista had assembled itself before their eyes.

Other features of the garden embody similar exquisite refinements and hint at the idleness of the idle rich who devised them. Early on in your tour you pass a thatch-covered bench where participants in the tea ceremony waited while the master made his preparations. Facing it is a low hillock planted with cycads, specially raised in order to block the view of the garden and prevent the surprise from being spoiled. A little further on is one of the garden's most famous allusions: a stone bridge and miniature spit of gravel intended to represent the coastline at Amanohashidate, a famous beauty spot on the Japan Sea coast. This is best viewed from the **Shokin-tei** (Pine Lute Pavilion), the most interesting of Katsura's tea houses. It faces water on three sides, and each of its four faces looks quite different so that each view of it seems to reveal a different building. Thus the garden designers expanded space and made four imaginary places out of just one. Within, the tea room arrangement of hearth and alcove is enlivened by the bold blue check *tokonoma* alcove. The entrance into the room is an unusually low narrow opening called a *nijiriguchi* (literally 'wriggle door'), which forced participants to prostrate themselves and enter the small room in an appropriately humble state of mind.

Large, shapely and well-cut pieces of stone were objects of great prestige and value; among the tributes given by *daimyō* to successive proprietors of the villa are many of the stone bridges and lanterns seen around the garden. The latter are especially interesting. A couple of them, which your guide may or may not point out, were given by the Christian garden artist Furuta Oribe, and bear an image of Mary and the Latin fragment 'Fili' on their bases.

The destination and focus of the path you follow is the *shoin* villa complex which, sadly, is rarely opened to tourists. The experience of sitting inside has been described as 'like looking at the world from inside cubist sculpture'. Even from the outside it's easy to see what has excited 20th-century architects about the place. The three distinct sections, which link corners in a diagonal zig-zag pattern said to imitate the flight of wild geese, were built separately over nearly 40 years, but they ripple gracefully into one another and, if steel and concrete replaced wood and bark, they would have a very modern air.

Saihō-ji (Temple of Western Fragrances)

Bus 29; buses 69 and 73 also go near, but a taxi from Katsura station is easiest. Permission to view the garden must be obtained in advance by post (see p.324).

The garden of **Saihō-ji**, also known as **Koke-dera** (Moss Temple), is one of the most extraordinary in Japan. Even if the eerie moss forest doesn't stun you, the admission fee will: ¥3000, as much as a night's accommodation in a modest *ryokan*. Is it worth it? If Japan is bleeding you dry, then forget it: Kyoto offers ten other unique temples for the price of this one. But if you've already seen the inner ring of famous sights, or just crave some megaphone-free peace and seclusion, then Saihō-ji is worth saving up for, especially during the June rains which are said to bring out its colours at their most beautiful. In fact, the high price is what preserves the special atmosphere of the place: there are no crowds, no school parties, no cheeping tour guides. Even if you have no interest in gardens, the spectacle is astonishing. Think of it as the horticultural equivalent of a night at the opera, priced accordingly.

Perhaps in order to reinforce the point that the ¥3000 fee is a 'donation', not an entrance charge, the temple also requires visitors to participate in a short religious service before being shown the garden. No one need feel intimidated by this, and plenty of your Japanese fellow worshippers will be just as baffled by the experience as you.

History

The original Saihō-ji was celebrated as much for its architecture as its garden. The famous Rurikaku, which stood on the very edge of the lake, provided the inspiration for both the great Ashikaga pavilions at Kinkaku-ji and Ginkaku-ji, but it was burned, along with countless others, during the 15th-century Ōnin Wars; today a simple tea house is the only architectural antiquity.

A temple originally founded here in the Nara period was rebuilt and landscaped in 1339 by Musō Kokushi, a famous Zen master and one of the earliest garden designers to be known by name. The story is told of a simple priest who would come to the temple every day to help with the back-breaking work of remodelling the hillside. No one, it seemed, knew who he was, and when Musō followed him one evening he disappeared into a roadside chapel to metamorphose back into a stone statue of Jizō, the ubiquitous *bosatsu* who guards roadways and travellers in the form of a tonsured monk.

Touring Saihō-ji

After presenting your appointment card and parting with your money, you will be ushered into a hall where you sit cross-legged before a low writing desk. Sutras will be chanted for twenty minutes 'for happiness and ancestors', and you'll be asked to write a short prayer on a wooden tablet with a calligraphy ink brush (a vague, non-denominational piety in English is fine). After that the congregation is led into the garden and for an hour or so you are left to your own devices.

Even without tales of stone jizōs that walk, the moss garden would be an enchanting spot with all the qualities of a secret garden: a place to meet fairies or— as was intended—Enlightenment. The layout is simple: a series of linked pools, said to model the strokes of the character *kokoro* (heart), and surrounded by hills on three sides. Above, the light is filtered and dappled by a thick forest canopy; below, every surface—earth, rock, the banks of the lake, the root boles of the trees—is coated with moss, a luminous green fleece of 120 different varieties. Between the leaf ceiling and the moss carpet it's almost like being indoors. You feel you should take off your shoes— indeed stepping off the paths onto the delicate moss is strictly forbidden.

Theologically, Saihō-ji is a bit of a mixture. The garden around the pond suggests an earthly realization of Amida's Western Paradise, the Pure Land of Jōdo Buddhism. But Musō was a Zen priest, and it was also intended as an aid to *zazen* meditation. The upper part of the garden in particular, northwest of the lake, is very Zen in spirit. Beyond a small thatched gate and up stone stairs the moss is left behind and the garden becomes rocky and austere. Behind the **Shito-an**, a small chapel enshrining a statue of Musō, is a dramatic cascade of boulders, one of the earliest examples of the so-called 'dry waterfall', and a precursor of the famous Zen gravel gardens.

Arashiyama and Sagano

The area is well served by public transport. Take the JR San-in Main Line to Saga station from Kyoto Station, or the private Keifuku Electric Railway's Arashiyama Line to Keifuku Arashiyama station. Buses 61, 62, 63, 71, 72 and 73 all stop at Arashiyama.

The flat land to the northwest of Kyoto narrows towards a ravine, and sandwiched between the Ōi River and the hills is an ambling, autumnal neighbourhood of expensive tea shops, little country temples and beautiful, timeless bamboo groves. Once this was a secluded village, the retreat of writers, abandoned court ladies and artistically-inclined emperors. Today it's still one of Kyoto's most pleasant suburbs, although the lazy, Sunday-afternoon atmosphere is hardest to enjoy at weekends when the restaurants and streets clog with yelling toddlers and wobbly 'office ladies' on rental bikes.

The heart of Arashiyama is the **Togetsu-kyō**, an attractive concrete incarnation of an old arched bridge. On clear days, eagles wheel above the wide river; below is **Nakanoshima**, 'Middle Island', once just a spit of river sand, but now home to some fine and expensive *kaiseki* restaurants.

Tenryū-ji

There's nothing special about the Meiji-period buildings at **Tenryū-ji** (Temple of the Heavenly Dragon) just to the northwest of the bridge, but it has an old garden and a history as interesting as its name. It was built in superstitious response to the death of Go-Daigo, the 14th-century emperor who famously attempted to restore direct imperial rule, and who was revered during the Meiji period as a revolutionary hero. Go-Daigo was aided and finally betrayed by Takauji, first of the Ashikaga shoguns, and the news of the Emperor's death in exile—clutching the Lotus Sutra and the imperial sword of office—caused great anxiety to the new regime. The Zen priest Musō Kokushi dreamed that the Emperor's spirit sprang from the Ōi River in the form of a golden dragon. In order to placate it, Heavenly Dragon Temple was built here in 1340 on one of the dead Go-Daigo's favourite spots; Takauji himself carried stones and timber to the site in a display of obeisance to the shade of his old enemy.

The **garden** doesn't compare with Kinkaku-ji or the Imperial Villas, but it's historically important in providing a link between the courtly Heian pond and the Zen contemplative garden. From the veranda of the **Hōjō** (Abbot's Quarters) one faces a cluster of tall, upright rocks representing the mythical Chinese Isles of the Blest and suggesting the influence of Sung Dynasty ink paintings which were admired in Japan at this time. It is also thought to be the earliest surviving garden to incorporate 'borrowed scenery'—the Arashiyama mountain behind. The temple kitchens serve Buddhist vegetarian lunches between 11 and 2.

Several lesser sights lie at the base of the hill east of Tenryū-ji. **Ōkōchi Sansō** is a 20th-century garden built for a celebrated actor of black-and-white samurai flicks. In **Rakushisha** (The Hut of the Fallen Persimmons), a straw raincoat and traveller's umbrella hat commemorate the *haiku* poet Bashō who holed up in this hermitage in the 1690s and composed his *Saga Diary*. Ten minutes' walk away is **Giō-ji**, named after a concubine of Taira no Kiyomori, the famously ruthless Heike leader. When Kiyomori tired of Giō, she retreated to this hermitage, leaving behind a sad little poem about the transience of love and beauty. It was discovered and read by the general's new girlfriend, who was so struck by it that she dumped him on the spot and joined her predecessor in the temple.

Seiryō-ji, a kilometre to the east, is worth visiting only on the 8th and 19th of the month when a secret image of Gautama Buddha (*Shaka* in Japanese), which gives the temple its popular name, **Shaka-dō**, is displayed to the public. The 1.5m sandalwood image, with its stylized drapery chiselled into thick grooves, is cruder than anything which exists in mainstream Japanese art but is considered profoundly holy. It was carved by a Sung Chinese sculptor as a copy of an Indian original said to have been modelled from the Buddha's own features. In the black days of the 12th century, the rumour spread that the statue, disgusted by the perpetual civil wars, was planning to do a runner back to China. Hordes of the panicking faithful turned up at the temple to beg for its continued protection; dozens of copies were carved just in case, and survive today all over Japan.

One kilometre northeast of Seiryō-ji, the five white bands on its outer walls and abundant chrysanthemum crests give **Daikaku-ji** away as an imperial temple. It used to be Emperor Saga's country villa and was converted into a Shingon temple in 876. Architecturally it's still closer to a palace, with a wide gravel forecourt before a **shinden** hall that was moved here by Emperor Go-Mizuno'o from the Imperial Palace. The style is identical to that of the Kyoto Imperial Palace—cypress shingle roof with a protruding central lip, and two trees (an orange and a plum) flanking the stairs. The interior has Momoyama period screens of hawks and peonies by Kanō Sanraku; behind it, a network of covered corridors (another feature of palace architecture) leads through the grounds to the **Worship Hall**. The **Godai-dō** enshrines the Five **Myō-ō**, the Fierce Kings of the Shingon sect, and its veranda faces the **Ōsawa Pond** where moon-viewing parties are still held in the autumn. The concrete octagon to the rear is a repository containing sutras inscribed by Emperor Saga in a successful attempt to avert plague. You'll see pilgrims following his example in the temple's halls today.

Kōryū-ji

By train to Uzumasa station, either by Keifuku Arashiyama Line or JR Sagano Line.

This lovely temple set in lush, informal gardens predates the founding of Heian-kyō, and has the oldest **Lecture Hall** (1165) in the city, as well as a 13th-century chapel to Prince Shōtoku. All these, however, are eclipsed in popularity by the modern concrete **Reihōkan** (Treasure House) and its statue of **Miroku Bosatsu**, the Mona Lisa of Japanese art, and one of the most celebrated oriental sculptures in the world.

History

The statue (the first object to be officially designated a National Treasure, in 1953) has always been considered remarkable, and the temple was purpose-built to shelter and enshrine it. It was almost certainly carved by a Korean (there are nearly identical pieces in bronze in the Seoul National Museum), but no one seems to know whether he lived in his own country or was one of the many immigrant settlers who thrived as weavers and craftsmen in central Japan. In 603, at any rate, the statue was given by the great Buddhist reformer Prince Shōtoku to the chief of the Sino-Korean Hata clan which occupied the Kamo River area. The temple was built around the time of Shōtoku's death in 623, and survived the next millennium relatively unscorched; its treasure house was constructed as a 1300th birthday offering in 1923. The statues and their admirers are constantly scrutinized by security men but even so—like the Temple of the Golden Pavilion and Michelangelo's David—the Miroku Bosatsu has suffered from the depredations of the mentally unbalanced. In 1961 an enraptured student reached out to touch it, and snapped a finger off its left hand.

Reihōkan (Treasure House)

Miroku is the Japanese version of Maitreya, a lesser *bosatsu* (Sanskrit: *bodhisattva*) who will one day be reborn as the *nyorai* (Buddha) of the future, the saviour of all beings. The statue here represents the deity's most familiar form: like the one in Nara's Hōryū-ji, it shows a slim, graceful boy (considered to be a likeness of the young historical Buddha) meditating on the nature of things, and exuding an air of profound gentleness.

He is a Christ-like deity, suggesting compassion, meekness and the absence of desire. Originally, the surface of the statue was covered in gold leaf. Thirteen and a half centuries later only the simple crested crown indicates the Buddha's royal origins. The red pine has been burnished to a deep irregular lustre. The 'half-lotus' pose—right leg folded across the left thigh, left foot on the floor—suggests the Miroku's dual nature: both in the world and outside it, human saviour and divine principle. The carving becomes simpler and purer as the eye moves up the statue: from the stylized but involved drapes of the skirt, to the smooth arms and impossibly slender torso, to the plain crown and beatific face. The upper body is sometimes compared to that other emblematic sculpture, *The Thinker*, although Rodin's modelling is crude and melodramatic next to this. The face inclines towards the fingers of the right hand but isn't quite supported by them, so that there is an unresolved quality to the pose: the tranquillity of enlightenment is set against the tension of deep concentration; the smooth plumpness of the shoulders and face is balanced by the sharp nose and pointed fingers. The statue is curiously lit, perhaps for conservation reasons: half of its face and body are in darkness so it is difficult to make out the warm archaic smile which the postcards reveal.

There are more than 50 other statues in the hall, many of them National Treasures. To the right as you face Miroku is an image of **Hata-no-Kawakatsu**, who received the statue from Prince Shōtoku and built the temple. He and his wife are carved in the simple, rather heavy style used for aristocrats and Shinto deities in the Heian period. To your left, seated on a large carved throne, is a posthumous rendering of the 16-year-old **Shōtoku**. Opposite are several huge and dramatic statues of multi-armed Kannons. The seated **Senju Kannon** in the middle, although in bad condition, is compelling. A crack visibly divides the middle of its face and body emphasizing the figure's powerful symmetry, despite the raddled and crumbling limbs flailing on either side.

Tōei Movieland (Tōei Eigamura)

Behind Kōryū-ji. Open 9–5; 9.30–4.30 in winter; adm adults ¥2000, children ¥1100/900.

Japanese theme parks can, as a general rule, be avoided like the plague, unless you take pleasure in long queues and egregious cuteness. **Tōei Movieland** is different, though: tatty enough to be charming, and with an amusing (and possibly unintentional) sense of irony, a refreshing oasis of tackiness in Japan's most elegant city.

The site still serves as a working studio for the Tōei Film Company. When the park is closed (and when they have the financial backing, an increasingly rare state of affairs) the recreated historical streets and façades are used for filming the samurai movies which are a staple of Japanese TV schedules. Something of the production values of these endeavours is conveyed by the sign which stands in front of a reconstructed Edo period bridge. 'Simply by changing the name on its signpost,' it explains, 'this bridge is magically transformed for the camera into any famous bridge in Japan.' As in movie museums all over the world, the sets are brought to life by energetic bands of out-of-work actors who mount bloodthirsty battles and displays of *ninja* stunts.

Attractions include a street of Edo period merchants' houses, a reconstruction of the famous Yoshiwara pleasure quarter of old Tokyo, and a room full of small screens showing excerpts from classic films and the careers of famous actors. Sadly, these are not subtitled, but press the bottom left-hand button in the central panel of the black and white section for a scene famous even in the west—the showdown in the rain from Kurosawa's superb *Seven Samurai* (*Shichinin Samurai*). Outside again there are several cinemas (one showing non-stop cartoons), a *kabuki* theatre, and a hilariously feeble special effects corner where fibre-glass monsters judder hydraulically out of murky paddling pools. All of these are included in the admission price, but there are plenty of ways of spending more money: shops selling photographs of old Japanese idols, remote-controlled boats, and a costume studio where you can pay large sums to be made up and photographed as a variety of historical characters. It's no Disneyland, but it's fun if this kind of thing is your cup of tea.

Ryōan-ji (Dragon Peace Temple)

Bus no.59.

Ryōan-ji is another temple eclipsed by its greatest treasure: its garden, the purest and most famous example of the *karesansui* rock and gravel style, as satisfying and suggestive a piece of abstract art as any in the world. Unfortunately it's one of the least well-kept secrets in Kyoto, and the covered veranda from which the garden is viewed frequently resembles a football terrace with standing room only. Arrive as close to the 8am opening time as you can, or choose a rainy day when it will be less crowded and just as enjoyable.

History

The old aristocratic estate which preceded Ryōan-ji passed in the 15th century to Hosokawa Katsumoto, a leading general in the Ōnin Wars which devastated Kyoto in the 1470s. On Hosokawa's instructions, the ravaged site was converted into a Zen temple after his death. The garden seems to have been constructed around 1500; of its origins, that is as much as we know.

Tradition attributes it to Sōami, but for no better reason than that he is conventionally considered the finest gardener of his age. Unusually, the long low rock by the back wall has two names—Kotaro and Jiro—carved on it, and it's conjectured that these might belong to *kawaramono*, the low-caste 'river bank workers' who became the first professional gardeners. Whoever put them in their place, the stones of Ryōan-ji have spent most of their existence in obscurity. For 400 years they quietly gathered moss, attracting almost no attention from outside. Then, in the 1930s, the garden was suddenly discovered. It became a popular subject for black-and-white photography, and the Western architectural theorists who were writing with such excitement about Katsura Imperial Villa found in it another example of brilliant spatial manipulation using the simplest of elements; it's as a precocious example of modern art that the garden has become famous. These days the temple is one of the most visited spots in Kyoto.

Despite its meteoric rise to fame, the site can hardly have changed at all in its 500 years. Zen gardens must be the most robust works of art in the world. In 1797, fire swept through the Ryōan-ji compound destroying screens, paintings, musical instruments, sculptures, scrolls and buildings. The rock garden survived unaltered.

Viewing the Garden

Because the garden is wide and can only be viewed from close up, it is impossible to photograph properly. Lenses inevitably chop the corners off or distort its flatness with neck-cricking camera angles. It has to be visited in person, and it is always a surprise.

The first surprise is its small size; the second its extreme plainness. The garden consists of a rectangular bed of raked gravel 31m by 15m, surrounded on three sides by a low wall. Set into the gravel are boulders, none of them particularly massive, none taller than a couple of feet. There are 15 of them altogether, arranged in five groups of (from east to west) five, two, three, two and three. They can only be viewed from the broad veranda of the **Hōjō** (Abbot's Quarters) on the garden's north side; no more than 14 of the stones can ever be seen from any one position.

The gravel is framed by a stone rim, a pebble-filled drainage channel, then the small flagstones from which the temple buildings rise. The walls to the south and west are made of clay baked in oil which over the years has oozed to the surface to form intriguing irregular patterns. At least three different kinds of tree overhang the shingle roof of the wall, and shed their leaves onto the gravel. Within, there are no plants at all, apart from tiny lichens on the surface of the rocks, and the haloes of moss into which they are set.

The garden is compelling, but its austerity and barrenness defy conventional notions of horticultural prettiness. Its appeal is intellectual, not sensual. Few people who take the time to contemplate it deny its unique power and fascination. But no one seems able to agree what its effects are or how they are achieved.

There's no shortage of interpretations. The more literal-minded see the rocks as mountain tops above clouds, curves of a dragon protruding from the water, a stylized Chinese character, or even a tigress leading cubs across a river. In truth, of course, you see what you want to: staring at the garden is as hypnotic as staring into the flickering flames of a fire.

The garden's shape and form suggest other archetypes. It shares, for instance, the 2:1 proportions of the standard *tatami* mat—the symbol of sleep, repose and the home. The long raked grooves might suggest the weave of the matting, or even the pattern of planted rice in the paddy—or the waves of the sea, or currents of a river, even the swirling patterns of iron filings around a magnet. Certainly, the rock groupings appear in some mysterious way to be locked into one another: to move even one would destroy the coherence of the whole. Countless other gardens have been constructed using the same materials. None has matched the tension of Ryōan-ji.

Like the Zen meditation which it was designed to aid, all this is very difficult to convey in words. The garden can be thought of as a Zen *koan*, a riddle or paradox designed to provoke and jolt the rational mind but without a straightforward answer. 'In Ryōan-ji, objects (the rocks) are so perfectly arranged in space (the sand) that the viewer eventually ceases to experience them as separate,' wrote the garden scholar Günter Nitschke. 'It symbolizes nothing, in the sense that it symbolizes *not*...It belongs to the art of the void.'

Kinkaku-ji (Temple of the Golden Pavilion)

Buses 12 or 59.

> *The Golden Temple, about which I had dreamed so much, displayed its entire form to me most disappointingly.*
>
> Mishima Yukio, *The Temple of the Golden Pavilion*

Every coach party in Kyoto passes through the Temple of the Golden Pavilion, and anyone visiting as the guest of Japanese hosts will almost certainly be taken here. Kyotoites are very proud of **Kinkaku-ji**, perhaps because its central attraction (a building coated in gold leaf) seems to correspond to Western ideas of grandeur and opulence. In fact, after a bizarre arson attack in 1950, the pavilion was completely rebuilt. It may have cost $7 million, but it's new, and it looks it—many visitors will experience the same first reaction as Mishima's narrator, Mizoguchi. Blasphemous though it is to say so, the Golden Pavilion can be skipped by anyone spending fewer than four days in Kyoto.

History

The 14th-century general Yoshimitsu led the life of an archetypal Ashikaga shogun: he succeeded to the title when barely an adult, held power for a few violent, famine-racked years, then retired gratefully in 1394 to rule from behind the scenes as a priest. Yoshimitsu was then 36; the son who succeeded him was ten. His last 14 years were largely devoted to the artistic activities which are his great legacy. He studied Zen and the tea ceremony, hosted boating parties and *nō* plays, collected the newly fashionable art of Sung China, and built a marvellous palace retreat for himself on the northwest outskirts of the city which was converted into a Zen temple on his death.

It was christened, and is still officially called, Rokuon-ji (Temple of the Deer Park). The Golden Pavilion (finished around 1398) was only one building among many, but it was the most splendid and, thanks largely to its position on top of a large pond, it was the only one to survive subsequent fires and dismantlings. Contemporaries compared its beauty to that of Amida's Western Paradise. Even the Emperor condescended to pay a visit there, just before Yoshimitsu's death in 1408. His grandson, Yoshimasa, sought to emulate it with his Temple of the Silver Pavilion (Ginkaku-ji) in the east.

The English pamphlet handed to foreign visitors explains that 'during recent years...the structure has become damaged, and has required extensive repairs.' Even by Japanese standards this is some understatement. In 1950 Kinkaku-ji was deliberately burned to its foundations. The arsonist gave himself up immediately, and was imprisoned after a sensational trial. He was a temple novice, a loner and a stutterer, who had become psychopathically envious of the beautiful pavilion. His intention had been to die with the building; at the last minute he lost his nerve and attempted suicide on a nearby hill. Mishima Yukio's claustrophobic novel was based closely on the case, and also provided material for Paul Schrader's 1985 film, *Mishima*. Fundraising for the new Golden Pavilion began immediately, and the building was opened in 1964. Even today, it's the most conspicuously guarded and security conscious temple in Kyoto.

Touring Kinkaku-ji

Viewed from a distance, in photographs or across the reflecting pond, the Golden Pavilion is a splendid sight: two broad sweeping roofs crowned with a copper-gold phoenix, the upper two storeys—pillars, hand rails and eaves—glimmering even in the thinnest light, perched on the brink of the water 'like some beautiful ship crossing the sea of time.' Closer up, you begin to have doubts. The woodwork is smooth and unweathered, the shingles are regular and free of moss. Even when new, it would never have looked like this. The gold (20kg in all) is, as the guides proudly boast, five times as thick as the original leaf, which would in any case have worn to transparency centuries before the fire. No expense has been spared and, undoubtedly, no replica could come closer to the original than this one. But it still looks ersatz.

For its time it was a bold and unusual building, an architectural hybrid which reflected the various roles of the retired shogun-priest Yoshimitsu. The first floor, **Hōsui-in**, is in the *shinden* style of an imperial residence with a broad veranda facing the pond and *tatami* rooms divided up by sliding screens; to its right is a covered pier for mooring pleasure boats. The middle floor, **Chōon-dō**, is more like a temple hall or samurai house. The small top storey has bell-shaped windows and swing doors in the style of a Zen cell. Each floor thus reflects one of Yoshimitsu's duties: on the first he was a courtier and aesthete; on the second, a politician; on the third, a priest. The bird on the roof is the phoenix, entirely appropriate for a building risen, literally, from the ashes.

Daitoku-ji (Temple of Great Virtue)

Buses 1, 12, 59, 92, 204, 205 or 206.

A mile west of Kinkaku-ji, on busy **Kitaōji-dōri**, is the greatest of Kyoto's big Zen temples, a monastic city within a city and an essential stop for anyone seeking to understand the social and political character of Zen. **Daitoku-ji** is popular with tourists, but its quiet avenues and twenty-odd sub-temples are broad and numerous enough for it never to feel crowded, and there isn't a vending machine in sight.

Zen was introduced into Japan from China in the 12th century and, like all successful foreign imports before and since, it was quickly modified to suit Japanese habits and traditions. The head temple of the typical Zen *garan* (monastic compound) was constructed on Chinese lines, with a Messenger's Gate, Main Gate, Buddha Hall and Lecture Hall formally aligned on a south–north axis, and a Bathhouse, Sutra Repository and Bell Tower to their west. At Daitoku-ji, these prominent public buildings still echo the Chinese Zen style, with diagonally laid flagstones and benches for the monks instead of the native *tatami* mats. The main doors swing on wooden blocks rather than slide, and the windows are curved arches, almost Islamic in shape, a style possibly imported into China from the Middle East.

The abbot's and priests' private living quarters, on the other hand, are Japanese in their *tatami* floors, sliding screens and irregular arrangement, and the same goes for the numerous sub-temples which form the true heart of Daitoku-ji and comprise most of its area. These lesser institutions were founded by priests of the sect after they had graduated from the main temple, usually at the behest of a rich patron. Where the head temple was formal, geometric and Chinese, they were personal, higgledy-piggledy and traditional. Like miniature Oxford colleges, they developed their own traditions, laid their own gardens, commissioned and collected their own works of art, and prospered or declined according to the wealth and taste of their individual patrons. Daitoku-ji should be thought of not as a single sight, but as a collection of fine temples behind one wall. You can easily pass the entire day here; a long morning is the minimum.

History

The great Zen master Daitō Kokushi founded Daitoku-ji in 1319, after 20 years living as a beggar under Gojō Bridge. Among his early converts were the Emperors Hanazono and Go-Daigo, and Daitoku-ji's prosperity was guaranteed in 1333 when it became an officially designated imperial temple.

It was razed in the Ōnin Wars, but rebuilt from scratch in the 1470s by the colourful priest Ikkyū. The popularity of Zen among the samurai class brought bountiful patronage during the Momoyama and Edo periods when many of Daitoku-ji's sub-temples were endowed. At one time there were as many as 80 of them; they dwindled to the current level during the anti-Buddhist persecutions of the Meiji period.

Visiting Daitoku-ji and its Sub-temples

Unfortunately, a number of the most interesting sub-temples, as well as the Abbot's Quarters of the main temple, are closed to the public for most of the year, apart from a ten-day opening for the autumn colour viewing season at the beginning of November. Serious aficionados can apply in advance for special permission at other times. Start with your nearest JNTO office and ask their advice.

Main Temple

The order and arrangement of the seven buildings of the classic Zen temple have been described above. The second and larger of the two gates, the orange-red **San-mon**, was rebuilt in 1526; the upper storey was added in 1589 by Sen-no-Rikyū, Hideyoshi's artistic mentor and (tea) drinking buddy. He made the mistake of placing inside it a statue of himself, an act of hubris which so angered the general that he forced Sen to commit suicide and nearly destroyed the entire temple.

To the north of the **Lecture Hall** is the **Hōjō** (Abbot's Quarters, usually closed) which dates from 1636 when ceremonies were held to commemorate the 300th anniversary of Daitō Kokushi's death. The rooms are decorated with ink screen paintings by the great

Kanō Tanyu. To the south and east are two Zen gardens. The smaller east one was designed to incorporate the 'borrowed scenery' of the mountains beyond, but smog and telephone wires have done for that idea. The larger garden contains two mysterious cones of sand. Opposite them is a lovely Momoyama period gate, intricately carved. It was brought here from one of Hideyoshi's Kyoto castles and is nicknamed **Higurashi-mon** (All Day Gate) because of its carvings—considered so flawless that one could spend all day admiring them.

Daisen-in (Temple of the Great Hermit)

The monks here are showmen and you may find the chirpy, Big Top atmosphere irritating, although at times it borders on the hilarious. A life-size cardboard cut-out of the chief priest adorns the temple shop and framed examples of his aphorisms, some of them translated, decorate the walls alongside stills of his TV appearances. 'Do not take the monastic for granted,' advises one proverb. 'For underneath that robe may be a badger in sheepskin.' The one benefit of this self-consciousness is the detailed, if wordy, English pamphlet which is sold here.

The temple has become famous on the strength of its **garden**, an extraordinary literal rendering of a Chinese Sung landscape, a collaboration between founding priest Kogaku and the artist Sōami, who painted some of the sliding screens in the **Abbot's Quarters**.

Gardens surround the **Hon-dō** (Main Hall) on three sides; their heart is the small and crowded section in the northeast corner. After more conventionally austere rock gardens, the number and variety of elements here appear chaotic. Hundreds of rocks bristle against a background of shrubs and white wall, overwhelming the white gravel between them. Many have individual titles and the best of these are brilliant; once you've heard the name it's impossible to see the stone in any other way. The **Darumaishi** looks just like the hunched figure of the Zen founder Daruma as he is always depicted in folk art; the **Tiger's Head Stone** is like the smooth head of a cat surfacing above the water. The most dramatic rock, and the one around which the garden was designed, is the **Treasure Boat Stone**, once the proud possession of the shogun Ashikaga Yoshimasa.

It's a dense, noisy scene with none of the pregnant emptiness of Ryōan-ji, and none of its inscrutability either. The garden, it's generally agreed, is to be read as an allegory for the course of human life. It begins at **Mt Hōrai**, the Chinese mountain of the immortals, represented here by the big camellia bush in the corner. In front of this are several upright and very obvious **foothills**, and to the right a **spring** (sand) plunges over a **waterfall** to fan out into the **island**-studded (rock-filled) **river** (gravel), suggesting the obstacles and difficulties which the soul encounters on its journey. The river flows to the west and south and in both cases empties into a broad empty **sea** of gravel, suggesting the void which comes with the end of life.

Kōtō-in (Temple of the Tall Paulownia)

Kōtō-in is a classic sub-temple, more like a private house than a place of worship, with a lovely moss lawn and spectacular autumn maple leaves. The **altar room** contains an image of Shaka, the historical Buddha, as well as members of the Hosokawa family, founders of the sub-temple and forebears of Hosokawa Morihiro, the Prime Minister who ended 38 years of rule by the Liberal Democratic Party in 1993. Kōtō-in's chief benefactor was Hosokawa Tadaoki, a gifted samurai who served all three of the great 16th-century warlords before ending up with Tokugawa Ieyasu in 1600. His wife, a famous beauty, took the name Gracia after becoming a Catholic in 1587. In 1600, in obedience to her husband, if not her priest, she killed herself to escape capture during a siege. The character of Mariko in the James Clavell novel *Shogun* was based on her.

Ryōgen-in

This is a compact and interesting sub-temple with good English captions and a pamphlet. It was built in 1502 and has five gardens. The **Totekiko**, jammed between a rectangle of verandas, is the smallest in Japan. The **Kodatei** was built out of rocks plundered from Hideyoshi's Jūrukutei villa, and has two stones representing the sounds 'a' and 'un', the alpha and omega, the passive and active principles of oriental religion.

Outer Kyoto

Kyoto's public transport network puts once out of the way places within easy reach of the centre. None of the following is more than an hour and a quarter from central Kyoto. **Uji's** Byōdō-in is an outstanding and ancient temple; **Ōhara** is an evocative old village, rich in history and anecdote; **Hiei-zan** should be visited as much for the pleasure of its forested slopes as for the historic monastic complex, Enryaku-ji, which it houses.

Uji

From Sanjō station take the Keihan Line to Keihan Uji, with a change at Chūshojima. From Kyoto Station take the JR Nara Line to Uji.

Uji was a Heian holiday camp, where rich courtiers built their villas and decamped in the summer to escape the heat of the capital. It was on the main road to Nara and became famous for two things: its green tea, still the best in Japan, and the strategically important Uji Bridge, the site of many bloody showdowns and last stands, several of them recorded in the 12th-century warrior epic, *Tales of the Heike*. In 1180, during the stewardship of the great general, Taira no Kiyomori, troops of the rebellious Minamoto family were pursued here as they fled towards Nara. The rebel leader, the 74-year-old Minamoto no Yorimasa, tore down the bridge and held off the army of 20,000 with a band of 200 loyal samurai. As his sons and comrades dropped around him, Yorimasa was finally persuaded to retreat to **Byōdō-in** where he laid down his fan, and composed his farewell poem:

> *How sad that the old*
> *Buried tree should die without*
> *A single blooming.*

There he committed *seppuku* on a spot still known as the Fan-Shaped Lawn.

Byōdō-in (Temple of Equality and Impartiality)

Byōdō-in is about 10 minutes' walk from the JR station in Uji, over a reconstruction of the famous Uji Bridge, widely signposted in English and Japanese.

Since the 1950s Byōdō-in's **Hōō-dō** (Phoenix Hall) has become one of the most famous buildings in Japan, but when Yorimasa spilt his guts here it was a lonely and neglected place. Its survival is almost inexplicable—few comparably important Heian structures made it much beyond the 1400s. For centuries at a time, and even until the war, the Hōō-dō was derelict; squatters sheltered here and lit fires beneath its wooden beams. Today, its fluttering roofs and fragile timbers are a nationally familiar archetype of Heian beauty. If you notice a lot of visitors reaching into their pockets and scrutinizing their small change, then this is the reason: the Hōō-dō adorns the flip side of the ¥10 coin.

History

The site of Byōdō-in was originally a pleasure villa owned by Minamoto no Tōru, a Heian courtier who probably inspired Lady Murasaki's hero, the shining Genji. (The final sequence of *The Tale of Genji*—the so-called Uji Chapters—is set around here.)

It came into the possession of Michinaga, the greatest of the Fujiwara regents whose policy of marrying off their daughters to successive emperors had made them the most powerful family in the land. In 1052 his son, Fujiwara no Yorimichi, converted the place into a huge private temple complex dedicated to the Fujiwara clan, with seven pagodas and 26 halls. The Emperor himself paid a visit here in 1067.

A century later the Fujiwara were history, their power broken by the contending Taira and Minamoto clans. With no one to tend it, the temple fell into disuse. Those melodramatic battles over the neighbouring Uji Bridge took their toll on the temple complex. Only the Phoenix Hall, surrounded and protected by its symbolic pond, survives to the present day.

The Hōō-dō (Phoenix Hall)

The hall has weathered over 940 years, the waters and garden around it have been altered beyond all recognition, but their combined effect is still uniquely majestic and delicate. It takes its name from a supposed resemblance to the great mythical bird, hovering above the pond with wings outstretched, in the act of taking off or landing, but never quite touching down.

In the time of the Fujiwaras, worshippers prayed from a floating platform on the water; musicians would perform from decorated barges. The far shore of the pond is still the best place to appreciate the **Hōō-dō**'s extraordinary construction, although these days you can also enter the Buddha hall. It's been described as sculpture, rather than architecture, because so many of its spaces are wholly unsuited for any human use. The famous wings, for instance, which unfurl from the central hall on raised stilts surmounted at their corners by roofed turrets, are purely ornamental. They lead nowhere, contain nothing, there is no access to them, and their ceilings are too low for a man to stand up, let alone worship. The 'tail'-corridor at the back (whose Zen-style bell windows give it away as a later addition) serves no purpose, and even the stone lantern in front of the hall is useless—its openings

are too wide to shelter a candle. In the best traditions of the Heian court, where an inappropriately coloured kimono sash meant social death to its wearer, appearances are all. The Hōō-dō may be as practical as a bottle of chips, but it looks out of this world.

Symbolically, that's just what it was intended to be. The temple's dedication ceremonies coincided exactly with the imagined onset of *Mappō*, the End of the Law, when worldly decadence outstrips all human bids for salvation, and the best that men can do is to put their trust in the mercy of Amida, Buddha of the Western Paradise. It's this heavenly realm which Byōdō-in represents and which forms the main theme of its famous paintings: the pond is the sea across which souls must journey to the Pure Land; on its far shore, Amida sits in his hall, facing east.

You can just make out his dully glinting face through the open doors of the central hall. The roof above it is raised, accentuating the opening and drawing the eye towards it. Inside, the 3m statue dominates the surprisingly small area. Amida looks down through drooping lids; the statue was designed so that only one man kneeling at the very base of his pedestal (i.e. Fujiwara no Yorimichi) can meet his gaze. The statue, together with the exquisite figures of the 52 heavenly musicians arrayed on the upper walls, is the only authenticated work of the priest-sculptor Jōchō who pioneered a new technique: instead of carving out of a single block, the figure was assembled from several smaller pieces of cypress glued together, allowing for much greater detail (see for example the delicate instruments and finely nuanced poses of the musicians).

Even if big, impassive Buddhas don't do much for you, the room itself is a pageant of decorative art. The arrangement of lotus leaves in the dais is unusual: instead of being staggered and interleaved, they are stacked in sets of four, reinforcing the impression of weightlessness. Amida's intricately carved halo dates from the Kamakura period; its flame-like peak laps at a flower-shaped medallion of great intricacy suspended from the square canopy above. The poles which hang from the latter would once have supported curtains.

The chamber still glints with the remnants of gold leaf replenished during various restorations. Once it would have shone: as well as the gold, the beams and pillars were studded with bronze mirrors which survive on a few of the roof beams. The base of the pedestal used to be inlaid with pearls and gold, which were picked off during the hall's period of service as a doss house; the coffered ceiling was gilt; and the panels, walls and pillars were painted with scenes of *raigō*—the moment of reunion between the dying man's soul and Amida in the Pure Land. There were nine of these, corresponding to the Western Paradise's nine levels (even Heaven has class distinctions). Some of these paintings have been skilfully reproduced, others can be made out amid the worn wood and centuries of graffiti, particularly to the immediate left and right of the statue.

Treasure Hall (Hōmotsu-kan)

The best of the surviving paintings have been moved here, along with the temple's famous bell, allegedly the most beautiful in Japan, and the original bronze phoenixes from the roof of the Phoenix Hall. The paintings are important to art historians as early examples of *yamato-e*—intimate, literary depictions inspired by the gentle, rolling landscapes of Yamato, the Japanese heartland, rather than by the craggy Chinese scenes which had influenced earlier artists. All of them show Amida and attendant *bosatsu* in action, sweeping down from the heavens to beam their celestial light at dying mortals of the nine classes. The heavenly host is conventional, but the earthly landscapes are warm and recognizable—horses gambol in the corner of one picture, and the buildings vary from an opulent winged villa (not unlike the Phoenix Hall itself) to humble thatched cottages still seen in mountain areas today.

Mt Hiei (Hiei-zan)

*Unnumbered **express buses** reach Hiei-zan in 1hr 10mins from stop no. 3 in front of the post office by Kyoto Station. They are infrequent in winter. **Trains** on the Eiden Eizan Main Line (from Demachiyanagi station) terminate at Yaseyuen station; from here a **cable railway and ropeway** transfer visitors to the top, some distance from the temple precincts. A more convenient centrally-placed cable car links the east slopes of the mountain with Sakamoto on the shores of Lake Biwa, a couple of miles north of Ōtsu.*

Note: at 2800ft, Hiei-zan is at least one layer of clothes cooler than the city below it.

Among the superstitious considerations which made Kyoto an ideal site for Japan's capital was Hiei-zan, the great mountain which dominates the northeast skyline. The northeast has always been an ill-omened direction in Japan, the *Kimon* or Devil's Gate, through which the forces of bad luck, fire and pestilence enter a house or city. This may be a folk memory of the early struggle between the Japanese settlers and the aboriginals who occupied large areas of northeast Japan before they were driven into Hokkaidō. Even the walls of the Imperial Palace have a notch in their top-right hand corner to confuse the evil spirits, and a guardian monkey just in case they break through anyway.

Emperor Kammu's solution for Kyoto was on a grander scale altogether. A temple on Hiei-zan, established by the priest Saichō, posthumously canonized as Dengyō Daishi, was formally appointed to protect and watch over the city. It was a fateful decision. The mountain temple, **Enryaku-ji**, soon became one of the most powerful and troublesome institutions in the country. The mountain location, far from isolating the bonzes, effectively fortified them against external control. Until the 16th century, violence and death often did visit Kyoto from the northeast—in the shape of the very monks who were supposed to guard it.

Enryaku-ji's long period of power ended, as you might expect, in devastating retribution. Today, most of the temple buildings are 17th-century and none has the individual charisma of the great city temples. Collectively though, they form one of the biggest temple complexes in Japan, scattered across a forested mountain with popular walks and fine views of Kyoto and of Lake Biwa to the east.

Enryaku-ji

History

Enryaku-ji, named after the historical period (782–806) of its founding, quickly became more powerful than any temple before it. Cunningly, the monks incorporated Shinto gods into their worship, claiming them as primitive avatars of existing Buddhist deities and thus establishing an authority over the 'descendants' of the gods, the imperial family. As the principal centre of learning, Mt Hiei became Japan's greatest university, having educated many of the great priests and thinkers of Japanese history and given birth to all the subsequent major Buddhist sects (apart from Zen which was imported directly from China).

Enryaku-ji was the founding temple of the Tendai sect, established by Saichō as an attempt to improve on the schools of Nara Buddhism which had become worldly and doctrinally slack. But by the 10th century, the same judgement was being made of Tendai. Successive splinter groups broke away, to the violent fury of the parent monastery. The first of these made its headquarters, unwisely, in Mii-dera on the shores of Lake Biwa, directly below the glowering peaks of Mt Hiei. For 600 years these two temples were the Tweedledum and Tweedledee of Japanese Buddhism, invariably taking opposing sides on any issue of contention. But Enryaku-ji had the strategic advantage of height and regularly stomped on its rival, razing Mii-dera to the ground 9 times in 250 years.

At the height of its power, Enryaku-ji comprised 3000 temples—a state-within-a-state, immune to external authority, with its own army and the power to tip the balance in secular as well as spiritual matters. Of the alternative sects which emerged in Kyoto during the Heian period—the Jōdo of Priest Hōnen, Shinran's Shin sect, Nichiren's Hokke—all endured persecution and suppression masterminded on Mt Hiei. Imperial authority was also flouted. When disagreements with the emperor arose, Enryaku-ji's private army would march on the palace—because they carried the portable shrine of the Shinto deity Sanno, no one dared to challenge them physically. 'There are three things which I cannot bring under obedience,' lamented Emperor Shirakawa (1056–1129) famously: 'the waters of the Kamo River, the dice of the *sugoroku* game, and the bonzes on the mountain.'

If anyone was going to put an end to this it was Oda Nobunaga, the notoriously brutal unifier of late 16th-century Japan. In 1571 he assembled an army at the foot of the mountain. Here, patently, was a man with no qualms about upsetting the odd portable shrine. 'Surround their dens and burn them,' he commanded, 'and suffer none within them to live.' The soldiers stormed the temples, torched their buildings and massacred their inhabitants, including a good many women and children besides the recalcitrant priests.

Nobunaga's successor, Toyotomi Hideyoshi, rebuilt Enryaku-ji, limiting the number of temples to 125, its approximate strength even today. But the stuffing had been knocked out of it and Kyoto's northeast front has been quiet for the last 400 years.

Visiting Enryaku-ji

Enryaku-ji's mountain top position hasn't saved it from crowds or commercialization, which are excessive. Grit your teeth through the recorded commentaries, bus fumes and souvenir emporia in the **Eastern Compound**, and escape at some point to the **Western Compound** and **Yokawa** down the road, which still maintain a measure of their ancient tranquillity. **Mudō-ji Dani** (Valley of the Still Temple), just below the eastern (i.e. Sakamoto) cable car station, lives up to its name; the half dozen modest temples have good views over Lake Biwa.

Eastern Compound (Tō-tō)

Adm ¥820.

Passengers from the express bus disembark in a horrible car park by the eastern compound entrance. The modern building on the left just after the ticket booth is the **Kokuhō-den** (Hall of Secret Treasures) where an early Heian statue of thousand-armed Kannon is housed. Further on, on the same side, is the **Daikō-dō** (Great Lecture Hall, originally built in 1634) which burned in 1956 and was replaced by the present building, carried up from the bottom of the mountain beside Lake Biwa. Just to the west of here (i.e. to the right as you walk south from the car park) is the **Kaidan-in** (Ordination Hall, 1604), with attractive curving gables and bell-shaped Zen windows. Saichō fought throughout his career for his own *Kaidan-in*. After his death permission was finally granted, and Enryaku-ji gained an important degree of autonomy from the Nara temples who had until then enjoyed exclusive rights of ordination.

The most important building is on a lower level, and the best overall view of it can be had from the back of the Great Lecture Hall where you can look down on the gable end with its intricately carved medallions and gold-fanged demons. This is the **Konponchū-dō** (Fundamental Central Hall), the first hall ever built by Saichō, and the cell from which the whole great monastery city grew. The statue of Yakushi Nyorai enshrined here (hidden— only a copy is displayed) was dedicated in 794 in a much simpler building.

The present hall dates from 1642 and is surrounded by an outer cloister with carvings of animals and birds beneath the eaves. Time, and centuries of candle and incense smoke, have done a good job in elegantly muting the once bold colours inside; the whole structure has an air of symmetry and purpose despite the intricate carvings on the transoms and the faded flower paintings in each panel of the coffered ceiling. The inner sanctuary is eerily beautiful. Its floor is much lower than that in the front worship area, so that the altar beyond seems to rise floating out of nowhere. The priests sat down there to conduct services, symbolically linking the void between man and god who, though on the same level, are unbridgeably separated.

The central image is Yakushi, Buddha of healing, a copy of Saichō's original which is hidden in the closed altar behind (complete with its own miniature roof and gables). He is flanked by Nikkō and Gakkō, deities of the sun and moon. Three gold lanterns in front of them contain flames said to have been kindled by Saichō and to have remained unquenched ever since—though they have certainly been swamped by greater fires in the intervening 1200 years.

West of the main buildings, paths and a fast road cut through the forest towards the Western Compound. The bright vermilion **Amida Hall** and two-storey **pagoda** are both 20th-century reconstructions. Past a small chapel to Kannon called **Sanno-in** (after the Shinto deity which the monks used to carry down the mountain on their punitive raids), steps lead down to **Jōdo-in**, a small sub-temple with a main hall, a phoenix-topped Amida hall, and the grave of Saichō. This beautiful and other-worldly place owes its unbelievable neatness to the curious austerities practised by the monks here. Nicknamed 'sweeping hell', they involve intensive brushing of the temple and its ground for up to six hours a day. Some monks spend 12 years on the mountain, never leaving and doing little else.

Western Compound (Sai-tō)

Beyond Jōdo-in, the Western Compound begins at **Benkei no Ninai-dō** (The Halls Benkei Lifted), two identical temples joined by a covered corridor which bridges the path. Benkei was the sidekick of the 12th-century hero Yoshitsune no Taira, renowned for his Herculean feats of strength: the story goes that he hoisted the halls by shouldering the bridge between them like a yoke. Both buildings are designed for religious walking cere-monies which play an important part in Tendai worship: monks pace around the outer corridors, chanting or reading from the sutras.

The next building, the **Shaka-dō**, is not so grand as the Konponchū-dō, but is much older. It was originally built in the Kamakura period as part of Mii-dera, the breakaway monastery at the foot of the mountain which naturally supported Oda Nobunaga against Enryaku-ji. Nobunaga's successor, Hideyoshi, had it rebuilt here—the interior layout is very similar to Konponchū-dō, but it enshrines instead a Saichō-carved statue of Shaka, the historical Buddha, flanked by the Four Directional Guardians.

On an isolated mound north of the Shaka-dō is a weird object, something like a pagoda that has sunk into the earth under its own weight leaving only the golden spire on the top. This is the **Sōrin-tō**, a rare example of a zero-storey pagoda, mounted on a stone vault containing sutras.

The road continues to **Yokawa**, the third and northernmost compound which has no buildings of particular interest. The two and a half mile walk is pleasant enough; intermit-tent buses link it with the main car park.

Ōhara

Bus 北 6 from Kitaōji Bus Terminal.

Like many naturally beautiful villages in this crowded country, Ōhara has become a little self-conscious over the years. Once it was famous for the 'Ōhara wenches', simple rustic maids with the endearing habit of walking round with bundles of sticks on their heads—these they would carry into Kyoto to sell in the markets. Nowadays, the *Ōhara-me* have neat little uniforms and jobs in the tasteful craft and souvenir shops which line the winding lanes. Apart from its lazy, rural atmosphere, the village is visited for the two lovely temples on either side of the Ōhara River: **Jakkō-in** to the west, and **Sanzen-in** to the west on the slopes of Gyō-zan—Fish Mountain.

Sanzen-in (Three Thousand Temple)

History

These days Sanzen-in is a *monzeki*, an imperial temple traditionally administered by an imperial prince; at its foundation, a thousand years ago, it was an altogether humbler place. A hall was built on the side of Fish Mountain by Eshin, a famous son of Enryaku-ji temple on Mt Hiei, in 985. This was a period of crucial intellectual change for Japanese Buddhism when the complex theology and rituals of the Tendai sect, accessible only to an educated few, were actively simplified and demystified for the benefit of the illiterate masses. Eshin was one of those who developed the doctrine of the **Nembutsu**, a chanted formula (*Namu Amida Butsu*, simply: 'Save me, Amida Buddha'), the mere utterance of which was said to guarantee the sincere worshipper's entry into Paradise. Amida, the merciful Lord of the Western Paradise, was depicted more and more in religious art, and the comfort which he offered after death to long-suffering souls became the great theme of late-Heian Buddhism. Simple rural temples, with only a few buildings and a single priest, were the places where this grass roots evangelism took place; because of the eminence of its founder Eshin, Sanzen-in—in spite of its remote location—became one of the most important and well-known.

Touring the Temple

Thirty years ago, Sanzen-in could only be approached on foot, but today a metalled road leads up Fish Mountain, to the right-hand side as you approach from Kyoto. The immediate approach to the temple runs beneath a fine wall like those built around 16th-century castles. In May, this approach becomes a tunnel of pink and white cherry blossom. Inside the **Goten-mon** gate is an extensive garden of cryptomeria trees rising like pillars out of a carpet of moss.

The three main temple buildings are linked by covered walkways which lead you first into the **Kyaku-den** (Guest Palace), a 16th-century structure built as a residence for the temple's Imperial abbots. Display cases contain treasures brought to Ōhara by these men (notice the ubiquitous imperial chrysanthemum embossed on swords and lacquerware). The interiors were comprehensively restored in the early years of the century, and the door paintings date from the same time, including an intriguing image of white-bearded

Shaka Buddha, praying fiercely on a mountain-top accompanied by a kneeling follower. A crazily distorted pine tree writhes beside them. Its branches form the shape of a dragon—look for the beady eyes in the top left corner.

The second building, the **Shinden**, burned, and was built anew in 1926, but the objects it contains are ancient. The west room enshrines the temple's abbots. On the left is a millennium-old statue of the 'Fierce King' Fudō Myō-ō, with much of the original colour of his cloak of flames preserved. In the centre is Amida, and to the right a lovely Guze Kannon with a metal crown, found to contain a letter inside its hollow body, dated 1246.

But it's the **Hon-dō** (Main Hall), also known as the **Ōjō Gokuraku-in** (Temple of Rebirth in Paradise), which you've really come to see. The plain, shingle-roofed building dates from the 12th century, but the main image of Amida Buddha was carved by Eshin at the time of the hall's original construction in 985. In themselves, the three sculptures are stiff, rather cool figures, but their state of preservation is remarkable, and they're beautifully set off by the snug, smoke-blackened interior. The ceiling is on two levels: the upper, accommodating Amida's head and halo, is shaped like an upturned boat and was originally painted with images of his 25 *bosatsu*—these can just be made out using the electric torch which is usually at the front of the altar. The lower beams are on a level well below Amida's head so that the statue, although far from huge, appears to loom impressively in the limited space. A few surviving fragments of mural survive behind protective frames, but at one time the walls teemed with the images of 3000 Buddhas, *bosatsu* and heavenly beings, plus countless flowers and geometric designs, all evocative of the Pure Western Land where Amida welcomes the souls of the dead. Seishi *bosatsu*, to the viewer's left, prays for the dying mortal; Kannon, on the right, proffers a lotus flower to scoop it up into paradise. The two flanking statues, possibly later than the main image, both kneel and lean forward slightly, adding to the dynamic, swooping quality of the whole composition.

The gardens extend above and behind the Hon-dō where a **tea arbour** stands, selling the ultimate beverage for the man who has everything: salty tea laced with flakes of gold dust.

Jakkō-in (Solitary Light Temple)

Adm ¥500.

This secluded little convent, reached by winding lanes on the west side of the Ōhara River, is a simple, unspectacular place, the scene of one of the most famous and pathetic scenes of Japanese literature. It is described in the *Tales of the Heike* (translation below by A. L. Sadler), a chronicle of the struggle at the end of the 12th century between the Minamoto (or Genji) clan and the Taira (Heike) who, under the powerful stewardship of their leader, Kiyomori, had in the space of a few decades become the rulers of Japan. Then, in 1181, Kiyomori died and the Taira's supremacy was challenged by the descendants of his old enemies, the Minamoto. The two sides played a cat and mouse game with one another on land and sea, until 1185 when the Taira fleet was destroyed in the straits of Dan no Ura at the westernmost tip of Honshū. At the climax of the battle, with the enemy closing in, Kiyomori's widow, Lady Nii, seized hold of her grandson, the infant Emperor Antoku, and jumped with him into the sea followed by her ladies-in-waiting.

All but a handful drowned. Among those dragged from the waves against their will was Kenreimon-in, daughter of Kiyomori and widow of the previous puppet emperor, Takakura. She had watched her mother, Nii, and child, Antoku, drown before her eyes. After the battle, the sole surviving member of her immediate family, she was taken to Kyoto, 'bereft of all her old companions like a fish on the dry land or a bird torn from its nest.'

> She was twenty-eight this year, and the beauty of her face was not
> yet dimmed; neither was the elegance of her slender form impaired;
> but what now availed the loveliness of her hair?

Kenreimon-in took the tonsure and offered the tiny robe of Antoku, still scented with his perfume, at Chōraku-ji temple. But the cell where she was living was destroyed in an earthquake, and the nun-empress resolved to escape from the capital and the gaze of curious passers-by. In the autumn of 1185 she was conveyed out of Kyoto to an obscure convent in the northern mountains.

> The place she had chosen to dwell in was ancient and surrounded
> by mossy rocks. The reeds in the garden were now covered with
> hoar-frost instead of dew, and when she gazed on the faded hue of
> the withered chrysanthemums by the wall, she could hardly fail to be
> reminded of her own condition...still the image of the late Emperor
> was impressed on her mind, and wherever she might be, and in
> what world soever, she thought she could never forget it. They built
> for her a small cell ten feet square beside the Jakkō-in, and in it were
> two rooms; in one she put her shrine of Buddha and in the other
> she slept.

In the summer of 1186, more than a year after the catastrophe that changed the whole course of Kenreimon-in's life, she received a visitor, the last old friend she would ever see. It was the retired emperor Go-Shirakawa, at various times the ally of both Taira and Minamoto, whose shifty power-broking had added much to the confusion of the civil war. Now, though, he came to Ōhara out of compassion. When Kenreimon-in first appeared, he didn't recognize her, such was her poverty and gauntness. All afternoon they talked about the unfathomable changes that had come to pass.

> Formerly she had lived delicately in the Jewel Halls, and couches of
> brocade had been spread for her in the Golden Palace, but now she
> dwelt in a hut of brushwood and thatch, and the sleeves of her robe
> were dishevelled and tear-stained.

When the Retired Emperor left with his retinue,

> the former Empress, her mind occupied in spite of herself with
> thoughts of bygone days and shedding tears she could not restrain,
> stood watching the Imperial procession until she could see it
> no more.

She lived for another 27 years. On her death bed she followed the convention of grasping a cord of five colours, attached at its other end to a painting of Amida in his Pure Land.

As the sound of her prayer grew weaker and weaker, a purple cloud of splendour unknown grew visible in the west, and an unknown perfume of wondrous incense filled the cell, while celestial strains of music were heard from above. Thus, in the middle of the second month of 1213, the former Empress Kenreimon-in breathed her last.

The Temple

It was the plainness and simplicity of Jakkō-in that made it such a poignant place for an empress to end her life; in 800 years, not a great deal has changed and the atmosphere of melancholy is still palpable. There isn't much to describe: a wooded garden with a waterfall cascading into a pond planted with azaleas, camellias, pines, cherries and maples; and a handful of worn old buildings, some open only intermittently to public view. The **Hon-dō** (Main Hall) was reconstructed in the early 17th century, but the rear part of the building contains timbers dating from the time of the Minamoto and Taira. Inside are statues of Kenreimon-in and her faithful lady-in-waiting, Awa no Naiji, a former concubine of Go-Shirakawa—who hurtfully failed to recognize her when he visited the convent that summer afternoon. The **Shoin** (Study), said to occupy the site of the empress's hut, is a 19th-century restoration; some of the interior screens are illustrated with scenes from the *Tales of the Heike*.

Traditional Arts and Crafts

For a lively survey of Kyoto regional crafts, visit the **Museum of Traditional Industry** (Dentō Sangyō Kaikan) in the southeast corner of Okazaki Park.

textiles

The Chinese immigrant family, the Hata, wove silk on the Kyoto plain even before the foundation of Heian-kyō in 794, but the Ōnin Wars drove the weaving guilds out of the city in the 15th century. After the wars petered out, the old military camps were colonized by the returning merchants. **Nishijin** (West Camp), north-west of the Imperial Palace, is the area with the greatest concentration of looms and textile shops and, although techniques have developed, it still produces some of the finest brocades in the world.

The **Nishijin-ori Kaikan** (Nishijin Textile Centre, *bus 9, 12, 51, 59 to Horikawa-Imadegawa junction; open 9–5; adm free, exc. certain exhibits*) has a museum of textile history, a shop, weaving demonstrations and displays of treasured fabrics. The **Orinasu-kan** (Weaving Centre, *bus 201 to Imadegawa-Jōfuku-ji*) has a smaller display, unstifled by coach parties, in a traditional Japanese house.

Kodai Yūzen-en (*Takatsu-ji-dōri, south of Ōmiya station*) demonstrates the techniques of **Yūzen dyeing**. Devised in the 17th century, this involves painstakingly painting silken garments by hand (or today by variously coloured stencils) and then washing out the excess dye in exceptionally pure water. The banks of the Kamo River used to be the place for this; it was said you could judge the prosperity of the city from the colour of the stained water as it passed out of Kyoto.

tea ceremony

Kyoto is home to **Omote Senke** and **Ura Senke**, the two most famous and influential tea schools in the world, founded in the 17th century by the great grandsons of Toyotomi Hideyoshi's tea master, Sen no Rikyū. Both contain historic gardens and tea houses, but permission to view them is difficult to get without connections or a demonstrable interest in the tea ceremony. **Ura Senke**, however, admits visitors for a tea ceremony demonstration on Thursdays at 1.30pm and 3pm. Make an appointment, ✆ 075 451 8516, or enquire at the tourist information centre.

Zen meditation

On the first and third Monday of each month, English-speaking monks at **Sōsen-ji** temple conduct *zazen* from 6pm. The evening begins with a lecture in English, followed by two hours of meditation. The temple is south of Gojō-dōri, three roads west of Kawaramachi-Gojō junction. Call Okumura-san, ✆ 077 162 3310, for further information.

Shopping

Like any other big Japanese city, Kyoto has its covered arcades, sunless underground malls and immaculate department stores, but it is also a major centre for the manufacture and sale of traditional Japanese goods. Small craft items are not expensive, but in the older shops you get what you pay for, and for the best you will pay a lot. Generally, the more venerable-looking the shop, the higher its prices. (Venerable in Japan doesn't necessarily mean opulent, just old and traditional-looking.)

For bargains the best places are Kyoto's **markets**. A full list of these can be found in the tourist information centre's monthly bulletin. Of the big ones, the most famous are on the 25th of the month at the **Kitano Tenman-gū shrine** (at the west end of Imadegawa-dōri, southeast of Kinkaku-ji); and on the 21st of the month at **Tō-ji temple**. The latter, held in commemoration of the Buddhist saint Kōbō Daishi, is particularly lively in January and December.

art

Nishimura, ✆ 075 211 2849, on the corner of Teramachi-dōri and Sanjō-dōri, two blocks west of Sanjō-Kawaramachi junction, is the oldest and most respected of Kyoto's **ukiyo-e** (woodblock print) sellers, with prices to match (there is very little priced under ¥10,000). Best for those who know what they are looking for.

Yamazoe Tenkō-dō, ✆ 075 561 3064, on Nawate-dōri, just south of Sanjō station, sells scroll paintings and calligraphy. There are reasonably priced pieces in boxes in front of the shop; more expensive scrolls are inside.

books

Maruzen (east side of Kawaramachi-dōri, 5 minutes north of Hankyū department store) devotes its entire sixth floor to foreign books; magazines are on the first floor. The **Izumiya Book Centre** has a smaller selection but it's a bit nearer the station, in Avanti department store, on the south side of the tracks.

ceramics

Asahi-dō, ✆ 075 531 2181, on the right-hand side of Kiyomizu-zaka (the slope leading up to Kiyomizu temple) towards the top, is the biggest dealer in Kyoto's local pottery, **Kiyomizu-yaki.**

Matsuda, ✆ 075 541 4009, on the left-hand side as you descend Sannen-zaka, below Kiyomizu temple, sells **Imari-yaki,** the distinctive blue and white pattern known in Europe as the archetypal Japanese porcelain.

Tachikichi, ✆ 075 211 3141, on Shijō-dōri, 7 minutes' walk on the right-hand side going west from Kawaramachi station, is a 250-year-old, large-scale vendor of Kyoto ceramics. The shop accepts many credit cards and will ship all over the world.

clothes and accessories

Two shops which stock kimono and accessories, new and second-hand, in a wide range of prices and conditions, are:

Kikuya, ✆ 075 351 0033. From Karasuma-Gojō intersection, walk a block north and then six blocks east. The shop is on the right.

Komachi House, ✆ 075 451 6838, is just southeast of the Nishijin Textile Centre—*see* 'Traditional Arts and Crafts'.

Kasagen, ✆ 075 561 2832, on Shijō-dōri at the Yasaka shrine end, sells hand-made oil-paper umbrellas in myriad designs.

crafts and toys

Yamato Mingei-ten, ✆ 075 221 2641, is next to Maruzen bookshop, on Kawaramachi-dōri, north of the Sanjō-dōri junction. This *mingei* (folk crafts) shop was opened shortly after the war by a member of the influential Folk Crafts Movement. It sells hand-made ceramics, glassware, lacquerware, basketry and textiles.

Maruzen bookshop (east side of Kawaramachi-dōri, 5 minutes north of Hankyū department store) has a floor devoted to traditional crafts.

Hirata, ✆ 075 681 5896, just north of Tō-ji temple, is a small, fascinating shop crammed with folk toys from all over Japan and owned by one of the leading authorities on the subject.

department stores

Hankyū and **Takashimaya,** on the southeast and southwest corners of Shijō-Kawaramachi respectively, are the most convenient of Kyoto's *depato.*

food

Murakami-jū, ✆ 075 351 1737, is on the block just to the southeast of Hankyū department store. For an edible souvenir that will keep in your suitcase, and *isn't* made of seaweed, try the delicious *tsukemono* (pickles) from this graceful old shop.

Hōrai-dō, ✆ 075 221 1215, on Teramachi, the fourth turning on the right as you walk west from Shijō-Kawaramachi junction, sells caddies, ladles, whisks, bowls and other tea ceremony utensils, as well as green teas in powder or leaf form.

Tsukimochi-ya Naomasa, ✆ 075 231 0175, is on Kiyamachi-dōri, the street running east of the Takasekawa canal, just north of Sanjō-dōri. If you really want **manjū**, those dreary sponge cakes stuffed with bean jam, this is *the* place to buy them. They make a good present for Japanese friends.

household and miscellaneous items

Aritsugu, ✆ 075 221 1091, in Nishiki Food Market, near the junction with Gokomachi-dōri, has traditional hand-made kitchen hardware—buckets, tureens, graters, strainers, steamers, and *sushi* knives as sharp as samurai swords.

Hirata, ✆ 075 561 1776, on Yamato-ōji-dōri, north of Shijō-dōri, and east of the bridge, is the place to buy beautiful bamboo and reed blinds, made to order.

Miura Shōmei, ✆ 075 561 2816, on the north corner of Shijō-dōri and Higashi-ōji-dōri, opposite Yasaka Shrine, sells hand-made lanterns, including some in bold modern designs.

Naitō, ✆ 075 221 3018, on the north side of Sanjō-dōri, between the Kamo river and the Takasekawa canal, sells brushes and brooms for every conceivable cleaning job—ashtrays, kettles, nostrils, shirts and desk-corners.

Kungyoku-dō, ✆ 075 371 0162, is on Horikawa-dōri, opposite Nishi-Hongan-ji temple. Here you will find countless flavours of incense, in sticks and chips, plus incense-burners and traditional *rōsoku* vegetarian candles.

Where to Stay

Compared to Tokyo, accommodation in Kyoto is varied, interesting and (relatively) inexpensive. If you haven't tried it already, this is one of the best places to stay in a Japanese-style *ryokan*. The cheapest of these are clean, friendly and elegantly simple. The most expensive are an extraordinary experience: like owning your own antique samurai house for the night, complete with world-class Japanese restaurant and full domestic staff. Old inn buildings were not designed for privacy: for sound-proofed rooms, as well as English-speaking staff and post-feudal gimmicks like faxes and international telephones, you'll be better off in a Western-style city or business hotel.

Remember to book in advance for Fridays and Saturdays, the autumn maple leaf season, and the evenings of big festivals (*see* pp.320–2). Kyoto, as you'll see for yourself, is used to foreigners and you shouldn't have too much problem making yourself understood. The tourist information centre can make reservations only for the (generally good) establishments listed in the Welcome Inn brochure.

The most convenient locations for transport and amenities are, in general, the most urbanized and noisy. If big cities oppress you, then consider seriously the possibility of staying in Nara, just 35 minutes away by train.

Japanese-style
luxury

Tawara-ya, ℃ 211 5566 (English spoken), is centrally situated on Fuyachō-dōri, two blocks west of Kyoto City Hall, on the south side of Ōike-dōri. This is probably the best *ryokan* in the world, patronized for over 300 years by international celebrities from the Rothschilds and the King of Sweden to Saul Bellow and Marlon Brando. No glitz here, though, just 19 rooms furnished with the finest antiques, private cedar baths and lovely gardens. Rates are from around ¥40,000+ per person, without meals. You will need to reserve weeks in advance.

expensive

Shiraume, ℃ 561 1459, in the east of the city on the south side of Shirakawa canal, is a former *geisha* house in the heart of Gion with rooms overlooking the gurgling Shirakawa river.

moderate

Kinmata, ℃ 221 1039 (English spoken), is centrally situated on Gokomachi-dōri, three blocks west of Kawaramachi station. Kinmata opened in 1801 as an inn for travelling quack doctors whose advertising boards still stand in the entrance. It has superb food and exquisite decor, although the nine rooms don't afford much privacy and only one of them has a private bath. Reservations required.

inexpensive

Gion Umemura, ℃ 525 0156 (English spoken), is in the eastern part of the city, south of Shijō station, two blocks east of Kennin-ji Temple. This popular Meiji period inn, run by an ex-sumo wrestler, specializes in *chanko-nabe*, the high protein sumo wonder food.

Sagano Satō, ℃ 882 0623 (English spoken), is in the northwest, just north of the main entrance to Tenryū-ji Temple on the opposite side of the street. This is a popular *minshuku* (family-run inn) with attached coffee shop in a house formerly owned by a famous samurai actor and his actress wife.

Kiyomizu Sansō, ℃ 561 6109, is in the east on Sannen-zaka. This tiny inn is on the street of craft and souvenir shops which is the traditional pilgrims' route to Kiyomizu Temple. Reservations required.

The best bargains in Kyoto are a string of simple *ryokan* on the banks of the Takasegawa stream, a picturesque trickle to the west of the Kamo River which used to carry trading barges to Fushimi and Ōsaka to the south. Ten minutes' walk from Kawaramachi-Shijō crossing, five minutes by bus from Kyoto Station, this is the quietest and most convenient neighbourhood in central Kyoto, with an authentic local atmosphere and a colourful local populace of mama-sans, sweet-potato vendors, curious children and squalling cats. A couple of doors south of Riverside Takase is a wonderful *sentō* (public baths of three different temperatures, plus sauna) where gentlemen with punch perms and dragons tattooed on their backs cackle villainously and soak away the strains of a hard day's...business.

Except for **Yuhara**, the following are members of the Japanese Inn Group. Rooms are plain *tatami* with communal bath or showers and meals are not generally served.

Riverside Takase, ✆ 351 7920 (English spoken), is three minutes' walk from Kawaramachi-shōmen bus stop, the third one after Kyoto Station on bus 205. It is the annexe of the slightly more expensive **Ryokan Kyōka**, nearer Kyoto station, ✆ 371 2709.

cheap

Ryokan Yuhara, ✆ 371 9583, is a few yards south of Riverside Takase.

Ryokan Hiraiwa, ✆ 351 6748 (English spoken), is between the last two, one block to the east.

temple accommodation

A number of Kyoto temples, generally the smaller ones, also serve as *shukubo* or inn lodgings for pilgrims.

Myōren-ji, ✆ 451 3527, buses 9, 12, 51, 59, 61 or 67 to Horikawa-Imadegawa. English is spoken but conditions are basic; use the local public bath.

Hiden-in, ✆ 561 8781 (English spoken), is a sub-temple of Sennyū-ji in the southeast of the city.

Daishin-in, ✆ 461 5714, and **Torin-in**, ✆ 463 1334, are both sub-temples of Myōshin-ji Zen temple. No one speaks English.

(✆ *075–*)   *Western-style*

expensive

Brighton Hotel, ✆ 441 4411, is two blocks east of the Imperial Palace on Nakadachiuri-dōri. It has a huge airy atrium with fountains and miniature trees.

moderate

Tōkyū Hotel, ✆ 341 2411, just north of Nishi Hongan-ji Temple, is a big, spacious hotel with decent-sized rooms and five restaurants.

Miyako Hotel, ✆ 771 7111, is in the east, by International Community House and the Keage stop of the Keihan-Keishin line. This is a famous old hotel on the edge of the eastern mountains which also has Japanese *ryokan*-style rooms.

Park Hotel, ✆ 525 3111, in the east, by Sanjūsangen-dō and Kyoto National Museum, has a great position, convenient for the station and Higashiyama.

Holiday Inn, ✆ 721 3131, lies on the Takano River in northwest Kyoto. There is a free shuttle bus from the station. The hotel has an out of the way position but is good value, with pools, gyms, saunas and tennis courts.

Hotel Gimmond, ✆ 221 4111, on Ōike-dōri is a smart convenient business hotel. It gives generous discounts to foreigners who book through the Welcome Inn Reservation Centre (Tokyo or Kyoto tourist information centres).

Sanjō Karasuma Hotel, ✆ 256 3331, is one minute southwest of Ōike subway station. A member of the Welcome Inn Group, it is a small new business hotel with public baths overlooking a garden (all rooms have private bathrooms).

Palaceside Hotel, ✆ 431 8171, can be found opposite the Imperial Park, north of Marutamachi subway station. It is a member of the Welcome Inn Group and gives a big reduction when rooms are booked through a tourist information centre.

cheap

Higashiyama Youth Hostel, ✆ 761 8135, is located on Sanjō-dōri, south of the Heian Shrine.

If you don't mind a 40-minute-plus bus ride from Kyoto Station, there are also Youth Hostels in **Utano** (near Ryōan-ji and Arashiyama, ✆ 462 2288) and **Kitayama** (in the countrified Takagamine district by the foothills of the northeast mountains, ✆ 492 5345.)

The cheapest places in Kyoto are its **gaijin houses**—dirt cheap communal apartments and dormitories with minimal amenities. They are often scruffy, seldom conveniently positioned, but still the best place for potential residents to pick up news of jobs and accommodation, meet travellers, and plug into Kyoto's large community of young *gaijin*. Places of this type scuttle on and off the scene as quickly as the cockroaches which infest their kitchens. For the latest list check the classifieds in *Kansai Time Out*; at the time of writing, the following were considered better than average:

Tani House, ✆ 492 5489, is near Daitoku-ji temple; take bus 206 to Kenkun-jinja-mae.

Green Peace, ✆ 791 9890, is east of Kitayama station.

Eating Out

Kyoto is the birthplace of **kaiseki ryōri**, the haughtiest of Japanese *haute cuisine,* but like every Japanese city it teems with cheaper establishments, serving food and drink in every style. The area around the station is poorly appointed; for a better choice start at **Shijō-Kawaramachi junction**, near Takashimaya and Hankyū department stores. Along the stretch of Kawaramachi-dōri north of here are numerous chain restaurants, pizza parlours and fast food joints, their plastic models displayed in the windows. The streets just south of Hankyū are calmer, and there are a handful of **nomiya** drinking places around there. A few yards east, towards the river, you cross the Takasegawa canal; bars, restaurants, noodle shops and clubs cluster on both of its banks. Many of the latter, especially in the area south of Shijō-dōri, employ 'hostesses' offering a variety of different services to their customers. They're harmless enough, except to your finances. If you choose to enter one of these places, make sure you know what you are spending.

(✆ 075–) **Japanese**

expensive

Nishiki, ✆ 871 8888, lies at the southeastern end of Nakanoshima, the river island at Arashiyama. It serves good value **kaiseki** courses in a very attractive area. The **oshukuzen** course, a cross between a *bentō* lunch box and a formal meal, is especially reasonable.

Nakamura-rō, ✆ 561 0016, is by the stone gate south of the Yasaka Shrine. The oldest buildings of this classic Kyoto *ryōtei* (first class *kaiseki* restaurant) are 400 years old, making it the oldest in Japan. Princes have eaten here, the architects of the Meiji Restoration plotted here, and there are screen paintings by the 17th-century painter Ogata Kōrin.

Minokō, ✆ 561 0328, is one block south of the stone gate of Yasaka Shrine. Minokō serves both regular and *cha* (tea) *kaiseki*, a highly formal accompaniment to the tea ceremony. Lunchtime *bentō* are served overlooking a beautiful garden.

Minokichi, ✆ 771 4185, in eastern Kyoto, just off Sanjō-dōri on Dōbutsuen-mae-dōri, the road that leads north to the zoo, is a big, popular restaurant with a relaxed and unintimidating atmosphere. It is popular with foreigners; English is spoken.

Kyoto's other cuisine, distinct from *kaiseki*, is **shōjin ryōri**, the delicate and surprisingly varied vegetarian food prepared by Zen monks out of tōfu, herbs and vegetables. The commercial restaurants specializing in this style are generally found in the vicinity of Zen temples, a number of which serve *shōjin ryōri* to their visitors at lunchtime. The most famous restaurant, and one of the most expensive, is **Ikkyū** (by the east gate of Daitoku-ji temple), although better value is **Izusen** (in Daitoku-ji's Daiji-in sub-temple). Both are closed by the early evening.

moderate

Okina-tei, ✆ 221 0250, opposite Vivre Hall (pronounced *Bibore Hōru*), one block north, then one and a half blocks west of Shijō-Kawaramachi junction, has *sukiyaki* beef dishes in a 120-year-old restaurant.

Okutan, ✆ 771 8709, in the Chōshō-in sub-temple of Nanzen-ji, is one of several restaurants around Nanzen-ji which serve *yudōfu: tōfu* (bean curd) stewed in a pot and dipped piping hot into flavoured sauces, with side dishes.

Hirano-ya, ✆ 561 1603, at the north gate of Maruyama Park, specializes in *imobō*, the dried and salted fish which were a staple of local cuisine until fast roads and refrigeration put the city within reach of the sea. It is authentic, but not to everyone's taste.

Izujū, ✆ 561 0019, on the corner of Shijō-dōri and Higashiōji-dōri, opposite Yasaka Shrine, is a century-old *sushi* shop decorated with Imari ceramics.

Kappa Nawate, ✆ 531 4048, is on the right-hand (east) side of Gion's Yamato-ōji-dōri, as you walk north from Shijō-dōri. It is a *robatayaki* grill: choose small dishes of fish and vegetables (from the English menu or by pointing at the counter) and watch them being cooked before your eyes. A snack here can be very inexpensive; it depends how many dishes you order.

These two restaurants, one in central, one in eastern, Kyoto, serve *bentō* box meals in the Kyoto style:

Tagoto, ✆ 221 1811, has a tiny entrance in an alleyway on the north side of Shijō-dōri, opposite Takashimaya department store.

Rokusei Nishimise, ✆ 751 6171 (English spoken), overlooks the canal on the west side of the Heian Shrine.

inexpensive

Matsuno, ✆ 561 2786, on Shijō-dōri, a few metres east of the Minami-za theatre, serves delicious broiled eels, painted with sweet sauce and served over a bowl of rice (*donburi*) or in a set (*teishoku*).

Kawamichi-ya, ✆ 231 8507 (English spoken), is a lovely garden-fringed **soba** shop, started 300 years ago to sell noodles to pilgrims climbing Mt Hiei. Walking east from Kawaramachi-Ōike junction, Fuyachō-dōri is the third street on the left. Turn down here; the restaurant is in the middle of the second block on the right.

Takasebune, ✆ 351 4032, is in an alleyway, just east of Hankyū department store. Look out for the large oar at the front of the building. This renowned **tempura** restaurant is run by an old Takasegawa canal boatman.

Tsukimura, ✆ 351 5306, situated south of Hankyū department store, is a small, friendly drinking spot which serves rice dishes cooked in the pot (*kamameshi*).

Agatha is a modern Japanese restaurant that serves anything—from meatballs to fruit—grilled on a skewer. There are two branches, separated by only a few yards, on the east bank of the Takasegawa canal south of Ōike-dōri. Main branch: ✆ 223 2379; northern branch: ✆ 255 2279.

(✆ *075–*)   *Foreign*

moderate

Finlandia, ✆ 351 7689, on the corner of Yanagonobanba-dōri and Gojō-dōri, a few minutes' walk east of Gojō subway station, is a Finnish restaurant decorated in cool, Scandinavian-style wood, serving reindeer and elk steaks.

inexpensive

Knuckles, ✆ 441 5849, on Kitaōji-dōri, 300 metres east of Senbon-dōri, is a cheap and popular foreign-run 'New York café', serving sandwiches, lasagne, cheesecake, Tex-Mex snacks, etc.

Pig and Whistle, ✆ 761 6022, on the 2nd floor of the Shobi Building, Sanjō-dōri, opposite Sanjō station, is a credible reproduction of an unpleasant British pub with vile, matted carpet and foreign beers. The atmosphere's noisy and cosmopolitan and it's definitely the place for anyone planning to stay in Kyoto to gather intelligence about jobs and accommodation.

Performing Arts

Japanese performing arts are disappointingly represented in Kyoto. *Kabuki*, was born on the gravel banks of the Kamo River near Shijō bridge, but the only major performances in the city now are the *Kaomise* season at the Gion **Minami-za** theatre in December. (The same venue hosts visiting Japanese theatre groups for the rest of the year.)

Most weeks, there are *nō*, and sometimes *kyōgen*, performances at the **Kanze Kaikan** (over the moat, just southwest of the National Museum of Modern Art and Okazaki Park). Less frequent are those at **Kongō Nōgaku-dō** (a few yards north and west of the Yasaka Shrine).

In April–May and October–November, Kyoto's surviving schools of *geisha* perform their traditional dances (*odori*) in theatres in different parts of the city. Most famous is the **Miyako Odori** of the Gion *geisha*, which runs throughout April in the **Gion Kaburenjō** theatre (on Hanami-kōji, south of Shijō-dōri on the eastern side of the river). For dates and times of all the above, consult the tourist information centre's **Monthly Information** bulletin.

Next door to here is **Yasaka Kaikan** which stages the twice-nightly **Gion Corner** show (*open Mar 1–Nov 29, exc. Aug 16; adm ¥2500; shows at 7.40pm and 8.40pm. ℂ 075 561 1119*). This tourist 'showcase' is unfortunately the only place in Japan where you can see several traditional arts in a short time for a reasonable price. To a moronic English voice-over, a couple of bored-looking ladies in kimono go through the motions of a tea ceremony and listless flower arrangement. A leaden *kyōgen* farce is followed by a twitchy performance of *bunraku* puppets. Go if you like, but don't let it put you off a proper performance of the real thing.

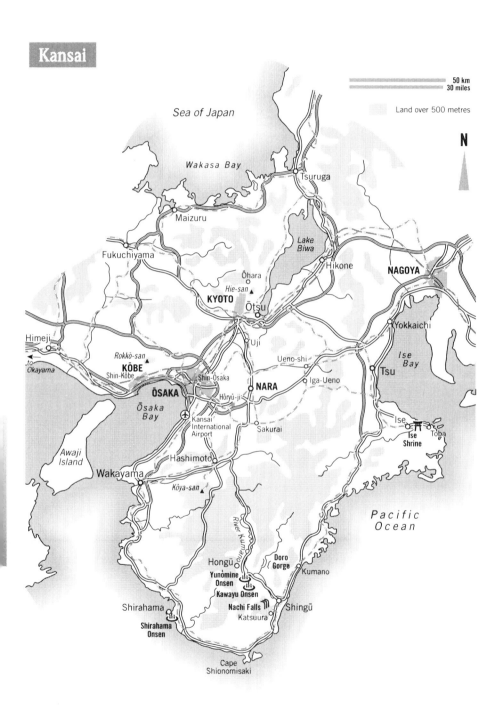

Kansai

Sea of Japan

50 km
30 miles

Land over 500 metres

N

Wakasa Bay

Tsuruga

Maizuru

Lake
Biwa

Fukuchiyama

Hikone

NAGOYA

Ōhara

Hie-san ▲

KYOTO

Ōtsu

Yokkaichi

Himeji

Uji

Rokkō-san

Ueno-shi

Ise
Bay

to
Okayama

KŌBE

Shin-Kōbe

Shin-Ōsaka

Iga-Ueno

Tsu

ŌSAKA

NARA

Hōryū-ji

Ōsaka
Bay

Kansai
International
Airport

Sakurai

Ise

Toba

Ise
Shrine

Awaji
Island

Hashimoto

Wakayama

Kōya-san ▲

Pacific
Ocean

River Kumano

Hongū

Doro
Gorge

Kumano

Yunomine
Onsen

Kawayu Onsen

Shirahama

Nachi Falls

Shingū

Shirahama
Onsen

Katsuura

Cape
Shionomisaki

Oh, what a beautiful land we have become possessed of!

Jimmu, mythical first emperor of Japan

When the rest of Japan was still a brigand-ruled wilderness, and Tokyo was a smelly saltmarsh, there had been civilization in Kansai for 1000 years. The old name for the region, Yamato, was a synonym for the whole country. It was here that an army of invaders from present-day Kyūshū arrived, sometime in the 1st century BC, to conquer and unite Yamato's disparate tribes under a single clan, the prototype of the later imperial family. To secure their legitimacy, they promoted the system of ancestor- and nature-worship later known as Shinto: the Yamato countryside is densely populated by the gods of mountain, river and rock, as well as the Buddhist deities who absorbed and supplanted them after the 6th century. All the main developments of Japanese history, politics, art, religion and society until the 17th century were focused on this small, teeming area. Lifetimes have been spent exploring and writing about it, and for first-time visitors with less time at their disposal there's really no need to travel anywhere else.

Kyoto, treated at length in its own chapter, is part of Kansai; so are the older capital of Nara, the great religious centres of Ise and Mt Kōya, and big modern cities like Ōsaka and Kōbe. With the opening of its own international airport on a man-made island in 1994, and an excellent inter-city transportation system, Kansai is now more accessible from abroad than Tokyo. It would be a shame to miss out on that extraordinary city, but if Japanese culture is your priority, then you should consider flying into Kansai and staying there.

Ōsaka

Japan's second city (pronounced 'OH-saka', with the first syllable long, not 'O-SAR-ka') is one of the most important in the world, and many visitors, especially businesspeople, will find themselves spending time here. It's a lively, rowdy, ugly place famous for its fierce dialect, *Ōsaka-ben*, and for its inhabitants, known throughout Japan as cheerful, warm-hearted, money-minded rogues, a world away from the cool Tokyoites or the refined denizens of Kyoto. There are a few interesting things to see here, but Kansai is too rich, and life too short, to spend more than half a day here (even then you could easily spend it in Kyoto or Nara, both less than 45 minutes away by train).

Getting There

Shin-Ōsaka is a major station on the Tōkaidō *shinkansen* **bullet train** line, under 3hrs from Tokyo by the fastest service, but it is some way north of the city centre: take a taxi or the Midosuji subway line.

JR lines pass through Ōsaka station, in the north part of town. This station merges with Umeda, the terminus for private **Hankyū line trains** from Kyoto. The comprehensive **Kintetsu rail network** converges on Namba station, a few kilo-metres south of Umeda.

Kansai International Airport, on a man-made offshore island 15km south of the city centre, has supplanted the old Ōsaka International Airport as the hub for most of the area's domestic and international flights. Trains and buses connect to the city centre in 30–60mins.

Getting Around

Ōsaka's **subway** system is one of the easiest to use in Japan. There's plenty of labelling in Roman characters, and the stops are all announced in English. Even if all else fails, the official municipal guide book is reassuring. 'Take joy in getting lost,' it urges. 'Like one in hell who happens across a Buddhist monk, you can expect only helpfulness and kindness from Ōsakans who will guide you back to the promised land.' The most useful line is the red **Midosuji** which (north–south) connects Shin-Ōsaka, Umeda, Shinsaibashi and Namba. The **JR Loop line** circles the inner city and connects with the subway at various points.

Ōsaka's single finest attraction is on Nakanoshima, a river island a few hundred metres south of Umeda station: the **Museum of Oriental Ceramics**, an outstanding collection of mostly Chinese and Korean pieces. These are ceramics raised to the level of high art and, even if you thought you weren't interested in pots, the wit and sensuousness of these will move you. Look out for the Tang Chinese dancer, with her elongated body and thin arms still bearing traces of gilt; and the towered pavilion, a metre tall, complete with miniature guards and slaves, which was buried with a dead nobleman. Especially appealing are the soothing, pale green celadons: one Chinese bottle, a National Treasure, is rendered diseased-looking by the bold application of brown iron splodges below the glaze.

Apart from this, conventional sightseeing is a bit limited. The **castle** is situated in a nice park, but the keep is a 1960s reconstruction, and the ancient temple of **Shitennō-ji** is a concrete job too. Ōsaka's great strength is its entertainments. The **National Bunraku Theatre** presents the best puppetry in the country. **Namba** is the teeming nightlife district of bars and restaurants alongside canals and beneath covered arcades; its focus is a bridge called **Shinsaibashi**, which is as good a place as any to start an evening. Anyone who has seen the Ridley Scott film *Black Rain* will recognize these streets and their atmosphere.

(✆ 06–) ***Where to Stay***

Ōsaka has hotels in every price range; even at busy times you should have no difficulties finding a room somewhere. In the *expensive* cate-gory, try the **Ōsaka Tōkyū Hotel**, ✆ 373 2411, near JR Ōsaka and Umeda stations, or the **New Ōtani**, ✆ 941 1111 overlooking the castle. *Moderately* priced are the **Riverside Hotel**, ✆ 928 3251, 10mins by taxi from the JR station, and the small **Hotel Ōsaka Castle**, ✆ 942 2401.

Eating Out

Like Nagoya, Ōsaka has a daunting range of places to eat, from world-class European restaurants in the big hotels to pushcarts serving seafood and noodles all night. The best strategy is to pick an area and wander around. **Namba** and **Shinsaibashi** are young, noisy and 24-hour. The area round **Umeda station**, in the north, is quieter and more grown-up, and closes earlier. Finding English speakers is never a problem.

Kōbe

Japan's second port, facing the Inland Sea, was until January 1995 a lively and pleasant city to live in, but never a first-class tourist attraction. Kōbe was one of the first ports to open to foreign residents in the late 19th century. Among its charms were wooden houses built in an Oriental-Victorian style, and a museum of prints and paintings depicting the arrival of the 'barbarians'. On 17 January 1995, however, the Kōbe area was struck by a powerful earthquake which destroyed buildings, roads and railways, and killed 5500 people. The reconstruction work is well underway, and normal life will undoubtedly be resumed in a few years. But there will be even less to bring tourists to Kōbe, and for the time being there's no reason to come at all.

Nara

Nara is what many first-time visitors expect, and are disappointed to find lacking, in Kyoto: a garden city of parks, ponds, turtles and deer, where the pagodas and treasure houses still hold their own against the highways and advertising hoardings. If you can live without flash hotels and nightclubs, then Nara has almost everything Kyoto has, in milder, small-town form: a National Museum, cultivated gardens, an ancient temple, and five of the oldest and biggest Buddhist temples in the world. Historically, Nara's treasures are older and, in many cases, better preserved than those in the later capital. The town is infinitely more compact and negotiable, and you can achieve in a few hours on bike and foot what in Kyoto would take days on crammed trains and buses. It's smaller, of course, and there's less variety, but there's enough to fill three or four days of anyone's time. If concrete and traffic repel you, and if you're prepared to make a day trip into Kyoto to see the essential sights, you should seriously consider making Nara your base.

Getting Around

Nara's attractions fall, by and large, into two areas: Nara Park and the downtown district, convenient for stations and hotels; and west of the city, in a straggling line from the side of the old Heijō palace down to Tōshōdai-ji and Yakushi-ji. The former can be walked or cycled around; the sights in the west are all close to local railway stations. Only Hōryū-ji, which no visitor to Nara should miss, is more than a few kilometres from the main transport termini.

There are two Nara stations, and this can be a source of confusion. The private **Kintetsu Nara station** is right in the centre of town, a few minutes from the

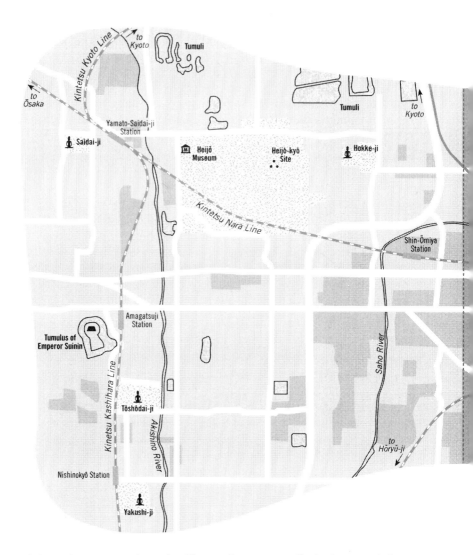

information centre and temples. These trains are generally the fastest and cheapest way around; they connect with Ōsaka Namba, Kyoto and Nagoya. The **JR station**, though central, is a little to the south and west, and here you can catch direct trains to Kyoto and Hōryū-ji. Fares on the public railway are usually higher, unless you've got a Japan Rail Pass in which case it's free.

Tourist Information

The **Nara City Tourist Centre** is a block east of JR Nara station; there's another information office, with the usual maps and English pamphlets, in front of Kintetsu Nara station.

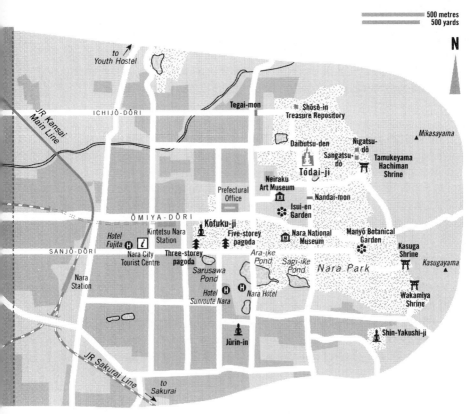

500 metres
500 yards

N

In front of Sarusawa Pond, there's a little office manned by the charming **Nara Student Guides** who will tour foreigners around the sights for nothing more than the price of lunch and admission tickets. Beware: the English-language map issued by the tourist centres in Nara is not to scale.

History

The Imperial City of fairest Nara
Glows now at the height of beauty,
Like brilliant flowers in bloom!

Poem from the *Manyōshū* (Sheaf of 10,000 Leaves), 8th century

By the beginning of the 8th century the so-called 'permanent' capital at Fujiwara had become too small for the court's growing population of bureaucrats, so in 708 the decision was made to relocate in present-day Nara, 16km to the north. The peasant population was cleared, and 321 acres (now occupied by **Heijō-jō**) were filled and levelled. Two old imperial tombs were excavated and removed to allow this, but in 709 the court got cold feet about disturbing the ancestral remains, which were restored to their original positions. The old Fujiwara palace was dismantled, and parts of it re-used. Timber was brought from Shiga to the north and Mie to the south; stones were carried from the area of present day Kōbe and Ōsaka. Kilns were established all over the Yamato region to bake tiles and *onigawara* (protective gargoyles) for the roofs. The demand for furnishings, metal and woodwork supported a full-time workshop; in 764 it was commissioned to produce one million wooden pagodas as an offering of thanks for the defeat of a rebel lord.

Seven thousand civil servants were employed in the new palace, which served as the centre of government as well as the imperial residence. With its monumental, symmetrical layout, the new palace was unmistakably Chinese in design, but it already embodied a principle that can still be seen in Japanese architecture. While the public precincts, the great halls of state, were foreign in appearance, with painted vermilion pillars and curving tile roofs, the Emperor's own personal living and sleeping quarters employed the plain domestic style—unpainted wooden pillars and a roof of cypress shingles.

But it was a religious building that immortalized Nara. Of the Heijō palace, nothing but a few museum pieces survive today. But Emperor Shōmu's great temple, Tōdai-ji, with its colossal bronze statue, still stands, in the same position, if not exactly the same form, as 1250 years ago. With universities, hospitals, orphanages, old people's homes, and dozens of monasteries and convents, Nara seemed destined to remain Japan's capital for centuries.

In the end, it was the temples and their ambitious monks who brought about its downfall. Shōmu was succeeded by his daughter, Empress Kōken, who later abdicated to enter a convent, where she fell under the influence of a monk named Dōkyō. Like Rasputin centuries later, Dōkyō won the Empress's trust through his powers as a healer; ribald rumours circulated concerning the nature of his relationship with his mistress. 'Don't sneer at monks for their flowing blouses,' went one song, 'for they have hammers in their trousers. When the bonze's hammer stands upright, he shines like a lord in all his might!'

Dōkyō persuaded the smitten Kōken to reascend the throne; after a power struggle, she succeeded, under the new name, Shotoku. The mad monk's next suggestion was that the Empress abdicate once again, this time in his favour. A messenger was sent to an imperial shrine to put this proposition to the sun goddess. When he returned with a negative answer, Dōkyō had the man's Achilles' tendons cut. He would, no doubt, have tried again, but the Empress died unexpectedly, and Dōkyō was swiftly sent into exile where he died three years later. The Fujiwara family, shaken by this challenge to their power, moved the court away from Nara and its troublesome monks in 784. After Kōken/Shotoku, no woman was to ascend the throne for 861 years.

Central Nara

Sarusawa Ike (Sarusawa Pond)

This small semi-circular pond, 400m around, has been here for centuries and forms the centre of historical Nara. On a clear day, the two pagodas of Kōfuku-ji temple are reflected in its waters to the north. To the west, along busy Sanjō-dōri, is the modern JR station, and to the east Nara Park and the Kasuga Shrine. A dragon, a small one presumably, used to live in the pond until it was driven away by a shameful incident, involving an unnamed emperor. One of his concubines (her name was Uneme) drowned herself here after being rejected by him. The tree on which she's supposed to have hung her clothes is signposted in Japanese at the east end: Coat Hanging Willow.

Kōfuku-ji (Happiness-Bestowing Temple)

Unusually for early Buddhism, this was a private establishment, the ancestral temple of the mighty Fujiwara family, who dominated Japan as statesmen, empresses and men of culture from the 7th to the 12th centuries. As they flourished, so did Kōfuku-ji, but after their eclipse in the late Heian period, it was consistently neglected until more or less the last half century. There are no original buildings: the oldest dates from 1426. But an outstanding collection of statuary, snatched countless times from burning halls, makes it an essential Nara stop.

History

The temple changed sites a couple of times as the emperors, and their Fujiwara ministers with them, moved around Kansai before settling in Nara. Kasuga Shrine, just up the road, had always been the Fujiwara shrine and in the 10th century the two were merged into one institution. There were many fires, and in 1180 the monks made the mistake of taking sides against the Taira family in the epochal Heike wars. The entire compound, plus that of Tōdai-ji, was razed.

This disaster had wonderful consequences however. After the defeat of the Tairas, the temple was rebuilt and became a kind of factory of Buddhist art as craftsmen from all over Japan converged on Nara to study its ancient masterpieces and create a generation of new ones. The result was Kamakura period sculpture, one of the most exhilarating and accessible of all Japanese styles. Great sculptors like Kōkei and Unkei learned their trade during this period and instituted their studios close to Kōfuku-ji.

At the end of the Kamakura shogunate, the temple fell on hard times. In 1717 there was another ruinous fire, and in 1868 the Shinto zealots of the Meiji Restoration forced the separation of Kōfuku-ji and the Kasuga Shrine. Halls were requisitioned and converted into schools and offices. Not until 1958 did the government properly come to its senses with the endowment of the new Treasure House.

Touring Kōfuku-ji

Fifty-two steps lead from the pavement opposite the Sarusawa Pond up the embankment to the edge of the precincts. Once the large site was thick with buildings; more than just a temple, it was a municipal facility with a hospital, orphanage, old people's home, public bath house and university. All of these buildings have been lost and many were never replaced, including the Great Southern Gate. On your right is the **Gojū-no-tō** (Five-storey Pagoda), the second highest in Japan at just over 50m, rebuilt in 1426. The **Tōkon-dō** (East Gold Hall), just beyond it, is a striking building with proudly uptilted eaves. The pagoda was endowed by Empress Kōmyō, and this worship hall was built 11 years earlier by her husband, Emperor Shōmu; the two buildings were at one time surrounded by a wall, symbolizing marital union. The **Tōkon-dō** (*open 9–4.50; adm ¥200*) is full of National Treasures; its central image of Yakushi (15th century) is flanked by a Gakkō (God of the Moon) and Nikkō (Sun), which originally belonged to Yama-dera, a temple outside Nara. After the destruction of their own temple in 1180, the Kōfuku-ji monks marched over to Yama-dera and requisitioned these statues by force.

Other prominent buildings include the **Chūkon-dō** (Central Golden Hall), an uninteresting 'temporary' hall erected in 1852, and two octagonal pavilions, the **Hokuen-dō** (North Circular Hall, 1210) and **Nanen-dō** (South Circular Hall, 1789). Both contain valuable statues but the former is open only on 17 October, the latter at certain times during the spring. Enquire at the tourist information office for precise details.

Kokuhōkan (National Treasure Hall)

9–5; adm ¥500.

This rather cramped concrete hall contains a higher percentage of masterpieces than almost any other collection; even the smallest book of Japanese art history will reproduce half a dozen of its sculptures.

Following the arrows as you enter, the first major piece is a metre-high head of the bronze **Yakushi**, stolen (along with his two attendants) from Yama-dera, and raised in the old Tōkon-dō. Being the heaviest statue, it could not be saved from a later fire: only the face, neck and one ear survived, hidden until 1937, under the new altar. It's one of the most perfect pieces of bronze sculpture in Japan, all the more fascinating for being viewed close up. The eyes have a far-seeing crispness which could only be realized in metal; the lips and nose are sharp but full, and the whole face seems to radiate intense concentration and sensual compassion.

The two **Guardian Kings** in the next case are among the most famous in Japan, small in size, but with magnificently powerful bodies, veins bulging in a rictus of rage. Adjacent to them is a case of exquisite Nara-period sculptures: four of the **Hachibūshu** (Eight Supernatural Guardians of Buddha), including the beaked Karura (from the Indian deity Garuda), and Asura, a ferocious three-headed, three-armed demon, here transformed into a graceful youth and rendered almost realistic despite his fantastic appearance.

Contemporaneous, but in a very different vein, are the **Ten Great Disciples**, luminously soft figures of human saints whose realistic qualities were taken up by later sculptors of the Kamakura period to produce characters in a nearby case: the **Six Patriarchs of the Hossō Sect**. Their lined faces, lumpy features and scowls of concentration convey the individuality of historical priests, and represented the closest that Japanese art had yet come to portraiture.

Tōdai-ji (Eastern Great Temple)

In Tōdai-ji, the two key threads of early Japanese history—the growth of Buddhism and the centralization of power under a supreme emperor—were knotted together in a single, brilliant building project. The famous Great Buddha may not be the loveliest bronze statue ever made, but it is certainly the largest; and, despite the usual run of fires and earth-quakes, the hall in which it sits is still the world's biggest wooden structure beneath a single roof. Other temples are neater and better preserved; but everything you need to know about the Nara period and its history is encapsulated here.

History

Tōdai-ji came to life on 9 April, 752. On that day a sumptuous ceremony, attended by the highest ranking men in the land and a congregation of 10,000 monks, was held in the courtyard in front of the Great Buddha. At its climax, the Indian priest Bodhisena stood on top of a platform alongside the huge statue and painted in its eyes. Long cords trailed from his brush; their ends were held by Emperor Shōmu, 45th Emperor of Japan, and his Empress Kōmyō, who thus shared in the symbolic completion of the grand project. The emperor was a sick man; in reality, the temple and its statue were far from finished, but the ceremony had been brought forward so that Shōmu could witness the dedication of the temple which had absorbed so much of his money and energy, and which epitomized his political and religious ambitions.

The construction of Tōdai-ji marked a crucial moment in Japanese history, not just as an expression of artistic ambition and religious devotion, but as an astute piece of political strategy. The new temple was dedicated to the Kegon sect, one of half a dozen Buddhist variants which had filtered through to Japan since the 6th century; the choice was certainly no accident.

Kegon's central deity was Roshana Nyorai, the 'Cosmic Buddha', an ultimate and omnipresent being of whom all other deities, including the historical Buddha (Shaka), are manifestations. In the sutra on which Kegon based its teaching, Roshana is described seated on a lotus flower, the pose in which the bronze Great Buddha has been sculpted. The lotus has a thousand petals, each one representing a universe made up, in its turn, of myriad worlds. The petal 'universes' are each ruled by manifestations of Roshana, which manifest themselves in the 'worlds' as still smaller Buddhas.

To Emperor Shōmu, ruler of a young and still imperfectly centralized state, this compli-cated theological diagram had immediate parallels with the new political structure which he was keenly propagating: a central, universal ruler (Roshana and, by analogy, the emperor) ruling in his satellite territories through authorized representatives (Roshana's manifestations/the emperor's officers) over large numbers of lesser beings (the lesser Buddhas/common people). 'Of all the various laws,' Shōmu declared in an imperial prescript, 'the Great Word of Buddha is the most excellent for protecting the State.'

Shōmu, who had already been ordained as a Buddhist monk, was a deeply devout man and there is no doubting the genuine fervour and humility behind his grand scheme. But politically it represented a bold, almost arrogant, assertion of temporal power, a powerful symbolic act in the centralization of the Japanese state. Tōdai-ji was quickly established as *the* state temple, headquarters of a network that extended into every corner of the country. In each of the provinces, subsidiary local temples, called *kokubun-ji*, were set up as spiritual counterparts to the local government departments. The building project was both a symbol of state authority, and an example of it. By the 790s when the temple complex was finally finished and fitted out, 50,000 carpenters, 370,000 metal workers and 2,180,000 labourers had been employed. The levels of taxation and forced labour demanded by this great undertaking brought hardship and starvation to many parts of the country, and exhausted Japan's meagre supplies of gold and copper.

The Tōdai-ji project raised another ticklish problem—the future role, in the Buddhist state, of the native Shinto religion. Although it never had the organizational and theological sophistication of Buddhism, Shinto was still the native religion of Japan, observed in various forms by many Japanese, from the peasants to the aristocracy; the Emperor himself, after all, claimed descent from the Sun Goddess. The problem was solved by an eminent Buddhist priest called Gyōgi (who is also credited with the invention of the potter's wheel). In 742, at the age of 72, the ingenious bonze travelled to the shrine of the Sun Goddess at Ise where, after seven days and nights in prayer, he received an oracle. The Goddess, speaking curiously in Chinese, declared herself well pleased with Shōmu's plans. Shortly afterwards the Emperor himself had a dream in which the Sun Goddess appeared as a fiery disc and explained that the Buddha and the Sun are the same.

Touring Tōdai-ji

The formal approach to the temple begins just to the east of the National Museum, and runs north through the heart of Nara Park, the most thickly touristed area of town: expect to be molested by giggling school parties and foraging deer in equal numbers. The precincts begin where the souvenir stalls end, at the **Nandai-mon**, the 18.8m high Great South Gate, rebuilt in 1199 after the original was levelled by a typhoon. Behind the protective bars are the two guardian kings, 8m tall, carved for the new gate by Unkei and Kaikei, two of the greatest Kamakura-period sculptors. Beyond the temple offices is the **Kagami-ike** (Mirror Pond) with a Shinto shrine on a small island; 500m to either side of here are the sites of the two seven-storey pagodas, each one 100m high, which were burned down by lightning and never replaced.

At the **Chū-mon** (Middle Gate) you pay an entrance fee and enter the inner courtyard, divided from the outer grounds by a cloister-like roofed wall called the *kairo*. Large scale Buddhist ceremonies are held here; in 1994 the temple hosted an international music festival with hundreds of musicians including Bob Dylan, Joni Mitchell and Jon Bon Jovi. As well as the usual water trough and tubs of smoking incense for ritual purification, a bronze octagonal lantern stands in the approach to the main hall. This is one of the few originals in Tōdai-ji, dating from Emperor Shōmu's time; the fine lattice work and airy scenes of floating *bosatsu* and heavenly musicians in flowing garments are characteristic of the supple, sensuous Nara style.

Daibutsu-den (Great Buddha Hall)

The double-hipped roof of the Great Hall, with its golden *shibi* (owls' tail finials) jutting up above the trees, is the symbol of Nara, visible from vantage points all over town. The current building dates from 1709—however imposing it appears now, in its original version it was even vaster: 88m along the front (as opposed to 57m today), but about the same depth (50m) and height (49m). The difference would have shown itself mainly in the length of the roof ridge (today's Daibutsu-den is narrow and rather squat compared to the original), and in the curving, Chinese-style gable over the main entrance, which the 8th-century building did not possess.

Inside, time, disaster and inept restoration have taken their toll on the **Daibutsu** (Great Buddha). These days he's a bloated, clumsy figure with chubby cheeks and rubbery lips who looks every ounce of his 400 tons. Cracks in his body, and different shades of metal (the head, for example, is much blacker than the torso) betray the hybrid form of the present statue. After a couple of decapitations and several near melt-downs, he's a bit like the knife which has had three new blades and two new handles. The giant lotus leaf petals on the left-hand side are original, as—apparently—are the Buddha's knees. But the point about this statue isn't its state of preservation so much as its size: 15m high (1.5m shorter than Emperor Shōmu's original), with a 5.3m face, a 2.4m ear, a metre-long eye and a nostril which a man can climb inside. The right hand is held up in the *mudra* (sacred hand gesture) signifying peace of mind; the left is held flat, indicating that all wishes will be granted, and five monks can stand together on this palm when the statue is being cleaned.

The construction of the statue was, for its time, an extraordinary technological achievement which cost many fortunes and not a few lives. Nothing this big had ever been attempted before. As well as mining the tons of tin and copper necessary for the alloy, the craftsmen also had to construct an immense mould. They built the statue in sections: first a mould was built for the Buddha's feet and legs, then a mound was raised around the cooling metal and the next few feet of statue were moulded and cast, and so on.

The disadvantage was that, until the covering mound was removed and the completed statue revealed, no one had any idea of how well the parts were forming a whole. Between 747 and 749 there were eight false starts, when the resulting Buddha turned out lopsided or unbalanced. The project seemed to be jinxed. Then, in 749, gold—the first ever to be mined in Japan—was discovered in a remote province. The Shinto gods, it was inferred, were smiling on the project, and at long last a satisfactory statue emerged to be gilded with the spoils of the new mine. A mystery disease killed many of the metal workers employed on the statue—modern evidence suggests they were poisoned by mercury used as an amalgam for the gold.

Roshana Nyorai, the Cosmic Buddha represented by the great statue, is flanked by two *bosatsu*: Kannon, on his left, holding a mystic jewel; and Kokūzō, on his right, the *bosatsu* of wisdom and happiness. Behind this trio are two of the Shitennō, the Directional Guardians. The one on the west side with the brush and scroll is Komoku-ten, popularly considered the patron of writers; until recently, it was thought lucky for those engaged in literary employment to flick chewed up pieces of tissue paper into the deity's belly button, a practice now strongly discouraged.

At the rear of the Buddha's podium is a scale model of the original Daibutsu-den. One of the pillars to the east has a square hole in it of limited dimensions: anyone who can crawl through it is guaranteed a place in paradise.

Other Buildings

There's more to Tōdai-ji than just one hall: the smaller sub-temples are full of sculptures, infinitely finer than the fat monster in the Daibutsu-den.

The **Kaidan-in** (Ordination Hall), due west of the Great Hall, was a crucial part of Tōdai-ji. Until it was built, the only authorities capable of investing new priests were in China—an obvious obstacle to the rapid Buddhification of the country sought by Emperor Shōmu. Accordingly, the famous monk Ganjin was invited from China to inject some continental rigour into Japanese Buddhism. Five disastrous attempts were made to cross the treacherous Japan Sea; by the time Ganjin arrived in 754, he had lost his sight as well as numerous disciples. But he brought with him earth from the sacred Chinese mountain Wu Tai Shan, and on this the ordination platform was built.

The present Kaidan-in dates from 1731 and contains a superb set of the **Shitennō** (Four Heavenly Kings), guardians of the four points of the compass. Their stern but astute faces and surprisingly dainty bodies still bear traces of the original pigments, particularly on Zōchō-ten, the staff-wielding guardian of the south.

On the opposite, east side of the Daibutsu-den, are several interesting buildings at the foot of the Kasuga Hills. Steps and a path lead up to a group of minor buildings closed to view apart from the **Shoro** belfry containing the temple's original 4m bell, its body 25cm thick.

Above and to the left of here is the **Kaisan-dō** (Founder's Hall), enshrining a statue of Priest Rōben, Tōdai-ji's first abbot, but the most interesting places are a little further on. The southernmost one is the **Tamuke-yama Hachiman-gū** (Mt Tamuke Hachiman Shrine) dedicated to the Shinto god of war, who gave his blessing to the construction of Tōdai-ji by means of an oracle. A little to the north is the **Sangatsu-dō** (Hall of the Third Month), immediately recognizable for its elegant roof with its wave-like 'double-exposure'—the result of one structure being built onto an older one. The latter is the oldest building in Nara, predating the Daibutsu-den by 15 years. Inside, via the outer worship hall, is a dimly lit collection of priceless Buddhist statues.

The most ancient and remarkable of Tōdai-ji's great buildings is on the other side of its grounds, northwest of the Daibutsu-den. The **Shōsō-in** is a treasure house, built by Emperor Shōmu to house the thousands of priceless objects which found their way to Nara along the Silk Route (this stretched from the Mediterranean through the Near and Middle East, before passing into China, and trickling onward through Korea to Japan). Sealed for hundreds of years, and opened only on the rare orders of the emperor himself, it represents a time capsule of the treasures of 8th-century civilization: musical instruments, glass, mirrors, textiles from China, Persia and Southeast Asia. The building's distinctive design—it looks like a log cabin on stilts—seems to have contributed to the preservation of these objects. The old theory used to be that it was the walls of interlocking cypress logs that held the secret: swelling in damp weather and shrinking in dry conditions, they allowed just enough air to circulate in and around the treasures.

These days, the Shōsō-in's contents are housed in purpose-built concrete buildings. Once a year, a selection of them is displayed at the Nara National Museum. For this reason alone, late October and early November is the best time to visit Nara.

Nara Park

East of Kōfuku-ji and the Sarusawa Pond, a large *torii* gateway marks the entrance to the sacred territory of the Kasuga Shrine, a 213-acre forest parkland stretching over the lower slopes of Mt Mikasa. This is the home of the thousand or so deer who crop up all over Nara and add so much to its charm. They are sacred animals, messengers of the Shinto gods, and for centuries killing them was a capital offence. Extremely appealing on first acquaintance, they soon become irritating: they're spoilt rotten, and extremely cheeky. These days the emissaries of the divine are more likely to steal your lunch than bring tidings from heaven. During the October rutting season, the stags can become aggressive and unpredictable and are de-horned in a special ceremony; all the same you might want to steer clear of them at this time, and keep an eye on young children.

Nara National Museum (Kokuritsu Hakubutsukan)

Open 9–4.30; adm ¥400 (more for special exhibitions).

This small but richly endowed museum has more treasures than it can display at once: because of this, and for conservation purposes, exhibits are rotated, making it difficult to give a detailed commentary.

The **Main Gallery**, a Gallic-looking building opened in 1894, contains a variety of archaeological relics excavated from temple sites and burial mounds, and a showcase of pieces from the museum's finest collection: Buddhist sculpture. The statues are superb (many of them were compulsorily 'lent' by temples during the Meiji period) and are arranged chronologically; with the help of the excellent English books and pamphlets you can trace the development of styles. An **underground passage** leading from the back of the first gallery makes this even easier. It contains a unique educational display of models and panels which demonstrate in detail the basic types and techniques of Buddhist art: the various kinds of statue, the pedestals on which they're mounted, and the different ways of carving, casting and constructing an image. The passage leads to the modern **Annex Gallery** with sections on statues, paintings, calligraphy and documents, and applied arts such as metalwork, bells and ritual implements. It is here that an exhibition of treasures from the Shōsō-in is held every autumn.

Kasuga Taisha (Kasuga Grand Shrine)

East of the deer park, on the slopes of Mt Mikasa, is the Kasuga Shrine, founded by the Fujiwara family in 710. The four deities worshipped here, known collectively as the Kasuga Myōjin, were carried to Nara on the backs of deer: the animals which these days pinch tourists' ice-creams are their descendants. Rows of tall stone lanterns line the main approach to the shrine buildings, donated by businesses as well as by devout individuals. Off the path to the left is the pleasant **Manyō Botanical Garden**, a collection of flowers and herbs dedicated to the *Manyōshū*, an 8th-century poetry anthology, and said to contain every one of the three hundred plants mentioned in its verses.

The inner shrine begins at the **Nandai-mon** (Great South Gate), beyond which is a courtyard containing booths selling talismans. The **Chūō-mon** is the next gate. You can't pass or take photographs beyond here, but you can see through, past the **Haiden** (Oratory) to the four individual shrines of the Kasuga Myōjin: from left to right, Takemikazuchi, Futsunushi, Ame-no-Koyane (legendary forebear of the Fujiwara), and his wife, Himegami. Traditionally the halls here were rebuilt every 20 years, but the last time was in 1957, and after a gap of decades the buildings need a lick of paint here and there.

Left of the oratory is a **dance platform** where sacred performances are dedicated to the deities on festival days or on payment of a donation by a worshipper. The dances offered here are among the oldest in the country, and the **Hōmotsu-kan** (Treasure Hall, *open Apr–Oct 8.30–4.30, Nov–Mar 9–6*), a little further down the hill, contains masks and a pair of giant drums played on special occasions. The most impressive of these is the On-Matsuri, from 16–18 December, held at the small **Wakamiya Shrine**, south of the main shrine. Wakamiya means 'young prince': the deity worshipped at this festival, with *nō*, sumo and ancient dances, is the child of the married *kami* from the senior shrine.

Western Nara

Heijō (Castle of Peace)

Kintetsu line to Saidai-ji station, then a 15-minute walk east to the museum (open 9–5) which is in the northwest corner of the site.

Today, the site of the 8th-century Nara Imperial Palace and Heijō-kyō, the city that surrounded it, is a bleak and lonely place of overgrown fields and semi-excavated avenues.

The archaeologists began working in earnest in 1958, and only about one quarter of the site has been completed. Still, with a stroll around the site and a visit to the **Heijō Shiryōkan** (Museum), it's possible to get a feeling for the scale and magnificence of the first great city of Japan.

Miraculously, given Japan's hunger for real estate, the site has remained more or less intact. A railway line crosses it, but the National Highway was expensively routed to swerve west just before the southern perimeter. The excavated areas can be visited: the raised concrete base was the **Daigoku-den** (Imperial Great Council Hall); lawns, bushes and gravel indicate the position of the main buildings, pillars and avenues respectively.

The **museum** has models, aerial photos and sample artefacts showing the techniques of excavation and preservation, and some remarkably fresh-looking Nara-period coins, nails and even leaves.

Tōshōdai-ji (Temple of T'ang)

By Kintetsu Line train to Nishinokyō (change at Saidaiji) or buses 52, 63, 70, 97 or 98. Open 8.30–4.30; adm ¥300.

This magnificent and matchlessly well-preserved temple complex was founded in 759 by the Chinese priest Ganjin, who had a profound influence on Nara Buddhism.

In 733, in the first flush of enthusiasm for the Tōdai-ji building project, Emperor Shōmu dispatched envoys to China. Their task appeared relatively straightforward: to bring back a Buddhist master, a trophy holy man to go with the monumental temple which Shōmu was busy constructing. Almost nothing went according to plan. After ten years of searching, they finally struck lucky with a famous abbot called Chien Chen (Japanese pronunciation: Ganjin), then in his fifties, who accepted the commission and began preparations for the dangerous crossing to Japan. Ten years, six separate attempts and many disasters later, he arrived in Nara in 754. By this time, Shōmu had abdicated and Ganjin himself had become blind. He was immediately installed at Tōdai-ji with a brief to inject some Chinese discipline into the somewhat languid Nara monasteries. In the end, Ganjin's zeal exceeded all expectations. He quit Tōdai-ji in disgust at its laxness, and with his surviving Chinese followers set up his own monastery here at Tōshōdai-ji, at a disdainful distance from the capital. Five of those original 8th-century buildings, and many smaller treasures, survive.

Touring Tōshōdai-ji

The finest of the halls is the **Kon-dō** (Main Hall) which can be seen through the **Nandai-mon** (Great South Gate), a 1960s reconstruction. Its magnificent tile roof has been rebuilt higher and heavier than it would once have been (there are plans to reinstate the lighter, flatter roof in future restorations), and the hall's imposingly weighty, stern form belies the subtlety of its construction. The seven bays of its long sides are narrower at the ends of the building than they are in the middle. This helps in supporting the roof (whose weight rests largely on the outer pillars), but also concentrates the eye on the centre bay and the statues which are visible through it.

At this early stage in Buddhist architecture, a temple's worship hall was itself out of bounds to lay worshippers. They prayed from the outside (the portico provided shelter), and the interior was reserved for the sculpted deities and their priests. The statues within have been toppled by earthquakes and battered by war, but they're still in remarkable condition. Carved by Chinese artists from Ganjin's entourage, they mark a fresh spirit in Nara sculpture, consistent with his newly rigorous approach to worship and discipline. Compared to the warm, humane sculptures carved 140 years earlier for Hōryū-ji, these are austere, mysterious, awe-inspiring figures. At their centre is the cosmic Buddha, **Roshana**, constructed out of dry lacquer on a wood and metal base, and surrounded by a halo of 1,000 lesser beings (864 of them survive). To the right is a very cross-looking **Yakushi**, God of Healing, and to the left an extraordinary **thousand-armed Kannon** with 953 of its eponymous limbs intact. A thick and mysterious fog once cloaked this hall for ten days, the story goes. When it had cleared, the monks re-entered to find this statue, carved and gilded by heavenly hands.

The **Kō-dō** (Lecture Hall), directly behind the Kon-dō, began life in 710 as a hall of the Heijō Imperial Palace, donated to Tōshōdai-ji by Empress Kōken in 759. The doors, brackets and Miroku statue inside are from the 12th and 13th centuries, however, and more than anything else the building looks like a Kamakura period hall. Among the temple's lesser buildings are a number of 12th and 13th century additions: the **Kaidan**, a three-tiered stone ordination platform, the **Shoro** (bell tower), the **Korō** (a drum tower also said to contain relics of the Buddha) and a long narrow building on the east side of the two main halls, containing priests' quarters and an altar. Behind this are two early 8th-century **treasure and sutra houses**, built in the same log cabin style as Tōdai-ji's Shōsō-in, and predating it.

The modern **Shin-Hōzō** (New Treasure House) apes this style in fire-proof concrete. As well as a set of illustrated scrolls describing the perilous adventures of Ganjin, and various wooden and dry-lacquer *bodhisattvas*, there's an 8th–9th-century **headless Buddha**, carved out of a single piece of nutmeg—more fascinating as a torso, one suspects, than it would ever have been as a perfect statue. In the absence of feet, hands or a face, attention is focused fully on the plump, muscular legs and torso and on the voluptuous, clinging drapery of the robe.

The temple's most famous statue is shown, unfortunately, for only one day a year, on the anniversary of Ganjin's death, 6 June. It's displayed in the **Miei-dō** in the northeast corner of the precincts: still clad in his original colours, blind eyes closed, the old sage himself sits in deep meditation on the verge of death. A quiet grove in the northeast contains his **grave**, beneath a stupa-topped mound.

Yakushi-ji

By Kintetsu Line train to Nishinokyō (change at Saidaiji) or buses 52, 63, 97 or 98. Both the station and the bus stop are closest to the back (north) entrance to the temple. Open 8.30–5; adm ¥400.

Modern reconstructions are a depressing feature of Japan's fire and earthquake-wracked temples and shrines, and the results are almost always disappointing. Yakushi-ji, though, is an inspirational exception. This 8th-century temple was almost completely destroyed by fire in 1528; sensitive modern restoration, based around the single surviving pagoda, has created a picture of how a big Nara temple would have looked at the height of its fortunes.

If you've entered from the north, make your way through the precincts to the humble **Nandai-mon** (Great South Gate), erected as a temporary replacement and still doing the job after 300 years. From here you can see the layout of the complex as the planners intended. Yakushi-ji was first built in Fujiwara-kyō, Japan's capital from 687 to 710. When the court moved to Nara in 710, the big monasteries went with it; the reconstruction of Yakushi-ji on its new site was complete by 730. It was the first temple to be built with two pagodas which stand, as they did then, on either side and slightly in front of the main hall.

The **Tō-tō** (East Pagoda), finished in 730, is the only survivor of the 1528 fire, and the only surviving structure of its period in Japan. Its western twin (**Sai-tō**) was rebuilt identically in 1984. Both show an unusual style, since the three true roofs each have beneath them a smaller lean-to roof which shelters the outer balcony. They look as if they have six floors, or rather as if a smaller and a larger three-storey pagoda have magically fused into one another. Critics are fond of describing the staccato effect of this interleaving as 'contrapuntal' or 'rhythmic'; it's suggested that the architecture of the pagoda may have been influenced by the growth of Japanese music which was taking wing at the same time.

The **Kon-do** (Main Hall)—a 1976 reconstruction—has a similarly complicated roof arrangement above its three great doors. Inside are three bronze statues, originally gilded, but glazed to an ebony lustre by the smoke and heat of the 1528 fire which they, but not the hall, survived. The central figure of the triad represents the eponymous Yakushi, Buddha of Healing, a solid and serene figure sitting on a large medicine chest. Much more striking are his attendants, Gakkō and Nikkō, deities of the Moon and Sun, on the left and right respectively; here again the temptation is to talk in terms of music. With muscular torsos but slender arms and feet, they have an almost feminine delicacy, sashaying their arms and inflecting their hips as if dancing to unheard music. Those square slots in their forearms would once have been threaded with billowing scarves.

As interesting as the statues, and something of a puzzle to art historians, is the plinth/chest on which Yakushi sits and the mysterious reliefs visible around its rim. They're best examined from behind, through the window in the rear corridor. On the upper edge is a grapevine motif, held to be West Asian or even Greek in origin, and imported via India and China along the Silk Road. The ovals and squares are considered Persian, and the dragon, phoenix, tiger and tortoise on each of the four sides are T'ang Chinese. Most puzzling are the 12 hairy fanged barbarians peeping out from arched cave entrances. They resemble figures from Hindu temples, but there is nothing else like them in Japanese art.

Other Buildings

The **Kō-dō** (Lecture Hall), behind the Main Hall, dates from 1852 and is slated for replacement by a reconstruction of the original. Beyond the **East Pagoda** (the original one) is the **Tōin-dō**, a 13th-century hall containing a **Sho-Kannon**, a flawlessly cast, standing figure with a beautiful, almost arrogant expression. For a week or two in the New Year, and a bit longer in October–November, the modern **Daihōzō-den** (Great Treasure House) is open to visitors. Three objects stand out from its collection: an oil painting on hemp of the goddess Kichijo-ten as a plump, seductive looking court lady in multi-layered diaphanous robes; and two rare 8th-century paintings of Shinto deities, guardians of the temple whose shrine is over the road, just south of the Nandai-mon.

Hōryū-ji (Temple of Noble Law)

Buses 52, 97 or 98 take 53mins; bus 60 takes 39mins. All depart from Kintetsu-Nara station; alight at Hōryū-ji-mae bus stop (announced in English). The JR

Kansai main line takes 12mins from JR Nara station to Hōryū-ji station, a couple of kilometres from the temple. Open 8–4.30; 10 Nov–10 Mar, 8–4; adm ¥700.

Hōryū-ji, 10km from Nara in the otherwise insignificant village of Ikaruga, is a landmark of Japanese history, a cradle of Buddhism founded 1400 years ago, containing many of its most important works of art as well as the oldest wooden buildings in the world. It's less accessible, and correspondingly less crowded, than the central Nara temples; but to the student of art or history, it must rank among the top three sites in Japan.

History

Hōryū-ji owes its existence to Prince Umayado, known to posterity as **Shōtoku Taishi** (572–622), a seminal figure of Japanese history who, although he never actually ruled as emperor, is credited with several of the most important reforms of the Asuka Period (538–645), the earliest of Japan's historical eras.

Shōtoku was deeply impressed and influenced by Chinese culture and by its religion, Buddhism, which he instituted as Japan's state faith. He dispatched the first ambassadors to China, adopted its calendar, established a fixed hierarchy of 12 court ranks, and in 604 promulgated the Seventeen Articles, Japan's first national constitution. 'A country does not have two lords, the people do not have two masters,' he declared. As a politician, Shōtoku's genius was to use Buddhism, with its conception of a universe ruled over by the single cosmic Buddha, Dainichi, to assert the power of a single emperor, and to dissolve the power of the clans which still divided Japan.

For all this, Shōtoku was deeply and sincerely devout, and the first great Japanese scholar of Buddhism. He studied the scriptures under a Korean master and wrote commentaries on the sutras which were used as teaching aids in Chinese seminaries. But his greatest legacy is Hōryū-ji. Despite being rebuilt after his death, its subtle spiritual atmosphere still embodies the innocence and delicacy of the earliest Japanese Buddhism.

In 601 Shōtoku had built a palace at Ikaruga, the birthplace of his favourite consort, and in 607 he founded a temple here, originally known as Wakakusa-dera or Ikaruga-dera. Its principal image was a statue of Yakushi Nyorai by Tori Busshi, a sculptor who, like many of the craftsmen on the building project, came from the Korean kingdom of Paekche.

The years following the completion of the temple were sad ones for Shōtoku who died, soon after his mother and consort, in 622. Worse was to follow for his descendants. The heirs of Soga no Umako, Shōtoku's great adviser and statesman, fell out with the Prince's son Yamashiro, who had made a claim for the throne. When Yamashiro retired to Ikaruga it was taken (perhaps rightly) as a sign that he was plotting rebellion. The Soga family sent an army to storm the Ikaruga Palace. Outnumbered, Yamashiro, along with the last of Shōtoku's blood relatives, committed suicide in the palace grounds. In 670 the temple complex was struck by lightning and burned down.

Fearful that Shōtoku would seek ghostly revenge for the snuffing out of his line, succeeding generations of rulers rebuilt and expanded Hōryū-ji. A personal cult developed around Shōtoku, who was thought to have been reborn as a Buddha in the temple's statues. Until recently the Prince's image adorned the ¥10,000 note.

Hōryū-ji tip: many of the treasures of Hōryū-ji, Japan's finest, are displayed in the deepest murk, pointlessly obscured by crude bars and wire mesh. Remember to bring a torch (if you haven't got one of your own, borrow one from your lodgings: hotel rooms are required to have them by law.)

Sai-in (West Precinct)

From Hōryū-ji-mae bus stop, an avenue leads north to the **Nandai-mon** (Great South Gate), built in 1439, which frames the temple beyond it. The **Chū-mon** (Central Gate) gives onto the main compound and forms part of the **Kairō** (Corridor), actually a roofed wall, which encloses it. The **Chū-mon** dates from the early 8th century; its pillars swell in the middle, a technique know as *entasis*, used in Greek temples to eliminate the illusion of concavity, which may have reached China from Europe along the Silk Route. Unusually, only two bays provide ingress to visitors. Normally there would have been a third, reserved for members of the aristocracy. This arrangement is said to reflect an egalitarian streak in Shōtoku's thinking. In the outer bays are two **Ni-ō** (Guardian Kings), carved in 711; note the monstrous webbing under their muscular shoulders.

The inner courtyard is unusual in its layout too. Shōtoku's original temple was built on a north–south axis with the pagoda in front of the Main Hall as the worshipper approached them. Here they stand side by side.

Gojū-no-tō (Five-storey Pagoda)

This is the most fascinating structure in Hōryū-ji. Over a hundred feet tall, its five roofs diminish in size as they ascend in the following proportions—10:9:8:7:6. The roofs get steeper too, so that the entire building appears even more soaring than it is, as if about to lift gently off the ground. Like all the oldest pagodas, the primary purpose of this one is as a marker for relics of the Buddha. A chamber 3m below the ground contains plaques, a copper bowl, beads, pearls and a glass relic bottle inside two larger gold and bronze containers. Unfortunately, the excavation of 1949 revealed the relic jar to be empty.

The earliest pagodas were monuments, not buildings; it was only in later years that they were built with internal space and sanctuaries and images of their own. Hōryū-ji's marks a transitional period. There is no 'inside' to this pagoda, but instead four grottoes at ground level between the corners of the base. These contain remarkable tableaux of famous moments from Buddhist history, modelled out of clay with individual statuettes. Coarse mesh masks the dim interiors; this is the moment to switch on your torch.

The **south tableau** depicts the Paradise of Miroku, Buddha of the Future. The one to the **west** shows the disciples dividing up the historical Buddha's relics after his death, kneeling on either side of his coffin. More interesting is the **east tableau** in which Monju, a saintly disciple of the Buddha, and Yuima, a celebrated scholar, engage in learned debate. The latter is depicted as an old man who, rather than achieve Buddhahood, has opted to remain on earth to expound the sacred teachings. His frail limbs and slack features are poignantly and realistically modelled; on his knees rests a tripod desk from which he reads.

Finest of all is the **north tableau** which shows the moment of death of the historical Buddha, Shaka. This is a recurring image in Buddhist art but rarely has it been depicted with quite such passion and drama. The background represents the beetling cliffs and swirling clouds above Mt Sumeru, the centre of the earth in Buddhist cosmology. Dead Shaka himself, larger than life and still bearing traces of gold leaf, lies on a low bed; behind him *bodhisattvas* sit in calm attendance. But attention focuses on the human disciples kneeling in front. Their bony, elderly bodies are contorted with grief—heads thrown back, fists pummelling their chests, mouths frozen in screams of despair. The detail—from the disordered drapes of their robes and their pierced ears, to their bulging necks and tiny, individually shaped teeth—is perfect. Just one figure, to the left of the Buddha's head, remains impassive, withdrawn, it almost appears, into catatonic shock.

Kon-dō (Gold Hall)

The main hall of Hōryū-ji was rebuilt sometime after the fire of 670, probably around 710, making it the oldest wooden building in the world. Wider, squatter, and more monumentally magnificent than the pagoda, it shares its steep roofs and smaller upper storey. The middle roof juts out as much as 14 feet, and supports, carved in the shape of lions and dragons, have had to be added at a later date to prevent it sagging.

Several of the statues within date from the temple's original founding by Shōtoku Taishi, or just after his death, making the oldest nearly 1400 years old. They were commissioned by the temple's patrons and cast in bronze, probably by naturalized Korean craftsmen from the kingdom of Paekche. Historians differ on the artistic heritage of these figures. Certain details of the carving, particularly the dignified, rather stiff regularity of the folds and drapes, suggests an effort to reproduce in bronze the look of stone carvings of the Chinese Northern Wei Dynasty. Exotic details, like the elaborate open-work crowns and jewellery and the intricate honeysuckle borders, point to a Korean provenance. The situation isn't made any clearer by the reluctance on the part of some Japanese scholars to attribute their National Treasures to foreign, and especially Korean, genius.

The hall contains three separate groupings of statues, each topped by an elaborate canopy, plus the **Shitennō** (Four Guardian Kings) at each of the cardinal points. The left-hand statue is the least important, a statue of **Amida Nyorai**, carved in the 13th century at a time when Amida was emerging as the pre-eminent Japanese deity. At the right-hand side is **Yakushi**, Buddha of Healing; on his back is a date (607) and an inscription, explaining that the statue was cast in memory of the late Emperor Yōmei by his son, Shōtoku, and his sister, later Empress Suiko.

The central space is occupied by a **Shaka Triad** (the historical Buddha, Shaka, flanked by two unidentified *bodhisattvas*) commissioned by Suiko as a prayer for Shōtoku's recovery from illness, but completed as a memorial the year after his death (623). Both are attributed to a sculptor called Tori Busshi and share obvious characteristics. They are composed, dignified, trustworthy figures: static but graceful, radiating calm and impersonal benevolence. Yakushi and Shaka hold their hands in identical *mudra* or symbolic gestures: the open right palm banishes fear while the extended fingers of the left grant wishes. Both sit cross-legged atop plinths which are completely covered by their flowing robes. The drapes are one of the most striking and characteristic elements of Tori's style. They fan out in a broad flat plane, almost, but not quite, symmetrical. The impression is of neatness and order—'rhythmical' is the word sometimes used to describe them. The figures flanking Shaka stand on lotus blossoms and hold in their left hands mystic jewels called *centamani.* Their head-dresses are ornate and unusual; they've been compared to Persian crowns worn by the Sasanian kings, and the headgear of Korean shamans. Behind each statue is a pointed halo with twining honeysuckle designs on the inner circle, and flickering flames on the outer edge, suggesting the power and passion which lie behind the serene faces of the deities. The seven miniature buddhas in the haloes of the principal figures represent their previous incarnations.

The hanging canopies are unique works of art in themselves, although they may incorporate later restorations and repairs. To their upper edges are attached beautiful miniature carvings of angelic musicians surrounded by haloes of blossoms, each painstakingly chiselled out of the thinnest wood. Below these are several wooden phoenixes, stylized in form (their combs come so far over their heads as to cover their eyes), but with realistically bony, bird-like feet.

The final set of statues represent the **Shitennō**, the directional Guardian Kings, familiar in other temples for their ferociously irate expressions and bellicose poses. On these Shitennō, however, attention focuses on the accoutrements of worldly rank, not physical prowess: the elaborate robes, clasped by a stylized knot, the rich cords encircling the ample bellies, the high-necked collars and minutely-detailed crowns. Stocky and pillar-like, standing on the backs of comically crude demons, they look more like dignified mandarins than burly warlords.

Sometime after the rebuilding of the Kon-dō following the 670 fire, its inner walls were painted with elaborate frescoes of the Four Paradises acclaimed for centuries as 'some of the noblest examples of religious art in Asia.' As artists were copying the pictures in January 1949 a heater which they were using to warm themselves short-circuited during the night. The fire was put out before it could damage the structure of the building—but the delicate pigments were ruined forever. The present frescoes are reproductions. They depict: the Western Paradise of Amida (on the west wall), Yakushi (on the northwest), Miroku (northeast), and Shaka (east).

Other Buildings Around the West Precinct

The **Ko-dō**, built into the back wall of the West Precinct, was brought to Hōryū-ji from Kyoto in 990, and contains a 10th-century Yakushi triad. In front of it are two smaller structures: a **bell tower** with an 8th-century bell, and the **Kyōzo** or sutra repository.

Immediately to the east of the West Precinct are two long low buildings running north–south: dormitories for the temple's monks. The one closest to the West Precinct, the Higashi-muro, dates from the Kamakura period; its south end (entrance opposite a pond) is the **Shōryō-in** (Hall of the Prince's Soul), a temple to Shōtoku containing scroll paintings and statues of him and his doomed family. Even the Prince's horse is honoured, in a small shrine to the east.

Daihōzō-den (Great Treasure Hall)

The **Treasure Hall** (*open 8–5; 20 Nov–10 Mar, 8–4*), a concrete fireproof structure built to supplant the log-cabin original, contains enough masterpieces to fill a book all of its own. It consists of two separate buildings joined by a covered corridor. The first room contains archaeological finds from the original temple, Wakakusa-dera, and the second displays **images of Prince Shōtoku** himself at various stages of life. There's an appealing 13th-century statue of the two-year-old Prince, looking realistically childish despite his praying hands and earnest expression (he was a precocious boy who was born with the power of speech, and read Chinese while still a child). The most famous picture is of the adult Prince, with a thin moustache and youthful beard fuzz, flanked by his two sons. The father carries a wand of office and jewelled long-sword; the boys have miniature swords and dinky, Asuka-period bunches. This is the picture which was reproduced on the ¥10,000 note and gave rise to the expression 'a Shōtoku', meaning 'a tenner'.

The next room contains miniature, personal images of the kind that priests might carry in the sleeves of their robes; and the **Yumechigai (Dream-Changing) Kannon**, a small, smiley statue credited with the power of turning nightmares into sweet dreams. The final room of the first building displays the celebrated **Kudara Kannon**, a mysterious and intriguing statue, unique in Asian art. Little of its origins is known but it seems to have turned up at Hōryū-ji only during the Edo period. Its traditional name indicates Korean manufacture ('Kudara' was the Japanese name for Paekche), but Japanese scholars dispute this; certainly nothing like it survives in Korea or China today.

It is a slim, tremendously tall statue (over 2m), both mild and imposing, with unnaturally long arms and legs. On its head and neck it wears a bronze crown and collar and it holds a long-necked vase or water jar in its left hand. The lacquer surface of the camphor wood, once colourfully painted, has become cracked and faded over time, adding to the aura of age and sanctity, although the date of its creation can only be estimated. In its flat, planar composition, the symmetry of its drapes and the long, elegant sleeves which flow to the ground in stylized curves, the Kannon resembles other statues of the Asuka period. But the relaxed set of the body, the dreamy, faraway expression and unmuscular, almost round-shouldered physique impart quite a different impression from, say, the Tori Busshi statues in the Kon-dō (this statue also used to stand there but, being wood, it was moved out after the 1949 fire).

The second building of the museum contains drawings and scrolls, carved angelic musicians, a variety of statues of Buddhist deities from the 8th to 11th centuries, and two miniature Buddhist temples, its greatest treasures.

The **Tamamushi Zushi** (Jewel Beetle Altar) is named for its most striking feature, long since rotted to dust. When the seven and a half foot tall shrine was built in the 650s, the bronze open-work around the edge of the base covered the iridescent wings of 9000 *tamamushi*—the *Chrysochroa elegans* beetle. It contains a miniature statue, and the roof is a precise model of a tiled hip-and-gable roof, complete with owl's tail finials. The outer doors of the shrine bear painted *bodhisattvas*; the base panels are decorated with famous scenes from the scriptures. At the front, angels hover above two monks who make offerings to the relics of the Buddha; at the back, dragons and phoenixes flap about the legendary Mt Sumeru as it rises from the sea. The side panels are more celebrated: both depict the young Shaka (the historical Buddha) engaged in heroic self-sacrifice. In one he is shown calmly hanging up his robe on a tree, then plummeting through space down the cliff he has jumped off, and finally being eaten by the hungry tiger whom he has chosen to feed with his own body. The various figures are slim and youthful, with long delicate necks— even the guardian kings on the upper doors who usually have imposing, bulky physiques.

Tradition ascribes ownership of the Tamamushi Shrine to Shōtoku's aunt, the Empress Suiko, although no one knows for sure. The **Tachibana-zushi**, however, is named after its owner, Lady Tachibana, the mother of Emperor Shōmu's consort. It was built probably a century or so after the time of Shōtoku and enshrines a beautiful trinity of Amida and attendant *bodhisattvas.* They sit on lotus leaves which rise out of a piece of bronze realistically carved to look like the surface of a pond.

Tō-in (East Precinct)

The land to the east of the pagoda and Gold Hall was the site of Shōtoku's Ikaruga Palace, demolished by the Soga family after the bloody ructions which snuffed out his line. It was rebuilt as a temple a century later when the cult of Shōtoku started to take wing.

The two precincts are quite different in layout. You enter through the **Tōdai-mon** (Great East Gate) which marks the boundary between west and east, and the first building you see is the striking, octagonal **Yume-dono** (Dream Hall) standing on top of a thick stone base, with a dramatic flaming jewel mounted on the apex of its roof. The East Precinct has no Gold Hall or pagoda, the Yume-dono serving as a combination of the two. The name comes from an old story about Shōtoku: it's said that as he sat on this spot, pondering the Sanskrit scriptures, a mysterious old man would appear in his dreams and explain the meaning of the most difficult passages.

Within is a fine Nara-period dry lacquer statue of the priest Gyōshin, who supervised the construction of the Tō-in, and the **Kuze Kannon**, holiest of the Hōryū-ji masterpieces. It predates the Yume-dono, and is the statue most intimately associated with Shōtoku himself; tradition variously has it that he worshipped the statue during his lifetime, was the model for it, carved it himself, or was reborn as the deity after his death.

The statue is miraculously well preserved with almost all its gold leaf intact. It is only displayed to the public twice a year, from 11 April to 15 May, and then in the autumn from 22 October to 20 November. Until late in the 19th century, it was completely hidden from view; not even the temple's abbots had laid eyes on it for centuries. Then, in the 1880s, an American art historian named Ernest Fenellosa undertook a survey of Buddhist art works on behalf of the Meiji Government. Since the Restoration of the Emperor in 1868 and the promulgation of 'State' Shinto, Buddhism had been treated with, at best, indifference and frequently with official hostility. Fenellosa had no trouble obtaining letters which gave him access to any temples he wished. In 1884, against the wishes of the Hōryū-ji priests, the closed central shrine of the Yume-dono was opened and its contents removed. 'I shall never forget our feelings as the long disused key rattled in the dusty lock,' wrote Fenellosa. 'Within the shrine appeared a tall mass closely wrapped about in swaddling bands of cotton cloth, upon which the dust of ages had gathered. It was no light task to unwrap the contents, some 500 yards of cloth having been used, and our eyes and nostrils were in danger of being choked with the pungent dust. But at last the final folds of the covering fell away, and this marvellous statue, unique in the world, came forth to human sight for the first time in centuries.'

To Fenellosa, there was no question that the Kannon was of Korean manufacture. In style it has much in common with the serene stiffness of the Tori bronzes in the Kon-dō, but heightened and rendered more monumental and magnificent. The splayed drapes which jut out symmetrically on either side of the figure's skirts are particularly bold. The face is fleshy with traces of the 'archaic smile' of the Kon-dō's Shaka playing on the thick, almost negroid lips. In front of the chest, Kannon holds a flaming jewel in an unusual and compli-cated hand gesture. The filigree crown and halo teem with minute detail.

Chūgū-ji

Open 9–3.45; adm ¥300.

This small nunnery, east of the Yume-dono, was originally built several hundred metres away as the palace of Shōtoku's mother. On her death in 621 (the year before the Prince himself) he had it converted into a memorial nunnery which was moved and recon-structed on this sight in the 13th century. The treasure hall, built in the 1950s over a shallow pond, contains Hōryū-ji's most beautiful and accessible work of art, usually referred to as **Miroku bosatsu**, Buddha of the Future (although there's disagreement as to the exact deity represented). It's very similar to the statue in Kyoto's Kōryū-ji temple: a slim, smiling youth, his right hand beneath his chin, his arm resting on his knee which is folded in the 'half-lotus' position. The neck, arms, fingers and naked torso (carved out of camphor wood, once gilded, now deeply tanned) are long and delicate; the face bears an expression of profound calm and benevolence. Despite the stylized proportions and the curious spherical buns on top of the head, there is something very human and realistic about the figure. It's an object of personal prayer and devotion, of sensuous, intuitive communion with the divine, in stark contrast with the monumental, ritualistic statues of the Western Precinct.

Also in this building is a reconstruction of fragments of a 7th-century tapestry, the **Tenjukoku Mandala**, embroidered by Shōtoku's consort and depicting the Prince in Paradise. In its time it must have been bold and impressive, but too little survives to form a picture of it today.

(✆ 0742–)   ***Where to Stay***

Nicest of all, and *moderately* priced for a single room, is the 80-year-old **Nara Hotel**, ✆ 23 5252, 5 minutes by taxi from the Kintetsu Nara station, towards the eastern end of town. It has big, Western-style rooms (plus a few Japanese) in an old tiled building, with restaurants and gardens, and a modern concrete wing. The **Hotel Sunroute Nara**, ✆ 22

5151, is a fine modern city hotel, about the same price as the Nara, and much more conveniently situated. The **Hotel Fujita Nara**, ✆ 23 8111, and **Nara Royal Hotel**, ✆ 34 1131, have good, modern facilities, beginning at around ¥10–12,000 for a single.

There are three good members of the Japanese Inn Group: **Ryokan Hakuhō**, ✆ 26 7891, and **Ryokan Matsumae**, ✆ 22 3686, are both *inexpensive*, and close to the centre of town. More interesting, but a bit more of a walk, is **Ryokan Seikan-sō**, ✆ 22 2670, a *cheap* old wooden inn in a former *geisha* house.

Eating Out

For all its art treasures and history, Nara has the nightlife of a small Japanese town—decent but modest restaurants, bars and *izakaya* (where you can drink or eat) which close early. If your hotel or inn is half-serious about food, eat there. Otherwise Sanjō-dōri, which runs west from Sarusawa Pond towards the JR station, has plenty of places open after dusk.

Ise

In more ways than one, the ancient twin shrines at Ise are central to Japanese culture and identity. Dedicated to the sun and rice deities, and enshrining the Three Sacred Treasures of the Imperial Family, they are the biggest and most important centre of the native Shinto religion, and the controversial emperor cult which survives—discreetly—even today. Architecturally, the magnificent cypress wood halls represent the earliest form of native building, before the curves and tiles of Chinese Buddhism. Most interesting of all, the rituals practised here embody ideas which still lie at the the root of much Japanese thinking—ideas of the internal and external, of cleanliness and purity, decay and renewal. If you've ever wondered why train and taxi drivers wear white gloves, or why Japanese families throw out perfectly good TVs when they are just a few months old, clues to the answers lie here.

Getting There and Around

Ise City, a nondescript place with few other attractions, is served by the Kintetsu line, connecting with Ōsaka and Nagoya, and the JR Sangū line which links up with the rest of the JR network. Ise-shi station is the most convenient, but some Kintetsu trains stop only at Uji-Yamada; both stations are a few minutes' walk from the Ge-kū (Outer Shrine). For the Nai-kū (Inner Shrine), 7km beyond, take a taxi or the half-hourly bus from the station.

Ise Jingū (Grand Shrine of Ise)

To Ise, the province of the divine wind, roll the endless waves, the waves of the Eternal World. There I will live, in that pleasant and secluded land.

The Sun Goddess, Amaterasu Ōmikami,
in the *Nihongi chronicles,* written in AD720

History

The origins of Ise Jingū are clouded by myth and unreliable chronologies, but from the very beginning the shrine was intimately associated with the Imperial Family. Amaterasu Ōmikami, Goddess of the Sun, direct ancestor of the emperors, was originally enshrined within the precincts of their palaces which were demolished and rebuilt on a fresh site with each new ruler. Under the semi-legendary Emperor Sujin, in the first century BC, she was installed in a permanent residence at the bottom of Mt Miwa near Nara. The present site at Ise was selected in 4 BC, and in AD 478 Amaterasu was joined by the Goddess of Cereals, Toyouke no Ōmikami, worshipped in the nearby Ge-kū (Outer Shrine).

These are profoundly important deities: the Sun, identified in myth with the Emperor himself, which gives life and light to the earth; and the Rice which nourishes his subjects. For centuries Ise Jingū was the private ancestral shrine of the Imperial Family, but the ceremonies conducted there were directed towards the well-being of the whole nation.

As the power of the emperors waned in the 12th century, the Shrine priests were forced to follow the example of the Buddhist temples and encourage devotion and offerings from the population at large. A shrine pilgrimage was established and became astonishingly popular, especially during the Edo period (1600–1867) when the country was periodically brought to a halt by Ise 'epidemics'. In 1705, three and a half million Japanese congregated at the shrine; similar explosions of mass hysteria occurred as late as 1830.

The Meiji period (1868–1912) saw the rise of State Shinto with its renewed emphasis on the divinity of the Emperor. The Grand Shrine became the heart of this aggressively nationalistic movement; it was refurbished with lavish government support. State Shinto was banned under the US Occupation, and today the Shrine exists as a private religious organization, maintaining strong links with the Emperor and Imperial Household Agency.

The Ceremony of Shrine Renewal (Jingū Shikinen Sengū)

Reverently the ground is levelled
At this Shrine on the Isuzu River;
And, the levelling accomplished,
The country of Japan will flourish,
The regions of Japan will prosper
Through the endless generations
Unto ages everlasting.

Song of the Levelling Ceremony, Ise Jingū

Among the many traditions and mysteries associated with Ise Jingu, the most profound and elaborate of all is the Ceremony of Shrine Renewal. Every 20 years (the last occasion was October 1993; the next will be 2013), the halls of the Ge-kū and Nai-kū, amid great and elaborate ritual, are dismantled and identically reconstructed on an adjacent site. Not just the buildings, but all their contents, are recreated from scratch: 2500 votive objects crafted from the finest materials as offerings to the resident deities. The rites were first perfomed in AD 690. With a single break of 124 years during the civil wars of the middle ages, they have been performed without interruption ever since.

The origins and meaning of the ceremony are mysterious, but plainly there is a practical aspect to it: in humid, typhoon-blighted, earthquake-wracked Japan, 20 years is a respectable span of life for any wooden building, especially one constructed on posts driven directly into the ground without the protection of stone foundations. Secondly, and most importantly from the historian's point of view, it is a means of preserving from oblivion the skills which created the shrine in the first place. After two decades, the young apprentices who worked on the previous reconstruction are master craftsmen, capable of passing on the techniques to the next generation.

It's also an aspect of the cult of purification and renewal which lies at the heart of many Shinto ceremonies. Architecturally, the shrine buildings are stylized palaces of the kind inhabited by the earliest human emperors. For centuries, until the establishment of the permanent capital of Heian-kyō (Kyoto) in the 8th century, it was traditional to move the site of the palace with each new ruler, to avoid the impurity associated with death and mourning. Above all, as indicated by the quotation above, it's a mystical celebration of rebirth and renewal of the kind found at the heart of so many religions—renewal of the sun, renewal of the rice crop, even renewal of the nation. 'People revere the august glory of the deity,' explains the guide book published by the shrine, 'and once every 20 years, they come into contact with the newly reborn divine light, thus being filled with new vigour and energy for the next 20 years. In order to maintain the eternal life of this land and make it forever new, at regular intervals new shrine structures are built alternately on the east and west plots of land, and people greet the new brilliance of the divine glory.'

The Ceremony of Renewal actually consists of more than 30 separate rites climaxing with the solemn transfer (*Sengyō*) of the divine symbols of the deity from the old shrine to the new. The next ceremony will be the 62nd. If all goes to schedule, prayers (to the deity of the mountain where timber for the construction of the new shrine will be felled) will begin in May 2005. Each stage of the building project—felling, transportation of timber, carpentry, ground-breaking, erection of foundations, doors and pillars, thatching, decoration of the completed shrines—is marked by solemn ceremonies presided over by Shinto priests, and celebrated by local people. The *Sengyō* itself is held at night. In torch-lit darkness, a long train of white-robed priests (including the High Priestess, a princess of the Imperial Family) processes to the accompaniment of drums and *koto*, carrying the box which contains the Sacred Mirror, the symbol of Amaterasu, from the old Nai-kū to the new. Simultaneously, an identical rite is held at the Ge-kū for Toyouke no Ōmikami.

As you would expect, none of this is cheap: the total cost of the 1993 ceremonies was a staggering ¥32.7 billion (almost $300 million at the time), raised entirely from private sources. ¥20 billion came from the Jingū organization, ¥4 billion from banks, and the remaining ¥8.7 billion from shrines across the country. The Emperor himself makes a donation, but strictly as a private individual from his personal funds (one of the laws enforced by the post-war American Occupation was a strict separation of state and religion). If the number of visitors it attracts (between five and six million a year) were not sufficient, these figures would be ample demonstration of the enormous power and importance of Ise in the Japanese mind.

The Architecture of Ise Jingū

The design of the Ise shrines—both the Nai-kū, Ge-kū and the fourteen auxiliary halls—is uniform; minor variations are noted under the descriptions of individual buildings. It's known as the *shimmei* style and represents one of the earliest and purest styles of native architecture. Small foreign elements have undoubtedly crept in, but the remarkable effect of vicennial reconstructions has been to preserve the shrines almost exactly as they would have looked 1300 years ago.

The immediate impression is of profound simplicity and purity, strikingly different from the elaborate style which Buddhism brought with it from China. Continental temples were typically tiled, with curved gables and gaudy vermilion paintwork; the Ise buildings are composed of plain, golden cypress wood, straight lines, and rich, heavy thatch. During the aggressive period of State Shinto, from the Meiji Restoration to the end of the Pacific War, the halls were encrusted with ostentatious decoration, eliminated during the reconstruction of 1953. The few non-native elements which survive today appear out of keeping with the tone of the rest of the architecture: the flaming orbs on top of the uprights, and the ornate metal caps on the end of the beams and posts (a practical measure, to prevent the ends of the wood crumbling before the 20 years are up).

There is disagreement as to what the form of the buildings represents, but the consensus seems to be that—with their heavy, insulating roofs, and floors raised on stilts off the damp ground—they are stylized versions of the kind of repositories used to store treasures or grain. Several originally functional elements have become merely decorative, but add greatly to the uniqueness of the buildings: they include the *chigi*, the distinctive 'horns' which project upwards from the roof ridge in line with its beams; the *muchikake*, eight truncated spikes which jut out from beneath the gable ends; and the *katsuogi*, smoothly polished logs resting horizontally on the roof ridge which once served to hold it down during storms and earthquakes. The Nai-kū has ten *chigi*, while on the Ge-kū there are only nine; the reasons for this discrepancy, if they exist, are lost in the mysterious past.

Touring Ise Jingū

The Nai-kū, as well as enshrining the principal deity, is the more interesting of the two shrines, although the Ge-kū is nearer to the stations, and visitors with a limited amount of time should go there. A description of the **Nai-kū** will serve for both.

For all their formal beauties, the great charm of the Ise shrines lies in their setting, an ancient cypress forest many centuries older than the oldest shrines established here. The entrance to the Nai-kū is across the **Uji-bashi**, a curving bridge. A very plain, austere *torii* gateway stands in front of the bridge: this is the first of several barriers or threshholds through which you will find yourself passing, each one marking a deeper level of sanctity. The second of these is the river itself: pilgrims are believed to be cleansed by the rushing waters of the Isuzu River below. The bridge, made of cypress and zelkova, is reconstructed along with the rest of the shrine at 20-year intervals. Sometimes storms and high water threaten to dismantle it prematurely: hence the pillars buried upstream, to stop typhoon-toppled tree trunks and other debris striking the bridge and damaging its foundations.

Through another *torii*, you turn right and pass a number of buildings, including the **Saikan** (Purification Hall) where priests spend the night before participation in shrine ceremonies. At the river bank below here are gravel steps: this is a designated point for further lustration. By now you've passed over another bridge and a small stream, and entered a still more sacred area of the Nai-kū.

The path bends round to the left. You pass through further *torii* and see a small stable, housing the sun goddess's sacred horse. The large building with the curved roof is the **Kagura-den**, where sacred dances are performed. Finally, you reach the **Nai-kū** itself. Visitors are allowed within the first gate, but three more palisade fences lie between here and the shrine itself. Even the gravel on the ground becomes finer, the closer you get to the inner sanctum. There are three buildings altogether within the enclosure, identical in design, but varying in size. The two to the rear are treasure houses; the central one is the shrine itself containing the holy of holies, the Sacred Mirror of Amaterasu.

Rather disappointingly, only the roofs of the inner buildings can be glimpsed. For an overall picture of the Ise style, you must turn to one of the smaller auxiliary shrines which are built in exactly the same style, such as the nearby Aramatsuri-no-Miya, which enshrines a more ferocious version of Amaterasu.

Kōya-san (Mt Kōya)

Kōya-san is the Mt Athos of Japan, an eleven-hundred-year-old temple city on a holy mountain in the Kansai heartland. Until a century ago women were forbidden; nowadays thousands of visitors of both sexes come here, but noticeably few foreigners. A small modern town of 4000 people has sprung up in their wake, but this is still principally a religious centre: a quarter of the population are monks, many of them students at the Buddhist Kōya University; many of the tourists here are genuine pilgrims, and accommodation is provided by 53 *shukubō*—temple-inns serving unique vegetarian food. There are few vending machines, and no neon: at night, walking past the temple walls and trees, it's still possible to imagine yourself in another age.

History

Kōya-san owes its fame and existence to one remarkable man, a 9th-century monk known during his lifetime as **Kūkai**, and posthumously awarded the title **Kōbō Daishi**, or simply *O-Daishi-sama* (Great Master). As well as being an outstanding scholar and founding priest of the Shingon (True Word) Sect of Esoteric Buddhism, Kūkai is remembered as a founding father of Japanese culture—a civil engineer, artist, sculptor, calligrapher, educator, and the linguist who invented the *kana* syllabaries used to render Chinese characters in Japanese pronunciation.

Kūkai was born in 774 in Shikoku, where he later achieved enlightenment and established the famous Pilgrimage of the Eighty-eight Temples. As the promising son of a local governor, he was educated in Kyoto by the greatest monks of the day, and ordained a priest. In 804 he travelled to China to study under the great master of Esoteric Buddhism, Hui-kuo. Kūkai excelled in his studies, picked up yet another name (*Henjo Kongō*,

'Universally Illuminating Adamantine One') and was confirmed as his master's successor. At the age of 32, he became the 8th patriarch of the Shingon Sect of Buddhism.

On Hui-kuo's death in 806, Kūkai began the dangerous sea voyage back to Japan. Before embarking, legend has it, he raised his *vajra* (a three-pronged implement used in Buddhist ritual) and flung it out over the ocean towards Japan, bidding it to 'go before me and find the place where Esoteric Buddhism may flourish.'

The new sect went down well in Japan and Kūkai soon found imperial patrons willing to build temples and endow universities. But the glamour and politicking of the capital were a distraction. True to the mystical traditions of both Esoteric Buddhism and the earliest Japanese religion, Kūkai sought a mountain retreat where the practice of Shingon and the training of its followers could be carried out in peace. In 816 he began scouting for a suitable spot among the mountains of the Kii Peninsula, south of Kyoto. Wandering alone one day, he met a hunter, seven feet tall, with a red face, carrying a bow and accompanied by a marvellous dog with two heads—one black and one white. The lofty hunter directed Kūkai towards Mt Kōya and gave him his dog to accompany him.

A little further on priest and hound met a woman, who announced herself as the guardian of the mountain and mother of the hunter. Deeper still into the mountain, Kūkai noticed a familiar object glinting in a tree—the pronged *vajra* which he had thrown from China all those years before. The mysterious dog-loving hunter and his mum were, of course, the guardian deities of the mountain: Kariba Myōjin and Niutsu Hime Myōjin, honoured today in the **Myōjin-sha** Shinto shrine. Kūkai knew that he had found the destined place.

Kōya-san had probably been a holy mountain for many years before the Daishi found it, but it suited his purposes in plenty of ways. It was remote from the capital, without being entirely inaccessible, and the peaks surrounding the high plateau protected it from the worst of the wind and snow. There are eight of them in two concentric rings, fancied to resemble the petals of a lotus, with the monastery at their centre. In 817 Kūkai was granted the land by imperial decree; within a few years, it was the site of a prosperous monastic centre, rivalling Enryaku-ji on Mt Hiei, to the northeast of Kyoto. Kūkai's business often took him to the capital, but it was Kōya where he chose to 'die' and where he is buried, along with many other great names from Japanese history, in Okuno-in cemetery.

Like Mt Hiei, Kōya's fortunes rose and fell. During the middle ages its private armies became notorious for their unruliness, and it was also used as a place of house arrest for high-class exiles. By the late 16th century, lay workers had wrested control of the mountain and its rich resources; they were bloodily quelled by Oda Nobunaga. At its peak, Kōya-san boasted 1500 temples; today there are 117. In 1872 women were at last admitted as pilgrims.

Getting There

The journey to Kōya-san is as thrilling as anything about the place; even in the bullet train-era, it still feels appealingly inaccessible and remote.

Ōsaka is the most convenient transport hub. From Namba station, special Kōya-bound trains run every 20–30mins on the private Nankai Kōya line. The express takes 1hr 40mins; the super express is only 25mins quicker and is more expensive. In both cases, you can buy a ticket all the way from Namba to the top of the mountain, including the cable car.

From Kyoto and Nara you must travel by JR lines to Hashimoto station, and there join the Nankai Kōya line for the last, spectacular leg. From Hashimoto the little train squeals round steep bends and through tunnels, along a forested valley punctuated here and there by terraced rice paddies and tiny settlements with gleaming tile roofs. The stations have long elaborate names, and nobody gets on or off.

The line ends at Gokurabashi, where a funicular railway accomplishes the final, near vertical ascent. The cable cars are extraordinary: like a set of steep steps mounted on wheels with the body of a tram built around them.

The upper cable car station has a taxi rank. From 5am to about 9pm buses connect with the town of Kōya.

Orientation and Tourist Information

The layout of Kōya-san is simple enough. The town is centred on a main street, running roughly west–east, on which most of the sub-temples are located. The **Kōya-san Tourist Association**, which provides maps, pamphlets, timetables and a booking service for temple accommodation, is located on the junction of this road with a north–south road; this crossing is the centre of the town.

West of this junction, on the north side of the main road, is **Kongōbu-ji**, the central monastery. Further west, and to the south, is the Garan compound, and south of there, the **Reihōkan museum**.

North of the junction, a road turns off west towards the cable-car station, the Tokugawa Mausoleum and the Nyōnin-dō.

At the eastern end of the main road are the entrances to Kōya-san's greatest attraction, the **Okuno-in cemetery and sanctuary**.

Buses connect all these places. Apart from the Okuno-in, they can all be covered in a day of hearty walking.

Kongōbu-ji (Temple of the Diamond Peak)

Open 8–5; Nov–Mar, 8.30–4.30; adm ¥350.

Kongōbu-ji was the name originally given by Kūkai to the entire mountain site; these days it refers to a single monastery, the most important on Kōya-san, chief temple of Shingon Buddhism. The main hall is 19th century, but the temple in its present form was founded in 1593 by Toyotomi Hideyoshi, the second of the great warlords who, not without bloodshed, united modern Japan.

Then called Seigan-ji, the temple was the scene of a particularly messy episode involving Toyotomi Hidetsugu, Hideyoshi's nephew, who for a long time enjoyed his uncle's favour and was named as his heir and first minister. In the early 1590s though, Hidetsugu fell from favour: first, he refused to lead Hideyoshi's campaign against Korea; later he irritated his uncle with various breaches of protocol, including a visit he made with his wife and daughter to the monasteries of Hiei-zan, which at that time excluded women. The last straw came in 1593 when Hideyoshi finally had a son of his own. Hidetsugu, by now nothing but an embarrassment, was accused of plotting his uncle's death, and confined to Seigan-ji. In August 1595 he was ordered to commit ritual suicide. His head was mounted on a spike in Kyoto; a few weeks later his wife and daughters were also decapitated.

The rooms are richly painted and coated in gold leaf in the Momoyama style of Hideyoshi's age. The **Yanagi no ma** (Willow Room) inside the **Main Hall** still contains paintings by the famous artist Kanō Tansai before which Hidetsugu is said to have sat as he performed the gory deed. The **Ōhiroma** (Great Room) is where religious ceremonies are held; the sliding screen paintings here are by a later member of the Kanō family. Tea is sometimes served to visitors here, along with a crumbly pilgrim's sweet included in the entrance fee. In front of the **Okuden**, a later building for VIP visitors, is a large modern gravel garden said to represent a pair of dragons in the clouds.

One of the most interesting rooms is the gymnasium-sized **kitchen** furnished with huge ovens, a great sooty chimney and an arsenal of fire extinguishers. Notice also the great wooden water casks on the thatch on the outside roof, poised for release onto fire.

By the entrance to Kongōbu-ji, mounted on a fortress-like base of dry stones, is the **Rokuji-no-kane** (Six o'Clock Bell), rung at 6am, and then every two hours until 10pm. It was erected in 1618 as an offering for the repose of his dead mother by one of Shogun Ieyasu's feudal lords; the present structure went up 17 years later after a fire.

Garan (Main Compound)

A thousand years of fires and reconstructions have made rather a jumble of Kōya-san's **Garan**. The wide gravel compound contains temples, shrines, bell towers, pagodas, ponds and trees but it has none of the monumental grandeur of the great Zen temples. Nonetheless, this was the historical heart of Kōya; when Kūkai hurled his bronze prong all the way from the shores of China, it was in these trees that it lodged, and here that he established the first monastic settlement. Many of the buildings are disappointingly modern; apart from the pleasant park atmosphere, the great attraction is the **Reihō-kan** (Treasure Hall), just south and over the road, a matchless repository of Esoteric Buddhist art.

The Central Buildings

The most arresting structure is the **Kompon Dai-tō** (Fundamental Great Stupa), a two-storey pagoda with square hipped roofs below and above a round core, suggestive of the original circular stupas of India. From a distance it's impressive, nearly 50m high and 25m wide, and the mist-shrouded silhouette, jutting above the dawn mountains, has become Kōya's most famous photographic image. Close up, it's obviously concrete (reconstructed in 1937); with its fenced-in upper balcony, it bears an unfortunate resemblance to a medieval version of Tokyo Tower.

Drop ¥100 in the collection box if no one is on duty. Inside are five seated buddhas, a symbolic rendering of a Shingon principle: the balance between the worlds of the Womb and the Diamond Mandala. Dainichi Nyorai, seated at the centre, inhabits the former; surrounding him are four representatives of the Diamond world. Painted on the pillars are the sixteen *bosatsu*, or lesser buddhas; the monks painted in pairs in each corner of the hall are the eight patriarchs who transmitted the teachings of Shingon. Opposite the Kompon Dai-tō is a **white tower** containing a 16th-century bell sounded daily at 4am, 1pm, 5pm, 9pm and 11pm. There are two lesser stupas, the **Tō-tō** and **Sai-tō**, at the eastern and western ends of the compound respectively.

The **Kon-dō** (Golden Hall) is the big hall with a tiled hip-and-gable roof in the middle of the compound. This was where Kūkai lectured, but in 1925, along with priceless statues, it burned, to be rebuilt six years later. The hexagonal structure, ahead and to the left as you exit the Kon-dō, is a **sutra repository**, built in the 12th century by Bifukumon-in, the consort of Emperor Toba, who spent her life copying out sutras—3568 of them—in memory of her dead husband. The scrolls, exquisitely written in gold ink on deep blue paper, were stored in this building; a few are sometimes displayed in the Reihō-kan.

Western Buildings

North of the Kon-dō (i.e. towards the main road and Kongōbu-ji) are three smaller halls with thatched roofs: from east to west, the **Mie-dō, Juntei-dō** and **Kujaku-dō**. None of them is old, but the **Mie-dō** (Hall of The Honourable Shadow) is one of the holiest sites on Kōya, containing a secret painting of Kūkai, modelled by the saint himself, which only the most eminent priests are permitted to view. In front of it, behind a protective fence, is a tree, described as the 'descendant' of the one in which Kūkai's priestly prong landed after its miraculous flight from China.

At the west edge of the Garan, south of the Sai-tō pagoda, is the **Sanno-in** (usually closed to the public), a monastic debating chamber where novices were formally tested on the tenets of Shingon. Behind it, strikingly at odds with the sober buildings nearby, is the **Myōjin-sha**, a Shinto shrine dedicated to the god and goddess of the mountain who led Kūkai to this spot.

Eastern Buildings

Behind the Kon-dō a set of steps leads down to a lower level of the compound, and the **Fudō-dō**—the oldest surviving structure in the Garan, although not an original component of it. With its low, undulating roof in a delicate late-Heian-period style, it was built in the last years of the 12th century by the Retired Emperor Toba, then dismantled and rebuilt here during restoration work in 1910. Next to it is a small **pond**; the island, reached by an orange bridge, contains a small Shinto shrine to the goddess Benten.

Reihō-kan (Treasure Hall)

The Reihō-kan is south and slightly to the east of the Garan. If you are walking from the Tourist Association, turn left at the Six o'Clock Bell and follow the road around; the museum is on the left. Open 8–5; adm ¥500.

With its rich and complicated symbolism, and a colourful cast of bizarre and ferocious deities, Shingon Buddhism is a religion more than usually suited to visual representation.

Kūkai himself was a master painter and calligrapher and, for over a thousand years, many of the finest artists in Japan have produced work for Shingon temples—especially during the Heian period, an era of exceptional artistic creativity which coincided with Shingon's greatest power and influence. Kōya's Reihō-kan isn't a large or architecturally impressive museum, but its collection numbers 2880 Prefectural Cultural Assets, 14,129 Important Cultural Assets and 4607 National Treasures. 50,000 more remain to be classified.

Most of the holdings are still owned by the temples, who entrust them to the museum for the purposes of conservation and protection from fire. Many pieces have collecting boxes or lit incense in front of them, and you will see visitors praying to them; one of the appealing things about the Reihō-kan is that these are very much living objects of pilgrims' veneration, not frozen artefacts of cultural history.

There are paintings, sculptures, mandalas, illuminated scrolls, calligraphy, and bronze ritual implements. The exhibits are rotated, and at any one time the majority of the museum's holdings will be mothballed in the concrete **storehouse**, built in 1984. This makes it hard to describe the display (in addition, there are five special themed exhibitions a year), but certain images central to Shingon Buddhism will always be in evidence. The most splendid of these is Fudō Myō-ō, Immovable Brilliant King, a ferocious character with fangs (one pointing up, one down) and a swinging pony-tail, inevitably depicted in a state of incandescent rage. Fudō's role is to discipline the faithful and chastise the wicked; for these purposes he carries a long sword and a lasso for ensnaring and hacking demons, one of whom is often shown writhing beneath his feet. He comes in various unnatural colours: a famous statue held by the museum is known as the Red Fudō for its vermilion paint.

Fudō Myō-ō is revered by several sects, but in the Shingon art of Kōya-san he's particularly prominent. He's often shown attended by two young boys: a white one carrying a long-stemmed lotus, and a red one holding a staff. Among the museum's most appealing statues are a set of eight of Fudō's young disciples, six of them carved by the great 12th-century sculptor Unkei. The beautifully observed, affectionate figures have fierce scowls on their plump, childish faces.

Mandalas are another key element of Shingon worship. With their minutely detailed, diagrammatic representation of the divine hierarchy, they amount to a Who's Who of the Buddhist pantheon. Dainichi Nyorai, the Cosmic Buddha, inevitably sits at the centre, wearing a crown; every other being on the mandala is an aspect of him. Lesser buddhas of various ranks surround him in the outer rings (sometimes concentric squares) of the pictures. The beastliest, and most entertaining, are generally to be seen at the edges: demons, animals, raddled old priests and patriarchs. Copying a mandala was believed to earn spiritual credit; the Reihō-kan has one commissioned by the doomed 12th-century general Taira no Kiyomori, said to have been painted with his own blood.

Okuno-in

The heart of Kōya-san is the **Okuno-in**, not a temple but a necropolis, a vast forest park overflowing with more than 200,000 moss-encrusted tombs and memorials, and, set into the mountainside beyond a pilgrim approach of paths, bridges and fences, the final resting place of the Daishi himself. Many of Japan's most famous dead—priests, emperors, shoguns, lords, samurai, politicians, writers, artists, craftsmen, their families and servants, plus numberless common citizens—are commemorated here. In a light mist (early morning and dusk are the best times to visit) it's a timeless and spine-tinglingly numinous place, enough to satisfy anybody's fantasies of the mysterious east. Even the few incursions of the 20th century are interesting and remarkable—more of these below.

The Okuno-in and the Life to Come

Devout Buddhists refer not to Kobo Daishi's death, but to his 'repose'. In 835 the 61-year-old priest announced the day that his earthly life would end. After prayers at the Kyoto Imperial Palace for the prosperity of the nation, and a formal farewell to the emperor, he returned to Kōya where he chose his burial place, wrote his will and named his successors. One of his disciples, a royal prince, painted his portrait, and Kūkai himself completed it by filling in the eyes.

He then entered a state of deep meditation and on 21 April, the day he had predicted, 'his fuel became exhausted and his fire was extinguished.' The contemporary account continues: 'Alas! Mt Kōya turned grey; the clouds and trees appeared sad. The emperor in sorrow hastily sent a messenger to convey his condolences. The disciples wept as if they had lost their parents. Alas! We feel in our hearts as if we had swallowed fire, and our tears gush forth like fountains.' But, like that of Christ's disciples, their mourning was premature. Shingon doctrine holds that the Daishi, as he became, is not dead but in deep meditation, a buddha in his own body. With the coming of Miroku, the great Buddha of the Future, he will rise from his resting place to lead the souls of men into Nirvana. In the inner sanctuary of the Okuno-in, a few metres from the rows of praying pilgrims, the 'resting' body of the Daishi himself, 1100 years old, still sits, presumably in a state of mummification. Once a year, the most senior of the Kōya priests has the task of entering the sanctuary to change his robe.

It was as a result of these beliefs that the forest around the Okuno-in has become the most famous and prestigious graveyard in Japan. Few of the tombs actually include whole bodies or a full set of ashes. Rather, distinguished Japanese would be interred in their home temples; later, their relatives would undertake a proxy pilgrimage to Kōya, bearing a portion of the deceased's remains (teeth, often, or a fragment of bone or cartilage). The wealthiest would enshrine these in expensively endowed tombs; paupers could add their loved one's ashes to a communal urn or simply scatter them over the forest. Emperors and the most senior priests are interred by the sanctuary itself, for it is proximity to the sleeping Daishi that is important. On the last day, when the Daishi awakes, they will, it is believed, be in pole position for the entrance into Paradise.

Touring the Necropolis

There are two entrances to the Okuno-in, both within walking distance of town, but since the approach to the sanctuary in any case involves a 2km walk, you'll probably want to take a bus or taxi there and back.

Get off at the stop called **Ichi-no-hashi** (First Bridge) where the traditional approach begins. Even today it is very much a place of serious devotion; among your fellow visitors will be pilgrims in white robes and straw sandals; others wear anoraks and trainers, but still carry the traditional staff. All along the way are signs of their passing: offerings in the form of origami cranes, coins wedged into the fissures of tombs, tiny Jizō statues wearing red bibs and knitted bobble hats. Many of the tombs here are individual, but there are a number of monuments to the collective casualties of war and disaster. Near the entrance is a stone for the victims of the Great Tokyo Earthquake of 1923. It's common to see old soldiers praying at the various cenotaphs to the war dead, some of which bear engraved maps showing the location of the campaigns. The striking modern monument by the Ichi-no-hashi, a patterned white cylinder with two wing-like crests, is dedicated to students who died during the Second World War. Another prays for the souls of 'all the soldiers, both on our side and that of the enemy, who died during the war in Korea'. The conflict in question was Hideyoshi Toyotomi's bloody and abortive invasion of 1597.

Deeper inside the forest, the tombs become older. The earliest legible inscription is from 997; every period since then is represented. The **largest tombstone** (Ichiban Hi) can be found about two-thirds of the way up, after the **Middle Bridge** (Naka-no-hashi), on the left-hand side. Dedicated to the mother of a 17th-century shogunal official, it's 6.6m high, 14.2 square metres at its base but, scale apart, its form is typical. Five stones (from top to bottom: a cube, a sphere, a 'roof' shape, a half-sphere with a flat top, a sphere with a pointed tip) are mounted on an ornate base, resembling a stylized lantern without the hollow for a candle. Each layer is marked with a Sanskrit letter denoting one of the five elements (void, wind, fire, water, earth). Other tombs are in the form of stone pillars, tablets and even ornate miniature shrines, with a Shinto-style *torii* gate, stone enclosure and tile-roofed sanctuary.

Except for the most modern tombs, all these man-made artefacts exist according to the Japanese ideal of perfect harmony with nature. Nothing could be further from the typical Christian cemetery with its grim rows of stark crosses and carefully cropped turf. Just as in a Japanese garden, nature and artifice blend indistinguishably with each other: split and toppled tombstones lie alongside the boles of the ancient trees and moss gathers like green snow on the tops of wood, rock and cut stone. There are smells of candle wax, incense, damp earth, and smoke billowing from the gardeners' leaf fires. Sounds are muted beneath the canopy of cryptomerias: calls of birds and insects, streams and springs, the clink of coins, the clapping of supplicants and the tapping of their shoes on the flags.

The Inner Sanctum

A third bridge, the **Mimyo-no-hashi**, marks the threshold of the most sacred area of the mountain. Just before the bridge is the **Gokushō** (Offering Hall) where meals are offered twice a day to the sleeping Daishi (in death, as in life, he is a vegetarian). Next to it is a small shrine containing the **Food-Tasting Jizō** who receives the offerings an hour before, just to check that there's nothing funny about them.

Priests and visitors are expected to tidy themselves up before crossing the bridge. It's said, moreover, to admit only those who are capable of entering paradise. When Toyotomi Hideyoshi paid a visit to Kōya after his bloody Korean campaign, his guilty conscience made him fear a public humiliation at this spot. The night before his official visit, he paid a secret visit to the bridge and nervously tried it out on foot. Reassured that the bridge would bear the weight of his war crimes, he returned to his lodgings and the next day made his grand entrance without incident.

Having crossed safely to the other side, the pure in heart will find themselves before the **Tōrō-dō** (Hall of Lamps), two large halls containing lamps (some of them electric) offered by the faithful. Two are said to have burned since the 11th century: one kindled by Emperor Shirakawa, the other by the hall's founder, a Daishi follower called Shinzen. When the hall containing them later caught fire they were snatched to safety. Another favourite story tells of an old woman who sold the hair on her head to raise funds for a lamp. 'A single lamp from a poor woman, ten thousand from a millionaire,' runs the slogan. The octagonal structure to the right is an **ossuary** where, even today, hair and bone fragments are deposited by the families of the devout.

A narrow path runs between the back of the Hall of Lamps and a stone fence. Before it there is an offertory box, beyond it a no-man's-land of big pebbles on which huge golden lotus leaves stand in green jars. Beyond these is a gate, and beyond that the barred doors of the **Gobyō** (Inner Sanctuary) itself, resting place of the Daishi. Exactly what lies beyond them, very few men alive know or are prepared to say.

The Return Walk

Take the path to the left on your way back from the **Inner Sanctuary**. This rejoins the main road at a point further east than the Ichi-no-hashi entrance, but takes you past some of the most interesting modern tombs on the mountain; huge, gaudy cenotaphs erected by rich individuals or even big corporations (look out for the one by the Yakult milk drink company). Presumably this is another of the perks of working for a big company: car, golf club membership and priority salvation on the Day of Judgement. The most famous monument, which everyone wants to photograph, was endowed by an aerospace corporation: it consists of a gleaming silver rocket.

(☎ 0736–)   *Where to Stay*

There are few Western-style hotels on Mt Kōya; visitors stay in *shukubō*, temple lodgings where the cooks, servers and chamber maids are monks. 53 of the 117 temples on the mountain provide this service. The usual conventions of staying in a *ryokan* apply, except that the food is *shōjin ryōri*—vegetarian Buddhist cuisine including many different kinds of *tōfu* (*Kōya-dōfu*, the chewy, dried-out kind, was invented here). Japanese guests are generally pilgrims who retire early (no great hardship: there's nothing to do on

Kōya after the sun goes down) to rise at dawn for a service before breakfast. But foreigners of any or no religion are also welcome and may sit in on the ceremonies. Many of the sub-temples are treasures in themselves. The experience of going to sleep in one to wake in the breaking light to the sound of bells, gongs and chanting is uniquely lovely. Try to arrive in Kōya in the evening, spend the next day sight-seeing, and leave the following morning after a two-night stay.

The cost of a night in a *shukubō* is generally at the top end of *inexpensive* to *moderate*, but includes two meals. For those who can't face rice and fish for breakfast, there are a couple of coffee shops on the main road near the Tourist Association. Accommodation can be booked on arrival at the Kōya Tourist Association. At busy times make a reservation in advance by ringing them on ✆ 0736 56 2417, or via the tourist information centres in Tokyo or Kyoto. The following have received good reports:

moderate

Sainan-in, ✆ 56 2421, at the far west end of Kōya, near the Daimon gate, has a fine modern rock garden.

Sekishō-in, ✆ 56 2734, is at the other end of town close to the Ichi-no-hashi bridge—very convenient for the Okuno-in.

Shinnō-in, ✆ 56 2227, north of the Garan, is a famously friendly old temple, especially welcoming to foreign visitors.

Tentoku-in, ✆ 56 2714, has a beautiful Momoyama-period garden and a rich wooden interior.

inexpensive

Henjōson-in, ✆ 56 2434, is south of the Garan, next to the Reihō-kan museum, and is a bit cheaper than the average.

cheap

Haryō-in, ✆ 56 2702, is a temple which doubles as a *kokuminshuku-sha* or people's lodge: no frills here, but all the elements of a night in a *shukubō* for well below the going rate. Haryō-in is close to the cable car station and a bit of a walk from the town centre.

(✆ *0736–*) **Eating Out**

As you'd expect in a monastic community, Kōya-san has little in the way of entertainment. There are a few modest restaurants serving rice and noodle dishes on the main road near the tourist centre, but these close early. The culinary centres of the mountain are its *shukubō*. Even if you don't spend the night at one of these you can eat lunch there if you book in advance—ask at the Tokyo or Kyoto tourist information centres or the main Kōya-san tourist office, or call the Shukubō Association, ✆ 56 2616. Lunch courses cost around ¥3000.

Himeji, a big industrialized city of iron, chemical and electrical works, is famous for two things: it produces 80 per cent of Japan's matches; and it contains its biggest and most beautiful fortress, the Castle of the White Egret, one of the five most worthwhile tourist attractions in the whole country.

Getting There

The **shinkansen** reaches Himeji in about 3hrs 45mins from Tokyo, an hour from Kyoto, and 50mins from Ōsaka. The rapid JR service from Kōbe's Sannomiya station takes 50mins. A Himeji-bound **night bus** leaves from Tokyo's Shibuya station, taking approximately 9hrs.

A wide avenue called Ōtemae-dōri leads north from the plaza in front of the station: the castle, illuminated by night, rises spectacularly at the far end, about one kilometre away.

Himeji-jō (Himeji Castle)

Open Sept–May, 9–4; Jun–Aug, 9–5; adm ¥500.

James Bond fans will recognize Himeji Castle. In *You Only Live Twice* it is transformed into a *ninja* camp, which Sean Connery choppers into for a rendezvous with an oriental temptress. Dozens of Japanese films and TV samurai dramas have also been shot here, and several times a year the grounds are filled with camera crews and actors in topknot wigs. On the most superficial level, knowing nothing of its history and purpose, Himeji is great fun, a place for indulging boyish fantasies of sieges and duels and samurai high jinks. At the same time, it's an architectural masterpiece of defensive cunning, technical ingenuity and strategic design, although an untested one. In reality, Himeji never saw action, and might not be here today if it had.

History: Himeji-jō and Japanese Castles

The remains of ancient stone walls in southern Japan suggest that fortified encampments were built there as early as the 6th century. By the 1400s, regional rulers were building homes at the bottom of mountains, and wooden forts at their summits, where they could scarper in time of war. But the first true castles developed during the interminable wars of the 15th and 16th centuries. A high mountain top was an inconvenient headquarters for the feudal lord with taxes to raise and fiefs to administer, and castles were increasingly built on flat land or, like Himeji-jō, on hills or rises on lowland plains.

Arquebuses had been copied from the Portuguese as early as 1543, but it wasn't until 1575 that the brilliant general Oda Nobunaga used them to significant effect in a siege. Castle architecture quickly adapted to the new weapon, with thicker walls (always wood; the risk of earthquakes made stone unviable), plastered exteriors and an inner core of sand and pebbles to repel fire. Square and round slits for muskets supplemented the rectangular arrow holes. Entire towns were designed around the central keep, with two or three sets of concentric walls and moats, containing narrow and winding streets to confuse and trap enemies *en route* to the castle. Temples and shrines were clustered at key entry points so that superstitious attackers would be deterred from further progress by the fear of blasphemy. When peace came to Japan in the Edo period (1603–1868), castles took on new functions: as administrative centres, and as symbols of the shoguns' might and authority.

Himeji Castle, in its various incarnations, has experienced many of these changes. The first simple structure was built in 1346, and in 1581 Toyotomi Hideyoshi raised a three-storey defensive castle on the same site. Finally, after uniting the country at the Battle of Sekigahara in 1600, Ieyasu, the first of the Tokugawa shoguns, appointed Ikeda Terumasa as hereditary *daimyō* (feudal lord) and permitted him to build the present castle. The Castle of the White Egret, as it is nicknamed for its delicate, bird-like appearance, was eight years in the making, finally finished in 1609. 18,000 labourers worked on the castle for a total of 30 million man-days, sculpting the foundations, transporting and shaping stones (103,396 tons), slate tiles (351,200 of them), and timber, and diverting the rivers into the freshly cut moats (2.7m deep). Ikeda was succeeded in 1617 by the Honda family whose son married the daughter of a shogun, winning with her a rich dowry, which was spent on further enlargement and decoration.

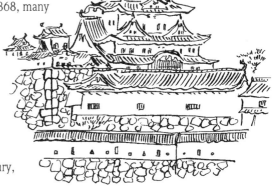

Its survival into the 20th century is almost miraculous, aided by the great loyalty which the castle inspires in its admirers. At the Meiji Restoration in 1868, many castles were dismantled; Himeji was spared by the Emperor on the personal recommendation of an officer in the Imperial Army. The city was a big military, as well as industrial, centre during the Second World War, and suffered intense bombing: plaster or no plaster, a single incendiary would have been enough to send the whole thing up in flames. But, soon to begin its fifth century, Himeji's luck has held out so far.

English-speaking Guides

The Volunteer English Guide Association (VEGA) offers free tours of the castle to foreigners, well worth taking advantage of, since so many of its secrets are invisible to the casual observer. They have an office by the castle ticket office, but at busy times guides may not be immediately available. Try to make an appointment a few hours in advance, and spend the intervening time in the excellent **Prefectural History Museum**. Call in person, or phone VEGA's President, Mr Takei, in English on ✆ 0792 85 1146.

Touring Himeji-jō

The moat which you cross to enter the castle grounds today was only the innermost of several lines of defence which protected the castle town. The outermost moat, long since filled in and built over, was as far from the keep as the present day railway station, and the intervening territory was filled with houses of the different social classes, the highest ranking samurai and retainers closest to the castle.

You enter by the **Hishi-no-mon**, a fortified gate with a guard room, from which spear throwers could snipe at attackers. The area beyond this is laid out according to a principle called *nawabari*, literally 'stretching the rope'—the art of putting as much distance and inconvenience as possible between the enemy and the defenders. From the gate to the main keep is 150m as the crow flies. On the ground, invaders had to take a zig-zagging course of more than 500m through gates, past turrets, up and down slopes, running the gauntlet of spears, arrows, bullets and vats of boiling sewage.

The castle is divided into two *maru*, or citadels. The *daimyō* and his family lived in the outer **Nishi-no-maru** (Western Citadel), the keep itself being unoccupied except during wartime. This is the park-like area which you enter through the Hishi-no-mon. When his son, Tadatoki, married the shogun's daughter, Princess Sen, Honda Tadamasa built a palace for them here, long torn down.

The turrets and walls of the castle buildings have many interesting details. The walls (wood, covered by thick plaster) are penetrated regularly by loopholes: rectangles (*yazama*) for arrows, squares (*jūgan*) or circles (*teppōzama*) for muskets. Alongside the tightly barred wooden windows are open chutes which bulge out just above the stone walls where attackers might try to scale them. These are called stone-drops (*ishi-otoshi*); through them rocks, spears and fluid could be dropped.

Various characteristic decorative details are also incorporated: angular dormer gables, as well as the 'Chinese-style' cusped ones. The snarling, spiny-backed fish on the finials of the roofs and gables are fantastic dolphin-like creatures called *shachi-gawara*, said to repel fire (if they've worked so far for Himeji, there are a thousand other castles where they failed dismally). Tiles at the ends of the eaves are often decorated with the crests of the various *daimyō* families who acted as its stewards. Your guide will point out the cross-shaped crest of the Christian Kuroda clan, which somehow escaped the persecutions of the 17th century. One wall contains a millstone. This is said to date from the time of the second castle, built by the great Toyotomi Hideyoshi. His architects requisitioned stone from all over the region, but still they were short. The millstone was donated by an old peasant woman who sacrificed her livelihood out of admiration for the bloodthirsty Hideyoshi.

The gates become smaller the closer you get to the **Honmaru** (Inner Citadel). Inside is the **Daitenshū** (Main Keep) and three lesser keeps, connected to it by fortified corridors. There are six levels within the main keep although, from the outside, it appears to have only four. A basement, built into the stone foundation, contains toilets and sinks, the only Japanese castle to have these (at the others, presumably, they used the stone-drops), and a second secret floor is concealed below the top storey. Including its foundations, it's 46m high and rests on 200 mighty pillars of Japanese cypress, each supporting 100 of the keep's 5000 tons. The rest of the weight is shared between 200 lesser pillars. On the first floor of one of the lesser keeps, a skeletal model, like a giant wooden birdcage, illustrates the intricate carpentry which went into these.

The Honmaru contains a large courtyard area. If war had ever come to Himeji, the *daimyō* would have set up camp here with his family and retainers. The well just south of it features in a famous *Kabuki* play about a young serving woman who was tortured and killed after being falsely accused of breaking a valuable plate. Her ghostly voice is said to echo from it, cursing the enemies who framed her. A gloomy corner nearby is known as the place of *hara kiri* (disembowelment), although it was used mainly for target practice by idle samurai and there is no evidence that any actual suicides took place there. This is what you have to remember about Himeji Castle: for all its dastardly defensive measures, the principal reason it has survived so long is that it never saw action. If it had, and if one well-aimed burning arrow had hit its target, the story might have been very different.

Hyōgo-kenritsu Rekishi Hakubutsukan (Hyōgo Prefectural History Museum)

Open Sept–May, 10–5; June–Aug, 10–6; adm ¥200.

Just north of Himeji-jō, in a soaring building by the contemporary architect Tange Kenzō, is this excellent museum which is worth visiting before you enter the castle. Interesting displays, well-labelled in English, trace the development and styles of military architecture all over Japan, with scale models of 12 of the great castles. At 11am and 2pm every day, visitors are invited to try on beautiful reproductions of Japanese costume: a suit of samurai armour, or a *jūni-hitoe*, a twelve-layered court lady's kimono.

(© 0792–)   ***Where to Stay***

It's not worth staying overnight in Himeji, if you can avoid it: with an early start from Ōsaka or Kyoto, you should be able jump off the *shinkansen*, spend a few hours looking round the history museum and castle, and catch a later train on to Kurashiki and points south.

moderate

Hotel Sunroute Himeji, © 0792 85 0811, **Hotel Sunroute New Himeji**, © 0792 23 1111, and **Himeji Washington Hotel**, © 0792 25 0111, are branches of two reliable business chains, all close to the station.

Higasa Ryokan, © 0792 24 3421, is a traditional inn between the station and castle. Without meals it's just ¥5000 per person.

inexpensive

Business Hotel Kishin, © 0792 22 4655, is a few blocks west of the station.

Eating Out

Surprisingly for a city close to the Inland Sea, Himeji makes almost nothing of itself as a gourmet centre, although there's no shortage of pizza, spaghetti and curry houses, and friendly inexpensive Japanese restaurants with models of noodles and rice dishes in the window. East of the main Ōtemae-dōri (i.e. to the right as you come out of the main exit at the station) is a grid of quieter streets and covered shopping arcades with some homely red lantern bars. The hotels around the station have more formal restaurants.

Shikoku

Shikoku is the last place in Japan which foreigners visit, and this is its attraction. The islands of the Inland Sea, off the north coast, have temples, leper colonies, rural *kabuki* and *bunraku* stages, but it is the sea crossings—on jetfoils or ponderous ferries—which make them worth visiting. Three small regional cities boast a great shrine, a great garden, and two and a half castles between them—but more compelling are the connecting journeys, along empty cliff sides and soaring, Himalayan valleys. Shikoku's temples are, in themselves, modest and uninteresting, but collectively they mark the points of the greatest Buddhist pilgrimage in Japan. Like a lot of backwater areas, neglected by history as well as tourism, there isn't much to arrive at; the pleasure is all in the travelling.

Shikoku is an escape, recommended to Japan veterans, and to anyone in search of peace and quiet, local oddities (roosters with 10m tails, sumo dogs), and the crumbling remnants of a rural culture which in 20 years' time will have passed for ever.

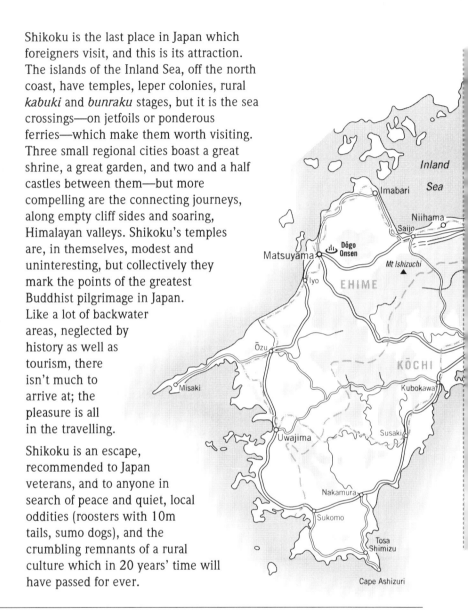

History

Next they [Izanagi and Izanami] gave birth to the island of Iyo-no-futana. This island has one body and four faces, and each face has a name. So the land of Iyo is called Lovely Princess; the land of Sanuki is called Prince-Good-Boiled-Rice; the Land of Awa is called the Princess of Great Food; the Land of Tosa is called Great-Good-Youth.

Kojiki, translated by Basil Hall Chamberlain

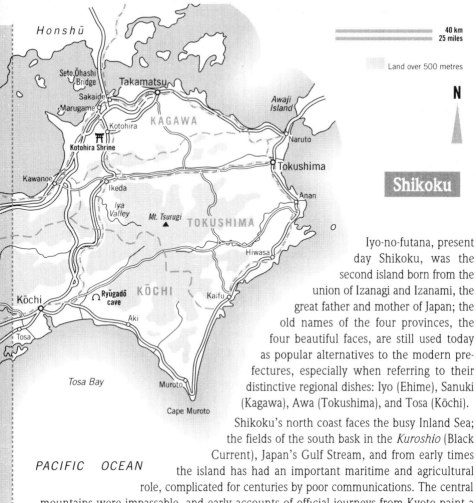

Honshū

Seto Ōhashi
Bridge
Takamatsu
Sakaide
Marugame
Kotohira
KAGAWA
Kotohira Shrine

40 km
25 miles

Land over 500 metres

N

Awaji
Island

Naruto

Tokushima

Shikoku

Kawanoe
Ikeda

Iya
Valley
Mt. Tsurugi
TOKUSHIMA

Anan

Hiwasa

Kōchi
Ryūgadō
cave
KŌCHI
Kaifu

Aki

Tosa

Tosa Bay
Muroto
Cape Muroto

PACIFIC OCEAN

Iyo-no-futana, present day Shikoku, was the second island born from the union of Izanagi and Izanami, the great father and mother of Japan; the old names of the four provinces, the four beautiful faces, are still used today as popular alternatives to the modern prefectures, especially when referring to their distinctive regional dishes: Iyo (Ehime), Sanuki (Kagawa), Awa (Tokushima), and Tosa (Kōchi).

Shikoku's north coast faces the busy Inland Sea; the fields of the south bask in the *Kuroshio* (Black Current), Japan's Gulf Stream, and from early times the island has had an important maritime and agricultural role, complicated for centuries by poor communications. The central mountains were impassable, and early accounts of official journeys from Kyoto paint a hair-raising picture of flimsy boats dodging pirates, and shipwreck in treacherous seas.

In the 12th century, the doomed Taira clan skirmished with their enemies, the Minamoto, off the northern coast. But Shikoku's most colourful historical character was Chōsogabe Motochika (1539–99), a lord of Tosa (Kōchi Prefecture) who rose to power during the late 16th century, the so-called Period of the Country at War. He was a brutal warrior, in the mould of his master, the great Japanese warlord Oda Nobunaga; temples all over the island commemorate him either as founder or destroyer.

Shikoku, like the rest of the country, survived peacefully through most of the Edo period (1615–1868) until the 1860s, when Tosa samurai, like Sakamoto Ryōma, were active in the overthrow of the shogun and the restoration of the Meiji Emperor. Change came most recently to the island in the form of a bridge, long debated, which finally linked Shikoku and Honshū in 1988. The Seto Ōhashi (Seto Great Bridge) is the longest two-tiered bridge system in the world, spanning five islands over a distance of 13.1km. Two more routes will open over the next few years, putting the island within easy reach of travellers and pilgrims—as well as lorries, tourist coaches and heavy industry. 'A bridge to Shikoku would be the end,' wrote Donald Richie in 1971 in his elegiac travel book, *The Inland Sea*. The end hasn't come yet but the landscape and culture of Shikoku will have changed irrevocably by the end of the 20th century.

The Shikoku Pilgrimage

Shikoku is a subtle place and to some first-time visitors it will be a disappointment, with none of the monumental excitements of the other islands. Kyūshū has active volcanoes, Hokkaidō has bears and wilderness, Honshū has matchless temples and shrines and electrifying modern cities. Shikoku, the smallest of the four, has beautiful countryside, but its great historical and religious treasure can never be seen or photographed or touched: an ancient pilgrimage along a thousand miles of arduous trails, between 88 Buddhist temples.

There are other pilgrimages—like the 33 temples of Kannon in Kansai—but none as long as this one. The numbers are significant. In Buddhist theology, 88 represents the number of passions or defilements which man is subject to. Penance for sins committed has always been one motive for pilgrims, but there are others: a prayer for divine favour, thanksgiving for favour granted, an escape from urban existence and—especially in the Edo perod when pilgrimage was the only kind of travel permitted to ordinary people—simply for fun.

Inextricably bound with the history of Shikoku is **Kōbō Daishi**, the Buddhist saint known in his lifetime as **Kūkai**. He was born in 774, 30km from present-day Takamatsu city, and spent many years wandering the island before finding enlightenment at Cape Muroto on the southeast coast. For the legend of the pilgrimage's origins, and the Daishi's part in it, see the description of Ishite-ji temple in Matsuyama. Actually, it was his successors, monks from his mountain headquarters on Mt Kōya, who became the first pilgrims or *henro*. As well as being the spiritual headquarters of Shingon Buddhism, Mt Kōya was also an important centre of fundraising for temple building projects. Monks were sent out all over the country to preach and beg for money, and in Shikoku the paths they trod, linking many of the places associated with the Daishi, were followed by other holy men and lay people. Older, local pilgrimages were incorporated and in time the temples were given numbers. Today, the pilgrimage begins at temple number one, near Tokushima city in the northeast of the island, running clockwise right round to temple eighty-eight in Kagawa Prefecture. On foot, for centuries the only feasible form of transport, it takes about two months.

Authentic, pedestrian *henro* are rare these days, but air-conditioned pilgrimage buses still whisk thousands of believers around the temples, which now provide car parks and comfortable lodging houses. You'll certainly see them in the distinctive *henro* kit: hip-length white robe, coloured shoulder band, huge umbrella-like straw hat, rosary, brass bell, staff and an album of blank sheets on which the stamp of each temple is marked. Some *henro* stamp their white coats as well. The characters written on robes, hats and staffs sum up the meaning of the pilgrimage to devout Buddhists: *Dōgyō Ninin*, 'We Two—Kōbō Daishi and I—Pilgrims Together'.

Takamatsu, the most accessible city in Shikoku, has one of the great feudal-era gardens, a beautiful outdoor museum of rural architecture, and easy access to a big old mountain shrine. One or two nights are all you need here. The bridge makes it so easy to reach from Honshū that, for just a taste of Shikoku, you could easily incorporate it into a journey along the Kyoto–Hiroshima *shinkansen* line, or even as a day trip from Kurashiki or Okayama.

History

The Sanuki region (these days called Kagawa Prefecture) contains the island's only sizeable plain, but it's always been a marginal region, a narrow ledge beneath the mountainous hinterland of Shikoku, with one of the lowest rainfalls in Japan. What little water does filter down from the hills is carefully shepherded into countless irrigation ponds and reservoirs. The biggest of these was constructed in 821 by none other than Kōbō Daishi who, as well as mystic, sculptor, poet and linguist, was also a first-rate civil engineer.

In the 12th century, Sanuki acquired incidental significance when Retired Emperor Sutoku was banished to a remote temple here after a struggle over the succession; in 1164 he was murdered. His curse on the treacherous imperial court marked the beginning of the end of the Heian period, and the rise of the rival warrior clans, the Minamoto and the Taira. In 1185 the latter were defeated in a sea battle at Takamatsu's Yashima peninsula, just two months before their epic annihilation in the straits of Dan no Ura to the far west.

Takamatsu itself was established as a castle town at the end of the 16th century by Toyotomi Hideyoshi. Two consecutive feudal clans were appointed and then dispossessed in the space of 55 years; the fief finally came into the competent possession of the Matsudaira family who held it until the Meiji Restoration. Only a couple of turrets remain of their castle which burned, along with most of the city, during an air raid in 1945.

Getting Around

The **JR station** is at the north end of town, right next to the harbour. Trains depart from here for Kotohira, for Matsuyama and Kōchi on the opposite sides of Shikoku, and for Okayama on the other side of the Seto Ōhashi bridge.

Opposite the JR station, behind the Takamatsu Grand Hotel, is Kotoden Chikkō station, terminus of a kind of **inter-city tram** network which serves Ritsurin Kōen (Park), Yashima and Kotohira.

In front of the Takamatsu Grand Hotel are numbered **bus** stops. Any bus from stop no.2 stops at Ritsurin Kōen. A few buses a day go to Yashima from no.5.

From the piers along the harbour **ferries and jet foils** sail to the islands and ports on both sides of the Inland Sea, plus Ōsaka and Kōbe.

Takamatsu's main street, **Chūō-dōri**, runs from the stations and ferry terminal in the north down to Ritsurin Kōen, a mile to the south. **Nightlife** and **restaurants**, as well as plenty of shops, are concentrated around the covered arcades to the east of the upper end of Chūō-dōri, and around Kotoden Kawaramachi station.

The small **Tourist Information Centre** in front of the station provides an English guide map and written instructions on how to reach the sights.

Ritsurin Kōen (Ritsurin Park)

Bus from stop no.5. 20 minutes' walk from the station down south-bound Chūō-dōri. Tram to Ritsurin Kōen station on Kotoden Kotohira line. Open during daylight hours; adm ¥310.

Ritsurin Kōen isn't numbered among the Three Beautiful Gardens of Japan, but if you've seen the ones that do make the list (especially Okayama's disappointing Kōraku-en) you'll wonder why. It falls into two distinct sections. The **Hokutei** (North Garden), with its lotus-filled ponds, was built during the late 17th century as a duck-hunting park and re-landscaped a hundred years ago. The **Nantei** (South Garden), on the other hand, was begun by one of the early *daimyō* of Sanuki, Ikoma Takatoshi, before he was banished to the far north for incompetence. The work was continued by the Matsudairas, and finally reached its present form in 1745.

At 750,000 square metres it's the biggest garden in Japan, and the most beautiful outside Kyoto, minimally marred by the post-war city which has spread out around it. Its greatest beauty is its position and the 'borrowed scenery' which looms above it to the west. Mt Shiun is neither a large nor a famous mountain, but it blends so seamlessly with the garden that from below they appear to be extensions of one another. At certain times of day the rays of the sun turn its slopes a famous purple.

The Matsudairas were a distinguished family, and the park contains many of the playful details and touches of artifice long prized in the gardens of Kyoto aristocrats. One famous tree (there are 29,190 altogether, of 157 different species) is called the **Byōbu Pine** because its artfully trained boughs are said to resemble a tree in a *byōbu* (folding screen) painting. The largest and most beautiful of the several tea houses is the **Kikugetsu-tei**— 'Scooping-The-Moon-Pavilion', a quotation from a Tang Chinese poem about moon-viewing by a lake ('Scoop up the water and the moon is in your hands'). One of the wings of the tea house thrusts out into the lake so that courtiers drinking tea before the open screens were given the illusion of being in the prow of a boat. You can try this for yourself: the more expensive admission price entitles you to a cup of *matcha* tea in this same room.

In form, Ritsurin Kōen is a stroll garden, designed to unfold before the eyes of the individual stroller, rather than present itself from a single fixed vantage point. There are many superb views, the best of them from **Hirai-hō**, a Fuji-like hill, one of 13 such artificial mounds. From here one sees the Kikugetsu-tei, floating above the lake on its stilts, and before it the **Engetsu-kyō**, a long, gracefully curved bridge. Don't underestimate the amount of time you'll want to spend just wandering round.

The park also houses a small **zoo** (*extra adm*) and the **Sanuki Mingeikan** (Folk Craft Museum (*adm included*), with several rooms displaying basketwork, furniture, ceramics, and—best of all—locally produced versions of **onigawara**, the grotesque tile gargoyles which surmount traditional buildings.

Yashima

A bus (no number—ask the driver, Yashima sanjō iki?*) departs from stop no.5 opposite Takamatsu JR station a few times a day, and goes to Yashima sanjō at the top of the peninsula hill. Otherwise take the Kotoden Line to Yashima station, and ascend on foot (a steep walk) or by cable car.*

Yashima was the site of an epic confrontation between the Minamoto and Taira clans, as the latter staggered towards their doom at the battle of Dan no Ura. As rocky promontories go, it's attractive enough—there are quiet cliffside paths, wonderful views of both the Inland Sea and the city of Takamatsu, and the **Yashima-dera**, temple number 84 on the Shikoku pilgrimage, with a handsome new treasure house and a mixed bag of screens and paintings depicting the famous battle. But the only sight worth coming out of your way for is at the bottom of the hill, near Kotoden Yashima station and the bus stop called Tōshō-gū-mae. This is the **Shikoku Mura** (Shikoku Village, *open 8.30–5; in winter 8.30–4.30; adm ¥500*), an outdoor collection of traditional rustic architecture, and the finest 'museum' on the island. The subtly landscaped park, designed by a well-known landscape gardener, is a work of art in its own right. Markers pointing out the recommended route are in the form of *henro* stones, which marked the ancient pilgrimage paths and were found, until recently, all over Shikoku. The lush greenery and glimpses of the city below are counterpointed everywhere by the trickle of water, flowing from pool to pool down specially created streams, and channeled down bamboo conduits into rocky basins.

Lovely though it is, the park is a symptom of irrevocable change. The 20th century may have come late to Shikoku but, having arrived, it has made its presence felt in all the usual ways. The buildings here are refugees from the old Shikoku—for every one dismantled and expensively transported here beam by beam, hundreds have fallen to the bulldozer.

You enter the park across a hair-raising vine bridge (there's an alternative, unadventurous way in for those with high heels or vertigo), built by the same craftsmen who maintain the one over the gorge in the Iya-dani Valley (*see* pp.440–1), but cheatingly reinforced with steel cables. Although the materials employed in the buildings here—wood, thatch and bamboo—are seen in traditional dwellings all over Japan, many of these structures have peculiar local characteristics—like the village bell made from a piece of rare resonating stone, quarried nearby. The steep terraces of the Shikoku gorges left little room for construction, so many of the houses are wide and very shallow, their backs hard up against the ascending slope behind. The finest is the dwelling of the Kore family: within, an unusual bamboo floor; outside, a steep roof with gable ends in the ancient style on which the shrine buildings of Honshū's Ise are still based. One of the most striking is a theatre from nearby Shōdo-shima island, built by farmers for a rustic form of amateur *kabuki* which can still be seen there—on 5 May every year a performance is given on this stage by Shōdo children.

Kotohira

45mins by JR or one hour by Kotoden Railway. Both services deposit you in Kotohira on the east side of the river. To reach the famous shrine, and other sights, you must pass through a large stone shrine gate and across the bridge. A small information booth beside the JR station has guide maps in English.

Kotohira-gū (Kotohira Shrine)

At Kotohira-gū—popularly called Kompira-san—the strands of Japanese religion form an inextricable tangle. At various times in its obscure history it has been a Shinto shrine, Buddhist temple, and both at the same time. For most of the four million pilgrims who visit here every year, it doesn't matter: above all, to a people isolated from civilization by risky seas, Kompira-san became important as the protector of sailors, a constituency which has recently been stretched to include travellers in space.

History

Kotohira-gū, like just about everywhere else in Shikoku, was visited in the 9th century by Kōbō Daishi, who is said to have instituted a place of Buddhist worship on the site of an older, primitive shrine. The resident deity, Kompira, seems to have reached Japan from India where he was worshipped as Kumbhira, the Hindu crocodile god of the River Ganges. Both the Shinto and Buddhist pantheons absorbed him, and the shrine-temple achieved its greatest popularity in the Edo period when pilgrimages were the only kind of travel allowed to the ordinary citizen, and a visit to Kompira-san literally was the journey of a lifetime. Those who lacked the funds or permission to travel themselves made the pilgrimage by proxy: a common ploy was to fill a barrel with rice or money, seal it and set it afloat on the sea with a label indicating its destination. Fishermen who picked it up would earn themselves spiritual credit by transporting it to the shrine. Even odder stories are told of pet dogs dispatched by their land-bound masters with pouches of coins and Kotohira-or-bust labels round their necks. Human pilgrims would point the animals in the right direction and pay for their food and ferries with the money in the pouch.

Theological complications began in 1872, when the engineers of the Meiji Restoration (pro-Emperor and therefore pro-Shinto) began their campaign to cleanse Japan of the 'foreign' Buddhist taint. Cohabitation between *kami* and buddhas was outlawed and the unfortunate half-breed Kompira was 'evicted' from his home to be replaced by a pantheon of squeaky-clean Japanese deities, including the Emperor Sutoku who died in exile nearby in 1164. The zealots quickly calmed down, however. Today, although technically a shrine, the curved Chinese-style roofs give away Kompira-san's Buddhist roots.

Touring Kotohira-gū

With ¥4000 to burn, you can hire a pair of **kago** (palanquin) bearers to carry you up the 785 steps which lead up to the main shrine. It's a waste of money—the steps aren't steep, and there are plenty of resting spots and (a few too many) souvenir, noodle and coffee shops along the way.

The stairs and paths leading off to the right of the main approach also have a number of interesting halls displaying some of the offerings made over the centuries. The **Gakugei Sankō-kan** contains interesting 20th-century paintings on Buddhist themes, plus toys, model boats and planes, and a room of big *ema* (votive plaques) bearing pictures of horses, heroes and beauties; Kompira's Hindu ancestry is honoured by the presence of a giant stuffed Ganges crocodile. In the **Hōmotsu-kan**, alongside many older scrolls, paintings and statues, is a black-and-white photograph of the Brooklyn Bridge offered as a thanks-giving *ema* by a troupe of dancers who'd returned from a successful visit to New York.

The **Ō-mon** (Great Gate) marks the beginning of the precincts proper. Built in 1649, it's unmistakably Buddhist in design—except for the courtly Shinto archers in the alcoves where the Buddhist *Ni-ō* guardian kings should be. Further up on the right is the **Shoin** (Study), with a broad veranda fronting onto a garden, and screen paintings of charmingly cat-like tigers, painted by an artist who had never laid eyes on the real thing.

The **Asahi no Yashiro** (Sunrise Shrine), a fiddly but imposing structure with a green copper roof, dominates the gravel platform just above here. It was built in 1837 and presently enshrines the Sun Goddess, Amaterasu, who supplanted Kompira in Meiji times. Paths continue to the very top of the mountain, but most pilgrims satisfy themselves with the next stage, an **elevated wooden platform** 251m above sea level, which supports the **Hon-gū** (Main Shrine, built 1879), a few lesser shrines, and the **Ema-dō** (Votive Plaque Hall), a fascinating story-board of Kotohira's history. Most of the plaques have been presented by the crews of ships in the hope that their presence here will bring the gods' favour on the ships and their mariners. The variety is amazing—there are pleasure liners, ferries, customs patrol boats, dredgers, warships, submarines, tankers and tugs. The shrine has even entered the space age: a prominent plaque depicts the country's **first cosmonaut**, a Tokyo television journalist who took a place as a paying passenger on the Russian *Soyuz* in 1990. 'I returned home safely by the grace of Kompira-san,' he told the head priest after his triumphant touch-down.

Other Sights in Kotohira

South of the main bridge is **Sayabashi** (Sheath Bridge), so called because of its copper green roof. Above it, on the slopes leading up the shrine mountain, is the **Kanamaru-za**, built in 1835 and thus the oldest **kabuki stage** in the country. In front is a gravel court-yard and a row of red lanterns and *sake* barrels bearing the names of sponsors. For ¥300 you can enter the beautiful timber interior with raked *tatami* seating and two *hanamichi*, the projecting walkways along which the lead actor makes his dramatic exit. Beneath the stage is a musty cellar containing the *kabuki* special effects department: a mighty mecha-nism of perpendicular beams and handles used to rotate the circular centre of the stage.

Where to Stay

Takamatsu has nothing spectacular in the way of accommodation. The top *ryokan* is the **Hotel Kawaroku**, © 0878 21 5666, a 10-minute walk from the JR station, with Western- and Japanese-style rooms from about ¥13,000 with two meals. The grandest of the Western-style hotels is the **Kokusai Hotel**, © 0878 31 1511. It has singles from around ¥8000, but it's inconveniently placed in Kita-chō, a 10min taxi drive from the centre of town, half way to Yashima. For friendly, English-speaking service, 1 minute from the station the **Takamatsu Grand Hotel**, © 0878 51 5757, is probably the best deal: singles start at ¥6500, doubles at ¥12,500. Takamatsu's branch of the **Washington Hotel** chain, ✆ 0878 22 7111, has similar prices, although it's a 20-minute walk from the station in the Kawaramachi entertainment area.

The road leading to the right and to the back (southwest) as you exit the station has lots of business hotels with tiny cheap rooms (all around ¥5000–7000)—you can book these through the information booth or just walk in. **Pearl ('Pāru') Hotel**, ✆ 0878 22 3382, and—bigger, but shabbier rooms—**Hotel Gekkōen**, ✆ 0878 51 7525, are on this street.

There's just one **Youth Hostel**, ✆ 0878 41 2318, near Takamatsu, next to the Shikoku Mura in Yashima.

Kotohira has a lot of pricey hotels and *ryokan* catering for coach parties of Japanese pilgrims—prices vary widely depending on the season. The **Bizen-ya**, ✆ 0877 75 4131 (*expensive*), is a famous old *ryokan*, and there are two Welcome Inns, both bookable in advance at Tokyo, Kyoto and Narita tourist information centres: **Kotobuki Ryokan**, ✆ 0877 73 3872 (*expensive*), and the business-style **Kotohira Riverside Hotel**, ✆ 0877 75 1880 (*expensive*). **Youth Hostel Kotohira**, ✆ 0877 73 3836.

Iya-dani Valley

On the JR Dosan Line between Kotohira (connections go from Takamatsu) and Kōchi, get off at Awa-Ikeda and take a bus from there to Kazura-bashi. Or, if you can find a train slow enough to stop at Iya-guchi, pick up the bus there.

The first 20 minutes of the journey from Awa-Ikeda seem lovely enough but then, at Iya-guchi Bridge, the bus suddenly crosses the river into Iya-dani, a valley of legendary remoteness and beauty, and one of the most unspoiled spots in Japan.

Before the days of modern roads and engineering, served only by a few narrow tracks and flimsy vine bridges, Iya was literally impenetrable to outsiders. Its settlements were said to be *ochiudo mura*, 'fugitive villages' where the surviving members of the Taira family holed up after their defeat at the hands of the Minamoto at the Battle of Dan no Ura in 1185. Today there is one small dam and a reasonably disguised hydro-electric plant. Apart from that there's just the sheer-sided valley, covered by mixed forest right down to the river's edge, and a snaking road that clings precariously to the slope hundreds of metres above.

Other than admire its dramatic beauty, there isn't much to do in Iya-dani. The only trail through the area is the main road, a narrow, winding walk, especially uncomfortable when traffic is passing. There's the grotty looking **Iya-dani Onsen** (get off at the bus stop of the same name), but most visitors make for **Kazura-bashi**, where you can cross a famous bridge of bamboo planks and vine creepers for ¥410. The bridge, or rather the know-how required to construct it, is classified as an Important Ethnic Cultural Property. It's rebuilt every three years by a dwindling band of rural craftsmen out of a tough mountain vine called *shirakuchi*. The Shikoku Mura near Takamatsu has a similar bridge, identical but for the addition of cheating metal cables. Make a point of avoiding the wretched 'park' (10 minutes' walk on the other side of the bridge), a bizarre juxtaposition of plaster Buddhas, pornographic tableaux of plastic mannequins and caged monkeys.

(✆ 0883–) **Where to Stay**

There are five well-spaced buses a day between Awa-Ikeda and Kazura-bashi, so it's quite easy to make a day trip of it. If you do need somewhere to stay, there are several *ryokan* on the far side of the bridge. Try **Kazurabashi Ryokan**, ✆ 87 2038 (*moderate*), or **Kazuraya**, ✆ 87 2242 (*moderate*). Inexpensive *minshuku* are on the near side, below the bus stop. Try **Minami**, ✆ 87 2342, or **Iya-sō**, ✆ 87 2242. **Yasuoka**, ✆ 87 2203, has rooms and if they can't put you up themselves they'll find someone who can.

South Shikoku

Until big ferries and road and rail tunnels opened it up, Kōchi Prefecture—the old Province of Tosa—was an awkward region, a mountain-locked arch of coast on Shikoku's Pacific underbelly. The sophisticated Kyoto types who were sent there to keep an eye on the place couldn't wait to get out. In the 10th century the poet Ki Tsurayuki was sent here as provincial governor and wrote a fictionalized *Tosa Diary* about the grim return journey through pirate-infested seas.

Tosa people developed a reputation for truculence too, especially among the *henro* (pilgrims) who converged on Shikoku to visit the 88 temples. Many natives regarded the pilgrimage ambivalently since it attracted beggars and cozeners as well as the genuine faithful, and in Tosa these suspicions were encoded into a strict set of regulations governing the conduct and treatment of *henro*. Entry was permitted only through speci-fied check-points, pilgrims were frisked, passports were frequently checked, and anyone caught sneaking in or out by an unauthorized route was whipped and deported. Excessive hospitality to pilgrims was forbidden. 'Tosa is the devil's land,' ran one *henro* ditty, '—no lodging there, we understand.'

In more sympathetic form, this reputation for stubborn practicality has stuck with Tosa people to the present day, and established them as the Yorkshiremen of Japan. The figure of the *igossō*—the proud, independent, unpredictable local stalwart—is commemo-rated in statues and plaques throughout Kōchi city. The first of these was Chōsokabe Motochika, the 16th-century Tosa *daimyō* who ruthlessly united the Four Provinces; more recent were Itagaki Taisuke, leader of the short-lived People's Rights movement; 'John' Manjirō, who became the first Japanese to study in the United States; and Sakamoto Ryōma, the swordsman and arms-dealer beatified as a leader of the Meiji Restoration.

Kōchi

This sunny southern city, with its castle and palm-planted avenues, hasn't got much to occupy the tourist, but serves as a natural focus for travels in south and central Shikoku. If you're going to spend a day in Kōchi, try to make it a Sunday so that you can visit the charming market.

The station is at the north end of town. Just in front, to the left as you walk out of it, is the **tourist information centre** which usually has an English-speaking volunteer. Two useful **tram lines**—one going north–south from the station to the port, the other running along the main east–west avenue—intersect at the Harimaya-bashi junction, where **department stores** and **bus stops** are also concentrated. The quarter immediately northwest of Harimaya-bashi is packed with **shops**, **bars** and **restaurants**, and bounded along its northern side by Ōtesuji avenue which leads to the castle.

Every Sunday, from dawn to sunset, Ōtesuji's 1km length is packed out with the stalls of the weekly **market**. Most of these sell food (not all of it dead), including locally caught fish and delicious local oranges in season. The western part, near the castle gate, is the most interesting, with antique shops and stalls displaying plants, coins, ceramics, pipes, iron bottles, inkstones, drums and even samurai swords and armour.

Kōchi-jō (Kōchi Castle) is just beyond here, its grounds surrounded by smart modern civic buildings. Chōsokabe Motochika had a fortress here, but his son made the mistake of siding against Tokugawa Ieyasu and was dispossessed and eventually executed. Tokugawa installed his own supporters, the Yamauchi family, who rebuilt the castle and ruled uninterruptedly until 1868. Almost all the castle buildings had to be rebuilt in the 18th century after a big fire, and all but the main keep were dismantled after the abolition of the shogunate (Tosa men, proud of their active participation in the Meiji Restoration, were particularly zealous in expunging traces of the old regime).

Nowadays, the grounds are a free public park. At the bottom of the stairs leading to the keep is the statue of a bearded demagogue in sharply-creased trousers—**Itagaki Taisuke**, founder of the People's Rights Movement which, for a short time, threatened to bring genuine democracy to Meiji Japan. At the height of the struggle, he was attacked by a knife-wielding assassin and, as the blood pumped out, he uttered the famous cry which this statue commemorates: 'Itagaki may die, but liberty never!' Wrong on both counts: effective democracy was unknown in Japan before the Pacific War, and Itagaki himself survived his wounds, living to the age of 82. The dagger used in the incident is still preserved in the (otherwise uninteresting) **People's Rights Movement Memorial Hall** (Jiyūminken Kinenkan) in the south of the city on the way to the port.

Apart from impressive, rough cut stone embankment walls, nothing much remains of the outer enclosures of the castle. The 18.5m high **keep** is still there, but apart from the great view from the top there's no need to pay ¥350 to go inside. Within are the usual undistinguished feudal relics and a dull exhibition eulogizing the local heroes of the Meiji Restoration. One unusual feature is the *shoin*-style living quarters on the first floor of the castle proper. In most castles, the lord lived in the outer citadel during peacetime, retreating to the keep only in an emergency.

Chikurin-ji, number 31 on the Shikoku Pilgrimage, is the only one of Kōchi's temples worth seeking out. It's at the top of Godaisan Hill, to the east of the city, which also has a Botanical Garden (buses take 25 minutes from the Toden bus terminal, next to Seibu department store on Harimaya-bashi crossing). The pagoda dates from the 1970s and looks it, but the halls are from the Muromachi period, and the overgrown grounds with their mossy stone statues and fine view of the sea and city below make this a worthwhile excursion. For ¥200 you can enter the **Treasure House** with its somewhat wormy selection of Important Cultural Properties, wooden statues from the late Heian and Kamakura periods. Most striking are the snarling figure of the **Myō-ō** (Fierce King) mounted on an ox, and the splendid Heian dog, carved with a lotus leaf on its back to support a now lost buddha.

Other Attractions

Among Kōchi's contributions to the outside world are two unlikely animals. The doughty **Tosa mastiff** (*Tōken*) is bred as a fighting dog. Competitors are awarded the same ranks as sumo wrestlers whom they resemble with their jowly faces and lumbering walks; champions even wear embroidered sumo aprons. On fine days, a retired champion often basks in the porch of Kōchi Castle in his regalia where he can be photographed for a fee (be sure to pay this: the owner is said to be fiercer than his hound). Enquire at the tourist information centre for the timing and location of tournaments, or visit the Tosa Tōken Centre at **Katsurahama**, a popular gravelly beach, 35 minutes by bus from Harimaya-bashi. The dogs are on display, and exhibition fights are staged here if more than 30 spectators are prepared to pay ¥1000 each.

An hour's bus ride from the Harimaya-bashi Seibu terminal is **Ryūgadō** cave (*open 8.30–4.30; adm ¥850*), a 150-million-year-old cavern of which 1km is open to tours. Traces of Yayoi era habitation have been found inside, include a **ceramic pot** placed by a prehistoric troglodyte to catch water dripping from the ceiling. Astonishingly, it became petrified and can still be seen, melded irrevocably with the stalactite.

Admission to the cave includes a taste of Tosa's other great animal invention, the **long-tailed cock** (*onagadori*) whose great plumes, the result of an in-bred mutation, have grown up to 10m long. There's an **Onagadori Centre** (*adm ¥500*) on Route 55, a taxi ride west of Kōchi city. Devoted rooster enthusiasts should ask at the tourist information centre for the less commercialized farms where the beautiful birds can be handled by visitors.

(*℡ 0888–*)

Where to Stay

Japanese-style

The poshest *ryokan*, both ¥20,000 plus with meals, are away from the city centre in the west of the city.

Jōseikan, ℡ 75 0111 (*expensive*), is the choice of emperors.

Sansui-en Hotel, ℡ 22 0131 (*expensive*), is an Edo-period mansion once owned by a retainer of the lord of Kōchi.

The following more modest establishments are all in within walking distance of the downtown area; roughly ¥7000 with meals.

Ryokan Tōgen, ✆ 82 688 (*inexpensive*); **Tosa Bekkan**, ✆ 83 5685 (*inexpensive*); **Wakakusa Ryokan**, ✆ 73 2151 (*inexpensive*).

Western-style

Shin Hankyū Hotel, ✆ 73 1111 (*moderate*), is south of the castle.

Washington Hotel, ✆ 23 6111 (*inexpensive*), is on the avenue leading to the castle. Rooms are about ¥8000.

Business Hotel Tosa, ✆ 25 3332 (*cheap*), is south and east of Harimaya-bashi, with singles for about ¥4000. This is the cheapest of its type.

Kōchi Ekimae Youth Hostel, ✆ 83 5086 (*cheap*), is a 7-minute walk due east of the station.

Eating Out

The culinary speciality of Tosa is fish, and includes **tataki**: steaks of bonito lightly broiled over a fire of pine needles, beaten with straws, and served in garlic-flavoured soy sauce.

Tosa-han (near Harimaya-bashi) is famous for this and other dishes. In Obiyama-machi, the shopping arcade below Daimaru department store, is **Tsukasa**, a cheaper Japanese restaurant. The **Shin Hankyū Hotel** has a reasonably classy Western-style restaurant.

Outside Kōchi

Two rocky prongs—Cape Muroto to the east, Cape Ashizuri to the west—jut out into the Pacific on the south coast of Shikoku. Between them is Tosa Bay, a 320km crescent of sandy shores with Kōchi city at its centre. Beyond them the coastline pulls back dramatically to the north; due south of here there's nothing but ocean until New Guinea, 4000km away. The capes are sub-tropically warm (both are washed by the *Kuroshio*, the 'Black Current' which washes up from the south seas) but they hold the records for the windiest and wettest spots in Japan. They have always attracted mystics and ascetics, since before the beginning of the Shikoku pilgrimage. Roads have found them now, along with mass tourism and its tacky baggage, but it's still possible for visitors to recapture a feeling of being at the end of the world. Don't expect anything more than rocks, wind and water: the point about these places is that there's nothing here.

Muroto Misaki (Cape Muroto)

2hrs 15mins by bus from Kōchi city's Harimaya-bashi terminal. 1hr by bus from Kannoura in Tokushima Prefecture which connects by rail with Tokushima and, finally, Takamatsu.

Neatly laid-out pathways link the cliff top with the rocky shore below. **Hotsumisaki-ji** stands on the top of the cliff terrace and there are two more temples just west of it;

although none of them is worth the visit in itself, they indicate the importance of this spot to Shingon Buddhism. A 25-minute walk along the beach brings you to the grotto called **Shimmei-kutsu** where the Shingon founder, Kōbō Daishi, magically invoked Kokūzō, Buddhist deity of space and wisdom, and achieved enlightenment after years of trying. Stones are piled up inside by believers. 'From that time on, I despised fame and wealth and longed for a life in the midst of nature,' he wrote, after the planet Venus, manifestation of Kokūzō, appeared in the dawn sky.

(✆ 08872–)   ***Where to Stay***

The temple on the cliff administers the **Higashi-dera Youth Hostel**, ✆ 2 0366 (*cheap*). The **Hotel New Muroto**, ✆ 2 1333 (*moderate*), has a couple of Western- as well as Japanese-style rooms. **Muroto**, ✆ 2 2345 (*inexpensive*), is a simpler, Japanese-style establishment.

Ashizuri Misaki (Cape Ashizuri)

By bus: 2½hrs from Kōchi JR station; 1½hrs from Nakamura station which connects with the Shikoku rail network. Infrequent local services also connect up the west coast to Uwajima and Matsuyama.

Three hairpin roads approach the cape through a bulging peninsula, not high but steep-sided, with sloping villages, thickets of wood and spectacular views of the depths around. Tiny islets jut out of the waters and on top of them perch pairs of fishermen casting into the surf. The drive to Ashizuri Misaki is an experience and, off-season, the chances are that you'll have the bus to yourself.

Once you've arrived, there isn't a great deal to see apart from the elements, although there's plenty of interesting lore about the cape and the people who have come here.

History

Ashizuri developed a curious role in the worship of Kannon, gentle *Bosatsu* of Mercy, which reached its peak between the 9th and 12th centuries. Indian belief had it that Kannon dwelled at India's southernmost point, Cape Comorin, on a mountain called Potalaka—Fudaraku, as it became in Japanese. The idea of a divine place, far to the south, associated with a rocky cape became so deeply rooted that literal-minded believers started trying to sail there. Ashizuri, along with the Kii peninsula south of Ōsaka, was their favourite port of embarkation. Chronicles record numerous holy men who cast off in tiny boats, like Katō who set sail in 1002 'and, breasting the waves which stretched for thousands of miles, departed as if he were flying.' A few were washed up on distant islands, as far south as Okinawa; most were never seen in this world again. The cape is notorious too as the place for secular suicides—look out for the signboards erected by the Salvation Army tactfully requesting visitors to *Chotto matte kudasai*—'Please wait a moment.'

A related legend explains the etymology of the name Ashizuri which means, literally, 'foot-stamping'. An old monk came to the temple here with a young disciple. One day another young monk appeared, and the disciple, seeing that he had nothing to eat, unhesitatingly shared his own portion. After a while, the master noticed this and chastised his servant for wasting food on a stranger. That night the newly-arrived monk led his generous young friend to the edge of the cliff. 'The kindness you have shown me is unforgettable,' he said. 'Please come with me and see where I live.' They climbed into a little boat and began rowing south through the stormy seas. The miserly old monk, who had been secretly watching all this, cried after them, demanding to know where they were going. 'We're going to the realm of Kannon,' they replied, and before his eyes they were transformed into *bodhisattvas*. Mad with envy and disappointment, he stamped his feet so hard that they left marks in the rock.

The present day temple, **Kongōfuku-ji** (dedicated, of course, to Kannon) is no architectural treasure, but has a pleasantly exotic atmosphere with its two-storey pagoda and cycad palms. You can take the steep stairs down to the rocky beach below, where there's a natural grotto framed by an arch of rock.

But the most intriguing of Ashizuri's not very considerable tourist attractions is on the main road, a few hundred metres west of the temple. **John Mung House** contains a small exhibition on the extraordinary career and travels of a Japanese Gulliver. In 1841 an American whaling ship anchored off Tori-jima, an uninhabited volcanic island 580km south of Tokyo. 'At 1pm,' the captain recorded, 'I sent in a boat to see if there was any water. Found five poor distressed people on the isle not understanding anything from them more than that they were hungry.' They were fishermen from the town of Tosa Shimizu near Ashizuri; five months before, their open fishing boat had been cast hopelessly adrift by a storm. They drifted for seven days until a miracle washed them up on Tori-jima, where they had been living ever since on the edge of starvation.

Among them was a 14-year-old boy named Nakahama Manjirō whom the captain of the ship, John Whitfield, nicknamed John Mung. When the whaler docked at Honolulu the four older fishermen staggered gratefully ashore, but Mung stayed. For four years he served in Whitfield's crew, then returned with him to Bedford, Massachussetts where the captain educated him. He embarked on further whaling trips to Africa, Australia, Java, New Guinea, the Philippines and Taiwan and became a vice-captain. He panned for gold in California during the Rush of '49, and with the money he saved returned to Honolulu to track down his old crew mates. One had settled down. One had died. Manjirō/Mung and the other two decided to return home.

In 1851 they reached Okinawa where they quickly attracted attention. The lords of Satsuma and Manjirō's home province of Tosa summoned him to tell them about life and conditions overseas. Instead of being executed, as previous returnees had been, Manjirō was elevated to samurai rank and eagerly sought out by those for whom *detente* with the West now seemed an inevitability. When Commodore Perry steamed into Tokyo Bay in 1853, Manjirō was whisked up to the capital, and when the first of the treaties was being concluded in 1860 he was sent back to the United States as part of the delegation. He died in 1898 at the age of 71 after a distinguished career at the Kaisei School for Western Learning, later incorporated into Tokyo University. Many Japanese had set sail from Ashizuri in search of Fudaraku. Few apart from Manjirō had returned—and none had ever brought the Southern Paradise back with them.

Matsuyama

Matsuyama, the gateway to western Shikoku, is the biggest city on the island, well-endowed with banks, airline offices and travel agents, but the only way to approach it directly is by boat across the Inland Sea. Soon the seven-bridge Onomichi–Imabari Route will put Matsuyama within a 2-hour drive of the Honshū expressways. But for now the town still retains a pleasing air of insularity, and the clanking trams and *yukata*-clad visitors to the hot springs add to the comforting feeling of being a decade or two behind the times.

The plain on which Matsuyama sits has been settled since ancient times. The resort of **Dōgo**, now a suburb, was already a sacred spot when the Shinto gods Ōnamuji and Sukuna-bikona bathed in the hot spring there, and numerous emperors and exalted persons followed their example. There was a provincial fortress in Dōgo from as early as 1335, but Katō Yoshiakira, the *daimyō* dispatched to northwestern Shikoku by the Tokugawa shogun, raised his castle on Katsuyama hill, a mile southwest of Dōgo, and the town has flourished quietly around it ever since.

Getting Around

Matsuyama's tourist spots and transportation facilities are dispersed across at least three different neighbourhoods, making orientation tricky at first.

The castle park is in the approximate middle of town and if this is taken as the centre of the clock face then **Matsuyama JR station** (*JR Eki*) is one and a half kilometres to the west at 8 o'clock. There is a second railway station, **Matsuyama City station** (*Shi Eki*) to the south of the castle at half past six—however this serves local commuter lines and is useful to the visitor only as a tram terminal and the centre of the downtown area. **Dōgo Onsen**, location of the famous old bath house and many resort **ryokan**, nestles under the hills to the east at 2 o'clock. Ferries for Honshū arrive and depart from the **port area** which is several kilometres to the northwest.

Buses shuttle between the port and Dōgo Onsen, via the JR station and castle. Several **tram** lines link both the stations, the main road south of the castle where **hotels**, the **Mitsukoshi department store** and government offices are found, and Dōgo Onsen.

There are **tourist information** desks at the terminal for the Hiroshima ferry, at the JR station, and in Dōgo Onsen (by the tram terminal). The **Matsuyama International Centre** by the Prefectural Office (immediately south of the castle by the tram stop called Kenchō-mae), ✆ 0899 43 2025, has a small library of English books and bilingual staff who can arrange **volunteer guides**.

Matsuyama-jō (Castle)

To walk up to the castle (it's steep) take the road by the tram stop Kenchō-mae. The cable car station is on the east side, equidistant between Ichiban-chō and Keisatsu-sho-mae tram stops. A return cable car ticket including entrance to the castle is ¥750.

Matsuyama-jō was damaged by lightning in 1784, arson in 1933 and bombing in 1945, but the reconstructions have been going on since 1820 and, even if there aren't many original structures left, it lacks the Airfix model appearance of more abruptly flattened castles. It was begun in 1602 by *daimyō* Katō Yoshiakira, who spent 25 years watching it progress, only to be sent off to Aizu in Tōhoku just as it was nearing completion. Anyone who walks—rather than taking the cable car—up the 132m hill will appreciate the labour that went into the transportation of all those tons of stone. The castle buildings are strung along the hilltop, which has great views of Mt Ishizuchi and the islands of the Inland Sea.

The **tenshukaku** (keep), rebuilt in 1854, only just qualifies as a feudal era castle and displays a few unusual features—an inner parade ground open to the sky, and a notable absence of the defensive stone-dropping chutes seen in most older castles. The northeast turret in Japan has no strategic purpose. Instead it enshrines the Shinto deity, Tenjin, as a protector against the evil influences traditionally thought to emanate from that direction.

Dōgo Onsen

Like many prosperous hot spring areas, Dōgo has succumbed to tackiness in recent years, with an excess of souvenir shops and flimsy modern inns. Still, every visitor to Matsuyama should spend at least a few hours here to poach themselves in the recuperative waters of the venerable public bath house; up the road are a pleasant shrine and temple too.

Dōgo Onsen Honkan

A few steps northeast of the tram terminal. Open 6.30–11; adm ¥250–¥1240.

The legendary origins of the Dōgo hot springs go back to a white heron which was seen to bathe its wounds in the naturally heated waters, and which lives on today as a civic emblem. The present building, a proud, multi-levelled structure with bristling grey tiles, was built in 1894. The inept hero of one of the most popular modern Japanese novels, Natsume Sōseki's *Botchan*, used to bathe here and is commemorated in the **Botchan room**. There are three floors, containing four different baths of increasing luxuriousness, each segregated by sex. The top price entitles you to a private chamber, cakes and *yukata* kimono, but more fun is the communal **Kami no yu**, 'Hot Water of the Gods', where you will still see old local men clapping hands in prayer in front of the great carved stone tap. The tile and wood interiors are in authentic 19th-century style; in the outer corridors are photos from the many historical costume dramas that have been filmed inside the building.

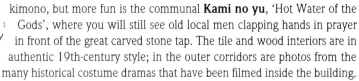

Other Attractions

On a hill above the *onsen* area is **Isaniwa Jinja**, a beautiful and little-visited shrine to Hachiman, the god of war, a semi-legendary character based on the historical Emperor Ōjin, son of a remarkable empress called Jingū. Ōjin was expected at the same time that his mother was masterminding an invasion of Korea in the 4th century. To forestall this inconvenience she bound a stone to her belly and put off Ōjin's birth until the war was over. She is said to have visited the *onsen* during her pregnancy.

The shrine dates from the 17th century and is in fine condition, with lively carvings of animals, fish, waves and leaves. From the side it displays the typical Hachiman architectural style: the oratory and main hall share the same walls but have two distinct roofs.

Ishite-ji (Stone Hand Temple), a 15-minute walk southeast of central Dōgo and number 51 on the Shikoku pilgrimage, is easily the most interesting temple in Matsuyama. Its curious name comes from one of the many legends concerning Kōbō Daishi, although to modern ears it reflects rather grimly on the Daishi's supposed saintliness.

The central figure of the tale is one Saburō Emon, a local landlord notorious for his greed and cruelty. There was famine in Shikoku, but Saburō had no compassion for his starving tenants and taxed them mercilessly. One cold winter day a simple priest came begging for alms, and Saburō had the man driven away. The next day he came back; Saburō had him beaten. Every morning, for eight days, the mendicant returned, each time suffering meaner and more sadistic punishments without complaint. On the eighth day his begging bowl—the source of his livelihood—was shattered by Saburō's staff. As it broke, it fell into eight fragments, like the petals of the lotus.

The nameless monk didn't return after that. But Saburō Emon's life had changed forever. On the first day his eldest son grew sick and died. Twenty-four hours later, the second son was dead. Every morning, for eight days, another heir was gone. By the end of the week he was childless, and ruined with grief.

Saburō realized that he was being punished for his blasphemous cruelty to the wandering priest. He gave away his lands, distributed his possessions among the poor, and set out as a pilgrim to track down the holy man and beg his forgiveness. He circled the entire island, but his object always eluded him. Peasants would tell Saburō that the man had been in their village, but had left a few hours before. So he walked around the island again, and again—20 times altogether, over four years.

On the 21st attempt, Saburō travelled in the reverse direction: instead of following the priest he would confront him head on. But half a decade of suffering had worn him out, and he was dying. Ascending a mountain path in a blizzard, he finally collapsed in the snow. Kōbō Daishi appeared to him, for the ninth and last time in his life. He told the dying man that by walking so far in faith, he had absolved himself of his sins. The saint blessed him and granted him a last wish; Saburō Emon asked to be reborn as a great man in the next life so that he would have the power to do good which he had come to recognize so late in this life. The Daishi picked up a stone, inscribed it and pressed it into Saburō's hand, and at that moment he died.

Nine months later, the Lord of Iyo (present day Matsuyama Prefecture) was presented with a fine baby boy. But the child was handicapped—his left hand was gripped in a fist, and no doctor or midwife could unclaw it. Finally, a Buddhist priest was summoned; as he prayed, the hand spread open. Grasped within was a stone bearing the inscription: *Saburō Emon reborn*. The child, naturally, grew up to be a great and benign ruler, and the local temple was renamed 'Stone Hand Temple' in commemoration of the strange events of his birth.

Ishite-ji has several dignified Kamakura-period buildings, including a three-storey pagoda and a main gate with distinguished *ni-ō* guardians, a National Treasure. But the temple's most bizarre feature is a dimly-lit tunnel several hundred metres long, a kind of Buddhist haunted house of deities surrounded by flickering stroboscopic lights. The hill which the tunnel penetrates has a large standing statue of Kōbō Daishi on its summit and the grounds also contain a dusty **museum** (*adm ¥300*) containing grubby statues and faded screens.

(✆ 0899–)   *Where to Stay*

Matsuyama hotels are split between **Dōgo Onsen** and the downtown area—principally **Ichiban-chō**, the main road immediately south of the castle. The latter is a little more convenient and most hotels here are Western-style; the former has the advantage of hot springs and Japanese-style *tatami* rooms.

Dōgo Onsen consists of numerous alleys crammed into a small area: for directions ask at the station, or have someone from your inn meet you at the tram station.

Top of the list here is the extraordinary **Dōgo-kan**, ✆ 41 7777 (*expensive*), 10 minutes' walk uphill from Dōgo tram station, a sumptuous luxury resort *ryokan*, purpose-built in 1989 by the avant-garde architect Kurokawa Kiso. The project cost 5 billion yen, and it's easy to see why. Behind the stern concrete façade lies a rich man's fantasy. Streams and waterfalls cascade through the huge entrance hall. A 16th-century tea room has been reconstructed in the third floor garden. There are saunas, *rotenburo* and regular tubs of many sizes, all drawing off the ancient springs. An experience in tasteful excess, but not a cheap one. Japanese-style rooms from ¥18,000 skywards, Western-style from ¥13,000 including breakfast.

Funaya Ryokan, ✆ 47 1278 (*expensive*), is the next best of the expensive inns. More moderate is **Midori-so**, ✆ 21 3807, and there's a *minshuku* called **Miyoshi**, ✆ 77 2581 (*inexpensive*), near Ishite-ji temple. The **Youth Hostel**, ✆ 33 6366 (*cheap*), is near Isaniwa Shrine.

Downtown, facing the castle in Ichiban-chō, is the top city hotel, **Matsuyama Zennikku (All Nippon Airways) Hotel**, ✆ 33 5511 (*moderate to expensive*). In Sanban-chō, a few streets to the south, is **Ehime Kyōsai Kaikan**, ✆ 45 6311 (*inexpensive*). There are several cheaper business hotels around Heiwa-dōri, north of the castle. Enquire at the tourist information points or try **Business Hotel Taihei**, ✆ 43 3560 (*cheap*).

(✆ 0899–)   *Eating Out*

Kaiseki Club Kawasemi, ✆ 33 9697 (*expensive* except for lunch sets which are *inexpensive*) presents traditional *kaiseki ryōri*—tea house cuisine served in tiny dishes—with a modern, nouvelle twist. At **Tōun**, ✆ 51 1571 (*expensive*), wriggling seafood is cooked in front of you by the chef. **Kappa Aburaya**, ✆ 21 2888 (*moderate*), has all kinds of seafood including (in season) the *fugu* puffer fish.

Chūgoku—Western Honshū

Chūgoku means 'middle country', although these days it's not the middle of anything very much. The name reflects a time when the centre of the Japanese nation was further west than it is today. When Nara and Kyoto, rather than Tokyo, were capital cities, the islands and channels of the misty Inland Sea were crucial hubs of trade and transportation. Since the war, heavy industry has robbed them of some of their charm, but there are still spots of great beauty: on the eastern shores, in Okayama prefecture, and the shrine island of Miyajima to the west. Hiroshima, until 1945 an unexceptional medium-sized castle town, is notorious as the first city ever to suffer atomic attack, a symbol and place of pilgrimage of the international peace movement. The mountainous inland areas of Chūgoku and the Japan Sea coast to the north are bleak, rugged and sparsely populated.

Okayama Prefecture

Okayama City is a bit of a disappointment, although it shouldn't be. There are several shiny modern museums and a reconstructed castle, but the town has a fussy, superficial atmosphere, and the much hyped **Kōraku-en** is far less interesting than many more modest gardens. The area east of the prefectural capital produces **Bizen-yaki**, one of Japan's most ancient and esteemed pottery types—a reddish-brown ware, undecorated apart from a natural ash glaze which can be coloured and manipulated by wrapping the vessels in straw during firing. Unfortunately, the pottery 'village' of **Imbe** where the kilns are located has become an unpleasantly drab and industrialized place. Committed ceramophiles can take the train to Imbe station and visit several museums, the best of which is the **Fujiwara Kei Memorial Hall**, dedicated to the greatest of the Bizen potters.

Kurashiki

Like Kansai's Himeji, Kurashiki is a sprawling modern city which has managed to preserve at its centre a tiny area of great beauty and interest. During the Edo period (1600–1868) it was an important centre for the shipping of rice. The grain was kept in black and white, earthen-walled storehouses called *kura*, which gave the town its name. Today, a number of these, as well as some distinguished Western-style buildings, have been converted into private museums and galleries. Ranged along the edges of a willow-lined canal, they attract thousands of visitors, mainly young Japanese women, to shop, stroll and enjoy the 'cute', quasi-European atmosphere.

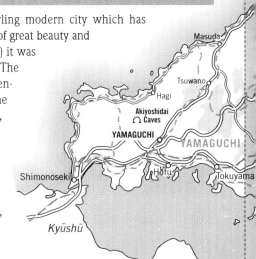

There are two principal stations: **Kurashiki** on the JR San'yō line, which is very close to the historical area; and **Shin-Kurashiki**, a stop on the Tōkaidō *shinkansen* line, which is a bus ride away from the places of interest. The quickest route is probably to take the *shinkansen* to Okayama and the connecting San'yō line from there to Kurashiki.

A **night bus** leaves from Tokyo's Shinagawa station to reach Kurashiki in 11hrs. It costs just over ¥10,000.

Bicycles can be hired at the station.

Tourist Information

Get an English language map from the information office in the station. The historical area, a few minutes' walk south, contains the copper-roofed **Kurashiki-kan**

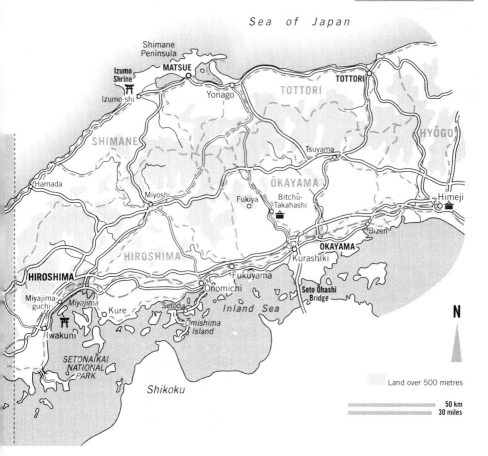

Western Japan

Sea of Japan

Shimane Peninsula

Izumo Shrine

MATSUE

Izumo-shi

Yonago

TOTTORI

TOTTORI

HYŌGO

SHIMANE

Tsuyama

ŌKAYAMA

Hamada

Miyoshi

Fukiya

Bitchū-Takahashi

Himeji

Bizen

HIROSHIMA

Kurashiki

OKAYAMA

HIROSHIMA

Fukuyama

Onomichi

Seto Ōhashi Bridge

Miyajima-guchi

Miyajima

Kure

Setoda

Inland Sea

Iwakuni

Ōmishima Island

N

SETONAIKAI NATIONAL PARK

Shikoku

Land over 500 metres

50 km
30 miles

Tourist Information Office (*open April–Sept, 9–5.30; Nov–Mar 8.30–5*), which has further pamphlets and staff who speak English.

Don't come to Kurashiki on a Monday or on a Tuesday after a national holiday: most of the museums will be closed.

Ōhara Museum of Art

Open 9–5; adm ¥800.

The admission price looks high, but covers four separate museums, all founded by Ōhara Magosaburo, businessman and Christian philanthropist, who opened his private collection to the public in 1930. Ōhara's agent, Kōjima Torajirō, travelled around war-scarred Europe during the early 1920s, snapping up works by famous artists which attracted huge crowds when they were displayed here. It was the first museum of Western art in Japan, at a time when things foreign were being viewed with increasing suspicion by nationalist politicians. The Rodin bronzes outside the front door narrowly escaped being melted down for gun metal during the war.

By international standards, however, the Western art here, displayed in a pastiche Greek temple, is extremely disappointing. Big names seem to have attracted Kōjima, regardless of the quality of the work in question. Apart from decent minor paintings by Gauguin, Pissarro and de Chirico, many of the pictures here seem to be token examples of a style or painter, not fully realized works in their own right: inferior and unambitious pieces by Degas and Toulouse-Lautrec, second-rate Sisleys, Seurats, Chagalls and Cézannes. Some of the pieces by lesser known artists are plain kitsch, Japanese fantasies of cute Westernness with lots of cats, puppies, big eyes, pastoral scenes and renderings of furniture and interiors in lush colours. The present curators seem to have more taste than their predecessors, and the galleries improve as they progress chronologically. There are some interesting European and American abstracts (Christo, Rothko, Jasper Johns and Jackson Pollock) as well as token works by Warhol and Lichtenstein.

An adjacent set of rooms, included in the admission price, make up for this disappointment. The **Craft Gallery** devotes a room to each of the four artists associated with the Japan Folk Arts (*Mingei*) movement: Hamada Shōji (1894–1978), Kawai Kanjirō (1890–1966), Tomimoto Kenkichi (1886–1963), and the great British potter Bernard Leach (1887–1979) who set up a workshop with Hamada in St Ives and also lived for several years in Japan. The objects they created, mostly ceramics, range from simple versions of folk pots, bowls and bottles (favoured especially by Hamada) to the more experimental, abstract sculptures in stoneware of Kawai. All four rooms are in a beautiful wooden annex.

Adjacent are rooms honouring two other men of the same generation: Seizawa Keisuke (1875–1984), a textile dyer and painter who created beautiful simple designs, many using the Japanese *hiragana* syllabary, on fans, theatre curtains, kimono, belts and lengths of plain linen. Munakata Shiko (1903–75) is perhaps the most ambitious and compelling of all: the highlights here are the strange, almost cubist woodblock prints of Buddhist deities.

On the other side of the canal, across **Imabashi Bridge** (the stone dragons carved on the outside are by the museum's first curator Kōjima Torajirō) is the old **Ōhara House**, built by the same family. It's closed to the public, but a similar merchant dwelling, the **Ōhashi House**, also built in 1796, will open in 1995. This one is a few hundred metres to the west, across Kurashiki Chūō-dōri, the main road you walked down from the station.

Other Museums

Two minutes' walk southeast of the Ōhara Museum of Art, on the bend in the canal, are two more museums, principally of occidental art. The **Kurashiki Ninagawa Museum**, on the same side as the Ōhara, also called the **Ancient Greece Museum** (*open 9–5; adm ¥800*), contains a huge collection of marbles, statues and reliefs from the Mediterranean and Near East, none outstanding, but many attractive. Over the curved stone **Nakabashi Bridge** is the **Kurashiki Kōkōkan**, an archaeology museum (*open Mar–Nov, 9–5; Dec–Feb, 9–4.30; adm ¥400*) in a white *kura* storehouse. It has a lot of local objects, but also Chinese and South American relics, nothing to get excited about.

Your priority should be the two museums round the corner, south of the **Kurashiki-kan Tourist Information Office**. The **Kurashiki Mingei-kan** (*open Mar–Nov 9–5; Dec–Feb 9–4.15; adm ¥500*) is one of the best folk art museums of its kind. Instead of focusing on individual artists (like the Ōhara Craft Gallery), the objects displayed here are anonymous. Again, it is the combined effect of the exhibits and the wood and plaster interior of the old granary that is pleasing, rather than any individual pieces. There's a working loom, a case of plain, dignified Bizen ceramics, fabrics, old household shrines, and antique chairs that you can sit in. Most are unlabelled, except by place of origin, because the craftsman and date of manufacture are simply not recorded.

Next door is the **Japan Folk Toy Museum** (*open 8–5; adm ¥310*), Kurashiki's most appealing attraction, with thousands of toys from all over Japan, and a few hundred from all over the world. Even if Japanese cuteness turns you off, you will enjoy this. Many of the exhibits are fine folk objects in their own right, including masks, dolls, animals, birds, cars, carts, floats, kites and tops. Among the most charming are the *aka-bekko* lucky cows from Aizu-Wakamatsu in Tōhoku, with red *papier-mâché* bodies and swaying heads. There are gaudy, snarling tigers made to the same design, and numerous representations of the children's hero, Momotaro the Peach Boy, bounding dynamically out of his fruit. A lot of these characters have appeared on specially issued stamps, displayed alongside. Among all this gay innocence, look also for the franker objects: the miniature of two ardently mating dogs; and the extraordinary painted plaques of a mother decanting her breast milk. The museum has an excellent shop selling hand-made versions of the toys on display.

Shopping

The canal teems with souvenir and craft shops. Planning laws require them to maintain a reasonable appearance, but that doesn't apply to the merchandise and there is plenty of over-priced tat. The most popular products are folk crafts and antique furniture, toys, pottery and *sake*. Shops facing directly onto the canal pay higher rents which are reflected in their prices. Try the quieter streets towards Tsurugatayama Park, the wooded hill to the north. The Folk Art and Folk Toy museums both have fine shops.

Ebisu-dōri is a covered arcade leading from the bottom of the park towards the station. Half way along here is a shop called **Tobidō**, which sells Bizen ceramics at better prices than the tourist shops. The owner speaks a bit of English, and an English pamphlet is available.

Dotemori is a lovely old *sake* shop, on the north side of the canal, with shelves of good luck charms, and all kinds of *sake* in beautiful bottles.

Ivy Square, a complex of brick warehouses built around a central quadrangle, used to be the Kurashiki Spinning Mill, the business which made the fortune of the Ōhara family. Now it's been converted into a village of cultural halls, elegant shops and an expensive hotel.

(✆ *0864–*)　　　　　　　　　　　　　　　　　*Where to Stay and Eating Out*

Kurashiki Kokusai (International) Hotel, ✆ 22 5141, is a modern Western-style hotel behind the Ōhara Museum, with suites and Japanese rooms also available. Singles range from *moderate* to *expensive*.

Kurashiki Ivy Square (Aibi Sukuea), ✆ 22 0011, in the Ivy Square complex, is *expensive*.

Convenient Japanese-style accommodation ranges from **Ryokan Tsurugata**, ✆ 24 1635, and **Ryokan Kurashiki**, ✆ 22 0730, both *expensive*, both facing the canal, to the *inexpensive* **Kokumin Ryokan Ōguma**, ✆ 22 0250, a minute from the station. The best deal in town is the simple **Minshuku Kamoi**, ✆ 22 4898, in an old wooden building, run by a charming family, from ¥5000 per person per night.

Kurashiki Youth Hostel, ✆ 22 7355, bookable via the Welcome Inn service, is the *cheapest* lodging (10 minutes by bus and a 10 minute walk).

As far as dining goes, the options are very limited after 6pm, and you will be best off eating in your hotel or inn. There are numerous coffee shops, the best of which, **El Greco**, is right next to the Ōhara Museum.

Okayama International Villas

Foreign visitors are important to the Japanese prefectures, and they put a lot of money and effort into courting them. Some build gleaming international centres with libraries and databases, others subsidize home-stay programmes and Japanese language courses. Okayama has had the best idea of all: a network of self-catering villas in sequestered rural spots, for the exclusive use of foreign visitors and their Japanese friends.

The Japanese countryside can be inaccessible, especially if you're short of time. The closest many visitors get to it is the view through a train window. As well as being one of the best accommodation deals in the country, the International Villas are the perfect way to catch a glimpse of rural Japan. The villages where they are sited have no big temples or famous museums—just farms, fishing, traditional architecture, and accommodation (as the prefecture quaintly puts it) 'at a price that reflects a more traditional time'—in other words, as cheap as the cheapest youth hostel. The Okayama International Villas Group started in 1988 and so far has six properties. All have bedrooms, self-catering kitchens, laundry and washing facilities, and bicycles for the use of guests.

Shiraishi is a small island in the Inland Sea. From Okayama take the San'yō Main Line to Kasaoka, and from there make the half-hour ferry crossing to the island. The villa is a purpose-built modern structure on a hill just above the town. Five rooms accommodate up to 12 people; there's a stereo CD player and a patio with a fine view of the Inland Sea. The island has forest hiking trails, local temples and curious granite rock formations. The villa phone number is ✆ 0865 68 2095.

Ushimado is a small fishing village on the mainland coast of the Inland Sea. From Okayama you drive the 30km, or take a bus (1hr), or a local train to Oku station, and then a bus. The villa is a modern wooden building on a steep rise high above the village: pick up the key from the Ushimado Town Hall (there will usually be someone to drive you up the hill). The village has an interesting history. The name is supposed to mean 'Thrashing Bull', after a legend concerning a supernatural beast which used to churn up the waters. The sea god, Sumiyoshi, subdued the bull, which was transformed into a string of islands. During the 18th century Ushimado was a stopping-off place for feudal *daimyō* and Korean diplomats, journeying by sea to Edo (Tokyo) to see the shogun; a small history museum commemorates these exotic visitors. There's a temple with a pretty three-storey pagoda, and a shrine honouring Sumiyoshi, the bull conqueror. Maejima island, a short ferry ride over the water, has beaches and sequestered walks. Quite unnecessarily, Ushimado insists on comparing itself to an Aegean village (various gimmicks have been manufactured to reinforce this tiresome analogy). The villa phone number is ✆ 0869 34 4218.

Fukiya is a beautifully preserved old village, worth visiting even if you don't manage to stay in the villa. Without a car, it's time-consuming to get to. Take the JR Hakubi Line from Okayama to Takahashi and from there catch the infrequent buses which reach Fukiya in an hour. The two-storey wooden villa itself is modern, but built in the style of the surrounding houses—wood, plaster and tile walls of the late 19th century. During that time Fukiya grew rich on two commodities: copper, mined from a defunct shaft which can be visited today; and *bengara*, a red mineral oxide used for staining wood in traditional architecture. One of the finest of the village houses, built by a *bengara* tycoon, has been converted into a **historical museum** (Kyōdō-kan). The **Hirogane Residence**, 4km to the south, is another fine merchant house, built on a hill like the fortress of a petty lord. The village also has several restaurants specializing in rural *sansai ryōri*, mountain vegetable cuisine. The villa phone number is ✆ 0866 29 2222.

Takebe is not in such a lovely setting as the other villas—a hot spring town on the banks of a rushing river—but the villa has one great advantage: its own *onsen*, hot spring bath. Trains or buses take about an hour from Okayama to Fukuwatari Station. The villa is a modern, wooden structure, with private showers in each of the five rooms. The villa phone number is ✆ 0867 22 2500.

Hattōji has the oldest villa of all, the thatch-roofed former home of a 19th-century village elder. Drive from Okayama, or take the train to Yoshinaga and then an infrequent bus to Hattōji village. The house has *tatami* matting, an open hearth, and an old-style cauldron bath. It's built on the slopes of Mt Hattōji (539m), a 1200-year-old centre of Buddhist asceticism, with old local shrines and temples, and mountain walks. A car would make sight-seeing much easier. The villa phone number is ✆ 0869 85 0254.

Koshihata is another 19th-century thatched farmhouse, though not such an old one. Take the train from Okayama or Himeji to Tsuyama, and the bus (four every day) to Koshihata. The modern kitchen and laundry adjoin *tatami* living- and bedrooms. The village is quite high (nearby Mt Tsunagosen is 1153m) and there are heavy snowfalls in winter. The surrounding countryside has fishing, walking, roadside shrines and waterfalls. The villa phone number is ✆ 0868 56 0207.

Booking the Okayama International Villas

The International Villa Group can be phoned or faxed in English on ✆/✆ 0862 34 3311, or write to 2-4-6 Uchisange, Okayama-shi, Okayama-ken, Japan 700. Colour brochures are available from Tokyo and Kyoto Tourist Information Centres. Membership, which is available only to foreign nationals, costs ¥500 per person. There's no special procedure: you can join at the office in Okayama, or as you check in. Japanese can stay at the villas, but only as the friends of foreign members. The current rate is ¥2500 per person per night for members, and ¥3000 for non-members. Solo occupancy of a twin room incurs a surcharge of ¥500. You may find yourself sharing the villa's communal facilities with other guests (part of the idea is that foreigners of different nationalities mix and get to know one another). At some villas you can guarantee sole occupancy by payment of an additional fee.

The Japan Sea Coast

The San'in coast, from the straits of Dan no Ura in Honshū's extreme west to Wakasa Bay, is one of the loneliest, least explored areas of Japan. For most of its length it's hypnotically empty: Route 9 and the JR San'in Main Line follow the coast past small fishing villages and occasional off-shore islands, empty but for sea birds and unmanned lighthouses. There are, however, two gems, little frequented by foreign tourists, but fascinating detours for those with the time to travel there: Izumo, an ancient region studded with traces of early Shinto; and Hagi, a seaside town of temples and crafts where the plotters of the 19th-century Meiji Restoration hatched their plans against the shogun.

Izumo

Izumo is the old name for a region now absorbed into Shimane Prefecture. **Matsue** is the prefectural capital, a castle town where the 19th-century writer Lafcadio Hearn settled and married. **Izumo Taisha** is one of the oldest and most important Shinto shrines; the modern **Izumo City** is nearby.

Matsue

Built on a narrow strip of land between two tidal lagoons, Matsue is a more than usually interesting regional town, with an original 16th-century castle, feudal architecture, and a fascinating crop of ancient shrines and burial mounds in the countryside to the south. It is nationally famous as the home of one man: Lafcadio Hearn, a one-eyed manic depressive, and the first and greatest foreign Japanophile, ranked (in Japan at least) alongside Shakespeare, Poe and Somerset Maugham as one of the greatest of all writers in English.

Getting There

Matsue is on the JR San'in line. Express **trains** run direct from Ōsaka, Okayama, Kyoto and Hiroshima. From Tokyo there are two trains every night, but they take 13hrs and cost over ¥20,000. It's quicker and almost as cheap to fly by Japan Air Systems to Izumo **airport**.

Night buses from Tokyo's Shibuya station run to Matsue and then on to Izumo for ¥11–12,000. The journey takes 12–13hrs.

Local buses and San'in line trains operate all day between Matsue and Izumo City.

Tourist Information

The station is in the southern part of town; the Hearn relics and other attractions are clustered around the castle to the north, across the wide Ōhashi River. Walk or cycle around Matsue (rent a cycle near the station). The town has a corps of English-speaking Goodwill Guides who will act as unpaid escorts to parties of visitors. Enquire, at least a day in advance, at the tourist information office in Matsue station, ✆ 0852 27 2598.

Lafcadio Hearn in Matsue

Whatever you make of his writing, and the awed respect with which he is regarded in Matsue, there's great interest in the life story of Lafcadio Hearn, and the lessons it seems to offer about Japan and the expatriates who settle there. Hearn was not the first Westerner to write about Japan, or even the most accomplished. But few, before or since, have expressed their feelings for their adopted country with such desperate sincerity and humility. In the strangeness of Japan, Hearn was able to forget (almost) the inner feelings of strangeness and alienation which had troubled him all his life. A century later, every Japanese city has its little colony of Lafcadio Hearns.

He was christened Patrick Lafcadio, after Levkas, the Ionian island where he was born in 1890. His mother was Greek, his father a Dublin-born doctor in the British army. The marriage was annulled within a few years and Lafcadio, virtually kidnapped by his Irish relatives, received a disjointed education in England, France and Ireland. Even as a boy he was restless and vulnerable. At the age of 16 he lost his left eye in a schoolboy fight, and the disfigurement compounded his feelings of self-disgust. Throughout his life he refused to let himself be photographed face on; the pictures displayed in Matsue invariably show him in right profile, with his bad eye hidden.

At 19, he was sent to America where he drifted for a few years, before starting as a crime reporter on the Cincinnati *Enquirer.* Later, he moved to New Orleans where he became fascinated with Creole culture, and wrote several books on the subject. After two years in French Martinique, Hearn sailed to Japan in 1890 as a correspondent for *Harper's Weekly.*

As usual, he quarrelled with his editors, and was forced to work as an English teacher to support himself. In any case, as his breathless essay *My First Day in the Orient* demonstrates, he had already fallen in love with the country. He never left.

Hearn's career took him to different parts of Japan—to Kumamoto, to Kōbe, where he edited an English newspaper, and finally to Tokyo as Professor of English Literature at the Imperial University. But it was Matsue, where he first taught at a secondary school, that he always thought of as home. Hearn wrote 11 more books before his death in 1904, including folk tales and analytical journalism, but *Glimpses of Unfamiliar Japan* (1894), a collection of essays based mainly on his experiences in Matsue, is his best-known and best-loved work. He wrote sketches about his students; about aspects of Japanese religion, such as *Jizō* statues and the fox messengers represented at Inari shrines; essays entitled *Of Women's Hair*, *The Japanese Smile*, and *In a Japanese Garden*, about his own house in Matsue. In later years he wrote popular English retellings of traditional ghost stories, published as *Kwaidan*, and filmed in 1964 by the director Kobayashi Masaki. His writing can be overripe and sentimental, irritatingly susceptible to the quaint and picturesque. But the detail which he packs in (despite a limited command of Japanese) is remarkable, and there's no doubting his love and unfashionable reverence for the country he adored. At a time when foreigners were welcomed as modernizers, Hearn recognized and recorded the value of what was being dismantled, and loved Japan for what it was.

In Matsue he married the daughter of a samurai family. They had four children, and in 1896 he was adopted by his wife's family, and took on Japanese nationality. He also took on his wife's name, Koizumi, and the given name Yakumo, which means 'Eight Clouds'. In 1904, after years of painful illness, he died in Tokyo. He was buried in a temple cemetery under a posthumous Buddhist name which means, exactly translated, 'Man of Faith, Similar to an Undefiled Flower Blooming like Eight Rising Clouds, Who Dwells in the Mansion of Right Enlightenment'.

Hearn's books, including *Kwaidan* and *Glimpses of Unfamiliar Japan*, are published by Tuttle, and sold in the English-language sections of big book shops. An anthology, edited with a sensitive introduction by Francis King and published by the Penguin Travel Library, provides the best introduction to his writing.

Around Matsue

Matsue-jō (*open 8.30–5; adm ¥310*) with its small, crisp, attractive keep set in the pleasant Jōsan Park, was built in 1611 and is one of the few original castles to survive the Meiji Restoration and Pacific War. A **Kyōdō-kan** (Local History Museum) within the grounds contains the usual armour, swords and feudal relics, and a street called **Shiomi Nawate**, curving along the far north bank of the castle moat still retains a little of the atmosphere of the town Hearn knew. A pretty **Buke Yashiki** (Samurai House) with a rest house serving refreshments, by a quiet bamboo grove, displays household objects from the feudal period (*open 8.30–5; adm ¥250*). The **Tanabe Art Museum** (*open 9–5; adm ¥500*), a little further on, is a private collection of ceramics and tea ware in a subtle modern building designed, in steel and concrete, to resemble a traditional tea house. Up a slope, between the museum and samurai house, is an authentic tea house, the **Meimei-an** (*open 9–5; adm ¥200*), a tiny, simple building built by a Matsue *daimyō* in 1779, moved here from its original site 20 years ago.

Herun Kyūkyō, Hearn's old house (*open 9–4, closed Wed; adm ¥200*) and the **Koizumi Yakumo Kinenkan**, a memorial museum to Lafcadio Hearn (*open 8.30–5; adm ¥250*) are close by one another, north of the castle moat. The house has been maintained exactly in the state described by Hearn in his essay *In a Japanese Garden*, even down to the shrubs and stones in the garden. A pamphlet, written in 1919 by Hearn's former students, who purchased and preserved the house after his death, quotes from this account at length. The modern museum is virtually a shrine: Hearn's comb is displayed, as are his pipes, penknives and brushes, and photographs of him as Koizumi Yakumo, cross legged in kimono in front of a low table, more Japanese than the Japanese. In 1971 some hair clippings believed to belong to Hearn were discovered. They have been solemnly buried beneath a stone to the left of the entrance.

Izumo Taisha (Izumo Grand Shrine)

From Izumo City, buses for Izumo Taisha depart several times an hour from the stop in front of Ichibata department store, on the right as you exit the station. There's also a clanky local railway line run by the Ichibata company.

Mythology and History

The complicated mythical origins of Izumo Grand Shrine seem to encode, in legendary form, fascinating information about the early history of the Japanese islands.

According to the ancient chronicles, Izumo was settled by the Shinto deity Susano-o, the brother of the sun goddess Amaterasu, expelled by her from the High Plain of Heaven for his violent and unruly behaviour. Susano-o's descendant was Ōkunikushi, a wise and benevolent ruler who spread prosperity throughout the country. When Amaterasu asked him to hand sovereignty over to her grandson, he agreed, and was rewarded with a palace at Izumo, the original Grand Shrine where he is now worshipped as principal *kami*. The legend seems to allude to an ancient encounter between two powerful tribes, one worshipping Amaterasu, the other worshipping of Ōkunikushi. When the latter yielded peacefully to the former, their loyalty was cemented by the construction of an elaborate shrine, and the elevation of Ōkunikushi's place in the pantheon.

These days he's honoured as the god of marriage (hundreds of weddings are held in the precincts every year) and protector of the nation. Every October, according to Shinto belief, the eight million *kami* leave their home shrines and converge on Izumo for an annual get-together. Daikoku, one of the seven lucky gods of folk superstition, is the most popular of Ōkunikushi's many alternative names and forms. Statues of Daikoku as the god of wealth, seated on bulging rice sacks and clutching a mallet, crop up all over the area.

There has been a shrine building at Izumo since before records began, but what relation the present structure bears to the original is uncertain. One theory holds that earlier versions were immense, towering on pillars 100m tall, with a massive staircase leading up to them. At one time the shrine seems to have been closer to the sea than at present. The large white stones in the precincts would once have been pebbles of the shore.

The halls used to be rebuilt at regular intervals (as they still are at Japan's other great shrine, Ise Jingū) but this practice was discontinued during the Edo period, and the original appearance of the shrine has therefore been lost. Most of the present buildings date from 1668; the main hall was rebuilt in 1744.

Touring Izumo Taisha

A small town, Taisha-machi, has grown up around the road leading up to the shrine which is straddled by huge *torii* gateways. The **Sei-mon** gateway marks the entrance to a long avenue of ancient pines which lean into one another to form an evergreen tunnel. A final copper *torii* marks the entrance to the shrine proper.

As at Ise, the most sacred buildings are inaccessible to casual visitors, partially concealed behind palisades. The first building you come to can be recognized by the ogre-sized *shimenawa* (sacred rope) suspended above its entrance. This is the **Haiden** (Oratory). Prayers can be offered here or at the steps leading up to the **Yatsuashi-mon** (Eight-legged Gate) which give onto the inner sanctum. At most Shinto shrines, supplicants clap twice; at Izumo, as the patron shrine of marriage, they clap four times: twice for themselves, twice for their spouse (actual or potential).

Even if it is just a quarter of the size of the original, the 24m-high **Honden** (Main Hall) is still the biggest in Japan. It lends its name to the Taisha style which differs from the Ise style in several respects. The entrance is under the gable end, and the steps leading up to it are covered by a roof. The horn-like finials (*chigi*) are, unlike the Ise style, purely ornamental, forming no intrinsic part of the roof's construction, and they are mounted towards the centre of the roof ridge rather than above the gable. The Taisha's stone base protects the wooden supports from damp and decay, so it has not had to be rebuilt as frequently as Ise. As a result, though, it represents a less pure version of an ancient style.

Beyond the Shrine

Buses follow a lovely coastal road to **Hinomisaki**, a fishy little town where you can buy sharks' teeth, dried *fugu* (puffer fish) and dozens of different kinds of beautiful sea shell. A functioning lighthouse (*open 8.30–4; adm ¥200*), built in 1904 by British engineers, is the oldest of its type in Asia. The 17th-century **Hinomisaki Shrine** is a complete contrast to Izumo Taisha: vermilion painted wood, graceful curves and elaborately carved animals.

Where to Stay

Matsue

Matsue Tōkyū Inn, ✆ 0852 27 0109, and **Matsue Washington Hotel**, ✆ 0852 22 4111, are *moderate* Western-style hotels. **Matsue Plaza Hotel**, ✆ 0852 26 6650 is a business hotel in the cheap category.

As far as *ryokan* go, **Horai-sō**, ✆ 0852 21 4337 is *expensive*; **Naniwa Bekkan**, ✆ 0852 21 4132 is *moderate*. **Taisenkaku**, ✆ 0852 21 7355, is a *cheap ryokan*-style hostel, 15 minutes' walk from Matsue station—phone ahead to be picked up. It can be booked through the Welcome Inn service.

Izumo

Izumo City has a few *minshuku* and Western-style hotels, but Taisha-machi is more convenient for the shrine, even if its lodgings are a bit modern and character-less. **Takenoya**, ✆ 0853 53 3131, is probably the nicest *ryokan* with rooms from *moderate* to *luxury*. **Business Hotel Taisha**, ✆ 0853 53 2194, is Western-style and *cheap*. The **youth hostel**, ✆ 0853 53 2157, is *cheapest* of all, but a bit grim.

The nicest place to stay if you have the time would be at **Hinomisaki**. There are several *minshuku* and a **Kokumin-shukusha** (People's Lodge), ✆ 0853 54 5111, which is *inexpensive*.

Eating Out

Izumo's speciality is *Izumo-soba*, buckwheat noodles in a rich, almost meaty soup, served in small bowls stacked one on top of another. The approach to Izumo shrine in Taisha Town has several little shops serving bowls for a few hundred yen.

Matsue is livelier: the few blocks between the station and the river comprise a rather raffish neighbourhood of restaurants and hostess bars. Traditional restaurants, serving eels and seafood from the Shinji lagoon, tend to cluster on either side of Ōhashi bridge, especially on the north bank.

Hagi

Hagi is a small relaxing seaside town with reasonable beaches and its own distinctive pottery, **Hagi-yaki**, a flesh to sand coloured stoneware much favoured for use in the tea ceremony. **Ito Hirobumi**, one of Japan's first modern prime ministers, and **Yoshida Shōin**, a teacher and samurai who inspired several of the leaders of the 1868 **Meiji Restoration**, were both from Hagi. Ito's childhood home, and a shrine to Yoshida, who was executed by the shogun for his beliefs, can be visited in the hills to the east of the town. Closer to the centre is an old-fashioned neighbourhood of **samurai houses** and the ruins of a small **castle**.

Higashi-Hagi is the name of Hagi's principal station, and this is what the town is called on the JNTO map. The slow, scenic JR San'in main line runs from Shimonoseki, on Honshū's westernmost point, through Hagi and on to Izumo and Matsue. But the quickest route from most parts of Japan is to take the *shinkansen* to Ogori (5–6hrs from Tokyo, 3hrs from Kyoto) and a JR **bus** (1hr 35mins, free to Japan Railcard holders) on to Hagi.

(✆ *08382–*)   *Where to Stay and Eating Out*

The best choices in Hagi are *minshuku*—family-run inns. Try **Minshuku Higashi-Hagi**, ✆ 2 7884, or **Minshuku Suzume-no-Oyado**, ✆ 2 0614, or ask the tourist information centre for their recommendation (you shouldn't pay much more than ¥6000–6500 a head, with breakfast and dinner). The **Hagi Grand Hotel**, ✆ 5 9595, is *moderately* priced and right at the centre of town. The **youth hostel**, ✆ 2 0733, is convenient, just south of the ruins of the old castle.

Like most Japanese seaside resorts, Hagi is disappointingly lacking in beachside restaurants, and very quiet at night. Eat at your inn, and take an evening stroll.

Hiroshima

For the post-war generation, Hiroshima has become such a powerful icon, a complicated and embattled symbol of both peace and war, that it is sometimes difficult to think of it as a real place at all. But for 350 of its 400 years, it was an important but unexceptional castle town which entered world history for the most mundane of reasons. Hiroshima was selected as the first city to be destroyed by an atomic weapon because of its weather.

It stands in a flat delta (the name means 'broad islands'), sheltered on three sides by mountains cocooning the port from the storms and high seas which pelt the northern seaboard, at this narrow point just 72km away. The countryside and islands adjoining Hiroshima produce *sake*, persimmons and satsumas; the tranquil lapping of the Inland Sea and the absence of prevailing winds foster a languid, Mediterranean atmosphere.

The B29 bomber, Enola Gay, which left its base in the Mariana Islands on 6 August 1945, had three possible destinations: Nagasaki, Kokura or Hiroshima. The last was chosen late on in the mission when reconnaissance planes confirmed that it had the clear skies necessary for accurate sighting of the new weapon.

The parachute-borne bomb, 'Little Boy' as it was nicknamed by its American creators, exploded 580m above the ground at 30 seconds after 8.15am. It was a Monday morning, and the pavements and streetcars were jammed with commuting soldiers, workers and schoolchildren. Nobody knows how many were killed by the immediate effects of the blast, but by November 1945, more than 140,000 of the 350,000 present in Hiroshima at the time were dead. More than 60,000 have since died from leukaemia, cancer and radiation-related diseases.

Today Hiroshima is a clean and modern prefectural capital, with airy parks and broad, well laid-out streets, old-fashioned trams, delicious seafood, and the famous Hiroshima Carp, the Liverpool FC of Japanese professional baseball. It's sometimes thought that there is only one reason to come to Hiroshima: actually, the city is well worth a relaxing day or two before moving on to the Inland Sea or Kyūshū, especially after the bedlam of Tokyo or Ōsaka. But, realistically and rightly, it is the atomic bomb, its memorials, ruins, and the peace movement which has grown up around it, which will preoccupy the traveller, and which form the bulk of this section.

The Atom Bomb and the Japanese Peace Movement

Enter the Hiroshima Peace Memorial Park on any warm afternoon and, along with the strolling families, immaculate teenage fashion victims and occasional crazy tramps, you will see posses of Junior High School children, identically dressed in Prussian army tunics (for the boys) and sailor suits (for the girls), clutching clipboards on which they record the results of interviews with the many foreigners who visit the park. After routine enquiries about your age, nationality, favourite food and purpose of visit, comes the tricky one: 'What do you think of world peace?'

How do you answer such an earnestly posed question? You might reply that you thought world peace a very good thing, that you were all in favour of it. You might equally ask: 'What world peace?' To many Japanese there is nothing abstract or elusive about the word: like 'beauty', peace is not so much an ideal to be debated and aspired to, as a concrete quality which is either present or absent. Opinion polls show the Japanese to be almost unanimously pacifist and anti-nuclear in their politics. Nonetheless, in the shape of the euphemistically titled Self-Defence Forces, they possess one of the largest standing armies on earth. During the 1980s, there was strong evidence that the non-nuclear policy was being systematically flouted by visiting US warships and with the government's compliant approval. Apart from a few noisy leftwingers, nobody raised an eyebrow.

Outsiders often criticize Japanese complacency in global matters, and the peace memorials in Hiroshima have often been cited as an example of this. In some ways, the simplicity of the ideals expressed here is touching. What makes the annual 6 August Peace Festival such a moving occasion is its innocence, its gaiety despite its grim origins, and the absence of political drum-beating. On the other hand, the ignorance of many Japanese people about the guilt of their own leaders during the war (undoubtedly the result of a highly selective and uniform national curriculum) is almost sinister. Seldom, in the extensive bomb museum, in the surrounding memorials or in the peace festivals, is any mention made of the context of the Hiroshima holocaust: the bloody Pacific War, instigated by the Japanese bombers at Pearl Harbour and pursued with terrifying tenacity and frightful loss of life until 12 August, three days after a second bomb destroyed Nagasaki. The thousands of Allied soldiers imprisoned and tortured in Burma and Thailand, the hundreds of thousands of Chinese, Korean and Singaporean civilians who fell victim to Japanese military adven-turism before 1945 go unrecorded here. Even the non-Japanese victims of the bomb were for years unremembered, although a monument to the Korean dead has recently been unveiled.

Despite these caveats, the Peace Memorial Museum must be seen. Faced with the realities of radioactive warfare, political and historical distinctions shrivel. The arguments over whether the bomb was necessary, and how much longer the imperial army could have held out before their inevitable defeat, are unlikely to be settled. But if, as President Truman claimed, the bomb was a last resort, a show of force intended to demonstrate to the Japanese the futility of resisting, why were the targets chosen two of the most densely populated cities in the country? To devastate the forests of Hokkaidō, to permanently deform the centuries-old silhouette of Mt Fuji—these would have given the necessary warning while keeping casualties to a minimum. The evidence suggests that senior members of the US military wanted to see the effects of their new weapon on a 'soft' target, and that the warning delivered at Hiroshima was not aimed at the ailing Japanese junta, but at a far darker and less tangible enemy: the Soviet Union, renewed by its recent defeat of the German army, and thought to be developing its own version of Little Boy. The incineration of Hiroshima marked not so much the end of the Second World War, as the beginning of the Cold War.

History

Hiroshima's claim to being a city of peace is undermined by a typically bloody feudal past, although, for obvious reasons, few traces of this are visible today. For the first thousand years, the political and mythological excitement was concentrated in Nara and Kyoto, but the region came into its own in the 12th century as the power base of the warrior Taira family and their patriarch, **Taira no Kiyomori** (1118–81), one of the most ruthless and bloodthirsty figures of Japanese history.

Like many inconveniently ambitious members of the military, Kiyomori was farmed out to the west to keep him out of trouble. Instead of acquiescing in the mundane tasks of oyster taxation and clan in-fighting, he proved to be an energetic regional governor, dredging the straits between the islands of the Inland Sea and establishing a profitable trade with China—and financial independence from his Kyoto-based masters. In 1156, the head of the rival Minamoto family attempted to restore a retired emperor in a clan coup. Kiyomori, assisted by Minamoto's oldest son, Yoshitomo, sided with ruling emperor Go-Shirakawa, and successfully defeated the rebels. After some celebratory blood-letting in Kyoto, Kiyomori ordered Yoshitomo to behead his own father. Not surprisingly, their alliance became somewhat strained after this, and four years later Yoshitomo himself died in his own unsuccessful uprising, leaving Kiyomori as the country's undisputed military master.

For the first time, a warrior rather than an aristocrat was effective ruler of Japan. Ignoring the claims of Emperor Go-Shirakawa, in whose name he had taken up arms in the first place, Kiyomori insinuated his family into the imperial family by a series of strategic marriages. By the time he died of a fever at the age of 63, however, none of his possible successors was old enough to muster the necessary military support. Appropriately, it was the sons of Yoshitomo, the former ally Kiyomori had so brutally humiliated, who destroyed the remnants of the Taira clan at the famous sea battle of Dan no Ura near Shimonoseki.

But even if his family had been destroyed in the process, the effect on Japanese history of Kiyomori's brief rule was profound. Imperial rule, by aristocratic courtiers in the name of

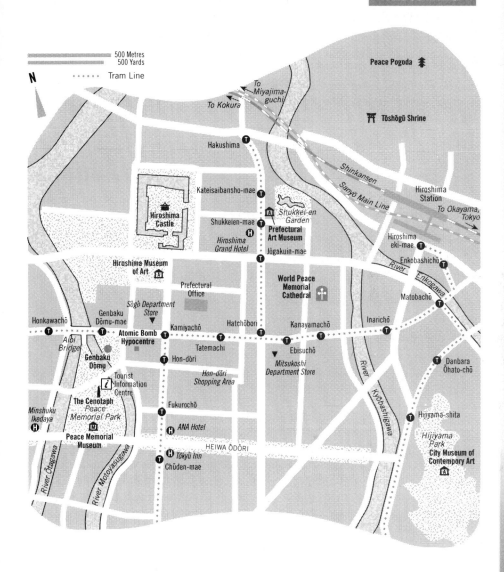

an emperor, was over. With brief interruptions, the warrior class controlled Japan until the restoration of the Emperor Meiji in 1868. As a patron of the arts, Kiyomori commissioned Sanjūsangendō in Kyoto, and, most lavishly of all, his own personal favourite: the sea shrine of Itsukushima on Miyajima island, a boat ride from Hiroshima and even today one of Japan's most famous treasures. Even after Kiyomori's power base moved towards the Kyoto heartland, the Hiroshima area remained his spiritual home, and many of the works of art displayed on Miyajima (Bugaku dance masks, Lotus Sutra scrolls) were commissioned, possibly even crafted, by the general himself, in an attempt to prove that aesthetic excellence was not a prerogative of the pampered aristocrats in the capital.

The shrine and surrounding region prospered quietly until 1589, when a business-minded *daimyō* named Mori Terumoto founded Hiroshima-jō (Castle of the Broad Island). Over the next 300 years, the city consolidated its position as the mercantile hub of the Chūgoku region. The Imperial Army was based here during the victorious Sino-Japanese War of 1894–5, and the Emperor Meiji spent two years in the castle, overseeing the campaign. Until 1945, Hiroshima housed a large garrison and served as a mustering station for conscripts from all over the region. Since the war, the city has been sensibly and conveniently reconstructed. With a population of 1,066,000, it is Japan's tenth largest city.

Getting There

Hiroshima is connected to Hakata in Kyūshū and to eastern Japan by the Tōkaidō **shinkansen**. Kyoto is 2hrs away, Ōsaka 1hr 40mins. From Tokyo to Hiroshima costs ¥17,700 by *shinkansen* and takes 5hrs. By **plane** it costs about ¥4000 more and takes 1½hrs, plus a 40min transfer from the airport into town. The **night bus** from Tokyo station takes 12hrs and costs ¥11,840.

A network of **ferry** services sails to and from Ujina, Hiroshima's port. The Beppu–Hiroshima crossing through the mists and islands of the Inland Sea is one of the nicest and most convenient: 9½hrs and ¥4000 for a second-class berth. Both ferries (2hrs 45mins) and hydrofoils (1hr 10mins) connect to Matsuyama on Shikoku.

For pleasure cruises to the smaller islands, *see* 'The Inland Sea' below.

Getting Around

Hiroshima's buses take a bit of getting used to, and the best way of getting round the city is by tram. The key stops are Kamiya-chō, opposite the Sōgō department store at the centre of the downtown area, and Genbaku-dōmu-mae (opposite the Atomic Dome), the disembarkation point for the relics and monuments associated with the bomb. Both are on Aioi-dōri, the road leading from just south of the station all the way to the Peace Park. Ujina, to the south of the city, is the port for boats to Kyūshū and Shikoku. From Miyajima-guchi, to the west, ferries shuttle to and from Miyajima island.

Four tram lines begin from the busy transport plaza in front of the station at the east end of town. Tram line no.1 goes to Kamiya-chō, before turning south and terminating at Ujina. Nos.2 and 6 both go through Kamiya-chō and Genbaku-dōmū-mae and then head off into the suburbs. No.5 heads directly south for Ujina.

Get on at the back of the tram and pay the driver as you disembark. If you're transferring onto another line, tell him where you're going and purchase a transfer ticket—you make up the difference at your final destination. Day tickets are available from the tram office in front of Hiroshima station.

There's an information desk in Hiroshima station, but more geared up for foreigners is the **Rest House** in the Peace Park, which has leaflets and magazines in English and bilingual volunteer staff. It's over the water from the Atomic Dome, across Motoyasu Bridge and near the Children's Peace Monument. The **International Exchange Lounge**, next to the Bomb Museum, is a gathering place for the foreign community, with newspapers and satellite TV.

Festivals

1 Jan	**Ancient court dances** and music mark the start of the new year at Itsukushima Shrine, Miyajima.
15 Apr	**Hiwatari**. Fire festival on Mt Misen, Miyajima. Priests and onlookers walk barefoot over glowing embers.
16–18 Apr	**Nō drama** performed on Itsukushima Shrine's open-air stage.
mid-June	(17th day of the lunar calendar) **Kangensai**. A beautiful festival when priests from Itsukushima Shrine parade the deity around the bay in torch-lit sacred boats. Afterwards, the crowd carries torches between the shrines on Miyajima.
6 Aug	Ceremonies marking the **anniversary of the atomic bombing** in Hiroshima Peace Memorial Park. Doves are released from the Cenotaph, and lanterns set afloat on the river in the evening.
15 Nov	**Hiwatari**. *See* 15 April.
15 Dec	**Ceremonial purification by fire** to mark the end of the year at Itsukushima Shrine, Miyajima.

The Atomic Dome

Tram no.2, 3 or 6 to Genbaku-dōmu-mae.

Hiroshima's Industrial Promotion Hall, built by a Czech architect in 1914, had no great distinction during its lifetime, but it stands almost exactly at the hypocentre of the blast and was one of the few structures within 2km to remain standing. Since 1945, the crumbling concrete cladding and distorted metal frame have been scrupulously preserved as an eerie memento of the physical effects of the blast: Genbaku Dōmu, the Atomic Dome. In the natural course of things, it would have disintegrated long ago. Restoration and reinforcement cost 200 million yen in 1989, but carefully cultivated decay has long played an important part in Japanese aesthetics, and the required sum was raised almost twice over. Grimly blasted though it is, the fact that the Dome is standing at all is a reminder that the one megaton Little Boy was a quaintly antiquated squib compared to the 2000 megaton monsters lurking in underground silos today.

You can walk around the Dome, but not inside. The most dramatic time to see it is at dawn and dusk, when the sun transforms the charred and mottled building into a pristine silhouette.The concrete pagoda just south of the Dome is the **Memorial Tower to the**

Mobilized Students. Reliefs behind it depict civilian war work—weaving and manufacturing—which conscripts were forced to carry out. Three million students, aged as young as 12, were used for compulsory labour during the course of the war. Six thousand died in Hiroshima, many of them caught in the open where they were constructing fire breaks to protect the city against conventional bombing.

Memorial Peace Park

Opposite the Dome is the **Heiwa Kinen Kōen** (Memorial Peace Park) on a long island formed by deltaic branches of the Ota River. Enter it at its north tip, across the T-shaped **Aioi Bridge**. The bomber on board Enola Gay used its distinctive shape to aim Little Boy, which actually fell a few hundred metres to the east over a clinic behind the Dome.

The first peace memorial ceremony was held here on 6 August 1947, when the area was still little more than a heap of ashes. Nowadays, the well-tended park is a place of pilgrimage, attracting 70,000 foreigners alone every year, and containing many touching memorials to the victims and their suffering.

In the centre of the park is a huge saddle-shaped vault, the **Memorial Cenotaph for A-Bomb Victims**, built by the architect Kenzō Tange in imitation of a mysterious clay object found in prehistoric tombs and intimately associated with mortality and remembrance. Beneath it sits a casket containing the names of all those known to have died directly or indirectly as a result of the bomb. New names are added every year; by 1992, the 59-volume register contained 176,964 names. Many thousands more, including large numbers of foreign forced labourers and prisoners of war, died unknown and unremembered. 'Rest in peace', an inscription on the front reads, with desperate confidence, 'for

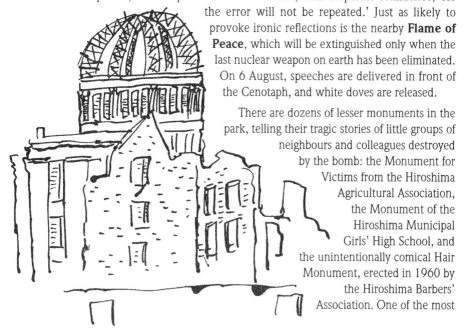

the error will not be repeated.' Just as likely to provoke ironic reflections is the nearby **Flame of Peace**, which will be extinguished only when the last nuclear weapon on earth has been eliminated. On 6 August, speeches are delivered in front of the Cenotaph, and white doves are released.

There are dozens of lesser monuments in the park, telling their tragic stories of little groups of neighbours and colleagues destroyed by the bomb: the Monument for Victims from the Hiroshima Agricultural Association, the Monument of the Hiroshima Municipal Girls' High School, and the unintentionally comical Hair Monument, erected in 1960 by the Hiroshima Barbers' Association. One of the most striking statues is that of a girl with her hands outstretched, holding a golden crane. The **Children's Peace Monument** is draped in rainbows of origami cranes folded in coloured paper by school children. The famous true story concerns a girl named Sasaki Sadako who had been in Hiroshima as an infant at the time of the bombing. In 1955 she suddenly became sick with leukaemia, ten years after the event. The crane is a symbol of health and longevity, and Sadako believed that if she could fold 1000 of them, she would recover. She was working on the second thousand when she died, at the age of 12.

Over the Honkawa Bridge, on the west side of the park, is the **Monument in Memory of the Korean Victims of the Bomb**. There were 20,000 of these (10 per cent of those who died) including a Korean prince, Lee-Woo; many were labourers forcibly conscripted from Japan's then colony. The memorial, a monolith mounted on the back of a turtle, was built in Korea and stands, significantly perhaps, outside the Peace Park proper. An inscription reads: 'The Korean victims were given no funerals or memorial services and their spirits hovered for years unable to pass into heaven.'

The **Peace Memorial Museum** (*open May–Nov, 9–5.30; Dec–April, 9–4.30; adm ¥50*) is the long concrete gallery, raised on stilts, at the south end of the park. If you are in Hiroshima for only an hour, this is where you should spend it: the collection of photographs, models, diagrams and fragments that fill it are a relentless record of the short-, medium- and long-term effects of the bomb. It's a harrowing experience, but there is a bleak comfort to be had in emerging from the grim chronicle of destruction into the modern city of Hiroshima, unscarred and good as new, 50 years later. Millions of visitors, including countless schoolchildren and foreigners, pass through every year.

Pitilessly factual though the exhibition is, it hasn't escaped controversy. It describes the Manhattan Project, the genesis of the bomb and the sequence of events which led to its detonation. But little reference is made to the wider context of the Pacific War, and Japan's bloody 15-year history of aggression in Asia. It would be possible, coming to the museum with no historical knowledge, to leave it with a very one-dimensional picture of the bomb as an impersonal agent of destruction, tossed out of the sky one day almost at random. This state of affairs has been the object of much criticism: as Hiroshima prepares for the 50th anniversary of the bombing in 1995, it may be rectified. *The Economist* recently reported that the exhibit was going to be revised. We'll see.

The exhibits are well labelled in English, but be sure to pick up one of the portable earphone guides, available in 15 languages. At the centre of the gallery is a large 1:1000 scale model of the city immediately after the blast; along with the many aerial photos, this leaves an extraordinary impression: block after block levelled to within a few metres of the ground, the moats and flattened keep of the 16th-century castle, beneath a red billiard ball suspended above the model at the point where the bomb exploded. Standing bleakly alone, almost directly below it, is the warped dome of the Industrial Promotion Hall. It's easy to understand the resonance this building still has for the people of Hiroshima, as a symbol of survival as well as destruction.

The most unforgettable section of the museum documents the fate of the victims and the varieties of horrible death that fell upon them. Surprisingly few were lucky enough to die immediately, like the nameless individual whose famous silhouette is thermally etched onto the stone steps of a bank building. Many more were trapped under fallen buildings to perish hours later from burns, broken limbs, asphyxiation, fire, thirst and blast-induced haemorrhaging. Those caught in the open were blinded by the flash and deafened by the shock wave. Many escaped apparently healthy and unscathed, carrying with them latent injuries caused by huge doses of radiation. Days or months or years later, they lost their hair, their skin, their gums and their sense of balance; cuts healed slowly into thick, ugly keloid scars, and cataracts clouded their eyes. Later came tumours and leukaemia. Unborn children whose mothers were exposed to the bomb were born with small deformed heads and brain damage. Thousands of country people who didn't even see the explosion were fatally contaminated by the 'black rain' of radioactive ash as they congregated in Hiroshima in search of friends and relatives.

There is nothing sensationalist about the museum: the exhibits speak for themselves. Many of them are personal mementoes, kept by families in memory of those they lost in the blast: the fingernails of a dead schoolboy; the buckled tricycle being ridden by a three-year-old. A series of velvet cushions bear tiny shards of glass and a card with a name and a date. These bullet-like fragments lodged inside the bodies of survivors to emerge intact, decades after the event.

There is a good book shop selling literature relating to the bomb on the lower floor of the Peace Memorial Museum.

Other Sights

Hiroshima is a modern city, as you would expect. Nonetheless, the Japanese passion for reconstruction has restored a few traces of the pre-war town.

Hiroshima-jō (*open 9–5; adm ¥200*) is a concrete reconstruction, only worth visiting if you won't have the chance to see an original castle. It stands in an attractive park and houses a local history museum. The **Shukkei-en garden** (*open April–Sept, 9–6; Oct–Mar, 9–5; adm ¥200*) is a beautiful pond garden, originally built by a 17th-century *daimyō*. Photos of snapped trees and scarred ground show what a transformation has been achieved, but the gentle atmosphere is infuriatingly shattered by piped music from hidden speakers.

(✆ 082–) *Where to Stay*

The **ANA Hotel Hiroshima**, ✆ 241 1111 (*expensive*) and the **Tōkyū Inn**, ✆ 244 0109, are close to one another near Heiwa Ōhashi (Peace Bridge) southeast of the Peace Park.

The **Hiroshima Station Hotel**, ✆ 262 3201, in the station terminal, is at the low end of *expensive*; posher is the **Hiroshima Terminal Hotel**, ✆ 262 1111.

Minshuku Ikedaya, ✆ 231 3329, is an *inexpensive* member of the Welcome Inn Group, a stroll from the Peace Park and handy for trams in all directions. **Hotel Kawashima**, ✆ 263 3535, is a simple business hotel a minute from the JR station.

Hiroshima is famous for seafood and *okonomiyaki*—a cheap and cheerful cross between a pizza and a pancake, made of eggs, vegetables and meat or fish, and cooked on a hot griddle DIY style. The **ANA Hotel**, east of the southeast corner of the Peace Park, has an elegant restaurant; otherwise, take your pick in the covered arcades south of the Kamiyachō tram stop.

Miyajima

Of Japan's officially designated Three Most Beautiful Scenic Places, Miyajima is the only one that lives up to the billing these days. The vermilion *torii* gate rising out of the sea in front of the 'floating' corridors and platforms of Itsukushima Jinja, the family shrine of Kiyomori and the Taira clan, is one of the most photographed images in Japan. But even at weekends when the town is thronging with tourists, there's an unquenchable sense of mystery about the place: the tame deer, messengers of the deity, who wander freely up and down the beach; the walks up the mountain, through monkey-infested forest; the view from the summit of the dozy bays and islets of the Inland Sea.

Getting There

From Hiroshima station, JR **trains** reach Miyajima-guchi in 26mins. The JR **ferry** to the island operates from about 6am to 10pm from the pier just over the road from Miyajima-guchi station, and the crossing takes about 10mins. Both are free to holders of the Japan Rail Pass. A slightly cheaper private line, the Hiroden, takes an hour to Miyajima-guchi. An English timetable for ferries and trains is available from the Rest House in the Peace Park.

Walking is the best way to get around, although taxis are available; infrequent buses from the town to Suginoura, a popular beach on the north side of the island.

Tourist Information

There's an **information desk** with English language pamphlets in the ferry terminal building—they can tell you about the free tea ceremonies performed for visitors in one of the nearby temples by a shaven-headed old nun. Remember that the shrine and town are on, roughly, the north side of the island. Most of the tourist maps are oriented upside down to give you a picture of the island as you face it from the mainland. Thus the area west of the shrine is on the right-hand side as you face it through the red *torii* gateway.

Itsukushima Jinja (Shrine)

Open 7–5; adm ¥200.

Miyajima (Shrine Island) is properly called Itsukushima, and a sea deity of the same name has been worshipped here since 593. It was Taira no Kiyomori, however, who built the shrine in its present form, in 1168. It's an exhilarating and dream-like work of architecture, at its best at high tide, when the vermilion painted halls and walkways, built into the sand on wooden piles, appear to float, reflected on the surface of the sea. Walking around the roofed, unwalled corridors as the water laps beneath you is a unique sensation, like being inside and outside at the same time. When the tide is out, the deer root around the crabs, flotsam and seaweed that gather on the stone foundations. As it comes in you can watch the sea eddying around the feet of the stone lanterns. The shrine's Canute-like position, on the threshold of land and sea, has its risks: in 1991 it was devastated by a typhoon, and for a couple of years the famous gateway was cloaked in scaffolding.

The **Ō-torii**, at the mouth of the small bay, 16m tall with a cross bar 24m wide, is noticeably more elaborate than most shrine gates. The style indicates the syncretic nature of rites performed here which, until the Meiji Restoration of 1868, were as much concerned with the worship of Buddhist deities as Shinto *kami*. At one time, boats approaching Miyajima would have passed through the *ō-torii*, as they still do during the shrine's spectacular festivals. Its position, at the mouth of the bay and one time harbour, emphasizes that the whole island is considered a shrine, not just the collection of buildings at the water's edge. The present *ō-torii* is the seventh replacement since 1168; it was built in 1875.

You enter the shrine at the northeast corner, the left-hand side as you face it through the *ō-torii*. The **shrine** itself is a blend of styles and influences unlike anything else in Japanese architecture. The halls, linked by corridors, and symmetrically arranged in front of a body of water, suggest the *shinden* villas built by Heian-period aristocrats in the 11th and 12th centuries, which were themselves imitations of Chinese Tang palaces. Shrine and temple elements are cheerfully combined: the *ō-torii* is predominantly Shinto, but the exit to the complex, on the southwest side of the bay, is Buddhist.

The *nō* **stage** is one of the most famous structures. It follows the classical canons in all respects but one: instead of being surrounded by white pebbles it projects directly into the sea. Members of the audience stand along the adjoining shore or, if they are especially honoured, watch the plays from boats moored in front.

West of the Shrine

You exit the shrine onto **Nishi-matsubara**, a spit of sand planted with pines, divided from the island by a narrow gulley. In warm weather this is a good spot for bathing. A strong swimmer could swim out to the *ō-torii* (but don't try to clamber onto it) or even walk at low tide. The water here seems less soupy than at the popular Suginoura beach. At the end of the strand is a small **shrine** to Kiyomori no Taira, the island's patron and protector.

Cross the bridges onto the island proper instead of walking along the strand, and you find yourself in a little square opposite **Daigan-ji**, a temple dedicated to Benten, a Buddhist goddess of water, music and islands, who became associated with the female sea deities of the main shrine. To the left of this, in a red and white modern building, is the **Hōmotsu-kan** (Treasure House, *open 8–5; adm ¥300*) containing a superb collection of illuminated scrolls, costumes, armour, swords and Nō masks, commissioned, created or owned by the Taira family. The originals are so precious that many of the objects displayed are replicas, brilliant ones nonetheless. The *Keike Nōkyō* are a set of sutra scrolls, written and illuminated by hand in opulent coloured inks and gold leaf; even the bronze cases in which they were rolled are works of art. There's also a wonderful painted panel of a crazy *yamauba* or 'mountain hag', with cracked teeth and long curling toe nails. Until recently an old female hermit like her lived on the island.

There's a 16th-century **Tahō-tō**, a two-storey pagoda, behind the Treasure Hall. **Ōmoto Park** has a shrine and pleasant strolls. The **Miyajima History and Folklore Museum** (*open 8.30–5; adm ¥200*) contains an interesting jumble of tools and objects in the converted house of a soy sauce merchant. Look for the boats used in the annual Kangen-sai festival, including the *Goza-fune*, a floating platform which supports the festival musicians.

East of the Shrine

Between the ferry terminal and the entrance to Itsukushima Jinja are several temples and halls of moderate interest. The **Senjōkaku** (Hall of a Thousand Mats) is a giant wooden hall built in 1587 by the warlord Toyotomi Hideyoshi, and the main building of the Hokoku .Shrine. He died before it was finished and the entrance and inside ceiling still show signs of incompleteness. The **five-storey pagoda** nearby dates from 1407.

Mt Misen

A path leads up Mt Misen from behind the shrine through **Momiji-dani** (Maple Valley), especially beautiful during the November autumn colour season. From here you could keep walking (the climb to the top takes a couple of hours), or take the two-stage **ropeway** (cable car) to within 25 minutes of the summit. Don't forget to check the time of the last ropeway down.

There's a **monkey park** here (don't get too close to the apes, they have a nasty bite), and the scattered buildings of a Shingon sect temple. Follow the signs to Mt Misen to reach the first of these, a smoke-blackened hall containing an **eternal flame** kindled, it is said, by the 9th-century saint Kōbō Daishi, and kept alive ever since. Fire is something of a preoccupation at this temple: on 15 November and 15 April, priests and onlookers perform a miraculous walk over the glowing embers of wooden tablets (persons of faith, and those who walk quickly enough, don't get burned). Many of the images—on rocky ledges along the path, as well as in the halls—represent Fudō Myō-ō, the benevolent demon who is always pictured in a corona of flickering flames.

More and more of these images crowd the rocky path as you climb higher. The summit, atmospherically rocky, contains an observation tower with sweeping 360-degree views of western Honshū and the Inland Sea.

| (© 0829–) | *Where to Stay and Eating Out* |

Miyajima can easily be treated as a day trip from Hiroshima, but try to stay overnight to see the island in the early morning before the tourists arrive. At festival times, high season and weekends, inns fill up weeks in advance: small groups might be lucky on the day, but book ahead if possible.

The **Grand Hotel**, © 44 2411, and the **Royal**, © 44 2670, are *expensive* resort hotels with both Western-style and *tatami* rooms. **Iwasō**, © 44 2233, is the island's finest *ryokan*, *expensive*, but with great seafood, right in the centre of Maple Valley. There are two dozen moderate *minshuku*, but prices are inflated, and there's no youth hostel. Cheapest is the **Miyajima Lodge**, Ⓒ 44 0430, with simple individual rooms at a *moderate* to *inexpensive* price.

Miyajima is a culinary disappointment. The best food is in the inns, though plenty of places serve overpriced fishy snacks along the waterfront near the ferry terminal.

The Inland Sea (Seto Naikai)

> *The islands of the Inland Sea are among the last places on earth where men rise with the sun and where streets are dark and silent by nine at night. Here is the last of old Japan, this valley-like sea where the waters turn green or blue with the season, where the islands stand black against the horizon or lie like folded fur under the noonday sun, where the blue and silver of towns and villages merge with the rich yellows, browns and greens of the patchwork land.*

Donald Richie, *The Inland Sea*, 1971

Seto Naikai, the 'sea within straits', is often described as the Aegean of Japan, but, apart from countless islands and an ancient history, the two have little in common. Japan's Aegean is smaller, for a start—500km long, from Awaji Island in the east to Shimonoseki in the west, but only 64km wide at its widest point, 6km at the narrowest. And the atmosphere is thoroughly un-Greek. Where the Aegean islands are flinty and sharply-defined, those of the Inland Sea are rounded and feminine, veiled by frequent sheets of transparent mist. The distances separating them are small and the cradling mainland islands, Honshū, Shikoku and Kyūshū, are close at hand to the north, south and west. Since Donald Richie travelled there a quarter of a century ago, plenty has happened to impinge on the idyll he described. Quiet rickety towns have been transformed by shopping malls and power stations, or have dwindled as young people left the islands for the mainland cities. Cranky old ferries have been replaced by impersonal car transporters and fleet hydrofoils, and a huge brilliant bridge now links Honshū and Shikoku. The 'real Japan' lurks undisturbed in the smaller bays and islands, but it is increasingly elusive, and time-consuming to get around. With so much else to visit, only a very unhurried or specialized traveller would devote more than a day or two to the Inland Sea. But many people will pass through it; and a sight-seeing cruise puts the better known islands within a day trip of Hiroshima.

Getting Around

Passenger **boats**, **ferries** and **hydrofoils**, run by numerous different companies, criss-cross the Inland Sea joining all the principal cities and inhabited islands. Enquire at a local tourist information office for up-to-date details.

Exploring the Inland Sea

Awajishima is the biggest of the Seto Naikai islands, and lies between Tokushima on Shikoku and Kōbe on Honshū, forming its eastern boundary. The Kōbe earthquake of January 1995 had its epicentre under Awajishima. Thanks to the sparseness of its population, loss of life was less than on the mainland, but many roads and buildings were destroyed or seriously damaged, and reconstruction is likely to take many months.

Even before the catastrophe, there was little to tempt foreign tourists on Awajishima. There are some good beaches, and, at **Senkō-ji**, a big modern temple to Kannon with a 90m statue. The island is most famous as the birthplace of the *bunraku* puppet theatre. The **Awaji Ningyō-za** in Fukura, in the south of the island, puts on several daily performances. From Fukura you can also see the **whirlpools** of the Naruto Straits; at high tide, water rushes in at 20km an hour. A bridge now crosses the straits; a second one, to link the northern tip of the island with Kōbe, had to be redesigned after the earthquake which drove Awaji and Honshū more than a metre further apart.

Apart from the road connection from Shikoku, Sumoto, on the east coast of Awaji, can be reached by high-speed boat from Ōsaka and Kōbe. Akashi, west of Kōbe, has ferry and boat services from the narrowest point to Iwaya.

Shōdoshima, between Takamatsu and Okayama, is a much smaller island, disproportionately rich in tradition. A miniaturized, 160km version of the Shikoku pilgrimage of the 88 temples was set up here in the 17th century, for pilgrims incapable of making the full 1,600km circuit. Twice a year, on 3 May and 3 October, an old style of village *kabuki*, originally done all over the island, is performed on outdoor stages. Apart from monkey and peacock parks, and a spurious fake Greek temple, the other main attractions are pretty **beaches**, and a ravine of **dramatic rock formations** at Kanka-kei. Tonoshō is the port; ferries and hydrofoils sail there regularly from Okayama and Takamatsu. From Himeji a ferry sails to the village of Fukuda, on the north coast.

The Seto Naikai National Park

The most popular area of the Inland Sea, between Shōdoshima and Miyajima, is a National Park, although this hasn't prevented unsightly heavy industry developing along the Honshū coast around Hiroshima. A dense web of local ferries serves the islands but, for travellers with limited time, the easiest way to get a taster of the Inland Sea is on the **guided cruises** run by SKK (Setonaikai Kisen).

These run from 1 Mar–30 Nov every year. The high-speed cruiser picks up passengers at Miyajima, Hiroshima port and Kure, and goes as far as Onomichi, stopping at Ōmishima and Ikuchishima islands where time is allowed for sightseeing. A one-way ticket costs about ¥6000. The one-day round cruise, departing Hiroshima at 9am and returning at 5.30pm, costs about ¥12,000. Both include lunch at an island restaurant and biscuits, booze and soft drinks. SKK also operates lunch and dinner cruises in Hiroshima Bay. The dining boat departs from Hiroshima port and sails around Miyajima; at night you can see the Itsukushima Shrine illuminated. Depending on the grade of menu, the lunch cruise costs ¥6000–8000, the dinner cruise ¥10,000–20,000. Reservations essential. Call SKK on ✆ 082 255 3344 and ask for Tom La Tourette.

The Cruise from Hiroshima to Onomichi

Etajima, the first big island, contains a big naval academy, a red brick building visible at the foot of the mountain. Formerly this was the principal training college of the Imperial

Navy, euphemized since the war as the Maritime Self Defence Forces. The narrow **Ondo Strait**, just after the port town of **Kure**, was cut out of the rock in the 12th century on the orders of the Taira clan chieftain, Kiyomori. Beneath the bridge on the right-hand side, a stand of pines marks an ancient mound commemorating Kiyomori. The **Cat Straits**, between the mainland and the next small islands, are visibly churned by powerful, conflicting currents: at times the turbulence looks almost like a set of undersea rapids.

Your boat next sails in and out of the **Geiyo archipelago**, a tight queue of islands seldom separated by more than a few hundred metres of shallow sea; already a sequence of bridges has begun which will eventually link Shikoku and Honshū. Between the 12th and 16th centuries, the Geiyo Islands were ruled by a clan of pirate-princes who taxed and tolled the islanders and the ships which passed between them before being unmercifully routed by Hideyoshi Toyotomi. **Ōmishima**, where the boat stops for 2hrs of lunch and sightseeing, was the base for these corsairs. The **Ōyamazumi Jinja** a few hundred metres from the quayside was their tutelary shrine, dedicated to the god of mountains, and revered by warriors who left votive offerings of arms. As a result, the shrine **Kokuhōkan** (Treasure Hall) contains the finest selection of weapons and armour in the country, including big name objects owned by characters like Yoritomo and Yoshitsune, rival brothers of the Minamoto clan, and a mighty 1.8m-long sword. At the end of one display case is a rather distinctive suit of armour: small, unmistakably curvy, it was said to have been owned by Ōhori Yasumochi, the warrior daughter of a corsair chieftain. The smaller **Shinyoden Museum** next door contains an exhibition of objects associated with maritime science, including a research boat used by the 'peace-loving' Emperor Hirohito, posthumously known as Shōwa. The glass cases include pickled sharks, helmet crabs, deep sea manganese nodules, and two of the emperor biologist's publications: *Some Hydroids of the Amakusa islands*, and its sequel, *Some Hydroans of the Bōnin Islands*.

On leaving Ōmishima, the boat passes on its port side a small island called **Ōkunojima**, which the guide may not tell you about. Incredibly, given how close it is to the mainland, this was for many years a chemical weapon production site. After decades of isolation the decontaminated beaches have been converted into a holiday resort—not one you'll feel a great urge to visit. **Setoda**, on the island of **Ikuchijima**, is the next stop and the home of an extraordinary temple complex built by a local lad, Kanemoto Kōzō. Despite making millions in the steel tubing business, Kōzō never forgot his roots, and in 1927 constructed a *shoin* style villa for his mother. When the old lady died, he started work on the **Kōsan-ji temple** dedicated to Mrs Kanemoto, who is worshipped as an incarnation of Kannon, Goddess of Mercy. The buildings, moreover, are facsimiles of famous temples of the Japanese mainland. Mother's ashes are interred in a five-storey pagoda alongside copies of Hōryū-ji temple's Dream Hall (Nara), Byōdō-in's Amida Hall (Kyoto), and Nikkō's Tōshō-gū. The absurdity and arrogance of the enterprise rather detracts from the fine quality of the copies. It's instructive, also, to look on these great buildings in their original gaudy colours, as they would have been before the patina of time softened and faded them.

The one-way cruises go on to the uninteresting town of **Onomichi**, where they terminate. The day cruise returns after a couple of hours to Kure, Hiroshima and Miyajima.

Kyūshū

For much of its history Japan was cut off from the rest of the world by isolationist policies, but foreign influence crept in nonetheless, and it was through Kyūshū more than anywhere else that the great personalities and movements of world history filtered into the country. St Francis Xavier, Mongol invaders, Western medicine, the matchlock pistol—all made their Japanese debuts here, often via the port of Nagasaki, a fascinating city which saw some of the fiercest Christian persecutions, and then in 1945 became the second victim of the nuclear age. Kyūshū is a centre of myth and legend, the place where the legendary forebears of the Japanese people are said to have touched down after their descent from heaven. Active volcanoes, bubbling hot springs, remote mountains and a balmy subtropical climate reinforce a sense that Kyūshū is different from the rest of Japan: older, warmer and more authentic.

Northern Kyūshū

Kokura, part of the sprawling metropolitan mess called **Kita Kyūshū**, is the gateway to Japan's southern island, but there's no reason for tourists to disembark there. The *shinkansen* terminates at **Fukuoka** (confusingly, the station is called **Hakata**, but it's the same city), where onward connections can be made to other parts of the island.

Gotō Islands

Fukuoka has a lively atmosphere, and a few attractions of its own. **Nakasu** is the city's famous riverside nightlife district, with an agreeably seedy ambience, and a famous street of *yatai*, tiny covered restaurant carts serving delicious *al fresco* seafood. The beaches north and west of the city were the scene of dramatic events during the 13th century, when a massive naval force of Kubla Khan's Mongol warriors threatened to invade Japan. They were finally seen off by a series of fortuitous typhoons, the original *kamikaze* or 'divine winds'. A few unimpressive remains of the anti-Mongol wall can still be seen along the coast, and in Fukuoka itself there's a **Mongol Invasion Memorial Hall**. The rapacity of the child-murdering, wife-ravishing Asian horde is made much of; there are displays of Mongol armour and weapons, and paintings of the bloody battles. Nearby is a huge statue of the Buddhist saint, **Nichiren**, who claimed to have secured their defeat by his prayers. Fukuoka also contains Japan's first Zen temple, **Shōfuku-ji**, founded in 1195, and rather run to seed now, hemmed in as it is by the encroaching city.

Dazaifu (40 minutes south of Nishitetsu Fukuoka station by the private Nishitetsu line) was an ancient regional capital which achieved its present fame in the 9th century as the exile of Sugawara no Michizane, a brilliant scholar, artist and calligrapher. Jealous enemies in Kyoto poisoned his reputation with the emperor, and he was dispatched here in disgrace to die of homesickness a few years later. A series of unexplained illnesses and disasters began to afflict the imperial court, and it was concluded that they were caused by Sugawara's unhappy spirit. He was posthumously pardoned, and eventually deified as

Kyūshū

50 km
30 miles

Land over 500 metres

N

Honshū

Kitakyūshū

Kokura

Iki
Island

FUKUOKA
(HAKATA)

Nakatsu

FUKUOKA

Daizaifu

Karatsu

Yufu-
dake

Hirado
Hirado-guchi

SAGA

Yufuin
Beppu

Hirado
Island

Imari

Arita

Kurume

ASO
NATIONAL
PARK

OITA

Sasebo

SAGA

Yanagawa

Kujū-san

Usuki

Kūjūkūshima
Islands

Ōmura
Bay

Ōmuta

OITA

Saiki

NAGASAKI

Ōmura

Isahaya

Ariake
Sea

Aso

NAGASAKI

Shimabara

Aso-san

Takachiho
Gorge

East
China
Sea

Unzen-dake
Unzen

KUMAMOTO

Takachiho

Nobeoka

UNZEN-AMAKUSA
NATIONAL PARK

Yatsushiro

MIYAZAKI

Amakusa
Islands

KUMAMOTO

Pacific
Ocean

Minamata

Ebino Plateau

Kobayashi

Kirishima-dake

Takachiho-mine

MIYAZAKI

Kirishima
Onsen

Aoshima

Sendai

KAGOSHIMA

Miyakonojō

Mt Sakurajima
SAIKAI
NATIONAL
PARK

KAGOSHIMA

Chiran

Kagoshima
Bay

Kushima

Makurazaki

Ibusuki

Kanoya

Lake
Ikeda

Cape Sata

Tenjin, Shinto god of scholarship and learning. Dazaifu's **Tenman-gū** shrine is one of thousands scattered across the country, popular above all with Japanese students and schoolchildren in the run up to their many taxing entrance examinations. The earliest buildings here date from the 16th century, but the huge plum tree on the right of the shrine is believed to be as old as the god himself. Sugawara loved the plum above all; when he was exiled to Kyūshū, this one magically uprooted itself from his garden and *flew* from Kyoto to Dazaifu to be with its master.

Western Kyūshū

The Pottery Towns

The prefectures of Saga and Nagasaki sprawl out into the East China Sea, along curling peninsulas and off-shore islands.

Because of its proximity to the continent (the Korean port of Pusan is just 200km away), this area has always been a repository for the crafts and skills of continental immigrants. In the 1590s the megalomaniac warlord Hideyoshi Toyotomi launched two inconclusive invasions of Korea from here. Among the slaves he brought back with him were Korean potters, one of whom, Ri Sanpei, discover the kaolin clay necessary for porcelain manufacture in 1615. Manufactured in the town of **Arita**, and exported via the nearby port of **Imari**, 'Imari porcelain', with its pale white undercolour and blue patterns, became extremely popular in Europe. Apart from pottery there's nothing in either of the towns to draw visitors today, but if ceramics are your interest then you shouldn't fail to stop in Arita, preferably during the **Arita Pottery Fair** between 29 April and 5 May when collectors and craftsmen from all over Japan gather to buy and exhibit. The information centre can provide maps and introductions to the many kilns still operating in the area. Of several museums, the **Kyūshū Ceramic Museum** is the most general and educational.

Karatsu, east of Imari, is another pottery town with more than just pottery to enjoy. Perched upon a pretty bluff, it has a pine-studded beach, a reconstructed cliff-top castle, and the **Karatsu Kunchi** (2–4 November), a famous festival of traditional floats which are displayed for the rest of the year in their own exhibition hall.

Nagasaki

Even if it had never been atom bombed in August 1945, Nagasaki would be famous among Japanese cities. For more than 400 years the beautiful natural harbour, nestled on the seaward flank of a convoluted, mountainous peninsula, has fostered one of the country's brightest and most cosmopolitan ports. Much of Nagasaki's charm lies in its relative isolation: even with the *shinkansen*, it's eight and a half hours by train from Tokyo, and in the 16th century, when captive Christians were transported to Nagasaki for martyrdom, the painful journey—across the foggy Ariake Inland Sea and the steep volcano of Unzen—was part of the torture. Even today, Nagasaki prefecture is a remote corner of Japan, 45 per cent of it detached and inaccessible islands where mainland Japanese are outsiders, and where descendants of the persecuted *kakure* (hidden) Christians still practise the distorted rites passed down from their ancestors. Aside from the relics and memorials associated with the bomb, Nagasaki has no single great tourist attraction and it's probably more interesting as a place to live than to visit. But it has an unusual, distinctive atmosphere. For many people, it's their favourite Japanese city.

History

Nagasaki, people will tell you, is the only place in the country where Japanese visitors will stop and ask a foreigner for directions. Uniquely among Japanese cities, it was built by and for foreigners to whom it was a home, not just a stop-over. There was nothing but a small fishing village here until 1568, when Ōmura Sumitada, the local *daimyō* and a Christian convert, invited Portuguese Jesuits to set up a mission. Within a few years the deep harbour, sheltered by small islands and flanking mountains, was attracting merchants from Macao trading Chinese silk, gold, porcelain, musk and muskets for Japanese silver. The duties on this trade were so important to Ōmura that he ceded control of the

Nagasaki

Map labels:
- Urakami shako-mae
- Ōhashi
- Peace Statue
- Peace Park
- Urakami Cathedral
- Atomic Bomb Hypocentre
- Matsuyama
- International Culture Hall (Atomic Bomb Museum)
- Hamaguchimachi
- Daigaku byōin-mae
- Urakami Station
- Urakami eki-mae
- Morimachi
- Zenzamachi
- Skyway
- Ropeway
- Mt Inasa
- Takaramachi
- Nagasaki Information Centre
- Yachiyomachi
- 26 Martyrs Memorial
- Fukusai-ji
- Youth Hostel
- Suwa Shrine
- Siebold Memorial Museum
- Suwa jinja-mae
- Shindaikumachi
- Nagasaki Station
- Nagasaki eki-mae
- Shōfuku-ji
- Sakuramachi
- Prefectural Art Museum
- 3,4,5
- Shinnakagawamachi
- Hotarujaya
- Harbin
- City Hall
- Kōkaidō-mae
- Gotōmachi
- Wakamiya Shrine
- Nigiwaibashi
- Kōfuku-ji
- Ōhato
- Harbour Inn Grand Hotel
- Prefectural Office
- Meganebashi (Spectacles Bridge)
- TERAMACHI AREA
- Mitsubishi Shipyard
- Ōhato Pier
- Dejima
- Nishihamanomachi
- Hamanomachi Shopping Arcade
- Kankō-dōri
- Dejima Pier
- Washington Hotel
- Shianbashi
- Sōfuku-ji
- Iriemachi
- Tsukimachi
- Chinatown
- Shōkakuji-shita
- Shiminbyōin-mae
- Nagasaki Harbour
- Ōura kaigan-dōri
- Hotel New Tanda
- Oranda-zaka (Dutch slope)
- Matsugae Pier
- Ōura tenshūdō shita
- Tokyū Hotel
- Kōshi-byō
- Chinese History Museum
- Glover Garden
- Ōura Catholic Church
- Ishibashi

N

········ Tram Line

500 metres
500 yards

city to the Jesuits. With 80 missionaries and 200 churches, it was an almost completely Christian city. In 1609 the Protestant Dutch set up their own trading post on the nearby island of Hirado, where they were joined by the English four years later.

Nagasaki has always been a city of firsts, and it was during this period that European technology and novelties began to make their presence felt in Japan. Matchlock arquebuses and navigational instruments like the astrolabe, imitating Portuguese originals, had been produced in the 1550s. In the early 17th century Europeans imported the first metal type printing press and the first pumpkins. Delicacies like *tempura* and Castile sponge cake (still sold in Nagasaki as *casutera*) date from this period, as does the Japanese fascination with Western fashions, manifested at the time in an enthusiasm among local dandies for crucifixes, breeches, and Mediterranean wines drunk from glass goblets.

The fun was short lived. As stability returned to the war-torn country, its new leaders began to regard the prosperous foreign outposts with growing greed and suspicion. In 1587 the volatile warlord, Hideyoshi Toyotomi, seized Nagasaki (after an initial show of sympathy towards the Europeans) and placed it under the supervision of his personal envoy. In 1597, gathering anti-Christian feeling culminated in the crucifixion of European and Japanese Christians on Nishizaka Hill—the famous Twenty-six Martyrs. There was an uneasy impasse until 1614, when the first of the great Tokugawa shoguns, Ieyasu, formally outlawed Christianity. Converts from all over Japan sought refuge in Nagasaki, and those who refused to apostatize met their deaths there. The tortures devised by the inquisition were exceptionally gruesome: men, women and children, priests and lay people, were burned, drowned, branded, mutilated, decapitated, crucified, and left to die of exposure in the mountains or lashed to stakes in the open sea. Men were branded on the genitals; women were sexually tortured and forced to couple with their own sons. Some were suspended upside down over pits of excrement where they slowly bled to death through opened veins; others were boiled alive in steaming hot spring 'hells'. Those who recanted had to confirm their rejection of Christianity by walking on metal plaques bearing an image of the crucified Christ. The plaques, called *fumi-e* (trampling pictures) were manufactured in large numbers. The trampling ceremony became an annual event. One by one, the foreign traders left or were expelled, until by 1640 only the Dutch and the Chinese were left, confined to purpose-built settlements from which their movements were strictly controlled.

After the trade treaties of the 1850s, Nagasaki came into its own again as sailors, diplomats and merchants from Europe, Russia and China converged on Nagasaki with their wives and children. Once again the city led the rest of Japan: the first Western-style schools, the first sundial, first mobile printing press, steam locomotive, telephone, photography, stone bridge, iron bridge, coal mine and slip dock were all seen in Nagasaki. In fashionable salons in Europe, 'Japonesque' porcelain, decoration and woodblock prints were all the rage. Nagasaki became a by-word for this romanticized and exotic world, and colourful letters, books and journals survive from the expatriate community. Pierre Loti, the novelist and French naval officer, visited Nagasaki, and his caddish treatment of the *geisha* he 'married' for the summer is related in his novel *Madame Chrysanthème*; a more gallant treatment of the same theme, *My Japanese Wife* by the Englishman Clive Holland, was the best seller of 1895. The most famous love story of Nagasaki, however, was not so immediately successful. Puccini's *Madama Butterfly*, an Italian opera based on a British play based on an American short story, flopped dismally at La Scala in 1904 and had to be revised before its brilliant revival the following year, when the tale of the doll-like Japanese whose heart is broken by the heartless foreigner became a legend. Nagasaki earned the nickname 'the Naples of the Orient', although the real city seems to have been a much coarser, more disreputable place than Puccini's wonderland. 'The principal productions of Nagasaki,' wrote one visiting journalist, 'are tobacco, *jinrikishas*, desponding commission agents, unripe plums, ships' chandlers, tomatoes, bow-legged Custom House officials, bankrupts, water melons, intoxicated sailors, tortoise-shell bracelets, mosquitoes, grog-shops and stagnation. The prevalent epidemics are dysentery and insolvency.'

In the early 20th century Nagasaki became an important industrial centre. The Mitsubishi Shipyards around the harbour were the target for the world's second and last atomic attack on 9 August 1945. Since the end of the war Nagasaki, like Hiroshima, has established itself as a focus for peace and anti-nuclear activism. The city's energetic and long-serving liberal mayor, Hitoshi Motoshima, has travelled the world making public apologies for Japan's aggression during the war which national politicians have steadfastly resisted. In 1989 a right-wing fanatic attempted to kill him after he suggested publicly that the Emperor should bear some personal responsibility for the Pacific War.

Getting There

Rail travellers from Honshū take the *shinkansen* to Hakata (Fukuoka) from where the expresses take about 2½hrs.

From Tokyo, seven flights land daily at Nagasaki's **airport**, constructed ten years ago on a man-made island in Ōmura Bay, one of the most spectacular landings in the world. There are also connections from Kansai International Airport. The limousine bus from the airport to Nagasaki station takes just under an hour.

Getting Around

For those with the patience to submit to an organized **bus tour**, the tourist information centre has a list of a dozen itineraries which pack a lot into a few hours. The best way to see Nagasaki, however, is a combination of walking and **streetcars**. Single rides cost ¥100 to go as far as you want—get on at the back, drop your money in the driver's offertory box as you disembark from the front. The city tourist information centre (*see* below) and some of the big hotels sell all-day passes for ¥500.

The four streetcar lines (numbered 1 to 5, there's no no.2) form an approximate triangle in the centre of town, with arms extending from each of its points. Line no.5 serves the Glover Garden, Dutch slopes and the relics of foreign settlement in the south of the city. The eastern arm (lines 3, 4 or 5) takes you towards the Prefectural Museum, while the northernmost arm (lines 1 and 3) extends from the railway station past the atomic bomb memorials, and up the Urakami Valley.

Harbour tours depart from Ōhato Pier (two tram stops down from Nagasaki station, line no.1) twice a day for a 50min chug around the harbour and bay with commentary in Japanese.

Tourist Information

In the station area alone there are three tourist information centres: a busy counter in the station building itself which will reserve accommodation; the **city tourist information centre** (by the police box, to the right as you face the station) which dispenses streetcar and tour bus tickets; and a 2nd floor resource centre directly above the bus terminal (opposite the station), with English-language pamphlets, magazines and timetables which the patient staff will photocopy for you. Anyone spending more than a few days in the city would do well to call on the Tourism Section of **Nagasaki City Hall**, ✆ 0958 25 5151, equidistant between tram stops Kōkaidō-mae (lines 3, 4 and 5) and Sakuramachi (line 3 only), which publishes excellent booklets and newsletters aimed at visitors and foreign residents.

South Nagasaki

Head—on foot or on board streetcar no.5—in the direction of the slender **Nagasaki Sky Tower**, a 135m, $10 million civic folly constructed for an international Expo in 1990. The glass doughnut which spins sedately up and down is an observation room with fine views of the town and harbour (*opens 9am, closes between 5pm and 9pm, depending on season; adm ¥600*).

Ōura Tenshu-dō (Ōura Catholic Church)

Ōura Tenshu-dō tram stop. Open Mar–Nov 8.30–5.45; Dec–Feb 8.30–4.45; adm ¥250.

A street lined with glass, cake, and souvenir shops ascends to the palm trees and white-washed façade of this appealingly tatty church, one of the oldest in Japan and the scene of a famous incident commemorated in stone relief inside.

After the trade treaties of the 1850s opened Japan up to European visitors, Catholic missionaries returned to Nagasaki to re-establish churches in the once great Christian city. In 1862 a Frenchman named Father (later Bishop) Bernard Petitjean began to travel among the outlying villages and islands in a vain search for relics and practitioners of the secret Christianity which was rumoured to have survived the persecutions. Meanwhile, the wooden Ōura Church was finished. On 19 February 1865, it was dedicated, in the presence of the French Consul, and the captains of Russian, British and Dutch warships moored in Nagasaki harbour. A month later Petitjean found a group of men and women standing outside the locked church. Inside they sought out the image of the Virgin. 'The heart of all those present,' they told the astonished Petitjean, 'is the same as yours.'

They came from the village of Urakami, a few miles to the north. A further 60,000 *kakure Kirishitan* (hidden Christians) were discovered over the next few years, all of them in remote areas where shogunal control had been weak. For more than two centuries, they had practised their religion, without Bibles or pastors, in small, tightly organized village

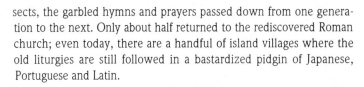

sects, the garbled hymns and prayers passed down from one generation to the next. Only about half returned to the rediscovered Roman church; even today, there are a handful of island villages where the old liturgies are still followed in a bastardized pidgin of Japanese, Portuguese and Latin.

Apart from the stained glass windows (blown out by the A-bomb) the church survives in its original state. The large, poorly-lit oil painting depicts the crucifixion of the Twenty-six Martyrs, commissioned by Petitjean on a visit to Rome. The next-door **Latin Divinity School** displays a small collection of crypto-Christian relics, including some Maria-Kannon images (mirrors reveal the carved crosses on the back), Japanized holy water bottles, and some well-trampled *fumi-e*—flat metal images of Christ employed by the shogunal officials to root out secret Christians. The faith was illegal for Japanese until well after the Meiji Restoration in 1868, and the New Year custom of lining up the town's population and having them tread one by one on the *fumi-e* was described by Western residents in Nagasaki. Afterwards, the devout would wash their feet and drink the bath water as a penance for their unwilling blasphemy.

Gurabā-en (Glover Garden)

Turn left at the bottom of Ōura Church steps for the entrance to Gurabā-en. Open Mar–Nov 8–6; Dec–Feb 8.30–5; adm ¥600.

This well-tended jumble of 19th-century Western-style houses and memorabilia, in the smartest quarter of the old foreign settlement, is *almost* (but not quite) authentic. The buildings here are all of 19th-century construction, but several have been moved from their original sites, and some touches, like the hillside escalators with their repro colonial-style roofs, do mar the historical interest with the atmosphere of the theme park.

Like much of Nagasaki, the garden is littered with quirky firsts, including the first asphalted road (built to give access to rickshaws), the first stone roller used on Japan's first tennis courts, and the home of Robert Walker, the British mariner who marketed the nation's first modern soft drinks, Banzai Cider and Banzai Lemonade, under the auspices of the Banzai Aerated Waters Co. The **Jiyū-tei Restaurant**, now an overpriced tea shop, was Japan's first European-style eating place, and a stone gateway marks the entrance to an early Japanese Masonic Lodge, founded in 1865—look for the compass and ruler emblem still visible on the pillars.

A lavish brochure in English is on sale at the ticket office. The wood and stone merchants' bungalows are identified by the names of their first occupants, whose moustachioed portraits frown from the walls of the restored interiors: the houses of Frederick **Ringer** (built in 1864), William **Alt** (1865), as well as 'Banzai' **Walker** (1877). The biggest, oldest and most interesting of the houses was built in 1863 by **Thomas Glover**, a Scot who had arrived in Nagasaki four years earlier to establish a trading company. He married a local *geisha*, and had a daughter and a son who Japanized his name to Tomisaburo Kuraba and took over the business when his father retired to Tokyo. The house, erected by the master carpenter who built Ōura Church, is filled with period gewgaws. The **Steele Memorial Academy**, the old American mission school reconstructed in the top corner of the garden, contains vivid snapshots from the lives of the 19th-century European community.

Beneath the decorous expatriate routine, however, great intrigues were being hatched. As well as his shipbuilding, coalmining and railway businesses, Glover was an arms dealer who played a key role in the overthrow of the shogun, equipping the rebels of the Satsuma and Chōshū clans, and smuggling out several of their young leaders to receive military training in Europe—including a future prime minister, Ito Hirobumi. A tableau, featuring life-size mannequins and hidden tape recorders, enacts their dramatic meeting in one of the front rooms. In 1908, on the recommendation of his protégés, Glover became the first foreigner to receive the Order of the Rising Sun (Second Class). He died three years later in Tokyo at the age of 73. Few of the Nagasaki foreign businesses survived the xenophobic purges of the Pacific War, however. Poor Glover Jr was hounded for his mixed blood, forced to sell up, and (although the official brochures remain conspicuously silent on the subject) killed himself in August 1945.

The garden commands great views of the bay and contains fountains and statues (including one entirely spurious monument to the fictitious Madame Butterfly) well worth a couple of undemanding hours. At the bottom of the slope, on the way out, is the smart new **Nagasaki Museum of Performing Arts** (*same hours as garden; admission included*) which houses the gorgeous floats used in the Nagasaki Kunchi, the autumnal Chinese Festival; a screen at the end of the spacious hall continuously shows an excellent film of them in action, including a giant whale, carp, 16th-century Dutch ship and a cohort of brilliantly choreographed dragons.

Kōshi Byō (Confucian Shrine)

On the north side of streetcar track no.5, off a side street half way between Ōura Tenshu-dō-shita and Ishibashi stops. Open 8.30–5; adm ¥515.

Chinese merchants had been trading and settling in Nagasaki since before the Europeans. Their influence is gaudily apparent in the yellow tiles and leaping curves of the Confucian Shrine. The basic elements may be the same, but this flamboyant giraffe of a building, constructed in 1893 and refurbished 90 years later, has as much in common with the traditional Japanese shrine as a Rococo chapel with a Norman church. The roof ridges are densely ornamented with flowers, birds and effigies, with rampant dragons on each corner and mythical Kirin guarding the sanctuary, which is tiled (no need to remove shoes). The courtyard contains marble statues of the 72 disciples of Confucius; the walls of the cloister are inscribed with the master's analects. The attached **Museum of Chinese History** houses a remarkable collection of treasures, renewed annually, from the Beijing National Museum of History, including horses and warriors from the famous Xian terracotta army. Even today this land is technically Chinese territory, administered by the Tokyo embassy.

North of the shrine are signposts for **Oranda-zaka**, the Dutch Slopes, a pleasant but strenuously steep promenade of flagstones, stone embankments, brickwork and wooden houses. This area, Higashi-yamate, was one of the most attractive addresses in pre-war Nagasaki and the location of several consulates, churches and Western-style buildings.

Central Nagasaki: Dejima

Dejima streetcar stop.

'Jutting-Out Island', as the name literally translates, is one of the most historically interesting sites in Japan, but these days you could easily walk across it without noticing. Sandwiched between the Nakajima River and streetcar tracks 3 and 4, it was absorbed into the mainland by a harbour landfill program during the Meiji period. For more than 200 years before, the fan-shaped, man-made island and the 20 or so Dutch merchants confined there, remained the only official point of contact between Japan and the West.

Dejima was originally built in 1636 for the confinement of Portuguese traders. After their expulsion, the Nagasaki merchants who had put up the construction money pressed the shogunate for new tenants, and in 1641 the Dutch East India Company was moved to Dejima from its old headquarters on Hirado Island. Throughout their 214-year tenancy, the Dutch were treated with characteristic (and sometimes justified) paranoia by the shogunal representatives. No Japanese were allowed onto the island, except for city officials and the *geisha* of the nearby Maruyama pleasure quarter who were the merchants' only female company. No Dutchmen were allowed off, save for the annual pilgrimage to Edo when the newly arrived factor presented his credentials to the shogun. Despite these rigours, and the harsh punishments inflicted on transgressors, the Dutch became expert smugglers, especially the captains who, exempt from body searches, would stuff their coats with every kind of contraband. One chronicle records the embarrassing case of the petty officer who entered Dejima with a live parrot stuffed down his breeches. The inevitable happened: as the man was being searched his cramped pet began chattering loudly.

But Japan depended on the Dutch far more than its disdainful treatment of them might suggest. The yearly reports which the factor prepared for the Japanese authorities became the country's only source of international news, and after 1745, when Dutch books were finally permitted to Japanese scholars, Dejima became the centre for a wide range of subjects grouped under the heading *Rangaku*—Dutch Learning. Native interpreters attached to the Dejima community introduced a range of European discoveries in maths, Newtonian physics, Copernican astronomy, geography, botany, warfare and, on the eve of the Meiji Restoration, photography. Dutch physicians, eager to relieve the monotony of their isolation, taught anatomy, pharmacy and surgery to Japanese students who had previously had access only to traditional Chinese herbal remedies (on several occasions a Dutch doctor was discreetly whisked off to Edo to minister to a member of the shogun's family).

Today, nothing survives of the old Dejima except a few stones, but the layout of the streets is unchanged and a 1:40 scale model of the island gives a good idea of just how tiny a place it was. The small museum, **Dejima Shiryōkan** (*open 9–5; adm free*) has an interesting display of Dutch memorabilia, including prints and paintings of the big-nosed, red-haired barbarians by contemporary Japanese artists.

Teramachi and the River

The sides of the harbour valley rise steeply to the east of Nagasaki, and around their base is strung a necklace of Buddhist temples. The outstanding examples are Chinese: **Sōfuku-ji** (*Shōkakuji-shita streetcar stop, the last station on lines 1 and 4; open 8–5; adm ¥200*), built in 1629 by an immigrant priest of the Ōbaku Zen sect, is in the Southern Ming style. Much of it was prefabricated in China and shipped over piecemeal; its red buildings, curling eaves and roof corners, stacked steeply on top of one another, are palpably exotic. The sturdy lower gate has a plain, square base of red plaster, topped by excitably curvy roofs. The inner gate, **Dai-ippo-mon**, transplanted from China in 1696, is a National Treasure—the intricate joinery under the eaves is characteristically Chinese, as are the geometrical, painted handrails around the halls and the wooden gong in the shape of a fish, used to summon monks to food and prayer. In 1681 a Chinese priest named Qiandai saved the city from rice famine when he cooked up gruel for thousands of starving citizens; the gargantuan kettle in which this miracle was performed still sits in the precincts.

At the top of the many steps are two halls. The left-hand one contains the main image of Shaka. Flanking him are 18, highly individualized *rakan*—human beings who have achieved Buddhahood. The hall to the right (**Masa-dō**) enshrines the mysterious Ama, Chinese sea goddess and patroness of sailors, whose guardians are two blue-robed bruisers, the left (with hand to eyes) all-seeing, the right (with ear cupped) all-hearing.

From Sōfukuji the road runs northwest, lined by smart boutiques. After a hundred metres is a turning to the right, just after a shop selling Buddhist household shrines. This is **Teramachi**, 'Temple Town', a street of shops selling drums, harps, *biwa* lutes, masks, dolls, gravestones, traditional furniture, and Buddhist funerary objects. The quarter sprung up during the Edo period, a typical example of overkill by the shoguns who decided that the way to cleanse Nagasaki of its Christian taint was to saturate the place with temples, whose gateways line the east side of the street. Six hundred metres to the north is the beautiful **Kōfuku-ji** (*open 8–5; adm ¥200*), also founded by Chinese in 1620, but a visual contrast to Sōfuku-ji, with wide springy lawns and tuberous cycad trees. Here too are fish gongs, and halls to Shaka and the sea goddess, as well as gates moved here from Chinatown and from the old Confucian Shrine.

Two blocks into town and parallel with the Teramachi thoroughfare is the **Nakashima River**, with its famous **stone bridges**. In 1982, torrential rains achieved what even the atomic bomb couldn't manage, washing six of them away: now fastidiously reconstructed, and flanked on the northwest bank by a tree-lined promenade, they're a reminder of what Japanese cities can do with their waterways, when they don't fill them with rubbish or build expressways over them. The famous **Megane-bashi** ('Spectacles Bridge', named from its reflection in the water) was stripped to its bare arches, but retains its status as an Important Cultural Property, built in 1634 by the second Chinese abbot of Kōfuku-ji.

East of the Station

In 1596, Hideyoshi Toyotomi, driven to characteristic fury by the insolent captain of a shipwrecked Spanish galleon, rounded up a group of Franciscan friars and their Japanese flock (including two boys of 12 and 13) and marched them from Kyoto to Nagasaki, where they were lashed to crosses, and, after the first of them had asphyxiated, pierced with spears. The martyrs were canonized in 1862 and the site of their crucifixion, Nishizaka, overlooks the present day railway station. Today it is marked by a memorial wall and a church, designed in a horrible derivative style by a Japanese student of the Barcelona architect Gaudi. Worth a brief look is the **Twenty-six Martyrs Museum** (*open 9–5; adm ¥250*) which includes original letters (by Francis Xavier, among others), *fumi-e*, blood-stained relics and gruesome prints of gurgling torturees.

East of the church are two more Chinese temples. **Fukusai-ji**, flattened by the bomb, is a good (i.e. bad) example of contemporary Buddhist architecture: a gargantuan Kannon and a group of monstrous supplicant children stand atop a hall in the shape of a huge turtle. Further down the road (second temple on the left after the Ikoma love hotel) is **Shofuku-ji** (not to be confused with the more famous Sōfukuji; the common element *fuku* signifies good luck), another lovely Chinese temple, calmer and less touristed than its more famous Teramachi sisters, with a fat, ho-hoing god of fortune and an unusual wall mosaic of broken tiles bearing ceramic faces of animals and fish. Above is a soothingly quiet hillside cemetery. If you keep going up, beyond the red-bibbed Jizō statues, you can climb almost to the summit, past steeply terraced family graves, to another stirring view of the city, especially fine at dusk.

Urakami

For the first few centuries of Nagasaki's existence, Urakami was a separate village on the banks of the river from which it takes its name. Under the shogunate it was a centre of crypto-Christianity, and in the 1870s a group of local Catholics chose it as the site of the church, 30 years in the making, which succeeded the one at Ōura as Nagasaki's cathedral. It was 500m above here that the second and larger of the US Air Force's atomic bombs exploded at 11.02am on 9 August 1945. As well as a prison, a hospital, half a dozen schools and 74,000 human beings, the plutonium bomb (nicknamed 'Fat Man' in honour, supposedly, of Winston Churchill) destroyed the largest Christian church in Asia.

In fact, strange though it sounds, the destruction could have been worse. The bomb run from Tinian had been a shambles from the start. The official photographer missed his flight after forgetting his parachute, and the B29, Bock's Car, virtually crash-landed on its return to Okinawa having completely run out of fuel. The first destination, Kokura in northern Kyūshū, was obscured by the smoke from a previous air raid, and when the secondary target, Nagasaki, was also covered in cloud the nerve-ragged airmen decided to ditch the monster in any case. At the last minute, a gap appeared in the clouds and the bomb was released not, as intended, over the shipyards and flat harbour area, but 3km to the north, where the steep sides of the Urakami valley absorbed much of the blast.

Whatever your position on nuclear weapons, the specific circumstances of these events give plenty of reasons for worry: if doubts hang over the bombing of Hiroshima, they are redoubled in the case of Nagasaki. True, in the three days since the first bomb, no word had come from Tokyo suggesting imminent surrender. But American intelligence was perfectly aware of the confusion which reigned in the Japanese High Command—the issue under debate was not whether, but *how* to submit to the inevitable. It knew, too, that with the Soviet Union's invasion of Manchuria, Japan's decline was irreversible. Effective communication had broken down between Tokyo and western Japan; even at the time of the surrender on 12 August, the Japanese Cabinet, bickering in their underground bunker, probably did not appreciate the full horror of the new weapon. Three days was hardly time for the news of Hiroshima to have reached Tokyo, let alone wrought its psychological impact.

Nagasaki's collection of photographs, relics and documents relating to the bomb isn't as slick or extensive as Hiroshima's, but it is superior in one important respect. Through the efforts of Mayor Motoshima, and to the discomfort of many of his compatriots, the Nagasaki peace movement places as much emphasis on the victims of Japanese cruelty as on the sufferings caused by the atomic bomb. 'People from Korea and China and the Allied powers were brought to Japan under force and subjected to inhumane treatment,' the official Nagasaki Peace Declaration points out. 'We must think deeply about the history of Japanese aggression in Asia and the Pacific, pray for the more than 20 million victims at home and abroad, and make reparations on the basis of our sincere self-reflection.'

Matsuyama streetcar stop (lines 1 or 3, eight stops north of Nagasaki railway station) is right opposite the small, flowery **Gembaku Kōen** (A-Bomb Park) whose black monolith, draped with bouquets and origami cranes, marks the point, 500m above the ground, where the bomb exploded. Scattered among azaleas and cherry trees are lumps of masonry from Urakami Cathedral and iron watchtowers, buckled into crazy shapes by the heat.

Above here is the **Atomic Bomb Museum** (*open winter 9–5, summer 9–6; closed 29–31 Dec; token adm*) temporarily housed on the first floor of **Nagasaki City Peace Hall** while its old home, the next door International Culture Hall, is lavishly rebuilt. The aim is to have it completed for the 50th anniversary of the bombing in 1995—but no one is holding their breath.

Queen Wilhelmina of the Netherlands is said to have fainted during her official tour; plenty of people leave the museum in tears. What the simple, artlessly displayed exhibits bring home is the *detail* of the suffering, the thousands of small individual tragedies which made up the whole. Mundanely familiar objects acquire an awful significance: clocks and watches stopped forever at 11.02; a pair of bent spectacles which were a family's only means of identifying their dead son; a tiny, stained cotton bonnet bearing the following label: 'This hood is a relic relating to a baby whose name was Yoshigitsu Ide, killed when he was 2 years and 7 months old. Though he was an innocent baby, he feared the air-raids and never parted with the mammy-made hood even for a moment. (Donated by Mrs Yae Ide, mother of the dead baby, in Ieno-machi, Nagasaki.)'

Parts of the exhibition, especially the large number of black and white photographs, are pure horror—the skinless bodies of the dead and fatally wounded, a burnt mother suckling a burnt baby, waxwork models of the keloid scars which disfigured the bodies of those caught in the blast. In one photograph two young brothers gaze into the camera, one supporting the other. The elder had carried the younger to safety on his shoulders, but he died anyway a few hours later.

There are also drawings and paintings by survivors, including Allied prisoners of war. The professional attempts to paint the inferno are not a success, appearing either melodramatically graphic or ladenly symbolic, as if the subject itself defies visual representation. This becomes embarrassingly clear in **Heiwa Kōen**, the Peace Park (*open April–Oct 9–6; Nov–Mar 9–5; adm free*) and its 'World Peace Symbol Zone' cluttered with donated statues from all over the world. It's well meant, but embarrassingly hackneyed, with an abundance of doves, olive branches and jubilant mothers holding aloft gravity-defying infants. At the centre of the park, and in a league of its own, is the **Peace Statue** by the Nagasaki-born sculptor Kitamura Seibō, all 10m and ¥30 million of it. The statue's posture is explained thus: 'the elevated right hand points to the threat of nuclear weapons, while the outstretched left hand symbolizes tranquillity and world peace. A prayer for the repose of the souls of all war victims is expressed in the closed eyes. Also the folded right leg symbolizes quiet meditation, while the left leg is poised for action in assisting humanity.' As you can imagine, all this makes for a pretty constipated-looking statue, although its size alone is impressive. The basalt box in front contains the names of all the victims as well as those survivors who have died since 1945. Every year a few more are added to the list.

Signposts in English lead up the hill to **Urakami Cathedral** (*open 9–5; donation*), rebuilt in 1959. The statues at the front are from the old church, and the original bell-tower still lies where it was hurled by the blast, on the grass embankment below the walls.

Just north of the cathedral (350 metres) is a tiny building called **Nyōko-dō**, literally **'Love-Your-Neighbour-As-Yourself House'** (*open 9–5; adm free*), the final home of Nagai Takashi, a Roman Catholic doctor in the medical school of the University of Nagasaki, who lost his wife and home in the attack. Despite suffering leukaemia (ironically he contracted it *before* the bomb, during his research into radiology), he and a band of volunteers struggled to treat the victims and made first-hand observations of the effects of the new weapon. As an invalid he wrote 20 books before his death in 1951, including the famous *Bells of Nagasaki* (Kodansha International), a famous account of his wartime experience and the mystical Catholicism which it inspired. It was finished in 1946 at the time of the International Military Tribunal of the Far East. Reluctant to sanction a book focusing on their own war crimes, the American authorities refused publication, then gave way on condition of an appendix about Japanese atrocities in the Philippines. The tiny Nyōko-dō, where Nagai did his writing, contains the doctor's death mask and simple relics of his life.

Where to Stay

There are several dependable, Western-style hotels in the *moderate* price bracket: the **Tōkyū Hotel**, ✆ 0958 25 1501, close to Ōura Church and the Glover Garden, is the nicest; the **Grand Hotel**, ✆ 0962 23 1234, is a 5-minute taxi ride from the station, and the **Hotel New Nagasaki** is opposite the station. A bit cheaper is the **Washington Hotel**, ✆ 0962 28 1211, close to Chinatown.

Minshuku Tanpopo, ✆ 0962 61 6230, is a *cheap* Welcome Inn, opposite the Urakami River. The **Oranda-zaka Youth Hostel**, ✆ 0962 22 2730, is on the Dutch Slopes, close to the Confucian Shrine.

Three streetcar lines meet at Nishi Hamanomachi stop in front of Chūō-bashi bridge, and the road leading away from it to the east is Nagasaki's consumer downtown, lined with banks, department stores and entertainment-crammed multi-storey buildings. On the north side is the entrance to the **Hamanomachi Arcade**, a cross-shaped covered shopping centre filled with restaurants, bars and souvenir shops—cheap, convenient and soulless. Opposite the arcade entrance, to the south, is the inevitable MacDonald's ('Makudonarudo'); the road alongside leads to a big gateway built by craftsmen from the Chinese city of Fuzhou, the entrance to **Shinchi-machi** (Chinatown), the liveliest and most accessible of Nagasaki's night-time quarters. The restaurant windows are full of clearly-priced plastic models of characteristic Nagasaki delicacies, including *champon, sara udon* (from ¥450 a bowl) and, for groups of four or more, *shippoku ryōri*, a Japano-Portuguese-style Chinese banquet (from about ¥2500 a head). There are many shops in this area selling tortoiseshell jewellery, and flowers, ships and even insects frozen in amber, prices from the mundane to the astronomical.

Yossoh, ✆ 0958 21 0001, is a long-established Japanese restaurant on a street just outside the Hamanomachi arcade, not far from Okamasa department store. It is inexpensive and serves sushi, tempura and Nagasaki cuisine.

On the road at the top of Hamanomachi arcade which runs towards Teramachi is **Ginrei**, ✆ 0958 21 2073, a restaurant decorated with objects recalling Nagasaki's history of contact with the West. The food is good and *moderate* in price.

Nearby is **Bharata**, ✆ 0958 24 9194, an Indian restaurant run by Dan Patel and his wife Uiko. It has a good atmosphere and *inexpensive* prices. Try the pumpkin mousse in season.

For French and Russian cuisine, try **Harbin**, ✆ 0958 22 7443 (*moderate*), 2 minutes' walk south of the City Hall. The food is excellent and the service friendly. Harbin serves (and sells) good home-made bread.

Sakura House, ✆ 0958 26 0229, situated on the road between Sōfukuji and Hamanomachi, recreates a Western-style restaurant of Taisho-era Japan. The food is excellent and the prices *inexpensive*.

Caveau, ✆ 0958 25 9387, on the small road below the Grand Hotel is a lively bar (some food is served) with a large selection of drinks and music. Live bands often perform here and the bar is a favourite with the expatriate community.

Hirado and the Kyūjūkyūshima (Ninety-nine Islands)

By train to Hirado-guchi station, then a bus to Hirado town.

Hirado island, divided by a narrow strait from the northwest tip of Kyūshū, contains interesting relics of the foreign merchants and missionaries who lived and traded here from the mid-16th to mid-17th centuries. St Francis Xavier came here with Portuguese traders in

1550, the Spanish in 1584. In 1600 a Dutch ship was wrecked off southern Kyūshū; its pilot, the Englishman Will Adams, who became an adviser to the shogun, lived here for a while. In 1609 and 1613 respectively, the Dutch and English set up trading posts, but within ten years the latter had gone bankrupt, and the former had been moved to tiny Dejima island in Nagasaki harbour. After the outlawing of Christianity and contact with foreigners, all Japanese wives of Europeans were exiled with their childrento Jakarta. Pathetic letters from these refugees, written to their relatives in Japan, survive in the **Matsura Historical Museum**, along with secret images and scriptures, handed down from generation to generation by covert Hirado Christians. There's also a bridge and remains of walls built by the Dutch, more crypto-Christian relics in the nearby Hirado Tourist Museum, and a strange Disneyland church of pseudo-Gothic plaster built in the 1930s. The town itself has an affable seaside atmosphere with arty coffee and craft shops selling paintings by local artists. An infrequent bus ride away is the **Hirado Christian Museum** (*Closed Wed; adm ¥200*). Beautifully laid out, in a handsome modern building facing a windswept bay, this is the finest museum on the island, situated in Neshiko, an ancient and remote haunt of secret Christians.

Central Kyūshū

Aso-san (Mt Aso)

Sprouting out of the centre of Kyūshū is the biggest volcanic caldera in the world, an egg-shaped concavity 24km long, 18km wide and 128km in circumference, containing two railway lines, a dozen towns and villages, and 100,000 people. There is no single Mt Aso, but rather a cluster of five volcanoes at the centre of the crater. Naka-dake, the only one still active, is one of the liveliest volcanoes on earth. As recently as 1979 it erupted violently, spewing out ash and rocks, and killing tourists and locals. The area has its share of tacky tourist absurdities, and the mountains are grimly impressive rather than picturesquely beautiful. Like many volcanic regions, it's rich in agriculture; the small farming villages south of Naka-dake have beautiful scenery and natural hot springs.

Getting There

Public transport is infrequent, and it may be easiest to hire a **car** in Kumamoto or Beppu: enquire at the tourist information office in either town.

Aso Station is connected by **train** on the JR Hōhi line. Expresses run three times a day taking 1hr from Kumamoto, or 1hr 50mins from Beppu. Slower local trains run more frequently.

Every day two **buses** run from Kumamoto station to the cable car station below Naka-dake.

In and Around Mt Aso

With absolute incongruity, **Aso station** has been built on a wild west theme, with mock timber façade and jaunty saloon-style lettering indicating the toilets and (English-speaking) information centre. Once a day in season an *ersatz* Western steam train, 'Aso Boy', ferries in wagon loads of over-excited children and their families.

Aso Town has nothing to keep you, although if you find yourself stuck here for a few hours you might look in on the **Aso Jinja**, an ancient shrine rebuilt in the early 19th century. For the volcanoes, take the bus from outside the station; six leave every day, the last at a little after 3pm, and the journey takes half an hour. As it climbs, the view from the bus dramatically reveals the outer rim of the great crater with its steep rocky sides. The sensation of being enclosed on all sides by it is curious, a bit like finding yourself in H G Wells's Valley of the Blind. The Five Peaks of Aso loom ahead: **Kishima-dake, Eboshi-dake, Taka-dake** (1592m), **Neko-dake,** and **Naka-dake,** the active one. *En route* the bus stops at Kosasanri, a flat green plain with a puddle-like lake in the crater of Eboshi-dake, which you can pay to trek across on a horse. The **Aso Volcano Museum** opposite contains (none too interesting) displays on vulcanology. Before it, on the right, you will see **Komezuka** (Rice Mound), a small, classically shaped volcano covered in velvety green vegetation.

The bus terminates at the cable car station below Naka-dake. From here, the ride takes 5 minutes and deposits passengers on a blasted plain of grey pumice and volcanic hillocks. It's a harsh, unbeautiful landscape, still potentially vulnerable to eruption at any moment. The area is dotted with domed concrete pillboxes, erected after the 1979 eruption when several tourists were killed in a sudden rain of volcanic boulders. (If you hear a big bang, run for cover.) The centre of attention is the mighty crater hole from which subterranean fumes and heat still issue. The edge is fenced off, and signs warn sufferers from asthma, blood pressure, respiratory diseases and cardiac conditions to keep back. It's more of a craggy gash than a clean crater, and the view of the bottom is often obscured by protruding ledges of rock and billowing smoke. But from certain vantage points the fumes part occasionally to reveal their seething source, an evil green lake 160m below.

Beppu

Beppu, the most famous hot spring resort in Japan, is an exhilaratingly tacky place, an oriental cross between Las Vegas and Blackpool, with neon-lit streets, resort hotels, and hundreds of establishments catering for lovers of hot water and the seedier activities associated with it. Apart from these, the town's 'attractions' are over-priced, and rather scattered, making it hard to get round them unless you spend still more money on taxis.

Getting There

By **train**, 3hrs from Kumamoto and 1½hrs from Kokura. Six **flights** a day from Tokyo Haneda airport to Ōita airport. A daily **boat** departs Beppu for Hiroshima; there are also sailings to Ōsaka and Kōbe.

Tourist Information

The **foreign tourist information service**, just south of the station, ℂ 0977 23 1119, dispenses pamphlets and advice in English.

Beppu Jigoku (Beppu Hells)

Taxi, buses 16 or 26, or sightseeing coach. Open 8–5; adm ¥250 each or ¥1500 for a ticket covering eight of the hells.

The exceptional thinness of the earth's crust beneath Beppu gives rise to a number of curiosities, apart from the abundance of natural hot mineral water. Tropical plants such as palms and cycads thrive in the heated soil. And there are the *jigoku* or 'hells', geysers and cauldrons of boiling water and mud in various dramatic hues, a symbol of Beppu. There are nine hells altogether. Eight are owned by the same company and an inclusive ticket to see the lot costs ¥1500. But only four are really worth seeing, and one of these is not on the all-in ticket; individual entry costs ¥250.

Most tours start at **Tatsumaki Jigoku** (Tornado Hell). For nearly half an hour nothing happens here. Crowds gather in front of a stone niche, fidgeting. Then, every 25 minutes, regular as clockwork, a geyser of water explodes upwards at high pressure, 720 litres altogether. Cameras click, people gasp, and then it stops. 25 minutes later the same thing happens again.

Chinoike Jigoku (Blood Pool Hell), next door, is, as you'd expect, a lurid red, due to iron oxide in the water which was once used to dye fabric. The next four *jigoku* are a bit feeble, although efforts are made to render them more hellish by placing models of demons in the undergrowth. **Kinryū Jigoku** (Golden Dragon) is named after the fearsome serpent which is supposed to be visible in the billows of steam. **Oniyama Jigoku** (Mountain Demon Hell) contains 100 crocodiles. **Kamado Jigoku** (Oven Hell) is so named because eggs can be boiled in its vapours. The waters of **Shiraike Jigoku** (White Pond Hell) are—big deal—white. **Yama Jigoku** (Mountain Hell) has nothing special about it at all; some disconsolate-looking hippos live nearby.

Umi Jigoku (Sea Hell) is worth a look, if you've come this far. The waters of this, the biggest hell of all (5000 sq m), are aquamarine, and impenetrably deep. The bottom is said to be 120m down with a temperature of 98°C. **Bōzu Jigoku** (Bonze's Hell) is not on the inclusive ticket but is one of the more entertaining hells. It's a bubbling mud pool of the kind seen in New Zealand and Iceland: the name comes from the resemblance of the fat bubbles to the scalps of tonsured monks.

Other Attractions

Beppu has plenty of other tourist traps—a monkey park, a zoo, cable cars—none worth making a special trip for. Students of the strange might want to look into the **Ashiya Sex Museum** (*open 9–11; adm ¥1500*), opposite the Ashiya Hotel, just before the Kinryū Jigoku: phalluses, fertility charms, action tableaux of fornicating marionettes. Just what Beppu deserves.

More wholesome family entertainment can be had in the eight separate hot spring areas. Many inns have their own *onsen*, free to guests, but there are plenty of places open to transitory visitors. The **Takegawara Onsen** is an old 19th-century wooden bath house where patrons can also have themselves buried up to the neck in geothermally heated sand, as at Ibusuki. The **Suginoi Palace** hotel, on a hill above Beppu, admits day guests to its temples of kitsch: tropical foliage, fake Buddhist architecture, and *risqué* after dark entertainment.

(✆ 0977–) **Where to Stay**

Beppu hot spring *ryokan* are tacky, almost by definition, and not cheap (generally rising from the *moderate* to the *expensive* category in high season). **Hotel Shiragiku,** ✆ 21 2111, is close to the station. The **Suginoi Hotel,** ✆ 24 1141, is the kitsch grand-daddy of them all. The town's one Welcome Inn, with its own hot spring, is the **Minshuku Kokage,** ✆ 23 1753. The **youth hostel,** ✆ 23 4116, is a 30-minute bus ride.

Eating Out

Beppu's commercialization is most obvious in its tacky and expensive restaurants. There are many of them, but none seem particularly worth recommending. Eat in your lodgings if meals are included. For lunch, don't be ashamed to go to one of the Western-style spaghetti houses and pizza parlours on the street leading down from the station. If you take the ferry to Hiroshima then be sure to pop into a convenience store for a picnic of crisps, rice balls etc.—there are kiosks on the ferry, but they are overpriced and often sell out.

Usuki

JR Nippō Line to Usuki station.

Just outside Usuki, a little coastal backwater south of Beppu and Ōita, is the **Usuki Sekibutsu,** a gallery of stone Buddhas carved a millennium ago out of the raw cliff face. Such images are more common to China than Japan. In this corner of Kyūshū, there's a scattering of them; the examples at Usuki are the finest and best-preserved of all.

From Usuki station take a bus or taxi (*open 8.30–5; adm ¥420; if no one's there to take your money, just walk in anyway*). There are several sets of carvings, reached by a pathway that climbs up alongside the rock face. It's a still, mysterious place—for a long time, the statues were hidden from view by thick stands of bamboo, and little is known about their history or purpose. They seem to have been carved at different times, beginning around AD 1000. Stone is a little-used medium in Japan; perhaps this is why the statues appear to have a distinctly Chinese feel to them, a stern, almost bureaucratic air, compared with the warmer wooden sculptures of the temples. The drapery of their robes and the 'snail curls' of their hair are exquisitely shaped. One or two retain traces of the thousand-year-old pigment with which they were originally painted.

Takachiho

Takachiho is a Japanese Glastonbury, a place of legend and ancient religion, and the setting for several key scenes of Japanese mythology. When Amaterasu Ōmikami, sun deity and mother goddess of the Japanese nation, was tormented by her brother, the storm god Susano-o, she retreated into a cave on the Iwato River. And it was to Takachiho that her grandson, Ninigi no Mikoto, descended from heaven as Japan's first political leader, bearing the sacred mirror, sword and jewel which are still the hereditary emblems of the imperial family. Every night at the central shrine and, during the winter, in rural farm-houses, troupes of performers enact these famous deeds in a cycle of ancient *kagura* dances.

Getting There

Beautiful empty mountain roads connect Takachiho with Aso to the north, Kumamoto to the west, Kagoshima to the south, and Nobeoka to the east. From Nobeoka a JR branch line cuts a dramatic course above the vertical sides of the Takachiho Gorge. Sit by the window for plunging views of the seething river; the railway bridges on this line are said to be the highest in Asia. There are also bus connections from Nobeoka, Kumamoto and Aso (Takamori).

The sights are divided between two main areas: Mitai, a village containing the Takachiho Shrine, station and bus terminal; and Ama no Iwato Shrine, a 7km bus or bike ride to the northeast.

Around Takachiho

At 8pm every night, *kagura* dances are performed for tourists beneath the cryptomeria trees of **Takachiho Jinja** (*adm ¥300*). Behind the shrine, a fragrant path leads up through woods and along a particularly interesting stretch of the **Takachiho Gorge**. Over the centuries, the soft volcanic rock has been eroded by the river into patterned ridges, like the surface of a giant washboard. A demon named Kikuchi was said to inhabit the many caves; *oni-no-chikara-ishi* (demon-strength rock) is a huge boulder which he used to perform his exercises. Boats (*¥1000 for 40mins*) are available for hire.

Ama no Iwato, a bus ride away from Mitai, is the site of one of the most famous of the Shinto myths. Amaterasu, the sun goddess, went into a holy sulk after her younger brother Susano-o, god of storms, broke into her fields and skinned one of her ponies. She hid herself away in a cave on this river, and refused to emerge; deprived of the light of the sun, the world was plunged into darkness. Nothing that anyone could say or do would bring Amaterasu out again. The other gods convened a meeting in another cave nearby to discuss the problem. Finally, on the river gravel in front of the cave, a goddess named Ame-no-uzume performed an erotic dance. The spectators cackled uproariously at this and, as they had intended, Amaterasu peeped out of her cave to see what was causing all the merriment. A waiting god pulled aside the boulder, and two more tied a rope across the cave mouth to stop Amaterasu slipping back in. So the sun returned to the world.

The cave itself appears to be completely inaccessible, but opposite, on the north bank of the river, is a shrine (**Ama no Iwato Jinja**) containing a sacred tree—Ame-no-uzume used a sprig of this in her naughty dance. A few minutes' walk upstream, along the river bank, is **Ama-no-yasugawara**, where the gods hatched their cunning plan. It's a big cave; the path to the small shrine leads through a forest of stone cairns, entirely covering the rocky floor, like a congregation of tiny people.

Kagoshima

Kagoshima is one of Kyūshū's most interesting cities, with a semi-tropical climate fostering palms and satsumas (recalling the province's former name), and a long tradition of independence from the distant capitals of Kyoto and Tokyo. Tanegashima island, part of modern Kagoshima prefecture, was the site of the first known contact between Japan and the West, when Portuguese traders were shipwrecked there in 1543. The Jesuit missionary St Francis Xavier made 600 converts in a 10-month stay in the city six years later. In the late 19th century, the Satsuma clan were instrumental in the defeat of the shogun and the restoration of the Emperor Meiji. Today, though, Kagoshima's most striking feature is Sakurajima—a huge, beautiful, and spectacularly active volcano which faces the city across a blue bay, and regularly chokes its air with billows of fine grey ash.

Getting There

From Hakata (Fukuoka), the terminus of the *shinkansen* from Tokyo and Ōsaka, the limited express **train** takes 4½hrs. From Tokyo and Ōsaka it's marginally cheaper to take the daily sleeper; this is non-stop, but takes 20½hrs as opposed to about 11hrs for the *shinkansen/*express option. Eight **flights** from Tokyo and six from Ōsaka land every day at Kagoshima airport, which is an hour by limousine bus from downtown.

Long-distance **ferries** sail to Ōsaka and Okinawa in the Ryūkyū chain. Tanegashima and Yakushima are two islands forming part of Kagoshima prefecture, both of them unspoiled nature reserves. Ferries and jetfoils depart daily, taking 4–4½hrs.

Getting Around

Kagoshima and **Nishi Kagoshima** are the two principal JR stations. The city's attractions are pretty much equidistant from both of them, although Kagoshima is more convenient for the Iso tei-en garden and Sakurajima Pier. A **streetcar** track joins the two stations.

The JR Red Liner **sightseeing bus tours** of the city itself are rather perfunctory, but they are recommended on Sakurajima which is big and time-consuming to get around, even on a bike. They leave from the Sakurajima ferry terminal at 9.30am and 1.30pm, return 3hrs later, and cost ¥1700 (free to Japan Rail Pass holders). The commentaries are in Japanese only.

Ferries to Sakurajima go every 10 or 15 minutes from Sakurajima Pier, on the shoreward side of Sakurajima Sanbashi-dōri streetcar stop.

Tourist Information

Both **Kagoshima station** and **Nishi Kagoshima station** have tourist information desks where English is spoken. Best of all is the **Update Visitor Centre** on the first floor of the white I'm (*Aimu*) Building half way between Takamibaba and Tenmonkan streetcar stops—plentiful maps and pamphlets and helpful English-speaking volunteers.

A Note on Sakurajima

Sakurajima is one of the most dramatically restless volcanoes in the world. After a quiet first half to the 20th century, it roused itself in 1955, and has been continuously active ever since. During that time there have been more than 5700 separate explosions. At their peak in 1985, 29 million tons of ash were expelled from the crater. Much of that ash lands on Kagoshima.

It gets everywhere—in shoes, hair, swimming pools, under finger nails and contact lenses. On days of light ash fall, you might notice no more than a greasy, grey residue on your skin and hands at the end of the day. On the heaviest days, it's like standing downwind of a sooty bonfire—without an umbrella, you'll be black in a matter of minutes. Crops in the area are periodically blighted and fish poisoned. Houses have to be fitted with dust-proof windows and air-filtration systems. Several times a day the yellow municipal road sweepers chug past marshalling and vacuuming little heaps of ash.

This isn't to say that you shouldn't visit Kagoshima, just that you should be prepared. The volcano is a capricious creature and the density of the ash fall is difficult to predict—you might enquire at Tokyo or Kyoto tourist information centre a few days before you go. Dress as you would on a visit to a coal mine, in durable and washable fabrics. If you have to go somewhere in your Sunday best, be prepared to take a taxi. Contact lens wearers may prefer to wear glasses.

Around Kagoshima

The best place to start is at the statue of the city's most famous son, the brilliant leader of the Satsuma clan, **Saigō Takamori** (1827–77). After the successful overthrow of the shogun and the restoration of Emperor Meiji, Saigō took a senior place in the new government which his military leadership had brought to power. Five years on, however, he resigned—partly out of loyalty to the growing numbers of unemployed and discontented samurai, partly out of pique after his colleagues rejected an alarming plan to invade Korea. For three years he bided his time in Kagoshima, building an army of disgruntled samurai from all over the country, and training new recruits in the *Shi-gakkō*, a military school. In 1877, the tension finally erupted into a war. Cornered by large numbers of government troops, the injured Saigō finally committed suicide on a hill overlooking the city. Despite technically being a traitor, his loyalty to the samurai code and unblinking sacrifice in the face of impossible odds turned him into a patriotic symbol after his death. Emperor Meiji pardoned him; during the Pacific War, he was held up as a paragon of martial virtue. A famously determined-looking statue of him with his dog, Tsun, stands near the entrance to Tokyo's Ueno Park. The one here (*walk north from Asahi-dōri streetcar stop*) shows a similarly doughty figure, with crop-hair (the samurai's traditional topknot had been outlawed by the Meiji government), firm, fleshy jaw, and uncompromising expression.

Behind the statue is a modern building housing the **Kagoshima City Museum of Art** (*open 9–4.30; adm ¥260*), more than usually interesting for the large numbers of Western-style oils painted by Japanese artists in the late 19th century. As Western ideas spread through Japan's undeveloped industries and social institutions, a number of artists travelled overseas or studied under Western tutors in their own country. European Impressionism was at its peak, and a group of painters from Kagoshima found a particular affinity with contemporary French artists—more than anywhere else in Japan perhaps, the sunlight and blue skies of their city corresponded to the conditions which inspired their exemplars, and the brooding shape of Sakurajima, with its clouds of smoke and unpredictable aspect, offered the perfect subject, as potent and recognizable as Cézanne's St Victoire. As well as some minor European originals by Monet, Renoir, Rodin, Utrillo and Picasso, the galleries also contain fine examples of Kagoshima's distinctive regional crafts. Satsuma-yaki is a local stoneware with a fine crackle in its glaze. White pieces were the preserve of the aristocracy; handsome everyday objects in black Satsuma-yaki were produced for everyday peasant use; both are now prized by collectors, and can be seen on sale in shops all over town.

The **Reimeikan** (Prefectural Museum of Culture, a few hundred metres north of the Art Museum, *open 9–4.30; adm ¥260*) is a good museum of history and culture, behind walls and a moat which used to defend **Tsurumaru-jō**, Kagoshima's castle, dismantled after the Meiji Restoration. Three floors of galleries cover local history from prehistoric times. There's a reconstructed thatched house, and representations of Tanokami, a small green Shinto leprechaun who protects the rice fields of Satsuma farmers. There are also panels on an extraordinary incident in 1863 after the murder of an Englishman living in Yokohama by samurai of the Satsuma clan. The British government insisted on financial compensation; when this failed to materialize, a fleet under the command of Admiral Kuper was sent to Kagoshima, where it bombarded the city from the bay. The Satsumans paid up, and relations between the two sides became so cordial that several students were sent to study in England. Even today, British citizens are assured an even friendlier than usual reception in Kagoshima.

Above the museums is **Shiroyama**, the hill where Saigō and his 300 surviving retainers made their last stand against a government army of 40,000. You can enter the gloomy cave near the top where, gravely wounded, he committed *seppuku*, the fatal blow being administered with a long sword by a loyal retainer. A few blocks to the north is a large **cemetery** containing a memorial hall and more than 2000 graves of the casualties of the pointless Satsuma War.

Northern Kagoshima

North of Kagoshima station and the pier where the boats leave for Sakurajima, nestling against the hillside opposite the volcano, is a beautiful garden, the **Iso Tei-en**, built for the Shimazu family who ruled the area until the Meiji Restoration. The stone **Shōko Shuseikan**, by the entrance, was Japan's first Western-style iron works whose furnaces were used to produce ships, ordnance, and other western novelties like glass.

Sakurajima

It came at high noon, when the people were at lunch. At first they seemed to hear a dull rumble of distant thunder. Then a sudden ear-splitting detonation. Houses shook, windows rattled. People panicked and ran into the streets, where they beheld a black column of smoke rising into the sky beyond the bay. The top of the column expanded into a shape like the round head on a sprig of cauliflower ...'It's like the cloud of the atomic bomb,' they said.

A two-kilometre stretch of open water lies between the volcano and the city. When they saw that the smoke was rising straight up, the people sensed that there was no immediate danger. They went back to stuffing their mouths with gobs of rice and watched the display while munching their food.

Endō Shūsaku, *Volcano*

Sakurajima, which means 'Cherry Blossom Island', has actually been a peninsula for the last 80 years, joined to the eastern shore of Kagoshima Bay by a narrow isthmus of lava. The mountain had been exploding intermittently for hundreds of years when the biggest eruption of all occurred on 12 January 1914, a day still marked by solemn disaster procedures and evacuation drills. The first signs that something was up were observed in the farming hamlets around the base of the volcano: the ground shook, the water in the wells boiled, and shoals of dead fish floated up, ready cooked, from the sea. Altogether 35 people were killed and 112 injured in the eruptions which followed; over 2000 homes were burned or buried. The smoke ascended 2500m into the air; the ash rained down as far away as Russia.

The story of the Taishō Eruption, as it's called, is told in the **Sakurajima Visitor Centre**, a short walk to the right as you exit the ferry terminal. Apart from this, and a spurious **Dinosaur Park**, you need to take a **bike** (*¥400 for an hour's hire*) or **tour bus** to get an overall picture of the mountain. (The map of Sakurajima included on the English *Tourist Map of Kagoshima* makes it look small and negotiable, but is hopelessly out of scale.)

The Red Liner sightseeing bus (*see* 'Getting Around') travels clockwise around the peninsula from the ferry terminal, and stops first of all at a village called Kurokami which was inundated with lava. The top of a stone *torii* (shrine gateway) projects out of the ground, demonstrating how the ground level has risen since 1914. Apart from the damage caused by the layers of suffocating ash, the heat generated by the volcano fosters giant radishes, early fruiting loquats, and bountiful satsuma oranges. Overpriced examples of these are sold in a souvenir shop, along with pumice at ¥100 a bag.

Just beyond here lies the field of raw lava which welded the island to the rest of Kyūshū; a purpose-built **Observation Point** gives good views of its chaotic ridged surface (only from a distance do volcanoes have that pristine, crystal-cut appearance). The greatest threat to the peninsula's 7600 inhabitants is not lava, which moves slowly, but heavy rain, which dislodges the mountain's loose skin of scree and sends it sliding down the slope in muddy landslides. Broad concrete flood channels have been cut to alleviate this danger. A scientific observatory operated by Kyoto University has been built high on the north slopes; the bus sometimes goes up here, but only when volcanic activity is low.

(✆ 0992–) **Where to Stay**

moderate

Tōkyū Hotel, ✆ 57 2411, is a comfortable resort hotel, with an outdoor swimming pool, a little way south of the town centre, but with a striking view of Sakurajima. It is 10 minutes by taxi from Nishi-Kagoshima station.

Kagoshima Hayashida Hotel, ✆ 24 4111, is an efficient business hotel in the centre of downtown Kagoshima, near Takamibaba and Tenmonkan streetcar stops.

inexpensive

Nakazono Ryokan, ✆ 26 5125, is a wooden Japanese-style inn, five minutes' walk from Kagoshima station, one minute from Shiyakushō-mae streetcar stop. Japanese breakfast and dinner, Western-style breakfast extra.

Business Hotel Union, ✆ 53 5800, is a simple business hotel, two minutes from Nishi Kagoshima station.

cheap

Young Inn Kagoshima, ✆ 23 1116, is a small friendly hostel-type inn, with Western and Japanese rooms, near the waterfront and the Sakurajima Pier.

Sakurajima Youth Hostel, ✆ 93 2150, is underneath the volcano, five minutes from the ferry terminal.

Eating Out

Kagoshima cuisine, *Satsuma ryōri*, bears a distinctive Chinese influence, the product of centuries of maritime trade with Taiwan and the sinified islands to the south of Kyūshū: seasonings are spicy, and there are several deep-fried dishes such as *tonkatsu*, delicately seasoned stir-fried pork cutlets, very different from the greasy breaded version served in the rest of the country. *Satsuma-age* is deep-fried fish, and *sake-zushi* is raw fish and rice soaked in *sake* rice wine. One of the best places to sample these is in the **Hayashida Hotel**, which contains a floor of small restaurants specializing in different styles. The streets of Tenmonkan where the hotel is located contain many red lantern bars and *izakaya* serving similar food.

Chiran

Best done as a day trip from Kagoshima or en route to Ibusuki. Direct buses from Yamagataya bus station in Kagoshima, near Asahi-dōri streetcar stop. Bus connections from Ibusuki: enquire at the tourist information desk.

Chiran, a small town in the middle of the Satsuma Peninsula, has two unconnected attractions. The first, in the town centre, is a well-preserved quarter of old **buke yashiki** (samurai houses) built during the 18th century by the Sata family, chief retainers of Kagoshima's Shimazu clan. In order to discourage any of their vassal lords from becoming too powerful or independent, the Tokugawa shoguns in Edo (Tokyo) permitted only one castle to be built in each province. Satsuma already had one fortress, Kagoshima's Tsurumaru-jō (now a ruin), but the Shimazus overcame the prohibition by establishing their most trusted servants in over a hundred fortified villages, of which Chiran is the best surviving example. The local headman's residence was built at the centre, surrounded by a tight protective skirt of fortified samurai houses with features which could, in an emergency, be turned to defensive use. They are ranged along a lane and privately owned but, at any one time, about half a dozen are usually open to the public. (*Entry to each of the gardens costs ¥310; ask for a copy of the English translation of the useful commentary.*)

The houses are cunningly constructed to hinder a direct assault. Their sturdy gatehouses open onto a stone baffle wall which attackers would have to negotiate in order to gain entry to the grounds. Just inside the stone walls and high hedges were the houses' latrines, positioned (it is said) so that their occupants could eavesdrop undetected on conversations in the lane. In reality, these ingenious defence mechanisms were never tested by any serious military action. In the absence of any challenge to their martial prowess, the samurai cultivated the gentle arts; the houses have beautiful gardens, artfully positioned so that the undulating bushes at their backs seem to merge with the mountains behind.

Chiran Tokkō Heiwa Kaikan (Chiran Special Attack Peace Hall)

A lonely impulse of delight
Drove to this tumult in the clouds

W B Yeats, *An Irish Airman Foresees His Death*

Chiran's most fascinating tourist attraction is made very little of in the English-language pamphlets put out by the local tourist organizations, in fact some of them omit mentioning it altogether. Perhaps this isn't surprising. The 'Special Attack Forces' (*Tokkō-tai*), commemorated in the Chiran Peace Hall are known to English speakers by a different word: the *kamikaze* suicide bombers, who flew from Chiran on their one-way missions against American aircraft carriers in the dying months of the Pacific War.

Glorious suicide in the face of imminent defeat had an ancient and exalted place in the codes of the samurai. As early as 1942, individual pilots had deliberately steered their burning planes into enemy shipping, and during the battle for Saipan in July 1944, cornered soldiers were seen to hurl themselves at American troops, laden with explosives which they would detonate at the last moment. But it wasn't until October 1944 that a programme of suicide bombing raids was systematically organized by the high command, the first and only time this has occurred in the history of warfare. As one of the southernmost airfields on the Japanese mainland, Chiran came into the picture in 1945 as the American forces advanced painstakingly north through the Ryūkyū Islands, Okinawa, and towards Kyūshū.

The characters used to refer to the new policy mean 'divine wind', an allusion to the typhoons which fortuitously saved Japan from Mongol invaders in the 13th century. The pronunciation *kamikaze*, however, had inappropriately crude overtones, being used to refer metaphorically to reckless drivers or breakneck skiers. At the time, the alternative reading of the same characters was always used: *shinpū*, derived from the Chinese pronunciation, with a pure, classical, appropriately dignified ring.

In the conduct of the *shinpū* missions, superficially at least, there was nothing frantic or bestial, as the displays in the museum demonstrate. The collection of photographs, letters and memorabilia of the dead pilots is desperately moving but, in the way they are presented, and in the taped English commentary which can be hired from the ticket desk (¥100), there is something disturbingly upbeat. The emphasis is all on the 'bravery' and 'purity' of the young men; reference is made to 'successful' suicide missions (as if the expression had any meaning); there is no attempt to paint in the savage background of Japan's dreadful war, or to consider the equally brave young Americans who were on the receiving end of the flying coffins. Among the distinguished grey-haired gentlemen who guide Japanese visitors around the exhibits are actual survivors of 'unsuccessful' *shinpū* missions who were forced to turn back by mechanical failure. By the end of each tour, plenty of visitors, too young to remember anything of the war, are in tears. You can't help worrying about what exactly they are crying for.

The pilots—few of them older than 26, many in their teens—were all volunteers, and came forward in large numbers. There are stories of young airmen weeping with shame and frustration on being passed over for the fatal missions ahead of them. Skill and experience was unnecessary, as were good aircraft—by the end of the war, the most rickety old crates were being loaded up with explosives and sent off.

Once they had been selected, the pilots were treated with the greatest reverence and consideration as 'living gods', destined to die for the nation and reunite as Shinto *kami* at Tokyo's Yasukuni Shrine. The personal motives of the pilots themselves seem often to have been more homely. Final letters to family and friends speak of dying for the honour of sisters and parents and villages, as much as for the Emperor. Girls in a pilot's home town would each add a stitch to a belt specially made by the mothers of the doomed boys. Along with their white silk scarves (symbols of purity), these 'belts of a thousand stitches' were among the pilots' most prized possessions on their flights.

On their last night, the pilots were billeted together in a special bunker where they wrote their farewell letters which were sealed with a lock of hair and nail clippings. Their last meal was simple and emblematically traditional—boiled rice, red beans, sea bream and *sake*. The next day, they were saluted by their officers and ground crew, posed for a photograph, and drank a last *sake* toast before climbing into the cockpit. These final photographs line the walls of the Chiran Museum and are among its most moving exhibits: a face, a name and a (pathetically young) age. The most affecting of all shows a group of pilots who have just been handed a tiny puppy. For a moment, the pose of impassive solemnity is broken, and they look exactly what they are: teenage boys, grinning as they stroke a dog.

It is hard to believe the museum caption writer's assertion that 'at the time of the sorties they all took off with smiles'. But all of them were volunteers, and all of them knew exactly what they were doing. Militarily, the effect of the *kamikaze* campaigns was almost negligible. If anything they hastened the end, by hardening President Truman and his generals in their resolve to use the atomic bomb. Amazingly, some of the pilots seemed to understand this. They knew that defeat was only a matter of time, and that their deaths could not divert this inevitability. It was as a spiritual gesture that they died, and it is this persuasive insistence on the 'sincerity' of the dead pilots that makes the museum such a heartbreaking, spine-tingling, and for foreign visitors, disturbingly ambiguous place. 'I am a human being and hope to be neither saint nor scoundrel, hero nor fool—just a human being,' wrote one of them, 22-year-old Sub-lieutenant Okabe, in his final diary. 'The world in which I lived was too full of discord. As one who has spent his life in wistful longing and searching, I die resignedly in the hope that my life will serve as a human document.'

Ibusuki

Because it has beaches and bikinis, the tourist brochures predictably refer to it as 'the Hawaii of Japan'. Actually, Ibusuki feels more like Deauville or San Sebastian than Honolulu, with palms, beaches, ramshackle beachfront hotels, and sleepy, siesta-loving locals. If Japan's pace and efficiency and fastidious politeness is beginning to get on your nerves, this might be just the place to release some stress—on the beach, in the water, or under steaming piles of geothermally heated sand which are the town's most famous feature.

Getting There and Around

Trains reach Ibusuki in 1hr–1hr 25mins from Nishi Kagoshima station. Ibusuki is situated on Surigahama, a strand of beach curving north to south. The station is 10 minutes' walk inland, to the west.

Ibusuki isn't a big place, and the best way to get around it, especially on a sunny day, is by **bike**. There are numerous hire shops all over town, including those by the station and in the Kankō Hotel.

Tourist Information

Pick up English maps and pamphlets from the **station information desk**.

Around Ibusuki

There are **sand baths** in other parts of Japan, including Beppu, but none are so much fun as Ibusuki's. Cheapest is the public facility on the beach (*adm ¥510*).

Admission includes the hire of a *yukata*, the light cotton kimono which you change into before stepping out onto the beach. The scene, on a busy day, is rather surreal: rows of faces emerging from the sand, like pink zombies rising from the dead. You are led to your own grave where a beefy old age pensioner shovels the sand on top of your *yukata*-clad body and, in sunny weather, adjusts a parasol to protect your face. The sand is coarse and gravelly, and it takes a while for the heat to permeate the cotton and start its sweaty work.

After a
while,
though,
the strength
of the heat
becomes clear. It's
buttock-searing,
and all the weirder for
being completely dry.
Twenty minutes is as much
as most people can take.

Afterwards you'll feel as light as a feather. Shake off the sand, and shower and wash thoroughly before soaking in the big communal baths inside.

Just as famous but more expensive is the **Jungle Bath** in the Kankō Hotel, at the southern tip of Surigahama, which also has its private stretch of hot beach, included in the admission price. The main building is smart and modern, with broad grounds containing palms, azaleas, tennis courts and private beaches. The Jungle Bath (*free to guests, ¥1000 to non-residents*) is a huge conservatory of tropical vegetation, with dozens of pools of varying shapes, sizes and temperatures. The sexes are segregated, but there is a family area where they can mingle—in bathing costumes.

Next door to the hotel is the private **Iwasaki Art Museum**. The 1979 building by the architect Maki Fumihiko far outshines the collection: Japanese artists imitating every kind of Western style, from post-Impressionism to Francis Bacon.

(✆ *0993–*)   **Where to Stay**

Ibusuki lodgings are on the expensive side. Twin Western-style rooms (no singles available) at the **Ibusuki Kankō Hotel**, ✆ 22 2131, cost from about ¥13,000, but vary with the season; there are Japanese *tatami* rooms, ¥1000 or so cheaper per person. **Ryokan Ginshō**, ✆ 22 3231, is *expensive*, but very elegant. *Cheap*, but homely, is the **New Yunohama-sō**, ✆ 23 3088, a few minutes' stroll from the beach. There are two **youth hostels: Tamaya**, ✆ 22 3553, right next to the sand baths; and **Ibusuki**, ✆ 22 2758, which is made of concrete and a bit less convenient.

Japanese isn't much like any other language in the world, and no one seems to have much of a clue where it comes from, or how it arrived where it did. Linguists relate it to the Hungarian-Magyar and Finnish (Altaic) languages, and suggest that all three may have originated in Central Asia. Modern Japanese has similarities with Korean; Turkish speakers are said to find it a very easy language to learn.

Nobody else does. The technical difficulties posed by Japanese are enough to deter the most fanatical linguist. The language has multiple levels of politeness, depending on who is talking to whom, about what, and where. The written language possesses two phonetic systems (three if you include the Roman alphabet) and more than 50,000 *kanji* or Chinese-derived characters. 2000 of these are necessary to read a daily newspaper; the knottiest of them consist of more than 30 individual strokes, which must be individually memorized, in the correct order. There are no short cuts: full literacy in Japanese requires years of patient study.

The good news is that short-term visitors don't need to worry. Without a doubt, the more Japanese you know, the more you will get out of Japan and the easier your travels will be. But with initiative, patience and some forward planning it is quite possible to have a full and rewarding holiday in the most out of the way places without any Japanese at all.

Communicating without Japanese

All Japanese study English for years at high school. Many of them are taught from standardized text books, by Japanese teachers who may never have travelled abroad themselves. Quite understandably, most of them have no confidence and are as embarrassed by their English as you would be by creaky schoolboy French or German. But, with patience and encouragement, simple questions and answers can be made understandable to most Japanese under 30.

The first trick is to choose a likely looking candidate. University students are the best bet (since they are required to study English to a fairly high standard), and after them business-types (who might use English in their work). Don't start jabbering questions immediately. Try first to establish eye contact, with a smile and a nod of the head and then a polite, 'Excuse me...do you speak English?' Most Japanese, even bilingual ones, are constitutionally incapable of answering yes to this question (modesty forbids), but don't be put off. Phrase your questions simply and directly, avoiding complicated tenses or figures of speech. Remember that most Japanese find written English much easier to follow than the spoken form; and that your pronunciation of Japanese names may bear very little resemblance to their native form. Carry a notebook to write down words, simple questions and maps.

Language

Japanese Phrases

The key to using and being understood is pronunciation, which is technically much simpler than in English. This, ironically, is the difficulty—Japanese has fewer sounds, and English-speakers often try to introduce diphthongs and stresses where there are none.

There are just five vowel sounds in Japanese, similar to those in Spanish and Italian. Pronouncing the following sentence, keeping the vowels short, gives you their approximate sound, in order:

Ah, we soon get old.

A   I   U   E   O

Avoid pursing your lips for the **U**.

A macron over the vowel 'ā', 'ū', 'ō' etc) doubles the length of the vowel. Macrons are used throughout this book with two exceptions. The two most famous Japanese cities—Tōkyō and Kyōto—are not macronized, and nor are words—like judo and shogun—which have effectively entered the English language.

Syllables are pronounced evenly and in full, with no syllable bearing more emphasis than any other. This is difficult for English-speakers to get used to, and causes a lot of confusion when they come to Japanese names. The famous city which suffered the first atom bomb attack, for instance, is usually pronounced by foreigners as 'huh-ROSH-uh-muh'. The correct pronunciation stresses each syllable equally—'Hee-Roh-Shee-Ma'— and a Japanese will genuinely not understand its English pronunciation. The same goes for Ōsaka: correct pronunciation—something like 'oar-sucker', with a lingering first syllable; incorrect pronunciation—'uh-SARK-uh'. Tokyo is 'tour-cure' or 'talk-your', not 'toe-key-oh'.

The exception to the rule about emphasis is the 'u' sound which is often swallowed in the middle of, or at the end of words. Thus *arigatō gozaimasu* (thank you) and *sukiyaki* (meat stew) sound more like 'arigatō gozaimass' and 'ski-yacky'.

Basic Phrases

hello, good day	*konnichiwa*
hello (on the telephone)	*moshi moshi*
good morning	*ohayō gozaimasu*
good evening	*konbanwa*
good night	*oyasumi nasai*
goodbye	*sayonara*, or to children and between young women *bai bai.*
excuse me	*sumimasen* (all purpose); *shitsurei shimasu* (on leaving or pushing past someone)
I'm sorry	*Gomen nasai*
thank you	*arigatō* (neutral), *dōmo* (casual), *dōmo arigatō gozaimasu* (formal)
thank you very very much	*dōmo arigatō* (*gozaimasu*)
don't mention it; it's nothing	*dō itashimashite*

how are you?	*ogenki desuka?*
I'm fine	*genki desu*
do you speak (English)?	(*Eigo*) *ga dekimasu ka?*
French	*Furansugo*
Japanese	*Nihongo*
I speak a little	*sukoshi dekimasu*
I don't speak (Japanese)	(*Nihongo*) *wa dekimasen*
say that again please	*mō ichido itte kudasai*
is there someone here who speaks English?	*Eigo ga dekiru hito wa irasshaimasu ka?*
menu	*menyū*
chopsticks	*hashi*
knife and fork	*naifu to fōkku*
water	*mizu*
coffee	*kōhī*
tea	*ocha* (green tea)
	kōcha (black tea)
how much is (coffee)?	(*kōhī*) *wa ikura desu ka?*
this	*kore*
that	*sore*
that (over there)	*are*
(I want) that one, please	*sore o kudasai* or *Sore onegai shimasu*
the menu, please	*menyū o kudasai* or *Menyū onegai shimasu*
the bill, please	*okanjō o kudasai*
please (meaning 'please go ahead', 'please help yourself', 'after you')	*dōzo*
where is (the station)?	(*eki*) *wa doko desuka*
bus station	*basu tāminaru*
taxi rank	*takushī noriba*
hotel (western style)	*hoteru*
one	*ichi*
two	*ni*
three	*san*
four	*shi* or *yon*
five	*go*
six	*roku*
seven	*schichi* or *nana*
eight	*hachi*
nine	*kyū*
ten	*jū*
eleven	*jū-ichi*
twelve	*jū-ni*

twenty	*ni-jū*
thirty	*san-jū*
one hundred	*hyaku*
two hundred	*nihyaku*
three hundred	*sanbyaku*
six hundred	*roppyaku*
one thousand	*sen*
ten thousand	*man*
twenty four thousand, six hundred and seventy three	*ni-man-yon-sen-roppyaku-nana-jū-sen*
what platform is the train to Ōsaka?	*Ōsaka yuki densha wa nan ban sen desuka?*
what time is the train to Ōsaka?	*Ōsaka yuki densha wa nan ji desuka?*
platform number (eight)	(*hachi*) *ban sen*
ticket office	*kippu uriba*
really? (lit. '[is it] true?')	*hontō?*
what a pity	*zannen desu*
too bad/it can't be helped	*shikata ga nai* (informally *shō ga nai*)

Forests have been levelled to produce the thousands of books in print on Japan. Most of them are rubbish, or simply wrong and boring. In particular, cast a sceptical eye on anything promising 'instant' Japanese, anything offering to reveal 'the real Japan', and anything by former foreign correspondents. Most of the following books can be found in a specialist oriental bookshop like the ones listed in **Practical A–Z** on p.15. Publishers may vary from country to country: in Japan, Tuttle, Kodansha and Weatherhill specialize in English language titles. In the following list, family names precede given names.

History

Barr, Pat: *The Deer Cry Pavilion* and *The Coming of the Barbarians* (Penguin). Witty, gossipy histories of the foreign communities in the great period of Westernization in the late 19th century.

Buruma, Ian: *The Wages of Guilt* (Cape). Compares the way in which Germany and Japan have digested and rationalized their experiences of the Second World War.

Cook, Haruko Taya and **Cook, Theodore F.**: *Japan at War: An Oral History* (New Press). Compellingly dramatic first person accounts by combatants and civilians.

Morris, Ivan: *The Nobility of Failure* (Secker & Warburg). Brilliantly indirect study of Japanese thinking through its many martyrs, underdogs and suicides. *The World of the Shining Prince* is a study of the halcyon Heian period, through the medium of its most famous book, *The Tale of Genji.*

Plutschow, Herbert: *Historical Kyoto, Historical Nagasaki,* and *Historical Nara* (Japan Times). Workmanlike, factual accounts of three of Japan's most interesting cities.

Sansom, Sir George: Japan: *A Short Cultural History* (Stanford University Press). First written in the 1930s and still the standard work—thorough, scholarly and not as short as the title suggests.

Seidensticker, Edward: *High City, Low City* and *Tokyo Rising* (Penguin/Tuttle). Heartfelt, elegiac, beautifully written accounts of Tokyo from the Meiji period to the great earthquake, and the earthquake to the 1980s.

Statler, Oliver: *Japanese Pilgrimage* and *Japanese Inn* (Tuttle). Part scholarship, part travelogue; superbly digestible accounts of Japanese history through the stories, respectively, of the Shikoku Pilgrimage and an old *ryokan.*

Storry, Richard: *A History of Modern Japan* (Penguin). The best place to start: concise, readable, with fine preliminary chapters on the early history too.

Waley, Paul: *Tokyo: City of Stories* (Weatherhill). Anecdotal histories of all the main areas; brings fascinating life to the concrete and expressways.

Further Reading

Rice, Jonathan: *Doing Business in Japan* (BBC Books). A sensible and unpretentious introduction.

Tasker, Peter: *Inside Japan* (Penguin). Accessible introduction to contemporary society and economics by a securities analyst who writes like a journalist. A bit out of date in some respects (1987) but still the best general introduction.

Van Wolferen, Karel: *The Enigma of Japanese Power* (Macmillan/Tuttle). Controversial but brilliant analysis of what makes Japanese society so different.

Bashō, Matsuo: *The Narrow Road to the Deep North* (Penguin Classics). Classic *haiku* travelogue by the 17th-century poet who was never happier than when he was completely miserable.

Birnbaum, Alfred (ed.): *Monkey Brain Sushi* (Kodansha). Short stories by young Japanese writers.

Collins, Clive: *Misunderstandings* (Marion Boyars). The best English fiction writer on Japan—sad, understated, unpatronizing short stories.

Endō, Shūsaku: *Silence* and *The Final Martyrs* (Peter Owen/Tuttle). The most accessible of contemporary Japanese novelists; his classic novel of Catholicism and conscience in 16th-century Nagasaki, and a selection of short stories summing up many of his themes.

Keene, Donald (ed.): *Anthology of Japanese Literature* (Penguin Classics). Representative selections of all the greats up to the 19th century.

Mishima, Yukio: *Confessions of a Mask* and *The Sea of Fertility* (Penguin/Tuttle). The first and last works of the most famous (and infamous) of Japan's novelists who committed ritual suicide after an attempted military coup in 1970. The first is a short, intense autobiographical story about the wartime childhood and youth of a homosexual man; the second a huge, sweeping tetralogy of the Japanese 20th century, taking in militarism, philosophy and reincarnation.

Murakami, Haruki: *A Wild Sheep Chase* (Penguin). Droll, melancholy, bizarre novel by the most successful living Japanese novelist.

Lady Murasaki: *The Tale of Genji* (Penguin Classics). One of the great works of world literature: a long, delicate, poignant tale of life in the 11th-century Heian court.

Ōe, Kenzaburo: The Silent Cry (Serpent's Tail). The best-known novel by the winner of the 1994 Nobel Prize for Literature, a painful and unflinching story of a man and his disabled son.

Tanizaki, Junichirō: *The Makioka Sisters* (Tuttle). Moving novel about struggling Japanese gentlefolk in pre-war Kōbe and Ōsaka.

Thwaite, Anthony: *Letter from Tokyo* (Hutchinson). Mild, elegant poems about Japanese life and history.

Brown, Jan: *Exploring Tohoku: A Guide to Japan's Back Country* (Weatherhill). Solid, practical guide to the deep north.

Durston, Diane: *Old Kyoto* (Kodansha). Illustrated guide to hundreds of fascinating old shops, inns and restaurants.

Guest, Harry: *Traveller's Literary Companion: Japan* (In Print). Short excerpts of many good books on and of Japan. Extensive bibliographies.

Hotta, Anne: *A Guide to Japanese Hot Springs* (Kodansha). *Onsen* all over the country.

Kennedy, Rick: *Good Tokyo Restaurants* (Kodansha). Lives up to its name.

Martin, John H.: *Nara: A Cultural Guide* (Tuttle). Solid but informative temple guide.

Moriyama, Tae: *Tokyo Adventures: Glimpses of the City in Bygone Eras* (Shufunotomo). Gossipy, garrulous guide to walks and days out in Tokyo, by a likeable old lady.

Mosher, Gouverneur: *Kyoto: A Contemplative Guide* (Tuttle). Written in 1964, and never updated, but still the best book about the ancient capital, full of charm and historical anecdote.

O'Sullivan, Jerry: *Teaching English in Japan* (In Print). Well-organized manual for those inclined to stay a bit longer.

Treib, Marc and **Herman, Ron**: *A Guide to the Gardens of Kyoto* (Shufunotomo). Practical information on what to see and how to get there, plus stimulating essays on the history, craft and semiotics of the gardens.

Living for Less in Tokyo and Liking It (Kodansha). Good practical advice on everyday matters. Mainly for long- to medium-term visitors.

Barthes, Roland: *Empire of Signs* (Cape). Essays on Japan by the playful structuralist semiotician. Not everyone's *tasse de thé*, but stimulating nonetheless.

Bird, Isabella: *Unbeaten Tracks in Japan* (Virago). Indefatigable Victorian gentlewoman braves fleas, saddle sores and bad service in pursuit of the hairy Ainu of Hokkaidō.

Booth, Alan: *The Roads to Sata* (Penguin). The best modern travel book about Japan— refreshingly sarcastic and irritable.

Buruma, Ian: *A Japanese Mirror* (Penguin). Subtle analysis of Japanese pop culture.

Carter, Angela: *Nothing Sacred* (Virago). The five essays on Japan by the late novelist are the best imaginative journalism on the country in English.

Constantine, Peter: *Japanese Street Slang* (Tengu Books). Ever wanted to know how to say, 'Grandpa, don't fart when we've got visitors present'? It's all in here.

Downer, Leslie: *On the Narrow Road to the Deep North* (Sceptre). British woman follows in the steps of Bashō.

Hearn, Lafcadio: *Writings from Japan* (Penguin). Well-chosen introduction to the troubled 19th-century Japanophile from Matsue.

Kayano, Shigeru: *Our Land Was a Forest* (Westview). Fascinating personal memoir of the tragic suppression of the Ainu people of Hokkaidō by Japan's only Ainu member of parliament.

Morley, John David: *Pictures from the Water Trade* (Flamingo). Slight but touching tales of contemporary Japan.

Popham, Peter: *Tokyo: The City at the End of the World* (Kodansha). Earthquakes, crazy architecture, religious cults, rabbit hutch existence—captures the excitement and weirdness of life in the biggest machine in the world.

Richie, Donald: *The Inland Sea* (Century). Travels around Shikoku and Chūgoku in the late 1960s.

Ventura, Reynald: *Underground in Japan* (Cape). Gripping account of the life of an illegal Filipino worker in Yokohama. The side of Japanese life most tourists never see.

Arts and Architecture

Mitsuo, Inoue: *Space in Japanese Architecture* (Weatherhill). Dry but brainy theoretical work.

Nishi, Kazuo and **Hozumi, Kazuo**: *What is Japanese Architecture?* (Kodansha). Big, practical guide with lots of diagrams and illustrations.

O'Neill, P. G.: *A Guide to Nō* (Hinoki Shoten). Pocket guide to plays and terminology.

Visions of Japan (Victoria and Albert Museum). Based on a 1991 exhibition; less a book than an assemblage of photographs, essays and found objects bound in a cardboard folder. Genuinely evocative.

Chapter headings and main references are in **bold** type; page numbers of maps are in *italics.*

Index